# WINTER SPORTS

# THE NEW YORK TIMES ENCYCLOPEDIA OF SPORTS

THE NEW YORK TIMES
**ENCYCLOPEDIA OF SPORTS**

**VOLUME 9**

# WINTER SPORTS

EDITED BY
**GENE BROWN**
INTRODUCTION BY
**FRANK LITSKY**

**ARNO PRESS**
A NEW YORK TIMES COMPANY
NEW YORK 1979

**GROLIER EDUCATIONAL CORPORATION**
SHERMAN TURNPIKE, DANBURY, CT. 06816

**Library of Congress Cataloging in Publication Data**

Main entry under title:

SSH

Winter sports.

(The New York times encyclopedia of sports; v. 9) Collection of articles reprinted from the New York times.
 Bibliography.
 Includes index.
 SUMMARY: Traces the history of winter sports as presented in articles appearing in the "New York Times."
 1. Winter sports. [1. Winter sports] I. Brown, Gene. II. New York times.
III. Series: New York times encyclopedia of sports; v. 9.
GV565.N48 vol. 9 [GV841] 796s [796.9] 79-19932
ISBN 0-405-12635-2

Manufactured in the United States of America

Appendix © 1979, *The Encyclopedia Americana.*

The editors express special thanks to The Associated Press, United Press International, and Reuters for permission to include a number of dispatches originally distributed by those news services.

**The New York Times Encyclopedia of Sports**

Founding Editors: Herbert J. Cohen and Richard W. Lawall
Project Editors: Arleen Keylin and Suri Boiangiu
Editorial Assistant: Jonathan Cohen

Photographs on the following pages courtesy of UPI: X, 3, 26, 40, 46, 55, 81, 109, 126, 165

# CONTENTS

# CONTENTS

Many winter sports originated centuries ago. Primitive skis were made from animal bones at least 5,000 years ago. Iron skates were used in Scotland around 1572, and before that there were skates made of bone and then wood. A skating club was formed in Scotland in 1642.

Competition in these cold-weather sports is relatively new. Speed skating contests began in 1814 in Britain, skiing in 1860 in Norway, figure skating in 1864 in Vienna and bobsledding in 1877 in Klosters, Switzerland.

Winter sports have received wide exposure through the Winter Olympics. Before there were separate Olympic Games for winter sports, figure skating was part of the 1908 Summer Olympics in London and figure skating and ice hockey were contested in the 1920 Summer Olympics in Antwerp.

Their success prompted many members of the International Olympic Committee (IOC) to propose a separate Olympic Games for winter sports. Norway and Sweden, the most important winter sports nations, opposed the idea, fearing that a Winter Olympics would diminish the importance of their Nordic Games.

The 1924 Summer Olympics were held in Paris, and in connection with them the French staged an International Winter Sports Week in Chamonix. The IOC voted to call this competition the Winter Olympic Games, and the success of these games led the IOC in 1925 to sanction a separate Winter Olympics every four years, the same years as the Summer Olympics.

While more than 100 nations normally compete in the Summer Olympics, the record entry for the Winter Olympics is 37. The Soviet Union, since its Winter Olympic debut in 1956, has been the dominant nation. The United States has had considerable success in figure skating and speed skating and occasionally in Alpine skiing. The other sports on the Winter Olympic program are Nordic skiing, bobsledding, luge, ice hockey and biathlon.

The Winter Olympics have overcome many problems, notably commercialism. The late Avery Brundage of Chicago, president of the IOC, disliked the Winter Olympics because of commercial intrusions, mainly in skiing, and he advocated abolition of these games.

In 1972, Brundage wanted to ban 40 Alpine skiers he accused of accepting payments from manufacturers of skis and ski equipment. The International Ski Federation, much more tolerant of commercial influences, threatened to cancel Olympic skiing if Brundage carried out his threat.

In a compromise, one skier was banned—33-year-old Karl Schranz of Austria, a favorite in all three Olympic events. Schranz probably earned more money (about $50,000 a year) than the others, and he talked freely about accepting these illegal payments. Today, skiers are often allowed to accept money from manufacturers, and the best skiers collect up to $250,000 a year.

## FIGURE SKATING

One of the most asthetically pleasing sports is figure skating, which is a combination of acrobatics and ballet, performed on ice by athletes wearing skates. Men and women compete separately in singles, and teams of one man and one woman compete in separate pairs and dance contests.

In 1850, E. W. Bushnell of Philadelphia made the first steel-bladed skates and sold all he could manufacture for $30 a pair, a huge sum in those days. In 1864, Jackson Haines, an American ballet master and dancer, emigrated to Vienna and used waltz music for skating (previously, skaters wandered aimlessly on the ice). Haines's pupils spread the new sport, and the first skating clubs were formed in 1878 in Canada and 1887 in Philadelphia.

Meanwhile, a style of figure skating emphasizing precision rather than dancing was being developed in England. The competition consisted of tracing figures on the ice. Eventually, the two styles of figure skating were combined in one competition, and figure skating today involves both required and optional routines.

Women's figure skating was revolutionized by one skater, Sonja Henie. In 1924, at age 11, she won the Norwegian women's championship. A few weeks later, she skated in the Winter Olympics and finished last. She was never last again.

From 1927 to 1936, she won 10 straight world championships, eight straight European titles and three straight Olympic gold medals. In all, she won 257 cups, medals, plaques and bowls. In 1936, she turned professional and started skating in ice shows. Eventually, she owned her own show. She appeared in 11 movies, getting good reviews for her skating and bad notices for her acting. Between ice shows and movies, she is reputed to have earned $47 million.

Men's skating was revolutionized by Dick Button. When he was a 12-year-old boy in Englewood, N.J., his parents asked a club pro to work with him. The pro watched him skate and rejected him as too fat and too uncoordinated. From 1946 to 1952, a slimmer and well coordinated Dick Button won seven straight United States and five straight World championships.

In 1948, as a Harvard freshman, he won the Olympic gold medal. In 1952, as a first-year student in Harvard Law School, his professors allowed him to go to the Olympics only if he took his law books with him and studied when he wasn't skating. He studied and skated and won the gold medal again.

Button was the first man to emphasize athletic skating rather than simply dancing on skates. He invented jumps and spins and used them successfully while rival skaters tried vainly to perform them. In recent years, Button's expert commentary on television has helped make figure skating a popular sport.

Perhaps the most accomplished of female skaters has been Peggy Fleming. She worked out eight hours a day and from 1964 to 1968, won five straight United States and three straight world championships, and the 1960 Olympic gold medal. Then, like many champions, she turned professional and joined a traveling ice show. She is slender and appears fragile, and she skates with a dreamy balletic style. Lloyd Garrison of The New York Times described her Olympic success as "a victory of the ballet over the Ice Follies approach to figure skating."

Today, both men's and women's skating have participants who emphasize athletic jumps and spins and others who seem to perform ballet on ice. In the 1976 Winter Olympics, John Curry of England won the gold medal with a balletic approach and Toller Cranston of Canada won the bronze medal with a free-skating routine bordering on the exotic. Later, both formed professional ice shows and departed even further from the styles used by most male skaters.

## SPEED SKATING

People were ice skating long before figure skating was invented. The Dutch were known to have skated on frozen ponds and canals as early as the 16th century. The sport of speed skating evolved in the 19th century, and the first American championships were held in 1891 and the first world championships in 1893.

International competition is held on 400-meter oval rinks. Two skaters skate at a time, and final standings are based on time. The skaters remain in lanes to avoid contact, switching lanes at specified intervals so that they skate equal distances.

For years, the only international-sized rink in the United States was in West Allis, Wisconsin, outside Milwaukee, and the best American skaters often moved there or commuted long distances to train there. Another 400-meter rink was built in Lake Placid, N.Y., for the 1980 Winter Olympics.

Many Americans have learned speed skating on indoor rinks that measure 12 to 16 laps to the mile. These are three or four times smaller than 400-meter rinks, so races involve almost constant turning and instead of two skaters racing at a time, many compete simultaneously in what is called pack racing.

When the 1932 Winter Olympics were held in Lake Placid, New York, international officials decided, as a courtesy to the host nation, to use American pack rules rather than international rules. Not surprisingly, Americans won all four races. Jack Shea of Lake Placid, who had taken the Olympic oath during the opening ceremonies on behalf of all athletes, won the 500-meter and 1,500-meter races. Irving Jaffee of New York won at 5,000 and 10,000 meters.

Those victories were especially satisfying for Jaffee. In 1928, at St. Moritz, he seemed headed for a similar double. He won the 5,000, and he had the fastest time in the 10,000 with no strong skaters remaining. But when the ice became soggy, the officials canceled the competition.

The IOC overruled that decision. Twelve hours later, the International Ski Federation overruled the IOC and decided that the race must be rerun from the start. By that time, most skaters had gone home and there was no rerun, and thus there was no official race. Still, some record books list Jaffee as the winner. Jaffee was disappointed by the no-contest ruling and then by the failure to rerun the race, and said, "I will face them again on skates, skis or at foot-running."

In 1964, Lidia Skoblikova, a schoolteacher from Siberia, swept the four women's events, the first time any athlete in any sport had won four gold medals in one Winter Olympic games. In 1976, Sheila Young of Detroit, twice a world cycling champion, won one gold, one silver and one bronze medal in Olympic speed-skating.

The most successful American skaters in the modern era are Eric and Beth Heiden, brother and sister from Madison, Wisconsin. In 1977 and 1978, Eric swept the three world overall championships—senior, junior and sprint. In 1979, too old for the juniors, he won the other two titles again. Beth, only 5 feet 1 inch, won the junior championship in 1978 and 1979 and the senior in 1979. Each of these championships consisted of four races at varying distances, with the title decided on overall performance.

## CURLING

Curling, which is essentially lawn bowling on ice, probably originated in Scotland in the 16th century. A large stone, with maximum dimensions of 36 inches around, 4½ inches high and 42½ pounds is slid along the ice toward a fixed object. The rink is 138 feet long and 14 feet wide. The ice is sprinkled with warm water to achieve a pebbling effect, thus providing the stone with a grip. There are four men or women to a team, and the three not sliding the stone, use brooms to sweep the ice in the path of the stone to help guide it.

## LUGE

Luge is competitive tobogganing. ("Luge" is the French word for sled.) It began early in the 20th century and became an Olympic sport for men and women in 1964. The rider lies on his back, his head toward the back of the sled, and races down a twisting, curving course similar to a bobsled run. The sled is little more than two steel runners mounted on two rails, with a canvas seat between them. It is about 51 inches long and 18 inches wide in the rear, narrower in the front. Maximum weight is 44 pounds.

## SLED DOG RACING

Dogs have pulled sleds for centuries in the snowbound north country. Racing began in the 18th century in northern Europe, and the first North American race was held in Alaska in 1908. One to three dogs are used in European racing, usually seven to nine in Canada and the United States. The dogs in North American races are normally Siberian huskies or Alaskan malamutes. Races usually last several days, with daily legs ranging from 18 miles to hundreds of miles. Although the International Sled Dog Racing Association helped standardize rules in 1966, local rules often prevail.

## SKIING

Competitive skiing began in Europe in the late 16th century, and Norwegian emigrants brought it to the United States in the late 19th century. The 1932 Winter Olympics at Lake Placid brought it to the attention of many Americans.

That year, the rope tow, powered by a motorcycle engine, was first used. The J-bar was introduced in 1936, and the chair lift followed. These devices solved a vexing problem for skiers—how to get back up the hill so they could ski down again. Another problem—lack of snow—disappeared when snowmaking machines were introduced.

Thus, with snow guaranteed and an uphill ride assured, recreational skiing grew. Another type of skiing—ski touring over relatively equal amounts of uphill, downhill and flat land—became a popular participant sport in the 1970's.

Alpine skiing—competition down hill—has three divisions: slalom, giant slalom and downhill. A slalom course has up to 75 control gates, each gate consisting of two poles, and the skier must ski through each gate. The giant slalom has fewer gates set wider apart, so the skiers go faster than in the slalom. The downhill is essentially a plunge at speeds that reach 70 to 80 miles an hour, an exciting and daredevil race. In each type of competition, one skier skis at a time, with placings decided on time.

Nordic skiing consists of cross-country racing and ski jumping. The races, on the same type of ground used for ski touring, cover from 5 to 50 kilometers. In ski jumping, a spectacular and dangerous sport limited to men, the jumper builds speed by skiing down a steep hill, then soars perhaps 300 feet or more onto a landing area. He is judged on style and distance. In a variation known as ski flying, only distance counts, and jumpers have exceeded 500 feet.

Alpine skis, usually 6 feet 9 inches long and 3 to 4 inches wide, are made of fiberglass, metal, laminated wood or some combination thereof. The bottoms of Alpine and Nordic skis are waxed before races to improve speed, and the choice of wax often makes a difference in success.

The major annual competition in Alpine skiing is the World Cup series, which began in 1967. It consists of 25 to 30 events for men and a similar number for women, running from December to March in Europe, the United States, Canada and Japan. A similar World Cup competition has begun in Nordic skiing. There are also professional circuits for Alpine skiers, freestyle skiing (trick competition once known as hotdog skiing) and biathlon (an Olympic sport that combines cross-country skiing and rifle shooting).

Skiing has always been a backbone of the Winter Olympics. The United States has produced occasional women's Alpine champions; Gretchen Fraser of Vancouver, Wash., in 1948; Andrea Mead Lawrence of Rutland, Vt., in two events in 1952 and Barbara Cochran of Richmond, Vt., in 1972. While American men have never won an Olympic gold medal. Toni Sailer of Austria in 1956 and Jean-Claude Killy of France in 1968 won all three.

Americans have had less success in Nordic skiing, so there was great surprise during the 1976 Winter Olympics when 20-year-old Bill Koch of Guilford, Vt., fighting off an asthma attack, won the silver medal in the 30-kilometer cross-country race. The best previous Olympic showing by an American was a 15th place in 1932.

## BOBSLEDDING

Toboggans were too slow for exciting races, and toboggans with runners proved too fast, so Americans in Switzerland invented bobsledding in 1895. The first races were held there in 1898, and an artificial run was built in 1904. The only run in the United States is in Lake Placid. There are separate races for two-man and four-man sleds, streamlined missiles built of steel and aluminum. Each sled races four times against the clock, with final standings based on total time. Americans, often weighing up to 250 pounds, were once the best sledders. The most celebrated sledder was Eugenio Monti, a 5-foot-9-inch, 145-pound Italian. Between 1954 and 1964, he won nine world championships, and in three Winter Olympics he earned two gold, two silver and two bronze medals.

— Frank Litsky

# CHAPTER 1

# SCANDINAVIAN DOMINANCE

Sonja Henie was the women's world figure skating champion, 1927-1936; she won Olympic gold medals in 1928, 1932 and 1936. But beyond the bare statistics, she was the person who made figure skating a major winter sport.

# FIGURE SKATING BECOMING POPULAR

## Champion Irving Brokaw Tells of Graceful and Skillful Movements on Blades.

During the past few seasons figure skating has received more attention than ever before from the participants in this popular and healthful form of Winter sport. At the rinks in American cities during the past season there has been a noticeable improvement in the styles and performances of the number who have taken up figure skating. Irving Brokaw, the American champion of 1906, predicts that skating in this country will in a short time be almost as popular as it is in Europe, and that the Continental style of figure skating, with its long, swinging, curved figures, executed while the body assumes a graceful, natural poise, is increasing in popularity here, and will be generally adopted by fancy skaters on this side of the Atlantic.

Two years ago Mr. Brokaw made a study of skating in Europe, and in speaking of the differences in American and European styles says: "The difference between the Continental and the American skating is not so much a matter of schedule as it is of performance. Both schools have similar sets of moves and figures, the former making them larger and always in the form of eights, while the latter makes them smaller and more infield, each, however, demanding correct tracings on the ice and proper executions at all turns. The Continental style also demands ability to harmonize and combine all possible combinations of figures into a complete performance set to music. Here, originality and skill have an opportunity, for the skater may invent and combine any and all moves which he thinks will have the most telling effect.

"At one time the American schedule had a final section which corresponded somewhat to this, which was called specialties, but in recent years it has been dropped, as the programme was already too long. Foreign and American skaters have seldom met in figure skating, probably because of the difference in the two styles, but when they have met the Americans have given the better account of themselves."

In speaking further of figure skating Mr. Brokaw emphasized the importance of the proper kind of skates.

"The runner must not be too flat or too sharp rocked for a comfortable balance on long curves."

Nowadays, with the round toe, the stanchion skate which Mr. Brokaw was instrumental in bringing back to this country, whence it originated almost fifty years ago, and which was designed and used by Jackson Haines, a famous skater of the "sixties," the standard of skating is beginning to improve under the instruction of competent teachers, so that the recent carnival at Boston brought together skaters from the United States and Canada, and all skating in the same style and using the same style of skate. The question of skating shoes is of the utmost importance, for unless the ankles are properly supported and at the same time flexible the skater will be hampered by not being able to stand up, or if the leather is too stiff and tight ankle straps are used the ankle action will be impeded.

"America," says Mr. Brokaw, "which once led the world in the art of figure skating, beginning with the Philadelphia Skating Club in 1849, and followed by the New York and Boston skating clubs in 1863, and brought forth such famous old-timers as Col. Page, Peter Wever, and the Van Hook brothers from Philadelphia; E. H. Barney, John Berry, and the Fullers from Boston, and later E. B. Cook, Jackson Haines, Callie Curtis, and E. T. Goodrich from New York, is now given over to the game of hockey.

"Now, under the influence of some of the European countries who learned their skating from our early American skaters, the various branches of the art have been systematized and arranged so that we now have what are called the school figures, what might be called the grammar of skating; the free skating is like the 'rhetorical or literary expression of the performers' character and power in true artistic form.' The importance of the school or prescribed figures is therefore at once apparent; as rhetorical excellence is impossible without grammatical accuracy, so good skating begins with the mastery of the school figures. This is, of course, the international style of skating, meaning that style which obtains in all the European countries, America being the only country not in the International Skating Union. It is time for us to train skaters in the form where they may meet foreigners on their own ground and in their own style. The Canadians have adopted the international style and the skating of the Minto Four at the recent carnival in Boston was an interesting event."

The international style of free skating as performed by Mr. Brokaw includes spread eagles, pirouettes, spectacles, jumps, spins, dance steps, grapevines, original moves, waltz, and many other figures. Mr. Brokaw believes that in a few seasons the Continental style will be in vogue generally in this country. He is one of the leading exponents of this style in this country and a great skating enthusiast. Mr. Brokaw's extensive work on the sport, "The Art of Skating," (Scribner's,) traces the history and development of the sport from its beginning to the present day.

March 19, 1911

## SKATERS WIN TITLES.

### Miss Weld and Norman Scott Champions in International Competitions.

NEW HAVEN, Conn., March 21.—Miss T. Weld of the Skating Club of Boston won the ladies' championship of the International Union of America in the recently adopted international style of figure skating on the Arena Rink here to-day, and while this honor was retained for the United States, the figure championship of America went to a foreign competitor, Norman Scott of the Winter Club of Montreal being the winner. In both events the competition was keen, and the judges reached their decisions only after a long conference. Miss Weld defeated Miss E. E. Rotch, a fellow-club member, by a slight superiority in free skating, both having scored equal points in the prescribed figure skating. In this event Mrs. Raymond Townsend of this city, a novice entrant, was placed third and complimented by the judges on her skill in completing the figures.

For the men's championship, Mr. Scott won over E. W. Howland of Boston by the decision of two of the three judges and on scoring he had a half point margin. N. W. Niles, also of the Boston Club, was third.

The judges were Irving Brokaw and J. C. Cruikshank of New York and G. H. Brown of Boston. In the non-competitive exhibitions of figure skating, Louis Rubenstein of Montreal and Dr. A. G. Keane of New York, winner of the American championship in 1905 in the old style of skating, participated. Medals were the prizes.

The pair skating championship, the first contest of the kind to be held in this country was won by Miss Chevalier and Norman Scott of Montreal. Miss Weld and N. W. Niles of Boston took second place, and Miss Crocker and E. M. Howland of Boston third.

March 22, 1914

IRVING BROKAW
FREE SKATING MOVE

MR. & MRS. IRVING BROKAW IN PAIR
SKATING SPIRAL

Sherwin Badger was the U.S. figure skating champion for five consecutive years, 1920–1924.

U.S. women's figure skating champion Maribel Vinson, shown here in 1933, was killed in the 1961 plane crash that took the lives of the entire U.S. figure skating team. She won nine titles: 1928–1933, and 1935–1937.

# *Building Skating Rinks for the Latest Fad*

## Brine Circulating Through Coils of Pipe Beneath the Ice Gives a Firm Surface That Is Planed at Intervals and Sprayed with Water to Make It Smooth

These Pipes, Through Which Brine Circulates, Are Flooded with Water Which Freezes, Forming a Smooth Skating Surface.

THE finger of Society has turned a new page in its annals of amusements. Emblazoned on the top of the sheet one sees in icy letters the name of the present favorite — skating. That the new sport—new in the sense of being considered fashionable—has become popular may easily be seen by the growing number of advertisements calling attention to the accessories so necessary, and in many cases so becoming, to the ambitious débutante. And, according to snatches of conversation overheard in streets and public conveyances, the new fad not only has pushed its predecessor, the tango craze, into obscurity, but bids fair to be a strong rival of the all-powerful patent medicine as a panacea for bodily ills.

"Run down? No wonder. You work too hard. Why don't you come over to the rink some evening? All right. To-morrow at 8:30." Or, "Suffer from indigestion? That's too bad. I'll tell you what; you need more exercise. Come

over to the rink and I'll wager we'll chase that monster out." Again, "Headache, did you say? You're too lazy. Why don't you go in for skating?"

The only one who does not seem so enthusiastic about the new pastime is the much-abused weather man. At any rate, he cannot be depended upon to do his duty, which to the impatient possesser of ice skates means but one thing—the freezing of lakes and ponds within the city limits. Indeed, so badly has he failed in his part of the work and so loud has been the clamor of the would-be skater that science has had to step in to still the cry. The result is the construction of skating rinks.

Of course it is readily understood that the process of refrigeration, the same that is used in the making of artificial ice, is the basis of this work. With this knowledge in hand, the question arose how to make and maintain a large, smooth layer of ice that would constantly be under the influence of pressure and heat. After many experiments the brine

circulating system was the one that was found to give the desired result. The details of this system are not beyond the comprehension of the man of ordinary intelligence. First of all, the floor must be made of such material as will not absorb the heat from the ice. In the majority of skating rinks the insulating medium is made up of cement and cork, the cork forming the upper layer. Over this floor are fastened at regular intervals a number of narrow beams, the supports of the brine pipes. On these, at intervals of four inches, come the lengths of iron pipes through which the brine circulates.

This brine or salt water is cooled to a degree of many points below 32 degrees Fahrenheit, the freezing point of water in the refrigerating system in the engine room. It is then pumped up into a "header," which is a large pipe laid at one end of the rink, perpendicular to the brine pipes on the floor. This header is connected with each brine pipe, so that when the brine is pumped in it immedi-

This Photograph Shows the Same Rink After the Ice Has Formed Over the Pipes.

ately rushes through the openings leading into the pipes, or coils, as they are called. The brine is continually pumped down the length of the coils. When it reaches the other end of the rink it enters another large main and is returned to the engine room, where it is re-cooled and again made ready to enter the header.

While the brine flows through the pipes laid on the floor it cools them. For instance, if the brine pumped through them has a temperature of 15 degrees, it will, while rushing through the pipes, take away any heat they might contain and bring them down near to the 15-degree point of heat—or should we say cold? The coils are now ready to have the ice formed over them. This is a very simple procedure, involving only the spraying of water. As soon as the water comes in contact with the cold pipes it freezes, and after the coils are sufficiently flooded there is an even layer of ice, usually about three or four inches thick. The brine is kept circulating through these coils just as long as the floor is in use, keeping the ice firm and even.

Of course there is a great deal more to the work than is here described. The engineer must, for instance, take into consideration the weather conditions and the amount of bodily heat given off by the skater, which tends to melt the ice. According to experts, women give off more heat than men. The explanation of this may be found in the mode of their dress, the skirt directing the heat to the floor. This, however, does not present such a problem as the ice scraped up by the skates. Usually the problem is solved by having a shaving plane driven over the rink. After being swept in this man-

ner the ice presents a rather rough appearance. This is remedied by spraying a thin film of water over it, which freezes once more into a smooth surface. All this, of course, is done after a regular skating session.

There are three sessions daily—morning, noon, and evening—thus giving the business man or woman an equal chance for amusement with the pleasure-seeking daughter of the rich. The artificial ice skating season lasts from October to April; which causes one to wonder what is done to make the space and machinery pay during the Summer, for it does pay. The St. Nicholas Rink, for instance, uses its refrigeration plant for making artificial ice. The rink itself is used as a stage for boxing matches.

Apart from the mechanical side of the subject, it is interesting to note what led to the building of the first skating rink in the United States, just about twenty years ago. Skating was not a craze then, and those interested in the sport were willing to bide their time until the weather proved favorable to them. There were, however, a number of hockey clubs which needed a rink that could be frozen at will. This led to the construction of an artificial rink, which was opened to the public when not used by the professional players. Let it not be understood, however, that all rinks are capable of being used for hockey. The dimensions of a hockey rink are, roughly speaking, 80 by 200 feet. The average rink is about half this size. The rink that the Biltmore Hotel has built is about 50 by 80 feet.

It is believed that the Biltmore is but the first of many hotels to install skating rinks. With the hotels it is comparatively a simple matter. Inasmuch as

each large hotel is equipped with a refrigerating plant, the expense of machinery and labor is greatly reduced. With them the main outlay is in building the rink itself. It is only where the refrigerating system as well as the rink proper has to be considered that the matter becomes of large expenditure, perhaps $50,000 or more.

The fact that this is not appreciated is proved by the constant demand upon the refrigerating companies for rates and plans by men who have the hungry glint of gold in their eyes and but four or five hundred dollars in their pockets. There are others, however, who can take up the question of expense with perfect equanimity. Their attempts may not be as ambitious as that of the Biltmore, which made an open-air rink on the site of its Venetian gardens, but at any rate one can say with some promise of fulfillment that before long there will be a chain of skating rinks in New York almost equivalent to the tango parlors so popular and so numerous just a short time ago.

One feels rather sorry for those poor individuals who have spent their energy and weight in mastering the newest dancing steps, but how they can show off their country cousins, who might have missed several beats in a hesitation waltz but are variable will o' the wisps on the ice.

At all events, let New York welcome a sport which leads to such heights of ambition as prompted one ardent follower to say to one not yet infected with the virulent germ, "Beg, borrow, or steal a pair of skates—but learn! Even if you have to practice in the iceman's cellar—learn if you want to be in the swing!"

And here you have it all in a nutshell. Turkey trot if you would be up-to-date, tango if you would be fashionable, and now skate if you would keep in the swing. It is gratifying to note, however, that the trend of popular amusements is going upward in character. According to the duration of the other fads, one is inclined to say to this one, "Here's to a longer life, but just as merry a one!" and add with a smile or sigh, as prompted by our temperaments, not by our age, mind you, "What next?"

December 26. 1915

### ACTIVE YEAR FOR CURLERS.

**Scotsmen Hereabouts Devotees of the Ancient and Honorable Game.**

It is this season of the year, when the ice is plentiful on the public parks and private club grounds, that the true Scottish sportsman, emigrant or descendant, comes into his own. Winter provides for him the opportunity to indulge in that ancient and honorable game, curling. The game is both ancient, because it dates back at least five centuries, and just as honorable because Scottish gentlemen and royal families have been patrons of it, including Prince Albert, the late King Edward, and now, King George V.

Hereabouts in the metropolitan district the St. Andrews Golf Club of Mount Hope, and the Caledonia Club of this City have so far been prominent in the sport this Winter and last week completed the annual competition for the Utica Cup. Included in the Grand National Curling Club of America's schedule of events for the rest of the season, and several more matches for interstate, sec-

and not golf or soccer football, that is nearest and dearest to the heart of a Scotsman. From some of the words used in its play, such as kuting, rink, bonspiel, and tee, inference has been drawn that it was introduced into Scotland from the Low Countries, but this assumption is denied strenuously by historical facts. Although it is now played in almost every country where ice abounds, there is always a Scottish ring about the sport, much more so than golf, and curling is regarded correctly as the national sport, the title generally given to it by its devotees being "Scotland's gin game." tional and local titles, in addition to such fixtures as the W. Fred Allen Memorial Medal match at Utica and the Champion Rink Match at Schenectady for the Gordon Medal. The national organization is headed by F. G. Vaughen of Schenectady, and the other officers are Alexander Fraser, First Vice President, New York City; N. G. Gurley, Second Vice President, Utica; Andrew Gillies, Treasurer, New York City, and Francis Dykes, Secretary, New York City.

At first curling was a form of quoiting on the ice. A stone was used which had been rounded somewhat by the action of a river's current, and hence came the term "channel stone," still given to the device. This is known as the Kuting-Stone or Pilty-cock period of curling. Then followed the Giant or Boulder Age, when the player took a large rock from a river's bed, inserted a rough iron handle, and propelled it along the ice toward the goal. The variety of the stone in this period was wide, for although sixty-pound weapons were the minimum, many of those used weighed as much as 200 pounds. Toward the end of the nineteenth century, however, the size was reduced and a recent edict of the Royal Club in Scotland fixed the maximum weight of the stone and handle at 44 pounds, and the majority of stones now used are between 35 and 38 pounds. In Canada, and some parts of the United States, a weight of 60 to 70 pounds is the average, but many of these heavier stones have an iron or steel bottom.

The rink , or marked ice surface on which the game is played, is from thirty to fifty feet long and ten to twelve feet wide. A tee or toesse, or neitter is at each end, and inclosing this tee are two circles or broughs, one of a four-foot radius and the other of a seven-foot radius. A line, a few feet inside of each tee, is drawn across the rink; this is called the hog-score, and stones which are not propelled past this line are thrown out as useless in the scoring. Each team or side is composed of four players, one of whom, the captain is called the skip, and each player is equipped with two stones and a broom, for a broom or kowe is essential to every curling match. The lead or driver, who is the first man of the team, endeavors to propel his stone from one end of the rink to as near as possible to the opposite tee, and other members of the squad are burdened with the work of protecting the shots of fellow-players or to strike away the stone of an opponent. As the game advances it becomes more intricate, and as the stones nearest the tee are more and more surrounded and guarded it is all the harder for the opponents to strike them away from the scoring zone.

There are few winter amusements which

excite more interest among its devotees than curling, for it abounds in excitement, and a staunch curler, in the severest weather, feels no cold. It is claimed for curling that it is the healthiest of all sports, giving "birr and smeddum" to the body at the season of the year when it is most needed. And perhaps no other game, in its original form as played by the true Scot, has such a variety of technical terms and such a unique vocabulary of slang. The player will be urged by his skip to "some snoovin down the howe and chuckle gently to the patlid" or he may be ordered to "cuddle into Grannie's wing," or to "pit doon a bit sidelin' shot on 'ither side of the Wittyr." In desperation he may be implored to "come wi' a hair o' pith" or "redd the hoose." All these commands have done good service, and history relates how the last man on a team in Edinburgh once took his last stone, mindful of his orders, and with one shot knocked out of the scoring zone all five stones of his opponents and the same stroke brought five of his own team's stones within.

January 28, 1917

---

# McLEAN LOSES WORLD'S PROFESSIONAL SKATING TITLE TO MATHIESEN

## MATHIESEN BEATS M'LEAN FOR TITLE

**Outskates American at 1,500 and 10,000 Meters and Clinches Championship.**

### VICTORY BY THREE TO ONE

**Norseman Captures Every Race Except That at 5,000 Meters on Ice at Christiania.**

CHRISTIANIA, Feb. 8.—Oscar Mathiesen of this city defeated Robert McLean of Chicago, the world's ice skating champion, by two-fifths of a second in the 1,500-meter race here today. Mathiesen covered the distance in 2 minutes 27 4-5 seconds, while McLean's time was 2 minutes 28 1-5 seconds. Mathiesen also won the 10,000-meter contest in 18 minutes 39 1-10 seconds. McLean's time for this event was 19 minutes 2-5 second.

An enthusiastic crowd witnessed the events today. The King and Queen and Prince Olav were present.

McLean led throughout the greater part of the 1,500-metre race, but Mathiesen passed him near the end.

In the 10,000-metre race McLean got off first, but on the first lap he took the inner swing for the outer swing and seemed to stop for a moment. He continued leading, however, up to the last two and a half laps, when he appeared to become exhausted. Mathiesen then passed him and won by three-quarters of a lap.

The contests were held in cloudy weather, but the ice was in good condition. There was enough wind, however, today to prevent new world's records for the distances.

In the 1,500-meter event McLean started out like a whirlwind, making the first 500 meters in 0:40 5-10. This outclassed Mathiesen's world's record of Saturday, which was 0:43 3-10. But the American apparently overstrained himself in this burst of speed, and Mathiesen succeeded in passing him and winning by a fraction of a second.

In the 50-meter race on Saturday McLean led for three-quarters of the distance, but Mathiesen, with a powerful spurt, outstripped him near the end. McLean took the lead from the start in the next event at 5,000 meters, and kept it to the finish.

At the end of Saturday's contests both McLean and Mathiesen appeared to be tired. Some of the spectators loudly voiced their disappointment over the time made, as conditions for fast racing were most favorable.

According to the terms of the championship contest, four races were to be skated, and in the event of each contestant winning two events, a fifth race, at 1,800 meters, was to be held. As Mathiesen won three of the four events, it was not necessary to continue the competition, his victory in the 10,000 meter race earning him the titular honors.

McLean's failure to get more than one of the four races will surprise local followers of skating, and at the same time bear out the contentions of Mathiesen regarding his defeats by McLean in this country. The Norwegian champion

was decisively defeated by the Chicagoan in a series of races, and declared at the conclusion of the match that track conditions affected his stride, which is a bit longer than that of the American.

Mathiesen predicted at the time that he would turn the tables in a match with McLean in Norway, owing to the fact that the longer turns on the courses used there would allow him to get the full benefit of the longer stride. Mathiesen had anything but an easy time in the races of the past two days, judging from the time recorded. He won the 500-meter race with a great closing sprint, took the 1,500-meter event by

the fraction of a second, and was defeated at 5,000 meters. The only event in which he won decisively was the 10,000-meter race, in which he finished twenty seconds ahead of the American, however, while McLean held the home skater closely, the difference in course conditions undoubtedly had an effect, since McLean clearly outclassed the Norwegian in the races held in this country some time ago.

February 9, 1920

---

## CANADIAN CURLERS WIN BY TWO POINTS

*Special to The New York Times.*

UTICA, N. Y., Feb. 12.—In what proved to be the closest and keenest struggle ever waged in international curling circles, Canadian curlers today successfully defended the Gordon International Medal, winning from the United States by a score of 189 to 187. The superb play of the Heather and Lachine rinks in the afternoon round brought victory to the Canadians, the former outclassing the newly organized Syracuse club, 27—10, and the veteran Robert Lucas leading his rink to a 20—11 win over Brae Burn. By virtue of its score of 27 points, the Heather rink, skipped by N. D. McLeod, secures possession of the medal for the ensuing year.

The United States curlers led in the morning play, 1 up, 95 to 94. The morning games were evenly divided, each country taking two, while Jersey City and Victoria played a tie game at 17. The fight of the Victoria rink was one of the outstanding features of the day. Apparently hopelessly outclassed, 16 to 4, Captain McGreary and his fellow-soldiers, all ex-service men, one of whom was Captain Falkenberg, the famous Canadian ace, launched a strong attack in the closing ends and finished on even terms with the Jersey rink.

Scoring honors for the day were annexed by Dr. T. H. Farrell and his rink, composed of E. C. Hare, A. O. Foster and A. M. Johnston, who, playing against St. Lawrence, totaled the fine score of 35 in the afternoon round. The Uticans finished 21 up over their opponents, and the Country Club of Brookline ran a close second on a neighboring sheet of ice, finishing 11 up over Caledonia. Schenectady, Syracuse and Boston rinks fell behind, however, and Canada took the season's premier honors by one of the scantiest margins ever known in this great competition.

February 13, 1920

---

## Sports

### Cutting a Dash on Runners.

The revival of popular interest in figure skating, as reflected in the success that attended the championship tournament in the Iceland Rink on Friday, Saturday and yesterday, is of no small significance, especially to those men who have labored during the last fifteen years to place the United States on an equal footing with European countries in this sport. The fact that some twenty skaters, all of them trained and skillful in the international style of figure skating, were attracted to the title events from all parts of the country, is encouraging evidence of America's increasing proficiency in the most beautiful of ice sports.

In 1906 Irving Brokaw, then the leading figure skater of this country and now the honorary President of the New York Skating Club, returned to the United States from the international championships determined to make far-reaching reforms in the American figure skating style. Although he was the premier performer in this country, he had found himself handicapped in Europe by the fact that his experience had been gained under the restrictions that bound the sport here in those days. The area of ice covered was a circle not larger often than the top of a barrel; the skaters rivaled one another in their efforts to sink their blades into the ice; the hands and arms were kept strictly at the side, and the figures were small and miniature rather than broad and sweeping.

Mr. Brokaw received able assistance from other Americans in his campaign for reform, some of his most effective help coming from George H. Browne, of the Boston Skating Club, James A. Cruikshank of the New York Skating Club, and Bror Meyer, a European champion who has been teaching in this country for the last ten years. Finally, in 1914, the European, or international, style was introduced in this country and slowly standardized, from Cohasset, Mass., to St. Paul, Minn., two of the municipalities that were represented in last week's championships.

The emancipation of American skaters from the former restrictions occurred only six years ago and the ensuing time has been too short to develop any serious contenders for the world's title. Sweeden, Russia, Austria and Bavaria, among others, lead the world in this respect,

and doubtless will continue to lead it, even if figure skating is made a part of the Olympic program at Antwerp this Summer, as is now proposed. But with the United States on a nearly equal footing, the friends of figure skating in this country have reason to view the future with greater confidence than ever before.

March 22, 1920

---

Weld Is Second on Points in Skating, but Is Placed Third.

#### American Skaters Disappointed.

The Americans displayed considerable disappointment over the awards in the skating competitions for women last night. An examination of the judges' scores this morning showed that on the total points made Miss Therese Weld of Boston, Mass., should have had second place. Her total was 898 points against Miss Norin's 887 and Miss Tulin's 913½. However, by the complicated award system used, each judge picked first, second and third choices in addition to estimating the number of points scored, and Miss Weld was put third. Each of the competing nations had a judge except America.

Nathaniel W. Niles of Boston competed in the school figure skating this morning against ten of the best skaters in the world, including Ulrich Salchow, the champion. Norway, Sweden and England each had two entries, and Italy, Switzerland, France, Finland and America one each. The awards will be made after the free skating contests, which probably will be decided tomorrow.

April 26, 1920

# HOCKEY HONORS ARE WON BY CANADIANS

## Dominion Skaters Defeat Swedish Team in Olympic Final by Score of 12 to 1.

### SECOND PLACE IN DOUBT

#### Three Combinations, Including United States Entry, to Play for Runner-Up Position.

ANTWERP, April 26 (Associated Press.)—The Canadian hockey team tonight defeated the Swedish team in the Olympic games championship final by the score of 12 to 1.

In the competition among figure skating pairs Finland won first place, Norway took second, England was third and the United States placed fourth.

The American team was disappointed, but not chagrined, at its defeat by Canada last night.

"It was anybody's game until near the finish," said Manager Fellowes, "but the better team won."

One hockey expert declared Europe had "never seen a game equal to it."

All competitors are invited to a charity exhibition next Friday. King Albert probably will be present, but it is possible the members of the American team will not participate, as many wish to visit the battle zones of France and Belgium before returning to the United States.

The one-sided victory for the hockey players of the Dominion gives them undisputed title to the championship of the 1920 Olympic Games, the start of which was made with the matches at Antwerp on Friday. After having defeated the Czechoslovaks by 15 to 0 in the first elimination round, while the American seven piled up a score of 29 to 0 over the players from Switzerland, the Canadians came back Sunday night and defeated the United States team by 2 to 0 after the first half had gone scoreless.

Canada's team, composed of veterans and experienced players, was constituted as follows: Forwards, Halferson, Frederickson and Goodwin; rover, Woodman; defense, Benson and Johanneson; goal, Bryan.

Sweden came through to the finals through a brilliant exhibition of hockey ability. The Swedes have been coached by Raoul Le Mat, a former Georgetown University athlete, and he has been enthusiastic about their progress in practice for the Olympic Games. In the first encounter Friday night the Swedes trounced the Belgian ice stars by 8 to 0, and on Sunday, in the semi-final round, piled up a victory of 4 to 0 over the French seven.

Although the final battle for the title has been held and won, interest in Olympic hockey will not simmer down completely until after the matches for the second prize. Under the curious Belgian system employed the runner-up is not automatically the second best team. In other words, Sweden, by reaching the final and losing to Canada's team, is not regarded as the winner of second honors. Instead a series will now be held among Sweden and the other two losers to the champion seven, which are the United States and Czechoslovakia.

According to the draw made last night, the American team will meet Sweden tonight (Tuesday), and the victor will play on Wednesday the Czechoslovaks, who have drawn the one bye.

April 27, 1920

# NILES IN FIFTH PLACE.

## American Is Excelled in Olympic Figure-Skating Contest.

ANTWERP, April 27.—Grafstrom of Sweden won first place in the men's Olympic figure skating contest tonight. Krogh of Norway, was second, Strixrud of Norway, third; Salchow of Sweden, fourth, and Nathaniel W. Niles of Boston, Mass., fifth.

April 28, 1920

# BADGER STILL KING OF FIGURE SKATERS

## Boston Youth Retains National Title in Championship Meet —Niles Second.

### MRS. BLANCHARD SCORES

#### Former Miss Weld Wins Women's Senior Honors for Sixth Time— Greensiee Leads Juniors.

*Special to The New York Times.*

PHILADELPHIA, Feb. 26.—Sherwin C. Badger, 19-year-old star of the Boston Skating Club, retained his title as men's school figure and free skating champion in the tournament held at the Ice Palace tonight, according to the official announcement of the judges.

Nathaniel C. Niles, also of Boston, was awarded second place, and Edward M. Howland, another Boston Skating Club entry, was third. C. J. Christensen of St. Paul, up until the final figures, was a strong contestant for first honors. He was placed fourth by the judges.

Mrs. Theresa Weld Blanchard won the women's senior event for the sixth time when she was declared a winner over a field of only another competitor. Mrs. A. Cramer of New York was second. Mrs. Beresford, the former English junior champion, was the only entry to defeat Mrs. Blanchard in the last six years, winning in the season of 1917-1918.

George Ferris Greensice of Boston was the choice of the judges as the winner in the men's junior championship. Raymond Harvey of New York was second, Einar Josephson of New York and Charles A. McCarthy of Chicago were tied for third. Among other strong contenders who were not awarded places were Carl Berndle of Pittsburgh and Oliver P. Tatum of Philadelphia.

The women's junior, which was unofficially announced late Friday night, was reported officially by the judges tonight. Miss Beatrice Loughran of New York was the winner. Miss Guinevere T. Knott of Boston appeared to be the popular choice for the winning honors, but due to a few falls, as a result of a recently injured ankle, Miss Knott was not at her best. The experts predict that she has all the championship qualifications. Miss Rosalie Knapp of New York was third

February 27, 1921

# *SKI-PLANING BRINGS NEW THRILL TO SPORT*

## *Lawrence Sperry Tows Boys at Cherry Valley at Sixty Miles an Hour.*

GARDEN CITY, March 9.—A new thrill was added to American outdoor sport today when Lawrence Sperry, inventor of the Sperry messenger plane, demonstrated to "movie" camera men and newspaper photographers his latest sport —ski-planing. It's a new relative to aquaplaning, only one uses an airplane and a pair of skis instead of a motor boat and water sled. Spectators crowded the links of the Cherry Valley Golf Club this afternoon and watched boys of the neighborhood being towed on skis across the snow-covered inclines of the golf park by the diminutive messenger plane At times the skis were swept along at a speed of more than sixty miles an hour.

Sperry succeeded in holding his airplane as low as five feet above the earth as he sped along the course, but was forced to rise higher when approaching the grove that lines the outer bounds of the club's property. The skiers would release their hold on the ropes tied to the wings and tail skid of the plane as they approached the trees.

To demonstrate the unusual qualities of the small plane Sperry went down the side of a forty-foot embankment, almost perpendicular, without turning over. The machine was outfitted with skids during the demonstration.

The inventor conducted successful trials yesterday at Mitchel Field, where he demonstrated how the airplanes could come within a few feet of each other without collision.

March 10, 1923

# U. S. SKATERS THIRD IN OLYMPIC GAMES

## Finland Leads on First Day With 20½ Points, Norway Has 17½, America 11.

CHAMONIX, France, Jan. 26 (Associated Press).—The men from the North, steel muscled and deep lunged, led the nations of the world in points scored at the end of the first day's competitions in the Winter Olympic Games, but the stout-hearted American skaters hold the honor of having their flag as the first national emblem flying at the top of the Olympic mast.

The Finns and Norwegians proved supreme in the distance skating, but the Americans demonstrated they were unbeatable in sprints. Charles Jewtraw of Lake Placid, N. Y., the international champion, won the 500-meter event, covering the distance in 44 seconds. Olsen of Norway captured second place, and Thunberg of Finland and Larsen of Norway divided third honors.

In the 5,000 meters Thunberg of Finland, the world's speed skating champion, showed much superiority over the others, winning with comparative ease in 8 minutes 39 seconds, his time being the best of all the competitors.

Julius Skutnabb, also of Finland, took second place, covering the distance in 8 minutes 48 seconds in his heat with Valentine Bialis, America. Larsen of Norway was third.

The score by points as given out at the end of the contests was: Finland, 20½; Norway, 17½; United States, 11; Sweden 1.

**American Style New.**

The American sprinters, with less physical power than the hardy Northerners, Thunberg and Olsen, and somewhat short in their training, not only finished first and eighth in the 500 meters, but had the Norwegian, Finnish and Swedish coaches gaping at the new system of ice sprinting which was introduced in Europe today. The swing of the arms used by both Jewtraw and Joe Moore enabled them to gather momentum and get into their stride promptly, and is likely to cause a change in method among the European short distance men.

It is thought that perhaps a little more judicious rating of Bialis's race would have brought the American closer to Thunberg's mark and gained a few more points for the United States. He got away very fast and set a terrific pace, doing the 400 meters on the second and third laps in 40 flat, but was dead on his feet in the last 500 and finished by sheer grit alone.

The 1,500 meters and 10,000-meter events will be contested tomorrow. The men who made the fastest time in today's race will be matched in the longer distances. Thrills are promised when Jewtraw meets Olsen, and Thunberg meets Larsen in the 1,500, and when Thunberg and Skutnabb, Larsen and Moens fight it out in the 10,000-meter event.

The weather was cloudy and the temperature a little below the freezing mark. The ice was in fair condition, but had a tendency to soften.

Thirty-one men were entered in the 500-meter event, necessitating fifteen heats. The rules provided that the skaters start from the same line on parallel tracks ten feet apart, the competitor holding the inside track at the start switching to the outside on the back stretch and vice versa. Time alone is taken into consideration in figuring the winners of the Olympic ice events and the man finishing second in a fast heat is placed ahead of the winner of a slower heat for the final reckoning, as there are no semifinals. The track on which the speed events are contested measures 400 metres.

**Wins in Fast Finish.**

Jewtraw defeated Gorman of Canada in the fifteenth heat of the 500-meter event. His time of 44 seconds flat was the best of any heat skated and under the rules made him the winner of the event. The Canadian was very nervous, but after three false starts got away better than Jewtraw. The American, on the outside track, lost ground for the first 200 meters but began catching up to Gorman on the backstretch. The men raced around the last turn elbow to elbow and Jewtraw won with a terrific burst of speed down the stretch. The American victory was very popular.

Joe Moore of New York was the only other American to get among the first ten, finishing in a tie for eighth. Harry Kaskey of Chicago, American national champion, was twelfth, and William Steinmetz of Chicago, fourteenth, the latter being the only American to lose his heat.

Thunberg, the Finnish skater, who was the favorite for the event, stumbled at one turn and got out of his stride for something like ten yards. Without this mishap he would have been close to Jewtraw's time.

The Americans were all in good shape and their followers feel gratified at the good account they gave of themselves.

**Moore Wins Heat.**

Joe Moore of New York defeated Irik Blomgren of Sweden in the first heat, winning easily by twenty yards in 45 3-5 seconds; Harry Kaskey of Chicago beat Marcel Moens of Belgium, winning the sixth heath in 47 seconds; William Steinmetz of Chicago lost to Oscar Olsen of Norway in the twelfth heat in 44 1-5 seconds. It was the best time of the day up to the thirteenth heat. Steinmetz's time was 47 1-5 seconds.

Thunberg, the Finnish star, won the 5,000-metre race, the second event of the games contested here this afternoon. Thunberg's time, which won the event for him was 8 minutes, 39 seconds.

Julius Skutnabb, Finland, was second lowest in the time made; Larsen of Norway, was third; Marcel Moens, Belgium, fourth; Harold Stroem, Norway, fifth, and Valentine Bialis, America, sixth. The standing of the other Americans was: Richard Donovan, eighth; Charles Jewtraw, thirteenth and William Steinmetz, fourteenth.

**Donovan Also Scores.**

Donovan defeated Wanhazebroeck, Belgium, in the fourth heat. The time was 9 minutes 5 3-5 seconds. Donovan was all in at the finish and collapsed after crossing the line.

The heat between Skutnabb and Bialis was most boldly contested in the 5,000 meters. Bialis used himself up in the early stages, setting a terrific pace from the start as if the race were a mere sprint. He led until the next to the last lap. but had nothing left when Skutnabb challenged as the finish neared.

Jewtraw, America, was defeated by Harold Stroem, Norway, in the third heat. The time was 8 minutes 54 3-5 seconds. Stroem, holder of the world's record for this distance, won in easy style from the Lake Placid star, who apparently was tired from his hard race this morning. Jewtraw's time was 9 minutes 27 seconds

In the sixth heat Julius Skutnabb, Finland, defeated Valentine Bialis. America. The time was 8 minutes 48 seconds. The time of the Saranac Lake skater was 8 minutes 55 seconds. William Steinmetz of Chicago won the eleventh heat in 9 minutes 35 seconds. Leon Quaglia, France, defeated Gorman of Canada in the first heat. His time was 9 minutes 8 3-5 seconds. The Canadian skater quit after going one mile, apparently in distress.

January 27, 1924

# FINLAND'S SKATERS WIN OLYMPIC TITLE

## Triumph When Skutnabb Takes 10,000-Meter Race and Thunberg the 1,500.

## REGISTER 48½ POINTS

## Norway Has 39½ and America, Failing to Score on Last Day, Is Third With 11.

## MOORE DEFEATS CANADIAN

CHAMONIX, France, Jan. 27 (Associated Press).—Finland carried off first honors in the speed skating events of the Winter Olympic Games, Norway came second and the United States third.

There were four events contested yesterday and today. Charles Jewtraw of Lake Placid, N.Y., international champion, captured the 500-meter sprint in 44 seconds; Thunberg of Finland won the 1,500 and 5,000-meter events, while Skutnabb, also of Finland, took the 10,000-meter event.

The scoring of points was: Finland 48½, Norway 39½, United States 11, Sweden 1.

Today the Finns and Norwegians had it virtually all their own way in the 1,500 and 10,000-meter races. The American skaters failed to add a single point to their count of Saturday. America's 11 points were scored on that day through Jewtraw's victory and the capture of sixth place by Bialis in the 5,000 meters.

Thunberg, the world champion, was easily the star of the meet. He showed ease of motion and smooth action, reeling off lap after lap, apparently without exertion, in 42 seconds in the distance races, the laps being 400 meters around. His two victories came without his having to extend himself to the limit of his speed, and seemingly he finished second in the 10,000 meters only out of courtesy to his compatriot Skutnabb.

### American Stars Popular.

The American boys were very popular throughout the games, their unassuming behavior making them great favorites with the crowd. The games were a success from every standpoint, the attendance was large, the weather conditions ideal and the ice as hard as flint.

In the 1,500 meters the Americans made rather a poor showing, failing to get a single man in the point earning column. Norway and Finland divided the honors, Norway getting four men in the first six. In winning this event Thunberg covered the distance in 2 minutes 20 4-5 seconds, coming within four seconds of Mathiesen's world record.

Larsen, Norway, was second: Moens, Norway, third; Skutnabb, Finland, fourth; Stroem, Norway, fifth; Olsen, Norway, sixth; Harry Kaskey, Chicago, seventh; Charles Jewtraw, Lake Placid, and Joe Moore, New York, tied for eighth; Gorman of Canada was tenth and William Steinmetz, Chicago, eleventh.

Kaskey made the fastest time of the four Americans—2 minutes 30 seconds flat. Jewtraw and Moore tied for eighth place in 2 minutes 31 3-5 seconds, while Steinmetz covered the distance in 2 minutes 36 seconds.

### Moore Defeats Gorman.

Moore defeated Gorman of Canada, while Moens of Norway defeated Steinmetz. Olsen defeated Jewtraw in 21 minutes 29 1-5 seconds.

In the first heat of the 10,000 meters Joe Moore defeated Harry Kaskey, the winner's time being 19 minutes 36 1-5 seconds, against the loser's 19 minutes 45 1-5 seconds. Numerous scratches brought the two Americans together, and each fought as hard as though pitted against a representative of another nation. Both were very tired at the end.

Stroem of Norway defeated Valentine Bialis, Saranac Lake, with 18 minutes 183-5 seconds to his credit, as compared with Bialis's 18 minutes 30 4-5 seconds.

Paulsen, Norway, won from Richard Donovan's, Saranac Lake, with 18 minutes 13 seconds, against Donovan's 18 minutes 57 seconds.

The results of the 10,000 meters follow: Skutnabb, Finland, first. Time—18 minutes 4 4-5 seconds. Thunberg, Finland, second, 18 minutes 7 4-5 seconds; Larsen, Norway, 18:12 1-5; Paulsen, Norway, 18:13; Stroem, Norway, 18:18 3-5; Moens, Norway, 18:19.

The standing of the Americans in this event was: Bialis, eighth; Donovan, ninth; Moore, twelfth; Kaskey, thirteenth. France failed by two seconds to get into the scoring column, when Quaglia finished seventh, behind Moens. The entire stand cheered the Frenchman in his desperate effort to score a point for France, but he just failed to make it.

January 28, 1924

# U. S. HOCKEY TEAM BEATS FRANCE, 22-0

## Shows Fast Attack in Olympic Game at Chamonix—England Conquers Belgium.

## CANADA WINS BY 33 TO 0

## Scores Almost at Will in Defeating Switzerland—Norwegian First In Ski Marathon.

CHAMONIX, Jan. 30 (Associated Press).—Hockey, skiing, fancy skating and curling occupied the attention of contestants in the Olympic Winter sports today. The Canadian hockey team defeated Switzerland, 33 to 0; England defeated Belgium, 20 to 3, and the United States won from France, 22 to 0.

Thus Canada, by defeating the three nations opposed to her in the upper half of the draw, has already earned the right to play against the winner in the lower half, in which the United States and England are tied for first place with two victories each The tie will be broken tomorrow, when these two teams meet for a decision.

Canada has given an impression of irresistible strength in all the hockey matches. The United States team has done well, but in one period today. against France, faltered badly. Manager Haddock read the riot act to the boys, because he seemed to think they

were content to fight for second place, which he told them was thoroughly un-American. They promised to show a brand of hockey against England tomorrow that would keep the spectators wide awake.

The teams in the hockey games tomorrow are paired as follows: United States vs. England, 10 A. M.; Belgium vs. France, 11:30 A. M.; Sweden vs. Czechoslovakia, 2:30 P. M. The only other event on the program is the figure skating for couples, in which Niles and Mrs. Blanchard will represent the United States.

A feature of today's games was the ski marathon race, in which thirty-four contested, representing eleven countries. The Americans decided not to start because of lack of practice. The marathon was won by the Norwegian star, Thorlief Haug, who covered the fifty kilometers in 4 hours 44 minutes and 32 seconds, remarkable time in the great snowdrifts in the mountains. In this event four Norwegians finished in the first four places, while Sweden captured the fifth and sixth places.

### Boston Man Sixth.

In the fancy skating competition for men the final choice lay between Grafstrom of Sweden and Boeckl of Austria, who were in the lead yesterday when the set figures were contested. Today the competition comprised free figure skating, with the advantage on the side of the Swedish representative. Nathaniel W. Niles of Boston was awarded sixth place and thus kept the United States third in the point standing for the Winter sports.

Great Britain defeated France in the curling competition and won the Olympic championship. Sweden was second and France third.

The standing of the nations at the end of the fifth day was as follows: Norway, 71½ points; Finland, 67½; United States, 20; Sweden 19; England, 16 Austria, 15; Switzerland, 14; France, 11; Czechoslovakia, 6; Canada, 1—total 241. Nine points have been cancelled by withdrawal of fifth and sixth places in the military competition and fourth, fifth and sixth in the curling competition.

January 31, 1924

# NORWEGIAN SKI STAR WINS OLYMPIC RACE

## Haug Captures the 18-Kilometer Speed Test From 43 Opponents in 1:14:03.

## U. S. TEAM FAILS TO PLACE

## Overby Finishes 20th, Carleton Is 31st, Haugen 34th, and Omtvedt 36th.

## ENGLAND WINS AT HOCKEY

## Ties Count in Second Period After Sweden Led by 3 to 1 and Finally Takes Match, 4 to 3.

CHAMONIX, France, Feb. 2 (Associated Press).—Forty-four skiers representing eleven nations—the largest number of competitors in any single Olympic event disputed thus far started at intervals of one minute beginning at 9:30 o'clock this morning in the eighteen-kilometer speed race.

The United States was unable to place in the Olympic ski speed race. The event was won by Haug of Norway, whose time was 1 hour 14 minutes 3 seconds. The others in the order of their finish were: Grottumsbraten, Nor-

way; Niku, Finland; Maaderlen, Norway; Landvik, Norway; Hedlund, Sweden. The results added 20 points to Norway's total, 4 to Finland's and 1 to Sweden's.

The four Americans entered in the ski race finished as follows:

Sigurd Overby of St. Paul, twentieth; time—1 hour 34 minutes 56 seconds.

Johnny Carleton, American Rhodes scholar from Dartmouth, thirty-first; time—1 hour 43 minutes 49 seconds.

Anders Haugen of Minneapolis, American national champion, thirty-fourth; time—1 hour 53 minutes 4 seconds.

Ragnar Omtvedt of Grand Beach, Mich., thirty-sixth; time—2 hours 5 minutes 3 seconds.

Norway made a tremendous leap forward in the race for first place by earning 20 points out of the 25 allotted for the eighteen-kilometer ski race today. With only four events left to be decided and 100 points remaining to be distributed, Norway's victory is regarded as practically certain, as neither Finland nor the leaders are figuring in the hockey and bob sleighs, and Finland would have to win the great majority of the 60 points yet to be allotted for the two remaining ski events in order to tie Norway for first place.

### Norwegian Stars Excel.

This is unlikely, as the Norwegian ski jumpers have been beating, in the training, every Finlander engaged in the same event. Thams of Norway making one leap of 53 meters and clearing 50 meters regularly, while the best any of the Finlanders has done is around 45 meters.

The other ski events and two more heats in the bobsleighs remain to be disputed tomorrow. Switzerland's team came in first in the bobsleighs today, covering the 1,444 metres course in two trials in a total of 2 minutes 53.99 seconds. Major Broome's British crew was second. There was no American entry. Belgium was third at the conclusion of the two heats today, while France was fourth, Horton's British team fifth and Italy sixth.

Six crews were forced out of the race due to accidents. The chute has an 11 per cent. grade with eighteen sharp turns. Alfred Guldener, a member of the second Swiss crew, broke a leg when the bob overturned. It was the fifth accident on the chute, as four mishaps occurred while the crews were training. The British hockey team defeated Sweden this afternoon, 4 to 3. The match was the most closely disputed of the Olympic tournament, the British winning in the last two minutes after the score had been tied at 3—all in the second period. The Swedes at one time led by 3 to 1, but could not keep up the pace.

By its victory the British team gains third place in the standing of the eight nations entered in the hockey competition, while Sweden takes fourth. France and Czechoslovakia have decided not to play off their tie for fifth and sixth places, and will divide the three points allowed for the two places.

### Rival Teams Practice.

First and second positions will be decided by the American-Canadian match tomorrow. The Canadian and American teams took a final light workout after the Swedish-British match, merely practicing combination work and shooting at the goal. The odds against the Americans receded this afternoon from 2 to 1 to 7 to 5.

If comparisons mean anything, it may be pointed out that Canada defeated Great Britain, 19 to 2, while the Americans won against the same team, 11 to 0. The scores of both finalists against Sweden were practically identical—Canada 22 to 0, the United States 20 to 0.

The Americans' hockey is more spectacular, but is weaker because of that very fact. Although both Drury and Abel are considered individually to have no superior on the Canadian team—perhaps even no equal—their very individuality is their weakness, for the Canadians play like the proverbial well-oiled machine.

Harry Drury of Pittsburgh, star centre, is the leading scorer on the American sextet, having accounted for 22 of the 72 American goals scored in four games. Clarence J. Abel, brilliant St. Paul player, is second with 15 goals. Abel's great work in taking the puck down the ice single-handed and scoring from difficult angles has been one of the features of the American team's play.

Willard W. Rice of Boston is third in line for scoring honors, with 13 goals. Irving W. Small of Boston, captain of the American team, and Justin J. McCarthy of Boston, each have scored eight, and Frank Synnott of Boston, first line substitute, has scored six goals.

The weather, which threatened to become milder during the latter part of the Canada-England match, has hardened again. A northerly wind was blowing today and the forecast for the next forty-eight hours was "clear and cold."

February 3, 1924

# CANADA BEATS U. S. IN HOCKEY FINAL, 6-1

## Captures Olympic Championship in Fast and Furious Contest at Chamonix.

## TEAM PLAY BRINGS VICTORY

### Winners Co-ordinate Attack and Smother Brilliant Efforts of Americans.

## DRURY SCORES LONE GOAL

### Dashes Down Ice and Tallies Single-Handed—Switzerland Takes Bobsleigh Honors.

CHAMONIX, France, Feb. 3 (Associated Press).—Canada won the blue ribbon event of the 1924 Olympic Winter games by defeating the United States today, 6 to 1, in the final of the hockey series. It was a fast and furious contest from start to finish. Ten Olympic points are thus added to Canada's total.

The American team went down with flying colors when the referee, Paul Loicq of Belgium, blew his whistle at the end. The sixtieth minute saw the roughest hockey struggle ever fought in Europe. The Americans were physically exhausted and stumbling from fatigue.

The Canadians, victors though they were, fully realized they had been through a real hockey match, but the indomitable courage, brilliant individual play and uncanny stick handling of the Americans could not prevail against the smooth clocklike combination work of the sextet from the Dominion.

There was some claim that the Canadians scored three of their goals from offside, and that 3 to 1 in the score represented in reality the respective merits of the teams, but this was not the referee's view of it.

Small, Drury and Abel starred for the United States. No one stands out prominently among the Canadians. That is why they won. The Canadians were transformed into a well-oiled machine. Watson's name may appear oftener than those of his colleagues in the scoring column, but in each instance he was merely the last link in the combination, as Smith, McCaffery to Watson, or Munro, Smith to Watson, and into the net was the prevailing system.

**Drury Breaks Loose.**

On the other hand, Drury, who scored the lone goal for the United States, did so after a single-handed run down the ice, which ended successfully, unlike many other attempts. There was much clever handling of the sticks and artful dodging by the Americans, but Munro and Ramsay of the Canadians smothered a majority of the tries.

There was no love lost between the rival teams; that was evident from the moment play began. This was partly due, it was said, to the statement of one of the Canadians several days ago that the United States would be defeated by 10 or 12 goals to 0. The game had not proceeded more than two minutes when Watson was bleeding from the nose and Rice was stretched out by the stick in Smith's hand. Several of the men were ruled off for rough tactics.

The Americans were first to appear on the ice, at 2:35 P. M. They received a great ovation from the spectators numbering several thousand, the largest gathering of the games. A special train came from Paris last night with hundreds of Americans and British enthusiasts purposely for this match alone.

The Canadians received a noisier welcome when they came out five minutes later. Some of this was due to the vociferous encouragement from Great Britain's hockey team and its supporters, who were all gathered in one section of the stand.

The weather was ideal, clear and cold, and the ice was fast and hard. The Americans won the toss and chose to defend the western goal, the Canadians playing with the bright sun in their eyes in the first period.

Munro, the Canadian captain, and Small, captain of the Americans, received final instructions from Referee Loicq in the center of the rink. There was considerable wrangling over the referee's interpretation of body checking, which delayed the start for several minutes. Finally at 3 o'clock, Smith secured the puck in the first face-off and passed it to Watson, who charged Abel and went flying to the ice after twenty seconds of play. He was knocked out for a minute or two. There was blood in every player's eye after Watson resumed, and many of the European players shouted, "Rugby."

**Both Use Five Men.**

The play up and down the rink was lightning fast, and for five minutes neither team had any advantage. Both played only five men for two minutes, while Smith and Abel were off. Finally McCaffery and Smith got clear and went down the ice together. Smith passed to Watson, who shot a goal, the puck rebounding off McCarthy's skate as he was covering McCaffery in front of the net.

Watson was used up from body checking and was taken off. McMunn was substituted, and Synott replaced Rice, who was bleeding after a collision with Munro. Watson came back and scored after thirty seconds with an unstoppable shot on a pass from Smith.

Drury, the American centre, secured the puck from a face-off and eluded the entire Canadian team, scoring for the United States.

McCarthy grieved greatly in the dressing room owing to his responsibility, as he believed, for the first Canadian goal when the puck struck his skate, but Manager Haddock cheered the boys up. Big Jeff Abel already had a black and blue spot over his ribs and Rice was in a bad way.

The stands cheered as the teams appeared for the second period, but Rice was weak and had to be taken off after three minutes' play, Synott taking his place. Then followed ten minutes of furious struggles, in which the men came to grips at every turn. Watson slashed Abel over the neck, and Abel countered with one on the hip, sending his adversary sprawling. Both were ruled off for two minutes.

Then Smith scored on a pass from Watson after eleven minutes of fast and furious work. McCaffery repeated after one minute on another pass from Smith. Almost immediately McCaffery was laid out, McMunn substituting, and Synott relieving McCarthy, who was also in a bad way. Smith was warned by Referee Loicq for loafing off side. A lively mix-up between Smith and Abel in the centre of the rink brought both of them a two-minute penalty. Munro closed the period with a terrific shot into the upper corner of the net, against which the American goal keeper, La Croix, had no chance.

**Small Plays Well.**

The third period was a repetition of the second so far as style of play was concerned. Small attended strictly to business and played a great game in both defense and offense. Synott, who replaced Rice, again immediately mixed it up with Munro, and both were sent off the ice for one minute.

"Remember your Olympic loyalty oath," one fair spectator shouted from the grandstand.

Cameron, the Canadian goal keeper, was called upon to stop seven shots for the goal in rapid succession from the sticks of Drury, Synott and McCarthy. Then McMunn, for Canada, eluding both Small and Abel, passed the puck to Watson, who scored the last goal after fifteen minutes of play.

**Swiss Win Bob Title.**

In the bob-sleigh competition, Switzerland was first with Great Britain second. The time for the Swiss team for the four descents down the 1,444-meter chute was 5 minutes 45 54-100 seconds, averaging nearly forty miles an hour.

The British team was captained by Major Broome. Belgium was third; France, fourth; Captain Horton's British team, fifth; Italy, sixth. All the teams today negotiated the difficult chute twice without accident.

February 4, 1924

# NORWAY WINS TITLE IN OLYMPIC GAMES

## Takes Winter Sports Championship With 134½ Points—Finland, Second, Has 76½.

## UNITED STATES IS FOURTH

### Registers 29 Tallies, but Trails Great Britain—Victors Score Heavily on Skis.

CHAMONIX, France, Feb. 4 (Associated Press).—Norway made a runaway race of the last two ski events in the Olympic Winter sports today, winning first place in the whole series with a total of 134½ points, 58 points to spare over Finland, which finished second with 76½ points.

Great Britain took third place with 30, and the United States was fourth with 29.

The Norwegians showed splendid form in all the events in which they competed. They were in admirable physical condition and displayed a great efficiency in all branches of Winter sports, with absolute supremacy in the ski events.

The ski jumping contest has aroused considerable dissension and there is keen disappointment, certainly among the Americans, over the decision of the jury in placing Anders Haugen of Minneapolis, the American national champion, fourth—behind Thams, Bonna and Haug, all of Norway.

**Haugen Jumped Furthest.**

Haugen, the American star, led the field with a jump of 50 meters, while Thams and Bonna each covered 49 meters, and Haug 44½. In reaching the decision the judges took into account style and action, whereby Thams was allotted 18.96 points, Bonna 18.68, Haug 18.00 and Haugen 17.91.

General disapproval of the decision was voiced by a large section of the sporting fraternity assembled here, and Mayor Leach of Minneapolis has declared his intention of filing a protest. It was expected that Haugen would be placed after Thams, whose jump was perfect, but that he would receive no better than fourth was not contemplated for a moment. The jury was composed of a Norwegian, a Frenchman and a Czechoslovak.

Later Mayor Leach withdrew his expressed intention of entering a protest against the decision of the judges in the ski-jumping contest, remarking to The Associated Press correspondent: "I do not like the decision at all, but, after consideration, I have decided not to file a protest. There are rules and regulations governing such contests. A protest on the question of the interpretation of these rules by experienced men would not get us anywhere. But it certainly is tough."

Albert Stenge, the Czechoslovak judge, said, regarding the competition: "Haugen's form and style were very poor. He could not begin to compare with the three Norwegians placed ahead of him. The American threw all style aside and bent all efforts only upon distance.

"You saw what happened a few minutes after the competition, when Thams, jumping alone, cleared 57½ meters in an exhibition, and likewise Bonna. As far as Haug's jump of 44½ meters was concerned, itw as perfection itself."

Some of the Americans left Chamonix this evening. Haugen, Overby, Batson and Lein proceeded to Paris, and will return to the United States immediately. Batson and Lein came all the way from America to take two ski jumps.

Mayor Leach will remain here for a few days, and Carleton will go to London.

Haug of Norway won the combined speed and jumps contest, with Stromstad, Norway, second, and Grottumsbraten, Norway, third. Okern of Norway was fourth, Nilsson, Sweden, fifth and Adolf, Czechoslovakia, sixth.

**Overby Is Eleventh.**

Only twenty-two men were placed, Sigurd Overby of St. Paul, Andres Haugen and Johnny Carleton, American Rhodes scholars from Dartmouth, being eleventh, twenty-first and twenty-second respectively.

Le Moine Batson of Minneapolis was placed fourteenth, and Harry Lein of Minneapolis sixteenth in the distance ski jumps out of twenty-six placed.

The Olympic Winter sports just concluded are described by those who attended them and those who have taken part as a great success, the organization of the games meeting with much praise. The lesson to be derived from the contests is that the Northern nations, Norway and Finland, will bear watching in the athletic events next July at Colombes, for it is understood that their representatives are training hard, with a determination to win.

February 5, 1924

## OLYMPIC CHAMPION WINS.

Mme. Jaross Szabo, winner in the fancy-skating events in the Olympic games at Chamonix, France, has just won the European championship for couples. Skating on her home rink in Vienna with Louis Wrede, another Austrian, she won in the final with a total of 11 1-5 points. Mile. Andre Joly, champion of France, and Pierre Brunet of the French Federation of Winter Sports Organizations, were second with 11 points.

The competition in this event was the closest that ever has been seen in the European championships, the judges said. It was only after a long deliberation that they were able to come to a decision. The work on the ice was closely inspected, and only in the school figures was there the slightest difference in the skating, the officials stated.

Mile. Joly performed better than she did in the Olympics and gives promise of becoming the European champion in a few years' time. Mme. Szabo has had much more experience than her French rival, and remarked after the competition that Mlle. Joly stood a better chance of taking the European and world titles than any other skater.

March 1, 1925

### Electric Signals Will Protect Tobogganists in the Alps

GARMISCH-PARTENKIRCHEN, Bavaria, Germany, Nov. 27 (A).— Electric block signals, similar to those used on railroads, have been installed in the principal toboggan slides in this Winter resort in the Bavarian Alps.

Red and green lights operated by watchers along the slide will be used to notify the starters at the top when to allow the next toboggan-load to start down. Further safeguards have been provided by a private telephone system connecting stations along the line.

November 28, 1925

# Moore Wins, but Thunberg, Who Finishes Third, Breaks Three World's Records

**Finnish Skater Sets 3 Records, but Bows to New Yorker in 3-Mile Race in Garden.**

---

**TRAILS BY HALF A LAP**

---

**Gorman Also Finishes Ahead of Invader, Who Falters Badly in Last Half-Mile.**

---

**O'BRIEN CAPTURES TITLE**

---

**Takes 440-Yard Met. Laurels and Meyers the Half-Mile Honors Before 8,000.**

---

**By HARRY CROSS.**

Joe Moore, the New York speed boy, defeated the great Finnish skater, Clas Thunberg, in the three-mile invitation race at Madison Square Garden last night, humiliating Europe's sensational speeder by half a lap. Charley Gorman, the Canadian champion, was also a victim of Moore's speed and finished a quarter of a lap behind Moore. Thunberg was a sorry looking third and the crowd of 8,000 spectators broke into a riot of enthusiasm when Moore flashed over the line a winner.

Thunberg was a disappointment after the two-mile mark. The Finn made the pace and was leading at this point, establishing a new world's record for the distance in 6:13 4-5. The former record of 6:17 was made by Charles Fisher of Pittsburgh in 1916. Up to this point Moore laid behind the champion and did not extend himself.

The three-mile course covered forty-two laps of the Garden track. When six laps from the finish the foxy New York boy suddenly shot to the front, with Gorman following him. They rushed past Thunberg so fast that the Finn looked as if he were standing still.

**Moore Opens Big Gap.**

Moore's skating was so fast that he soon opened a big gap between himself and Gorman. Moore had just started. He had reserved all his stamina for this burst of speed, which was perfectly timed. On and on sped Joe, not once looking back to see where the other two champions were. Joe could tell by the outcry from the spectators that he was doing just what the crowd had expected of him.

Thunberg followed a steady pace all the way and did not uncover the sprint which Moore had hidden in his flashing skates. Moore's time for the three miles was 9:25, which was slower than the world's record of 9:13 3-5, held by Fisher.

The Finn, who was such a sensation at the last Olympic Games, did not show the fire or dash of a champion. Although he led in 36 out of the 42 laps, he did not have the driving finish which brought Moore home in front.

However, although tasting bitter defeat, Thunberg had the satisfaction of setting, in all, three new records. In addition to the two-mile record, he also established new figures for 1¾ and 2½ miles, his times at these points being 5:25 4-5 and 7:03, respectively.

Thunberg took the lead at the start and set the pace. Moore dropped in behind him and Gorman trailed along in third place. The Finn cut the first quarter in 47 3-5 seconds as all three paced along easily and gracefully with long strides.

Thunberg took the turns easily and did not appear to be troubled with the fourteen-lap track. He traveled the half in 1:31 4-5 and there was no change in the positions of the skaters. Thunberg, still out in front, passed the three-quarter mile post in 2:17 3-5, and he was still making the pace at the mile mark, when he flashed past the clockers in 3:02 2-5. All three skaters were taking it rather easy and Moore and Gorman were content to let the Finn set the pace.

At the two-mile mark Thunberg flashed past with a new record, while Moore slipped and fell a few yards behind, but quickly picked up the lost distance.

**O'Brien Wins "440" Title.**

Paul O'Brien of the 181st Street Ice Palace won the 440-yard senior metropolitan championship by a narrow margin from Donald Feiger of the Brodon Ice Palace. George Pickering of the Paterson Skating Club was third. Paul Forsman got away to a good start with the gun, but after one lap he fell and was out of the race.

Eddie Meyers of the Knickerbocker Hockey Club ran away with the half-mile title event when he beat Eddie Searles of Iceland by a big margin. Paul O'Brien was third. The other contestants for the title were Sam Goldberg, Irving Jaffe, George Pickering, Roy Swankamp, Allan Potts, Leslie Boyd and William Murphy.

Elsie Muller of Iceland took her second title of the evening when she easily won the 440-yard women's metropolitan title, defeating Dot Jackson of the Van Cortlandt Park Skating Club by more than 30 yards. Previously Miss Muller had triumphed in the 220-yard metropolitan event.

The mile metropolitan championship went to Irving Jaffe, a Van Cortlandt Park skater, who took the lead early and won handily from Paul O'Brien. Eddie Meyers was third. Of the nine skaters who started six were put out of the race by spills. The winner's time was 3:30 4-5.

January 15, 1926

---

### Olympic Crowd Rebels When Swiss Ski Race Utterly Exhausts Youths on 20-Mile Trail

ST. MORITZ, Switzerland, Feb. 12 (A).—Popular feeling was aroused to a high pitch at the utter state of exhaustion of the young soldiers finishing the twenty-mile military patrol ski race today and may cause an elimination of the event from future Winter Olympic sports.

France, it is understood, is preparing to present a motion to eliminate the race at the next meeting of the International Olympic Committee.

The rules provide that contestants, carrying a rifle, rations and other field equipment, must be soldiers in active service. Many of the nations with military service requirements of a year or eighteen months had mere youths of 20 and 21 years in the event.

Gendre, a French youngster who collapsed three miles from the finish and was carried on the shoulders of his comrades the rest of the way, is reported to be delirious and to have a high fever tonight. He is a slender youth of 20. The Finns recovered quickly from the effects of the long hike and were up and around after a few hours of rest.

Norway won the event, with Finland second and Switzerland third. Two of the four members of the Finnish team collapsed after crossing the finish line and had to be carried tot a hotel, where hot grog and other stimuiants were administered.

Some of the youthful soldiers dropped exhausted in the mountain passes and others staggered over the finish line to fall headlong in the snow.

Norway's winning time over the twenty-mile course, in which the difference of altitudes between the start and finish at some points was 3,000 feet, was 3 hours 50 minutes 47 seconds. The hardy men from the Northland, fresh and erect, finished, singing the national anthem of Norway at the top of their lungs, five minutes ahead of the Finns.

February 13, 1928

---

# U. S. SKATERS LOSE IN OLYMPIC RACES

**Ballengrud, Norway, Takes 5,000-Meter Test. With Farrell and Murphy in Ruck.**

---

**THUNBERG, FINLAND, IN TIE**

---

By The Associated Press.

ST. MORITZ, Switzerland, Feb. 13. —Blond and blue-eyed men of the north swept down upon the Olympic ice today and raced away with the major honors in the first day's events of the speed skating championships.

Norway's flashy band of speed stars captured the bulk of laurels when Ivar Ballengrud skated off with the 5,000-meter race after Bernt Evensen had tied with Clas Thunberg, the famous Finnish champion,

In the 500-meter event in record-breaking Olympic time.

All told, Norway took six out of the twelve point-scoring places in the two opening events, while the United States and Finland each gathered three. But while Finland's stars gave their Norwegian rivals a keen tussle in each race, the American contingent was able to land no better than third in either feature.

### Farrell Ties for Third.

O'Neil Farrell of Chicago, the chief American threat in the 500-meter race, which was won in the last Olympics by Charles Jewtraw of Lake Placid, finished in a tie for third place, and with better racing luck might have done even better. As it was, Farrell's time of 0:43 6-10 was only two-tenths of a second behind the record shattering pace of the two winners, Evensen and Thunberg, who were clocked in 0:43 4-10, breaking Jewtraw's old record by six-tenths of a second.

Farrell was unable to score in the 5,000-meter race afterward, but two Americans placed when Irving Jaffee of New York finished fourth and Valentine Bialis, the team captain, sixth.

While a blinding snowstorm swept the racing course the skaters staged their battle against time.

Farrell, a heavy favorite in the shorter race among the Americans, was handicapped by lack of such fast pacing as Thunberg had when he was paired for his heat with Larsen, one of the Norwegian aces. The American, drawn against Bertil Backman of Finland, took the lead at the start and was forced to make his own pace all the way.

In this race Eddie Murphy of Chicago finished eighth, Jaffee eleventh and Bialis sixteenth. Farrell and Murphy both were far down the list in the 5,000-meter event.

### Gorman Is Shut Out.

Charley Gorman, the Canadian ace, was shut out in the 500 meters after being thrown off his stride by his opponent's fall, but his protest was denied. Because of this fact Gorman withdrew from the 5,000 meters event. Ross Robinson, Gorman's team-mate, was shut out in the longer race.

February 14, 1928

# JAFFEE WINS CROWN AFTER U. S. PROTESTS

### Has Best Time for 10,000 Meters When Officials Cancel Olympic Race on Soft Ice.

### THEIR DECISION REVERSED

### International Body Votes Title to American When Canada and Norway Aid U. S.

### THUNBERG ALSO IS VICTOR

### Takes 1,500 Event, With Americans Finishing Down List—Point Scoring Plan Is Abolished.

By The Associated Press.

ST. MORITZ, Switzerland, Feb. 14.—A day of bickering and dispute ended tonight with the crowning of the United States' first champion of the 1928 Olympic games. That honor fell to Irving Jaffee of New York, who was officially recognized as 10,000 meters speed-skating champion by the Executive Commission of the International Olympic Committee.

The commission's action came after Augustus T. Kirby, official representative of the United States, had protested cancellation of the race because of the soggy condition of the ice at a time when six of the contestants already had completed their heats.

The furore over the 10,000 meters event came after Clas Thunberg of Finland had captured the 1,500 meters race, the only other event on the skating program today.

### Jaffee Well in Lead.

Jaffee, by covering the longer distance in 18 minutes, 36 5-10 seconds, was leading the field and considered an almost certain winner when the race was called off by an official of the International Skating Federation. Kirby, P. J. Mulqueen, the Canadian representative, and Norway immediately protested. Kirby pointed out that Eddie Murphy of Chicago had been forced to compete in the 500 meters event yesterday in a blinding snowstorm. Both Kirby and Mulqueen were agreeable to a postponement, but vigorously complained against cancellation.

Failing to obtain a reconsideration from the federation official, Kirby took his case to the International Committee.

"We don't want to raise a row," said Kirby. "We prefer to win the race on the ice, not in committees, but this action does not seem fair to us."

### Another Race Is Listed.

After due consideration the Executive Commission approved a proposal, advanced by the Marquis de Polignac of France, that Jaffee be recognized as champion in the event, but that another competition should be held before the close of the Winter sports program.

The Swiss Olympic Committee decided today to suppress official point classification by countries in the Olympics. Hereafter the winner of each event will be known as the Olympic champion, but the scores of the countries competing will not be added up.

Jaffee, competing in the first heat of the 10,000-meter race, was favored by the fact that he drew as a competitor the crack Norwegian, Bernt Evensen. The Norwegian extended Jaffee to the limit and finished only one-tenth of a second behind the flying American, who broke the tape in front by virtue of a sensational last-minute spurt.

Trailing Jaffee and Evensen were Otto Polacsek, Austria; Rudolf Riedl, Austria; Armand Carlsen, Norway, and Valentine Bialis of Lake Placid, N. Y.

### Thunberg Home in Front.

Thunberg's time in winning the 1,500-meters event was 2 minutes 21 1-10 seconds. Trailing him in order were three Norwegians, and then the four members of the American team. Their times: Bernt Evensen, Norway, 2:21 9-10; Ivar Ballengrud, Norway, 2:22 6-10; Roald Larsen, Norway, 2:25 6-10; Eddie Murphy, United States, 2:25 9-10; Valentine Bialis, United States, 2:26 3-10; Irving Jaffee, United States, 2:26 7-10; O'Neil Farrell, United States, 2:26 8-10. Charley Gorman, the Canadian ace, was twelfth.

The only other event on the day's program, the ski Marathon, was a walkaway for Sweden, which took the first three places, while Norway placed fourth and fifth. The United States was not entered.

Pete Hedlund won the event when he covered the 31 miles in 4 hours 52 minutes 27 seconds. Ole Jonson was second, 15 minutes behind Hedlund, and Volger Andersson was third.

February 15, 1928

# SKATING BODY TAKES TITLE FROM JAFFEE

### Overrules Olympic Committee and Says 10,000-Meter Race Must Be Skated Again.

### ACTS ON A TECHNICALITY

### States Protest That Gave the Crown to American Had Been Filed Too Late.

### KIRBY WILL FIGHT RULING

### But Rain May Force Cancellation of Games—Norwegians Congratulate Jaffee as Champion.

By The Associated Press.

ST. MORITZ, Switzerland, Feb. 15.—The United States today lost in committee the Olympic victory it won yesterday. It rained here today, the temperature went up and the ice has gone down so rapidly that the rest of the program may be abandoned.

Twelve hours after the executive commission of the International Olympic Committee had proclaimed Irving Jaffee of New York the 10,000-meter ice-skating champion the International Skating Federation overturned the commission's decision wiped yesterday's competition off the books and ruled that the race must be rerun.

The fact that most of the skaters already have left St. Moritz apparently precludes any satisfactory attempt to rerun the race, leaving cancellation of the event as the probably eventual course.

### Action is Believed Final

The federation's action, generally regarded as final, added one more chapter to a short but vigorous dispute which began yesterday when an official of the Skating Federaton canceled the 10,000-meter event because of unfavorable weather conditions after six of the contestants had completed their heats. Jaffee had made the besttime and was regarded as virtually certain to win first place. Cancellation of the race brought forth strenuous objections from Gustavus T. Kirby, official American representative.

An appeal to the executive commission of the International Committee ended successfully for the United Staes and Jaffee was recognized as the champion. His reign was short-lived, however, for the federation quickly overruled the commission and declared the race off.

The federations' decision was taken on technical grounds, it was revealed tonight, the American protest having reached the federation more than three hours after the race was canceled.

Kirby, however, has not accepted the federation's decision as final. Propped up in bed, the American delegate, who is suffering from a heavy cold, dictated later tonight to Dr. Otto Messerli, General Secretary of the Swiss Olympic Committee, demanding that the federation overruled and Jaffe allowed to retain the championship.

### Kirby Files "Real Protest."

"You may call this letter a real protest," Kirby told The Associated Press. "Yesterday's complaint was merely a friendly suggestion."

Kirby informed the Swiss committee that the Americans were prepared to rerun the event, but "it would be a travesty with the best competitors away."

Henning Olsen of Norway, who was responsible for the federation's action, said "it was all according to the rules and regulations of Olympic competition. I have nothing further to say."

Although Kirby's letter was taken under consideration by the Swiss Committee, members of that body said they were powerless to act, since the Skating Federation was supreme in any action taken on technical grounds.

Jaffee, who was present when Kirby's letter was transmitted, was asked whether he would race again.

### Ready to Race Again.

"This is a tough break," he replied, "but I will race them again on skates, skis or at foot-running."

Pending a decision on the latest American protest, the American skaters planned to remain in St. Moritz, but the Norwegians have returned to Oslo.

Although apparently doomed to lose his Olympic crown, Jaffee had the satisfaction today of being hailed as the champion by his closest competitors, the Norwegian skaters, who called at the American's hotel to congratulate him.

Even should arrangements be made for rerunning the race, the weather might have the final say. Unfavorable since the opening of the Winter sports competition last Saturday, the weather was worse than ever tonight. It was raining hard and there were indications that the entire Winter sports program might have to be called off.

Canada is scheduled to meet Sweden in the first of the hockey finals tomorrow, but the condition of the rinks made it extremely doubtful whether this program could be adhered to. The ski run and bobsleigh course has been badly damaged by the unseasonably warm weather.

Final decision on what is to be done probably will come at a meeting of the Swiss Olympic Committee tomorrow night.

February 16, 1928

# HEATON BROTHERS SCORE IN OLYMPICS

### Jack Takes Skeleton Bobsled Title, With Jennison Second, at St. Moritz.

### WINS BY ONLY ONE SECOND

### Speeds Almost a Mile a Minute and Misses World's Mark by 2 Seconds.

### U. S. LOSES IN SKI RACE

### Canadian Hockey Team Scores, 11 to 0, and Sweden Takes Men's Figure-Skating Crown.

By The Associated Press.

ST. MORITZ, Switzerland, Feb. 17.—Streaking down the ice at nearly a mile a minute, John Heaton of New York scored the United States' first official victory of the Olympic Winter sports competition today when he captured the skeleton bob sleigh race.

Heaton covered the distance in 60 2-10 seconds, two seconds slower than the world's record, held by the Earl of Northesk, Great Britain.

Jennison Robert Heaton, brother of the winner, was second and the Earl of Northesk was third. Entrants from France, Austria, Italy and Switzerland failed to place.

**U.S. Loses in Other Sports.**

Aside from this triumph, the first to go to America's credit in the official record books, the day saw United States competitors defeated at every turn.

Norwegians capture five of the first six places in the twelve-mile ski race, with the three American entrants far down in the list. Johann Grottensbraaten, Norwegian veteran, won first place, trailed by two of his countrymen. Then came the Finn, Veli Saarinen, followed by two more Norwegians.

Anders Haugen was the first American to finish in the field of fifty-nine. Rolf Monsen of Springfield, Mass., showed great grit in finishing the long grind although handicapped by an injured knee. The third American, Charles Proctor of Hanover, N. H., was outdistanced.

**Trail in Figure Skating.**

The Americans, Roger F. Turner, Sherwin C. Badger and Nathaniel W. Niles, failed ed to place in the figure skating, which went to Gillis Grafstroem, sole representative of Sweden, in the event. Willi Bockl, Austria, was runner up and Robert Van Zeebroeck, Belgium, was third; Karl Schaeffer, Austria, was fourth; Joseph Silva, Czechoslovakia, fifth, and Markus Nikkanen, Finland, sixth.

Canada's crack hockey team, the Toronto Grads, chosen arbitrarily for the finals, gave an impressive demonstration of strength in overwhelming Sweden in its first appearance in competition. The Canadians outclassed their rivals to win by 11 to 0. Dave Trottier, Canadian left wing, scored four goals.

Under the arrangement by which Canada was chosen for the finals, the twelve other competing nations were divided into three groups of four each, the survivor of each to

meet the Dominion sextet. Since Sweden is regarded as the best of the European teams, there appears little doubt that the Canadians will repeat their 1924 victory, in which they defeated the United States in the final. The United States was not entered in the competition this year.

England was put out of the tourney today when it bowed to Switzerland, 4 to 0.

**Miss Loughran a Favorite.**

Although America fared poorly in the men's figure skating competition, Miss Beatrix Loughran of New York is a popular favorite to win honors in the woman's division of the same event. Most of the women contestants have completed their trials.

On the basis of Heaton's victory in the skeleton event, the United States also has been made a favorite to win the team bob-sleigh race tomorrow morning.

The bob-sled races today were staged over a 1,460-yard course down the famous Cresta Run, which, with the return of cold weather, was a sheet of glittering ice. Each pilot made the trip three times, the total of the time required to negotiate the course determining the winners.

**First by One Second.**

The standing at the conclusion of the race was: Jack Heaton, 3 minutes 1 8-10 seconds; J. R. Heaton, 3 minutes 2 8-10 seconds, and Lord Northesk, 3 minutes 5 1-10 seconds.

At the end of the second run down the course the total times were; Jack Heaton, 2 minutes 4-10 seconds, and J. R. Heaton, 2 minutes 1 8-10 seconds.

Sweden's hockey team was unable to make any impression on the Canadian offensive. The losers put up a stubborn defense, however. The team work of the canadians was regarded as the best ever seen in Europe. Canada scored four goals in the first period, four in the second and three in the final.

February 18, 1928

---

## Count Kisses Jaffee Twice, Calls Him Olympic Champion

ST. MORITZ, Switzerland, Feb. 17 (P).—Sportsmanship had paved the way today for a new amity pact between the United States and France without the necessity of diplomatic intercourse when Marquis de Polignac championed America's protest at the cancellation of the 10,000 meters speed skating competition and demanded that Irving Jaffee of New York be declared the official winner. Count Clary, President of the French Olympic Committee, hailed Jaffee as the Olympic champion as far as France was concerned. The venerable and aged Count, with flowing patriarchal whiskers several inches long, kissed Jaffee on both cheeks.

"Gee, old top!" Jaffee expostulated aside. "This is worse than racing Evenson in the 10,000 meters."

February 18, 1928

---

# U. S. PLACES THIRD IN FIGURE SKATING

### Miss Loughran, Favorite, Fails to Take Olympic Crown at St. Moritz.

### 16-YEAR-OLD GIRL FIRST

### Miss Henie of Norway Is Victor, With Miss Burger of Austria Second.

### FISKE'S BOB IN THE LEAD

### Ski Jump Goes to Norway and Canada Advances in Hockey by Beating England.

By The Associated Press.
ST. MORITZ, Switzerland, Feb. 18.—The defeat of Miss Beatrix Loughran of New York, popular favorite to win the women's figure skating title, provided the chief sensation of the Olympic Winter sports program today.

The judges' decision, announced late tonight, awarded the figure skating title to Miss Sonja Henie, 16-year-old Norwegian girl, with Miss Loughran third. Second place went to Miss Fritzi Burger of Austria and fourth to Miss Maribel Vinson of Boston.

Miss Loughran's defeat was surprising in view of the fact that she finished second in the 1924 Olympics to Mme. Szaboplank of Austria, who was not entered in the competition this year.

**The Official Results.**

The results, announced tonight by the judges, follow:
1.—Miss Sonja Henie, Norway, 8 points.
2.—Miss Fritzi Burger, Austria, 25 points.
3.—Miss Beatrix Loughran, United States, 28 points.
4.—Miss Maribel Vinson, United States, 32 points.
5.—Miss Cecil Smith, Canada, 32 points.
6.—Miss Constance Wilson, Canada, 35 points.

Miss Vinson received the fourth place position over Miss Smith after three hours of deliberation by the judges. Each was credited with 32 points. Mrs. Theresa Blanchard of the United States was ninth.

Another title went to Norway today when Albert Andersen captured first place in the ski jump with a leap of 64 meters. Simund Ruud, another Norwegian, was second with a jump of 63 meters, while Rudolf Purkert, Czechoslovakia, placed third. Axel Herman Nilsson of Sweden was fourth and Sven Olaf Lundgrey, another Swede, was fifth.

**Monsen, American, Is Next.**

Then came the first American, Rolf Monsen, whose best leap was 59.50 meters. Charles Proctor and Anders Haugen, the other Americans, placed fourteenth and eighteenth, respectively.

Monsen was the star of the event. Suffering from an injured knee that would have kept most men out of competition, Monsen took the jumps in splendid form despite the pain they caused him.

Jacob Thams, Norway, leaped 73 meters, a meter beyond the world's record, but made a bad landing that disqualified him.

The United States got a half grip on its second Olympic title when the bobsleigh team, headed by William Fiske of Chicago made the best time in the first descent down the Olympic chute. Another descent will be made tomorrow, with total times determining the winner.

**Belgian Team Is Second.**

Fiske's team made its run down the chute in 1 minute 39 9-10 seconds. Belgium was second and Argentina third. England got fourth place and a tie for fifth with Switzerland, while John Heaton's American team was ninth.

Meanwhile the spectators were pondering whether the weather was going to permit completion of the Winter sports program. As the ski jump was completed the snow was melting fast and there appeared some doubt whether the competition could be finished tomorrow as scheduled.

Canada's hockey team romped through its second test, crushing Great Britain, 14 to 0. Yesterday the Canadians shut out Sweden, 11 to 0, and tomorrow will meet Switzerland, the last hurdle to be cleared by the Dominion sextet in its march to the championship.

**Six Goals at Start.**

The Canadians scored six goals in the first period, four in the second and four in the last. At no time were the Canadians extended to win. William Stanley Speechley, the British goal keeper, withstood a continuous bombardment, stopping at least 150 cannon-ball shots.

Sweden today beat Switzerland, 4 to 0. The match was regarded as one of the roughest Olympic games ever played. At one time three men of the Swedish team and two of the Swiss team were ruled off the ice, leaving only seven men on the rink. Mang of Switzerland was badly cut over the eye.

Belgium's bobsled team, which finished second to Fiske's, was led by Ernest Casimir-Lambert and Argentina's, third, was led by Arturo Gramajo. The English team led by Cecil Pim was fourth. Switzerland and Great Britain tied for fifth place.

"For a country seldom favored with snow, we didn't do so bad in ranking third out of twenty-five possible places," Gramajo of the Argentine team said.

Another Argentine team under Eduardo Hope finished eighth. It had an extremely rough trip and nearly shot off the course at one corner, but managed to right the sleigh and avert an accident.

February 19, 1928

---

# U. S. TAKES SECOND AS OLYMPICS CLOSE

### Norway Keeps Crown It Won in 1924, With Sweden Third and Finland Fourth.

### FISKE'S BOB TEAM IS FIRST

By The Associated Press.
ST. MORITZ, Switzerland, Feb. 19.—The Olympic Winter sports competition closed here tonight with Norway the winner for the second successive time, and the United States secure in second place, from which it had ousted Finland.

Canada again proved supreme in

hockey, but was ranked sixth in the complete scoring. Sweden, Finland and Austria finished in that order, after the United States and ahead of Canada.

Norway won the meet by all-around superior work in the skating and skiing events even though it did not compete in the hockey. The United States relied upon the so-called expatriates, the Heaton brothers, residing in Paris, who scored three-fifths of her points.

### Fiske's Bob in First.

William Fiske of the United States captured first place in the bob sleigh finals, with John Heaton second and Paul Kilian of Germany third. The Argentines, Gramajo and Hope, placed fourth and fifth, while Ernest Casimir Lambert of Belgium was sixth.

The fastest time in one descent made by Heaton today was 1 minute 38 7-10 seconds, exactly ten seconds slower than the world's record for the track held by Martineau of England.

When Canada defeated Switzerland, 13 to 0, today to take the crown, there were 7,000 spectators present, but at least 3,000 were "deadheads," standing on the slopes of the Alpine range.

The Canadian goal posts have been inviolate throughout the Olympic hockey competition. Canada met the best of the amateur teams of Europe and scored thirty-eight goals in all of their games. The name "Stonewall" has been given to Sullivan, the Canadian goalie, who permitted not a single disk to pass into his net.

### Sweden Gets European Crown.

Sweden's sextet gained the European championship today when it defeated England by 3 to 1. Sweden by this victory took second place in the Olympic tourney.

Miss Beatrix Loughran and Sherwin Badger of the United States took fourth place in the figure skating championship for couples today which was won by the French team of Mlle. Andree Joly and Pierre Brunet.

Miss Lilli Scholtz and Otto Keiser of Austria were second, with Miss Melitta Brunner and Ludwig Wrede, also of Austria, third. Miss Ludovica Jacobson and Walter Jacobson of Finland finished fifth; Miss Josy Venlerverzue and Robert Vanzeevroeck of Belgium, sixth.

Mrs. Theresa Blanchard and Nathaniel Niles of the United States were last. Thirteen couples competed.

The weather man proved the bitter enemy of Winter sports, while the cost of living scored heavily as the undisputed Olympic champion. There were times during the past week when the rink was flooded with thousands of gallons of water.

Canada supplied the fireworks on the closing day with an exhibition of hockey such as has never been witnessed outside of the Western Hemisphere. The combination of John Heaton and William Fiske of the United States took chances streaking down the bobsleigh chute that would make a man smoking a cigarette sitting over a powder magazine appear as a first rate insurance company risk.

"What nerve!" the spectators gasped as Heaton, traveling at the rate of sixty miles an hour, steered his bobsleigh around the sunny corners.

During the last few days tremendous competition developed between Old King Sol and Jack Frost, the latter winning, as there is still snow and ice tonight as the victors celebrate and the losers mourn.

### Norway Well in Lead.

If the official point scoring by the teams of various nations, such as was practiced at Chamonix in 1924, had been adopted here, the rankings of the events just completed would read: Norway, 90½ points; United States, 50½; Sweden, 40; Finland, 39½; Austria, 22, and Canada, 13¾.

Argentina, a land of little snow, scored five points, all in the bob sleigh events, while Switzerland, the nation that organized the Winter sports, must be content with 6 points. This is figured on a basis of 10 points for first place, with 5, 4, 3, 2 and 1 for the next five positions in all events.

In the bob sleighing events, the United States was the greatest winner, totaling 30 points, finishing first in both the skeleton and passenger sleighs. The Heaton brothers, with twenty points between them, were the individual leaders.

Norway captured six first places in thirteen events, the United States, Finland and Sweden, two first places each. The other blue ribbon event, hockey, went to the Canadian skaters without a struggle.

The American points may be figured as follows: Skeleton bob sleigh, 15; passenger bob sleigh, 15; 500 meters skating, 3, dividing points three ways with other nations for third, fourth and fifth places; 1,500 meters, 3; 5,000 meters, 4; figure skating for women, 6½; figure skating for couples, 3. Rolf Monsen won a single point for America by finishing sixth in the ski jump.

The point winners for the United States were:

The Heaton brothers and William Fisk in the bob sleighing; O'Neil Farrell, Eddie Murphy, Valentine Bialis, and Iring Jaffee in the speed skating events; Miss Beatrix Loughran, Miss Maribel Vinson and Sherwin Badger in the figure skating, and Monson in the ski jump.

Had the 10,000 meters race been allowed to stand with Jaffee's 10 points for first and Bialis's 1 point for sixth, America would have had a total of 61½ points. At any rate, the Americans' showing is considered magnificent by Burgomaster Nater and Dr. Nesserli, the two most active organizers of the Swiss Winter Olympics.

### Canadian Six on Attack.

In the hockey final the Canadians commenced scoring early in the first period when Taylor, defence player, rushed through the Swiss ranks for a goal. Hugh Plaxton made it 2 to 0 before the first rest.

The Toronto Grads, representing the Dominion, opened up somewhat in the second period and ran in six rapid-fire counters. At this juncture the Canadians showed the European spectators a flash of real hockey when they scored three of their six goals within the space of two minutes. One of them followed a snappy combination play by H. Plaxton and Trottier.

Trottier's roving disposition brought him three more goals in the final period, while H. Plaxton scored the other two.

The Canadians in all have registered thirty-eight goals in the Olympic series, at the same time holding their opposition scoreless. They defeated Sweden in the first of the final series on Friday by 11 goals to 0, and in a good-natured contest yesterday the Grads whitewashed England, 14 goals to 0.

February 20, 1928

## ST. GODARD WINS CUP IN QUEBEC DOG RACE

### He Is Victor by a Margin of 3 Minutes 13 Seconds Over the Veteran Seppala.

### ALASKAN SETS NEW RECORD

*Special to The New York Times.*

QUEBEC, Feb. 22.—Emile St. Godard of The Pas, Manitoba, won a closely contested sled dog race today from Leonhard Seppala of Nome, Alaska, thus completing three legs on the famous gold cup and giving him possession of it. The young dog-racer started with a slender margin over Seppala of forty seconds. He increased this to eight minutes, which Seppala, in a magnificent spurt in the homestretch, reduced to 3 minutes and 10 seconds.

Earl Brydges, also of The Pas, was a close third. In fact, it seemed that either of the three might be the winner in today's event of the three-day 123-mile dog derby until the judges reported.

Seppala had regained on the second day of the Eastern international classic all but forty seconds of the 10 minutes and 15 seconds he lost on the first. Seppala covered the last fourteen miles in a terrific burst of speed. It was not enough.

When the little man in forest green came down Grande Allee early this afternoon he was kicking with one foot behind his team with every pound in his body. He thought then that he had won.

### Mrs. Ricker Drops Out.

St. Godard, it was estimated, must finish within forty-two minutes behind him to compensate for the difference in starting time this morning, and St. Godard did it just as the gallery began to figure that he could not.

Brydges ran himself to the edge of exhaustion. He reached the finish line ready to drop.

Except for the New Hampshire race of two years ago, it was considered the most dramatic sled dog race ever held in the East.

Mrs. Edward P. Ricker Jr. of Poland Spring, Me., did not start the last day. She is the only woman who ever had courage or skill enough to enter this race against the best men drivers of the continent. Two of her dogs tired last night and she dropped out to save them. Fourth place went to Georges Chevrette of Quebec, who finished fifth, seven minutes behind Brydges.

Quebec won this race the first year and has won it only once since in six times. Francois Dupuis was only thirteen minutes behind Chevrette. Chevrette's old record for the course in one day was broken by St. Godard on Monday. Dupuis's record for the last fourteen miles from the Indian villages was broken by Seppala today.

### Gold Cup to St. Godard.

The gold cup went with the race. W. R. Brown of Berlin, N. H., gave it in 1922 to be won three times. Arthur Walden, who is to go with Commander Byrd to the Antarctic next year, won the first leg.

The time for the three days follows: St. Godard, 11:14:17; Seppala, 11:17:30; Brydges, 11:28:50; Chevrette, 12:26:10; Dupuis, 12:39:35; Russick, 12:52:58; Skeene, 12:29:50; Lavigne, 13:29:     ier, 13:43:45; Lapointe, 13:58:07; Channing, 14:24:46; Alain, 15:00:20 and Routhier, 16:40:30.

February 23, 1928

### Boeckl of Vienna Retains World's Figure-Skating Title

BERLIN, Feb. 26 (P).—Willi Boeckl of Vienna today successfully defended his world's figure skating championship at the Berlin Sport Palace. Schaefer and Dister, also Viennese, placed second and third. Roger F. Turner and Nathaniel W. Niles, American entries listed, finished in fifth and tenth positions, respectively, in the official score. Boeckl was credited with a score of 357.65. Grafstrom, Olympic winner, did not participate.

February 27, 1928

## SKI CONTEST TO GO ON IF SNOW FALLS OR NOT

### Major Welch of Palisades Park to Use Crushed Artificial Ice Jan. 20 If Nature Fails.

*Special to The New York Times.*

STONY POINT, Jan. 8.—Worried lest the lack of snow in the Palisades Interstate Park continue until Jan. 20, when the Eastern State ski-jumping tournament is to take place, and prevent use of the toboggan slides, Major W. A. Welch, chief engineer and general manager of the park system, announced today that if snow failed to fall he would manufacture some himself in Bear Mountain Park.

To prove that he was no rash optimist, he manufactured some today, and employes and guests enjoyed the day coasting down toboggan slides of home-made snow. The snow consisted of artificial ice, crushed and distributed in the path of the toboggans.

"We have been praying for days for snow," Major Welch explained. "We will need a lot for the ski-jumping contests, but none has come. So we made some of our own in our refrigerating plant. We made ice and ground it up. It's simple."

The ice is cut up as fine as powder in a grinding machine operated by employes in their spare time.

Major Welch also said that by an artificial refrigerating process skating is provided on an outdoor rink. Colonel Campbell B. Hodges, cadet commandant at the United States Military Academy at West Point, has given cadets permission to skate on this rink, and it is constantly in use. Sufficient artificial snow will be stored so that if natural snow is lacking, the ski contests can be held.

January 9, 1929

# 4 KEEP U. S. TITLES IN FIGURE SKATING

## Turner Scores in Men's Singles and Miss Vinson in the Women's Event.

### COOLIDGE-MISS VINSON WIN

#### Continue as Championship Pair— Hill, Mrs. Mapes, Hapgood-Miss Weld Junior Victors.

Four national figure skating champions retained their titles in the finals of the two-day competition which came to a close at the Ice Club atop Madison Square Garden last night. Challenged by some of the foremost skaters in the country, the quartet of champions overcame the hardest sort of competition to keep their crowns.

Four new figure skating champions and one dancing championship pair also were crowned. The former were in the junior events, the titles in which were not defended by previous champions.

The men's national singles championship was kept by Roger W. Turner of Boston; Miss Mirabel A. Vinson of Boston retained the women's singles title; Thornton Coolidge and Miss Vinson remained as the senior pairs champions.

### Hill Junior Champion.

George Hill of Boston was crowned the new men's junior champion; Mrs. Bruce S. Mapes of Brooklyn won the women's junior singles championship and Richard L. Hapgood and Miss Dorothy Weld of Boston captured the junior pairs crown.

Mrs. Frederick Secord and Joseph K. Savage of New York were crowned the national dance champions. This event was introduced last night for the first time in the national figure skating championships and proved popular and interesting and will be continued on future title programs.

In the singles competition Turner displayed a skill that won rounds of applause from the gallery. His form was declared to be as nearly flawless as any seen in recent title events. This was especially true in the school figures, consisting of the change loop and the change bracket, spins and jumps. His spins were remarkable and the complete assurance with which he ran through the figures attracted the eyes of the crowd as well as the judges.

Turner, in addition to being a two-time champion, also was a member of the last United States Olympic team.

Miss Vinson, who also was a member of the United States Olympic team in 1928 and who captured the women's senior title for the second time last night, excelled in the execution of the very difficult Jackson Haynes spin.

Miss Vinson is only sixteen years old but has been an actual competitor in amateur figure-skating ranks for twelve years, having been initiated into the graceful but difficult art at 4 years of age by her father, who was a famous figure skater some years ago.

The execution of the Jackson Haynes spin, which is named for the man credited with developing the modern American school of figure skating, by Miss Vinson was the outstanding factor in her performance, yet she displayed a well-rounded program, showing great speed and accuracy in both the school figures and the free skating, in which she brought forth a number of startling new figures.

Teaming with Thornton Coolidge in the senior pairs event, Miss Vinson again showed wonderful skill. This pair, repeating their victory of last year, excelled in speed, executed their figures in perfect unison and then produced a number of rythmic movements that were judged of the highest type.

The road to the pairs title was by no means an easy one for Miss Vinson and Coolidge, however, for they were forced to compete against that veteran pair, Nat W. Niles and Mrs. Blanchard, who was Miss Theresa Weld. Miss Vinson and Coolidge defeated this same pair a year ago, but Mrs. Blanchard and Niles had held the title for the previous eight years and they have represented the United States in the last two Olympic games as a pairs entry.

February 20, 1929.

---

# Players of the Game

## Miss Sonja Henie—Pavlowa of the Ice

### By JOHN RENDEL.

A NATIONAL figure-skating champion at 11, a world's champion at 14 and seeking a fourth world's title at 17. Add to that half a dozen miscellaneous crowns won at various times during her brief career, and you have the record of Miss Sonja Henie, pretty blue-eyed blonde from Norway. Any one wishing to tie her record is advised to start early, work hard and live in a cold climate. Sonja did, and the results were excellent.

Miss Henie will try to retain her world's championship at the tournament to be held at Madison Square Garden and the Ice Club next week. She'll do it, too, or her father, Wilhelm, is no prophet.

"Sure she will win," booms stout and jovial pater Henie, with his rich, rolling accent, glancing with pride at the lithe Sonja, skimming over the ice during a practice period.

### Seems to Defy Gravity.

Following his gaze, even one uninitiated in the mysteries of figure skating is inclined to agree at sight of the ease and grace with which the youthful champion traces the most intricate and difficult patterns on the ice and executes leaps and spins in the air with a lightness that appears to defy gravity. Though less than 18 years old—she was born April 8, 1912—Miss Henie's performance has all the beauty and verve of the great dancer, Pavlowa, to whom she has been likened.

Wilhelm Henie, who, by the way, won the cycling championship at Antwerp in 1893, explains that Sonja has ten pairs of skates, all identical in appearance and all specially made for her.

Nine pairs travel in a trunk made to order, but the tenth pair never leaves his possession. They are the "lucky skates," shining blades which

**MISS SONJA HENIE.**

have glided her to victory in every contest during the past three years.

### Most Valuable of Valuables.

Mr. Henie may forget his wallet, his keys, his railroad tickets, even his broad smile, but never will he forget those precious, irreplaceable skates. They are here now, so how can Sonja lose? His listener becomes convinced that she won't.

If those favored by fortune are born with silver spoons in their mouths, it can be said with equal truth that Miss Henie was born with skates on her feet.

She was but a tiny tot when her parents took her to St. Moritz to see an ice carnival. Little Miss Henie was greatly impressed with the pirouettes, jumps and sundry capers of the figure skaters and insisted, somewhat lustily she now admits, that she, too, wanted to be a beautiful ice queen. Nothing would do but that her mother design steps for her on a ballroom floor so she could go through the motions. Mrs. Henie promised that if Sonja worked hard and paid strict attention to her lessons she might some day become a great skater. She has.

### Survived Roller-Skate Test.

When she was 6 the child who was to be hailed as the Pavlowa of the Ice first ventured forth in her native Oslo on roller skates. By what the average mother would regard as a miracle, Sonja survived that hazardous stage and a few months later graduated to the equally uncertain surface of a near-by rink.

Sonja undoubtedly was gifted at the start, but even infant prodigies must learn before they become masters. Without the infinite pains taken by herself and her mother Sonja never would have won the Norwegian championship at the tender age of 11.

That was in 1924, the same year she entered her first Winter Olympics at Chamonix. Eleven-year-old Sonja Henie placed no better than eighth there, but the girl grew older. By the time she was 14 Miss Henie had developed to a point where she could claim the mantle of supremacy among women figure skaters. Claim it she did by winning the world's championship in 1927 at Oslo, and it has been hers ever since. She has defended the crown twice, in London in 1928 and at Budapest last year.

Miss Henie cannot be said to have been idle in the years intervening between her first and latest titles unless idleness consists of capturing five more Norwegian singles crowns, the Norwegian doubles title three times with Arne Lie, the all-Scandinavian championship and the 1928 Olympic laurels.

That left her just enough time to become the third ranking woman tennis player in Norway, an excellent swimmer, a daring equestrienne and a capable ballet dancer, accomplishments which won for her the first medal ever bestowed on a woman by the Norwegian Government for versatility and achievement in sport.

### Admirers Crush Car Window.

No one who meets her can doubt Miss Henie's popularity, but Sonja has found that popularity can be inconvenient and even dangerous.

In Gothenburg last Winter she narrowly escaped injury when the glass in her automobile was shattered by the pressure of crowds eager to hail their idol. A multitude followed even to her hotel, where big plate glass windows were smashed by the crush of humanity and order was restored only by the arrival of the militia.

The enthusiasm in Sweden was the most spontaneous since the days of Jenny Lind, but Sonja says she would far rather have had it less demonstrative. The plaudits of the crowd and attention from royalty in England, Holland and Norway have left her still a demure, modest, reticent little golden-haired miss who wonders a bit about the tumult when she thinks of it at all.

### Style Called Dancing on Ice.

Experts who have analyzed her technique state that her success is due to the fact that her figure skating is essentially dancing on ice. Sonja performs the hardest feats with the utmost ease. The Axel Paulsen, said to be the most difficult jump known to skaters, one so involved that few can do it at all, proves so simple for Sonja that spectators remark, "Why the fuss? It is nothing."

Yet the turn and a half in the air, landing with the left foot in back, is the despair of many able skaters and has shattered more than one championship hope.

Miss Henie's immediate concern is the defense of her world's title, and to that end she is training earnestly in the early morning, long before most schoolgirls are awake, and again late in the afternoon. She won't make predictions, but admits that she hopes those "lucky skates" will carry her through once more.

January 27, 1930

# FOURTH WORLD TITLE GOES TO MISS HENIE

## Norwegian Star, 17 Years Old, Takes Figure Skating Crown Before 13,000 in Garden.

## SCHAFER WINS MEN'S EVENT

### By VERNON VAN NESS.

Miss Sonja Henie, blond vision from Norway, for the fourth consecutive time was crowned world's amateur singles figure skating champion before an enthusiastic crowd of 13,000 at Madison Square Garden last night.

The world's singles title for men went to Karl Schafer of Vienna, runner-up for the honor last year, while the world's pair championship was captured by M. and Mme. Pierre Brunet of France. The championships were conducted under the auspices of the Skating Club of New York under sanction by Internationale Eislauf-Vereinigung and the United States Skating Union.

The little 17-year-old Norwegian star, who scored her first triumph in Oslo in 1927, repeating at London in 1928, and at Budapest last year, was in brilliant form and virtually surpassed herself by her beautiful exhibition in the four minutes during which she cavorted and twirled and spun before the cheering crowd.

Schafer, debonnaire, nimble, nearly as graceful as the little Norse girl, but in addition daring and bold in his figures and leaping spins, achieved a success for which he had striven for several years, though he is only 19 years old and a student in Vienna. Only by the narrowest of margins did he miss annexing the crown at London last year when Gillis Graistrom triumphed. The latter failed to come here to defend his crown last night.

### French Win Pairs Event.

In the pairs competition eight teams competed and the French representatives clearly led through an intricate and brilliant set of figures that bordered on the sensational.

Miss Cecil Smith of Canada was awarded second place in the women's singles and Miss Maribel Vinson of Boston was third. Roger F. Turner, national champion, was second to Schafer in the men's title event and Dr. George Gautschi of Switzerland third. In the pairs Miss Melitta Brunner of Austria and Ludwig Wrede of Austria were placed second and Miss Beatrix Loughran and Charwin C. Badger of New York won third place.

Mrs. Theresa Blanchard and Nat W. Niles of Boston, Mr. and Mrs. Melville Rogers of Canada, Mrs. Norman Samuel and Montgomery Wilson, Mrs. Frederick Secord and Joseph K. Savage of New York and Miss Maude E. Smith and Jack Eastwood of Canada were the other pairs competitors.

Miss Henie, appearing last among the six women competitors in the singles, showed the wonderful skill that won her the title in Budapest last year. The personification of grace, she performed a series of waltz steps, spins and glides punctuated by daring and sensational pinwheel pivots that had the crowd gasping. Dressed in a bewitching salmon-colored velvet skating outfit edged with fawn-colored fluffy fur, the ensemble topped with a fawn-colored turban clinging close to her head but failing to hide all of her blond curls, she made a charming picture as she came onto the ice.

### Glide Starts Performance.

She began her four minutes of work with a running glide that ended in a daring one-foot jump. From this she swung into a flowing waltz to a waltz-march time. It was apparent at once that she had caught the fancy of the big crowd, for her figures were made with a swiftly moving grace that carried her around the big rink with amazing speed. Her forte seemed to be in the more intricate swirls, pivots and pinwheels.

She nearly fell as she started a jump spin shortly after taking the ice, but caught herself on the tips of her fingers, smiling to the crowd as she straightened up. And then, as if to make amends for this slight miscue, she swung into a series of back glides, inserting sudden and unexpected pivots and swirls.

The most sensational of her efforts was her double pinwheel, the formation and execution of which produced the optical illusion of a flaming torch being rapidly turned in the air.

Miss Vinson, a slender vision in a light salmon-colored velvet outfit, topped by a black toque, came dashing into the picture in the next to the last exhibition, entering by way of a back swan glide that won instant applause. After a measure or two of waltzing movements, she started a pivot swirl, but fell as one of her skates slipped. She arose quickly and renewed her efforts, winning the crowd with her lithe grace, especially as demonstrated in her back glides and her one-foot swirls.

There was no doubt that the crowd wanted to see the American girl succeed in her quest of the title and her every movement won applause. She was brilliant in some of her figures and always graceful with the flare that marks her style distinctly. She had come upon the ice in the wake of Miss Cecil Smith of Canada, the charming, graceful and fawn-like former Canadian champion.

Miss Smith, who in her school figures had shown a subdued grace that won her the esteem of the critics, was dressed in a black velvet costume trimmed with white fur. To the measure of a two-step she made her bow with a long swan glide, ending with a one-foot spiral, and then set off to dance in complete abandon. Afterward the beautiful Canadian girl declared that she was startled for a moment as she looked up at the crowded galleries. Then, as the crowd, sensing her wonderful grace and poise, began cheering, she set forth to outdo herself. Her performance was received with loud applause. Miss Smith is a former amateur golf champion of Ontario.

Mrs. Norman Samuel, the former Constance Wilson, Canadian champion in 1926, 1927 and 1928 and the North American champion in 1929, was the first of the women skaters to appear. She sported a golden velvet outfit. Displaying fine balance in every one of her feats, she seemed to place chief dependence upon swirls and spins. Her back swirl spins were done with much brilliance. She was well received by the crowd and gave a sparkling performance.

### Miss Davis Well Received.

Miss Suzanne Davis of Boston, United States junior champion in 1927, was the second one on the ice. Lacking some of the experience of the others, she executed the simpler forms of spins and swirls in a commendable performance and was received with some warmth.

Miss Melitta Brunner of Austria, pair-skating champion of Austria, was the third to appear. She was greeted with much applause and immediately showed an amazing knowl-

## WINNERS OF WORLD'S FIGURE SKATING CHAMPIONSHIPS IN THE GARDEN LAST NIGHT.

Times Wide World Photo.

Miss Sonja Henie of Norway.

Times Wide World Photo.

Karl Schafer of Vienna.

edge of the various close figures in the spins and glides. She was particularly effective in the pivoting, in which she changed from one foot to the other, and on the one-foot back glide. She won the acclaim of the crowd in a manner surpassed only by the receptions accorded Miss Henie, Miss Smith and Miss Vinson.

### Daring Thrills Crowd.

Schafer showed amazing skill and daring, which captured the crowd. With dashing running starts, leaps through the air that seemed almost impossible and a continuity of motion that appeared hard to surpass, the young Austrian student went through his five minutes with an eclat that critics declared had never before been seen in this country.

Beginning with a back glide that carried him half way around the rink and then suddenly leaping into the air for a spin, again dashing off at breakneck speed for a circle glide and then a series of spins and loops, there was never a time that Schafer was still. He was a wildly but perfectly controlled whirlwind. Beyond all of the others in the men's singles, he possessed the grace and poetry of motion which marked the performance of the women skaters.

He followed both Turner and Wilson, United States and Canadian champions respectively, and while their performances had been of the highest order, it was apparent that the crowd had discovered for itself a skater who struck its fancy and did not hesitate to make it known by thunderous applause, all of which the handsome, slender Austrian youth received with a smile. His self-assurance was surpassed only by his complete mastery of the figures and feats he attempted.

Turner showed a sound knowledge of his work, but he did not seem quite so completely at ease and was far from being as spectacular as the Austrian. Wilson, tall and lithe, performed with great skill and yet, he, too, lacked the flair of Schafer. Dr. Gautschi, William J. Nagle of New York City; Wrede, J. Lester Madden of Boston and Gail Borden of New York put forth excellent performances.

February 6, 1930

## MISS HENIE RETAINS WORLD TITLE ON ICE

### Norwegian Girl Extended to Win Figure Skating Crown for Fifth Year in Row.

### VIENNESE GIRL MAIN RIVAL

Miss Vinson, Fourth, Also Loudly Acclaimed—Turner, Another U. S. Star, Men's Runner-Up.

By The Associated Press.

BERLIN, March 1.—For the fifth successive year, Miss Sonja Henie, little blond skating star from Oslo, Norway, won the world's figure skating championship for women tonight. But she had to share the crowd's applause with two rivals, Hilde Kolovsky, a 13-year-old Viennese girl, and Miss Maribel Vinson of Winchester, Mass.

The greater international experience and smoothness of Miss Henie gave her a victory over little Miss Kolovsky, whose flashing grace and skill came near wresting the title from the Norwegian star. Miss Vinson was placed fourth by the judges, but the award was little indication

New York Times Studio.

Miss Sonja Henie, Winner for the Fifth Successive Time.

Miss Maribel Vinson, American Entrant, Who Placed Fourth.

of her popularity with the onlookers, who shouted and stamped on the floor and all but raised the roof in appreciation.

Another American, Roger Turner of Boston, finished second in the men's competition to Carl Schaefer of Vienna, who retained his world's title with ease. Schaefer far outshone all competitors until Turner, the twelfth of thirteen entries, appeared on the ice.

The Boston star brought repeated applause from the thousands who packed the big arena, and none appeared surprised when the judges singled him out for second place.

Third place in the men's championship went to Ernst Beyer of Berlin and Hugo Distler of Vienna finished fifth. Miss Fritzi Burger, another Viennese star, finished third in the women's competition, while fifth place was awarded to Miss Vivian Hulted of Sweden.

March 2, 1931

## OLYMPIC TITLES WON BY SHEA AND JAFFEE

### Score for U. S. in 500 and 5,000 Meter Skating as Games Open at Lake Placid.

### By ARTHUR J. DALEY.

Special to The New York Times.

LAKE PLACID, N. Y., Feb. 4.—The gaunt pine shaft that stands silhouetted against the white background of the snow-covered Adirondack countryside twice bore the American flag today in the age-old custom that is the symbol of Olympic victory.

Governor Roosevelt officially opened the Third Olympic Winter Games this morning and before the assembled athletes of seventeen nations the firm young voice of Jack Shea rang out in the icy air as he took the Olympic oath of amateurism and sportsmanship. And a short time later this same Jack Shea outsprinted the fastest speed skaters in the world to capture the 500-meter final.

That triumph was staged under a benign sun, which served to take some of the nip from the frosty air. The joy of the Americans was evident as the Stars and Stripes were run up the central masthead. That seemed more than enough for the opening day.

But in the afternoon Irving Jaffee of New York raced through a flurry of snow to the 5,000-meter title, a distinct surprise that was intensified by the fact that Eddie Murphy of Chicago finished second and Herbert Taylor of New York came in fourth. So as the American flag was run up the pole for the second time, the mast to the right also bore the Red, White and Blue as a result of Murphy's performance.

### A Setback for Americans.

Only one drop of regret filtered into this picture of complete United States success. The Canadian hockey team turned back the Americans in the opening match of the Olympic round robin tournament by 2 to 1 in an overtime game.

Aside from this the crowd of 8,000 could find little cause for complaint. Norway had been a top-heavy favorite to annex speed skating laurels, and with this section of the program half over the United States rolled up 29 points toward the unofficial team championship, thus gathering together in two events as many points as this country had been able to gain in the entire 1924 Olympic Winter games.

Canada has 13 points and Norway, the defending team titleholder, the unexpectedly scant total of 8. Both of Norway's individual champions were dethroned, and with Shea eager for a triumph in the 1,500-meter test tomorrow, and Jaffee set to repeat at 10,000 meters, American hopes bear a distinctly rosy hue.

### Norwegian Stars Dethroned.

What is vastly encouraging is the fact that the 21-year-old Shea deposed the great Bernt Evensen of Norway in the 500-meter sprint and Jaffee accomplished a similar deed

Times Wide World Photo.

Irving Jaffee, United States, Winner of 5,000-Meter Championship.

in vanquishing the equally great Ivar Ballangrud. Two Olympic champions were encountered and both decisively beaten.

The 500-meter race was far more spectacular than the 5,000-meter battle. And it was singularly appropriate that Shea, a Lake Placid boy and the pride of the entire countryside, should emerge with the initial American triumph. He skated today as though no man alive could beat him.

With his coal black hair tucked beneath a flaming red beret and lips tightened in a grim jaw, Shea flew over the glistening ice like the champion he is. Right from the crack of the starter's gun Shea broke away from the field, determination written on every feature.

Arms flying wildly and legs pumping like pistons. Shea shook off the relentless pursuit of Evensen in the straightaway and snapped the red worsted that was strung out over the blue-crayoned finishing line a full five yards ahead of his Norse rival in the brilliant time of 0:43.4, figures which equalled the Olympic record but not acceptable as such since the race was skated in the American style.

### Long Vigil Rewarded.

Lake Placid had waited three years for the Olympic Games to start, and back in April, 1929, when the International Olympic Committee made its award the villagers pointed to this youth of 18 as the coming champion. Accordingly, keen is the exultation of the townsfolk tonight.

It was in impressive fashion that these long-awaited games were opened officially this morning. The Governor had just been seated in the stadium when the roll of drums and the sound of bugles announced the approach of the athletes. The band struck up the "Star-Spangled Banner" and the portals swung open to admit the contestants.

Through the gates came the red and white flag of Austria as the white-sweatered band marched onto the track. Then came the Belgians in blue ski suits, red and gold knit nats fitting snugly. Next came the huge group of Canadians, red maple leaves standing out strikingly against white coats.

Czechoslovakia, France and Finland in hues of dark blue followed. Germany's color was a bright red, but in the centre of the squad was the blue-coated figure of Captain

Werner Zahn, right arm in sling, a grim token of his bobsled smash on Sunday.

Behind the Germans came the four little English girls, all figure skaters, representing Great Britain's participation in the Olympics. Italy in light blue, Japan and Norway in dark blue, followed. A different note in the middle of the Norwegian delegation was the bright burnt-orange coat of Miss Sonja Henie.

### U. S. Squad in Striking Garb.

Poland's athletes wore maroon, and the color of Rumania and Sweden was dark blue. The Swiss were clad in red and white, but it remained for the team of the last nation to file through the stadium gates to present the most colorful picture of the entire ensemble.

It was the United States, ninety-four strong. Billy Fiske carried the American flag and right behind came Avery Brundage, president of the American Olympic committee; George W. Graves, its treasurer; Frederick W. Rubien, its secretary; Murray Hulbert, Gustavus T. Kirby, Dr. Graeme M. Hammond and Daniel J. Ferris, all high amateur sports dignitaries.

And in back of them marched the team. The athletes wore white-peaked caps, white coats and blue sweat suits, the latter bearing bright red collars. These with the red buttons on the coats and the American shield over the heart could leave no doubt but that the United States was entering the arena. So striking was the picture they presented that the Canadians gave their neighbors a rousing cheer as they passed.

Once around the track and into the hockey box in the centre of the track they paraded, the flags of every country dipping before the Governor in passing. In serried rows they lined up and then each standard-bearer stepped out in front in a semicircle.

### Governor Proclaims Games Open.

Dr. Godfrey Dewey, president of the organizing committee, extended Lake Placid's welcome in a short speech and then Governor Roosevelt addressed the gathering. At the close he delivered the long-awaited words, "I hereby proclaim open the third Olympic Winter Games, celebrating the tenth olympiad of the modern era."

**Jack Shea, United States, Winner of 500-Meter Championship.**

As the last word issued through the microphone a gun cracked and in slow majesty the white Olympic flag with its interlocking circles rose to the masthead. A brisk breeze that had swept from snow-capped Whiteface Mountain in the distance ballooned the standard out from the staff. The Olympic Winter Games were on.

There was a bustling of activity on the track and the skaters shot around the ice, warming up for the initial heat of the 500-meter sprint.

Five athletes lined up for the first heat. With feet braced and arms outstretched the call came for the start. Then the crack of the pistol. It was a little Japanese, Shozo Ishiwara, who first assumed the lead, but the strong Shea overtook him in the backstretch and coasted along into the straightaway with Frank Stack of Canada, the North American champion, at his elbow.

The two rode down the stretch, shoulder to shoulder, looked behind to see that they were off by them-

selves, and then eased up at the wire, Stack winning by inches, but Shea qualifying with plenty to spare.

### Murray Is Eliminated.

The second heat was productive of something of an upset. Ray Murray of the United States, one of the favorites, was shut out when Evensen won and William Logan of Canada barely nipped the American boy at the tape.

In the third heat Alex Hurd of Canada was the victor and O'Neil Farrell of the United States was second, a few inches ahead of his teammate, Allan Potts. Then, to allow an intermission, the first period of the Canadian-American hockey game was staged and after that came the final.

It was Shea from start to finish. The Lake Placid boy was too fast at the start for any of the others. His skates fairly danced on the ice at the getaway. He gained the pole without effort. This placed a tremendous burden on his rivals. Logan and Evensen strove mightily to slip into the second post.

The Norwegian edged in so quickly that Logan almost climbed up his back and had to catch himself to keep from falling. Around the backstretch they sped, Evensen still unable to gain on the fast flying American. Into the final curve they swung and Shea had a 3-yard margin on the Norseman. He even added to this in the stretch and streaked in the winner by five yards. Evensen was second, Hurd third. Logan fourth, Stack fifth and Farrell sixth.

### Recalls Jewtraw's Triumph.

The time of 0:43.4 equalled the Olympic record that Evensen and Clas Thunberg of Finland jointly set in 1928. Incidentally, his triumph brought back to the United States the Olympic crown that Charles Jewtraw won in 1924.

After the brilliant display of speed in this event the 5,000 meter race seemed dull by comparison. It bore much resemblance to a six-day bicycle race where every contestant is reluctant to take the lead. This was evident in heats and the final.

In the first heat Jaffee and Murphy finished one-two with Ballangrud third and Smyth of Canada fourth, the main casualty being Ossian Blomquist of Finland who failed to qualify. Some idea of the desultory manner in which the race was run may be obtained by a comparison of the winning time of 9:51.6 with the world's record for the distance 8:21.6.

The next heat was even slower. Evensen triumphed in 10:01.4 with Taylor second, Logan third and Stack fourth.

### Ballangrud Out in Front.

Then came the final. Ordinarily one might expect a far different manner of skating. But it was not to be. At the start all the athletes obviously dawdled along, each refusing to break for the trailers. Finally Ballangrud discovered that he was out in front and so stayed there.

On practically every turn the leader swung wide and let the second man show the way so that each of the starters found himself a pacesetter at one time or another.

It was not until nine of the twelve and a half laps had been traversed that there were some signs of acceleration. All eight were closely bunched, each alert for a real sprint from the other. But none was forthcoming. Murphy was in the lead with a lap and a half to go and Jaffee in fifth position behind Smyth, Stack and Ballangrud.

And then as the leaders swung wide in the backstretch, Jaffee saw a hole near the pole. He shot inside and in a few strides was right back of Murphy. Then a peculiar mixup assured an American triumph.

In an effort to save ground Smyth tried to slip inside Ballangrud on the last turn. Suddenly the white figured Canadian was driven inside the oval and the force of the collision knocked both Smyth and Ballangrud off stride.

Meanwhile Murphy and Jaffee

**Shea Leading the Field Around Turn in 500-Meter Speed Skating Championship Race, the First Event to Be Decided in the 1932 Olympics.**

were driving for the tape, side by side. It was not until ten yards from the finish line that Jaffee was able to forge the slightest bit ahead. And that was the extent of his margin of victory. The time was 9:40.8, far away from any sort of a record, American or European.

**Tie Score in Last Period.**

Tying the score in the last period and then coming through with another marker in the overtime, the Winnipeg sextet of Canada turned back the All-Star American combination, 2 to 1, in the opening hockey game.

In the overtime the Maple Leaf contingent tallied in spectacular fashion when Vic Lindquist swept down the ice alone, ploughed through the United States defense and swept the disk into the net while sliding on his back.

In the second game, Germany defeated Poland by a similar score, 2 to 1.

February 5, 1932

# 1,500-METER TITLE CAPTURED BY SHEA

## Lake Placid Ace Scores to Add to U. S. Sweep in Olympic Speed-Skating Tests.

## FOUR NATIONS IN PROTEST

### Officials Then Reinstate Disqualified Men and Rule 10,000-Meter Heats "No Contest."

## CANADA WAS READY TO QUIT

### Other Countries Join in Demanding That American System of Racing Be Sharply Revised.

By ARTHUR J. DALEY.
Special to THE NEW YORK TIMES.

LAKE PLACID, N. Y., Feb. 5.—An undercurrent of dissatisfaction—so serious that at one time Canada threatened to withdraw its teams—over the rules under which the speed skating races have been held thus far in the Third Olympic Winter Games broke sharply into the open tonight.

As a result, after a meeting with American and foreign officials, Joseph K. Savage, referee of the races, ruled that the trial heats held today in the 10,000-meter event be declared "no contest." They will be held again tomorrow. The final will take place Monday.

The meeting was a direct result of a formal protest filed with the International Skating Federation and with Count Henri de Baillet-Latour, president of the international Olympic committee, by representatives of Norway, Sweden, Finland and Japan.

**Skates to Another Crown.**

Tonight's developments dampened somewhat the enjoyment of the Americans, who have scored a sweep in the races held thus far, for young Jack Shea of Lake Placid skated to his second Olympic title today, adding the 1,500-meter championship to the 500-meter race which he captured yesterday.

The dissatisfaction first was evidenced when Irving Jaffee of the United States triumphed yesterday in the 5,000-meter test and it reached its climax today when four athletes—Alex Hurd and Frank Stack of Canada, Edwin Wedge of the United States and Shozo Shiwara of Japan—were disqualified.

The disqualifications, with the exception of that of Stack, came about as the result of a rule by the race officials that each lap in the heats be traversed in at least 45 seconds, and that each man bear his share of the pace setting. Hurd, Wedge and Shiwara were disqualified in the first heat after Norway, Sweden and Finland had protested that they had failed to take their turns leading the pack.

In the next heat Stack was disqualified on the protest of Bernt Evensen of Norway that the former had fouled him.

P. J. Mulqueen, chairman of the Canadian Olympic Committee, threatened to withdraw the entire Canadian delegation unless the disqualifications were lifted.

At tonight's meeting all four disqualifications were lifted and the men will be permitted to race again.

**Text of the Resolution.**

The following is the resolution signed by Sir Thomas Fearnley, Wilhelm Morgenstierne, Carsten Matheson, Cato Waall, Axel Greswig, Captain Smith Kelland, Sverre Weindelboe, Ingvar Bryn and P. Chris Anderson, all of Norway; Count Clarence von Rosen, Sixtus Jansen and Runar Ohman of Sweden, Walter Jakobson of Finland and Professor Sato of Japan:

"The undersigned leaders of the Finnish, Japanese, Norwegian and Swedish teams desire to draw your attention to the fact that, in their opinion, the rules under which the speed-skating events have been run have not proved a success, and they desire to express the opinion that these rules should not be applied to Olympic contests in the future.

"It was only reluctantly that the countries which we represent sent teams of speed skaters to compete in the third Olympic Winter games at Lake Placid under these rules, and the experience which we have gained during the first days of the games has further confirmed us in the view that we previously held regarding the desirability of adopting the rules of the Amateur Skating Union of the United States for the Olympic events.

**Find Rules Too Complicated.**

"We would like to point out that these rules are so complicated that they cannot, in our opinion, be strictly adhered to or controlled, and we have seen many examples of these rules having been violated without any consequences to the participants or to the results of the events except those unfavorable to the victims.

"It has been clearly demonstrated that these rules can lead to results which are not in accordance with our ideals of the sport, which, in our opinion, should be that the best man, that is, he who can run each particular distance at the greatest speed, should be the winner, whereas the American rules obviously give wide play to tactics which are contrary to these ideals.

"It seems evident, from what we have observed during the recent contests in the 5,000-meter and 1,500-meter races, that the American rules will permit tactics which practically eliminate the distance set for the longer events, inasmuch as they allow the competitors to run the major part of the race at a snail's pace, with a final spurt in the last round, and it is our opinion that this system is not only detrimental to the ideals and aims of fair sport but that the race run under these rules can actually become a parody on what a fine and fair speed race should be."

Shea's twin triumphs together with Irving Jaffee's 5,000-meter success yesterday gave the United States all three of the Olympic championships that have been decided to date and America's total mounted to 42 points in the unofficial team tabulation, with Canada second with 25 and Norway holding fast to its 8 markers.

It is a striking commentary on America's astounding progress in Winter sports. Yesterday in two events this country rolled up 29 points, as much as the United States tallied in the entire 1924 Olympic Games, and today this country is within eight and a half points of its 1928 total of 50½ points as runner-up to Norway's 90½. This is practically certain to be passed tomorrow.

In the 1,500-meter race the bell had sounded for the final lap as Shea glided along in back of Ray Murray, his fellow-American. "Better get going, Ray. I'm stepping on the gas," said the Lake Placid youngster to his team-mate. And then the glinting blades of Shea's skates bit into the ice and he was off in a headlong dash that continued unabated to the tape.

Three Canadians—Hurd, Bill Logan and Stack—followed him over, the foremost of them five yards behind, and then came Murray and Bert Taylor, the latter a victim of an unfortunate spill in the straightaway when he had second place as good as won.

**Rule Spurs Contestants.**

One thing that was very evident today was that the ruling in regard to minimum time for each lap was an excellent antidote for a slow race. Where the 5,000-meter clashes yesterday were from one minute to a minute and a half behind the record, the 10,000-meter heats today were completed expeditiously in fairly respectable clocking.

The order of finish in the first heat, exclusive of the disbarment proceedings, was Hurd, Bialis, Wedge, Ivar Ballangrud of Norway, Ishawara, Michael Staksrud of Norway and Ossian Blomquist of Finland, and the ranking in the second heat was Schroeder, Stack, Jaffee, Evensen and Tokuo Kitani of Japan.

The 5,000-meter test yesterday gave the foreign protests some momentum, but it remained for the 1,500-meter heats this morning to supply the final incentive to a meeting. In the second heat, in which the new champion, Shea, qualified, the skaters dilly-dallied so long and so persistently that Referee Savage stopped the race after about 1,000 yards had been covered, called it "no contest" and ordered them to skate it over.

Only once did any athlete attempt to set a fast pace. That was in the third heat when Carl Lindberg of Sweden started out to burn up the course. As a result every one clung to him and every starter passed him before the finish was reached.

**European Stars Shut Out.**

The order of finish in each heat bitterly disappointed the Europeans. Three Americans broke the tape first in each and three Canadians were second. Among those shut out were two of the best skaters in Europe, Evensen in the first and Ballangrud in the second. So the final was strictly a North American affair.

It was Hurd who led for the first lap and then he swung wide and let Shea set the pace. After one lap in the lead Murray sprinted past the Dartmouth sophomore and slipped into the van. He stayed there until Shea made his last lap sprint.

At this juncture Taylor was in the third notch back of Shea and in the backstretch the three Americans swung out abreast. The Canadians could not pass until the turn, when Hurd glided around Murray. Shea was well in front and Taylor was staying close to him when the latter's skates hit a bump in the ice and he went sprawling, climbed to his feet and finished last as Murray eased up near the wire and the other two Canadians shot past him.

Shea's winning time was 2:57.5. The world's record, European style, is 2:17.4 and the Olympic mark 2:22.8.

**Hockey Teams in Action.**

Only one hockey game was held in the Olympic tournament today, although two exhibition matches were staged. The United States conquered the much improved Polish sextet, 4 to 1.

John Bent took a pass from John Cookman to whip in a score in 2:15 of the first period and then passed to Cookman for the second tally, 35 seconds after the second session opened. Cookman registered unassisted in 10:15 of the same period.

Adam Kowalski went down the ice in a solo trip in 2:16 for Poland's only score in the final session and John Garrison shot in the disk in 14:16 for the last tally. Josef Stogowski was brilliant at the net for Poland.

## CANADIANS WIN AT CURLING.

### Beat United States, 12 Games to 4, in Exhibition Series.

LAKE PLACID, N. Y., Feb. 5 (AP).—Canada's rinks won their exhibition curling series with the United States, completed today, 12 games to 4. The exhibitions were arranged as a demonstration for visitors to the Winter Olympics.

Canadian rinks won all four games played this morning and split even in four games this afternoon.

February 6, 1932

# JAFFEE WINS TITLE IN OLYMPIC SKATING

## U. S. Scores Sweep as New Yorker Takes 10,000 Meters for His Second Victory.

## AMERICA'S FEAT UNIQUE

### First Nation to Capture All Four Speed Tests—Boblet Event Postponed.

## WOMEN'S RACE TO CANADIAN

### Miss Wilson Annexes 500-Meter Demonstration — U. S. and Canadian Sextets Win.

By ARTHUR J. DALEY
Special to THE NEW YORK TIMES.

LAKE PLACID, N. Y., Feb. 8.—Beams of sunlight broke through black, low-hanging clouds this afternoon and struck an American flag as it rose for the fourth time to the top of the central mast of the Stadium in token of Olympic victory. Irving Jaffee of New York had just scored a stirring triumph in the 10,000-meter final, giving the United States a clean sweep of the Olympic speed-skating championships.

It was for only a moment that the sun peered forth, but it illuminated a scene which marked the conclusion of a feat unprecedented in the annals of the Olympic Winter Games. With Jack Shea's 500 and 1,500-meter victories and Jaffee's twin successes at 5,000 and 10,000 meters, the United States became the first nation ever to win all four skating laurels.

It was no wonder then that American officials and athletes danced with glee on the ice, pounded Jaffee on the back and shook his hand before being joined in their rousing outburst of applause by the 5,000 spectators huddled in the stands, forgetful of cold and snow at the sight of this heart-warming spectacle.

Irving Jaffee, United States. Winner of 10,000-Meter Title.

Miss Jean Wilson, Canada, Who Won 500-Meter Demonstration Final.

As Jaffee and Eddie Wedge dived over the finish line to slide twenty feet along the track for first and fourth places, respectively, and as Val Bialas crossed for fifth position, the point total of the United States toward the unofficial team championship soared to 57, almost twice as many points as had been registered in 1924 and well beyond the complete 1928 aggregate of 50½. Norway's defense of its team crown has been a rather unsuccessful one to date, the Norsemen compiling 14 points to 29 for Canada.

Canada and the United States, the two top-ranking teams in the hockey tourney, continued their triumphs in evening games played in the Arena. The Americans turned back Poland's six by 5 to 0 and the Maple Leaf combination, still undefeated, won from Germany by the same score. The victory was Canada's fourth in the tourney.

For a time today it looked as if the weather conditions would halt the 10,000-meter final. It snowed all last night and the heavy fall forced the postponement of the opening round of the boblet championship competition until tomorrow. Tractors had cleared the track this morning, but just before noon the cold abated and the snow turned to rain.

The ice was soft and porous and a thin sheet of water covered the track. Along about 1 o'clock the rain reverted to snow once more and the cold tightened the racing strip to icy smoothness.

**Best Eight in Field.**

That was all that was needed and conditions were excellent by the time the eight who had qualified first on Friday and then repeated in the re-run on Saturday. That double test had demonstrated, beyond doubt, that these were the best eight in the entire field, and the race itself served to make this fact even more convincing.

In the final lap all eight were spread out over the track with less than three yards separating leader from tail-ender. Ivar Ballangrud of Norway was at the pole with Jaffee alongside of him on the outside. There could be no questioning the

American's sprinting powers. He outraced the Norwegian to the final turn and zoomed into the straightaway still ahead and in the last 100 meters increased his advantage to five yards.

But Jaffee took no chances. He fairly threw himself at the red worsted that was strung tightly over the finish line. The force of his lunge carried him off balance and he went sprawling onto the ice. Skidding along on his back the American became, for the second time in this year's games, an Olympic champion.

**Stack Follows Ballangrud.**

Ballangrud followed Jaffee over, a yard in front of Frank Stack of Canada, who had all he could do to beat Wedge, who also tried to gain extra ground by flinging himself at the tape. Bialas was fifth, a foot behind, and Bernt Evensen of Norway was sixth, less than a yard in back of the third American.

Quite a bit to the rear came Alex Hurd of Canada, the victim of Eddie Schroeder's fall at the last turn. As the Detroit boy went down the young Canadian had all he could do to keep from tripping over him and this disconcerting spill ruined whatever chance the Dominion youngster had of placing.

When Jaffee skidded along the ice willing hands picked him up and bundled the American into his training suit and robe. Triumphantly he was escorted to the pedestal of honor where Count Henri de Baillet-Latour, president of the International Committee, made his fourth presentation of an Olympic medal to a United States athlete.

As the blue plush box was passed over the American flag started to rise on the pole. The sun issued forth to light up the picture, made all the more spectacular by the panorama of white-covered mountains in the background. And to add to this perfect setting the wind whisked the banner out from the mast just as it reached the top.

**Jaffee Is Congratulated.**

On Jaffee's right stood Ballangrud, who smilingly offered congratulations. So did Stack on his left. Then the Norwegian and Canadian reached

across in front of the American in a firm clasp that denoted the termination of all the controversy of last week.

There was not the slightest bickering in evidence today. Clerk-of-Course Charlie Goldsmith had all the starters in line without any trouble. Although there was a little more manoeuvring and crowding than had occurred in any of the four heats, no one protested, even though there were collisions or near collisions on five occasions.

This was partly caused by the fact that the race was skated under a revised ruling. Instead of having the lead assigned to a certain individual at the end of each lap by Goldsmith, the contestants were told that each had to set the pace for two circuits. They then were free to take whatever position they wished. As a result, a man who had carried out his assignment frequently displayed some reluctance to slow down for a new leader so that the succeeding pace setter had to sprint hard to get in the van.

The two Norwegians, Ballangrud and Evensen, assumed their pacing burdens early in the race. After Hurd and Stack had shown the way for two trips around the track Evensen climbed up around the two Canadians and was out in front. He held the lead for two and a quarter laps and then dropped back as Ballangrud advanced to the lead.

**Arms Swing Together.**

The first mix-up came as Wedge tried to take the pole on the seventh lap. As he went to pass Ballangrud their arms swung together, both going off stride and the Norwegian evincing a show of anger at the accident.

The next came on the eleventh circuit as Bialas accelerated his pace when Hurd came up. The Canadian and the American brushed arms. Neither was visibly affected. The most serious of all occurred two laps later.

With Stack out ahead and Hurd in second place, Evensen advanced up the line and cut in ahead of Hurd so sharply that their skates entangled and the Dominion star stumbled off the track and onto the infield before righting himself. Two

laps further along Evensen and Stack came together in one more accidental brush. Just before the end Hurd was sent off balance once more as the sprint for places started.

By the twentieth lap everyone in the race had set the pace for the required two circuits and then the dawdling started. All the contestants spread out over the track, skating slowly down the entire backstretch.

At the turn Evensen was ahead so he led the parade around the bend. He stayed ahead for one complete tour of the track and then swung wide. So did every one else and no one would set the pace. Eventually Stack found himself in the van and held the lead for two circuits.

Coming around the bell lap Ballangrud had assumed first place with Jaffee in an ideal spot right behind him. Stack was third and Bialas fourth. The real sprint started around the penultimate turn and Jaffee surged abreast of the Norwegian.

They raced shoulder to shoulder along the backstretch, but Jaffee had too much speed and power and as he cut toward the pole for the last turn he had plenty of room to spare. He streaked down the straightaway an easy winner and thus certified his unofficial 10,000-meter championship gained at St. Moritz.

**Held Comfortable Lead.**

At that time Jaffee had a comfortable lead in a race held under European rules, when a thaw set in and prevented the remainder of the race from being run. Eventually Jaffee's triumph was deemed unofficial.

Jaffee's time of 19:13.6 today was well off the record, the world's mark being 17:17.4.

Although the United States triumphed in the men's race, the Americans suffered their second successive setback in a demonstration sport. Following closely on the heels of Emile St. Goddard's sled-dog success yesterday, Miss Jean Wilson of Canada nipped Miss Elizabeth Dubois of the United States with a closing homestretch drive to capture the 500-meter women's demonstration final today.

While the speed skaters were com-

Times Wide World Photo.

Ivar Ballangrud, Norway, Second in the 10,000 Meter.

peting in the Stadium, the men figure skaters were performing in the Arena where about 1,000 persons watched them this morning and an even larger number was in attendance at the afternoon session.

**Official Figures Withheld.**

No official figures were forthcoming on the standing and the order will not be known until about an hour after the free figures are completed tomorrow night. But experts in the stands were practically unanimous in their opinion that Karl Schafer of Austria, the world's champion, had made the best showing, with Montgomery Wilson of Canada second; Roger F. Turner, the American titleholder, third, and Gillis Grafstrom of Sweden, the defending Olympic king, fourth.

Grafstrom was patently nervous when he took to the ice and in one of the early movements went off balance and had to start over again. After this poor beginning, however, he settled down and was brilliant for the rest of the day.

One figure that caused a tremendous burst of applause was his change-double-three which was perfect in execution as to print, form, triple repetition and size.

Prospects of a heavy snowstorm outside in the Olympic Stadium forced the officials to switch the American-Polish hockey contest indoors to the Arena.

The United States sextet won with plenty to spare, hitting top speed in the third period. The blue-shirted aggregation presented a revised line-up, Ty Anderson being shifted from defense to the second-string forward line as several substitutes saw service for the first time.

It was only another superb exhibition by Jozef Stogowski in the Polish net which prevented an overwhelming score. The Americans peppered him from start to finish, and by the time the bell had sounded for the completion of the contest he had registered 46 saves, a sharp contrast to

the small number of 18 to the credit of Frank Farrel.

Stogowski almost was forced to withdraw from the contest in the second period when Ding Palmer unleashed a terrific drive that struck the Polish star squarely in the mouth. Despite the smash, Stogowski stayed at the net until the disk was knocked out of danger.

**Palmer Is Outstanding.**

Palmer once more was the outstanding player for the Americans, with Johnny Garrison and Anderson also performing brilliantly. Two unassisted goals went to the credit of Palmer as Anderson, Johnny Chase and Gordon Smith also tallied.

Smith hammered in the first goal in 6:42 of the first period after Garrison had circled around the cage and passed out to him in centre ice. It was not until 10:05 of the next session that the United States scored again, Palmer driving the rubber past Stogowski.

In the final session the Americans attacked at full speed. Palmer sent in the rubber on a rebound in 0:57 and in 3:53 Chase slammed in the disk from out near the sideboard. The concluding goal was made by Anderson in 9:01 after a solo flight down the full extent of the Arena.

The game was hard fought and remarkably clean. Only one penalty was called, Joe Fitzgerald being banished for one minute as a result of playing with a broken stick. This marked the third successive victory for the Americans and the fourth consecutive defeat for the Poles.

**German Defense Stubborn.**

The stubborn defense of the German sextet kept the Canadians from rolling up a high score even though they were always pressing toward the Teuton goal. The work of Walter Leinweber in the German net again was excellent.

Most of the shots of the Europeans were from out beyond the blue line and their passing had nothing of the smoothness and coordination of the Maple Leaf contingent.

The combination of Romeo Rivers and Vic Lindquist was especially effective on the Canadian attack, while Rudi Ball and Alfred Heinrich did splendidly in back ice for the Germans.

Lindquist took a pass from Walter Monson for the first score in 2:44 and then they reversed the order, Lindquist passing to Monson for the second in 4:52. An unassisted tally by George Garbutt in the second period was the extent of the scoring in this session. Rivers and Lindquist worked well together for a third-period score in 5:20. Duncanson went in alone for the final marker in 8:17.

February 9, 1932

# SCHAFER CAPTURES TITLE IN OLYMPICS

### Austrian Takes Figure-Skating Crown, With Grafstrom of Sweden Runner-Up.

### SWISS LEAD IN BOB EVENT

**By ARTHUR J. DALEY.**

Special to THE NEW YORK TIMES.

LAKE PLACID, N. Y., Feb. 9.—An iron-nerved youngster, the 19-year-old Swiss, Reto Capadrutt, and a graceful Austrian, Karl Schafer, dominated the Olympic picture today. The former twice bettered the

world's record for two-man bobsleighs down the winding silver strip of the Mount Van Hoevenberg run this morning to take the lead over the favored Americans, and the latter deposed the defending champion, Gillis Grafstrom of Sweden, in the men's figure skating competition in the Arena tonight.

It was a striking contrast these two presented, one daring in his piloting of the giant sleds, the other skillful and artistic in his perfect manoeuvres on the ice. But Capadrutt's task is only half completed, since he must face determined American rivals in the morning. Schafer's work, however, is over. He has added the Olympic crown to his title of world's champion.

Capadrutt's marvelous steering and other developments on the bob run today were the topics of conversation tonight, but Schafer's victory was immediately important, since the event was the first in which the United States had failed to win a title in the Third Olympic Winter Games. There were several changes also in the unofficial team standing.

**Turner Finishes Sixth.**

The Americans picked up a single tally as Roger Turner, the national champion, finished sixth and the United States total rose one notch to 58. Grafstrom finished second to Schafer and then came Montgomery Wilson of Canada, Marcus Nikkanen of Finland, Ernest Baier of Germany and Turner.

The Canadians' aggregate total advanced to 33. Then follow in order Norway with 14, Austria with 10, Sweden with 5, Finland with 3 and Germany with 2.

To achieve his distinction as new champion, Schafer turned in an almost perfect performance. He was chosen for first by five of the seven judges. Two picked him for second. Grafstrom took two firsts, three seconds, one third and one fifth.

Figure skating counted in the race for the team crown, but it really was the bobbing competition that attracted the greatest influx of visitors this town has seen to date. And it was Capadrutt and J. Hubert Stevens of the United States who stirred natives and newcomers.

**Shows Skill as Pilot.**

Holding firmly to the thongs of his rope-steered sled, the 138-pound capadrutt piloted his Switzerland II in masterful fashion as he was successively clocked in 2:05.88 and 2:07.21, both times being lower than the mark of 2:09 that Stevens made a year ago.

But it was Stevens, in a grand comeback on his second descent, who regained his record with a careening flight in 2:04.27 and thus forced himself into second place behind the dare-devil from St. Moritz, approximately four and a half seconds back.

On six occasions this morning the old mark was surpassed, twice by Capadrutt, once by Stevens and then by Jack Heaton of the United States, Lieutenant Alexander Papana of Rumania and Count Teofilo Rossi di Montelera of Italy, as the track kept getting faster and faster with every run.

Strung out over the mile and a half course as it reached up to the top of Mount Van Hoevenberg was the greatest crowd of spectators that has assembled here to date. Fully 10,000 persons jammed their way into the stands at the principal turns and when these were filled to capacity they stood along the snow-covered banks for the entire distance.

Unfortunately for the American cause, the two United States pairs drew the first two places and they made their initial trips while the snow in the straightaways was still soft. But it will be Capadrutt who

will be the second down tomorrow and it is only due to this that the chances of an ultimate American victory can be considered possible.

The final ranking will be on total time and as Erwin Hachman of Germany sent the last sled down at noon, Capadrutt was in the lead in 4:13.09, Stevens was second in 4:17.37, Heaton third in 4:22.53, Werner Huth of Germany fourth in 4:23.11 and Lieutenant Papana fifth in 4:23.33.

All except two of the twelve starters improved their time on the second run, Capadrutt was one of these. After coming down in the record time of 2:05.88, he made his second descent. As the white shirted Swiss pair zoomed into the Whiteface curve the clever little driver swung high to come slamming down into the trough.

At that point he already was traveling at a faster clip than in his previous trip. But the weight of Oscar Geier, his brake, pulled the sled around in a violent skid and two very precious seconds were lost before the boyish pilot regained control.

Capadrutt was greeted with a tremendous outburst of applause as he broke the string in the electrical timing machine at the bottom of the run. But it was the Stevens pair which shot down the slope amid the excited shouts of the crowd.

There was tenseness in the air from the moment that the loudspeakers boomed forth the announcement that they were ready to start. Frozen feet in this zero weather were forgotten as the spectators sought to catch a glimpse of the American hopes.

**Crouch Low Over Sled.**

Far up on the top of the mountain Hachman gave the signal to start. Hubert and Curtis Stevens crouched low over their sled, the U. S. A. I. They ran along the hard packed snow, and then vaulted into position, Hubert at the wheel and Curtis right behind him.

Through Eyrie they came in 29 seconds as the loudspeakers announced their progress. They hit Whiteface, a half mile from the start, in 52 seconds, rounded Cliffside in 1:09.2, and then the large crowd at Zig-Zag peered anxiously at Shady Corner a half mile above them.

In a moment a speck came rocketing down the mountainside, disappeared into the gutter of the run, and then was seen rounding Shady Corner. Into the straightaway they came, Curtis bobbing strongly and steadily.

One could almost hear him mutter through clenched teeth, "One-two-bob." Officially he was the brakeman, but he never forced the steel prongs into the ice. Hubert was hunched over his wheel, Curtis bobbing in back of him. The protecting glasses of both were perched jauntily on their foreheads.

Hubert wore the blue shirt of the American Olympic forces with the red U. S. A. monogram on the front. Curtis had on an old black pull-over. As they shot into Zig they hugged the middle line drive closely, jumped across the trough into Zag, and swept up near the top before the skillful Hubert pointed into the straightaway once more.

Then they were lost from view, but the amplifiers boomed forth news of their progress. "They have left Zig-Zag. They are nearing the finish. They are over. The time is 2:04.27."

Hardly had they split the tape before attention was switched to the top of the run once more. Heaton was about to start. He kept pace with the Stevens brothers through Eyrie and Whiteface, lost ground at Cliffside, but gained some of it back at Shady Corner. He was less than two seconds behind at this point, but in the approach to Zig-Zag the sled wavered in its path.

Bob Minton applied the brake to steady their flight. Bobsledders cannot afford to take any chances with the twisting reverse course of Zig-Zag. Everything has to be under control. Heaton went swishing into the turn four seconds slower than Stevens had a few moments before and that was almost the difference between them at the finish.

It was on the first run that the

two Americans lost ground. Stevens was first down the course and he was clocked in 2:13.10 and Heaton followed in 2:15.02.

Capadrutt, the University of Zurich student, held tightly to the controls on the only rope-steered sled in the race and there was a smile on his boyish face for the entire trip, on both descents, so that he looked like a schoolboy running away from a truant officer. So daring has he been in his practice runs that there was some anxiety on the part of the spectators as to whether he would be able to make the distance safely.

### Youth Is Clever Driver.

But for all his youth, Capadrutt is a clever driver. He was fourth at the world's championship races at St. Moritz in 1931 and first in the bobsleigh derby that preceded them, the same contestants competing in both. And it was with remarkable skill that this slight boy drove his queerly built sleigh with its sharp runners that curve into the framework of the sleigh itself.

In the free-figure skating that was held before a crowd of 3,000, Schafer and Grafstrom put on brilliant artistic displays to the continual applause of the spectators. The Austrian placed his entire dependence on an original program, while the Swedish star remained true to the old designs and twists.

One of the Austrian's best movements was one he had invented himself, the Karlisprung. He leaped into the air, twisted his body sharply around and then landed flat on his skates and glided away without a pause.

Grafstrom was exceptionally clever in his execution of the Axel Paulsen, the Salchow and the Brillen step. He also was excellent in slow toe spins and toe jumps. His performance came to a close with a spectacular Jackson Haynes whirl.

Schafer employed all these jumps and spins and then added a few more. His slow pirouette, the Langsam Sitz, was done marvelously and other steps that were perfectly executed were the Euler jump, the Lutz jump, the Mondaxel figure and the Rittberger.

The weather was ideal for the races this morning. It was below zero when the bobbers gathered at the Olympic run and the report for tomorrow again indicates perfect conditions, with increasing cloudiness and continued cold tonight.

The only definite decision of the afternoon came in the fifth consecutive victory of Canada in the Olympic hockey tournament with a 10-0 rout of the Polish sextet.

While the game was in progress another of the women's demonstration sports, which do not count toward the unofficial team standing, was staged. Skaters from the United States and Canada clashed in the 1,000-meter test. Miss Elizabeth Dubois of the United States triumphed in 2:04 to equal the world's record that her team-mate, Miss Helen Bina, had set a fortnight ago.

### New Mark for Mrs. Potter.

Miss Dubois, runner-up to Miss Jean Wilson of Canada in the 500-meter final yesterday, broke the tape when her Dominion rival fell in the last five yards. Prior to the final, however, Mrs. Leila Brooks Potter of Canada had been clocked in a heat in 2:01.2, time that supersedes Miss Dubois's effort for record consideration.

Meanwhile, in the Olympic Arena, the women figure skaters started in pursuit of the crown that the peerless Miss Sonja Henie of Norway now holds. Pursuit appears to be a vain one for the Norwegian girl's rivals.

Although no official score on their standing was forthcoming, there was not a spectator in the hall who left with anything but the impression that Miss Henie was certain to retain her crown. The graceful Norwegian girl was perfect with her school figures. Clad in a brown silk costume and with a rabbit's foot dangling from her Norwegian emblem, she skated firmly and retraced her previous figures with accuracy. Miss Fritzi Burger, the ebullient

little Austrian, who was a close runner-up to Miss Henie in the recent world's championship, also turned in a remarkable performance. She was not at her best during the early part of the program, but she did beautifully later and gave a splendid exhibition of counters and loops.

Miss Maribel Vinson, five times American champion, turned in an exceptionally even performance. She was steady and graceful and her executions were enthusiastically received. Miss Vivi-Anne Hulten of Sweden, Mrs. Constance Wilson Samuel of Canada and Mme. Yvonne de Ligne of Belgium also skated well.

February 10, 1932

# U.S. PAIR CAPTURES OLYMPIC BOB TITLE

### Stevens Brothers Snatch Victory From Swiss Team Led by 19-Year-Old Capadrutt.

### 10,000 SEE RECORD RUNS

By ARTHUR J. DALEY.
Special to The New York Times.

LAKE PLACID, N. Y., Feb. 10.— Seemingly beaten by the bob piloted by a mere slip of a boy, the gray-haired Stevens brothers came careening down the Mount Van Hoevenberg run today in two thrilling trips, shattered all records and virtually assured the Winter Olympic team

championship for the United States.

Snatching away victory from the very rim of defeat, the two Americans turned back the gallant bid of the 19-year-old Swiss, Reto Capadrutt, and Oscar Geier, whose last descent of this winding run failed by slightly more than one and a half seconds of gaining them the boblet title.

With the triumph scored by the Stevens pair and the third place captured by Jack Heaton and Bob Minton, the American total mounted to 72 points in the unofficial standing. When Norway's two ski stars, Arne Rustadstuen and Johan Grottumsbraaten, were unable to do better than fifth and sixth in the 18-kilometer Langlauf this morning, an ultimate United States triumph seemed assured.

The great Sven Utterstrom of Sweden, a long distance skier and never considered a factor over the shorter route, romped off with the 18-kilometer crown.

Even the victory of the five-time world's champion, Miss Sonja Henie of Norway, in defense of her Olympic figure, skating crown before a packed house at the Arena tonight could not alter the fact that the United States appears headed for the team title. Her triumph had been almost foreshadowed, although Miss Fritzi Burger of Austria pressed her right to the end and took second.

But the United States managed to add to its point total slightly, even though Norway's jumped considerably. Miss Maribel Vinson, five times United States titleholder, gained third place and increased the American aggregate to 76. Mrs. Constance Wilson Samuel of Canada was fourth, Miss Vivi-Anne Hulten of Sweden fifth, and Mme. Yvonne de Ligne of Belgium sixth.

The Norsemen, who won in 1928, face an almost impossible task now. They must make a clean sweep of the first four places in the three remaining ski events and there is hardly a chance of their doing that while the United States has certain points forthcoming in hockey and the four-man bobs.

There has not been a thrill in the entire Olympic tournament that could equal those two rides of J. Hubert and Curtis Stevens. Another crowd of 10,000 was strung along the serpentine path of the run. And the excited shrieks and cheers of the spectators turned the calm quiet of the mountain into a bedlam of noise from the moment the amplifiers boomed out "Clear the track!" until word came "They're over the finish."

Announcement of the time of the first descent could hardly be heard above the terrific din. Every one knew that Hubert Stevens had driven his sled to a new world's record even before it was confirmed officially. Then when he came rocketing down on his second trip it again was apparent that even the new universal mark had been surpassed.

There was magnificent competition on the run today and it was climaxed by another comeback by the Stevens pair when it seemed utterly impossible that they could win. When the bobbers took to the course yesterday the record was 2:09. Then Capadrutt did 2:05.88 to smash it and Stevens followed with 2:04.27 to regain the mark. During the day the old figures were surpassed six times.

### Stevens Regains Record.

Then when they started today Capadrutt once more slammed down the course to recapture the record for his team with 2:03.52, only to have Stevens regain it, with an amazing ride of 1:59.69, a flight that brought the brothers only fifty-five one-hundredths of a second away from the Swiss team.

But as startling as was that time, Hubert Stevens was even more perfect in his handling of the sled in the fourth and final heat. He shot down in 1:57.68 to break all records and give his 138-pound rival a target that could not be touched.

But Capadrutt did not give up without a fight. His sled was clocked for the last run in 1:59.67, slightly better than the Stevens's third-heat figures but still behind the last run of the Americans.

The once highly regarded time of 2:00 was turned into an empty set of statistics. Seven times in the third

Times Wide World Photo.

J. Hubert and Curtis Stevens, U. S. Team Which Won Bobsled Title, Heating Steel Runners Before Run.

Sven Utterstrom, Sweden, Victor in 18-Kilometer Cross-Country Race.

heat and six times in the fourth the daring band of bobbers went dipping below the old mark, so that for the two days of competition 2:09 was beaten nineteen times.

So superb was the piloting of the various drivers on this lightning-fast track that thrill followed thrill until it seemed that there could not be another one left. Capadrutt started it when he came zooming down for the new record of 2:03.52.

### Runners of Sled Heated.

As this clever little collegian was rocketing to the bottom the Stevens brothers stood at the top and watched a blow-torch heat the runners of their sled. Then the clarion call of "clear the track" issued forth from the loud-speaker. The words "Attention. please. No. 1 American team, Hubert Stevens driving," set the crowd on edge.

At the cry "they're off," every one stood in wrapt tenseness. When the time of 29 seconds at the Eyrie curve was announced the cheers broke forth, never to end until the tape was broken. They knew then that the Stevens brothers were record-bound.

But seconds later there was a gasp of dismay. News had come that the riders had spun around in the perpendicular Whiteface turn as Hubert, overanxious, had wheeled too sharply into the trough. Elation followed, however, when the announced time indicated that the Americans were still traveling faster than any one had before.

A black dot hove into view above Shady Corner, going at tremendous speed. "Crew bobbing—going into Shady—taking the turn high—they're out" was the staccato bark from the amplifier.

### Bobs Forward Violently.

Slicing down the mountainside they came, Curtis bobbing as no one had ever bobbed before. He jerked his body forward violently right into Zig-Zag. No one had ever done that, either. To the right into Zig, to the left into Zag they tore in 1:48, three seconds better than the Capadrutt team's best.

Over the finish they came and wildly enthusiastic spectators rushed up the hill where the sled had come to rest. They patted the two brothers on the back and hauled Curtis to his feet completely exhausted from his violent exertions on the way down.

There was a slight delay as the sleds were hauled by tractors back to the start and the same thing began all over again after another short stretch of anxiety and impatience. Then came the call to clear the track. The tension was terrific. It was on this run that the championship would be decided.

When the signal came for the start it seemed hours before the Americans reached Eyrie, but it was only 28 seconds, a full second better than the previous record time. There was no mistake at Whiteface on this occasion. Hubert hewed to the proper line, Curtis once more bobbing precisely.

In the stand at Zig-Zag stood Captain Werner Zahn of the German team near the spot where he had gone over a little more than a week ago, and with him was Paul Stevens, brother of the American standard-bearers. They peered up the mountain, seeking the speck that would reveal the descent.

### Whirl Into Straightaway.

After what seemed endless waiting the Americans came to light, etched darkly against the snow. They rounded Shady Corner high and whirled into the straightaway, Curtis bobbing and Hubert tightly clutching the wheel. There was not the slightest cessation in the brakeman's lunges. The brake, itself, was forgotten. Curtis never stopped until they swooped around Zig and as Zag was reached Hubert drove so close to the brink that Paul Stevens held his breath and then bellowed, "Ride 'em, Hubert."

In twelve seconds the U. S. A. I had covered the quarter mile to the finish. Keen was the jubilation when the time of 1:57.68 was announced, although the announcement was practically drowned out in the strident chorus of cheers. Every one felt that the dauntless Swiss pilot, Capadrutt, would never be able to touch that.

New York Times Studio.

**Miss Sonja Henie of Norway, Who Retained Her Olympic Figure-Skating Championship at the International Games.**

Capadrutt, aided by Geier, did his best, but the gallant little sportsman was unequal to the task. He was one-fifth of a second behind at Eyrie, took Whiteface low and lost four-fifths of a second more. He regained some ground going into Cliffside where he was only one-fifth of a second behind, dropped back two seconds at Shady and was three seconds behind at Zig-Zag. That finished him. His final time was 1:59.67.

Smilingly Capadrutt walked back to the bulletin board as his brake, Geier, spoke quietly to him. Capadrutt was learning a new word in the English language. It was "congratulations." The race was over.

The bobsledders supplied the thrills with their spectacular daring, but it remained for the women figure skaters to give superb exhibitions of grace and rhythm in the Arena tonight. More than an hour before the scheduled starting time hundreds were jammed on the stairways waiting for the doors to be opened.

So many were waiting outside that, long after the competition had started, spectators were still filing into the Arena. The early contestants received their share of applause, but it was not until Miss Henie skated to the centre of the ice that the moment had arrived for which all had been waiting.

It was a striking picture that this Norwegian girl presented. She was clad in shimmering white satin, flecked with rhinestones, and her jaunty toque, also made of rhinestones, was perched on her blond curls. Dangling from an ornament on her dress was a rabbit's foot, her omen of good luck.

Miss Henie stood bowing at the thunderous acclaim she received. The judges nodded and the band launched forth in a popular air. The applause was still heard as she started and it never ceased until she had finished.

### Stars With Paulsen Jump.

The Norwegian girl began with an Axel Paulsen jump and did this difficult leap so easily and so gracefully that it looked as if any novice could have done the same. Never for a moment was Miss Henie anything but assured of herself. She was the epitome of perfect control. By so much did she outdistance the field that only Miss Burger could be rated in her class.

Time after time the Olympic champion from Norway brought down the house with her sensational Paulsens, and the very difficult Lutz jump was also included in her repertoire. Her spread-eagles were smartly executed and were smooth and graceful.

When she dropped into the Jackson Haynes spin she rose slowly out of the whirl and switched her feet so rapidly that the change almost eluded the eye. Once she made the exchange four times without pause. Her slow top spins were superb and the storm of applause that greeted her concluding backward sweep down the ice was a fitting tribute to her exhibition.

The effervescent Miss Burger also caught the popular fancy. The instant she glided out on the ice she smiled and every one applauded. She was dressed in blue with silver pipings and a blue bonnet topped her ensemble. She, too, started with a Paulsen after several dainty sweeps around the surface of the arena.

### Receives Much Applause.

After a Brillen step Miss Burger darted into a spread-eagle and back to a Paulsen once more. She finished to applause almost equal to that received by her Norse rival.

The red-clad Miss Vivi-Anne Hulten of Sweden skated well. She was doing excellently when she attempted a Paulsen, but in coming down on the ice her ankle turned and she lost her balance.

While the bobsledders were flashing down the course in runs that took two minutes, sixty-one skiers were racing in the grueling 18-kilometer test that took some of the starters almost two hours to complete.

In this event Grottumsbraaten was deposed as titleholder and Rustadstuen, his chief rival, badly beaten. The Norwegians began to founder along about the twelfth kilometer when the warmth of the noon-day sun had melted the snow. The Swedish leaders, however, found the soft snow to their liking and had no trouble in taking first and second.

Also competing in the 18-kilometer race were thirty-three athletes who were using this as a means for gaining points in the combined event which will be concluded with the ski jump tomorrow. They started with the others, but those who were entered only in the combined test received no ranking in the other standing.

Among the combined skiers Grottumsbraaten was the leader in defense of the crown he had captured in 1928 at St. Moritz and he stands an excellent chance of winning, despite his dethronement in the Langlauf itself today.

### Zetterstrom Leads Americans.

The first American to finish in the 18-kilometer event was Olle Zetterstrom, twenty-third, and first in the combined standing was Ed Blood of New Hampshire, sixteenth.

In the afternoon the last of the women's demonstration tests, the 1,500-meter speed skating event, was held with an American triumphing. Miss Kit Klein was victorious in 3:00.6 when Mrs. Leila Brooks Potter fell as the field was closely bunched at the finish.

In the first heat Miss Jean Wilson of Canada broke the old world's record of 3:28 with the new figures of 2:54.2, only to have Mrs. Potter beat that time with a 2:54 performance in the second trial.

The United States hockey sextet gave a splendid display of team-work in rolling up its highest score of the tournament in the Arena this evening, turning back the German team, 8 to 0.

This completed the preliminary work for the final game with Canada in the stadium on Saturday. The United States combination now has registered four straight victories following the setback at the hands of the Dominion aggregation by a 2-1 score in the opening contest. A victory for the Americans Saturday will mean a play-off on Sunday.

February 11, 1932

# BIRGER RUUD WINS OLYMPIC SKI TITLE

---

## 19-Year-Old Norwegian Takes Jump Crown With Leaps of 218 and 226 Feet.

---

## COUNTRYMAN IS SECOND

---

## Beck, Fellow-Townsman, Sets Record of 234½ Feet, but Loses by 1.1 Points.

---

## 15,000 APPLAUD JUMPERS

---

### M. and Mme. Brunet of France Retain Pairs Figure Skating Laurels—U. S. Finishes Second.

### By ARTHUR J. DALEY.

Special to The New York Times.

LAKE PLACID, N. Y., Feb. 12.—Snow that had been stored in a shed today saved the greatest exhibition that the Third Olympic Winter Games have furnished to date. The barren tower of the ski jump was blanketed with a new surface at daybreak so that the Olympic jumping tests could be held in the afternoon.

With the weather still balmy and the sun beaming overhead, the crowds poured out in such numbers that there were 15,000 packed in the stands that reached upward to the starting tower and strung out along the surrounding countryside. They saw the new course record of 204 feet broken fifteen times and tied thrice. And they saw the 19-year-old Birger Ruud of Norway win the Olympic crown with successive jumps of 218 and 226 feet.

Hans Beck, another Norwegian 19-year-old, gave him a sturdy battle for the title, jumping 234½ and 208 feet. The former distance was the longest of the day and automatically became the new Intervales Hill record. Ruud and Beck were so close together in their duel that only a little more than one point separated them in the estimation of the judges.

### Ericsson in Fourth Place.

Ruud was awarded 228.1 and Beck 227, while still another Norwegian, Kaare Wahlberg, took third place with 219.5 points after leaps of 205 and 209 feet. Then came Ivan Sven Ericsson of Sweden, Caspar Oimoen of the United States and Fritz Kaufmann of Switzerland.

But this 19-point increase of the Norwegians in the team standing was partially offset by the results of the figure skating for pairs tonight when Miss Beatrix Loughran and Sherwin C. Badger of the United States finished second to M. and Mme. Pierre Brunet of France, the Olympic and world's champions. The American total mounted to 83, while the Norwegians had to be satisfied with 68. The placing of the other contestants in the figure skating had no important bearing on the standing. Hungary broke into the ranking for the first time when the pair of Laszlo Szollas and Miss Emilia Rotter gained third position, with another Hungarian combination, Sandor Szalay and Miss Olga Orgonista,

fourth. In fifth and sixth places were the Canadian teams, the brother and sister duo of Montgomery Wilson and Mrs. Constance Wilson Samuel, and Chauncey R. Bangs and Miss Frances Claudet.

### Chances Are Remote.

With colder weather tonight the chance of staging the four-man bobsled event on Sunday is much brighter, and Americans are certain to gain valuable counters there, and with the second place of the Miss Loughran-Badger combination tonight, the chances of a Norwegian triumph are very remote, even if the bobsledding is not held.

To its 83-point total the United States is certain to add at least five points from the hockey tournament. To beat this the Norwegians will be forced to oust the great Sven Utterstrom of Sweden and sweep the first four places in the 50-kilometer ski race tomorrow. The American team triumph still is not mathematically assured.

There was considerable confusion connected with the announcement of the ski jumping results. The competition was over at approximately 3:30 this afternoon and it was not until four hours later that any inkling of the order of finish was forthcoming. Then it was stated that Beck was the winner, no other places being given. A short time later there was an official reversal when the points were tabulated again, and the younger of the Ruud brothers was named as champion.

### Rivals From Same Town.

It was odd that the chief difficulty should centre on two youngsters who were brought up together in the mining town of Kongsberg. They learned to ski together and to-day they battled for the same title.

Ruud won because he elected to gamble on his second leap, while Beck jumped cautiously. The latter had set a new course record in his first flight, a grand 234½-foot journey through the air. Ruud had done 218 feet on his first try.

So the second time Ruud shot down from the top of the tower he risked whatever chance he had of overtaking his friend with a splendid leap of 226 feet. If he had fallen he would not have placed at all. But Ruud made the attempt with success.

On the other hand Beck was satisfied with his first jump and was unwilling to jeopardize his standing with a similar leap that might not have so happy an ending. His second effort measured 208 feet. In total distance there was not much to choose between them, Ruud being a little less than two feet ahead. Since several experts were of the opinion that the two were equal in form, this slight matter of less than two feet may have meant an Olympic title.

### Japanese Is Applauded.

Both jumps of Ruud and Beck drew vociferous applause from the huge crowd, but it remained for a little Japanese to evoke a storm of handclapping and cheers. He was Goro Adachi, another 19-year-old contestant. Every one had noted his name on the program as an entrant but no one really expected to see him come whisking off the slide into space.

Adachi is the youth who tried the Intervales Hill for the first time about a fortnight ago and went spinning into the grand stand. He was so badly injured that hospital treatment was required. Undaunted by his rather terrifying experience, Adachi went 196¾ feet on his first trip and the somewhat amazing distance of 216 2-5 feet on his second try, thus becoming the first Japanese ever to leap more than 60 meters.

Adachi's form was splendid in addition to his fine distances, and he was ranked in eighth place, less than five points behind Sigmund Ruud of Norway, in seventh position.

That was the biggest surprise of the day—the failure of the elder of the Ruud brothers to obtain a higher ranking. Although a favorite to win, Sigmund could do only 206 and 205 feet, both leaps longer than the old record, but still not good enough against so high class a field as was gathered together today.

Caspar Oimoen, the American champion, whose practice workouts had been very encouraging, when 206 and 219 feet in his two tries, and these were enough to bring him fifth place.

There was one very bad spill on the run when Yoichi Takata of Japan turned over twice in midair and crashed down on his back on the hillside. He rolled to the bottom, his skis dancing around crazily. He lay there unconscious until carried to the dressing room. At the hospital it was believed that he had a dislocated shoulder.

Roy Mikkelsen of Chicago, one of the foremost American hopes, did 226 feet in his first trip down the slide, but he fell in attempting to pull up and wrenched his right leg so badly that he was not able to continue.

Beck's record leap was made under conditions which, though alike for all the contestants, militated against a better performance. The upper stretch of the chute that comes out of the tower on Intervales Hill had become too slippery for safe use by the time the jumping event began and it became necessary to start the athletes from a rope stretched across the runway about thirty feet from the top.

As each contestant's turn came he slid rapidly down from the upper landing and stopped himself by grasping the rope. The start was made by loosing his grasp. On his record leap, the eleventh in the first round of jumps, Beck started down the chute with three rapid strides.

At the take-off Beck bolted upward in a mighty leap that was obviously sending him to a new record. Up shot his arms, then down like wings they came and he started propelling himself by churning the air with his arms. Approaching the precipitous incline, he straightened out gracefully to complete a performance that bordered closely on perfection.

### Tip Touches Midway Point.

The measurer at the side of the hill put down his bamboo pole, the tip touching the midway point between the toe of Beck's forward foot and the heel of his rear foot as he touched the ground. It was found that he had struck halfway between the 71 meter and 72 meter posts at the side of the landing hill.

The leap was officially adjudged one of 71.5 meters, approximately 234.5 feet. No attempt was made to draw the decision finer, as much depends upon the eye of the measurer and steel tape measurements are impracticable.

The Arena was more crowded tonight for the figure skating than at any other time to date. Hundreds were turned away and the onlookers were lined along the railings in back of the seats and were perched on any ledge that could afford them a view of the contestants. The windows at the front end of the ice were blocked with spectators.

Seven pairs took part and in comparison with the long delay that followed the other figure-skating events before results were forthcoming the judges acted quickly. They took no more than a half hour. The waiting crowd was entertained by the Olympic champions, Miss Sonja Henie of Norway and Karl Schafer of Austria, and by Miss Maribel Vinson of the United States and Miss Fritzi Burger of Austria.

The spectators received the exhibitions of the defending French couple, of the American team of Miss Loughran and Mr. Badger and of both Hungarian combinations warmly. So closely matched were they in the minds of the onlookers that there really was some doubt as to the eventual winner.

The Brunets skated with a marvelously developed sense of unity and rhythm. They skated to the strains of a waltz and presented a varied and original program.

The Hungarian pair of Miss Rotter and Mr. Szollas had a program that was as varied and as original as the Brunets and many Hungarians in the crowd were disappointed when their representatives failed to win. The skaters captivated the crowd with spectacular jumps and lifts.

The Americans were very striking as they took the ice. Miss Loughran was charming in white satin bordered with black. The national champions never skated better than they did tonight, keeping to a fast tempo at all times. Thunderous applause greeted them at the finish.

February 13, 1932

Times Wide World Photo.

**Birger Ruud of Norway, Who Captured Ski-Jump Title.**

# CANADA'S SIX KEEPS TITLE IN OLYMPICS

## Undefeated Hockey Team Plays 2-2 Overtime Tie With U. S. and Annexes Crown.

## FINNISH SKIER TRIUMPHS

## Saarinen Wins 50-Kilometer Race, With Liikkanen, Countryman, In Second Place.

By ARTHUR J. DALEY.
Special to The New York Times.

LAKE PLACID, N. Y., Feb. 13.— A crazily bounding disk that rolled past Goalie Frank Farrel of the United States team in the Arena today gave Canada the Olympic hockey championship as the Dominion sextet and the Americans played to a 2-2 tie. A deadlock was all that the Maple Leaf contingent needed to triumph since its slate was clear of defeats, while the blue-shirted squad had suffered one setback.

Never has the Arena been so packed with spectators as it was this afternoon. The normal capacity is 3,000, but there were more than 5,000 present, watching a spirited contest between two high-class sextets that played through a regular game and three overtime periods with relentless fire and spirit.

While the hockey tournament was completed in the comparative warmth of the Arena, the skiers were braving a raging blizzard on the fifty-kilometer ski trail. Veli Saarinen of Finland triumphed in the race and shut out completely any chance of a Norwegian victory for the team title.

**Mathematical Chance Gone.**

The United States thus won the Third Olympic Winter Games championship, with the present standing being 88 points to 77 for the Norwegians, twice winners of the international crown. The Americans had practically clinched the honors several days ago, but there was a slight mathematical chance of their being overtaken. Now no such chance remains, no matter what happens in the four-man bobsled competition tomorrow and Monday.

Although the closing ceremonies were held in the Stadium after the hockey game as thousands sat out in the snowstorm to watch the winners receive their rewards, the Olympics will continue for two more days. Twenty-four hours' grace is permitted in accordance with the terms of the international protocol, but an extra day's grace has been granted by the committee in order to complete the bobsledding.

The return of cold and snow has furnished assurance that the bobsledding will be held. All last night and today a corps of workmen carted snow up the mountainside, packed down the straightaways and built up the icy banks of the curves. The first two heats of the juggernaut derby will start in the morning and the final two on Monday. When the event is over the American total in the unofficial standing is likely to be increased. The Norwegians are not entered. As far as they are concerned, the Olympics are over.

**Blizzard Follows Warm Weather.**

The fickleness of the Lake Placid weather could not be better illustrated than it was today. After two days of rain and warmth a blizzard settled down on the countryside. The local committee was not quite prepared for this. It had marked out a course for the 50-kilometer race that doubled back on itself, so that the same trail was traversed twice. Instead of starting and finishing in the Stadium the terminal points were several miles out of town.

This did not meet with the approval of all the contestants and there was a three-hour delay while they argued back and forth, and instead of starting at 8 o'clock it was 11 before the first man was sent off the mark.

Saarinen had an excellent starting time. He was twenty-third on the list, right in back of the Norwegian star, Arne Rustadstuen. Sven Utterstrom of Sweden, the defending champion, was off early, thirteenth, and he was never in a position to know what time his competitors were making.

The winner was in an excellent spot, and the runner-up, Vaino Liikkanen, another Finn, was even more advantageously situated, since he was third from the rear. These two led at the half-way mark. At the finish they were twenty seconds apart. Saarinen was timed in 4 hours and 28 minutes and Liikkanen in 4:28.20. Rustadstuen was third, Ole Hegge of Norway, fourth; Sigurd Vestad of Norway, fifth, and Utterstrom, sixth.

While the skiers were trudging through the heavy snowfall the Americans and Canadian sextets were flashing the best brand of hockey that the tournament has seen to date. Germany had beaten Poland, 4 to 1, in the morning, and the afternoon game was to be the deciding test.

If the United States squad won it would mean a play-off tomorrow, and the Maple Leaf combination was determined that no such extra game would be forthcoming, but when Romeo Rivers of Canada swung at the disk with only thirty-three seconds of play left an American victory seemed certain.

However, the rubber bounced along erratically and skidded between the United States defense men. Before Goalie Farrel was aware that the disk was approaching it had skipped into the net, knotting the count.

The Canadian objective was achieved with that goal. Through three overtime periods they played defensive hockey, batting the rubber down the ice at every opportunity. The Canadians forced the Americans to start every foray from down near their own net.

Toward the close of the game, in the third overtime session, the blue-shirted players abandoned any pretense of protecting their goal and repeatedly sent five men down the ice, but Goalie Cockburn of Canada was always on the alert and firm efforts for a score were of no avail.

All the American first-stringers played brilliantly. Ding Palmer, Doug Everett and Johnny Chase in the front line were always scoring threats, and Johnny Garrison and Ty Anderson did yeoman work on the defense.

**Hundreds Wait in Snow.**

Long before game time the Arena entrances were jammed with eager spectators. They stood in the snowstorm, waiting to get in. Standing room only was being sold, and so anxious was the crowd to enter that even these tickets went rapidly.

Before the teams skated out on the ice there were huge gaps of empty seats that had been reserved, but up on top in dense packs were the standees. A signal was given for them to rush into the stands. When they poured down there were so many of them left behind the rail that no appreciable difference could be discerned by the advance of some of the standees to the seats.

Hardly had the game started when Mayor Walker of New York made his entrance, clad in ski trousers and a brown pullover sweater, with his white shirt open at the neck. So engrossed were the spectators by the game that his approach was hardly noticed. It was not until intermission that he received rousing cheers from the crowd.

At this time the American stick-handlers were not aware of the progress of the 50-kilometer ski race and for all they knew the Olympic team championship might depend on their victory. That is the way they played. But when the two Finns finished one-two, their triumph was not necessary to capture the team title for the United States.

The United States won the unofficial crown by any method of scoring. Even if first places alone were considered, the Americans still would emerge victorious. Of the thirteen events contested to date the United States has won five.

**Clean Sweep in Skating.**

There was a clean sweep of the speed-skating races as Jack Shea annexed the 500 and 1,500 meter honors and Irving Jaffee took the 5,000 and 10,000 meter laurels. Then J. Hubert and Curtis Stevens shot down the Olympic bob run to conquer the fastest drivers in the world in the boblet test.

Norway gained three first places, Miss Sonja Henie, won the women's figure-skating title; Johan Grottumsbraaten repeated in the combined ski event, and Birger Ruud annexed the ski-jumping laurels. The only other victors were Karl Schafer of Austria in the men's figure skating, M. and Mme. Pierre Brunet of France in the pair figure skating, Sven Utterstrom of Sweden in the 18-kilometer skirace, Saarinen and the Canadian hockey team.

Of the defending champions, few repeated. Among this number was Jaffee at 10,000 meters, Miss Henie, the Brunets, Grottumsbraaten and the Maple Leaf hockey sextet.

The dethroned titleholders included Bernt Evensen of Norway at 500 meters, Ivar Ballangrud of Norway at 5,000 meters, Gillis Grafstrom of Sweden in the men's figure skating, Grottumsbraaten in the 18-kilometer race and Utterstrom in the 50-kilometer event. In addition to these, Jack Heaton, victor in the skeleton bob test at St. Moritz, could do no better than third in the corresponding boblet competition.

**Teamwork is Excellent.**

The American team never showed to better advantage than it did today. It was aggressive and its teamwork was excellent. Not until the final bell did the Blueshirts stop trying.

For the first two minutes the rivals seemed to test one another's defense. Then Palmer started the Americans on their way. Deftly handling his stick, he swooped down the sideboards and carried the disk right in back of the cage. In an instant Everett was in position in front of the net and it was easy work for him to hammer it past the goalie in 2:17.

Garrison almost followed with another goal. He darted down the ice and was just inches away from a second tally when Cockburn made the save. Shortly after that sortie, however, the sterling defense man was sent to the penalty box and Canada launched its greatest drive.

Sending four men down the ice, the Canadians peppered away at Farrel, but the former Yale star was equal to every emergency and he turned aside drive after drive, holding the fort by his own individual prowess until Garrison returned.

It was right after this, when the Americans were at full strength, that the Maple Leaf sextet tied the score. Hack Simpson, centre on the second line, pierced the American defense and hit a terrific shot, not at the net but at the backboard. Farrel wheeled around to see if the disk had lodged in the drapes behind him, but the rubber bounced back to centre ice and Simpson found the cage totally unprotected, flicking the disk behind Farrel.

The Americans pressed into Canadian territory in the early stages of the second period. The United States teamwork was excellent and a half dozen perfectly executed plays issued being goals by a matter of inches.

Finally one of the plays worked. Johnny Bent skated along the sideboards in an individual rush with Palmer coming down on the opposite side. Bent eased his way through, but his drive went to the right of the cage and ricocheted off the wall to Palmer's feet, some thirty feet out and to the left.

The former Yale ace took his time and swung. The rubber rose waist-high in its flight and went whistling past Cockburn in 13:38 to give the Americans a one-goal lead.

This lead endured until just before the close of the game. But this time the Blueshirts were playing much more cautiously than they had at first. They sent the disk skidding down the ice to keep the Canadians back near their own goal with occasional trips to the Dominion net so that the Maple Leaf squad would not move up its back men.

**Makes Brilliant Save.**

The acrobatic Farrel made a brilliant save of one Canadian try when he dived head foremost for the disk as Monson skated with it behind the goal, but this merely postponed the inevitable. The deadlock came in 14:27, as Rivers's bouncing shot escaped Farrel and tied the score.

After that the Canadians played safe hockey. They kept at least one man down the ice in American territory to harass the American players as they swept past the Blue line. The closest call Canada had was in the second overtime period when Palmer and Chase came down together and found only Rivers between them and the net.

The Canadian wingman took a desperate chance. He attempted to poke-check the rubber away from the clever Palmer. Had he missed nothing could have averted a score. He did not miss.

As the bell clanged for the end of the game the two teams met in the centre of the arena, cheered each other and shook hands all around. The crowd filed out into the storm and entered the Stadium, where the athletes were reassembled for the closing ceremonies.

The closing of the games had none of the impressiveness of the opening ceremonies. For one thing, they were closed before all the competition was over. But, strangely enough, there were more persons present in the grandstands for the finale than there had been for the opening.

**Medals Are Distributed.**

Count Henri de Baillet-Latour, president of the International Olympic Committee, made the presentations of diplomas and medals to those who had not as yet received them and thanked the contestants for their fine display of sportsmanship.

The early bickering was forgotten. Differences had been settled to the complete satisfaction of every one and it was in true amity and international fellowship that the games were declared over.

February 14, 1932

# FISKE'S TEAM WINS OLYMPIC BOB TITLE

**No. 1 United States Four-Man Sled Returns Best Total Time for Four Heats.**

## HOMBURGER QUARTET NEXT

**No. 2 U. S. Crew Trails by 2.02 Seconds — Kilian's German Sled 3d, Capadrutt 4th.**

## 10,000 SEE CLOSING EVENT

**Americans, Winners of Team Crown, Finish With 103 Points—Norway Is Second With 77.**

### By ARTHUR J. DALEY.
Special to THE NEW YORK TIMES.

LAKE PLACID, N. Y., Feb. 15.—The Third Olympic Winter Games ended today as they had started almost a fortnight ago—with an American victory.

Holding fast to the remnants of a slight lead he had established in the initial two heats yesterday over Henry Homburger's No. 2 United States team, Billy Fiske, pilot of the winning team in 1928 at St. Moritz, drove the No. 1 United States sled down the Mount Van Hoevenberg run to the four-man bobsled championship, compiling the best total time for four heats.

The giant slide was a bit faster today than it was yesterday, when Fiske led the other American team by slightly more than three seconds, but it was not speedy enough to permit any unusually fast times.

To overtake the team led by the young Cambridge alumnus, Homburger would have had to equal his own world's record of 1:52 on his last run, but the best he could do was 1:54.28. Thus, Fiske's sled triumphed on total time by 2.02 seconds.

### Winners Receive Medals.

In sharp contrast to the official closing ceremonies on Saturday, today's climax was a simple one. The bobsledders gathered at the bottom of the course and Dr. Godfrey Dewey, president of the local organizing committee, presented each of the riders of the winning team—Fiske, Eddie Eagan, Clifford (Tippy) Gray and Jay O'Brien—with Olympic diplomas and gold medals.

Then Captain Werner Zahn of Germany, victim of one of the bobsled crashes, who still has his arm in a sling, advanced and handed Fiske the huge silver bowl, known as the Martineau Challenge Cup, emblematic of the world's championship.

That was all. There was no blaring of the band, no playing of the national anthem and no majestic ascent of the American flag over the Stadium ramparts. Instead of this, a few quiet words were spoken, and

Mayor Walker With the Team, Left to Right: Jay O'Brien, Clifford B. Gray, Edward F. Eagan and William L. Fiske.

*Times Wide World Photo.*

the Olympic Games were over.

With the capture of the first two places in the bob run the American unofficial total advanced to 103 points, the United States already having clinched the Winter Olympics team championship for the first time. Norway stayed in second place with an aggregate of 77, while Canada was third with 49.

### Attendance Falls Off.

The crowd today was far below its record proportions of yesterday, when 20,000 saw the first two heats. Those who witnessed the events came early, so that there were almost 10,000 present when the final heats were started. But there was no huge increase in the number of spectators later on, so that the initial attendance figures virtually stood for the day.

As was the case yesterday, the crowd was apathetic in its cheering. It was bitterly cold out in the unprotected stands, which probably accounted for the lack of applause. The only approach to real excitement came with the final descent of Homburger and his Saranac Red Devils.

To equal Fiske's time, the broad-shouldered young engineer had to drive his sled down the slide in 1:52.28, an infinitesimal margin over his world's record clocking. As the black-masked crew shot down the mountain it kept at least one second ahead of Fiske's best time at every point.

The team was bobbing strongly and was almost two seconds ahead of Fiske after leaving Shady Corner, but just before Zig-Zag was reached the bobbers hit a small set of curves, known as "little S."

### Rights the Sled in Time.

Homburger went so high on both of these that there was fear for a moment that he was going to plunge over the top. But he righted his sled in time at the cost of a precious fraction of a second and took Zig-Zag very high. When his time of 1:44 was announced it was evident that he would never be able to make the final quarter of a mile in eight seconds.

Homburger was beaten there and the crowd sensed it. He shot across the finish line in 1:54.28, the fastest clocking of the day, but not fast enough to win.

There was still a great deal of snow in the straightaways today, but the turns were much faster than they had been. The chief complaint on the part of the drivers was that the ruts of the previous day still were present. Once these deep ice paths were entered there was no chance of escaping from them.

Homburger lost a great opportunity on his first descent when he skidded badly after hitting a rut just before going into the Whiteface curve. It was hard to judge just how far behind he fell by his mishap.

He had passed Eyrie in 29 seconds and Whiteface in 56 seconds. Hanns Kilian of Germany made one trip in which he swept by Eyrie in 29 and then took Whiteface in 50. Perhaps Homburger lost 6 seconds. But whatever it was, he was almost on a par with the best clocking of the day at Cliffside and he finally ended in 1:58.56.

Kilian's sled had two good runs of 1:58.19 and 1:57.40 for a total time of 8:00.04, a little less than 5 seconds behind Homburger, to take third-place honors. The sled driven by Reto Capadrutt of Switzerland was fourth with 8:12.18 and Count Rossi di Montelera of Italy fifth in 8:24.21.

The most disappointed of all was Lieutenant Alexander Papana of Rumania, whose team missed tying the Italians by one one-hundredth of a second. The sled of Baron Walther von Mumm of Germany was seventh with 8:35.45.

With the Olympic Games over and the crowd rapidly disappearing from hotels and streets, Lake Placid is starting to return to normalcy. Interest here is centring on the North American bobsled championships, which will start tomorrow and finish Wednesday.

The four-man tests will be held in the morning with eight teams entered, while the boblet event will be gaged on the following day, also with eight teams on the entry list. Two heats daily will be run.

### Three Invaders Entered.

In the four-man competition there will be three foreign nations represented. Lieutenant Papana will drive a Rumanian sled, Kilian a German bob and Capadrutt a Swiss sled. Pilots of other bobs will be Raymond Stevens, Hubert Stevens, Curtis Stevens, Henry Homburger and Harry Grayson Martin.

In the two-man tests all these will be at the helm except Curtis Stevens, who again will ride with his brother, Hubert. The eighth driver will be Gilbert Colgate Jr.

February 16, 1932

At the 1932 Olympics, the U.S. swept all four speed skating gold medals. Irving Jaffee took the 5,000 and 10,000 meter events. John Shea, (foreground) shown here winning the 1,500 meter race, also took the 500 meter contest.

Ivar Ballangrud, shown here after winning the 5000 meter speed skating event at the 1928 Olympics at St. Moritz, achieved even greater glory at the 1936 games when he captured the 500, 5,000 and 10,000 meter events. He was the first to capture three gold medals at a Winter Olympics.

# MISS VINSON TAKES 6TH SKATING TITLE

## Again Annexes National Figure Championship at the New Haven Arena.

## TURNER WINS ONCE MORE

### Captures His Sixth Consecutive Crown in Men's Event— Young Robin Lee Third.

By LINCOLN A. WERDEN.
Special to THE NEW YORK TIMES.

NEW HAVEN, Conn., March 18.— Retaining the national figure skating championship in the same arena where she first scored in 1928, Miss Maribel Vinson of Winchester, Mass., captured her sixth consecutive title tonight.

While 3,000 followed the spinning blue figure of Miss Vinson on the ice, the Radcliffe College senior equaled the mark of Mrs. Theresa Blanchard in winning once more at the New Haven Arena.

Later Miss Vinson, with George E. B. Hill of Boston as her partner, annexed the senior championship for pairs.

A few minutes before Miss Vinson triumphed, Roger Turner, the Boston lawyer who began his string of conquests at the same time that the Massachusetts girl did, won the men's singles crown for the sixth year in a row.

Turner, profiting by his work this morning in the school figures, went through his free ice skating tonight without a mishap, while J. Lester Madden, 23-year-old Harvard Business School student, who loomed as a real threat, had the misfortune to tumble to the ice twice while attempting jumps.

Back of Turner and Madden came 13-year-old Robin Lee of St. Paul, who is a sensation of the skating world. Young Lee, competing in his first national senior championship, performed with confidence. After he had made some excellent jumps and an up-and-down Jackson Haynes spin, he fell, however, trying a Salchow jump.

Miss Suzanne Davis of Boston finished second to Miss Vinson, while Miss Louise Weigel of Buffalo was third and Dr. Hulda Berger of New York, fourth.

Miss Vinson overcame a handicap during her free skating, as she, too, fell at the start of her five-minute program, but otherwise her performance was of its usual high standard. She twirled and spun and did the orthodox and difficult jumps with a clear-cut smoothness. Miss Davis, too, added to the evening's splendid program, her split jumps being especially spectacular, and Miss Weigel was well poised in her skating.

The 18-year-old Buffalo girl, Miss Estelle Weigel, carried off the women's junior championship, suc-

ceeding her sister, Miss Louise Weigel, who held the title last year.

She included a number of spins in her free skating and won against some high-class competition. Miss Valerie Jones of New York, who won the novice honors last year, finished second, while Miss Grace Madden of Boston was third.

Miss Audrey Peppe, a member of the 1932 Olympic team, elected a difficult free-skating program. Unfortunately as she attempted to repeat the testing Axel Paulsen jump she fell, and the mishap affected her chances, as the competition was close.

The men's junior honors went to the mid-Westerner, William Swallender of Minneapolis, who was making his début in the championship. Swallander turned in a good performance in the school figures and his free skating was steady and well controlled, so that he went back home tonight with the laurels that graced the brow of the youthful Lee in 1932.

Bruce Mapes of Brooklyn accounted for second place and the intercollegiate champion, Lyman Wakefield of Dartmouth, finished third.

The junior pairs proved to be a colorful event, with the New York team of Miss Eva Schwerdt and William Bruns winning by virtue of their elaborate program that was well done.

The women's novice competition was one of the high spots of the two-day tourney, 13-year-old Miss Polly Blodgett of Boston performing with grace and confidence through a fine program. Despite the fact that more experienced skaters took part, Miss Blodgett's chum, 11-year-old Miss Joan Tozzer of Boston, won second place. In a red costume with her hair braided down her back she formed a pretty picture and when she did a marvelous split jump the gallery roundly applauded. Miss Nettie Prantel of New York, skating well, finished third.

Another New Yorker, Wilfred MacDonald, won the men's novice singles with Otto Dallmayr, also of New York, second, and Herbert E. Cook of Detroit, third.

March 19, 1933

## 50,000 SEE SKIERS PERFORM ON COAST

### Snow Brought in Box Cars— Wooden Platform and Slide Used at Berkeley.

BERKELEY, Calif., Jan. 14 (AP). —While 50,000 persons watched, a ski-jumping contest was held today on 43,000 cubic feet of snow brought here in box cars from the Sierra Nevada Mountains. It was Berkeley's first snow carnival.

Contestants took off from a wooden platform sixty feet high on the crest of a hill north of the University of California campus stadium after a run of 75 to 100 feet on a wooden slide. They landed in a slide of snow six inches deep, packed on straw for a distance of 450 feet, a thin white streak incongruously bisecting the green and brown hillside.

Roy Mikkelsen, national ski-jumping champion, jumped 125 feet, and although he had, under more favorable conditions, jumped 242 feet, his performance today was considered exceptional.

January 15, 1934

# Oimoen Regains U. S. Ski-Jumping Title; Fall Eliminates Mikkelsen, 1933 Winner

By The Associated Press.

CARY, Ill., Jan. 21.—Hurling himself through space in a 175-foot effort on his second trial, Casper Oimoen of Minot, N. D., regained the national ski-jumping championship today after a lapse of two years.

Oimoen, who won the 1929-30-31 championships while competing from Canton, S. D., but failed in 1932 and 1933, was in a difficult position as he faced his second and last jump off the giant Norge Club slide.

Sverre Fredheim of Minneapolis, who had jumped 171 feet with superior form to 170 for Oimoen, led in the point total. But with 25,000 spectators cheering him, Oimoen flashed off the slide to victory.

The victor's point total was 226.55 for two leaps. Fredheim, who had jumps of 165 and 171 feet, finished second with 220.15 points. Harold Sorensen of Norfolk, Conn., was third with 213.90 points and efforts of 161 and 164 feet.

Roy Mikkelsen of the Norge Club, Chicago, the defending champion, put up a mighty battle to retain the title, but fell on a 175-foot jump and was disqualified.

Jimmy Hendrikson of Wisconsin

Rapids, Wis., proved himself best of the Class B riders, leaping 157 and 165 feet for 208.80 points, to beat Walter Bietila, one of a group of skiing Ishpeming (Mich.) brothers, who had 208.60 points.

Class C honors went to Theron Place of Racine, Wis., who totaled 150.40 points on jumps of 119 and 124 feet. Frank Haltner of St. Paul was second with 140.09 points and leaps of 104 and 115 feet, while another of the Bietilas, Roy, who had a pair of 118-foot jumps, was third. Bietila's score was sharply trimmed when he fell on his second effort.

A pair of riders from the home club, Karl Nilsen and Harry Lien, finished one-two in the senior division, a classification for riders of 35 years or over.

The contestants operated at a disadvantage which led to a severe injury to Paul Bietila. The weather was warm, causing the snow, which was imported from Escanaba, Mich., to soften. Every rider found it difficult to keep his feet after landing and Bietila fell, suffering a fracture of his left hip.

January 22, 1934

# MISS HENIE KEEPS HER WORLD TITLE

## Royal Family Among 15,000 at Oslo Figure Skating— Miss Vinson Fifth.

By The Associated Press.

OSLO, Norway, Feb. 11.—Skating faultlessly to the cheers of a crowd of 15,000, including members of the royal family, Miss Sonja Henie, graceful Norwegian, retained her world's figure skating championship today.

The American star, Miss Maribel Vinson of Boston, fell during a spin in the free-skating competition, and was placed fifth.

Miss Henie was adjudged the winner by unanimous decision of the judges.

Second place went to Miss Megan Taylor of England, who turned in an excellent performance, marred only by a spill during the school figures yesterday.

Miss Liselotte Landbeck of Austria was third and Miss Vivianne Hulthen of Sweden fourth. Behind Miss Vinson were placed Miss Grete Lainer of Austria, Miss Nana Egedius of Norway, Miss Maxi Herber of Germany and Miss Mollie Phillips of England, in that order.

With the King and Queen, Crown Prince Olaf and Princess Martha watching, Miss Vinson opened the exhibition of free skating today at great speed, which she maintained to the end, but with a touch of recklessness which contributed to her spill.

Conditions were excellent, with sunny weather and good ice, although the wind bothered some of the competitors toward the end of the day.

A crowd of 12,000 jammed the stadium, with 3,000 more overflowing to the surrounding hills.

February 12, 1934

# CANADA BEATS U.S. FOR GORDON MEDAL

## Dominion Curlers Triumph by 194-135 in International Tourney at Brookline.

Special to THE NEW YORK TIMES.

BROOKLINE, Mass., March 10.— The combined forces of Canada's curling clubs conquered their United States rivals, 194 to 135, in the biennial competition for the Gordon International Medal at the Country Club today after ten hours of competition.

The medal is awarded on a basis of points scored in thirteen international matches. Seldom, if ever, has either side been able to win by so convincing a margin as did the Canadians today.

Canadians Take Lead.

In the first match the Thistle Club of Montreal routed the Brookline Country Club, 21 to 7. C. Doutre, Thistle lead, scored the first point and the Canadians were never headed.

The first royal Montreal team followed with an 18-to-8 triumph over the first Utica quartet. This gave the Canadians a 24-point lead at the conclusion of two matches.

The first counter stroke by the Americans forces was the 11-10 victory which the Utica second team recorded over the first Caledonia four in one of the most interesting matches of the tournament.

Other American victories were gained by the third Brookline team over Montreal West, by the third Utica team over Lachine and by Caledonian over Outre-Mont.

Tomorrow the semi-finals and finals for the Stockton and Clyde Park Cups will be staged.

March 11, 1934

27

# LEE, MISS VINSON WIN SKATING TITLES

## New York Schoolboy, 15, Gains National Senior Crown in New Haven Arena.

### TURNER IS THE RUNNER-UP

#### Miss Davis Second in Women's Event as Six-Time Champion Regains Her Laurels.

**By LINCOLN A. WERDEN.**
Special to THE NEW YORK TIMES.

NEW HAVEN, Conn., Feb. 9.—Robin Lee, 15-year-old New York schoolboy, won the men's senior championship and Miss Maribel Y. Vinson of Winchester, Mass., regained the women's senior title as the national figure skating championships were concluded in the New Haven Arena tonight.

The little fellow, whose home is in St. Paul but who has been studying in the metropolis for the past two Winters, inscribed his name in a unique place in the history of the sport. No one as youthful as Lee ever before has been able to master the technique, grace and skill which are required of a champion.

The boy skater showed all these qualities as he completed the free-skating part of the program following an excellent showing in the technical school figures on Friday.

**Crowd of 4,000 Attends.**

The gathering of 4,000 that occupied every available seat and sat in the aisles had heard much of Lee during the past three years. At the age of 12 he won the junior crown and during the past two seasons was an important competitor in the senior competition.

Only a year ago Lee finished second to Roger F. Turner, the Boston lawyer whose string of triumphs began here in 1928. They continued uninterrupted until Lee scored to-night.

Skating at a fast pace, Lee went through an exceedingly testing program without a moment's hesitation. From the instant the orchestra leader's baton swung into action Lee proceeded to show marvelous control of spins and jumps that had the audience constantly applauding.

His dance steps were rhythmic and he varied these with an up and down Jackson Haines spin to show his versatility. Added to these he did a full Lutz jump and a Boeckl jump.

All through an elaborate repertoire Lee gave a masterful exhibition. Not once did he make an error. His execution of the intricate spins, jumps and steps was faultless.

The crowd that had come to see Lee left no doubt of its pleasure as he finished. The cheers were so prolonged that he had to return to take a bow. Modest little fellow that he is, when he sat down on a bench to watch the other competitors that followed he was partly surrounded by a group of youngsters who lost no time getting his autograph.

Turner, the only seven-time champion in the men's ranks, was a close second. In third place was J. Lester Madden, also of Boston.

There was no official announcement concerning the other contestants, George E. B. Hill of Boston, William Swallander

of Minneapolis and William Nagel of New York.

Turner, whose forte has always been his perfection in the school figures, skated well but Madden unfortunately fell during his time on the ice. Madden attempted a series of brilliant jumps and was doing splendidly until he went down.

Among the first to congratulate Lee, who now undoubtedly will head the United States contingent in the Olympics, were Turner and Willy Boeckl, Robin's New York Tutor.

**Did Not Compete Last Year.**

In the women's championship Miss Vinson recaptured the title that she held for six successive years until she did not compete in 1934 at Philadelphia. Miss Vinson, who spent the greater part of last year skating in Europe, appeared to be skating even better than when she won her last American crown here two years ago.

In the school figures yesterday, her tracings were so excellent that she entered the free skating with a decided advantage over the other entrants. Wearing a turquoise blue ensemble she did a varied program with the grace and poise that has long been characteristic of her skating.

Miss Vinson divided her program into five parts, doing her half Lutz jump and toe spins admirably. There were also traces of European skating in the manner in which she did her steps.

There was no phase of the program, from the inner spreadeagle to the Paulsen jump, in which she did not display excellent timing, coordination and a grace of style. She ended with a beautiful fade-away down the centre of the rink and poised as she won the acclaim of the spectators.

Miss Suzanne Davis of Boston, the defending titleholder, was second and Miss Louise Weigel of Buffalo third. Miss Estelle Weigel of Buffalo was fourth and 17-year-old Audrey Peppe of New York, whose free skating was one of the most spectacular bits of the evening's program, was fifth.

Miss Vinson returned a few minutes later to carry off another national title. She and George E. B. Hill of Boston won the senior pair event following a brilliant performance which enabled them to supplant the defending champions, Miss Grace Madden and her brother. Miss Eva Schwerdt and William Bruns Jr. of Yonkers were third.

**Miss Blodgett Wins.**

The women's junior crown went to the 15-year-old Boston girl, Miss Polly Blodgett, who like Lee was scaling new heights. The young Massachusetts miss placed ahead of Miss Frances Johnson, the 16-year-old Minneapolis entrant, while Miss Ardelle Kloss of New York was third and Miss Katherine Durbrow, another New Yorker, was fourth.

The skaters from the East, however, were unable to keep all junior honors in this sector. Earle Reiter of Minneapolis, a 17-year-old high school student, triumphed in the men's junior group in a field of ten and the diminutive duo of Miss Jeanne Schulte, age 13, and Oliver Haupt Jr., 14 years old, carried the junior pair honors to St. Louis.

Reiter gave a finished performance in the free skating. The variety of his program was surprising for the junior class and his execution of it won salvos of applause.

It was Reiter's free skating that gave him the advantage over Bruce Mapes of the Brooklyn Figure Skating Club, who finished second. Mapes's school figures yesterday excelled.

Haupt, the St. Louis youngster, essayed a difficult program and did splendidly. Seventeen-year-old Eugene Reichel also demonstrated the improvement of the younger skaters, especially those from the

Middle West, when he finished fourth.

**Pair Form Striking Picture.**

The St. Louis pair of Miss Schulte and Haupt formed a striking picture. The little girl wore a white costume, a tiny white hat and gardenias were fastened to her shoulder. Haupt's black skating suit offered a contrast. Their dainty steps captured the attention of the crowd and they moved so gracefully through their program that they became popular immediately.

The women's novice competition attracted the most representative field that has yet taken part, eighteen competing. An exceptionally close victory was scored by another member of the Weigel family as Miss Mary Weigel, 14, received the first award.

Mrs. Mabel Thorns of Los Angeles, the first skater from the Pacific Coast to participate in the championships, was second. Third honors went to Mrs. Anson Beard of Westport, Conn., and New York.

In the men's novice there were only three entrants, Bernard Fox, Harvard freshman and a member of the Skating Club of Boston, being the winner. Fox gave a dashing exhibition in his free skating. Edward Berkson of the Manhattan Figure Skating Club of New York was second, and Marius Nelson of Philadelphia was the other contestant.

The Skating Club of New York quartet, consisting of Miss Ardelle Kloss, Miss Nettie Prantel, Joseph K. Savage and Roy Hunt, annexed the fours competition. The Skating Club of Boston was second and the St. Louis four third.

Miss Prantel and Hunt, members of the victorious New York four, gained further laurels by accounting for the waltz competition in which eleven teams were entered. Miss Ilse Twaroschk and Fred Fleischman of Brooklyn were second and Miss Vinson and Joseph K. Savage were third.

*February 10, 1935*

# MISS HENIE VICTOR IN CLOSE CONTEST

## Triumphs by Only 17.4 Points in Berlin to Keep European Figure Skating Laurels.

### MISS COLLEDGE IS SECOND

#### Young English Girl Makes an Excellent Finish—Miss Taylor Places Third.

**By ALBION ROSS.**
Wireless to THE NEW YORK TIMES.

BERLIN, Jan. 26.—Miss Sonja Henie, world's champion woman figure skater, again won the European title tonight at the Sport Palast. She was opposed by a field made up almost exclusively of girls in their teens. The youngest of all was Yetsuko Inada, Japanese miss, who is only 11 years old. She finished ninth in the field of seventeen skaters.

This year's competition was notable chiefly for the excellence of the British skaters, Miss Cecilia

Times Wide World Photo.
**KEEPS SKATING CROWN.**
Miss Sonja Henie.

Colledge and Miss Megan Taylor, and the German sports press was practically unanimous in asserting that the future of women's figure skating, as far as Europe is concerned, belongs to England.

**Miss Henie Acclaimed.**

The classical Viennese and Budapest schools seem to have been left far behind, although some critics asserted that the Viennese remained the only "dancers on skates" and that their successful English opponents were little more than "acrobats on skates," with no evidence of esthetic feeling.

The experts and the others who attended the competition are apparently in unity, however, in the enthusiastic conviction that Miss Henie is still the marvel she always has been, both as a dancer and an acrobat, without letting either tendency rule.

Karl Schafer of Austria has yet to find his master in the men's division. He placed first in the competition which ended last night, with Graham Sharp of England second and Hans Speir of Germany third.

**German Pair Triumphed.**

The Germans console themselves, however, with the fact that Ernst Baier and Miss Maxi Herber earlier in the week secured for the Fatherland the pair skating championship. In the men's singles Katayama of Japan placed seventh.

From Garmisch-Partenkirchen, scene of the Olympic Winter Games, come reports that elimination trials for the American ski team are expected to start Tuesday. The trials will determine which members of the team are to rate as contestants and which as alternates.

The American bobsledding corps of sixteen men, according to last reports, is still at St. Moritz. The trials on the Olympic run at Garmisch-Partenkirchen have not yet begun.

**Nazi Notables Attend.**

BERLIN, Jan. 26 (AP).—Miss Sonja Henie, who has been rated as the world's leading woman figure skater for nearly a decade, faced the closest competition of her career today.

The 24-year-old Norwegian girl, defending the European championship for what she said would be the last time, barely outscored Miss Cecilia Colledge.

Among those present were Dr. Paul Joseph Goebbels, Reich Minister of Propaganda and Public Enlightenment; Air Minister Herman Wilhelm Goering, Hans von Tschammer-Osten, Reich sports leader, and other Nazi officials.

The tall English girl earned second place, only 17.4 points behind Miss Henie, by flawless performance in today's free-skating figures. This, with her excellent composition and the difficult feats she chose to perform, enabled the 15-year-old Miss Colledge to overcome most of the advantage Miss Henie had gained in the compulsory school figures yesterday.

The Norwegian girl's perfect performance of the required turns was all that enabled her to win the title for the ninth time.

#### Makes Good Impression.

The 11-year-old Japanese girl Yetsuko Inada made a good impression as she appeared for the first time to compete with the stars of the Western world.

Although lacking the polish and style of the world's leading skaters, she skated, leaped and whirled through the most difficult figures in a confident manner, which made the European experts consider her a future title contender.

She was not placed among the leaders, however, because her performance of the compulsory figures was not good enough. Miss Anada, placing ninth on the competition, had a total of 372.7 points.

Miss Henie's performance was scored by the judges at 434.6 points, while Miss Colledge received 417.2. Miss Megan Taylor also was close to the leader with 413.9 points. Miss Liselotte Landbeck, former Austrian skater, now a Belgian citizen by marriage, took fourth place with 403.6 points, while Miss Vivi-Ann Hulten of Sweden, runner-up to Miss Henie last year, finished fifth with 400.2 points. Miss Hedy Stenuf, tiny Austrian star, was sixth with a score of 391 points.

January 27, 1936

# NORWEGIAN SKIERS WIN AT OLYMPICS

## Birger Ruud and Laila Schou Nilsen Take Downhill Races —Durrance Is Eleventh.

## U. S. SEXTET SCORES, 3-0

## Downs Swiss Team, Getting All Its Goals in Sensational 54-Second Drive.

**By ALBION ROSS.**
Wireless to THE NEW YORK TIMES.

GARMISCH-PARTENKIRCHEN, Germany, Feb. 7.—Plunging headlong down sheer mountain slopes and precipitous forest trails on their skis, some hundred competitors from fifteen countries today inaugurated the Alpine sport of downhill racing as an Olympic event.

Such Alpine racing evidently never will be a sport for the multitude. The scene of today's competition, Nauner Run, which drops 3,000 feet in its two-mile course from high, windy Kreuz-Joch to the floor of the distant valley, already has taken

a goodly toll of broken bones since training began here for the fourth Olympic Winter Games.

There was one casualty today. The English racer James Riddell had to be brought down to the valley on a stretcher for transportation to a hospital. He is suffering from internal injuries but is in no serious danger.

The racing ended with Norway and Germany covered with glory. Birger Ruud, Olympic jumping champion at Lake Placid in 1932 and possibly the world's greatest skier, won the men's event. Others equaled him in courage but none in skill.

In 4 minutes 47 4-10 seconds he covered the two-mile drop to the valley, making an average speed of around twenty-five miles an hour as he dashed in and out through the close forest, over rock-strewn slopes and rough pastures, down inclines where it would be impossible for a man to keep his footing without cleated boots and alpenstock.

The great Norwegian, who in ordinary life is just another sports goods salesman here in Garmisch-Partenkirchen, did not stem, hesitate or help himself by straddling. He shot down the steepest and most difficult party of the rocky run with his skis close together and his body swaying slightly from side to side, as if he were riding easily down broad, gentle paths before a Winter sports hotel.

Where the incline lost its precipitous character for any distance he drove himself with his poles, stooping low until almost squatting on his skis, then hurling his body forward as if he were going off the lip of the jumping tower.

Franz Pfnur of Germany, timed in 4:51.8, was second, and Gustav Lantschner of Germany, third, in 4:58.2.

Emile Allais of France made the day's most dramatic run. His compatriots here refer to Emile as "a congenital candidate for the Suicide Club." He lived up to his reputation. The red flags setting the run's theoretical bounds flew in all directions and Emile was on occasion badly out of control, but he stayed on his feet by a series of near-miraculous recoveries and his flying course down the mountain was recorded by outbursts of clamorous cheering from the thunder-struck spectators.

America's strongest entry was Dick Durrance, Dartmouth College sophomore, who seemed to be making a slow, conservative and almost effortless run. Nevertheless, he achieved eleventh place with 5 minutes 16 2-10 seconds.

Like Ruud, Durrance is a lightweight and small. Like Ruud, he showed perfect form and self-control today. America has apparently in Durrance a great skier who with opportunity may some time top the list in his specialty. He placed only eleventh today largely because of the splendid competition.

Another factor also played a rôle, however. His team-mates explained he was given to understand that the course was much the same glare ice proposition as yesterday and Wednesday when he practiced on it. The American team accordingly waxed for ice, and Durrance himself stemmed considerably at the beginning in order to avoid coming out suddenly at top speed onto an icy slope.

As a matter of fact the run was in better condition than expected, and it was not until he was half-way down that the American star discovered he had been taking unnecessary precautions against falling. Even at that he took only some 29 seconds more than the winner, whose performance today is a landmark in the history of ski competitions.

George H. Page, the European-American who trains in Switzerland, came in seventeenth, his time being 5:42.8. On the precipitous slopes he showed more brilliance

Birger Ruud.

and speed than Durrance, but lacked his form.

Robert Livermore Jr. of Boston, former intercollegiate slalom champion, arrived twenty-eighth, taking one and a half minutes more than the winner. A. L. Washburn, recent Dartmouth graduate, who was second in the downhill American Olympic trials last year, finished fourth among the Americans and thirty-fifth in the listing.

The race was featured by frequent falls but all the Americans kept upright throughout excepting Livermore, who fell on the most difficult steep slope. From the American viewpoint the race demonstrated that both Durrance and Page, who are European-trained, are completely out of the class of Washburn and Livermore, who have spent more of their time in their own fatherland. Evidently the price of ski excellence is exile.

The American women's team failed to make much of an impression in the downhill race. Evidently the era of top-ranking American women skiers has yet to dawn despite the solid training the American girl competitors received this

year at Saint Anton in Austria before coming to the games. One-third to one-half of all the women entered from all nations for the women's race were not of Olympic caliber.

The women's course was just as difficult as the men's. Laila Schou Nilsen of Norway was the winner, completing the distance in 5 minutes 4 4-10 seconds. Germany took second and third places and Switzerland fourth.

The event's heroine was an Anglo-Canadian girl who dashed down the course with a broken wrist in a sling and only one ski pole. In her eye was clasped her constant companion—a monocle. She made a perfect run but failed to register among the first ten.

Today's downhill competitions for both men and women were part of the combined slalom and downhill events. The final standing of the competitors will not be announced till after the slalom contests.

America won its hockey game with Switzerland, reputed to be the best of the European teams, 3–0.

February 8, 1936

# GERMAN GIRL WINS IN OLYMPIC SKIING; U. S. SIX IS BEATEN

## MISS CRANZ IS VICTOR

**By ALBION ROSS.**
Wireless to THE NEW YORK TIMES.

GARMISCH-PARTENKIRCHEN, Germany, Feb. 8.—Germany's women skiers presented the fatherland with the first victory for any nation in the fourth Olympic Win-

ter Games today when Miss Christel Cranz, Black Forest girl ski star, won the gold medal for the women's combined downhill and slalom event.

The German theory is that woman's place is in the home, but Miss Kaethe Grasegger also proved in this case that the German woman's place is on skis by finishing second, securing for Germany the silver medal. Hadi Pfeifer placed

**Miss Christel Cranz of Germany.**

fifth for Germany and Lisa Resch sixth, assuring the fatherland of a sizable block of points in the team standings. It is a question whether any other country will be able to earn an equal number of points in any given event scheduled. Germany's men are going to have a hard time equaling the accomplishments of their women.

Miss Cranz is a great slalom artist. She fell yesterday in the downhill race and accordingly came in nineteen seconds behind Miss Laila Schou Nilsen of Norway.

### Takes Bronze Medal.

On the strength of her plunging, courageous down-mountain victory yesterday, the 16-year-old blonde, blue-eyed Norwegian schoolgirl will carry back to her home in Oslo the Olympic bronze medal, having contributed largely to Norway's chances of achieving the highest place in the team standing. Fourth in the event was Miss Erna Steuri of Switzerland.

Miss Cranz is a 21-year-old brunette. She is a student of physical education, training for a career as a gymnastics and sports teacher. Born and reared in Switzerland, she has lived recently with her family in the old German cathedral city of Freiburg-in-Breisgau on the outskirts of the Black Forest. She wore skis for the first time at the mature age of four.

Partenkirchen is regarding with renewed contempt tonight its rival town of Garmisch since Miss Grasegger won the silver medal. All her nineteen years she has spent in her parents' peasant household on the outskirts of the town. Last year, assert the town boys, she was still wearing pigtails in the approved Upper Bavarian fashion. Now her startlingly black hair has been cut to practically a bob. She has a tomboy reputation and a freckled face that goes with it.

### Miss Woolsey Nineteenth.

America's women skiers undoubtedly did their best, but they did not do well competitively. Miss Elizabeth Woolsey of New York made the best showing. Placing fourteenth in the women's downmountain race yesterday, she reached only nineteenth place in the final scoring for the combined events in the field of twenty-nine. Making a very creditable run yesterday over the difficult and dangerous trail with its icy slopes and forest labyrinth, she did not do so well today, falling twice during her first descent of the slalom incline.

Mrs. Helen Boughton-Leigh was not up to the form she was reported to have shown in last year's International Ski Federation races, when she placed eighth. Today she took only twenty-first position.

### Brave in Face of Odds.

Miss Clarita Heath, who is a small blonde, gay and courageous in the face of great odds against a skier with so little experience, can hardly be classed as being of Olympic caliber. Yesterday the heavy demands of the downhill race proved too much for her and she fell repeatedly, climaxing her run with a headlong plunge into a gulley by the side of the narrow bridge at the bottom of the now famous "Steilhang." But she righted herself and dashed bravely off again to make the best time possible. Today she was among the trailers.

America's day of disappointments was topped off by the loss of the hockey game to Italy, which was easily defeated yesterday by Germany and is considered to be one of the weakest teams in the Olympic hockey tournament. Italy played a good game and its goalie rose to unexpected heights in steadily repulsing every American attempt to score.

Italy scored a 2-to-1 victory after playing two overtime periods, scoring the winning goal in the eighth minute of the second overtime session.

John Garrison, captain of the American team, scored once, but tonight was making no secret of his disgust with his own playing and that of his teammates. The two golden minutes yesterday, when America scored three goals one after another against an excellent Swiss defense, seemed today like some vision of another hockey world or a happy dream of things to come if the American collection of players ever decides to become one hockey team and settle down to the business of playing North American hockey.

The Italian goalie's excellence, the American players confessed, is an explanation of sorts but no excuse for the display of ragged and pointless play which they put on this afternoon.

For two periods the discouraged Italians held back, clinging to their own territory and covering up their cage, waiting for America to open up with another burst of hockey generalship and inspired playing such as it showed yesterday, and plainly hoping against hope they would be able to bear the brunt thereof more successfully than the skilled Swiss. The Americans repeatedly went down the ice, but, like the Germans on the games' opening day, they appeared to have no idea what to do when they did arrive at the Italian cage.

Finally, in 9:30 of the third period Garrison scored for his team on a perfectly directed shot. The Italians, facing defeat, saw a great light. They seized the fact that the American team was playing European quality hockey. In 12:30 Italy scored on the surprised American team that had intended to use the same stalling tactics it had employed in its opening game of the tourney.

The overtime periods were faster than the rest of the game, but even at that the Americans had developed apparently no plan either of offense or defense. Almost at the close of the second overtime period the puck bounced off the backboards and slithered to the front of the American cage. An Italian plunged forward and practically drove the disk past Goalie Tom Moone by main force.

The game was over and the puzzled American team went off the ice minus a good deal of its remaining prestige.

The United States team does not appear to be the crowd's idol. It is a rough team, because North American hockey is a rough game. On several occasions today the Americans were roundly booed and the Italian underdogs wildly cheered whenever they seemed to have a chance of scoring.

### Faces Threat of Elimination.

This rather unnecessary American defeat could have serious consequences. A three-way tie among Italy, Germany and the United States may result in the elimination group of four if Italy wins from Switzerland tomorrow. In that case the decision will be made on the scores. America has had low scores and is likely to be eliminated tomorrow in the first round of the Olympic contest in which it was expected to be Canada's chief rival.

America also suffered on the bob run today an injury to its crack four-man driver, Donna Fox of New York, whose sled upset coming out of the Bavaria Curve, making what looked like a record run. Fox's three companions came through with only bruises but he was removed to the emergency hospital by ambulance.

Later the doctors' report indicated he had a badly strained leg. Returning to the run, he said he will continue to train and certainly will take part in the Olympic events.

The Olympic bob run threatens to prove as dangerous as the Lake Placid run in 1932, which put two German teams in the hospital. Hans Stuerer's two-man Austrian bob went crashing out of the run this afternoon, but fortunately on the inside of the Bavaria Curve. The Austrian driver escaped with slight internal injuries.

Several four-man sleds overturned with no serious results except for Jean Stevenart of Belgium, who broke a wrist. Jean Schene also was treated at the emergency hospital for a wrist bruise.

J. Hubert Stevens made the best time of the American bob drivers today, going down the course in 1 minute 24 seconds, or six seconds over the course record. Pierre Musy of Switzerland made the run in 1 minute 26 seconds.

This afternoon the Americans discovered they will meet stiff competition in the two-man event. Fritz Grau of Germany made the run in 1 minute 28 9-10 seconds, Gilbert Colgate Jr. of America following in 1 minute 29 7-10 seconds. Frederick McEvoy of England competed sharply with 1 minute 29 8-10, Ivan Brown of America following with 1 minute 30 6-10. Stevens made a slow run in the afternoon trials for two-man bobs.

### Brundage Visits Team.

Lavery T. Brundage, president of the American Olympic Committee, visited the Americans at the bob run this afternoon. He explained that the protest against the presence of two suspended Canadians on the English hockey team has not been withdrawn.

He said the Canadians denied canceling their suspension order, and England appeared to be using her players without permission and against the specific instructions of the International Ice Hockey Federation. He expected that some more drastic action might be awaited in the affair.

February 9, 1936

# Germany, Close to Sweep in Men's Ski Event, Continues to Dominate Olympics

## PFNUER CAPTURES SKI CHAMPIONSHIP

### German Takes Down-Mountain and Slalom Combined Event —Durrance, U. S. Ace, 10th.

### U. S. SIX IN SEMI-FINALS

### Gains as Swiss Top Italians —Wilson and Schafer Star as Figure Skating Begins.

**By ALBION ROSS.**
Wireless to THE NEW YORK TIMES.

GARMISCH-PARTENKIRCHEN, Germany, Feb. 9.—Germany continued to sweep all before it today in the fourth Olympic Winter Games. Another pair of gold and silver Olympic medals fell to its lot when Franz Pfnuer and Gustav Lantschner finished first and second in the combined down-mountain ski race and the slalom.

Rudolf Cranz and Roman Woerndle also secured for Germany fifth and sixth position. The German men have thus barely succeeded in equaling the German women in the team scoring. The German women skiers yesterday took in the same competition the first, second, fifth and sixth positions.

All in all, however, the Germans now have a tremendous head start on the other twenty-eight nations competing in the games. They have a wide lead on points, according to the officially unrecognized but traditional Olympic scoring system, and have won two gold and two silver medals.

The third place captured today in the combined event by the dashing Emile Allais gave France a bronze medal and Norway secured one yesterday through the efforts of the 16-year-old Miss Laila Schou Nilsen. No other nation has won any medals as yet.

### Two Brilliant Runs.

Dick Durrance, the Dartmouth sophomore who has sacrificed a year of schooling to carry the American colors in Alpine competition in the Olympics, placed tenth. He ran two brilliant slaloms today that made up for his excellent but perhaps slightly too conservative performance in the plunging down-mountain race Friday.

George Page, the Swiss-reared and English-educated American skier, placed thirteenth and Robert Livermore of the Boston Hochgebirge ski runners, twenty-third. A. L. Washburn of New York, another Dartmouth-trained competitor, was eliminated in the second slalom trial after making too slow a run in his first trial.

America obviously has not yet arrived at the point where she can meet and equal first-class competi-

tion from European skiers.

The German colors were borne to victory today by a schoolboy, a woodcarver and a mountain-climbing cameraman. Franz Pfnuer, the gold medalist, is a 25-year-old Bavarian woodcarver and cabinetmaker from the village of Schuelleberg on the outskirts of Berchtesgaden. He was born and reared on the high mountainside across the valley from Wachenfeld, where Chancellor Hitler now spends much of his time.

Lantschner is no contented mountaineer following the trade of his fathers. He was born and reared in Innsbruck. A violent Nazi, he fled the country of his origin and joined the movies. Now, at 26, he makes mountain films such as "Flaming Peaks" and Nazi party films under the direction of the official film producer.

Garmisch now has been put utterly to rout by its rival, Partenkirchen. Not content with securing a silver medal yesterday through the 19-year-old Miss Kaethe Grasseger, the latter town now possesses in the 19-year-old shoemaker, Roman Woerndle, another Olympic scorer whose name will be engraved on the Olympic tablet with those of the first six in every competition. The tablet will stand permanently in the Partenkirchen ski stadium.

Garmisch will not be able to lift its head again until Hanns Kilian, proprietor of its fashionable Park Hotel, secures at least a bronze medal on the Olympic bob run.

### Youngster Has Stage Fright.

America's hopes were dampened again today by the failure of Robin Lee, 16-year-old national figure-skating champion, to impress the European judges as had been expected. He did well and will probably place well. The fact remains that Robin is 16 and he suffered from stage fright.

The judges got through only a part of the figure trials for men before nightfall, but it is clear that the event is to become a duel between Karl Schafer of Austria, the present world champion, and Bud Wilson of Canada for the Olympic gold medal. The sensation of the day on the ice was the perfect self-control and style of Wilson, who looks very much like the next world champion.

Since no official announcement of the results has been made the relative standings of the other competitors are difficult to determine. Erle Reiter, who was graduated from high school only last year, probably will place among the Americans ahead of George E. B. Hill, famous partner of the women's national champion, Miss Maribel Y. Vinson, in pair skating.

America, however, can hardly be regarded as a threat of any sort to the little group of European and Canadian skaters who really are competing for the Olympic title.

America's hopes for a gold medal outside of the speed skating continue to be centered on its bob run. With races scheduled for the

four-man sleds Tuesday morning, the final teams had been selected tonight. Avery T. Brundage, as head of the American Olympic Committee, entered J. Hubert Stevens of Lake Placid as driver of the United States No. 1 sled.

Donna Fox, who suffered a leg injury yesterday, was entered tentatively as the driver of the United States No. 2 sled with his old teammates, Richard W. Lawrence, Max T. Bly and James Bickford, composing one of the heaviest and most reckless combinations that has ever gone roaring down the ice for America. The American bob managers, however, reserved the right to replace Fox with Francis W. Tyler if the Bronx bobber's injury proves too serious.

### Tyler Fares Poorly.

Tyler made two practice runs today that were not very successful, because of a broken runner. The first time he went down the mile-long run in 1 minute 29.3 seconds, and the second time in 1 minute 28.2 seconds.

Stevens was making a very different showing on the fast track. The course record is 1 minute 18 seconds. The United States No. 1 sled, with Stevens at the wheel, did the run in 1 minute 20.3 seconds. This time was bettered only by Stevens's old rival of Lake Placid, Reto Capadrutt of Switzerland, who rode down in 1 minute 20 seconds.

In this afternoon's two-man trials Gilbert Colgate Jr. of New York,

Times Wide World Photo.

Nora Stromstad, Ela Petersen, Johanne Dybwad and Laila Schou Nilsen. Miss Nilsen won the 3,000-meter downhill race in 5:04.4 on Friday.

riding as usual with Lawrence, former Syracuse University oarsman, came within a fractional distance of the record time for the track. The record, made by Capadrutt last season, is 1 minute 25.2 seconds. Colgate rode down in 1 minute 25.6 seconds, coming within four-tenths of a second of Capadrutt's time.

### Rumanian Sled in Spill.

The track took its toll of broken bones again today. A Rumanian sled overturned and there now are only two Rumanians left in the race. This afternoon they borrowed for the trials Fox's much-discussed knee-action bob, which none except the owner ever dared to drive before. Another American sled has been lent to the Belgian team with the understanding it will be returned if America suffers a crash and finds itself short of a sled.

The readiness with which the American bobbers are willing to lend their sleds to any rivals who have had an accident was the talk of the track today. America is, in any case, not an unwelcome guest at the scene of the games, but the bob team has acquired a rather remarkable popularity. Of all the American competitors, they are the friendliest and the merriest, and evidently the happiest to be here. Brundage's suggestion to the American competitors that they should be very reserved in their behavior, notably in their relations with newspaper men, has not served to dampen the good spirits of the bobbers.

Switzerland's one-point victory over Italy tonight assured America of a place in the hockey semifinals which began next week. The Italian goalie, who was a tower of strength against the confused American players yesterday, proved no insurmountable obstacle for the Swiss tonight.

### An Unsolved Mystery.

The American-Italian hockey game is evidently to be one of the unsolved mysteries of the Winter Olympics. It has served to remind the Americans, however, that they are not yet a real team and that it is high time they did something about it.

A meeting of the jury of the International Ice Hockey Federation has been called for 10 o'clock tomorrow morning to reopen the question of the status of the two Anglo-Canadian players, James Foster and Alex Archer, whom the jury expelled from the Olympic Games and who have nevertheless been used by England in every game played so far.

The English spokesman claims the Canadian Amateur Hockey Association has withdrawn its suspension orders upon which the expulsion was based. The Canadian functionaries deny they have done anything of the sort.

The American member of the jury is Brundage and he is expected to support actively tomorrow the protest against England's rather highhanded move in ignoring the rulings of the international federation.

Perhaps the most notable event of the day now closing was the attendance at the slalom competition—55,000. No such attendance at such a competition ever had been approached before. The slalom is neither particularly interesting nor particularly thrilling for the layman. It is more than anything else a copybook exercise in the fine art of skiing.

### Wins by a Wide Margin.

By The Associated Press.

GARMISCH-PARTENKIRCHEN, Germany, Feb. 9.—Franz Pfnuer won the slalom race by a wide margin today. His two times both were faster than the best his nearest rival in the field of thirty-three could do and he received a minimum of penalties for form.

Pfnuer finished second to Birger Ruud of Norway Friday in the downhill race, but his sensational times of 1:12.1 and 1:14.5 in slalom enabled him to win the combined title with a point total of 99.25.

Dick Durrance, America's best performer, was well up on the list of slalom racers, but his comparatively slow down-hill time set him back to tenth place in the double event. He was timed in 1:26.4 and 1:26.9 for today's two trips down the slalom course.

### Points Are Averaged.

The points scored in the downhill race, starting with 100 for the winner, are averaged with those of the slalom race to determine the combined placings. Durrance was eleventh in Friday's down-hill race and ninth in the slalom.

Ruud spoiled his chances for a victory by falling near the start of his first run. He punted—worked his sticks to increase his speed—furiously for the remainder of the journey, but in vain, as the judges penalized him heavily for the spill. Ruud's official times were 1:31.9 and 1:17.1, giving him sixth in the slalom standing and fourth for the combined event.

Time-wasting spills on the icy course, which has thirty hairpin turns, cost the American, Canadian and Japanese teams heavily. Only three Americans were listed among the combined finishers. Durrance had a combined point score of 87.74, as his slalom performance was rated at 84.59 points.

February 10, 1936

# FINNISH QUARTET WINS BY 6 SECONDS

### Jalkanen's Great Final Lap Brings Triumph Over Norway in Olympic Ski Relay.

### BRITISH ACES REINSTATED

### Ban on Hockey Players Lifted for Duration of Games—U. S. Six Faces Czechs Today.

### By ALBION ROSS.

Wireless to The New York Times.

GARMISCH-PARTENKIRCHEN, Germany, Feb. 10.—America will make its strongest bid for Olympic gold medals tomorrow in the 500-meter speed-skating race and in the four-man bob races, which will start at the same time. The results of these events will determine largely whether the United States is to preserve the mythical Winter Olympic championship which it won from Norway four years ago at Lake Placid.

However, with its hockey team safe in the semi-finals, with Miss Maribel Y. Vinson and George E. B. Hill well under way to a bronze, silver or possibly gold medal in the pair skating later in the week, and with Gilbert Colgate Jr. of New York appearing in the trials as the likeliest two-man bob candidate for the gold medal, America is not in a hopeless situation.

The second round of hockey eliminations will open for the now rather humbled American team tomorrow afternoon when it plays

Associated Press Photo.

**Miss Cecilia Colledge of England, Miss Sonja Henie of Norway, who will defend Olympic crown; Miss Liselotte Landbeck of Belgium and Miss Maxi Herber of Germany.**

Czechoslovakia, the strongest Continental European team competing in the Olympics and itself one of the four seriously considered candidates for the Olympic medal. On Wednesday the United States will play Austria and on Thursday Sweden.

### Players Are Reinstated.

Great Britain succeeded at the final meeting of the International Ice Hockey Federation today in preserving its practically all-Canadian hockey team. It secured the reinstatement of its two Canadian stars who had been expelled from the Olympics by a vote of the international federation, but who had nevertheless played by orders of the British coach.

Today the Canadian federation's spokesman withdrew "solely for the period of the Olympic Games" the suspension from membership in the Canadian federation which had made the two allegedly British players ineligible for the Olympics. This solution of the question was accepted by most of the delegates on the board of the international federation. It did not prove as acceptable to the American delegate, Avery T. Brundage, who stated at the last meeting that America would just as soon play only one team of Canadians instead of meeting Canadians under all colors.

Mr. Brundage informed the other delegates he had "heard rumors" Great Britain would withdraw its two formerly ineligible players in recognition of the sporting attitude taken by the federation, which had been placed in a difficult position. Walter Hunter, chairman of the British Hockey Federation, allowed the meeting to understand Great Britain would do nothing of the sort.

### Makes Bid for Tourney.

Thereupon it was generally agreed that Great Britain was showing a really unsportsmanlike attitude. The British spokesman, in bidding later for the next world and European championship tourney, confessed his country needed to have

more native Englishmen playing hockey. This sort of frankness rather overwhelmed the rest of the delegates but indicated clearly enough that Great Britain was determined to play its Anglo-Canadian team in the face of all obstacles and irrespective of what is being said at Garmisch-Partenkirchen about British sportsmanship.

Finland enjoyed today one of those spectacular last-minute victories which become historic tales to be recounted in locker rooms throughout the world.

The event was the 40-kilometer relay, one of those grueling tests of endurance and speed which make up the classic répertoire of Scandinavian and Finnish ski champions. For three of the four laps Norway led. Oddbjorn Hagen, Olaf Hoffsbakken, Sverre Brodahl and Bjarne Iversen are a corps of racers such as apparently only Norway can develop.

### Event Attracts 6,000.

A scattered crowd of 6,000 in the ski stadium saw the start of the first lap and saw the relay baton change hands twice. The loudspeaker droned steadily on reporting the same fact, namely, that Norway had preserved its well-earned lead.

It was not until the Norwegian entry was well up the long hill leading out of the stadium on the race's last lap that Kalle Jalkanen of Finland received the baton from his team-mate, Matti Lahde, and the cold and somewhat disappointed spectators suddenly were made aware of the dramatic possibilities in relay ski racing.

Jalkanen may be a well known figure in Finland but he was an unknown entrant for the crowds milling about the streets of Garmisch-Partenkirchen. Tonight his name is in every conversation and he has become a public figure.

With one glance at the distant Norwegian ski runner, Jalkanen took the baton from his team-mate's hand and started to catch up to and pass the apparently certain victor. All up the long, winding trail, mile after mile over the snow, Jalkanen gained second by second on the racing Norwegian, Iversen. The battle of endurance continued.

Both the Finn and the Norwegian negotiated successfully the steep, icy hill which led the racers back onto the broad floor of the valley. It was not until both practically were entering the ski stadium to finish their heart-breaking effort that Jalkanen decided to call on his last reserves.

He skied as if possessed. His body flexible, his arms swinging steadily, the Finnish racer gained inch by inch to the very gates of the stadium. With a last effort of his will the Finn passed his rival and won the race. He was sixty feet ahead, and Finland was in possession of a new gold medal.

Finland's four competitors had taken only 2 hours 41 minutes 33 seconds, those from Norway 2 hours 41 minutes 39 seconds. The race had been lost and won by a matter of six seconds.

America made only a fair showing as a team. Warren Chivers of Dartmouth College and Richard E. Parsons of Salisbury, Conn., kept the American colors in eighth position for two laps. Birger Torrissen of Norfolk, Conn., leading off, had done no better than eleventh. Paul Ottar Satre, also of Salisbury, in whom great confidence had been placed, fell repeatedly on the icy trail and America ended the race as it had the first lap, in eleventh position.

Preliminary indications issued tonight by the judges of the men's compulsory figure skating are rather disappointing for America. Robin Lee, United States champion, is first among the Americans, but his name appears far down the list.

February 11, 1936

# BALLANGRUD WINS 500-METER TITLE

## U. S. Skaters Trail, Freisinger Taking Third, Lamb Fifth and Potts Tying for Sixth.

### By ALBION ROSS

Wireless to THE NEW YORK TIMES.

GARMISCH-PARTENKIRCHEN, Germany, Feb. 11.—Ivar Ballangrud, Norwegian, European and world speed-skating champion, took his revenge today for his defeat by the Americans at Lake Placid in 1932 at the last Winter Olympics.

The Americans skated out on the hard, slippery ice of Riessersee Rink this morning with visions of winning silver and gold Olympic medals in the 500-meter race. They left the rink glad that Leo Freisinger, 19-year-old Chicagoan, had been able to win for the United States even a bronze medal as the sole distinction achieved today in the fourth Olympic Winter Games.

Within the last month three Americans have defeated Norway's stars twice in 500-meter races at Oslo and Davos, the latter counting as the world's championship. Norway, whose skaters are popular

Ivar Ballangrud of Norway, winner of 500-meter race.

Keystone View Photo.

idols, was faced this morning with the possibility of another such defeat as overtook its colors four years ago. The American optimists reckoned, however, without the hard ice and the stubborn Norwegian character.

### Clocked in 43.4 Seconds.

Ballangrud, throwing his weight and strength into every stride, raced over the ice, cutting by main force into its granite surface, and equalled Clas Thunberg's and Bernt Evensen's Olympic record time of 43.4 seconds.

The Brooklyn filling station attendant, Allan Potts, had left the ice shortly before, bitterly disappointed. Only three weeks ago at Oslo, skating on ice which had a thin film of water over it, he established a new world record of 0:42.4. Today he either failed to recognize the fact that the ice was almost impenetrable or else he lacked the strength to follow Ballangrud's example and grind his way to victory.

He took 0:44.8, tying for sixth behind Georg Krog of Norway, Freisinger, Shotzo Ishihara of Japan and Delbert Lamb of the United States, who registered 0:44.2.

The Norwegian, Krog, was only one-tenth of a second behind his countryman and took the silver medal but was half a second ahead of Freisinger's 44 seconds, which won the bronze medal.

### No Explanation Offered.

The American defeat can almost certainly be laid to the use of natural instead of artificial ice. Riessersee presented this morning not only an uneven surface with

occasional air pockets but also a track so hard that the lighter skaters had the greatest difficulty keeping their feet, while some former world record holders fell.

Potts lost his stride and the race when he slipped on the first turn and had to make an effort to recover his balance.

The International Ice Federation frowns on the use of natural ice in deciding international championships and no explanation has been offered for forcing the world's best skaters to race on a mountain lake in these Olympics. Both functionaries and coaches after the race pointed out to any one who was interested that after all a speed skater is expected to concentrate on speed and not on keeping his balance, and in great races he is supposed to be provided with the best ice possible.

The race was skated against time in the European style, two competitors chosen by lot skating at one time and changing midway from the inner to the outer lane. As a contest this sort of a race does not prove very interesting for the spectators.

### Crowds at Bob Run.

Today was in reality four-man bobsledding day. Regular Olympic guests and Nazi "Strength Through Joy" excursionists from all parts of Bavaria alike ignored the classic speed-skating event on Riessersee Lake and crowded up the mountain to jam the stands and wait patiently along the barriers guarding the mile-long bob run with its sixteen curves, including the hairpin Bavarian Curve that gives the uninitiated a sinking sensation in the pit of the stomach when the bob hurtles through it.

Bobsledding has apparently come to stay as the greatest Winter Olympic sport from the standpoint of the spectators. All types and ages of humanity stood mesmerized

in the freezing morning air today as bob after bob bearing the colors of eleven nations whisked by.

The day's racing stripped America of its Olympic bob titles, unless J. Hubert Stevens, driving the United States No. 1 sled, and the Lake Placid policeman, Francis W. Tyler, driving the United States No. 2 sled instead of Donna Fox, perform in the remaining two heats scheduled for tomorrow some sort of a miracle. If the races were to end tonight the United States No. 1 entry would stand fifth.

Switzerland more than avenged Reto Capadrutt's sensational last-second defeat by Stevens in the two-man racing at Lake Placid in 1932. The best Stevens could do today as the No. 1 United States driver was 1 minute 19.17 seconds to 1:18.78 by Pierre Musy of Switzerland, whose time equaled the course record made by Hanns Kilian of Germany yesterday.

Stevens's clocking, although his sled came in second to Musy's on the second heat, was marred by a 1:25.61 run in the first heat. The loss of time could have been a more serious matter. Stevens's sled went for fifty feet scraping the walls of the straightaway below Bavaria Curve, occasionally raising one runner and going along on its side.

### Mishap on No. 2 Sled.

The United States No. 2 sled had the bad luck on the second run to throw out an anchor on the long straightaway called Waterwall while making an apparently record run. The "anchor" was James Bickford, the brake, who rode seventy feet on the floor of the run half in and half out of the sled, until Richard W. Lawrence noticed something was wrong and reached out his arm and pulled him back into the sled.

The driver and his team constitute a net weight of 840 pounds. As they came with a jerk out of Bavaria Curve a long-suffering rivet gave way in the guard rail and Bickford went half off the sled to be bumped for several yards on the floor of the run.

Bickford, although the brake, enjoys the title of "No Brakes" Bickford as a result of his feeling that the use of brakes is a procedure unworthy of a real American bobber. Having unconsciously been forced into a position of becoming an involuntary brake on a record run, "No Brakes" Bickford considers he has totally disgraced himself.

### Italian Bobbers Hurt.

The Italian No. 2 sled, driven headlong into Bavaria Curve in a false position by Francesco de Zanna, provided the day's thrill by overturning and hurtling twenty feet through the air before it fell with a crash on two Italian riders. One suffered crushed ribs, the other a broken nose, but neither would be considered to have been injured in the bobsledder's sense of the term "injury." Two more sets of broken ribs were contributed by a German bob which made a preliminary run to pack the course.

Tonight the talk of the town is that there is something wrong with the construction of the Bavaria Curve. It is the single dangerous feature of the Olympic run but it is deadly.

Two bobs were running today with runners over the curve's wall. Czechoslovakia's No. 1 sled rode around the curve in this exciting but inconvenient fashion and righted itself after the team had recovered its balance and its breath. Capadrutt of Switzerland also rode too high up the curve despite his skill and seemed for a moment about to go over.

It is on this curve, however, that America's two bobs will have to attempt tomorrow to break the course record if either of the two is to place in the race. The Americans have now fallen behind both the Swiss bobs, Britain's No. 1 and Germany's No. 1.

February 12, 1936

# SWITZERLAND GAINS FIRST TWO PLACES

## Musy Pilots Winning Bobsled at the Olympics—Capadrutt Finishes Second.

## U. S. IS FOURTH AND SIXTH

## Ballangrud of Norway Takes 5,000-Meter Skating Race in Record Time.

### By ALBION ROSS.

Wireless to The New York Times.

GARMISCH-PARTENKIRCHEN, Germany, Feb. 12.—Most of the United States' Winter Olympic ambitions now have been buried under an avalanche of failures and misfortunes.

America lost its Olympic four-man bobsled title to Switzerland today after eight years of almost undisputed supremacy. J. Hubert Stevens and Francis W. Tyler of Lake Placid went down to defeat before the skill and courage of Pierre Musy on Switzerland's No. 2 sled, winner of the gold medal, and Reto Capadrutt, on Switzerland's No. 1 entry, winner of the silver medal.

America did not take even the bronze medal, which has, in the past, been the consolation prize for some European teams. Third place went to the wealthy British sportsman, Frederick McEvoy.

### Substitutes for Fox.

Stevens and his 200-to-250-pound companions, John J. Shene, Robert P. Martin and Crawford C. Merkel, finished fourth. Tyler, driving as a substitute for Donna Fox of the Bronx, injured in practice, was sixth, behind Belgium's No. 2 representative. Max Houben was the driver, and he rode with his mates in a sled borrowed from the American team.

Not satisfied with routing America, Capadrutt topped off the four heats by breaking the record for the run, taking 1 minute 18.61 seconds for the mile-long course on his final effort. This was the last blow for Hanns Kilian, holder of the old record of 1:18.70, who went into the race the universal favorite on the ground that he was born and bred in Garmisch, helped build the run, knows it better from experience than any one else, and has twice won the Olympic bronze medal on strange runs.

The Fatherland's hopes were pinned on Kilian, and he dragged them down to the obscurity of seventh place. The other German team's driver, Walter Trott, was left sitting near Bavaria Curve yesterday, watching his sled slither on down the track unguided.

### No Excuses for Losers.

There are no excuses for the losers. Yesterday the track was a hard ribbon of ice, presenting so unyielding a surface that the two heats were a literal race with death in the worst tradition of breakneck bobsledding. Today the track was steady and fast.

The leaders were bunched within three seconds of one another in the first heat today and the spectators were treated to the finest display of skill and nearly perfect driving that has been put on anywhere, any time.

Yesterday the sleds bounced and crashed from wall to wall and hurtled up the edge of the Bavaria Curve in hair-raising fashion. Today they slid past silently in a cloud of silver snowdust that settled among the pines along the track. It was hard yesterday for the spectator who is not a bob fanatic to discover what pleasure there could be in plunging, swerving and bucking down the run in such headlong, helter-skelter fashion.

On the contrary, the bobs' rapid flights this morning were a pleasure to watch as they took the hairpin Bavaria turn, swinging up to the center of the ice wall and swinging down again while the crowd held its breath so that you could hear the creaking of the straps and the grinding sound as the runners bit firmly into the ice. Rumania's No. 2 overturned, but there were no injuries and the race continued.

### Second Best Time of Day.

After Capadrutt's record run, Stevens made the day's best time. Driving hard through the five curves of the labyrinth and taking the preliminary curve to the hairpin high, he drove over into the wall of the Bavaria Curve with his sled hardly quivering as it rode up to within three or four feet of the top. For a tenth of a second Martin and Shene appeared to be losing their balance, but the sled swept down into the trough of the track along the waterwall and crossed the line only fourteen-hundredths of a second behind Kilian's former record for the run.

In all four heats of the two-day event only Capadrutt, who set the new course record, and Musy were able to better Stevens's time. Capadrutt gained sweet revenge for his sensational defeat at Stevens's hands in the two-man race at Lake Placid four years ago.

Stevens made no secret today of his conviction that he owed his defeat in this year's race to one fatal blunder yesterday in his first heat. Making clearly record time, he went into Bavaria Curve too low and confident that he would make it easily. After hearing he had lost even the bronze medal today, he said:

"I deserved it. I was feeling too good yesterday and went in too low. If it hadn't been for my team's nerve we all would have been smashed to pieces. I'm done with bob racing. This is the end. My wife gets sick with fright every time I race. I've had enough. Let somebody else do it from now on."

There cannot be much doubt that Stevens is right about the consequences of his mistake yesterday. If his sled had not swerved and nearly upset, losing valuable seconds, in the first heat, America probably would have at least a silver medal to sweeten the taste of defeat.

Tyler lost his chance to place higher on another bit of bad luck when his guardrail broke yesterday and "No Brakes" James Bickford dragged for fifty feet on the run's floor before he recovered his position. Today Tyler drove a great race, his fast second heat being just about six-tenths of a second slower than the old course record.

The new Olympic titleholder, Musy, is 28 years old, a lieutenant in the Swiss Army and a son of a former President of the Swiss Republic.

The most remarkable happening today was the bettering of the Olympic record for the 5,000-meter speed skating race by nine contestants. The old Olympic record of 8 minutes 39.24 seconds was established by Clas Thunberg of Finland in 1924. The skaters of four nations bettered it today.

Ivar Ballangrud of Norway will soon have a private collection of Olympic gold and other medals. Winning today's 5,000-meter race, Ballangrud captured his second gold medal of the two available for the speed skaters to date in these games. He already has at home the gold medal for the same 5,000-meter event which he brought there from the St. Moritz games in 1928, not to speak of the silver and bronze medals he won in other events at St. Moritz and Lake Placid.

Ballangrud skated the distance in 8:19.6 to place first today, followed by Birger Vasenius of Finland in 8:23.3, the silver medalist, and Antero Ojala, also of Finland, in 8:30.1, the bronze medalist. Jan Langedijk of Holland, Max Stiepl of Austria and Ossi Blomqvist of Finland were fourth, fifth and sixth. The race was a masterpiece of speed, skated on perfect ice but with an oily film of water. The American competitors were completely outclassed. Both Americans, Robert Petersen, who finished eleventh, and Edward Schroeder, who was fifteenth, said they had skated the best 5,000 races of their careers.

Schroeder was more precise and pointed out that he had bettered his record in the 5,000 meters today by exactly one second. He appears to be recovering his 1933 form which he lost after returning to America and skating American style.

February 13, 1936

# MISS HENIE IRKED BY JUDGES' RATING

## Tears Down Chart, Terming It a 'Misrepresentation' of Her Performance.

## MISS COLLEDGE SECOND

## British Figure Skater Threat to Champion—Miss Vinson Sixth in School Designs.

Wireless to The New York Times.

GARMISCH-PARTENKIRCHEN, Germany, Feb. 12.—Miss Sonja Henie, twice Olympic champion and nine times world champion in women's figure skating, the most famous personality in the Winter sports world, had a tantrum today.

She objected to the estimate of the results of the compulsory figure competition issued by the press office of the Olympic organization committee here. The announcement indicated, on the basis of the mathematical averages of the judges' decisions, that Sonja was only 3 points ahead of Miss Cecilia Colledge of Great Britain. The sensation of the skating events has been the duel between Sonja and Miss Colledge, who threatens seriously to take away from her the Olympic title.

Tonight when the announcement was placed on the bulletin board at the Olympic ice rink Miss Henie looked at it a few moments, then went over and tore it down, stating it was a misrepresentation.

It appears from statements made here by specialists of the sport that she probably was right. It is believed that the system of taking a mathematical average doesn't give an adequate picture of the skaters' real standing.

### Free Skating on Sunday.

GARMISCH-PARTENKIRCHEN, Germany, Feb. 12 (AP).—Miss Sonja Henie of Norway finished with the highest average in the school patterns of the figure skating competition today. The free-skating part of the championship will be decided Sunday.

Miss Maribel Y. Vinson of Boston, premier American contestant, finished sixth.

The rankings according to the averages of values assigned by seven judges follow:

Miss Henie, 251.6; Miss Cecilia Colledge, Great Britain, 248; Liselotte Landbeck, Belgium, 235; Miss Vivi-Ann Hulten, Sweden, 234; Leigh Butler, Great Britain, 232.1; Miss Maribel Vinson, United States, 231.9.

Miss Audrey Peppe of New York came in seventeenth with 209.6 points. The other Americans, Misses Estelle and Louise Wiegel, placed twenty-second and twenty-third, respectively. Louise compiled 203.5 points and Estelle 198.5.

February 13, 1936

# LARSSON, SWEDEN, CAPTURES SKI RACE

## Scandinavians Take Five of Six Places Over 18-Kilometer Garmisch Course.

By The Associated Press.
GARMISCH-PARTENKIRCHEN, Germany, Feb. 12.—The Scandinavians' dominance of Olympic skiing competition continued today as Artur Larsson of Sweden set the pace for 115 skiers from twenty-two nations.

Larsson sped over the 18-kilometer course, that included every variety of Bavarian terrain, in 1 hour, 14 minutes, 38 seconds. Scandinavians swept five of six scoring places and finished eight men among the first eleven.

In asserting his supremacy over the world's best ski runners, Larsson beat Oddbjorn Hagen of Norway by 55 seconds. The Norwegian was clocked in 1:15.33 with Pekka Niemi of Finland third in 1:16.59.

Against the Scandinavians' combined display of endurance, fortitude and skiing, the Americans were outclassed. They all finished far back.

Magnus Satre of Salisbury, Conn., made the best showing, covering the course in 1:25:56 to finish in thirty-fifth place. Birger Torrissen of Norfolk, Conn., was forty-sixth in 1:29:08 and Richard E. Parsons of Salisbury forty-seventh in 1:30:09. Warren Chivers, Dartmouth student, was clocked in 1:30:25 for forty-ninth position. The placings of Edward Blood of Lake Placid, N. Y., and Karl Satre of Salisbury, were not determined although Blood was timed in 1:33:45.

Although considered a separate event in the Olympic competition, the results of the run also will be used in figuring the winners of the combined event, which will be concluded tomorrow when fifty-one of today's competitors compete in the jumping test. Of the leaders only Hagen and Olaf Hoffsbakken of Norway will go after the combined title.

The competitors started at half-minute intervals from the ski stadium.

February 13, 1936

# MISS HERBER, BAIER ANNEX PAIR TITLE

## Skate to a Brilliant Victory—Miss Vinson and Hill Are Fifth in Olympic Test.

**By ALBION ROSS.**
Wireless to THE NEW YORK TIMES.
GARMISCH-PARTENKIRCHEN, Germany, Feb. 13.—Europe continues to demonstrate in most disconcerting fashion its complete superiority to the New World in Winter sports, always excepting hockey.

The fourth Olympic Winter Games are drawing to their close and America has garnered to date only young Leo Freisinger's bronze speed-skating medal to prove it ever sent a team to the Winter Olympics.

Norway, with four gold, four silver and two bronze medals to date, leads the field, having 80 points in the unofficial but customary team scores. Germany follows with three gold and four silver medals and 47 points in the scoring.

Finland, with one gold medal, two of silver and one of bronze, rates 31 points. Switzerland, with both first and second in the four-man bobsledding, now has 18 points and one gold and one silver medal.

The United States is sixth in the team standings at present with only 15½ points, the fraction resulting from Allan Potts's tie for sixth place in the 500-meter speed-skating race.

### No Alibis Are Offered.

The United States suffered another blow to its hopes today when the national figure skating champion, Miss Maribel Y. Vinson, and her partner, George E. B. Hill, skated a courageous and brilliant pair program, but did it rather badly and landed in fifth place. It was generally agreed that the American pair presented the most difficult set of figures of any couple on the Olympic ice. Their program was original, daring, dramatic and well rounded, but for five out of the ten minutes it was badly skated.

Neither Miss Vinson nor Hill offered any alibis but probably their failure today was, in part at least, the result of the fact that they had only fifteen minutes of practice on the Olympic rink in the ten days since they arrived here.

Chancellor Hitler, Dr. Joseph Goebbels, General Hermann Goering and various other great Third Reich personages were in the seats reserved for honored guests when the Olympic pair skating began this afternoon.

They saw Miss Maxi Herber and Ernst Baier, the German champion, adjudged the gold medal winners by the nine referees representing nine nations. Miss Herber and Baier danced, pirouetted, did acrobatics and made their bow to music composed to fit their program.

### Perfect Rhythm Attained.

The German victory in this most theatrical of sports was the result of painstaking application of science to the art of figure skating. The German pair had a film made of their complete schedule of figures. This film then was placed in the hands of a composer, who undertook to fit notes to every movement and gesture. The result proved there is something new under the sun.

Baier and Miss Herber appeared moving in effortless response to the music itself and their program achieved a degree of perfect rhythm that has probably never been attained by any other two skaters.

It remained for a 15-year-old schoolgirl from Vienna and her 16-year-old brother to threaten the German champions with defeat before the eyes of their Fuehrer. Miss Herber and Baier are great skaters because they have prepared for every eventuality and labored lustily at their chosen task. The 9,000 spectators at the Olympic rink this afternoon knew Erik and Miss Ilse Pausin of Austria merely as names on the program.

They soon discovered the difference between labored and inborn skating. For a moment, standing alone on the ice, the two young Austrians presented a rather forlorn spectacle. In a moment they were off like dragonflies, skimming over the surface of the ice with the tempo, verve and abandon that the

Times Wide World Photo.
Miss Maxi Herber and Ernst Baier, who triumphed in figure skating.

crowd had been waiting for.

The two children went flying through their figures so easily and joyously, spinning and pirouetting furiously from one end of the rink to the other, that they brought the spectators half out of their seats. Applause volleyed from stand to stand. When it was over the judges, who failed to mark the young Viennese as high as the crowd expected, were roundly hissed and booed. In the final result they placed second.

Neither Laszlo Szollas nor Miss Emilia Rotter of Hungary is a first class single skater, and they were unable today to present a program that was fast or daring enough to attract much attention. They received the bronze medal, perhaps as a consolation prize. Their compatriots, the brother and sister pair, Attila and Miss Piroska Szekrenyessy, placed fourth with a more modern performance that demanded more from both skaters individually.

The second part of the classic Scandinavian ski test, the combined 18-kilometer race and jump, was performed today. Seven thousand persons, including Hitler and half of his Cabinet, came to town to see the jumping. The result was a sweep for Norway. Oddbjorn Hagen is the gold medalist, Olaf Hoffsbakken, the silver, and Sverre Brodahl, the bronze.

The Americans in the event placed quite hopelessly among the "also ran" group. Karl Magnus Satre was twenty-sixth, Birger Torrissen, twenty-seventh, Edward J. Blood, former intercollegiate ski star, thirty-sixth, and Paul Ottar Satre, forty-third. There were only forty-five competitors entered.

The star of the jumping, which took place on the smaller of the two Olympic jumps, was Laurl

35

**Ivan Brown and Alan Washbond, two-man team to compete today.**

Times Wide World Photo.

# Bobsled Mark Is Broken 12 Times

## BROWN-WASHBOND EXCEL ON BOB RUN

### Lead by More Than 3 Seconds in Olympic Race—Colgate-Lawrence in Third Place.

### SCHAFER RETAINS TITLE

### Triumphs in Figure Skating, With Lee of U. S. Twelfth—British Six Wins, 5-0.

**By ALBION ROSS.**

W.reless to THE NEW YORK TIMES.

GARMISCH-PARTENKIRCHEN, Germany, Feb. 14.—The American hero of these Winter Olympics evidently will be Ivan Brown, the six-foot Adirondack guide who today in the first two heats of the two-man bobsledding races bettered by more than three seconds the best that Europe had to offer. And Europe had a great deal to offer. Twelve times in the course of three hours of skillful, headlong driving the two-man record for the course—1 minute 25.2 seconds—was broken.

The display ended with the spectators on their feet shouting and throwing hats and mufflers in the air as Brown and Alan Washbond shot down the course in 1 minute 21.02 seconds only to be followed by Fritz Feierabend of Switzerland, who established a new and amazing record of 1 minute 20.31 seconds.

It is a historic experience in any sport to see an international record fall twelve times between breakfast and lunch. There were few spectators willing to climb the mountainside above Riessersee Lake and stand freezing in the morning air when the race began. It was not until the wealthy New Yorker, Gilbert Colgate, broke the course record the first time with a run of 1 minute 25.06 seconds that the news went down to the crowds in the warmer valley that something was afoot.

### Spectators Are Thrilled.

The stands filled slowly as sled after sled began to come down faster and faster. The announcer became increasingly excited. The stands seethed with excitement for the first time as Brown and Washbond, halfway through the first heat, went by with a rush. They hurtled along the Bavaria Curve's perpendicular wall barely three feet from its base to speed silently down the straightaway called Waterwall, Washbond bobbing with the full strength of his 230 pounds.

The loud-speaker broadcast the news that the run had been made in 1 minute 22.5 seconds, almost three seconds under the old record time. A hysterical demonstration began that continued until Feierabend capped the climax in his second heat.

With two heats over, the United States No. 1 sled is in first place with an advantage of 3.13 seconds over Feierabend, on Switzerland's No. 2. Colgate and Richard W. Lawrence, on the United States No. 2 sled, reached 1 minute 21.94 seconds in the second heat and placed third in the ratings for the day, only 35-100 of a second behind the Swiss driver. They were not as hard pressed by the fourth driver, Reto Capadrutt of Switzerland, who finished nearly two seconds behind them.

### Chances Are Excellent.

Unless Brown and Colgate should have the most outrageous bad luck tomorrow the United States seems well on its way to a gold medal won in fierce competition from a brilliant field. The Americans' chances of acquiring a silver medal for good measure can be regarded as excellent.

The last two heats in the race, which will be run off tomorrow, will either blast or realize the high hopes of winning at least one resounding Olympic victory to take the sting off the series of defeats and the loss of our Olympic championship title acquired at Lake Placid in 1932.

Both the 10,000-meter speed skating race and the men's free figure skating this afternoon left America as devoid of Olympic laurels as before. The American contestants in both events were completely outclassed.

Eddie Schroeder of Chicago placed eighth in the 10,000-meter skating event. Bob Petersen was eliminated when he collapsed on the track. The Milwaukee lad was overtrained. He explained after the race that his thigh muscles tightened until they were torturing him, and when he finally let go they bunched and he collapsed on the ice.

### Clocked in 17:24.3.

Ivar Ballangrud of Norway took the gold medal, being timed in 17 minutes 24.3 seconds. The Norwegian skater now has three of the gold medals awarded for speed skating. Birger Vasenius of Finland was second and Max Stiepl of Austria placed third to win the bronze medal.

The former Olympic record for the distance was bettered by the first nine skaters. This number includes Schroeder, who, despite his relatively poor showing, came within a quarter of a minute of his own best time to date. None of the racers came within striking distance of the existing world record.

The outstanding individual victor in the games is Ballangrud, who has won three gold medals and one of silver. He has proved a tower of strength for the Norwegians, who now seem to be re-establishing more strongly than ever their dominant position in international Winter sport.

Germany is still in second place in the unofficial but generally accepted national ratings and Finland third. The United States made no headway in the standing today and still is well down among the "also rans."

### Fall Hurts Lee's Chances.

Robin Lee, the schoolboy who is the American figure skating champion, lost whatever chance he may have had to place well when he fell while presenting his free figure program this afternoon. Erle Reiter fell thrice.

The young American champion, for some reason, added at the last

---

Valonen of Finland, who registered 52 and 54½ meters.

Ivar Ballangrud, who had been threatening to take all four Olympic medals for speed skating, courteously stepped down into second place today and his countryman, Charles Mathisen, took the gold medal in the 1,500-meter race. Ballangrud won the silver medal and Birger Vasenius of Finland the bronze one.

### Brown's Decisions Booed.

Freisinger of Milwaukee placed fourth. He bettered his previous record in the 1,500 meters by 1 2-10 seconds, but his achievement was not sufficient to place him among the first three.

Beating Sweden by 2 to 1 in a midnight hockey game, the American team came successfully through the eliminations. The Austrian and Swedish teams have been eliminated in one group and the Germans and Hungarians in the other, leaving for the next round Canada, Great Britain and Czechoslovakia and the United States.

Under Olympic rules America will not play Czechoslovakia again, however, facing only Canada and Great Britain. Also there will be no game between Canada and Britain and if only those two teams survive the final round the Anglo-Canadian team which represents the British Isles will become automatically the victor in the Olympic hockey tournament on the basis of its surprise victory over Canada two nights ago.

An essentially German crowd at tonight's games appeared not to be particularly friendly to the American officials and American players. Walter Brown acted as the referee for the game early in the night between Great Britain and Germany, in which Germany was defeated. Several of his decisions were booed. The Swedish team also played the rôle of favorite with the spectators in the second game.

### Breaks Olympic Record.

By The Associated Press.

GARMISCH-PARTENKIRCHEN, Germany, Feb. 13.—Charles Mathisen romped away with the 1,500-meter speed skating crown in 2 minutes 19.2 seconds today, shaving 1.9 seconds off the former Olympic standard hung up by Clas Thunberg, the great Finn, in the 1928 games.

Leo Freisinger could do no better than fourth, but forced all three men who led him in the final standings to better Thunberg's time. Ivar Ballangrud was caught in 2:20.2 and Birger Vasenius, who was third, in 2:20.9.

Freisinger, paired against Ballangrud in the third heat, gave the Norwegian ace, acknowledged king of world skaters, a stiff fight all the way and finished in 2:21.3.

Eddie Schroeder of Chicago finished in a tie for twelfth place with Karl Leban of Austria, each clocked in 2:24.3; Bob Petersen of Milwaukee was seventeenth in 2:25.4, and Allan Potts of Brooklyn wound up in the ruck with his time of 2:31.2.

Delbert Lamb of Milwaukee still was suffering from a cold and scratched.

February 14, 1936

minute an unexpected thrill to his program. The addition to his routine proved fatal when he tried to execute it and was unable to keep to his feet. He finished in twelfth position. Reiter was thirteenth and George E. B. Hill twenty-second.

Karl Schafer, world champion and Olympic gold medalist, retained his title. He was pressed by Ernst Baier of Germany and Felix Kaspar of Austria. The young Austrian was one of the day's sensations. His program was difficult but he executed it gracefully and capably. Schafer appeared to be tired and somewhat indifferent. He had, however, executed his compulsory figures earlier in the week with such great success he could not be beaten today.

**A Unanimous Choice.**

By The Associated Press.

GARMISCH-PARTENKIRCHEN, Germany, Feb. 14.—Austria's brilliant figure skater, Karl Schafer, successfully defended his Olympic crown in the singles today.

Schafer, the unanimous choice of seven judges after giving a marvelous performance, had a clear-cut margin over his nearest rival, Ernst Baier of Germany, who shared the pair title with Miss Maxi Herber. Robin Lee, 16-year-old American champion, finished twelfth.

It was with a total of 422.7 points that Schafer topped the field. Baier accumulated 400.8 points. Lee, best of the American trio, totaled 363 in his first bid for Olympic honors, finishing strongly after a somewhat shaky start. Erle Reiter of Minneapolis scored 352.9 and George E. B. Hill, Boston, 325.1 points.

Great Britain's hockey team took a commanding lead in the final round-robin by trouncing Czechoslovakia, 5–0, in today's only match. The British, already conquerors of Canada, will clinch the title if they beat the United States tomorrow night.

Despite their lead in the two-man bobsledding, Ivan Brown and Alan Washbond appeared tonight to be pondering the question: "What's three seconds among a bunch of maniacs?"

They considered their margin trifling, but compatriots disagreed.

"If you try to set another record tomorrow morning," said Edward Varno of Lake Placid to Brown, "I'll break your neck. Just take it easy and win with what you've got in hand."

"You might as well start breaking then," said Brown. "We're going to take nothing easy. If that run is like it was today and the sled doesn't jump the wall, just watch our smoke."

Although the oddly assorted pair —Brown, the high-strung, strapping guide, and Washbond, the stolid, slow-moving merchant — smashed the old record twice they were far from satisfied.

"Why I only bobbed four times on that last run," Washbond told The Associated Press. "We had one door open today. We'll open them both tomorrow."

**Autograph Hunters on Hand.**

He and Brown were besieged by autograph hunters, but Washbond's hands were so cramped from keeping a vise-like grip on the brakes it was minutes before he could wield a pencil.

The leaders' biggest worry was that they'll be the third sled down the hill tomorrow in the third heat. The first six today failed to break 1:30, but as soon as the ice got sure enough the slick boblets began shooting past with lightning speed. Incidentally, the Americans discovered one reason for Fritz Feierabend's smashing-record heat. Taking a tip from the Americans, he has equipped his sled with far sharper runners than any of the other Europeans.

---

The runners Brown and Washbond used today were the same that won them the Olympic try-outs and North American championships. They were rusty when they were dug out yesterday at the last minute, but a few minutes' work had them shined up and in shape again.

February 15, 1936

---

## ITALY MILITARY SKI VICTOR

**Four-Man Team Wins 25-Kilometer Run and Shooting Event.**

GARMISCH-PARTENKIRCHEN, Germany, Feb. 14 (AP).—Italy won the military ski patrol race of the fourth Winter Olympic games today. The race, a 25-kilometer ski run and shooting exhibition for four men—an officer, an under-officer and two enlisted men—was a demonstration and did not figure in the Olympic scoring.

Italy's team covered the course in 2 hours 28 minutes 35 seconds. Behind the Italians finished Finland in 2:28:49, Sweden in 2:35:24, Austria in 2:36:24 and France in 2:40:56.

Upon completion of the ski race, the competitors shot at small balloons at a distance of 150 meters. Fifteen rounds of ammunition were allowed and for each balloon not brought down with this amount, a penalty of three minutes was added to the racing time.

February 15, 1936

---

# BALLANGRUD GAINS AN OLYMPIC TRIPLE

**New Mark for 10,000 Meters Crowns Norwegian Star's Speed Skating Feats.**

---

**SCHROEDER OF U. S. EIGHTH**

---

**Also Betters Hurd's Standard for Games—Finn and Austrian Second and Third.**

By The Associated Press.

GARMISCH-PARTENKIRCHEN, Germany, Feb. 14.—Ivar Ballangrud rounded out the greatest individual Olympic performance in a dozen years today as Norway completed a clean sweep of the speed-skating championships of the fourth Winter Olympic Games.

The well-built blond speedster from the North, who already had equaled one Olympic record and cracked another in the 500-meter and 5,000-meter championships, added the 10,000-meter title to his collection and bettered Alex Hurd's Olympic standard for the distance by 31.9 seconds.

Hurd, Canadian ace, set the mark at 17:56.2 in a preliminary heat of the 1932 championship at Lake Placid. Ballangrud's time today was 17:24.3.

**Equaled Nurmi's Feat.**

Not since Paavo Nurmi ran off with the 1,500-meter and 5,000-meter flat races and the 10,000-meter cross-country event at Paris in 1924 had any Olympic athlete

---

won three individual championships.

Undisputed king of world speed skaters, Ballangrud allowed only the 1,500-meter crown to slip from his grasp. He finished second in that event to his team-mate, Charles Mathisen, in a close struggle in which both bettered the Olympic record.

So thoroughly was the old mark demolished by today's remarkable pace that Eddie Schroeder, Chicago's long-distance star, found himself in eighth place despite the fact he had skated the distance more than four seconds under record time. Schroeder was clocked in 17:52.

**Couldn't Stand the Pace.**

Bob Peterson of Milwaukee, the only other American starter in the 10,000 meters, fell on the twentieth lap and withdrew. Afterward he said: "My legs just went back on me. This is my favorite distance, but I just couldn't take it."

The showing of the Americans contrasted sharply with their 1932 record, when they captured all four speed-skating crowns with the competition conducted under United States "man-for-man" skating rules, instead of European style, against time.

America's team of five, which also included Allan Potts of Brooklyn, Leo Freisinger of Chicago and Delbert Lamb of Milwaukee, picked up only 9½ points in the four races.

Freisinger collected 7 with a third place in the 500 and a fourth in the 1,500 meters. Lamb, who scratched from three races because of a bad cold, was fifth in the 500 meters. Potts picked up the half point by tying for sixth in the same event.

Times Wide World Photo.
**Ivar Ballangrud.**

Second to Ballangrud today was Birger Vasenius of Finland, who was clocked in 17:28.2. Max Stiepl of Austria was third in 17:30, Mathisen fourth in 17:41.2, Ossi Blomqvist of Finland fifth in 17:42.4 and Jan Langedijk of Netherlands sixth in 17:43.7. Antero Ojala of Finland, clocked in 17:46.6, took seventh place, just in front of Schroeder.

February 15, 1936

---

# U. S. BOBSLEDDERS WIN AT OLYMPICS; HOCKEY TEAM TIES

**BROWN IS HOME FIRST**

---

**Riding With Washbond, He Registers Initial American Victory.**

---

**COLGATE-LAWRENCE THIRD**

---

**Record for Run Is Shattered 22 Times, With Final Heat Deciding the Placings.**

By ALBION ROSS.
Wireless to THE NEW YORK TIMES.

GARMISCH-PARTENKIRCHEN, Germany, Feb. 15.—The United States won its first gold medal of the fourth Olympic Winter Games this morning when Ivan Brown, guide, caretaker and policeman of Keene Valley, N. Y., drove to vic-

---

tory in the two-man bobsledding competition. Although the United States now has lost completely through these Olympics its short-lived leadership in Winter sports acquired at Lake Placid four years ago, this bobsledding victory is well worth having.

The four heats proved one of the great sporting events of the games. The previous record for the run was broken twenty-two times in the most desperate struggle for places the Winter Olympics have yet provoked in the sixteen years of their existence.

**American Lead Reduced.**

After bettering the record on his first run yesterday by nearly three seconds and then bettering his own time by another second, Brown found himself this morning nevertheless at a disadvantage in his duel with Fritz Feierabend of Switzerland, who established a final course record yesterday of 1 minute 20.31 seconds. America's position was serious. The run was, as usual, slow until half a dozen sleds had gone down. Brown was drawn in the third starting position and the ambitious Swiss driver in seventeenth place.

The American sled had acquired in the first two heats yesterday a three-second lead. The unfortunate effect of Brown's position in the starting list appeared in the results of the first heat today. Feierabend reduced the American lead to two seconds. This was not so bad. But the situation became acute when Feierabend accomplished a bobbing miracle and established in his second heat a new record of 1 minute 19.88 seconds.

America seemed well on its way to losing its gold medal after it had appeared to be secure. It became necessary for Brown to make the run in 1 minute 21.72 seconds if he were to keep his lead over the Swiss driver.

The spectators held their breath as the American No. 1 sled started down on its fourth and last heat. Brown made the run in 1 minute 20.38 seconds. America had kept its gold medal and Feierabend had to be content with the silver.

**Washbond Does His Part.**

Gilbert Colgate Jr. of New York won the bronze medal with a time of 5 minutes 33.96 seconds for the four heats.

All the talk about Brown's victory is rather unfair to his rider, Alan Washbond, general store proprietor and bobsled fanatic of Keene Valley. Washbond is not only the proud possessor of some 230 pounds of ballast but he is a living contradiction of the "sack of sand" theory in bobsledding. Like "No Brakes" Bickford of the four-man team, Washbond although a family man and a pillar of Keene Valley society, does not believe in brakes. He does his part, instead, by "bobbing" steadily eight times every 100 yards or so.

Colgate and Brown are old friends and old rivals. Colgate demands that his rider, Richard W. Lawrence of Branchville, N. J., behave literally like the proverbial sack of sand. He is convinced bobbing does more harm than good. The results obtained through Washbond's bobbing efforts this time ought to settle the argument.

Colgate drove a great race but Brown and Washbond not only drove but bobbed their way to the gold medal. As Washbond expressed it in a cablegram to his wife: "We brought home the bacon on the old tin runners."

America is still in the running for a possible second gold medal, as our hockey team played to a 0-0 tie with Great Britain in a night game that went three overtime periods and finished after midnight. The game apparently added new complications to the already hopelessly involved system of elimination scoring.

The German broadcaster at the stadium announced at the conclusion of the contest that Britain had clinched the gold medal. The announcement was promptly denied by the British coaches and hockey officials present.

Seen dimly through the smoke engendered by the hockey controversy now raging in every bar and café in the twin towns, it appears that America will have to defeat Canada tomorrow by some such score as 5 or 6 to 0 in order to win the tourney. As there is very little likelihood that the United States will be able to win at all, the stadium announcer was merely somewhat discourteously quick about broadcasting the demise of the American hopes for another gold medal.

It would appear, however, that our chances are excellent for obtaining second place. The United States, in any case, will take the bronze medal, as Czechoslovakia, the other competitor in the four-way finals, already has been eliminated by two painfully thorough defeats.

**British Goalie Kept Busy.**

Great Britain was kept almost constantly on the defensive tonight, its Anglo-Canadian goalie, James Foster, spending a good deal of his time on his knees struggling with three or even four American players who had gone in a huddle with the puck in front of his cage. Unfortunately, the Americans showed more ability getting into this advantageous position than they did in employing it for the purpose of goal-making.

The American combination fought its way successfully through the elimination round but it is not yet a genuine team with a plan and a technique of its own.

Great Britain, anxious to obtain at least a tie, played a defensive game and made only such raids on American ice as seemed necessary to stem the tide of the American advance.

The day's great event for Olympic guests has been the free figure skating competition for women at the Ice Stadium. Miss Sonja Henie of Norway, who had been so hard pressed by Miss Cecilia Colledge in the compulsory figures that the British enthusiasts were already hailing a new champion, definitely reestablished her threatened prestige by skating as well as she ever has in her long career and retaining her championship. Miss Col-

ledge is the silver medalist and Miss Vivi-Anne Hulten of Sweden the bronze medalist.

America's national champion, Miss Maribel Vinson, finished in fifth place after successfully presenting a difficult and well arranged program. Today Miss Vinson skated well. She was fast and confident, but apparently she lacked some element of perfection which the judges found in Miss Colledge.

The excitement has been intense here ever since it became known Sonja was in danger of defeat. Her performance today was a revelation to her self-appointed critics. Appearing in a carefully designed white and violet costume, she skated with all the vigor and much of the abandon of a girl just beginning rather than finishing the difficult career of a figure skater who has become a world figure. Opening with a Lutze jump, she performed her Axel Paulsen smoothly and the experts assert she showed in her spins, especially her cross-foot, more smoothness and complete mastery than ever before.

She had, as she always has in Europe, the crowd with her all the way, and her skating brought round after round of applause.

There was no doubt in the minds of the spectators about the identity of the world champion despite all the gossip that has been heard here during the last few days respecting Miss Colledge's chances. The English champion showed again today she is a great acrobat on skates but no dancer.

The Swedes made a clear sweep of the 50-kilometre ski race. They led all the way, taking all three medals. The American competitors fared poorly.

**Margin Is 1.35 Seconds.**

By The Associated Press.

GARMISCH-PARTENKIRCHEN, Germany, Feb. 15.—Ivan Brown and Alan Washbond successfully fought off the challenge of the great Swiss pilot, Fritz Feierabend, to win the two-man bobsledding competition today by the margin of 1.35 seconds and thus successfully defend the Olympic championship Hubert and Curtis Stevens won for the United States at Lake Placid four years ago.

It was a triumph for American ingenuity as well as speed and skill. A set of $2.48 runners of homemade spring steel they had made in their spare time carried Brown and Washbond to their spectacular victory.

Where Feierabend and other leading rivals were riding on Sheffield steel that set them back as high as $65 a set, the winners placed their

faith in their own handicraft.

The total elapsed times for the three leaders were: Brown and Washbond, 5:29.29; Feierabend and Joseph Beerli, 5:30.64; Gilbert Colgate Jr. and Richard W. Lawrence, 5:33.96.

**Colgate Praises Winners.**

Colgate had nothing but praise for the winners and their sled.

"I think I got everything out of my sled it was built to give," he said, "but it wasn't enough to beat that pair."

Brown, who admitted he didn't sleep a wink after 2 A. M., said he thought he had made only one real mistake in his four runs. In the third run, he said, he misjudged the bend just before the Bavarian horseshoe and as a result hit the big ice wall too late. Fortunately, however, he escaped serious loss of speed.

Although they knew on their last trip just what time they had to make to win, Brown said "We weren't half as nervous then as we were on our first run."

The victory came almost as a birthday present for Brown, who will be 28 tomorrow.

When he went to the breakfast table this morning he found at his place a big cake, inscribed "Good Luck." His team-mates had it baked during the night and found a pastry expert who could write English.

**Is Highly Superstitious.**

Brown, incidentally, is just about the most superstitious pilot of them all. His pet "mania" takes the form of hunting hairpins. His eyes seldom leave the sidewalk any day until he has found one. Up to today, by actual tabulation, he hadn't failed for twenty-four consecutive days.

Washbond has no superstition except one—he'll ride with no driver except Brown. He never has.

When they originally formed the partnership Washbond was the driver and Brown the bobber. Three years ago, however, Washbond stepped into a hole and injured a knee. So there was nothing for Brown to do but learn to drive. They intend to stick together at least until they have won the 1940 Olympic championship.

Although Reto Capadrutt's chute standard of 1:25:20 took a fearful beating, only one accident marred the record-breaking proceedings. Henri Koch and Gustav Wagner of Luxembourg cracked up on Bavaria Curve today and suffered injuries severe enough to send both to the hospital.

February 16, 1936

Associated Press Photo.

**Alan Washbond, brake, and Ivan Brown, driver, who scored for U. S.**

# Miss Henie Hard Pressed To Defeat Miss Colledge

### Wins Third Olympic Figure Skating Title With 424.5 Points to English Girl's 418.1—Miss Vinson Is Fifth.

By The Associated Press.

GARMISCH-PARTENKIRCHEN, Germany, Feb. 15.—Miss Sonja Henie, queen of the figure skaters for ten years, retained the Olympic crown today only after a lanky English girl, Miss Cecilia Colledge, gave the blonde Norwegian the closest contest of her career.

In winning her third Olympic title and beating twenty-two of the world's ranking skaters from twelve nations, Sonja was forced to give an exhibition ranked by experts as her best since she won

her first world title in 1926. She entered the free skating with a three-point margin over Miss Colledge and doubled it with a brilliant execution of spins, twirls and jumps.

The final figures gave the title-holder 424.5 points as against 418.1 for the newly risen English star.

Miss Maribel Vinson, the American titleholder, moved up one notch from her ranking in the school figures to take fifth with 388.7, behind Miss Vivi-Anne Hulten of Sweden and Miss Liselotte Landbeck of Belgium.

Of the three other Americans, little Miss Audrey Peppe of New York ranked the highest, finishing twelfth. The Weigel sisters of Buffalo were far down the list, Louise placing twenty-first and Estelle twenty-second.

From the start, the event was a battle between the champion and Miss Colledge. The English skater, first of the pair to appear on the ice, kept the crowd of 11,000 in a continuous uproar as she whirled through a program designed to force Sonja to give her best. The judges gave her an average of 5.7 points on both difficulty of program and performance.

### Receives a 5.8 Rating.

There was a dead silence when Sonja skated into the arena, appearing slightly nervous. She knew she dared not make one mistake. The nervousness soon disappeared, however. She swung into a répertoire of difficult figures, at one time executing a brilliant double Axel Paulsen jump, ending in a graceful split, to bring forth cheers from the crowd. At the end of her performance she received a 5.8 rating.

Miss Vinson's program was more conservative but she gave it perfectly to get a maximum rating on performance. Miss Peppe was popular, but, like Miss Vinson, her program was too conventional to gain a higher rating.

Miss Etsuko Inada, little Japanese skater, gave one of the most popular exhibitions as she sprang about the big ice stadium unconcerned and with all the fervor of youth.

February 16, 1936

---

### SWEDEN SWEEPS SKIING.

**Crown Prince Sees Viklund Win, With Three Team-Mates Next.**

By The Associated Press.

GARMISCH-PARTENKIRCHEN, Germany, Feb. 15.—Sliding along as though they were out for a morning constitutional, Sweden's tireless skiers carried off the first four places in the 50-kilometer Olympic marathon today.

In quick succession, Elis Viklund, Axel Wickstrom, Nils Englund and Hjalmar Bergstrom crossed the finish line, smiling and apparently fresh enough to cover the 31.7 miles of hilly terrain again without so much as batting an eye. Viklund, the winner, was clocked in 3 hours 30 minutes 11 seconds, an average of about nine miles an hour.

America's team of four again was outclassed. Karl Magnus Satre of Salisbury, Conn., who made the best showing, was eighteenth in 3:58:45. Birger Torrissen of Norfolk, Conn., was twenty-seventh in 4:07:44; Richard Parsons of Salisbury twenty-ninth in 4:11:08, and Nils Backstrom of Norfolk thirty-second in 4:29:30.

Thirty-six started and thirty-four finished. Fifth place went to Klaes Karppinen of Finland in 3:39:33 and sixth to young Arne Tuft of Norway in 3:41:18.

Crown Prince Gustav Adolf of Sweden witnessed his compatriots triumph.

February 16, 1936

---

### RUUD AGAIN NAMED SKI JUMP CHAMPION

*Norwegian Keeps Olympic Title With 232 Points—Eriksson of Sweden Runner-Up.*

GARMISCH-PARTENKIRCHEN, Germany, Feb. 16 (UP).—Birger Ruud of Norway, displaying great form under conditions that seriously handicapped all competitors, successfully defended his Olympic ski jumping title today as the fourth Olympic Winter Games came to a close.

An early rain wet the snow and partly melted it and the bright afternoon sun made conditions even worse. This precluded any long jumps, and Ruud did not make the longest of the day. His perfect form gave him a score of 232 out of a maximum of 240 points and enabled him to retain the title he won at Lake Placid in 1932. The Norwegian star leaped 75 and 74.5 meters (246 feet and 244 feet 5 inches).

Ruud's best was surpassed three times, twice by Sven Eriksson of Sweden, who took second place. Eriksson made 76 meters each time, the longest jumps of the event. America's jumpers, pressing for distance and losing points for poor form, could not threaten the leaders. The highest American ranking went to Sverre Fredheim of Minneapolis, who took eleventh place.

Third place went to Alf Andersen of Norway, fourth to Kaare Walberg of Norway, fifth to Stanislaw Marusarz of Poland and sixth to Lauri Valonen of Finland.

The three places added 17 points to Norway's total in the unofficial scoring and enabled that nation to take final honors by a good margin over Germany.

February 17, 1936

---

Times Wide World Photo.
Birger Ruud, who retained ski jump title.

---

### TALLY BY NEVILLE WINS FOR CANADA

**Lone Goal of Hockey Contest With U. S. Comes in Third Minute of First Period.**

By The Associated Press.

GARMISCH-PARTENKIRCHEN, Germany, Feb. 16.—The Olympic hockey championships, born of trouble, closed amicably enough today as Canada defeated the crippled American team, 1 to 0, and thus presented the crown to Great Britain.

The championship was decided in the third minute of play when Dave Neville, clever Canadian forward, weaved into the American defense zone after a face-off and easily beat Goalie Tom Moone of Boston who was partly blinded as he stood facing the hot sun.

Thereafter, the teams battled through 42½ more minutes before Reichsfuehrer Adolf Hitler, Dr. Joseph Goebbels and other guests of honor without another score.

The British, defeating Canada in the second series and tying the United States and trouncing Czechoslovakia in the final round robin, were credited with five points in the final standing. The United States, holding only a bare chance of taking the crown when today's game began, finished in third place with three points. Canada gained four points to capture second.

### German Team Fifth.

Czechoslovakia took fourth in the final standing, Germany fifth and Sweden sixth.

The American team was sadly handicapped today by the absence of its "spark plug," Jack Garrison of Boston, who injured his shoulder in last night's game against the British. Frank Shaughnessy, defense ace, and Frank Spain, a clever front-line performer, played despite painful charleyhorses.

Canada also was handicapped by injuries which kept Walter Kitchen and Ralph St. Germain out, but Raymond Milton and Maxwell Deacon performed creditably in their places.

In the closing minutes of the game when Francis Moore, Canadian net minder, had the sun in his eyes, the American coach, Walter Brown, withdrew Phil La Batte from the defense and put four forwards on the ice in a desperate effort to score a goal that would have given America second place.

### Milton Hurt in Mix-Up.

It was almost successful when Frank Stubbs broke loose thirty seconds before the finish and fired from ten feet out. But Moore dived out like a football player making a flying tackle and clutched the rubber.

Hitler, kept busy during the intermissions by American speed skaters who sought his autograph, appeared to have particular admiration for La Batte, the rugged Minneapolis player who drew three penalties in quick succession in the second period. Milton of Canada lost several teeth in one violent mix-up near his own net.

Brown had high praise for his team's performance.

"Considering their condition, I honestly expected them to get beaten a dozen to nothing," he said. "They put up a marvelous scrap and I, for one, am proud of them."

Tired as they are, the Americans leave tomorrow for Prague to play the Czechs, then a hard exhibition tour which includes four games in Switzerland and four in London before they sail for home March 11.

February 17, 1936

---

## Miss Henie Turns Pro; Tour May Net $150,000

### World Champion Figure Skater to Appear in Ten United States Cities Starting Next Week and Then Plans Career in Movies.

By LINCOLN A. WERDEN

Miss Sonja Henie, the 23-year-old Norwegian girl who recently won her third Olympic title, announced yesterday that she would embark upon a career in this country next week as a professional figure skater.

The foremost woman figure skater in the world, who reached

Sigmund Ruud (left) and his brother, Birger, are shown in a double jump at Seattle in 1938. Birger took the gold medal for the 90 meter ski jump at the 1932 and 1936 Olympics.

Dick Durrance, shown here competing in the 1936 Olympics, was the U.S. men's downhill champion, 1937, 1939–1940; men's slalom champion 1939–1941; and winner of the men's alpine combined, 1937, 1939–1940. In 1939, he was the men's four-event all-around champion.

Times Wide World Photo.
MISS SONJA HENIE

these shores last Tuesday, said that she expected to net between $100,-000 to $150,000 by the time she had completed a tour of ten cities.

Although Miss Henie said her guarantees amounted to $70,000, she pointed out that this sum would be increased because she was to share in a percentage of the gate receipts at each appearance she made.

Miss Henie's professional début will be made at New Haven next Tuesday, and according to her program she will make her New York appearances at Madison Square Garden on March 29 and 31.

However, she is scheduled to appear prior to that at Philadelphia on March 27 and Boston the following evening. On April 1 Miss Henie will skate at Buffalo and then four appearances at Chicago will follow, beginning April 2 and ending April 5.

The tour will continue at St. Louis on April 7, Minneapolis on April 9 and 10, St. Paul on April 11 and 12 and Detroit on April 14 and 15.

This schedule, however, will not interfere with plans for Miss Henie's participation in the charity carnivals at Madison Square Garden next Sunday and Wednesday, in which she has consented to skate.

In discussing her step from the amateur to the professional ranks Miss Henie pointed out that one of her greatest hopes is to become a motion picture star.

"I want to go into pictures," confessed Sonja, "and I want to skate in them. But the minute I skate in them I become a professional, so why shouldn't I go on this tour?

"What is my idea about pictures? Well, I want to do with skates what Fred Astaire is doing with dancing. No one has ever done it in the movies and I want to."

It is understood that Metro-Goldwyn-Mayer has an option on Miss Henie's services and that upon completion of her skating tour, she will take a screen test. The Pacific Coast office of the motion-picture organization is at present seeking a "suitable vehicle" for Miss Henie, it was learned yesterday.

As far as her skating is concerned, Miss Henie is apparently as enthusiastic as ever about it, although she is tired of competitive tournaments. "I have won everything," she added yesterday, "and the next Olympics are still four years off. But I understand they intend to stage an open championship in Europe next year and that ought to be fun."

Although Miss Henie, who is here with her parents, expects to be in this country for many months to come, she said that she intended to tour Canada next season and possibly Europe.

Just what sort of supporting cast Miss Henie will have in her exhibition work was not made known, but it is not likely that she will have her own entourage. Local skaters in each city undoubtedly will augment her program.

She outlined briefly what she thought would comprise her exhibition skating. The Olympic free skating program that she used at Garmisch-Partenkirchen, a mazurka or tango and her famous "Dying Swan" number, will be the features of her skating répertoire.

**Norwegian Champion at 11**

Miss Henie laughed when she was reminded of some of the incidents in the long career that has made her known wherever figure skating is popular. She started skating at the age of 6 and when she was 11, she became an idol of her native Oslo by winning the Norwegian championship. Her conquests in world tourneys started in 1927 and she has been world champion ever since. She also has been one of her country's leading tennis players and is an expert swimmer.

"Yes," she said smilingly, "that story is very true about my brother and me. When I was seven years old we had an awful fight so I could get a pair of skates like his. But now," she added, "I have a lot of work ahead and much practicing for my shows."

When the interview was concluded, Miss Henie and her parents, Mr. and Mrs. Wilhelm Henie, started for the nearest motion-picture theatre.

*Miss Henie's Record.*
**Titles Won**

| | |
|---|---|
| 1924 | Norwegian |

Finished eighth in Olympics (last place)

| | |
|---|---|
| 1925...Norwegian | 1932...World |
| 1926...Norwegian | European |
| 1927...Norwegian | Olympic |
| World | 1933...World |
| 1928...Norwegian | European |
| World | 1934...World |
| Olympic | European |
| 1929...Norwegian | 1935...World |
| World | European |
| European | 1936...World |
| 1930...World | European |
| European | Olympic |
| 1931...World | |
| European | |

March 18, 1936

# ROBIN LEE RETAINS NATIONAL LAURELS IN FIGURE SKATING

**Despite Knee Injury, 17-Year-Old Ace Wins Men's Crown for Third Year in Row**

By LINCOLN A. WERDEN
Special to THE NEW YORK TIMES.

CHICAGO, Feb. 13.—Blond-haired, 17-year-old Robin Lee of Minneapolis, representing the Skating Club of New York, continued his reign as men's national figure skating champion when he won the title

Times Wide World Photo.
Robin Lee, who repeated his 1936 victory

tonight at the Chicago Arena for the third year in succession.

Lee, who became the boy wonder of the sport when he first captured the crown at the age of 15, was faced with a stern test in his five minutes of free skating at the climax of his title bid.

In other years, it has been skill and grace that carried him to the top, but tonight he can add courage to the list and feel well satisfied that he bears the title of champion with all that the word signifies. Starting his skating at fine speed and doing some magnificent double salchow jumps (two revolutions in the air) Lee twisted his left knee. But no one guessed that he had aggravated an old injury—not even his close rival, 20-year-old Erle Reiter of Minneapolis, who sat on the sidelines.

**Forced to Make Change**

Lee continued his spins and, as he said later, he was forced to change from his left foot, on which he usually springs, to his right.

It was only on his final spin that it appeared that something might be amiss. And then when the organ music stopped and Lee bowed to the applause, he hobbled along the ice and off the rink, giving the first noticeable indication that he had hurt his leg. So well had Lee completed his exhibition under pressure that few of the officials were aware of what had happened until the youngster started to leave.

As it turned out, it was Lee's mastery of school figures yesterday that saved the title for him. Reiter,

showing grand style, followed Lee in the free skating and so effectively did his spin and leap that he was rated higher than the champion in this part of the championship.

However, as the school figures count as two-thirds in the final tabulation, Lee was able to triumph over his skating chum, who has been residing in New York during the past few months. The official point score gave Lee an aggregate of 977.09 and Reiter 964.92. W. J. Nagle, the 53-year-old New Yorker and the only other contender for the men's title, was roundly cheered as he went through his program.

**Another Notable Feat**

While Lee's plucky bit of skating will go down in the annals of skating, there was one more record which will have a place on the books. That was the skating of Miss Maribel Y. Vinson.

Few women skaters can expect to match Miss Vinson's proficiency at school figures and her high marks yesterday attested to that fact. Tonight she did a varied program. It included a standing flat-foot spin which developed into an arabesque one-foot spin, difficult jumps, dance steps of her own innovation and a stunning spread-eagle. And then, with her dashing costume of gold making a striking picture against the background of green-blue ice, she topped her performance with a cross-foot spin.

The 17-year-old Boston girl, Miss Polly Blodgett, carried off second honors, while Miss Katherine Durbrow of New York finished third.

The point score gave Miss Vinson 996.6, Miss Blodgett 934.3 and Miss Durbrow 911.5.

**Near-Perfect Performance**

Later Miss Vinson and George E. B. Hill retained their national pair championship against one of the best fields that has competed in recent years. Their rhythmic skating was so well coordinated that, when the judges raised their big cards designating the rating, the Vinson-Hill marking was close to perfection.

Another pair that made a hit with the spectators also represented the Skating Club of Boston—Miss Joan Tozzer, who yesterday accounted for the women's junior title, and her partner, Bernard Fox, Harvard undergraduate.

But the crowd did not approve of all the ratings that the judges made and, while some of the veteran observers sat by amazed, boos and catcalls greeted the officials during the competition.

So far as any one could remember this is an unprecedented occurrence at a championship.

Miss Grace Madden and her brother James, a well-known pair at the skating carnivals in New York, were awarded second place, while Miss Tozzer and Fox were third. Mr. and Mrs. William Bruns of Bear Mountain, whose low rating the crowd did not approve, and

Miss Blodgett and Roger Turner of Boston were the other pairs participating.

When Miss Vinson ended her free skating tonight she became the women's champion for the ninth occasion, a mark that is likely to stand for a long time in the sport.

The metropolitan duo of Miss Ardelle Kloss and Roland Janson of the Skating Club of New York won the national junior pair championship. Eight couples took part in the competition.

One of the finest exhibitions was given by Miss Helen Barrett and Ted Harper of Detroit, who danced to tango music and earned the commendation of the spectators for the even and flawless presentation of a pleasing program.

The Detroit pair was placed second, while Miss Marjorie Parker and Howard Meredith, also of the Skating Club of New York, were third. Mr. and Mrs. Eduardo Hellmund of Kansas City, another pair that caught the eye, were fourth.

The national dance title was also won by the New Yorkers. Miss Nettie C. Prantell and Harold Hartshorne of the Skating Club of New York were successful in this competition that is made up of waltz, fox trot, tango and fourteen-step. Their clubmates, Miss Marjorie Parker and Joseph K. Savage, were rated second and Miss Kloss and Janson annexed third.

February 14, 1937

## Allais Becomes Idol of France By Capturing World Ski Laurels

### He Wins All-Around Title at Chamonix, Victory in Slalom Giving Him Two Firsts in Combined Event—Miss Cranz of Germany Annexes Women's Championship—Americans Trail

#### By CLARENCE K. STREIT
Wireless to THE NEW YORK TIMES.

CHAMONIX, France, Feb. 15.— Emile Allais is the new world's all-around ski master and France's idol. His rise this year in skiing has been as spectacular as it was some years ago in tennis.

Allais won this most coveted ski title—open to both professionals and amateurs—by his victory here today in the slalom race of the International Ski Federation on top of his smashing victory in the downhill race Saturday. To win the title by taking firsts in both fast and fancy skiing is rare in ski annals. Rudolf Rominger of Switzerland, who lost the title today—he placed tenth—won the championship last year by capturing the downhill and placing third in the slalom.

Another French star, Cannonball Maurice Lafforgue, took second in the all-around competition. As Rene Beckert placed thirteenth, France took the team title too.

**Swiss Team Second**

Allais and Lafforgue were followed in this order by such famous skiing names as Willi Steuri of Switzerland, Heinz von Allmen, Rudi Cranz of Germany, Vittorio Chierroni of Italy, Rudi Matt of Austria, Roman Woerndle of Germany and Willi Walch of Austria. The Swiss team placed second, Germany third, Austria fourth, Czechoslovakia fifth and the United States sixth, defeating Great Britain.

Miss Christel Cranz, young Rudi's more famous sister, won the all-around championship for women even more decisively than

Allais topped the men. She took the slalom today as easily as she scored in the downhill Saturday. The men and women came down the same course today and the Olympic champion's class may be seen from the fact that only nine men made faster times than she did and the best was less than six seconds faster.

The Americans' inexperience showed up even more in the slalom, where good technique is more essential than in the downhill. Miss Clarita Heath again did the best of all the Americans, women or men, but today she placed only thirteenth. The best time in her two trials, 84 seconds, was better than any of the American men, though both Tony Page, who placed twenty-sixth, and Henry Woods, thirty-second, made better averages.

**The Other Finishers**

Miss Miriam McKean finished fourteenth, Miss Hannah Locke sixteenth and Miss Lilo Schwarzenbach seventeenth. The other two American men, Sunny Sceaber and Adams Carter, finished thirty-third and thirty-fourth.

It was reported erroneously in a previous dispatch that the American girls' team had beaten the British in the downhill contest. The British won by one second.

The slalom was run in bright sunshine and good snow conditions over the Argentieres course, facing the celebrated glacier. The distance was 2,500 feet, with a 700-foot drop and forty gates or turns to make.

The best time was made by Walch of Austria, 64 2-5 seconds—just two-fifths better than Allais's.

That was in the first trial and both sought to be more prudent the second time, as it is the average of two trials that wins. Walch was too prudent, however, taking 67 seconds for second place against the 66 Allais had just made.

**Two Great Performances**

Both came down beautifully, as if dancing around the 100-degree turns, making at one point six of these parallel "Christies" in succession within some 60 feet. Allais's victory was all the more acclaimed

since last year he placed only sixth in the slalom and eighth in the downhill. Matt of Austria, who won the slalom last year, was seventh today.

In the slalom teams Germany and Switzerland tied for first, with Austria and France only three seconds behind. The German women's team won both the slalom and the all-around title, with Switzerland second, Great Britain third and the United States fourth.

February 16, 1937

## HIGH SPEED ON THE DOG SLEDS

### An Increasing Number of Amateur Teams Have Been Training for Races in New England This Winter

#### By MARY LEE

THE growing enthusiasm for sled-dog driving as an amateur sport in New England is shown in the appearance of half a dozen or more new teams in the racing field this year. Thirty teams have been competing in the racing series of the New England Sled Dog Club this Winter and sled-dog fans have gathered 2,000 strong in the New England towns on race days.

The towns having race dates contribute, generally, through a local outing club to the owners' expense fund of the club, and this money is divided at the end of the season among the sled-dog owners in proportion to the number of races run by each. This enables owners of small means to compete on fairly even terms with the owners of large kennels.

The rules for the series are strictly amateur: whips may not be more than three feet long, and never used except to stop a fight; doping dogs is not allowed, nor is pacing from automobiles; drivers must keep one foot on the sled except at certain marked stretches along the trails, which allows women to compete on equal terms with men. A team must consist of at least four dogs, and may be as great as seven, eight or nine.

Training of sled-dog teams has gone on steadily in New England this Winter, in spite of poor weather conditions. The more northern drivers find that they can train on the surface of frozen lakes and ponds, keeping their leaders' ears attuned to their shouts of "Gee" and "Haw," while drivers of Southern New England, accustomed to bare ground for much of the Winter, even in normal years, have evolved clever wheel-gigs, made from motor cycles. The dogs pull these strange contrivances through bridle paths and wood roads on bare ground.

Better than nothing, so the drivers tell you, are these contraptions, but not the same as a sled skimming across white snow. The dogs know the difference, and when, after a light snow, they are hitched to the sled for an early morning's run they become different creatures, yapping with delight, bounding over the cold white surface, licking it with their tongues.

Because of the increased entry list this year it was decided to hold the races in two divisions, the Class A, or faster teams, racing in the afternoon, and the Class B, or

slower teams, racing in the morning. It was settled that while the Class B teams were out on the course, there would be held a sprint race for the Class A teams, and while the fast teams were holding their race, a load race would be held for the Class B teams.

Load races have come about as the result of a demand from New England drivers with experience in the Antarctic. These men felt that merely to race a dog team at top speed without any load save the driver's own weight was not to prove the real merits of a team of sled dogs. The first load race was held last Winter at Ashby, Mass. A South Pole freight sled, loaded with a burden of 800 pounds, is hitched to by each team in turn, and hauled a quarter of a mile out of the town and back again, against time.

A real South Polar race was planned for this season at West Ossippee, N. H. The drivers were to camp out in the snow overnight, packing their duffel next morning into their sleds and racing with it to the next night's stop. However, the race had to be canceled.

February 28, 1937

### SNOWSHOE MARK CLAIMED

#### Cote Sets Fast Time in 10-Mile Race at Montreal

MONTREAL, Jan. 29 (P).—Gerard Cote of St. Hyacinthe, Que., claimed a new world record for the ten-mile snowshoe marathon today as he won the feature race of the opening day's program held in connection with the international snowshoers' convention.

Cote covered the difficult course in 1 hour 3 minutes 46 seconds. The previous record was said to be 1:06:14, made by Walter Young of Verdun, Que. United States runners failed to perform impressively in the long race. Honore St. Jean of Manchester, N. H., placed tenth and was followed closely by Eddie Duhamel of Manchester.

In the shorter events racers from the United States were more successful. Edmond Hachey of Berlin, N. H., won the senior 100, 220 and 440 yard dashes. Bertrand Soucy of Manchester captured the junior 100-yard dash, was second in the junior 440 and third in both the senior 100 and 220 yard events.

Miss Becky Marcoux of Manchester, who was forced to drop out of the marathon, won the only women's event, the 60-yard dash.

January 30, 1938

## Neglected Cross-Country Skiing Slated for Revival This Season

### Events in Once-Popular Phase of the Sport Listed by Many Groups—College Coaches Aid Move

#### By FRANK ELKINS

Cross-country skiing, the most neglected phase of the sport in America, will be emphasized this Winter, according to Harry Wade Hicks, chairman of the National Ski Association cross country committee.

The veteran Lake Placid Club secretary, who has been influential in the development of community and regional skiing during the past five years, related yesterday the steps being taken by his organization to bring langlaufing back to the heights that it enjoyed from 1929 to 1934, when such capable athletes as Ole Hegge, Magnus and Olav Satre, John Parsons, Birger Torrissen and the late Johan Satre were battling for honors.

Since the introduction of downhill and slalom running, phases of the sport that enable the novice to learn fast and even feel able to take a competitive hand after one or two years, cross-country has been sadly neglected. Principally through the efforts of Mr. Hicks and several college coaches in the East, notably Ed Blood of New Hampshire and Walter Prager of Dartmouth, who realize the value of cross-country, langlaufing has begun to return to its rightful position.

#### Topic at Convention

"Never in twenty years had the subject of cross-country been so thoroughly and concretely debated and supported as at the last national convention," Mr. Hicks said.

A number of championship and regional tournaments have been arranged throughout the country by organizations, and recreational clubs have stressed the physical value and scenic attractions of touring on skis.

The remarkable achievements of the Finnish skiers in their warfare against the Russians also will create interest in cross-country running. The durable Finns have always dominated international langlaufing and dauerlaufing competitions and are now showing the value of their proficiency.

In this connection Roger Langley, president of the National Ski Association, writes: "I note with great interest the advance of the Finnish ski army and it looks as if skiing is proving a great help to the Finns. Much as I deplore war and fighting of any kind, I am pleased that skiing is proving such a benefaction to the Finns.

"Slow-moving Russians, who cannot ski and are utilizing cumbersome snowshoes that cut their speed to twenty miles a day, are no match for the fast-moving Finnish ski patrols, which can cover eighty miles a day over the deep snows."

Virtually every prominent Finnish cross-country skier is playing an important part in his country's battle for existence.

January 10, 1940

**WINNER OF NATIONAL DOWNHILL SKI TITLES**
Mrs. Grace Carter Lindley, who triumphed at Sun Valley yesterday

---

# SKI RECORD BROKEN ON SUN VALLEY RUN

---

### Durrance Takes U. S. Amateur and Open Downhill Crowns in Daring Exhibition

---

### EUROPEAN STARS BEATEN

---

### Mrs. Lindley Also Captures Two Titles—Slalom Will Be Contested Today

---

#### By FRANK ELKINS
Special to The New York Times.

SUN VALLEY, Idaho, March 22—Speeding down the steep mountainside apparently without regard for life and limb, Dick (Little Man) Durrance showed the way to the strongest field ever to compete in the national downhill skiing championships today. For many years one of the world's outstanding skiers, the American Olympian reasserted his supremacy by covering the two-mile course with its drop of 3,200 feet in the phenomenal time of 2:56.2, equivalent to a speed of about forty-eight miles per hour.

Thus the erstwhile Dartmouth ace, who has won virtually every major downhill and slalom championship in this country and gained additional prestige in competitions abroad, today captured the national amateur and open crowns.

Pitted against an international field of seventy-four selected aces, Dick came through in a fashion that will not soon be forgotten by the large crowd assembled at the hazardous run.

#### Many Stars in Field

Toni Matt, the 20-year-old Arlberg ace who won the national open last year and beat Durrance by a wide margin in doing so, and who had been undefeated in this type of racing since his arrival in the country; Friedl Pfeifer, Martin Fopp and Hannes Schroll, some of Europe's most distinguished skiers, were expected to battle among themselves for the titles.

But Durrance today was the same mighty figure that surprised the skiing world with a brilliant performance in the 1936 Olympics in Germany. He took one of the world's most trying and exacting descents wide open.

Despite the many pitfalls along the way such as trees, gullies, steep grades and rock gardens, last year's national amateur champion schussed the entire course. Just at the trail's finish he could not control his speed and went slithering through the woods. In ten seconds he was back, finishing fifteen seconds under Matt's old record.

#### Finds an Open Spot

Those who witnessed the performance, particularly at the "steilhang"—a 500-yard fallaway with a 37-degree grade—saw Durrance run it straight, the first time this has been done, and dash into the woods with only a prayer on his lips to save him. Fortunately, Dick found an open spot, returned to the course and continued zooming down without checking.

Veteran followers of the sport said that never in the history of skiing in America or abroad has a man performed so riskily and yet maintained such control.

Sharing the day's laurels with the 145-pound Durrance was his former Dartmouth coach, Walter Prager, and Mrs. Grace Carter Lindley of Sun Valley. Prager was the best man among the "restricted amateurs," or ski instructors, with 2:59.4, while Mrs. Lindley, American Olympic ace, won both the women's open and closed titles with 4:10.6.

#### Ideal Weather Conditions

Weather and snow conditions were ideal. The events attracted entries from forty clubs, eighteen States and eight foreign countries. So difficult was the run that only Prager, Fopp and William Janss negotiated it without a fall, while 15-year-old Miss Marilyn Shaw of Stowe, Vt., was the sole one to do it among the nineteen women skiers.

A number of contestants finished without poles and many almost collapsed from exhaustion. Such world renowned skiers as Alf Engen, Schroll, Charley Proctor and Sepp Benedicter did not even finish. Matt went tumbling twice, an unheard-of occurrence for him, to place sixth.

Miss Nettles De Cosson, British star, suffered a slight concussion of the brain.

Luggi Foeger, famous Arlberg instructor, will set the championship slalom tomorrow on the steep summit of 9,200-foot Baldy Mountain. The results will also decide the combined winners in both men and women's divisions.

March 23, 1940

---

# TORGER TOKLE SETS SKI JUMPING MARK

---

### Leaps of 243 and 238 Feet on Olympic Hill Win Honors at Lake Placid

---

#### By FRANK ELKINS
Special to The New York Times.

LAKE PLACID, N. Y., Feb. 22—Torger Tokle, dynamic 22-year-old Norwegian skier, continued his record-smashing career today when he soared through a snowstorm 243 and 238 feet, shattering the nine-year-old Olympic sixty-five-meter jumping record on both flights. These thrilling leaps gave him first place in the concluding event of the Lake Placid Sno-Birds four-day meet.

A record crowd of 4,000, the largest to view a jump since the 1932 Winter Olympics were staged here, saw one of the finest meets in the history of the United States Eastern Amateur Ski Association. Most of them had heard of the brilliant performances of the Norway S. C. star since he came to this country three Winters ago, and today they saw this marvel on three-grooved skis at the top of his form.

Last year, on this same hill, Tokle leaped 225 feet, the longest since the Olympics, but today he broke the 235-foot mark set by his countryman, Hans Beck, in the quadrennial games of 1932 on his first leap. Thus he captured the handsome Dunn Trophy for the second successive year.

The towering slide was in grand shape, with a new fall of snow leaving it as soft as a woolen blanket. While this surface naturally would tend to cut down the speed and the fall made for poor visibility, none of the contenders seemed to mind. There was unusual jumping all along the line.

### Thirteen Records Set

Tokle, in his three Winters in this country, has created thirteen hill marks, including the American long-distance leap of 273 feet, while winning twenty-six of twenty-nine competitions.

Before the meet it was felt that the two Lake Placid Club hopefuls, 18-year-old Arthur Devlin and 19-year-old Jay Rand, would turn the tables on the transplanted Norwegian on their own hill. They had been practicing hard for days and were out to put an end to the victorious march of Tokle. But the blue-shirted Norseman left no doubt of his superiority on his first leap. Swinging down from the top of the inrun at breakneck speed, Tokle timed his take-off perfectly and made a landing almost down to the flat of the snow-packed incline. The crowd sent up a cheer, for it sensed that the record that had withstood assaults from the greatest figures in the sport for so many years had gone the way of others.

All told, for distance and form, Torger got an impressive total of 230.3 points, while Devlin with 227 and 225 foot leaps for 224.5; Rand with 217, 225 for 218.4, and Harold Sorensen, veteran of the group, who now is located with the Forty-fourth Division Ski Patrol of the United States Army at Old Forge; N. Y., with 215, 210 for 213.3, followed.

The Class B victor was 20-year-old George Sherwood, another of the home club's talented youngsters. He had two almost flawless leaps of 207 and 202 feet for 219.9. The 15-year-old lad from Berlin, N. H., Kenneth Fysh, had the longest leaps in this group, two of 209 feet each, but had to be content with third place, behind Erhard Lindroth of Gardner, Mass.

Bjorn Lie, Norsemen S. C. athlete, retained his combined jump and cross-country honors for the famous Beck Trophy with a total of 430.9 points and successfully defended his Hendrix Ski-Meister award for being the best four-event entrant with 368.73 points.

February 23, 1941

# BUTTON CAPTURES U. S. SKATING TITLE

### Englewood Youth, 15, Annexes Junior Crown—Miss Merrill Leads in Women's Event

#### By BRYAN FIELD

Richard Button, 15-year-old youth representing the Philadelphia Skating and Humane Club, last night won the national men's junior championship as amateur figure skating returned to New York to an enthusiastic reception at Iceland.

There will be no men's senior championship this year because of the war and Button will take 1945 rank as the outstanding man in the four-day meet which began yesterday. It will conclude Monday night in Madison Square Garden.

Three championships were decided, the others being the men's and women's novice championships. The former went to John Lettingarver of the St. Paul Figure Skating Club, who is the same age as Button, and the other to 13-year-old Miss Barbara Jones of the Tulsa Figure Skating Club.

It was an appreciative group of several hundred that watched proceedings all day yesterday and last night on the first occasion when the national championships are being held in conjunction with the North American championships. This combination is a new departure caused by the war, but no North American titles will be decided until Monday night.

Miss Jones, as well as Button and Lettingarver, had the distinction of leading in the school figures in addition to the free skating. Experts who watched asserted that young Button essayed the most difficult routine.

Evidently the judges considered this strongly as the Englewood (N. J.) lad, who represents the Philadelphia club, suffered two spills. He took them with the grace of a good figure skater and was applauded for his sang froid as well as his skill.

Early arrivals had a view of the dashing skating of Miss Gretchen Van Zandt Merrill of the Boston Skating Club as she carried off the honors in the school figures for senior women. Miss Merrill is the defending champion, having also triumphed in 1943, and most favor her to become a three-time winner. In earlier years she was novice and junior champion.

### St. Paul Girls Contenders

How high she ranks toward the standard of perfection in the opinion of the judges is indicated by her score of 897.7, enough points to swamp her five opponents. St. Paul Figure Skating Club girls got the second and third honors, Miss Janette Ahrens and Miss Madelon Olson scoring 855.2 and 852.4 respectively.

It is possible, but not probable, that some other girl will surpass Miss Merrill tonight in the senior women's free skating. The championship goes to that girl who attains the highest combined score in both school figures and free skating.

Glamour and dash are two attributes of Miss Merrill, who is known as the "best dressed sportswoman." This Boston girl who trains in California is not likely to falter in the free skating. Many were outspoken in saying that she was the main American hope to turn back the Canadians Monday night in Madison Square Garden when the North American championship is decided.

March 3, 1945

Walter S. Powell, president of the United States Figure Skating Association, and Miss Barbara Ann Scott after the Canadian star triumphed at the Garden last night.

*The New York Times*

## Miss Scott Defeats Miss Merrill To Capture Figure Skating Title

#### By BRYAN FIELD

With a performance as crisp and showy as the snowy heights of her Canadian homeland, 16-year-old Miss Barbara Ann Scott last night won the North American figure-skating championship to the enthusiastic applause of 5,000 persons in Madison Square Garden.

It was one of the closest contests in the history of this competition between the United States and its neighbor to the north, and Miss Scott was strongly pressed by the two 19-year-old American girls, Miss Gretchen Van Zandt Merrill and Miss Janette Ahrens, who were placed second and third, respectively.

The girl who now wears the brightest skating crown in this hemisphere began skating when she was 6 and has twice won the Canadian title after being the novice and junior champion in that country. The only person to hold the gold medal in both countries for proficiency in skating, Miss Scott practices the year 'round and has made many appearances on tours for the armed forces.

### Skating Carnival Star

In the crowd last night were many men in uniform, some who had seen the Maple Leaf star in carnivals in the northlands.

Miss Scott, accompanied by her mother, received the congratulations of scores, but with all the honors that skating has brought she nevertheless is determined to make music her career. In sports she also is a capable horsewoman and swimmer and seemed not a bit fatigued after the arduous program on the final day of the four-day skating carnival.

In the morning and afternoon sessions the eight contestants went through the school figures, and Miss Scott gave an indication of what was to come by taking first in this preliminary stage of the competition. In the school figures Miss Scott led Miss Merrill by 1,653.3 to 1,638.9. Last night in the free skating Miss Scott maintained her advantage so that in the final compilation the score sheets of four judges showed her first and two placed her second.

Miss Merrill, skating with the dash of a champion, but carrying the handicap of the need to overtake her Canadian rival, was placed first by two judges and second by the four others. The Western star, Miss Ahrens, was placed third by all six judges.

### The Order of Finish

After that the order of finish was Miss Margaret Grant of the United States, Miss Marilyn Take of Canada, Miss Gloria Lillice of Canada, Miss Nadina Phillips of Canada and Miss Madelon Olson of the United States.

Officials of the Skating Club of New York and others devoted to skating were highly pleased by the success of their wartime effort, this being the first time the national and North American championships had been combined. War conditions prevented the running of a men's senior championship, but last night other honors were distributed.

In the championship for junior pairs the Skating Club of Boston scored when Lieut. Comdr. Lyman Wakefield and Miss Betty Higgins were placed first amid general applause. Second went to Robert Swenning and Miss Yvonne Sherman of the Skating Club of New York, while third fell to Peter Kennedy and Miss Betty Kennedy of the Seattle Skating Club.

War interfered to a degree in the championship for senior pairs as Navy's Walter Noffke was unable to compete. He and Miss Doris Schubach won in 1944. This championship went to J. P. Brunet

and Miss Donna J. Popisila of New York. The honors in fours went to the Chicago team of L. and E. Vanderbasch, brothers, and Miss Jackie Dunn and Miss Joan Yocum.

The senior dance championship was taken by Robert Swenning and Mrs. K. M. Williams of New York, upsetting the three-time winners, James Lochead and Miss M. M. Willis.

March 6, 1945

## Swedish Press Hits Award of World Title In Figure Skating to Swiss Over U. S. Star

Special to THE NEW YORK TIMES.

STOCKHOLM, Feb. 15—The award of the men's world figure skating championship to the Swiss champion, Hans Gerschwiler, over the 18-year-old Richard Button of New York is contested by the Swedish press.

One paper says:

"Sweden has never seen such elegant skating as Button's. He was superb and should have won, especially as the champion, Gerschwiler fell a couple of times while Button skated as though he were wearing ballet shoes instead of skates."

The judges held that Gerschwiler was superior in the fixed program.

In the women's championship Canada's Miss Barbara Ann Scott so far holds the leading position, followed by Miss Gretchen Merrill of Boston.

STOCKHOLM, Feb. 15 (AP)— The Stockholm press and public today criticized the referees for giving early entries in the world figure skating championship high scores which resulted in Richard Button of Englewood, N.J., losing the title to Hans Gerschwiler of Switzerland.

The Stockholm Tidningen said "the best skater lost the world championship."

Sportswriter Oscar Soederlund, former chairman of the International Amateur Boxing Association, wrote:

"The judges gave the first skaters too high points. Had Button started first he might have overtaken Gerschwiler's lead." Soederlund termed Button's skating "something revolutionizing in the art of figure skating—technically the most fantastic performance ever seen here."

Ulrich Salchow, longtime world and Olympic skating champion, writing in Dagens Nyheter, said Button "failed in nothing. The more difficult his task the surer was his performance." Salchow also said "the judges lacked experience without which they should not be allowed in an event of this importance."

When the competition closed last night Button had 352.86 points and the Swiss 350, but three of the five judges voted Gerschwiler the better skater. Under the international rules the United States skater thus finished second. Had United States or Swedish rules prevailed, Button would have been awarded first place.

STOCKHOLM, Feb. 15 (U.P.)— Miss Barbara Ann Scott of Ottawa, Ont., virtually clinched the women's world figure skating championship today by piling up a 78-point lead with only the free skating competition to go.

Miss Scott, who had only a four-point lead over Miss Gretchen Merrill of Boston at the conclusion of yesterday's events, won all six of today's compulsory figure competitions to pile up her all but insurmountable lead.

Although Miss Merrill, who retained second place with a total of 1,767.1 points against Miss Scott's 1,845.1, is considered superior at free skating, that 78-point margin was expected to be more than she can overcome in tomorrow's final competition.

In perfect form, Miss Scott never wavered in today's events at Stockholm Stadium. She explained later that she won all of them "by stern determination not to make a single mistake."

She admitted she expected difficulty in the free skating tomorrow "despite my fondness for it because it permits more chances for fantasy and variation."

Miss Merrill barely held second place at the end of the second day of competition.

Pressing her closely was Miss Daphne Walker of England with 1,765.9 points. Miss Jeanette Altwegg of England was fourth and Miss Shirley Adams, also of England, was fifth, while sixth and seventh places were held by two Czechoslovak skaters.

Miss Janette Ahrens of the United States was eighth with 1,670.1 points and Miss Aileen Seigh, another American, was eleventh with 1.648.4 points.

February 16, 1947

### AT WORLD TITLE EVENT IN SWEDEN

**Miss Barbara Ann Scott, 18-year-old Canadian, and Dick Button, United States figure skater, at Stockholm.** *Associated Press*

## WORLD TITLE GOES TO OTTAWA SKATER

### Barbara Scott Triumphs at Stockholm—Daphne Walker Second, Miss Merrill 3d

STOCKHOLM, Feb. 16 (AP)— Miss Barbara Ann Scott, 18-year-old Canadian star from Ottawa, today won the women's world figure skating championship. Miss Daphne Walker of England was second and Miss Gretchen Merrill of Boston, the United States champion, third.

When the Ottawa girl was declared the winner, the crowd, which had been entranced by her graceful maneuvers in the free-skating phase of the competition, poured on the ice to offer congratulations.

Miss Eileen Seigh of Brooklyn, who was far back in tenth place after yesterday's school skating, put on a sensational performance in the free skating today to take fourth place in the final reckoning. Miss Janet Ahrens of Minneapolis, Minn., finished sixth.

Miss Scott, winner of the recent European championship, at Davos, Switzerland, had piled up a 78-point lead—1,845.1 to 1,767.1—over Miss Merrill yesterday. The Canadian girl put on a dazzling performance in her free skating today and eight of the nine judges placed her first. Two sixes—the highest possible score—were posted after her performance.

In the final scoring for both the school and free skating, the Canadian girl received 348.37 points while Miss Walker had 334.09 and Miss Merrill, 327.76. Miss Seigh's total was 319.05 while Miss Ahrens had 317.52.

Miss Merrill, who had a slim lead over Miss Walker after the first day, fell in the middle of her dancing exhibition today and lost her chance right then and there. A murmur of sympathy and disappointment swept through the crowded stands as the attractive Bostonian, dressed in a white frock and with a silver diadem in her crown, fell to the ice.

February 17, 1947

# CHAPTER 2

# SKIING COMES OF AGE

Jean-Claude Killy swept to a triple victory in Alpine skiing at the 1968 Olympics. He took gold medals in the slalom, giant slalom and downhill events.

# Both U.S. Teams Barred From Olympic Hockey; Swiss Group Defies Ruling

## A. H. A. IS ELIGIBLE, HOST COUNTRY SAYS

### Backed by Switzerland After Olympic Executive Group Drops Both U.S. Sextets

---

### MORE ACTION SEEN TODAY

---

### Entire Committee Might Lift Olympic Stamp From Hockey, but Keep It on Program

---

ST. MORITZ, Switzerland, Jan. 28 (P)—The Swiss defied the authority of the International Olympic Executive Committee tonight by refusing to obey an order throwing both disputed United States hockey teams out of the winter games starting Friday.

"The Amateur Hockey Association remains qualified to participate in the ice hockey championship," the Swiss Olympic Committee declared in a formal statement. Nothing in the Olympic code covers the situation.

Meanwhile, the International Hockey Federation quashed reports that it might withdraw its teams from the Olympics and hold a world championship elsewhere by announcing it planned to stick with the Swiss Olympic Organizing Committee.

"I am proud of the Swiss Olympic Committee for sticking to us," Dr. Fritz Kraatz, I.I.H.F. president declared after his group had taken the loyalty stand in an emergency session, "and we should stick to them."

An informed source said one possibility was that the entire International Olympic Committee, meeting tomorrow, might remove the Olympic stamp from hockey but still leave it on the program with the Amateur Hockey Association team participating.

Avery Brundage, chairman of the United States Olympic Committee, has declared that if the A. H. A. team competes in the Olympics, his committee will withdraw all American athletes from the games.

But if hockey is struck from the official Olympic program, even if continued as an exhibition or a world championship, the way is presumably clear for the United States ski, bobsled and skating teams to compete.

Meeting as a "jury of honor," the International Olympic Executive Committee resolved, "owing to irregularities on both sides, not to allow either hockey team of the United States to compete in the winter games."

The hockey team selected by the United States Olympic Committee —which apparently gets the trip to St. Moritz just for fun—attended with other members of the United States team a dinner given by Brundage.

Informed of the Swiss decision, Brundage declared: "Now you have got a story," and J. Sigfried Edstrom, International Olympic Committee president, immediately interjected: "Well, we're going to sleep on it tonight. We're not going to do anything now."

As if the Swiss did not have enough to worry them, snow fell intermittently through the day. It is now waist deep on every mountainside and much more would throw the whole program out of kilter.

The whole angry international dispute which has marred the resumption of the winter olympics after a twelve-year war lapse began a year ago when the International Ice Hockey Federation declared that the Amateur Athletic Union no longer governed hockey in the United States.

Instead, said the federation, the Amateur Hockey Association was in charge.

Brundage declared the Amateur Hockey Association is under commercial sponsorship, and refused to certify its team for the Olympics.

The Swiss accepted the entry of the A.H.A. team and refused the team sponsored by the United States Olympic Committee.

It was in this tense atmosphere that the executive committee met this afternoon in a clean, sunny room of the Kurverein, or city hall.

#### Mayer Tells Decision

Otto Mayer, the chancellor, came out and explained slowly in English that the executive committee had met "as a jury of honor"— which it does for all non-technical Olympic disputes—and, after hearing both the United States Olympic and Swiss sides of the case, turned thumbs down on both teams.

A little later the Swiss spoke out, and after citing the verse and chapter of a variety of Olympic rules, wound up by declaring that "the Swiss Olympic Committee maintains its former decision, i. e. that the A.H.A. remains qualified to participate in the ice hockey championship within the fifth winter Olympic games."

At the emergency session of the I.I.H.F., Walter Brown of Boston, vice president of the A.H.A., said:

"Would it be possible to call a hockey tournament world championship instead of Olympic championship so that the A.H.A. would not be an instrument for forcing the rest of the team (U. S.) out?"

George Dudley, secretary manager of the Canadian Amateur Hockey Association, jumped to his feet and plastered the idea, declaring: "I came here with a team to compete in the Olympic Games and until some higher power stops us from that I propose we continue."

The innocent victim of all this wrangle is the United States Olympic Committee's hockey team. The international Federation already has declared no European team can play with it. So that means the fifteen boys, many fresh out of Dartmouth, Harvard, Princeton, Minnesota and Michigan, can relax and enjoy this picturesque mountain resort.

Hotel lobby gossip ranged all the way from a belief that the International Olympic Committee might give in to the Swiss to the suggestion it would make a new Swiss Organizing Committee—or even that the games might be taken away from Switzerland.

Informed opinion, however, seemed to be that the games would be held on schedule.

The athletes themselves took their final workouts. The skies cleared and a brilliant moon and stars came out, raising the hopes of the Swiss snow shovellers who have been hard at work the past week.

January 29, 1948

---

## NEW OLYMPIC MARK SET BY NORWEGIAN IN SKATING VICTORY

### Helgesen Takes 500 Meters as Bartholomew, Fitzgerald of U. S. Tie for Second

---

### SWISS BOBLETS ONE-TWO

---

By The Associated Press.

ST. MORITZ, Switzerland, Jan. 31—Americans finished as runners-up and in third place today in two events on which they had set their hearts as the fifth winter Olympic Games suddenly changed their complexion from one of verbal war to sturdy competition.

Norway's Finn Helgesen snatched the first gold medal to be awarded in this trouble-infested carnival by skating 500 meters (547 yards) in 43.1 seconds for an Olympic record.

His speed shunted Ken Bartholomew and Bob Fitzgerald, both of Minneapolis, to second, although their identical times of 43.2 seconds also surpassed the old mark of 0:43.4.

The United States No. 2 team in the two-man bobsled, Schuyler Carron of Ausable Forks, N. Y., and Fred Fortune of Lake Placid, N. Y., was third behind two Swiss teams. Felix Endrich and Friederich Waller slid through the mile-long tunnel of ice four times in the elapsed time of 5 minutes 29.2 seconds for their victory. Carron and Fortune needed 5 minutes 35.3 seconds.

But in the 18-kilometer (11 mile) cross-country ski race, in which the Americans expected little glory, they were simply outclassed. The first wearer of the Red, White and Blue to finish was Wendell Broomhall of Rumford, Me., who was in sixty-fifth place.

Martin Lundstroem of Sweden was first in one hour 13 minutes and 50 seconds. Nineteen of the first twenty places went to skiers from the Scandinavian countries.

#### Keep Right on Playing

Although the International Olympic Committee had said firmly that hockey was no longer on the Olympic program, the sextets of the world kept right on playing.

The American Amateur Hockey Association team, center of the controversy that for a time threatened the entire program here, crushed Poland, 23—4, in a game marked by occasional fighting.

In Olympic Games only individual championships count. An informal score, based on 10-5-4-3-2-1 points for the first six places, shows Sweden far out in front tonight with 21 points, all gained in skiing.

Switzerland is second with 15, Norway third with 14½, and the United States fourth with 14¼.

Other national standings: Finland 4, Belgium 3, Great Britain 2, Italy 1 and Canada ¼.

But tonight, in contrast with yesterday, there was every indication that the various countries would be able to add to those totals. Where twenty-four hours ago the very continuation of the games appeared problematical, today the athletes occupied the spotlight.

Their defeats in the skating sprint and two-man bobsled were sore disappointments to the Americans.

The boblet olive wreath went to the United States in 1936 and premeet indications were that the Americans would retain it. Uncle Sam's third place was taken by his No. 2 team, which stepped up its speed to climb from sixth place in today's final runs.

#### They Pack the Weight

Fortune and Carron are youngsters as bobsledders go, Carron being 25 and Fortune a year older. But they pack the weight—Carron boasts 276 pounds—and they have the daring that counts.

The American No. 1 sled, piloted by Tuffy Latour with Leo Martin as brakeman, had a couple of slow runs despite a change of runners and dropped from sixth to ninth place in the fifteen-team field.

# As 1948 Speed-Skating Title Was Decided at St. Moritz

Kenneth Bartholomew (left), Minneapolis, Minn., congratulating Finn Helgesen, Oslo, Norway, after the latter won the 500-meter event. Bartholomew finished in a three-way tie for second place.

Bob Fitzgerald, Minneapolis, crossing the finish line. He tied for second place in 500-meter race with Bartholomew and Thomas Byberg of Norway.    Associated Press Radiophotos

Originally, sixteen teams competed but Great Britain's No. 2 sled cracked up today without serious injury to Wing Commander Anthony Gadd and Flying Officer W. B. Wellicome.

Latour's sled came here equipped with long runners for the sweeping curves at Lake Placid, N. Y., where he and Martin both live, and he changed overnight to shorter runners for the sharp bends in the glazed slide here.

Bartholomew and Fitzgerald were only one-tenth of a second behind Helgesen in the 500-meter race. Tied with them was Tom Byberg of Norway and in fifth place came Ken Henry of Chicago. Henry's time of 0:43.3 also bettered the old record which was shared by four men, one of them John A. Shea of the United States team in 1932.

Coach Pete Miller of Chicago, although he had hoped for a victory, said he was pleased.

"After all, the boys are entirely unaccustomed to this style of skating. We are used to skating in a bunch with the best sprint winning in the stretch," he said.

### Race Weak Opponents

In the Olympics, two men skate at a time and each is clocked separately. Fitzgerald and Bartholomew skated against weak opponents and Henry's foe, Craig Mackay of Canada, fell 100 yards from home so none of the Americans was pushed.

Helgesen, today's skating winner, is 21, blond and pleased with himself. He has been skating for years. Back home in Oslo, Norway, he has been regarded as only promising.

"It was nice to win," he said. "I did not know that I could do it. But I was hoping, of course."

"Those Americans had me sweating for a while," the young Norwegian added. "They ran before it was my turn. Their times stood there on the record to scare me. I knew I had to run fast."

The world 500-meter record of 0:42.4 was set by Allan Potts of the United States at Oslo in 1936.

Corey Engen of Huntsville, Utah, captain of the ski cross-country team, had an answer for the Americans' showing in the 18-kilometer event.

"I am Norwegian-born myself, somehow that does not seem to be enough. This kind of skiing requires years of bitter training. I guess Americans are too easy going."

The American finishers and their times — Broomhall, sixty-fifth, 1:30:40, nearly 17 minutes behind the winner; Don Johnson, Salt Lake City, sixty-sixth, 1:32:03; Ralph Townsend, Lebanon, N. H., seventy-fourth, 1:37:12; Engen, seventy-fifth, 1:37:24, and Gordon Wren, Winter Park, Col., seventy-seventh, 1:40:12.

February 1, 1948

## Bott, Fishbacher Victors In Cresta Bobsled Tests

By The Associated Press.

ST. MORITZ, Switzerland, Jan. 31—R. E. A. Bott, 48-year-old London refrigerator dealer, won the Bott Cup on the Cresta bobsled run in the winter Olympics today, completing three courses down the treacherous 1,320-yard track in a total of 2 minutes 58.8 seconds. Bott's handicap was 3.9 seconds.

Christopher Fishbacher of Switzerland captured the open event for the Morgan Cup with an aggregate time of 3 minutes and six-tenths of a second.

Jack Heaton of New Haven, Conn., the United States' only previous Olympic champion competing in the current games, was second in the open run. His time was 3 minutes and 2.3 seconds.

Heaton, who won the Cresta in the 1928 Olympics, had the best single run of the day when he toured the track in 59.8 seconds. The track record is 56.7 seconds.

February 1, 1948

# Spurned Olympic Hockey Team Gains Only U.S. Victory in St. Moritz Games

## ITALIANS ROUTED BY A.H.A. SIX, 31-1

### Game in Switzerland Marked by Only One Penalty and Numerous Handshakes

### NORWEGIAN SKATER WINS

### Liaklev Annexes 5,000-Meter Race — Hasu of Finland Takes Nordic Ski Test

ST. MORITZ, Switzerland, Feb. 1 (AP)—Apologies, handshakes, a flash snow storm and a 31-to-1 hockey triumph by the United States over Italy marked this third day of the hectic fifth winter Olympics.

Ironically, the day's lone U. S, victory was scored by the Amateur Hockey Association sextet which is shunned by the U. S. Olympic Committee and was made in a sport that currently isn't on the official program.

In the sports that did count the Americans couldn't tally a point. The Scandinavians, as expected, dominated.

Reider Liaklev, a skinny Norwegian who is both a farmer and a mailman, triumphed in the 5,000-meter (3⅛ miles) speed skating event by traveling the distance in 8 minutes 29.4 seconds. Ray Blum of Nutley, N. J., was the first American, his 8:54.4 being good for seventeenth place.

Ken Henry of Chicago, Sonny Rupprecht of St. Louis and Dick Solem of Chicago, were even further back. The Americans, however, had to skate during the unexpected snow storm. Moreover, Blum complained of an old back injury.

### Long Jump Is Wasted

Gordon Wren of Winter Park, Col., made the longest ski jump of the day—224 feet 9 inches—but his poor finish in yesterday's 18-kilometer (11.2-mile) cross-country ski run kept him in twenty-ninth place behind Finland's Heikku Hasu in the Nordic combination. Hasu is the first non-Norwegian winner of the event.

After three days of competition, Sweden led the various nations with 32 points, computed on a basis of 10-5-4-3-2-1 for the first six finishing positions.

Norway was second with 30½. Finland third with 21, Switzerland fourth at 18 and the United States fifth with 14¼. Belgium and Holland each have 3 points, Great Britain 2, Italy 1 and Canada ¼.

All the handshakes and one of the apologies came in the lopsided hockey victory, though only one penalty was called.

Coach John B. Garrison of Lincoln, Mass., said he permitted his charges to pile up the score because it might mean the title for the U. S. team. If the orphaned hockey competition should end with teams deadlocked for first place on a won-lost basis, total goals will decide.

### Alphonse and Gaston

Every time two opposing players brushed each other in today's fray, they stopped and shook hands. And when Arnaldo A. Fabris of the losers accidentally banged Fred Pearson of Beverly. Mass., above the left eye with his stick, it was the Italian players who rushed to pick up the American and helped to patch him up for further use.

Bruce Cunliffe of New York City; Ralph Warburton of Cranston, R. I.; Bruce Mather of Springfield, Mass.; Robert Boeser of Minneapolis and Robert Baker of Thief River Falls, Minn., each scored five goals in the massacre.

The United States team now is in fourth place behind three unbeaten teams, Czechoslovakia and Switzerland, 3—0 each, and the Canadians, 2—0. The Americans have won twice and lost once.

In today's play the Czechs defeated Poland, 13 to 1; the Swiss blasted Austria, 11 to 2, and Canada blanked Great Britain, 3 to 0.

The Americans are idle tomorrow. The other apology was made by J. Lyman Bingham of Chicago, who is in charge of supplies for all American teams.

He told Dr. Albert Mayer of the Swiss Organizing Committee to drop the inquiry into the attempted sabotage of the U. S. bobsleds last Thursday night.

The steering wheel of one sled was loosened, the cowling of another had been damaged and the hand grip of a third had been battered by a hammer.

### Swiss Not Blamed

Bingham said Dr. Mayer felt the U. S. bobsledders were blaming the Swiss. "That isn't the case at all," he added, "I understand things like that happen among the bobsledders all the time." The Americans continued to post a guard at the bobshed, however.

Actually, there were only two disturbing incidents today and only one of those happened in view of the spectators who came to this Alpine village in sleighs complete with tinkling bells.

As Aake Seyffarth of Sweden, holder of the world record for the 5,000-meter skating test, zipped toward the finish he was brushed by a photographer who stepped onto the ice for a picture. The Swede, who finished seventh in 8:13.7, lost precious seconds getting back into stride.

The other incident involved the judges of the Nordic combination. They couldn't decide who was second to Hasu. At first they picked Sven Israulsson of Sweden, Then they decided on another Finn, Martti Huhtala. They conferred again. Finally they announced officially that Huhtala was the runner-up.

Corey Engen of Huntsville, Utah, was twenty-sixth in the Nordic with 346.8 points and Don Johnson of Salt Lake City, also finished ahead of Wren. Johnson was twenty-seventh with 345.1 points.

Of thirty-eight ski pilots on the hill, Wren tallied second highest points for jumps alone — 220.2, with Engen third. Israulsson beat out Wren by 1.7 points in this competition total.

Ralph Townsend of Lebanon, N. H., was thirty-third with 376.7 points, compared to the 286 points that brought Wilber Irwin of Canada the thirty-seventh spot.

Henry was eighteenth in the 5,000 with a clocking of 8.56; Rupprecht was twenty-first in 8:58.4 and Solem twenty-seventh in 9:10.4.

### Skates Through Snow

Pete Miller of Chicago, coach of the United States skaters, said that the snowstorm and the Olympic style of racing against time had handicapped his team. However, Liaklev was one of the last to take the ice and he had to skate through a blanket of snow.

It was the second straight skating triumph for Norway. Finn Helgesen yesterday won the 500 meters (547 yards) in Olympic record time.

Wren fell on his first jump in the combination but escaped injury. The competition's longest leap came on his second try and he closed with a third effort of 216 feet 6½ inches.

Gustav Allan Lindh, a Swedish Army officer, led the field in the shooting phase of the winter pentathlon by hitting 20 bullseyes for 194 points. He was second in yesterday's ski race. No Americans are listed in this competition.

Although trailing fifth for team honors, the United States gets its best chance at first place in an event tomorrow — men's figure skating.

Dick Button, 18-year-old Englewood, N. J., ice artist, is a slight favorite to beat Hans Gerschwiler, world champion from Switzerland. Button defeated Hans for the European title at Prague last month, and said, "I hope I can do it again."

American prospects also look good for high honors in the women's downhill ski race, in which another teen-ager, 15-year-old Andrea Mead of Rutland, Vt., is the leading United States hope.

Also on tap tomorrow are three hockey matches, women's figure skating, downhill skiing for men, and 1,500-meter (metric mile) speed skating.

February 2, 1948

# Button Takes Lead Over Gerschwiler in Olympic Figure Skating Contest

## NEW JERSEY STAR SEEN AS CHAMPION

ST. MORITZ, Switzerland, Feb. 2 (AP)—The husky sons of Norway swept into the lead tonight in the race for team honors in the winter Olympic games, but an 18-year-old American ice artist—Dick Button of Englewood, N. J.—kept the lagging United States team within sight of a championship.

Dick held a surprise advantage over his top rival, Hans Gerschwiler of Switzerland, at the end of the first half of the men's figure skating competition—compulsory figures. His official score was

994.7 points against Gerschwiler's 965.1.

"Unless Dick breaks a leg, he's the Olympic champion," said his beaming coach, Gus Lussi of Lake Placid, N. Y., "and take it from me, there will not be any accidents."

Button, already holder of the European title, surprised his most ardent admirers by outscoring Gerschwiler in today's compulsory figures. Experts considered the

youngster a cinch to excel in tomorrow's free-style, the concluding phase of the exacting event.

In previous meetings between the American and the Swiss, Gerschwiler has been better in the school figures, Button the master of free style. The lad from New Jersey gave one of the greatest exhibitions of his career in beating the Swiss artist at his own game today.

Most Olympic fans roamed the

snowy mountain landscape watching the exciting settlement of these three Olympic titles: /

1,500-meter speed skating—won by Sverre Farstad, 28-year-old Norwegian cartoonist, in 2 minutes 17.6 seconds, a new Olympic record and Norway's third straight speed skating triumph.

Men's downhill ski race—won by Henri Oreiller of France, who careened down the two-mile course in 2 minutes 55 seconds.

Women's downhill ski race—won by a Swiss miss, Hedy Schlunegger, on a shorter, less precipitous course, in 2 minutes 28.3 seconds.

America's money in the women's event rode on the baby of the team—15-year-old Andrea Mead of Rutland, Vt.—but she fell on an abrupt knoll and finished third from last.

Norway, with 44½ points, replaced Sweden as team leader on the Associated Press team score sheet, based on 10-5-4-3-2-1 points for the first six places. The Swedes finished the day with 39.

Switzerland had 37, Finland 24, Austria 16, United States 15¼, France 11, Italy 5, Belgium and Holland 3 each, Britain 2 and Canada ¼ point.

Of twenty-eight nations competing, sixteen had not scored at the close of the fourth day of the ten-day games.

### 1936 Champion Beaten

Czechoslovakia crushed Great Britain, 1936 Olympic champion, 11—4, in the ice hockey tournament, which is strictly unofficial in the eyes of the International Olympic Committee.

Canada beat Poland, 15—0, and Sweden defeated Austria, 7—1. The Amateur Hockey Association team of the United States was idle, along with two other entries, Italy and Switzerland.

Avery Brundage, head of the American Olympic Committee, who has fought the entry of the Amateur Hockey Association team in the Olympics, spoke, at a dinner last night given to the hockey team brought here by the American Olympic Committee. It has yet to play a game in Europe.

Following the dinner, Brundage declared that "there will be no more ice hockey in the Olympic games until this is cleared up. It is a very serious matter."

Asked what would happen if the Swiss give Olympic medals for hockey competition, Brundage said "that would put the Swiss in an indefensible position."

In today's balmy weather, cafe proprietors pushed tables on the sidewalks to serve the crowds.

Almost ignored by the fans were the sixteen men figure skaters, etching in dull monotony the ice of a small rink to do the five compulsory figures. Each skater performed his assignment and slipped to the sideline unapplauded, while the judges inspected the closeness of the lines.

### Final Contest Wednesday

Button's placing on top in this department was a bonanza, since his ace in the hole is free skating, the colorful ballet half of the competition, which comes on Wednesday.

John Lettingarver of St. Paul, runner up to Button in the United States senior men's championship last year, stood fifth tonight with 916.3 points. Ninth was 15-year-old James Grogan of Oakland, Calif., with 867.4.

Another Minnesotan turned in a good performance. John Werket,

Richard Button, Englewood, N. J., was the winner of the compulsory figure skating tests at St. Moritz yesterday. *The New York Times*

who learned to skate on the Powderhorn Park rink in South Minneapolis, won a point for the United States by placing sixth in the 1,500 meter speed skating.

His time of 2 minutes 20.2 seconds would have been good enough for second place in previous Olympics. But today the Scandinavians capitalized on the fast ice of the Olympic stadium and three of them submarined under the Olympic record of two minutes 19.2 seconds set by Charles Mathisen of Norway in 1936.

"That was the fastest I ever skated in my life," said Werket, who had set himself a mark of 2 minutes 18 seconds to shoot at.

"I was almost on schedule, but tired on the last curve. Still, it wasn't so bad," he consoled himself.

United States speed skating coach Pete Miller said, "I'm proud of the way our skaters are going. We were not given a ghost of a chance against the Scandinavians, but we have done well in both the 500 and 1,500."

Between races—run on the European style in pairs—spectators could look up and pick out the skiers speeding down an Alpine slope at 40 miles an hour.

### Many Defy Dangers

Men from the Alpine countries proved successful in the downhill ski race. It often was a question of taking chances—to take time saving shortcuts and risk dangerous jumps down the slope.

Most of the Scandinavians, who normally prefer to go straight down a slope and not check their speed by roundabout maneuvers, ran the race a little too wildly and fell, losing time.

The more accomplished and controlled skiers from France, Austria, Switzerland and Italy, who know their Alps, dominate the event.

The Americans came down rather carefully, on the whole, but some, too, showed a tendency to overlook, or at least to underestimate, the dangers. Dick Movitz and Robert Blatt each lost a ski after a heavy fall.

Jack Reddish of Salt Lake City, in twenty-sixth place, was the highest American finisher, with a time of 3 minutes 12.6 seconds. There were 125 listed starters.

Movitz, of Salt Lake City, finished forty-second; Steve Knowlton of Aspen, Col., was forty-third and Blatt, of Palo Alto, Calif., forty-fourth. Devereaux Jennings of Salt Lake City finished forty-

fifth and Barney McLean of Denver, forty-seventh.

Andrea Mead's fall was a tough blow to United States hopes of picking up points in the women's downhill, since she had been reckoned a worthy rival of the European aces.

"I hit a soft spot and lost my balance," she explained. "I got up, of course, but I lost an awful lot of time. They said I had a good chance of winning before that happened."

Another disappointment was Georgette Thiolierre-Miller, the G. I. bride who wore French colors but now lives in Boston. She finished far back in 2 minutes 52.4 seconds.

Best of the American girls was Brynhild Grasmoen of Mercid, Calif., who was twelfth in 2 minutes 36 seconds.

Olympic officials announced that the women's compulsory figure skating competition, originally scheduled for today, would be staged tomorrow. Shortage of judges was given as the reason.

ST. MORITZ, Switzerland, Feb. 2 (AP)—Richard Button of Englewood, N. J., put on one of the finest precision exhibitions of his career today in winning the compulsory phase of the Olympic figure skating competition for men.

Second to Button was his greatest rival, Hans Gerschwiler of Switzerland, who had beaten him in the school figures in other competitions. Since Button is considered without a peer in the freestyle skating, which will be held on Wednesday, it was considered virtually certain that the Olympic championship would go to the Jersey youth.

Third behind the two leaders today was Eli Rada of Austria, with Henry Sharp, the British champion, fourth and John Lettingarver, 18-year-old United States entry from St. Paul, fifth.

Button's score for the first three figures was 44.9, 47.0 and 46.9, against Gerschwiler's 44.6, 45.9 and 47.2. The American piled up his lead in the fourth and fifth figures, the loop change and the loop backwards outside.

The points listed for these figures do not take into account the factor, or number by which each must be multiplied to arrive at the final score. This varies, depending on how hard the required figure is, and can be as high as five.

Button received a plus-five score in each of the first three figures.

February 3, 1948

# Sweden Scores Two Victories and Regains the Lead in Winter Olympic Games

## SEYFFARTH WINNER IN SPEED SKATING

### Swede Annexes 10,000-Meter Title—His Countrymen Gain Ski Relay Race Crown

### A. H. A. SIX VICTOR BY 5-2

### Miss Scott Is Figure-Skating Leader—Heaton, U. S., Tied for Second in Cresta Run

ST. MORITZ, Switzerland, Feb. 3 (P)—Sweden again took over the winter Olympic leadership from Norway with smashing victories in skiing and skating today as United States athletes failed once more to hit the winner's circle.

A blazing sun brought pools of water to Alpine ice rinks and caused cancellation of part of the program.

The heat may make matters difficult when Dick Button, the 18-year-old Englewood, N. J., youth, makes his supreme bid for an Olympic championship tomorrow in figure skating.

The United States has never won an Olympic figure-skating title, and has yet to take a first place in the present games, now five days old.

Champions crowned today were:

Ake Seyffarth, Sweden, 10,000-meter speed skating, in 17 minutes 26.3 seconds.

The Swedish 40-kilometer ski race relay team (Nils Oestensson, Nils Taepp, Gunnar Eriksson and Martin Lundstroem), in 2 hours 32 minutes 8 seconds. America's entry was canceled because of skiers' fatigue.

#### Standing of the Teams

The Associated Press point total, with half the Olympic program completed, stands tonight:

Sweden 50, Norway 48½, Switzerland 39, Finland 38, Austria, 19, U. S. A. 15¼, France 11, Italy 6, Holland 6, Hungary 3, Belgium 3, Britain 2, Canada ¼ point.

Miss Barbara Ann Scott, Canada's figure skating idol, held a commanding lead on completion of two compulsory school figures today. But in the afternoon, with the temperature hitting the 50's, the ice became so soft the remaining three figures were postponed until tomorrow morning.

Seyffarth, one of the world's greatest skaters, in taking the fourth and last speed-skating title (Norway won the other three), had the advantage of an early start when the ice was crisp and fast.

It became so mushy by early afternoon that Richard Solem of Chicago, racing at the very end of the program after eight men had dropped out due to poor ice and the altitude, plowed through slush up to the tubes of his skates.

But he gamely finished, and his time of 26 minutes 22.4 seconds attested to the ordeal. He was cheered for nineteenth place almost as loudly as the victor.

#### Canada Now First

In hockey, which the International Olympic Committee considers as stricken from the program, Canada defeated Italy, 21—1, and moved into first place with four victories and no defeats. Czechoslovakia likewise has four victories and no defeats, but its goal average is poorer.

The United States defeated Sweden by 5—2 in a hard, fast game in which the Amateur Hockey Association team showed its best form so far.

The United States now holds three victories against one defeat in the hockey competition, played on a round-robin basis.

In the capacity crowd of more than 2,000 that filled the stands and perched on a cliff were hundreds of American soldiers in uniform, part of an Army excursion from Germany.

Their mighty cheers for American scores and boos for adverse officiating decisions caused raised eyebrows in the sedate European crowd.

Jack Riley of Medford, Mass., put the game away for the Americans when he scored two goals within thirty seconds in the second period to make it 4 to 0. From there on Sweden never seriously threatened.

In the first three heats of the Cresta one-man bobsled run, John G. Crammond, London broker, took a two-tenths of a second elapsed time lead over Jack Heaton of New Haven, Conn., the 1928 Olympic champion, and Nino Bibbia of Italy.

#### Chute of Solid Ice

Cresta is something than can be run off only here. The chute of solid ice with low banked curves twists down the mountain. At the end the tiny sleds, scarcely four feet long and only four inches off the ice, are going eighty miles an hour.

Today's run were from a "junction," and covered only two-thirds of the course. Tomorrow's three final runs will be from the top, 1,320 yards.

Two sleds hurtled of the course today, tossing up great clouds of chipped ice and snow. Neither rider was injured. One was Christian Fischbacher of New York City, competing for Switzerland. The other was Hugo Kuranda of Austria.

The United States should score heavily in the event, which has been on the official Olympic program only twice—in 1928 and again this year.

Heaton, with a total time of 2 minutes 23.2 seconds for the three runs of 956 yards each, is in good challenging position. Crammond's time was 2:23 flat.

In fourth and fifth places are Lieut C. W. Johnson, 31, Minneapolis, Minn., and Sergeant W. L. Martin, 19, Kalispell, Mont., who never saw a Cresta sled until two weeks ago. Their times were 2:24.1 and 2:25.2, respectively.

Fairchilds MacCarthy of Belmont, Mass., Cresta coach and competitor, did 2:26.5 for the three heats, tying for ninth place in the thirteen-man field.

Sergeant Martin flirted with the top of the embankment today, showering spectators with snow. He said afterward he hoped to have better control tomorrow. With Lieut. Johnson and others, he was detailed by the occupation Army to compete, and has made the run fewer than a half-dozen times.

America's ski relay entry was canceled because Coaches Walter Prager and Alf Engen felt that Wendall Broomhall of Rumford, Me., and Corey Engen of Huntsville, Utah, were too weak after Saturday's 18-kilometer cross-country run to participate.

Norway had a tough break in the ski relay. Its first man, Erling Evensen, broke a ski in the first rush over the half-mile clear space before the field had to form single file through the forest. He lost three minutes replacing it, and Norway finished third, three minutes behind second-place Finland, whose time was 2 hours 41 minutes and 6 seconds.

Martin Lundstroem of Sweden became the first double winner of the present games by virtue of the gold medal he will receive as a member of the winning team. He won the 18-kilometer ski cross-country race.

The Alpine weather, bitter cold at night and in the morning, but hot at midday, drew from Reidar Gudmundsen, president of Norway's Skating Association, the comment that "it may be only a question of luck who wins the games."

Commenting on today's 10,000-meter skating race which ended in such miserable conditoins, he said:

"It is irresponsible to arrange a competition that drags on hour after hour, like today's race. Particularly in this climate, where the temperature changes all the time, too early and too late starters are badly handicapped."

All of America's long-distance skaters started late, and all finished far down, due in no small part to the ice.

John Werket, 23, of Minneapolis, who was a sergeant in the Army and competed in the Army championships at Nuernburg, was eleventh in the 10,000-meter (6¼ miles) speed skating in 19:44.4.

In seventeenth place was Sonny Rupprecht of St. Louis, in 21 minutes 20.3 seconds; eighteenth came Francis Seaman of Minneapolis in 21 minutes, 34.8. Solem was last in the slush.

In women's figure skating, Miss Scott amassed 334.6 points for two school figures, with three more to be run off before the free-style skating starts.

Second was Miss Eva Pavlik of Austria, with 326.2 points, while Miss Gretchen Merrill, the vivacious champion of the United States, was in seventh position with 311.1.

Tomorrow morning, if the ice stays firm, the women's compulsory skating will be completed. In the afternoon Button, considered the greatest of all free-style skaters, who holds a commanding lead over his chief rival, Hans Gerschwiler of Switzerland, will perform chiefly in midair, for five minutes.

Unless he falls down he almost certainly will give the United States its first gold medal of the 1948 Olympic Games.

The first Olympic victory ceremonies were held today in the tiny stadium on a mountain ledge over which flames the Olympic torch.

February 4, 1948

# Mrs. Fraser Takes First Skiing Medal for U.S. in Olympic History

## AMERICAN ENTRANT JUST MISSES TITLE

### Mrs. Fraser Second to Austrian by .37 of Point in Alpine Combined Ski Event

ST. MORITZ, Switzerland, Feb. 4 (AP)—A pretty Western housewife, her pigtails flying, plummeted down a zig-zag Alpine snow course today to accomplish something no American ever had done before her —win a medal in an Olympic skiing event against Europe's masters.

Mrs. Gretchen Fraser, the 28-year-old Vancouver, Wash., star, was the toast of the American camp tonight as the mercury dropped, the ice froze over again and it became certain that it would not be necessary, after all, to abandon the winter games in mid-career.

Mrs. Fraser, a modest 115-pounder, scored her unprecedented personal triumph by placing second in the women's Alpine combined ski test. She was edged out of first place by Miss Trude Beiser of Austria by the nearly invisible margin of thirty-seven one-hundredths of a point.

The highest an American—man or woman—ever placed before in an Olympic ski event was eleventh. Sverre Fredheim of St. Paul, Minn., attained that mark in the ski jump of the 1936 winter games at Garmisch-Partenkirchen in Germany.

#### Eleventh in Downhill

The combined is a ski event in two sections, the first a downhill race and the second the slalom, in which the contestants speed in and out between markers set on a precipitous slope. Mrs. Fraser finished eleventh in the downhill on Monday, but her speed and grace today all but carried her to the championship.

She flashed down the course twice in 61.8 and 59.2 seconds for the second-best elapsed time of the day—2 minutes 1 second. Miss Beiser, the winner, totaled 2 minutes 10.5 seconds for the two runs but her better placing in Monday's downhill enabled her to squeak through over the American competitor.

"I had no idea I could do it," Mrs. Fraser said happily after the result was announced. "My husband will be very happy." Her husband, Donald Fraser, competed for the United States in the 1936 winter Olympics.

Figure skating and cresta sledding were postponed today because of the unseasonable thaw, but toward evening the temperature dropped and the information bureau announced that all ice events would be held tomorrow.

The day's results left Sweden still on top on The Associated Press scorecard and pushed France above the United States despite Mrs. Fraser's brilliant showing.

#### Standing of the Teams

The team standing tonight: Sweden, 60 points; Norway, 48½; Switzerland, 45; Finland, 38; Austria, 36; France, 27; United States, 20¼; Italy, 11; Holland, 6; Belgium, 3; Hungary, 3; Britain, 2, and Canada one-fourth.

The sixth day's champions:

Men's Alpine combined — Henri Oreiller of France, who also won the downhill championship, thus becoming the first double individual winner of the games.

Women's combined—Trude Beiser of Austria.

Tomorrow Mrs. Fraser will race in the special slalom, which counts in itself as a championship, and she has a good chance to win.

The United States, in fact, has a chance for two titles tomorrow. The men's figure-skating crown seems a certainty for Dick Button of Englewood, N. J. Dick led the field by a wide margin at the end of the compulsory part of the competition on Monday and only free style remains — at which he is without peer.

The Cresta run, put off from today, may well go to Jack Heaton of New Haven, Conn., winner of the event in 1928. He was only two-tenths of a second behind the leader at the end of the first three heats yesterday. Three more remain to be run.

Three hockey games were played on mushy ice today and a fourth— Canada vs. the United States—was postponed. Switzerland and Czechoslovakia, two of the leaders, defeated Britain and Austria, respectively, 12—3 and 17—3. Poland defeated Italy, 13—7.

#### Gloom Is Dispelled

For a time gloom enveloped the figure skaters. It looked as if Olympic championships in their division might have to be called off because of the thaw, thereby robbing Button and Miss Barbara Ann Scott of Canada of almost certain victories.

But a chill came down from the mountains, making things as they ought to be. The heat at lower levels had no effect on the skiers.

Oreiller, the brilliant Frenchman, had already won the downhill race, which counted as an individual event as well as part of the men's alpine combined, and all he needed to do today was to ski with caution.

As a result, his countryman, James Couttet, made the best times, 68.7 and 66.2 for a total of 2:14.9. Oreiller's times were 72.3 and 70 seconds flat.

Oreiller, a member of the underground movement in France during the war, took his victory with nonchalance.

"I had expected to win," he said, "after winning all the championships last winter at Chamonix where I defeated Europe's best skiers."

Tomorrow he will try for his third Olympic gold medal in the special slalom.

"I think I have a good chance," he said. "I consider my best opposition Couttet of France, Karl

Mrs. Gretchen Fraser of the United States after she finished second in the Alpine combined ski event yesterday.
Associated Press Radiophoto

Molitor of Switzerland and Zeno Colo of Italy."

Colo fell in the downhill Monday, so he did not bother to ski today.

With the Cresta run and figure skating postponed, several thousand fans ploughed their way through the slush of St. Moritz up to the Suvretta Hill, where the men's and women's skiing events were run off side by side.

Among the spectators was Major Gen. Frank W. Milburn, commander of American troops in Austria. He was the first to congratulate Mrs. Fraser.

"Your boys are our best rooters," she told the General. She was cheered by crowds of United States occupation forces.

Still breathing hard from the perilous descent, Mrs. Fraser explained she learned to ski in Sun Valley, Idaho, but neglected to mention she was the national downhill and combined champion in 1941 and the national slalom champion in 1942.

"This is our best performance," said United States ski coach Walter Prager. "Now we have very much of a chance in the special slalom."

Dr. Jean Carle of Paris, president of the International Ski Federation, had high praise for the United States representatives.

"Gretchen Fraser is great," he declared, "and Jack Reddish will be one of the best in the slalom in the world in the near future." Reddish, from Salt Lake City, Utah, finished twelfth in the men's Alpine combined.

The American girls generally did well. Andrea Mead, the 15-year-old from Rutland, Vt., placed eleventh in the slalom with a total time of 2 minutes 15.5 seconds despite a fall at the start of her second descent.

Miss Ruth-Marie Stewart of Hanover, Vt., did 2 minutes 16.4 seconds for twelfth place and Miss Rebecca Cremer of Lacrosse, Wis., was timed in 2:21.9 for twentieth place in the field of twenty-seven.

Gustav Allan Lindh of Sweden won the Olympic pentathlon, an exhibition event, with a total of 14 points. Two other Swedes, William Grut and Bertil Haase, placed second and third.

The competition included cross-country skiing, shooting, downhill skiing, fencing and horsemanship.

In the men's combined skiing event the Americans to a man did much better in the slalom than in the downhill racing. In placing twelfth in the final standing Reddish earned 9.71 points in the downhill and 3.53 in the slalom for a total of 13.24.

The lower the point score, the higher the ranking. Oreiller of France, the victor, posted a combined score of only 3.27 points.

Steve Knowlton of Aspen, Col., finished twenty-fifth with 23.75 points; Barney McLean of Denver, Col., was twenty-sixth with 25.15 points and John Blatt of Palo Alto, Calif., was twenty-ninth with 27.83 points.

February 5, 1948

# *Button Wins Olympic Skating While Mrs. Fraser Takes Slalom for Americans*

## U. S. RISES TO THIRD AS SWISS SET PACE

### Button's Near-Perfect Skating and Mrs. Fraser's Surprise Ski Triumph Help Team

### HEATON SECOND IN CRESTA

### Canada's Miss Scott Leads in School Figures—Swedes Fall to Olympic Runner-Up Spot

ST. MORITZ, Switzerland, Feb. 5 (AP)—Climaxing an amazing comeback, America's men and women athletes dominated the seventh day of the Winter Olympics as they swept to clean-cut victories in two events, placed second in another and vaulted from seventh to third place in team standing.

It was an historic day for the red, white and blue from the moment Mrs. Gretchen Fraser, flying housewife from Vancouver, Wash., flashed across first in the women's special slalom until Dick Button of Englewood, N. J., won the men's figure skating as the sun set over the snowclad Alps.

Their triumphs were the first ever scored by Americans in skiing or figure skating since the inception of the winter games in 1924. Mrs. Fraser's surprise victory followed her almost equally spectacular second place yesterday in the women's combined ski event.

Unofficial team scores, based on 10 points for a first place, 5 for second, 4 for third, 3 for fourth, 2 for fifth and 1 for sixth, follow: Switzerland 69, Sweden 62, United States 52¼, Norway 48½, Austria 46, France 39, Finland 38, Italy 24, Britain 7, The Netherlands 6, Hungary 5, Belgium 3 and Canada ¼.

#### Martin Fourth in Cresta

Between Mrs. Fraser's two breathless descents of Mount Piz Nair and Button's almost flawless performance in free skating, Jack Heaton of New Haven, Conn., presented a second-place silver medal to Uncle Sam in the dangerous Cresta one-man sled race. Will Martin, a GI with the occupation forces in Germany, slammed across fourth.

Possibly the most dramatic moment occurred as Hans Gerschwiler of Switzerland, world figure skating champion, was trying desperately to overcome the lead Button had taken over him on Monday in compulsory figures. In the midst of a graceful, original maneuver, the Swiss star slipped, his skates flew up—and he fell.

At that instant the 18-year-old Button became the Olympic champion. No other competitor had a

Richard Button of Englewood, N. J., during a practice session at St. Moritz.
The New York Times

hope of catching him. His parents were at the rinkside to witness his triumph by the most one-sided margin ever.

Pretty, shy Mrs. Fraser was first of thirty-one girls to plummet down the zigzag slalom course in the cold early morning, and she threw an additional chill into her opponents by making her first run in 59.7 seconds. The nearest any rival approached to equaling it was Erika Mahringer of Austria—one-tenth of a second slower.

#### Swiss Woman Runner-Up

On her second run, the 28-year-old American matron really opened the throttle. Cutting the corners crisply, she sped down under perfect control in 0:57.5. When her total time of 1:57.2 was announced, every one of several thousand spectators knew a champion had been crowned. Antoinette Meyer of Switzerland finished second with a total of 1:57.7 for her two descents.

Gretchen of the pigtails was so happy she was virtually numb. "How am I supposed to feel?" she asked, honestly. "It beats me. I don't know. At some of the gates (flags) it was too close for comfort, but I got through."

Andrea Mead, 15-year-old star from Rutland, Vt., finished eighth in 2:08.8 for her two runs. Brynhild Grasmoen of Merced, Calif.,

was ninth in 2:09.6, and Paula Kann of North Conway, N. H., eleventh in 2:09.8.

Two of Button's team-mates, 18-year-old John Lettingarver of St. Paul and James Grogan, 16, of Oakland, Calif., gave figure-skating performances good enough to place them "in the points" under the unofficial scoring system. Lettingarver's fluid grace in the free style gained fourth place behind Gerschwiler, who salvaged second honors, and Edi Rada of Austria. Grogan placed sixth.

#### Reinalter Captures Slalom

In only two events, the men's slalom and non-Olympic ice hockey, did the Americans fail to make their presence felt. Edi Reinalter of Switzerland won the slalom with two runs totaling 2:10.3 as his country wrested team leadership from Sweden.

Jack Reddish of Salt Lake City, best of the Americans in the slalom, finished seventh in 2:15.5. Dr. Jean Carle, acting president of the International Ski Federation, still thought Reddish looked like a future world champion.

The Amateur Hockey Association team representing the United States in the ice hockey tournament caught a 12-to-3 thrashing from Canada—its second defeat of the tournament—and virtually was

eliminated. Canada, Switzerland and Czechoslovakia are deadlocked for the leadership, each with five victories and no losses.

Nino Bibbia, an Italian grocer, won the Cresta event with six runs totaling 5 minutes 23.2 seconds for approximately 3.8 miles. Heaton had a total time of 5:24.6. John G. Crammond, a London broker, finished third in 5:25.1 in this most dangerous of winter sports in which the sleds hit up to 80 miles an hour.

Martin, 19-year-old GI, was the youngest of the top finishers. The first three have years of experience. Heaton won the event in the 1928 Olympics, the last time it was held.

Another American soldier, William Johnson of Minneapolis, hurtled over a ten-foot snowbank in his fourth run and was eliminated. He was not hurt.

When asked how the lanky Italian had beaten him, Heaton, an importer, said: "He was just better."

Following the four leaders were, in order, Gottfried Kaegi of Switzerland, R. E. A. Bott and Lieut. Col. J. S. Coats of Britain and Fairchild McCarthy of Belmont, Mass. Fairchild's time for eighth place was 5:35.5.

Already the United States has made a stronger showing than in any previous winter games. Of the remaining five events, Americans are almost certain to score in the four-man bobsled, women's figure skating and figure skating pairs, with even an outside chance for a place in the ski jump.

Button entered the final freestyle skating event with a commanding lead earned in the compulsory or school figures—and he is rated the greatest free-style skater in the world.

He did not disappoint the capacity crowd in the Olympic Ice Stadium. Up and down over the crackly surface he glided as surely as if it had been the best of ice. He did five leaps and spins that no other skater attempted, and made everything look easy.

#### Button Smiles Brightly

At times he seemed to hang poised in the air. At others he spun with such rapidity as to be only a blur. From the most exacting maneuvers he would emerge with a broad smile.

There was a tense moment when the nine judges walked out on the ice and reached in their little score boxes for the numbers that would give Dick's score.

Six is perfect. Five is thumping good. Nine numbers went up. The lowest was 5.5, a score only barely reached by any previous competitor. The highest was six—perfection. That was given by the American judge, M. Bernard Fox of Boston.

The first score announced was for content of his free-style program. The second, for performance, was even more sensational. Four judges gave 5.9; the lowest again was 5.5.

His jubilant coach, Gus Lussi of Lake Placid, N. Y., said that never before in Olympic history had such a score been made.

Dick Button dominated men's figure skating in the late 1940's and early 1950's. He won the Olympic gold medal in 1948 and 1952 and was U.S. men's champion, 1946–1952.

Winner of the Olympic gold medal in 1948, Barbara Ann Scott was also the women's world champion in 1947 and 1948.

When Gerschwiler, who followed Dick and who was in second place at the end of the school figures, sat down heavily almost at the start of his program, it was obvious to all that a new championship had been won by the United States.

This morning the women's school figures were completed. Barbara Ann Scott of Canada, the world champion took a strong lead to draw close to the crown won in 1936 by Sonja Henie. Barbara Ann made 858.1 points to 842.1 for Jeanette Altwegg of Great Britain, in second place.

Gretchen Merrill of Boston, the American champion, placed highest of the United States contingent—sixth place with 798 points. Yvonne Sherman of New York was eighth with 783.9 and Eileen Seigh of Brooklyn twelfth with 755.8. Twenty-five are competing.

In the men's slalom, American entrants placed well in addition to Reddish's seventh. Steve Knowlton of Aspen, Col., was sixteenth in the sixty-six-man field; Colin Stewart of Hanover, N. H., was twentieth and Barney McLean of Denver was twenty-fourth.

The fifty-kilometer cross-country ski race, an event dominated by men from the North, and the finals in women's figure skating will be staged tomorrow. The first two heats also will be held for four-man bobsleds, among which the team piloted by James Bickford of Saranac Lake, N. Y., is highly rated.

Figure skating pairs had been scheduled for tomorrow, but officials postponed that competition until Saturday. Main United States hopes are pinned on Peter and Karol Kennedy, Seattle brother-and-sister team.

February 6, 1948

# *Miss Scott Wins in Olympic Skating; Sweden Regains Team Lead From Swiss*

## BROKEN WATER PIPE STOPS BOBSLEDDERS

### Slide Flooded With U. S. Four Driven by Tyler Second to Swiss After First Heat

### CANADIAN SKATER SUPERB

### Miss Scott Easy Victor, While Yvonne Sherman Is Sixth— Ski Marathon to Swede

ST. MORITZ, Switzerland, Feb. 6 (AP)—Blonde, blue-eyed Barbara Ann Scott, Canada's superb ballerina of the ice, won Sonja Henie's olympic figure skating crown today with a dazzling exhibition of grace and beauty that left her rivals nowhere.

Wearing No. 13 on the sleeve of her white fur-trimmed costume, the pretty Ottawa girl defied that "hoodoo" to be hailed as a worthy successor to the Norse star who took three olympic titles before the war.

Barbara Ann's victory, on top of Dick Button's triumph for the United States in the men's figure skating final yesterday, carried the Western Hemisphere to a sweep of a specialty which always before had been dominated by Europe's ice eartists.

The Canadian beauty, already the world's champion, returned a motor car to her admirers last year in order not to endanger her amateur standing. She declared tonight after realizing her life's ambition that she would not turn professional.

Four European girls, headed by Eva Pawlik of Austria, supplied what little opposition Miss Scott encountered. Yvonne Sherman of New York was sixth, while Gretchen Merrill of Boston, the American champion, gained eighth place after taking two spills.

#### Barbara Obliges Cameramen

A not too happy note was struck when the victorious Canadian girl, at the behest of photographers, re-

Barbara Ann Scott, who won figure skating crown
The New York Times

turned to an end of the rink. Miss Scott exhibited fragments of her routine then while Miss Merrill was in the midst of her competitive free-style gyrations.

While the United States contingent was being halted temporarily after its banner two-victory splurge of the previous day, the hardy Swedes swept back into first place in the team standing by finishing first, second and fifth in the 50-kilometer cross-country ski race, most grueling of all Olympic events.

Nils Karlsson, solemn-faced and tireless, sped over the course of more than 30 miles in the excellent time of 3 hours 47 minutes 48 seconds. Harald Eriksson, his team-mate, was a strong second in 3:52:20. No American even attempted to compete in the grind.

The 17 points picked up in the snow marathon jumped Sweden to the top among the 28 competing nations with a total of 79 points, with two days to go in the games. Switzerland dropped to second place with 70 points, and the United States clung to third with 53¼.

#### Austria Has 51 Points

Other totals under the unofficial scoring system were Austria 51, Norway 48½, Finland 45, France 39, Italy 24, Great Britain 11, Canada 10¼, The Netherlands 6, Hungary 5, Czechoslovakia 5, Belgium 3. Ten points are given for each first place, 5 for second, 4 for third, 3 for fourth, 2 for fifth and 1 for sixth.

A broken water pipe flooded the bobsled run at mid-morning and halted competition among the four-man bobs after the first of four scheduled heats had been completed and a good start made on the second heat.

The American No. 2 sled, piloted by Francis Tyler of Lake Placid, N. Y., had the second best time in the opening heat and was leading in the second when the accident occurred. Workmen frantically repaired the chute, and it was announced that the contest would be resumed tomorrow, starting with the second heat.

A bob piloted by the Swiss, Fritz Feierabend, made the best time of the first heat—1 minute, 16.9 seconds—followed by Tyler's time of 1:17.1. A Norwegian and a Belgian sled tied for third and fourth at 1:17.3, followed by the American No. 1 bob, driven by James Bickford of Saranac Lake, N. Y., at 1:17.4.

#### Eight Sleds Make Two Runs

Only eight sleds had taken their second dashes when the water pipe broke. Tyler's 1:17.4 was best, but none of the other leaders—Feierabend, Bickford, the Norwegians and Belgians—had made their second runs.

Tyler was upset about the decision to start the entire second heat over, thus throwing out his good effort. The big New Yorker declared that an "injustice" to him and his crew, but Coach Donna Fox of the American team remained calm.

T"omorrow the second heat will be run over again, according to the rules," he said. "Of course, that wipes out Tyler's good time for the second run. Naturally, he is pretty upset about it."

Curtis Stevens, manager of the American squad, said that, as Tyler would have to lead off in the second heat tomorrow, he would like to have six or seven sleds go down the chute ahead of the American bob to "break it in."

The Amateur Hockey Association team representing the United States scored a 13-2 victory over Austria. Having suffered two defeats, however, the A. H. A. was out of the running for the title.

The Swiss forged into the lead with their sixth straight victory, routing Poland, 14—0. Their chief rivals, Canada and Czechoslovakia, battled to a scoreless tie, leaving each with five triumphs and one tie. The Swiss have yet to play both Canada and the Czechs.

In the event of a tie the title will be decided on goal count. The Czechs have scored 69, the Swiss 68 and Canada 54.

The biggest crowd since the Fifth Winter Olympic Games opening ceremony packed the bleachers and perched on terraced cliffs to see Miss Scott add the last great title to her skating honors. She poised on her toes and took off in a twirl with the first note of the music. Respecting the ice, chewed into ruts by two morning hockey matches, Barbara Ann picked the smoother ends of the rink for the riskiest parts of her repertoire.

A fall might have meant taps, despite her big lead after the compulsory figures yesterday. Growing confident as she mastered the rink, she performed more and more in the middle.

Always, on the saw-toothed tip toes of her silver blades, or flat out, she was the ballerina. Almost every second she was dancing, twirling, leaping.

She glided off the ice on one foot amid applause that bespoke her triumph even before the judges confirmed it a minute later with the marks, ranging from 5.3 to 5.9. Six is perfect.

### Trainer Runs Interference

Then 200 photographers rushed for Barbara Ann, but Sheldon Galbraith, her trainer, caught her arm and ran interference to the dressing room.

Miss Merrill was downcast about the two falls which cost her so heavily.

"The ice was bad and I was nervous," she said. "I was worried about my double loop. I practiced it before and went O.K., but I probably shouldn't have put it in. Afterward I thought how disgraceful to fall—and it also was a mighty hard plop."

Her explanation was no alibi. She added: "I think Barbara Ann is simply terrific."

Pretty Miss Sherman topped the three American entries with a beautiful show that drew shouts from GI's in the stands. It was a gallant comeback for the 17-year-old miss, who had finished eighth in compulsory figures. Eileen Seigh of Brooklyn fell three times, spoiling any hope of a good placing.

Second in figure skating was Fraulein Pawlik. Third was Jeannette Altwegg of Britain; fourth, Jirina Nekolova of Czechoslovakia, and fifth, Alena Vrzanava of Czechoslovakia.

February 7, 1948

opened the scoring in the first period on a pass from Ralph Warburton of Cranston, R. I. But Austria rallied with two quick goals. Warburton then tied the count and the United States went on to a comparatively easy triumph.

The Americans tallied four goals in the second period and five in the third while blanking their rivals. Warburton led in the damage with four goals. Cunliffe and Bruce Mather of Springfield, Mass., scored three apiece.

February 7, 1948

# TYLER'S SLED TAKES FOUR-MAN CROWN IN OLYMPIC GAMES

## U. S. Now 2d in Team Standing With 3d Title—Bickford Annexes Third in Event

### BELGIAN SKATERS VICTORS

## Miss Sherman-Swenning Gain 4th Among Pairs—Hugsted of Norway Ski Jump Winner

By The Associated Press.

ST. MORITZ, Switzerland, Feb. 7—Arguments and snow failed to stop the Americans today as they pulled into second place in the winter Olympic Games with a championship in the four-man bobsled race.

It was the United States' No. 2 team, piloted by Francis Tyler of Lake Placid, N. Y., that streaked four times down the mile of sheer ice in the total time of 5 minutes 20.1 seconds to add more gold medals and points to the American aggregate.

Only last night Tyler threatened to withdraw. Officials had ruled that all second runs yesterday were not to be counted because some of the teams had not been able to compete when a water main burst and flooded the tunnel of ice. He still was angry this morning.

The United States' No. 1 team, guided by James Bickford of Saranac Lake, N. Y., was third.

The biggest feat of the day, however, was the somersault taken by the International Olympic Committee which restored hockey to the Olympic program. The Swiss had insisted all along that hockey was a part of the Olympics even though the I. O. C. ruled it out in the squabble over United States representation.

### Other Champions Crowned

In addition to Tyler's championship, other titles decided were:

Figure Skating by Pairs—Won by Micheline Lannoy and Pierre Baugniet of Belgium. Yvonne Sherman and Robert Swenning of New York were fourth and the Kennedy children, Karol and Peter, of Seattle. Wash., were sixth.

Ski Jumping—Won by Petter Hugsted of Norway. Gordon Wren of Winter Park, Colo., took fifth place—the first time an American male ever scored a point in an Olympic ski event.

With only the hockey championship to be settled, Czechoslovakia is tied with Canada, followed by Switzerland and the United States

## Hockey Tourney Is Ruled Official By International Olympic Body

### All Teams but A. H. A. of U. S., Which Cannot Finish in First Three Anyway, Eligible for Medals—Americans, Swiss Victors

ST. MORITZ, Switzerland, Feb. 6 (Reuters) — The International Olympic Committee today decided that after all the ice hockey tournament being played here should be regarded as an Olympic event, with the exception that the American Hockey Association team should be regarded as outside the competition.

The decision means that the winners will get Olympic gold medals, the runners-up silver medals and the third team, bronze medals.

The International Olympic Committee is saved any embarrassment by the fact that the American team will not finish in the first three.

It is understood that the delegates felt that it was rather unfair that teams of countries who came to St. Moritz in all good faith to play in an Olympic tournament should have to suffer as the result of an internal American dispute.

### Swiss Win Sixth in Row

ST. MORITZ, Feb. 6 (/P)—The United States A. H. A. hockey team defeated Austria, 13 to 2, today while Switzerland was forging into the lead in the tournament.

The Swiss won their sixth straight by downing Poland, 14 to 0. Their chief rivals in the three-team race for the championship—Canada and Czechoslovakia—meanwhile played a scoreless tie.

The scramble for the title is still wide open, with Switzerland yet having to play both the Canadians and Czechs in the round-robin.

In case of a tie the championship will be determined on a goal count. The Czechs have the most goals, 69, to 68 for the Swiss and 54 for Canada.

In the only other hockey game

played, Sweden defeated Great Britain, 4—3.

The United States' victory kept the team in fourth place in the standings with four triumphs and two defeats.

Although superior in all departments, the A. H. A. team had to rally halfway through the first period.

Bruce Cunliffe of New York

The United States four-man bobsled team, which captured the title yesterday. Left to right: Francis Tyler, Pat Martin, Edward Rimkus and William D'Amico.

Associated Press Radiophoto

—The Associated Press scorecard, based on 10-5-4-3-2-1 for the six places shows:

Sweden 79 points, United States 73½, Switzerland 73, Norway 69½, Austria 51, Finland 49, France 39, Italy 25, Belgium 18, Canada 14½, Great Britain 13, Hungary 10, Holland 6, Czechoslovakia 5. Only fourteen of the twenty-eight competing nations have scored in the competition that ends tomorrow.

The victory in the bobsledding gave the American team its third Olympic championship. Dick Button of Englewood, N. J., won one in men's figure skating and Mrs. Gretchen Fraser of Vancouver, Wash., triumphed in the women's ski slalom.

Over-all, this is the strongest showing the United States ever has made in the winter Olympics. The Americans won at Lake Placid, N. Y., in 1932 but it was a hollow victory because the depression and travel distances cut sharply into European entries.

"A magnificent showing. It is beyond our fondest hopes," said J. Lyman Bingham of Chicago, boss of the team.

Snow fell thickly all day, causing delays and anguish. Hockey teams sometimes lost the puck. Figure skaters wobbled and fell. Ski jumpers slowed down. Only bobsledders rocketed down their icy course, oblivious to the elements.

Never before, perhaps, has a team wavered so close between winning a championship and just sitting on the sideline. Last night it was touch and go if Tyler's sled would compete.

What happened was this: The second heat of the bobsled was interrupted yesterday when the track caved in due to a leaky pipe. Tyler had already made a fast second run.

Bobsledding authorities ordered the entire heat canceled and rerun. Tyler said "no" emphatically. Then he declared if the heat was canceled, he would not lead off in rerunning it unless four or five pilot sleds were sent down to smooth out the course.

**Petter Hugsted of Norway, who took first place in the ski jump.**

Donna Fox, Larchmont, N. Y., undertaker and coach of the American bobsled squad, stepped in to mediate—and Tyler made the first run of the day.

"The rules are the same for everyone," Fox said, "and fair all around."

Tyler is a veteran of the hazardous sport. He was on the 1936 team. He also was chosen for the 1940 team that did not compete because of the war.

Tyler weighs 202 pounds and is an insurance investigator and adjuster. Back of him was a hefty trio. Pat Martin, No. 2 man, from Massena, N. Y., weighs 250. From Schenectady, N. Y., came Edward Rimkus, 225 pounds. At brake was William D'Amico of Lake Placid, N. Y., at 210 pounds. He also was chosen for the 1940 team.

"Luck and a wonderful team did it," said Tyler jubilantly.

On the argumentative side of the Olympics, even after the International Olympic Committee welcomed hockey back after spanking it earlier in the week, Dr. Fritz Kraatz, International Ice Hockey Federation president, refused to sign the communiqué announcing the settlement.

Of America's other jumpers,

Sverre Fredheim of St. Paul, Minn., placed eleventh, just as he did in the 1936 games. He made leaps of 216 feet 6½ inches and 213 feet 3 inches.

Paul Perrault of Ishpeming, Mich., after a comparatively poor first jump of 200 feet 2 inches, made 219 feet 10 inches on his second for fifteenth place. Walter Bietila of Iron Mountain, Mich., did 200 feet 2 inches on his first jump. He fell on his second and escaped injury.

In figure skating America's hopes for a championship were curtailed by the scarred ice and the heavy snow. This slowed down the Kennedy kids so much they landed in sixth place. Last year they were runners-up to the Belgian pair for the world championship.

Yvonne Sherman and Bob Swenning were fourth with an interesting program performed with grace although probably too slow for the taste of the judges.

As the round-robin hockey tournament drew to its close, Czechoslovakia knocked off the strong Swiss team, 7—1, the American team defeated Great Britain, 4—3, by virtue of a penalty shot, only one called so far at St. Moritz. Canada crushed Austria, 12—0, and Sweden swamped Italy, 23—0.

Norwegians finished one, two, three in the ski jump. The victor, Petter Hugsted, won not only on form, but soared out into the snowstorm for the day's longest jump of 70 meters (229 feet 8 inches).

Attesting to the durability of the Norsemen was Birger Ruud. He won the Olympic ski jump in 1932 and again in 1936 and was second today.

Wren, who stands 5 feet 6½ inches and weighs only 145 pounds, flew off the runway with the best of the great northerners.

Both his jumps measured 68 meters (216 feet 6 inches), but his second had more style. His landing on the first, the judges ruled, was a little too stiff and not quite balanced, and he carried his skis too broadly for European taste. But there was dash and daring in his jumps. He got 17 points for his first jump, a trifle under 18 for his second. Twenty is perfection.

It was a jubilant American team that looked back on a week of competition against the best the world had to offer in sports that for the most part are not Ameri-

can specialties.

Here's the score card:

Figure skating—Button won the men's championship with John Lettengarver of St. Paul, Minn., fourth, and Jimmy Grogan of Oakland, Calif., sixth.

Miss Sherman of New York was sixth in women's singles, in addition to her fourth place today, with the Kennedys sixth. The United States never before won a figure skating title.

Skiing—Mrs. Fraser won the women's slalom, and placed second in the Alpine combination event, which is both slalom and downhill. The United States had never before won a skiing medal. Mrs. Fraser, by virtue of her double scoring, became the leading point winner on the American team.

Wren was the only American to place in the first six in a men's skiing event.

Bobsledding—In addition to today's championship and third place, the No. 2 bob in the two-man event, piloted by Fred Fortune Jr. of Lake Placid, won second place.

Skeleton bob—Jack Heaton of New Haven, Conn., the champion in 1928, the only other time the event has been run, placed second this time, with Corp. W. L. Martin of Kalisall, Mont., fourth.

Skating—Ken Bartholomew and Bob Fitzgerald, both of Minneapolis, tied for second in the 500 meters. Ken Henry of Chicago was fifth, with Del Lamb of Milwaukee, a veteran of the 1936 team, tied for sixth place. John Werket of Minneapolis was sixth in the 1,500 meters.

Hockey—The team brought by the United States Olympic Committee never got to play because the Swiss refused its entry. The Olympic Committee refused to endorse the Amateur Hockey Association team, which the Swiss accepted. The A.H.A. team went on to play. The Olympic Committee's team has already gone home. And now hockey, after being off the Olympic program, is back on it. The A.H.A. will probably wind up fourth or fifth in the nine-team field.

Tomorrow the fifth winter games come to an end. The final victory ceremonies will be held and the flag lowered, not to be raised again until the 1952 games start in Finland.

February 8, 1948

---

# Sweden Wins Winter Olympic Games With Switzerland Second, U. S. Third

## NINE MEDALS WON BY AMERICAN TEAM

ST. MORITZ, Switzerland, Feb. 8 (AP)—The United States finished third in the turbulent fifth winter Olympic Games which closed today with all the informality of a country church picnic.

The games, which opened with a verbal war and were plagued by hot sun and heavy snowstorm on alternate days, were won by Sweden. Switzerland was second, keeping the United States from the place on the final day by taking third in the trouble-pocked hockey tourney.

The hockey championship was decided today when Canada defeated Switzerland, 3 to 0, and gained just enough points to edge out Czechoslovakia on a goals-average basis. The United States Amateur Hockey Association sextet, center of all the controversy, lost to the Czechs, 4 to 3, in its finale.

Although the AHA team finished fourth in the tourney, the three points thus gained were not added to the United States total of points.

That produced this table of points.

Sweden 82, Switzerland 77, United States 73½, Norway 69½, Austria 51, Finland 49, France 39, Italy 25, Canada 24½, Belgium 18, Great Britain 15, Hungary 10, Czechoslovakia 10, Holland 6 and Poland 1. Thirteen of the competing nations did not score.

Even if the American hockey points had been counted, the United States would have remained in third place by a fraction of a point—the best showing of a Red, White and Blue winter team on this side of the Atlantic.

Although the AHA team has been disowned by the U. S. Olympic Committee, the Swiss said today they would award Olympic participation certificates to the players.

Despite the tempers of the past ten days, pleasantries and informality marked the closing of the contests.

Barely 5,000 spectators perched themselves on mountain ledges and pelted the officials with snowballs during the final hockey games. When decisions went against the Swiss in the vital game with Canada, a chorus of shrill whistles would echo through the Alps and a barrage of snowballs would come down from the hillside.

During the solemn closing ceremonies the spectators straggled across the rink for autographs and an exchange of greetings with the flag carriers.

### In Contrast With 1936

That was all in sharp contrast with the closing of the 1936 games at Garmisch-Partenkirchen in Germany, where 100,000 spectators were held in rigid check as a show for Nazi bigwigs.

Today the flags of the twenty-eight nations were paraded part of the way around the rink and lined up below the mountain ledge. The American flag was carried by Jack Heaton, bobsled veteran, of New Haven, Conn. He was conspicuous in his white American parade jacket.

The little military brass band played a monotonous, rhythmic piece which is the Swiss Flag March. Down came the Olympic flag. Down came the flag of Switzerland. Down came the flag of England, host for the big summer games.

It was the last Olympic flag left. The first of the three was stolen by a souvenir hunter the day the games began. The second was stolen last night.

When the flags were all in line, the Olympic medal winners were announced over a rasping loudspeaker.

Gold, silver and bronze medals were awarded to athletes who won first, second or third places, respectively. Participants from Sweden and Norway each took home four gold medals and three

medals each for second and third places. Representatives from the United States and from Switzerland also had identical records. Each country won three firsts, four seconds and two thirds.

Three second place medals were awarded in the 500-meter speed skating because of a tie. Third place was omitted.

Although the American team included some 250-pound bobsledders and big, tough skiers and skaters, it was a 5-foot 4 inch, 115 pound bride from Vancouver, Wash., who led the United States scoring with 15 points.

Mrs. Gretchen Fraser, with rosy cheeks, pig tails, and a shy smile, was the darling of the squad. She won the women's slalom event and placed second in the Alpine combination — a gold and silver medal. She was the first American ever to win a skiing medal in the games.

This was also the first time an American had won a figure skating championship. Dick Button, 18, of Englewood N. J., captured the men's title. The third champion was Francis Tyler of Saranac Lake, N. Y., pilot of the four-man bobsled winner.

The Olympic torch, a two-foot high flame springing from a bowl atop the modest tower in the main stadium, was extinguished and the games were over.

The mountain shadows deepened and the wet snow came down thicker than ever. The crowd straggled out. Some used sleighs with jingling bells. Others plodded on foot in the slush.

### Britain Defeats Italy

In the final hockey games Great Britain also defeated Italy, 14 to 7, and Sweden downed Poland, 13 to 2.

There was a military ski patrol event this morning, but it was only

an exhibition and no Olympic medals were awarded.

Switzerland won it, followed by Finland and Sweden. It was a 27-kilometer (17-mile) race, with some shooting at toy balloons midway. The American team finished last in the eight-nation field.

Many of the American teams have already departed for home. Others will leave tomorrow and Tuesday.

Of the 4,500 persons who came to St. Moritz for the games, 30 per cent were Swiss. Next in number came the Americans, 10 per cent being from the United States. Another 5 per cent were American soldiers from Austria and Germany.

February 9, 1948

## SWISS TEAM TAKES 16-MILE SKI PATROL

### Finns Are Second in Olympic Exhibition—U. S. Military Squad Finishes Eighth

ST. MORITZ, Switzerland, Feb. 8 (UP)—Ill luck attended the United States' first venture in international competition among military ski patrols as the Olympic games ended today as the Americans finished last in a field of eight teams.

Lieut. Donald L. Weihs of Sherman, Tex., who led the four-man patrol from Camp Carson, Colo., broke a ski shortly after the takeoff on the 27-kilometer (16¾-miles) race. Under regulations the

ski could not be replaced and the entire patrol had to remain together to complete the contest.

"I hit a hole where someone else had fallen, my ski cracked off behind the heel and I turned completely over," said the 25-year old Texan, "but I kept going."

At this point the American patrol had taken about 50 minutes to do the first eight kilometers. If they had kept up that pace they could have finished in about three hours and twenty minutes. Retarded by the broken ski, however, they finished in four hours 35 minutes 58 seconds. The winning Swiss team completed the maneuver in two hours 34 minutes and 25 seconds.

The military ski patrol race—an Olympic exhibition only—consisted of Alpine ski patrol over 27 kilometers with a total climb of one thousand meters and a test in marksmanship at the halfway point.

There three members of the patrol were allowed a maximum of three shots at a toy balloon. If he hit on the first shot, a total of three minutes was deducted from the total running time of the patrol. Two minutes was allowed for the second and one minute for the third.

The Americans got credit for only three minutes from their running time as against a perfect score—nine minutes—registered by the Finns, who placed second.

Tech. Sgt. Stanley Walker, 25, of Lynn, Mass. scored a bullseye on his first shot.

The other riflemen—Henry Dunlap of Lindsay, Calif., and Lorentz Eide of California Springs, Calif.—failed to connect.

February 9, 1948

---

# *Button Wins World Figure Skating Title, With Gerschwiler Second at Davos*

## NEW JERSEY YOUTH IN SUPERB DISPLAY

### Button Is First American to Capture World Laurels Among Figure Skaters

### SWISS ACE IS DETHRONED

### Gerschwiler Beaten in Free Style Phase—Lettengarver Is Fourth, Grogan Fifth

DAVOS, Switzerland, Feb. 13 (UP) — Dick Button, 18-year-old skating marvel from Englewood, N. J., in one of the most brilliant performances ever seen on European ice, today became the first

American ever to win the men's world figure skating championship, while Miss Barbara Ann Scott of Ottawa made a good start in defense of her women's crown.

The handsome young Olympic champion turned in a near-flawless exhibition in the free skating events to overcome the narrow lead which defending champion Hans Gerschwiler of Switzerland had assumed in yesterday's compulsory figures and thus made it a clean sweep of the "big three" figure skating titles.

Button previously had won the European crown at Prague, Czechoslovakia, on Jan. 14, and the Olympic crown at St. Moritz last week.

#### Gains Substantial Lead

Miss Scott, who also holds the European and Olympic titles and is an odds-on favorite to win the world championship, glided off to a 5.8-point lead over Miss Jeanette Altwegg of Great Britain in the first two of six compulsory figures events. The remaining four school figures will be skated tomorrow and the free skating events on Sunday.

Button, bringing the astonished crowd to its feet time after time,

was marked 5.9 (6.0 is perfect) by four of the nine international judges for both performance and content to finish with a total of 11 placements and 220.3 points, or a total of 1,980.7 points to 1,948.5 for the Swiss start.

Gerschwiler, who was second to Button in the European championships and the Olympics, again placed second in today's meet with 19 placements and 216.5 points. Ede Kiraly of Hungary was third with 28 placements and 213.0

points; John Lettengarver of St. Paul, Minn., was fourth with 212.2 points and Jimmy Grogan of Oakland, Calif., fifth with 200.8.

Although Button said that "the ice was fine and everything went perfectly," Gerschwiler, Kiraly, Edi Rada of Austria and Grogan all took spills in the midst of their performances.

#### St. Paul Youth Excels

Lettengarver outshone everyone but Button in today's free skating

## AMERICAN ACE NOW THE WORLD'S CHAMPION

Dick Button at St. Moritz during the Olympic Games

The New York Times

competition, but was unable to make up the deficit left by his mediocre performance in the school figures yesterday. His fourth placing was the same he had gained in the Olympics, while Grogan's fifth was one place better than his showing in the winter games.

Despite the fact that Button's exhibition left no doubts in the minds of the spectators that he had won the title hands down, the New Jersey youngster was worried to distraction during the hour between the end of the meet and the judges' official announcement. He spent most of the waiting period futilely trying to pry information from the judges.

After he had jubilantly received official confirmation of his victory, Button told The United Press he had no interest in ever turning professional.

"For ten years that life may be okay," he said, "then you just get to be a part of an ice ballet show.

"If my skating would somehow help me pay my way through college I would gladly make use of it," he added. "I would like to go to Yale and later get into business."

In the women's competition, Miss Scott unofficially placed first with 341.9 points, to Miss Altwegg's 336.1. Miss Yvonne Sherman of New York was sixth at the end of the first two compulsory figures with 318.7 points.

Miss Jirina Nekolova of Czechoslovakia was third with 329.6, Miss Eva Pavlik of Austria, Olympic runner-up, was fourth with 327.9 and Miss Shirley Adams of Great Britain fifth with 320.6.

A victory for Miss Scott would mark the first time since the world skating championships were inaugurated in 1896 that the two titles ever were won by North American competitors.

February 14, 1948

## Barbara Scott of Canada Retains World Laurels in Figure Skating

### Ottawa Girl Completes Triple Crown by Victory at Davos—Miss Pawlik of Austria Second—Yvonne Sherman Is Sixth

DAVOS PLATZ, Switzerland, Feb. 15 (P)—Miss Barbara Ann Scott of Canada gave another dazzling performance today, despite soft ice, to retain her women's world figure skating championship.

Thus the 19-year-old blonde from Ottawa completed a sweep of the sport's three major titles. Besides capturing the Olympic crown at St. Moritz, Barbara Ann won the European championship at Prague last month.

A crowd of 4,000 watched silently as the Canadian ballerina of the ice, clad in a white costume trimmed with silver, danced to the tune of "Beautiful Island of Somewhere," in her four minutes of free skating.

Then the fans gave her a thundering ovation. They poured onto the ice to offer her congratulations, chocolates and handshakes.

Smilingly she greeted them all and signed countless books and papers for the autograph hunters.

Among those who greeted her was Dick Button, the 18-year-old star from Englewood, N. J., who won the men's world title as well as the Olympic laurels.

Surprisingly, two of the nine judges— the Hungarian and Austrian officials—voted against the champion. They awarded her second place while the other seven all agreed that she had won.

Miss Scott accumulated a total of 1,643.4 points for a 42.3 margin over Miss Eva Pawlik, 22-year-old Viennese medical student and Austrian champion. Miss Pawlik's total was 1,601.1.

Third place went to 16-year-old Jirinia Nekolova of Czechoslovakia with 1,580.4 points. The British champion, 17-year-old Miss Jeannette Altwegg of Liverpool, scored 1,578.6 points. Fifth place went to Miss Alena Vrzanova, 16, of Czechoslovakia, 1,568.7 and sixth to 17-year-old Miss Yvonne Sherman of New York, 1,523.7 despite her fall on the mushy ice.

Delayed by the soft ice, the twenty-nine competitors from eight nations completed their last two school figures before engaging in the free skating today.

Barbara Ann finished first in the compulsory figures with 970.5 points. She added 672.9 in the free style.

After finishing her dance, Miss Scott, known as "B.A." to her friends, said "I just want to go home to Canada. The ice is getting softer and softer."

She said she had no thought of going into the movies where her predecessor, Sonja Henie of Norway, made good in fabulous fashion.

"I want to go to a university and learn domestic science," added the Ottawa girl. She is a licensed plane pilot and an all-around sportswoman.

February 16, 1948

## Italy's Colo, Miss Burr of U. S. Annex Downhill Laurels at Banff

### Schopf of Austria Next in Men's Division of North American Ski Meet—Dagmar Rom Fourth in Women's Race

By FRANK ELKINS
Special to THE NEW YORK TIMES.

BANFF, Alberta, Feb. 25—Zeno Colo, one of the greatest Alpine skiers of the modern era, today turned in a performance as sharp as his axes. The Italian woodcutter from Abetone again showed his gleaming skis to a brilliant international field in winning the North American downhill championship over the steep course carved out of rugged Mount Norquay.

But the day's surprise was furnished by 22-year-old Miss Janette Burr, Seattle, Wash., who came roaring down an eight-gate controlled course on the face of the mountain under perfect control to capture the gold medal in a field of sixteen representatives.

This triumph, most stunning and equally as surprising to the bespectacled University of Washington graduate, was loudly received by the thousands who could watch the girls racing down their trail, unlike the men, who thrashed down the tree-lined mountainside.

"I can't believe it," declared the personable former United States national queen, who at first had been made to believe that she was fifth, due to a mistake in calculation. Hers was a well-merited triumph, one that should give the United States a terrific lift in this phase of skiing after the disappointing performance in the world title games at Aspen, Col.

A smart figure in blue, Janette

came streaking down from the wide open fields starting at a 6,850 feet altitude in good control. She hit the straightest line possible approaching Memorial Bowl and swung to the left of Exhibition Bowl where control gates forming a sharp "S" made her check momentarily.

Still in front of her singing boards, the physical education student went into the long traverse that averaged 32 degrees at good speed, and from there on she was a picture of extreme confidence and assurance.

Timed in 1:30.8, Miss Burr was two-fifths of a second better than Austria's Erika Mahringer, Olympic slalom winner and most consistent performer in the recent world championship.

Canada also had something to be proud of when Sandra Tomlinson of Vancouver placed third, followed by Austria's 21-year-old Dagmar Rom, who captured both the giant slalom and slalom world titles last week. Miss Jacqueline Martel of France was fifth, then came Switzerland's Rosemarie Bleuer and Sally Neidlinger of Hanover, N. H.

Miss Andrea Mead of the United States took a spill and this prevented her from doing better than eleventh, two and two-tenths seconds better than Italy's Celini Seghi. Miss Katy Rodolph, figured to be our best bet, was ill with a cold and could not compete, while Austria's Trude Beiser-Jochum tore a muscle in her right thigh in training over the men's course yesterday. She won the world downhill crown at Aspen.

Colo. 30-year-old athlete who virtually turned in a one-man show in sweeping two of the three world title events, just barely losing the regular slalom at Aspen, Colo., last week, was a steady, driving blue figure as he took the natural hazards and the difficult snow conditions in stride to handily trim a field of fifty-one stars from eleven nations with the sparkling time of 2:03.3.

Three-tenths of a second behind was Austria's Egon Schopf, blond-haired Innsbruck student. Christian Pravda, another wearer of the deep red sweater and the Hapsburg eagle of Austria, was third in 2:04.5.

Then came the first member of the Swiss array, which, as things turned out, performed as the strongest unit of any nation. Rudolph Graff, mountain guide from Wengen, was clocked in 2:05.1 for fourth place to show the way to his team-mates, who came in sixth, seventh, eighth, eleventh and fourteenth, for the best balanced squad in the inaugural event of the nine-day competition in the Canadian Rockies.

A close struggle ensued for the No. 5 spot, which Carlo Gartner, Italian, snared in 2:06.4 from Fernand Grosjean, 2:06.6; Georges Schneider, winner of the world slalom crown, 2:06.8, and Bernhard Perren, 2:07.5, all wearers of the deep field red shirts and the white cross of the little Alpine nation of Switzerland.

Yugoslavia's Valentin Mulej, 26-year-old barrel-chested locksmith who holds his country's title, came in ninth, 2:07.8. He beat by six-tenths of a second France's George Panisset, defending the slalom and the combined North American crowns.

Andy Tommy, 17-year-old Ot-

tawa junior, gave his Canadian admirers lots to be cheerful about as he dashed down the sporty course in what looked to be the straightest line possible in 2:10.9 for the fifteenth spot, the first to finish for the Dominion. George Macomber, 22-year-old West Newton, Mass., athlete, who holds most of the United States titles, broke through for the Americans in 2:12.4 for the No. 18 spot.

**Skis Are Too Slow**

Like his colleagues, Dean Perkins and Jimmy Griffith, Macomber appeared to be quite slow. "Just poor wax" commented our lads, who would certainly have done faster work since their performances were clean. None had trouble except that their "skis weren't fast enough."

This Canadian hamlet was buzzing with excitement just before the sun even broke as queues of cars and buses made their way from distant points—especially Calgary, almost ninety miles away—to Mount Norquay, whose snow-capped peak at 8,275 feet stands out vividly with Banff, three and a half miles away, just a speck in the south.

There was real holiday spirit. Indians, natives and foreign skiers mingled freely in making the trek up the mountain. Everything was in readiness, it seemed, except the fact that new snow had added to the difficulties of the mile-and-a-half course that drops away close to 2,500 feet.

For days, the tournament officials, headed by Harvey Clifford, have been packing, side-stepping and side-slipping the downhill trail that had a slight crust which, when broken out, led into several feet of sugary snow. This was the toughest problem facing the brilliant array of skiers, who knew all about the steep turns, the sharp falling away curves, the dangerous trees that bordered the course and the quick "schussees" that made control absolutely essential for safety.

It was the new snow, however, that brought concern. This was especially true for the Italian coach, Otto Menardi, technical adviser for the event, who insisted that the race be delayed forty-five minutes, that the course at the so-called "flats" be packed and that the best possible be done since the stand-out skiers were among the first twenty to take off from the top of the Alpine fields of the chairlift terminus. Since Italy's Colo had drawn No. 1, it was obvious that Menardi would be insistent upon having everything as well prepared as possible.

However, to be fair to the late starters, too, the course at the essential parts, where control flags had been placed to keep the athletes on a safe line down the wooded trail, was packed out after every tenth skier had finished. As things developed, the snow and course stood up unusually well.

Having drawn No. 1, Colo lived up to advance expectations. His was a smooth run, characterized by lots of judgment of pace, understanding the best line over the bumps, checking slightly when the steep and narrow turns demanded such action and riding low in his pronounced vorlage at the straightaways.

He finished under terrific power despite the long flat coming into the "apron" that marked the end.

The ovation that greeted the Italian, credited with more than 100 miles an hour on natural skis

three years ago in the flying kilometer lance in Plateau Arosa in the Italian Alps, echoed throughout the mountainside. For the favorite came through as expected with a performance that has marked his skiing in America, one of grace and élan, not the wild, reckless running as associated with his exhibitions in the past.

Today's course, typical of the ones skied in Eastern United States and Canada, was short, steep and falling away throughout its mile-and-a-half descent and lined with trees at the last two-thirds. The trail called for keen perception and understanding while running at breakneck speed. The bumps were of the short, "chattery" type. Yet, spills were unusually few and only three failed to finish with none hurt. France's Jean Pazzi, defending the "straight-down" crown, took a cropper at the "steilhang," broke his skis and finished under his own locomotion—walking the remainder of the course by foot.

*February 26, 1950*

# BUTTON AGAIN WINS IN FIGURE SKATING

### Takes U. S. Title Fifth Year in Row—Tenley Albright Is Junior Women's Victor

WASHINGTON, March 24 (AP)—Fabulous Dick Button proved tonight that he is still America's top figure skater.

The handsome Harvard sophomore completely overshadowed the field in the finals of the national figure skating championship to win the men's title for the fifth straight year.

The World and Olympic champion did not ring up a perfect 10 in performance as he did at the world title meet in London two weeks ago. But the 20-year-old Englewood, N. J., star did get 9.9 ratings from two judges. From the other three judges in the free-skating phase of the title chase he was

credited with 9.8, 9.6 and 9.7.

On the composition of material, Button received 9.9, 9.8, 9.7, 9.5 and 9.3.

The final point totals gave Button 1,621.8. The possible point total was 1,750.

Blond-haired, blue-eyed Tenley Albright of Boston capped a three-year battle to recover from polio by winning the women's national junior championship.

The 14-year-old Lassie was stricken by the disease in 1947. Her legs, one arm and back all were paralyzed. This came when she was working toward the Eastern junior title. Her doctor told her to try to continue to skate to overcome polio.

The game little girl did. Five months later she won the Eastern juvenile title and now has her heart set on ascending not only to the American crown but the world championship.

In the silver dance competition two local skaters, Carol Ann Peters and Dan Ryan of Washington, carried off with top honors.

In the men's National junior championship, the two top favorites, Dudley Richards of Boston and Washington's Donald Laws, were only two and a half points apart at the midway point.

Richards, runner-up in the National junior in 1947 and third in the same event last year, was credited with 643.9 points of a possible 800 at the end of the compulsory school figures.

Laws, a 20-year-old local skater and the capital's top entry in the Nationals, is close behind with 641.3.

In the men's and women's novice finals tomorrow afternoon, Ronald Robertson from Berkeley is favorite. Robertson, who finished second in the same division in 1949, is more than eleven points ahead of David Jenkins of Cleveland at the end of the school figures section. He has 374.6 to Jenkins' 363.0.

In the novice women's, Nancy Mineard of Akron, Ohio; Patricia Quick of Berkeley and little 10-year-old Carol Heiss of New York City are expected to battle it out for the title. Miss Mineard leads with 384.2. Miss Quick is second with 383.4 and Carol Heiss third with 360.7.

*March 25, 1960*

## *Miss Altwegg Gains World Title In Skating; Button Sets Record*

By The Associated Press.

MILAN, Feb. 24 — Miss Jeannette Altwegg of Britain captured the 1951 world figure-skating title for women tonight at Milan Ice Palace and Dick Button of Englewood, N. J., set an unofficial world mark for superiority in the compulsory competition.

The 20-year-old Miss Altwegg, European titleholder and four-time British champion, defeated twenty-two rivals from nine countries. Mlle Jacqueline du Bief, four-time French champion, was second and American titleholder Miss Sonya Klopfer of Brooklyn, N. Y., was third. Miss Suzanne Morrow, Canada's best, wound up fourth.

Miss Altwegg outscored the big

field after gaining a wide point advantage in yesterday's compulsory figure skating. Her 57-point margin was narrowed in tonight's free skating event by Miss Du Bief's fine performance.

Miss Barbara Wyatt of England placed fifth. Miss Tenley Albright of Boston was sixth, Miss Andra McLaughlin of Colorado Springs, Colo., seventh and Miss Margaret Ann Graham of Tulsa, Okla., eighth.

Rounding out the first ten were Miss Valda Osborn of England and Miss Gundi Busch of Western Germany.

The brown-eyed British winner

## THE NEW WORLD FIGURE SKATING CHAMPION

Miss Jeanette Altwegg of Britain, who triumphed yesterday at Milan. This picture was made when she won the European crown at Zurich three weeks ago.

Associated Press

thus took over the world title vacated by Czechoslovakian champion Aja Vrzanova, now a professional.

Miss Altwegg's title was the second to be decided in the current competition. Yesterday, Ria Baran and Paul Falk of Western Germany won the pairs crown by outscoring defending champions Karol and Peter Kennedy of Seattle by a narrow margin.

At the end of today's program for men, Button, the young Harvard student, had 730.7 points against 658.6 for Hallmut Seibt of Austria, the runner-up.

This is a margin of 72.1 points, the greatest known edge a title contender ever has taken into the final half of the program. Tomorrow each of the eleven contestants will skate the figures of his choice, but it is probable that Button could fall three times and still retain the world crown he won a year ago.

After Seibt came a trio of United States skaters. Third, and in a good position to take second, is James Grogan, 19-year-old Colorado Springs athlete with 651.8. Hayes Alan Jenkins of Akron, Ohio, is fourth with 635.6 and Dudley Richards of Boston fifth with 599.4.

Scores of the other contenders: Carlo Fassi of Italy, 591.2; Michael Carrington of England, 587.2; Don Laws of Washington, D. C., 573.4; William Lewis of Canada, 563.4; Freimut Stein of Western Germany, 518.0, and Ryusuke Arisaka of Japan, 513.1.

Immediately after completing his skating today, Button returned to his hotel. He is competing despite a severe respiratory ailment. The known biggest margin of superiority at the start of the final half was the 42 points Button had a year ago at this point.

February 25, 1951

## WOMEN'S CURLING DEFIES TRADITION

Special to THE NEW YORK TIMES.

MOUNT HOPE, N. Y., Jan. 15—The curling rink at the historic St. Andrews Golf Club presented an unfamiliar scene today.

The skip-calls of "sweep" and "up" echoed in high pitch. Absent were the deep masculine voices heard regularly in this cavern of curling.

The gaily attired, comely participants at this centuries-old Scottish sport belied the sign which hangs just inside the doorway, announcing to all who enter that "We're Brithers A'."

For the girls had taken over the ice at old St. Andrews. The first bonspiel for women curlers ever held in the metropolitan area was in progress.

It was strange to find St. Andrews succumbing to the feminine influence. The weather-darkened clubhouse, situated just above the rink, has been exclusively a "gentlemen's club since it was founded in 1888. Nevertheless, here were the women taking over, and playing at a sport reserved for men for generations.

This modernization—bordering on the heretic in the eyes of many of the more conservative addicts of the sport—lost none of its fascination because the players were of the fair sex.

### Clad in Gay Tartans

The distaff curlers were clad in gay, colorful tartans. They sported plaid shirts and skirts, wool suits and jackets of assorted hues. Their headpieces were, for the most part, regulation curling bonnets, Balmoral or Glengarie, with tassels of ribbon down the back. Some of the players, however, preferred a ski-type peaked cap. Most of them wore an array of the little curling buttons which each club gives to the rival players after a match.

Quite naturally, the players were skilled in the art of "sweeping," an essential factor in the sport. But the brooms have longer corn, and they are tied tighter than the ordinary kitchen variety. The finesse and accuracy with which the ladies delivered the forty-pound granite stones down 140 feet of smooth, fast ice won the applause of many a curling veteran.

The bonspiel, which will continue tomorrow, is an invitation meet. The teams are the host Westchester Wicks, the Nashua (N. H.) Country Club and the Utica (N. Y.) Curling Club. Westchester visited the other clubs a year ago. The Wicks, with four rinks participating, must refrain from using the club name St. Andrews during the play here "by courtesy." There are two Utica and two Nashua rinks. The victor will be the squad scoring most points, or stones, in six matches.

### Title Play Next Month

The caliber of play exhibited today presages excellent competition here on Feb. 5 through 7, when the first Northeastern district women's championship bonspiel is held.

There was one double winner. The Utica No. 1 quartet, skipped by Mrs. Edith Smith, defeated Nashua No. 1, guided by Mrs. Lucille Spaney, 10—5, and later halted Mrs. Dot Hahn and the No. 3 Wicks, 9—8. The other Utica entry, skipped by Mrs. Mary Clark, split even, although scoring 10 points in each match, so that Utica has a 39-stone total, one more than Nashua, with two matches remaining for each. Westchester has 28.

January 16, 1952

Teams from Utica and Westchester that competed on the ice at Mount Hope yesterday measuring their stones to find out which one scored.

The New York Times

# Mrs. Lawrence Takes Giant Slalom for U. S. to Start Sixth Winter Olympics

## FAST SKI RACE PUTS AMERICANS IN LEAD

Mrs. Lawrence's Victory and Miss Rodolph's Fifth Place Give 12 Points to U. S.

### GERMAN BOBLET IN FRONT

Benham-Martin Upstate Sled Is Runner-Up After 2 of 4 Heats in Oslo Olympics

**By GEORGE AXELSSON**
Special to THE NEW YORK TIMES.

OSLO, Feb. 14—The United States got off to a scintillating start in the sixth winter Olympics today when Mrs. Andrea Mead Lawrence of Rutland, Vt., won the women's giant slalom at Norefjell in supreme style, more than 2 seconds ahead of her nearest competitor.

Two American teams engaged in the two-man bobsled event at Frognersaeteren also gave good accounts of themselves. Team No. 1, with Stanley Benham of Lake Placid and Patrick Henry Martin of Massena, N. Y., was second to Germany after two heats and will start tomorrow's deciding runs with a possibility of capturing first place for America.

Mrs. Lawrence's slalom gold medal and the fifth place earned by Miss Katy Rodolph of Hayden, Colo., placed America at the top of the unofficial point score for the first day with 12 points to Austria's 8, Germany's 4 and Norway's 1.

### Soldiers Shovel Snow

The course of the women's giant slalom had been shortened because of a lack of snow on the lower half of the Norefjell course. It was barely two-thirds of a mile, and the drop accordingly was cut to 350 meters. However, snow-shoveling by detachments of the Norwegian Army pioneer units had put the course in fairly good condition.

No spills or accidents marred the race. Only one of the forty-five contestants, Sweden's Margareta Jacobson, did not finish the race, having run off the track en route.

Mrs. Lawrence was fourth to start, and her time of 2 minutes 6.8 seconds made her look like the probable winner. Not stopping to acknowledge the applause of royalty in the persons of Princess Ragnhild of Norway and Princess Josephine-Charlotte of Belgium at the finish line, 19-year-old Andrea rushed to her waiting husband, David, also a member of the United States ski team. Half a minute later her record-breaking time was computed and announced.

Austria's Fraeulein Dagmar

AT OPENING OF GAMES IN NORWAY YESTERDAY

Mrs. Andrea Mead Lawrence of Rutland, Vt., with her husband, David, after winning the women's giant slalom for the United States in the Winter Olympics.

Rom took second place, 2.2 seconds behind Andrea. Germany's Frau Anne Marie Buchner was third with 2 minutes 10 seconds flat and Austria's Gertrude Klecker fourth in 2:11.4.

### Miss Opton Fifteenth

Miss Rodolph was clocked in 2:11.7 and Norway's Borghild Niskin was sixth in 2:11.9. Miss Imogene Opton of North Conway, N. H., was fifteenth in 2:15.8 and Miss Jannette Burr of Seattle was twenty-first in 2:19.2.

In a 17-year-old bob appropriately named Cognac, a German saloon keeper, Andreas Ostler of Garmish-Partenkirchen, with a compatriot, Lorenz Nieberl, as his brakeman, lorded it all over the opposition from eight other countries. Germany's No. 2 bob, crewed by Theodor Kitt and Ludwig Kuhn, was only thirteenth of eighteen at the halfway point.

The two American crews were handicapped by the fact they had arrived so late they had little time to familiarize themselves with the Frognersaeteren course. Although designed for the occasion by Swiss specialists, the course is not ideal in construction from an American point of view.

Some remodeling of curves was required to meet complaints by competitors, but Benham and Martin, in America's No. 1 bob, set off in great style. They were timed in 1 minute 22.03 seconds for their

first run and 1:22.12 on their second, making a total for two runs of 2:24.15.

### Germans Have Good Lead

German No. 1 times were 1:20.76 and 1:21.64, placing this German team 1.75 seconds ahead of Benham and Martin, a lead that may prove impossible to overcome. The Swiss No. 2 and Swiss No. 1 were third and fourth, respectively, fractions of a second behind America.

The United States No. 2 bob, crewed by Fred J. Fortune Jr. of Lake Placid and Hank Whisher of Ausable Forks, N. Y., finished seventh with an aggregate time of 2:47.94. The average speed during

today's runs was around 42 miles per hour, with the maximum approaching eighty.

America has a decided disadvantage tomorrow in that the No. 1 bob must start first over a track "unproperly" plowed, which is likely to prove a factor, especially if snow falls during the night.

In the United States speed skating camp there was some gloom because of an epidemic of intestinal flu. Two men are convalescing and there is some doubt about their finding top form for Saturday's competition.

February 15, 1952

# Germans Win Olympic Two-Man Bobsled Race; Norwegian Annexes Slalom

## AMERICANS RETAIN OSLO GAMES LEAD

**Benham-Martin Place Second in Bob Run—Dodge Sixth in Ski Event in Norway**

**U. S. HALF-POINT AHEAD**

**Austria, Germany, Norway Next in Scoring—Our Hockey Team Registers 3-2 Victory**

**By GEORGE AXELSSON**
Special to THE NEW YORK TIMES.

OSLO, Feb. 15—The United States winter Olympic team held a half-point lead after the second round of competition today.

In the giant slalom race at Norefjell they got a sixth place and in the two-man bob run at Frognerseteren they finished second to the Germans. The American ice-hockey team just barely nosed out a Norwegian sextet.

Norway's Stein Eriksen won the slalom easily with almost two seconds to spare over the runner-up, Christian Pravda of Austria.

Eriksen's time was 2:25 against Pravda 2.26.9. The men's contest was run over a course with a descent of just under 2,400 feet in a mile and a half.

Joseph Brooks Dodge of the United States got sixth place in 2:32.6. Jack Reddish of the United States tied for twenty-fourth at 2:39.5 with Italy's Roberto Lacedelli; Jack Nagel was twenty-ninth in 2:42.

First to congratulate Eriksen was Katy Rodolph, the girl from Hayden, Colo., who finished fifth in yesterday's women's giant slalom. The 24-year-old Eriksen is no novice. He placed third in the last world championships at Aspen, Colo., and has won several Norwegian championships in slalom, downhill and combined, including that of Holmenkollen.

**David vs. Goliath**

There weren't many in the crowd of 9,000 fans who would have conceded Norway's red-jerseyed team even a fighting chance against the American Blues when the teams skated into Jordal Stadium for the Olympic ice-hockey tournament opener this afternoon.

But David took a lead over Goliath and four minutes from the end the score was tied. Then in a scrimmage before the Norwegian goal, Arnold Oss Jr. of the United States shot the deciding goal. Up to that moment it had been nip and tuck. Even so the match ended with heavy Norwegian pressure on the frantically gum-chewing United States goalie Donald Whiston.

Some of the spectators were overheard saying that the Americans played sloppily. This may be admitted but, on the other hand, they were playing against a determined Norwegian team that had nothing to lose and so surpassed itself. The Americans were faster but the Norwegians had superior strategy.

The United States pulled out of this tight squeeze through luck as much as through ability. Norway's Oivind Solheim opened the scoring after ten minutes in the first period. Oss equalized after one minute in the second period and in the fifteenth minute John Mulhern made it 2—1 for the United States. Norway tied the count in the fourth minute of the third period on a beautiful shot by Bjoern Gulbrandsen on a thrilling solo dash through the American defense. Then came Oss's deciding goal.

In other ice hockey matches today, Sweden defeated Finland, 9—2; Czechoslovakia beat Poland, 8—2, and Canada downed Germany, 15—1.

There was nothing the American bobsled team of Stan Benham and Pat Martin could do about Germany's Garmisch-Partenkirchen saloon-keeper Andreas Ostler, driving his 16-year-old bob, appropriately named Cognac, assisted by Lorenz Nieberl as brakeman. Not even in training had this pair strayed much from the 1-minute-21-second mark for the 1,500-meter course at Frognerseteren and this proved enough to assure victory.

The bobsled competition was delayed today on a protest from several of the European teams. They complained that the course was "all ice." When the race finally got under way, about an hour late, and after snow had been shoveled onto the course, Benham and Martin made the first run. This was a handicap, since it gave the "plowing job" to the Americans. Nevertheless, both Americans and Germans displayed remarkable skill and their times were close. In today's two descents the Germans were clocked in 1:21.07 and 1:21.12 while Benham and Martin made 1:21.21 and 1:21.12.

In the first day's two heats the German had built a lead of one and three-quarter seconds. Benham and Martin were well aware that it was a difficult handicap to overcome.

Today, the course was sprinkled with water and the surface was not to the liking of the lighter American crew. But they did not complain.

"We just couldn't beat them," they said.

The No. 1 Swiss team finished third, almost one second behind the Americans and less than two seconds ahead of the No. 2 Swiss sled. The No. 2 French team was fifth and the No. 1 Belgian sled, sixth.

*February 16, 1952*

## HENRY TAKES 500 IN SPEED SKATING AT OLYMPIC GAMES

**McDermott Finishes Second as U. S. Team Widens Lead —Hockey Six Triumphs**

**BECK FIFTH IN DOWNHILL**

**Ski Event Won by Colo, Italy —Misses Albright, Klopfer 2d, 3d in Figure Skating**

**By GEORGE AXELSSON**
Special to THE NEW YORK TIMES.

OSLO, Feb. 16—The Star-Spangled Banner was played in Bislett Stadium this afternoon in honor of Kenneth Henry of the United States who won the Olympic gold medal in the 500-meter speed-skating event.

It became a double triumph for America when Donald McDermott placed second, only seven tenths of a second behind Henry's time of 43.2 seconds, only a tenth of a second off the winter Olympic record set in 1948 at St. Moritz. His performance stands out the more because the ice had developed kinks in spots from an overnight sprinkling.

Elsewhere on the Olympic front the Americans were not so fortunate but on the whole the performances were good. The United States team widened its lead in the unofficial point score, with a total of 34½ to second-place Austria's 26.

In the first round of compulsory figure skating, Miss Tenley Albright of Newton, Mass., placed second to Britain's Jeanette Altwegg, while Miss Sonia Klopfer of Long Island City, N. Y., was third. In the downhill ski race at Norefjell, William Beck of the United States placed fifth. The winner was Zeno Colo of Italy. In the ice hockey tournament the American sextet kept its slate clean by defeating Germany, 8 to 2. It was not a great performance but it added two points to the over-all score.

In the 500-meter skating event Henry was drawn for the fourteenth heat with Canada's Craig Mackay. Henry went off like a bullet. Mackay kept up with him for about 100 yards. Then Henry parted company with the Canadian in a seemingly effortless but powerful glide. At the finish there was at least forty yards separating them. American officials who had clocked Henry rushed out on the rink to congratulate him.

**First by Tenth of Second**

McDermott was paired against Norway's Arne Johansen in the third heat. The Norwegian gave McDermott an exceedingly good race and for a moment it seemed that he would finish first. But the American managed to keep in front and finished a tenth of a second ahead.

John Werket of the United States had a bad day. He obviously was still suffering from the effects of stomach flu from which Henry also had suffered. Werket's time was 45.5.

In the ice hockey game against Germany the Americans did not have to work very hard. They didn't put on any real attack until the third period.

The Germans scored a goal each in the second and third periods. The Americans got one in the first, two in the second and five in the third.

Experts in the stands were agreed that the United States will have to produce better hockey against Switzerland on Monday, not to mention the Czechs, Swedes and Canadians. Norway, downed by the Americans, 3 to 2, yesterday, was routed today, 6—0, by the Czechs.

**Large Field in Skating**

OSLO, Feb. 16 (UP)—Only three of the five compulsory figures in women's figure skating were run off today with the remainder postponed until tomorrow because of the size of the field.

Zeno Colo, colorful lumberjack skier, gave Italy its first gold medal of the games with a daredevil run of 2 minutes 30.8 seconds in the mile-and-a-half men's downhill event, winning over a field of eighty-seven before a crowd of 10,000.

He skied in characteristic style, bowed forward with knees almost touching the tips of his skis.

Othmar Schneider of Austria was second at 2:32, Christian Pravda of Austria third with 2:32.4, Freddy Rubi of Switzerland fourth with 2:32.5, Beck fifth with 2:33.3 and Norway's giant slalom winner, Stein Eriksen, sixth at 2:33.8.

Beck was a squad replacement for James Griffith of Ketchum, Idaho, who was killed in a ski-training accident in Utah last December.

Other Americans found the going tougher. Dick Buek of Soda Springs, Calif., finished twelfth in 2:39.1, Jack Reddish of Salt Lake City tied for fourteenth in 2:41.5, and Brooks Dodge of Gorham, N. H., tied for thirty-second in 2:52.2.

**Gets Mark of Nine**

Miss Altwegg, who gave Britain the European as well as world figure-skating crowns, won the lowest placing in all three figures on the program today — forward inside counter, three change and three backward and the forward outside rocker—for a mark of nine.

But clearly the surprise of the early skating was Miss Albright, who skated into second place with twenty-six place marks ahead of other world favorites. Wearing leopard skin briefs, she flitted through her figures with the poise and skill of an international veteran and supplanted Jacqueline Dubief of Paris as the glamor girl of the competition.

Miss Klopfer, 17-year-old U. S. champion, compiled forty-one place points to snare third place in the standings from Miss Dubief, who was superior on points but higher in place marking with forty-nine.

Barbara Wyatt of Britain was fifth with 51.5 marks and Suzanne Morrow of Canada sixth with 54.5.

With twenty-four skaters entered from twelve nations, the compulsory phase of the event was broken into two days, with the remaining two Sunday. Then on Wednesday comes the final portion —five minutes of free skating for each contestant—after which the champion will be crowned.

Andrea Mead Lawrence of Rutland, Vt., who gave U. S. its first gold medal by winning the women's giant ski slalom on opening day, will bid for her second medal in the women's downhill event tomorrow.

Also scheduled are the 5,000 meter speed skating event in which Norway is likely to excel, and the jumping portion of the classic combined ski event, also an event in which Scandinavians are strong, as well as continued action in the round-robin hockey tournament.

The United States sextet scored its second straight victory today by downing Germany, 8 to 2.

February 17, 1952

# Austria Takes Lead in Winter Olympics at Oslo as U. S. Is Blanked for Day

## ANDREA LAWRENCE IN SKI NEAR-SPILL

### U. S. Star Finishes 17th in Downhill—Wegeman Hurt in Jumping — Henry Trails

### NORWEGIAN BREAKS MARK

### Andersen Skates the 5,000 in 8:10.6—Mrs. Beiser Paces Austria to Olympic Lead

**By GEORGE AXELSSON**
Special to The New York Times.

OSLO, Feb. 17—The traditional winter sports nations shared the spotlight in today's Olympic competitions. Especially did Norway shine. Three Norwegians topped the Holmenkollen ski-jumping list in the so-called combined event to be decided by a cross-country race later.

Norway also captured first and third places in the 5,000-meter speed-skating. Austria, Germany and Italy shared in the order named the medals awarded in the women's downhill ski race at Norefjell.

Aside from the Misses Tenley Albright and Sonya Klopfer, who finished second and third, respectively, in the first leg of the women's figure skating, that involving compulsory figures, America's colors did not show up front at all.

Austria moved to first place in the unofficial team standing with a total of 41 points. The United States is second with 34½, Norway third at 32 and Germany fourth with 19.

By far the most graceful event today was this figure skating event, in which Britain's Jeanette Altwegg easily maintained the points lead she had piled up yesterday. Now it all hinges on the fancy figure skating and in this department Miss Altwegg faces particularly stiff competition. But today this graceful British girl,

dressed in a little black skirt, black sweater and tiny black hat, had it all her own way over her twenty-four competitors from a dozen nations.

**A Flawless Performance**

Her execution of the maneuver of thrice superimposing twin circles, one on top of the other, most difficult of the world's sixty-nine recognized figures in the specialty, was so perfect that it seemed afterward as though she had cut the ice only once.

Nine times she had to turn in her tracks and each time she broke the surface so cleanly that the nine judges could hardly see where she had reversed.

Miss Albright strove valiantly to duplicate that performance but couldn't quite make it, though her performance was beautiful, too.

Jacqueline Du Bief, the attractive French girl who took fourth place, was actually in tears over having to suffer comparison with the Altwegg girl, who skated ahead of her. But Jacqueline and the German girl, Gundi Busch, now in tenth place, are likely to prove formidable in the fancy skating tomorrow.

**12,000 "Skate Him In"**

A display of enthusiasm reminiscent of the baseball world series greeted the performance in the 5,-000-meters speed-skating event of Norway's Hjalmar Andersen, who won this race "hands down."

The 24,000 Norwegian fans were on their feet throughout the eight-odd minutes of the race urging him to victory. Barring accident Andersen was considered a certain winner on past performance before the race started. This record-breaking long distance skater, who twice in a short time had lowered his own world record over the 5,000 meters, did not disappoint his public.

Paired with the Netherlands skater Van der Voort, with whom he parted company soon after the start, Andersen moved away swiftly with long, powerful strides. He had to go twelve and a half times around the 400-meter track.

Loudspeakers announced the times for each lap separately and for the 600 and 3,000-meter marks. In each case Andersen bettered the clockings of the old Olympic champion, Ivar Ballangrud, also a Norwegian. Shouting and cheering from the stands greeted each announcement. The whole stadium was in a turmoil. When the "cowbell" installed at the finish line for the occasion clanged to denote the last lap, everybody, or so it seemed, rose to "skate him in."

His time was 8 minutes 10.6 seconds, a new Olympic record but more than his own world record set at Trondheim of 8:07.6.

The United States competitors, notably Ken Henry, found the distance unsuitable. Ken and his three American team-mates finished in the ruck.

**Broeckman Is Second**

There was some excitement when it appeared that Norway's Sverre Haugli would beat the Netherlands' Kees Broeckman for second place, but he failed by eight-tenths of a second. Broeckman was clocked in 8:21.6 and Havgli in 8:22.4.

Associated Press Radiophoto

Hjalmar Andersen of Norway en route to victory in the Olympic 5,000-meter event at Oslo yesterday. His time was 8:10.6, nine seconds under the old mark.

An accident to one of America's young ski-jumpers marred the competition at the famous Holmenkollen, just up the hill from the capital. In his third jump, Alvin Wegeman lost control of his left ski after landing and as a result he turned over and skidded on his body. He was unconscious when picked up by an ambulance crew. Luckily he got away with only a minor concussion and will be in action again very soon.

Norway's Simon Slaattvik, Sverre Stenersen and Per Gjelten were the top men in this jumping phase of the "classic combined." In this contest each man is judged not only on the length of his jump but also on style. Thus it happened that Stenersen, who produced 69½ meters in distance which is only "good" at Holmenkollen, was moved down for having less beautiful style than Slaattvik, who jumped only 66½ meters.

But as already mentioned the jumping is only half the story. The other half on which points are also awarded, is the cross-country run in which the Finnish competitors excel, particularly Heikki Hasu, who carries many service stripes in the specialty. Today Hasu finished fifth, but he shouldn't have too much trouble in making up the points in the cross-country that he lost in the jumping.

Ted Farwell was best of the American team, placing thirteenth. Thomas M. Jacobs placed twenty-first and John Caldwell twenty-fifth.

There was a crowd of 45,000 watching the Holmenkollen event —half of them free of charge on adjacent hills. Three times as many are expected next Sunday for the free jumps.

The technical loudspeaker announcements here were punctuated by frantic appeals for a boy program vender to come forth and collect a hundred krone bill for which he had given change. Whether the person who had the hundred krone bill and the ninety-nine kroner change plus the program ever got together with the boy was not determined late tonight.

### Skids Into Soft Snow

OSLO, Feb. 17 (UP)—Mrs. Andrea Mead Lawrence, the 19-year-old Rutland, Vt., competitor who went hurtling after her second gold medal, lost her balance during the women's downhill ski race today when she made a daring jump and skidded into soft snow.

Trude Jochum Beiser of Austria, young mother of two, won the women's downhill ski race after Mrs. Lawrence almost fell.

Mrs. Lawrence, winner of the women's slalom championship last week and determined to become America's first double ski winner in winter Olympic history, might have made it but for the poor condition of the course—and her daring.

Normally, the downhill is a straight mile-and-a-half downward run. But today Olympic officials, after realizing how dangerous the ice-streaked course might be at top speed, erected twenty-eight gates through which the skiers had to pass. This was to control their speed.

Mrs. Lawrence was in no mood for controlled speed. Hurtling fearlessly down the slope, she took a great gamble at the twenty-third gate. To cut her time, she made a leap. Her momentum carried her through the gate at top speed and she skidded into a patch of soft snow. She teetered, fighting for her balance, and barely managed to stay up. That cost her precious seconds and she finished in 1:55.3 —a chagrined seventeenth in the race.

Miss Betty Weir of Omaha, Neb., the only American not to suffer some similar mishap in the race, was nineteenth in 1:55.7; Miss Katy Rodolph of Hayden, Colo., was twenty-third in 1:57.4, and Miss Janette Burr of Seattle was twenty-sixth in 1:59.1.

Annemarie Buchner of Germany was second to the victorious Mrs. Jochum Beiser, Guiliana Minuzzo of Italy third, Erika Mahringer of Austria fourth, Dagmar Rom of Austria fifth and Madeleine Berthod of Switzerland sixth.

February 18, 1952

# Three First Places Lift Norway Into Winter Olympics Lead

## U. S. SQUAD BLANKED SECOND DAY IN ROW

Falls to 3d Place as Norway Rolls Up 74-Point Total— Austria, 2d, Shut Out

### ANDERSEN SKATING VICTOR

First to Gain Olympic Double— Slaattvik and Brenden Set Pace in Skiing Events

#### By GEORGE AXELSSON
Special to The New York Times.

OSLO, Feb. 18— Norway swept the boards in the Olympic events contested today, taking all three first-place Gold Medals, one for the 18-kilometer cross-country ski race, one for the best of the participants who had also scored in yesterday's ski-jumping at Holmenkollen, and another for the 1,500-meter speed skating competition.

This string of victories, two of them complete surprises, gave the Norwegian team a comfortable lead over all the other nations in points scored thus far. The American team was blanked for the second day in a row. Norway now has 74 points, to 41 for Austria and 31½ for America.

The only Norwegian success ever in doubt was, oddly enough, one that was generally discounted beforehand, the speed skating. The Norwegian star, Hjalmar Andersen, who had won the 5,000 meters yesterday, was considered a certain winner of the 1,500 before the race started, indeed it was heresy in Norwegian circles to have a contrary opinion.

The race itself was to justify the heretics—almost. The draw favored Andersen, when he was named for the first of the twenty heats. He began in beautiful style, covering the first 300 meters in 28½ seconds—half a second below the corresponding mark of the Olympic record for the distance set by Norwegian Sverre Farstad. But then he began to sag for some unexplained reason and at the 700-meter mark he was half a second behind Farstad's time, at 1,100 meters he was one and a half seconds behind and he turned in an exceedingly slow last lap to finish at 2:20.4, which is 2.8 slower than Farstad's mark.

With the United States' Johnny Werket and other strong competi-

Associated Press Radiophoto

Halgeir Brenden of Norway winning the 18-kilometer cross-country race of the Sixth Winter Olympic Games at Oslo yesterday. His time was 1:01:34.

tors to follow, notably Vim Van der Voort of Holland. Andersen's time seemed easy to beat. But luck favored him.

Werket muffed his start, losing valuable seconds, and could do no better than 2:24.3, while Van der Voort, who got off well and ran a wonderfully planned race, lost more time than he had estimated on a "breather" just before the last lap, and his magnificent sprint could not repair the damage; he finished in 2:20.6.

Then luck with a capital L took over. Just after Van der Voort's race, a heavy snowfall began and there was not the slightest chance, except for a superman, to beat Andersen.

dersen's time. The snow slowed every performance thereafter, but several men turned in times close to Andersen's.

Norway's Raald Aas got 2:21.6 and the bronze medal for third place. Sweden's Carl Eric Asplund at 2:22.6 placed fourth. Werket placed twelfth with 2:24.3, Ken Henry of the United States seventeenth at 2:25, Pat McNamara eighteenth, 2:25.5 and Donald McDermott twenty-eighth, 2:28.1.

**Prophets All Wrong**

In the cross-country ski race, the "experts" had it all worked out as an affair between the Swedes and Finns—with the Swedes decided

favorites for the "straight event" and Finland's Heikki Hasu the choice in the so-called combined because of the points he had scored in yesterday's jumping and his speed on the flat. The prophets proved radically wrong. The Norwegian youngster Halgeir Brenden won the straight event easily in 1:01.34, and his countryman, Simon Slaattvik the "combined" race. The latter placed fifteenth in the general classification, but the points lead he obtained by his brilliant jumping sufficed to put him up top in the "combined" ahead of Hasu, who got fourth place in the straight race only fifty seconds behind the winner. The favorite for

the cross-country, Sweden's Nils Karlsson, could do no better than fifth.

Scenes of joy unequaled here since the end of the occupation in May, 1945, greeted the news of Norway's victories. Many quit work in droves and stepped out in the streets to shout their joy and slap each other's backs.

At the Hotel Viking, where the international press is quartered, more than half of the waiters walked out. It took more than an hour to order food and another two hours to get it.

February 19, 1952

# Andersen of Norway Sets Olympic Mark With Third Skating Victory in 3 Days

## BUTTON'S BIG LEAD RAISES U. S. HOPES

### He Paces Figure Skating as American Team Stays 3d at Oslo With 34½ Points

### NORWAY IN FRONT WITH 94

### Andersen Sets World, Olympic Marks in 10,000-Meter Test —Austrian Wins Slalom

**By GEORGE AXELSSON**
Special to The New York Times.

OSLO, Feb. 19—Norway's drive on the winter Olympic awards continued successfully today. The harvest was one first-prize gold medal for the 10,000-meter speed skating and second-place silver and third-place bronze medals in the men's slalom, which was won by an Austrian.

The United States men's figure-skating team turned in a fine performance. Dick Button captured top place easily in the compulsory figures phase and his team-mates James Grogan and Hayes Jenkins ranked third and fifth, respectively. Button has virtually clinched first place, with the free-style phase to be skated Thursday.

The United States team remained in third place in the Olympic standings with 34½ points as Norway continued to lead the unofficial team scoring with 94. Austria was second with 51.

**Dutch Skater Second**

The Norwegians had another chance to cheer themselves hoarse over their skating idol, Hjalmar Andersen, who took the 10,000-meter ice race in the world and Olympic record time of 16 minutes 45.8 seconds. Andersen thus became the first athlete ever to score three

Associated Press Radiophotos
**Hjalmar Andersen of Norway raising his hands to acknowledge cheers from the crowd after he won the 10,000-meter ice skating race.**

Winter Olympic victories on consecutive days. He previously won the 1,500 and 5,000-meter races. The runner-up today was Kees Broekman of the Netherlands, in 17:01.6. A Swede, Carl-Erik Asplund, captured third place in 17:66 for the first medal won by the highly regarded Swedish team in six days of Olympic competition.

Figure skating is not much of an attraction in Norway since Sonja Henie turned professional, so only a few hundred spectators attended the competition, and most of those

were relatives and friends of the participants.

Figure skaters from nine nations competed, including a 12-year-old French boy named Alain Giletti, who was so light on his skates the nine judges almost needed magnifying glasses to trace his impressions on the ice. He placed seventh.

**Position Seems Secure**

The rink just outside Jordal Stadium was perfect. Button went through all five figures in supreme fashion, piling up 111.1 points. An Austrian, Hellmut Seibt, was next

with 106.4. Then came Grogan, with 103; Canada's Peter Firstbrook, with 99, and Jenkins with 97.5. Since these points count two-thirds as against one-third for free-style performances, Button's position would seem secure.

Brooks Dodge of the United States gave an excellent account of himself at Roedkleiva. Pitted against the world's top slalom artists, he turned in a remarkable performance to place ninth. His total time for the two descents was 2:04.7, about four seconds behind the Austrian winner, Othmar Schneider.

Jack Reddish finished eighteenth for the United States with 2:09.0, and Darrell Robinson, 2:10.2, was twenty-second among the ninety competitors.

Arnold Lunn, British referee and foreman of the jury, protested violently but in vain against the excursion of two-thirds of the slalom competitors from having a second chance. He held up proceedings for nearly a half hour registering his protest. Only the thirty best got two chances.

There was more trouble in connection with this slalom event. The Italians protested against the last "gate," which had been placed at such a difficult angle that most of the racers fell or stumbled at that flag. The gate was removed for the second try.

More persons had bought or received tickets today than could be conveniently taken care of in the stands and the result was an indescribable crush, producing many accidents.

February 20, 1952

# *Mrs. Lawrence First American Ever to Win Twice in a Winter Olympic Meet*

## RUTLAND GIRL FIRST DESPITE SKI SPILL

### Mrs. Lawrence Takes Slalom With a Stirring Comeback After Olympic Fall

### U. S. SECOND IN STANDING

### Norway Holds Lead at Oslo— Miss Altwegg of England Wins Figure Skating

OSLO, Feb. 20 (AP)—America's 19-year-old ski queen, Mrs. Andrea Mead Lawrence, picked herself out of the snow after a jarring tumble in the Olympic slalom today and staged a remarkable comeback to win her second gold medal of the winter games.

The victory, believed impossible after the daring Rutland, Vt., housewife skidded and fell on the first of two runs down Rodkleiva's hazardous slope was the climax of the best showing in history for a United States ski team in the Olympics.

The slender New Englander became the first American skier, man or woman, to win two winter Olympic titles in one meet and she established herself as the world's greatest in her specialty.

The triumph broke a three-day scoring famine for the Americans and the United States picked up other precious points in the women's figure skating, won by England's world champion, Miss Jeanette Altwegg.

**Austria Drops to Third**

The American team, with a total of 56½ points, moved into second place in the unofficial team standing as Austria dropped to third with 51. Norway continued to lead the way with 101 after fifteen of the twenty-one events.

Miss Tenley Albright, 16-year-old schoolgirl from Newton Center, Mass., took second place behind the 22-year-old Miss Altwegg with a dazzling performance in today's free figure phase.

The United States and North American champion, Miss Sonya Klopfer of Long Island City, N. Y., fell and finished fourth as Miss Virginia Baxter of Detroit placed fifth.

The only other championship of the day went to Finland, its first, when Veikko Hakulinen, a young woodcutter, won the gruelling 50-kilometer (31 miles 120 yards) ski race in 8 hours 33 minutes 33 seconds.

But these developments were

Andrea Mead Lawrence was the first American skier to win two gold medals at one Olympics. She took the slalom and giant slalom in 1952.

overshadowed by Mrs. Lawrence's spill and her bold rally that won her the two-heat slalom championship in 2 minutes 10.6 seconds. The American girl won the giant slalom last Thursday. On Sunday two bad falls probably cost her the downhill championship.

Racing down the 508-yard slope today at blinding speed, Mrs. Lawrence tried to make a difficult right turn at one of the forty-nine control gates near the top of the hill. She skidded and went spinning into the soft snow while the crowd of 15,000 lining the hillside groaned.

**Fourth After First Run**

The United States star quickly got up and continued the run with a wild recklessness that brought cheers from the spectators. She finished in a creditable 1 minute 7.2 seconds, good for fourth place at the halfway mark, 1.2 seconds behind the leader, Fraulein Ossi Reichart of Germany.

But Mrs. Lawrence came back to the summit with grim determination. She again swept down the steep slope. Flawlessly, she wove in and out of the turns and then skied into the arms of her

husband, David, a member of the men's ski team. She was timed in 1:03.4. Others in the field of forty-two from fourteen countries, representing the best women skiers in the world, failed to match the pace.

"I knew I had to do it so I just cut loose," said the young housewife from Vermont, who was an Olympic performer at 15.

"I was scared stiff with Andy in front of me," said Fraulein Reichert, starting her last run. The German girl finished second with runs of 1:06 and 1:05.4 for a total of 2:11.4, followed by Mrs. Anne Marie Buchner Fischer of Germany, in 2:13.3; Signorina Celina Seghi of Italy in 2:13.8, and Miss Imogene Opton, 19-year-old student from North Conway, N. H., with 2:14.1. The surprising Miss Opton had runs of 7:07.4 and 1:06.7.

America's two other ski representatives, Miss Jannette Burr of Seattle and Miss Katy Rodolph of Hayden, Col., suffered spills and finished out of the running. Miss Burr was fifteenth in 2:20.5, and Miss Rodolph was twenty-first in 2:24.

America's skiers, badly beaten in the 18-kilometer race Monday, decided to withdraw from the 50-kilometer test to save their strength for Saturday's 40-kilometer relay. Team members are John Caldwell, Putney, Vt.; John Burton, Wayzata, Minn.; George Hovland Jr., Duluth, Minn., and Wendell Broomhall, Rumford, Me.

Hakulinen wearily slogged home 4 minutes 38 seconds ahead of his countryman, Eeron Kolehmainen. Two Norwegians, Olav Oekern, with 3:38.45, and Kalevi Mononen, with 3:39.21, were third and fourth.

Mrs. Lawrence's fall came about a third of the way down the hill at a wide turn where the descent is not particularly steep. She was going too fast and her skis slid sidewise. She landed on her hip but pushed herself up quickly with her hands and was off again.

Falls bothered many in the field but most of them came at a "coffin corner" near the stands. It was here that Dagmar Rom, the Austrian favorite, saw her hopes ruined on the first run. This treacherous curve also threw Misses Burr and Rodolph.

...

# Button Keeps Olympic Figure-Skating Title, With U. S. Also Third and Fourth

## ENGLEWOOD YOUTH DEFEATS AUSTRIAN

### Button's Daring Skating Beats Seibt With Ease—Grogan Is Third and Jenkins Fourth

### GERMAN 4-MAN BOB LEADS

### Benham's American Sled Next After Two Heats—Sweden Halts U. S. at Hockey

By GEORGE AXELSSON
Special to The New York Times.

OSLO, Feb. 21—Dick Button of Englewood, N. J., won a fourth gold medal for the United States, as generally expected, in the men's figure skating decided tonight at Bislett Stadium, but otherwise this eighth day of the sixth winter Olympics was not favorable for America.

The ice hockey team dropped back in the round-robin tournament, losing two valuable points to Sweden, and after the first two of the four heats in the four-man bob event down the Frognerseteren course, the "meat trust," as the American sled No. 1 affectionately is nicknamed because of its aggregate weight, was second to the German No. 1 driver who had downed them in the boblet event.

Sudden springlike weather, raising the mercury above 60 degrees Fahrenheit at noon, was a source of worry to officials and competitors. The thaw rendered the bob-sledding course, which faces due south, soft on top, so the third heat will have to be staged one hour earlier than originally scheduled tomorrow morning before the ice starts melting.

### French Youth Applauded

Button's figure-skating victory had been forecast by his magnificent showing in the compulsory figures earlier in the week, so only a small crowd showed up to watch him and thirteen other contestants from eleven nations compete for the Olympic title. As in yesterday's free skating for women, the bulk of the applause went not to the winner, but to a representative from France.

In this case it was diminutive Alain Giletti, the 12-year-old boy who skates like a true champion and can show most of the adults among the world's elite a trick or two, as he did today.

Placings after the compulsory figures were unchanged by today's performances. Austria's Hellmut Seibt was second, with an American, James David Grogan of Colo-

rado Springs, taking third place. A third member of the United States figure-skating team, Hayes Alan Jenkins of Akron, added three points to America's over-all point score by taking fourth place.

The four-man bob situation after the first two heats is analogous to what it was at the same stage in the boblet category. The German No. 1 sled is leading America's No. 1 by a fraction of one second, but a smaller fraction than in the boblet.

### Swiss Third and Fourth

The combined times for the morning's two runs were for Germany 2 minutes 34.43 seconds and for the United States 2:35.22. Switzerland's No. 1 was third with 2:36.75 and the Swiss No. 2 fourth with 2:37.20. The American bob was driven by Stanley D. Benham of Lake Placid, N. Y., who was accompanied by Patrick H. Martin of Massena, N. Y.; Howard W. Crossett of Bradford, N. H., and James N. Atkinson of Hamilton, N. Y.

The United States No. 2 bob, driven by James J. Bickford of Saranac Lake, N. Y., and manned by Hubert G. Miller of Saranac Lake, Maurice R. Severino of Saratoga Springs, N. Y., and Joe Scott of Ausable Forks, N. Y., had an unlucky day. In the first heat, a stirrup on the left front broke on the first curve. Bickford had difficulty in holding the sled on the track.

The stirrup was welded during the intermission, but broke again on the first curve in the second heat. In spite of that, Bickford was ninth among fifteen sleds with a two-heat time of 2:39.10.

The Germans, with Andreas Ostler driving, lopped valuable fractions of a second from their running time with perfect starts and expert taking of curves.

### Canadians Stay Unbeaten

In the ice hockey tournament, Canada and Sweden continued undefeated and were tied for first place, each with five victories in as many games. Canada trounced Switzerland, 11 to 2, in a dull game that looked more like an exhibition than an Olympic contest.

Then the American team, which had won its first four games, skated out o nthe Jordal rink a decided favorite over the Swedes, but Sweden won, 4 to 2. The game hadn't been in progress many minutes before it was plain where the victory was headed.

The American boys seemed to have mislaid their passing somewhere and hence became easy prey to a Swedish defense which easily broke up most attacks. The Swedes scored their first goal — by Hans Oeberg — after 12 minutes of the first period.

While the match at no point got rough, the usual minor incidents occurred. In the first period, Sweden's Goesta Johansson and the United States' John Noah clashed and went to the penalty box for two minutes each for high sticking.

The second period was scoreless. Play was swift and the puck trav-

eled back and forth, but mostly in United States territory. The Swedes made a goal in the seventh minute which was disallowed because a Swedish player was inside America's cage when the puck was netted. America's Gerald Kilmartin drew a 2-minute penalty for holding.

The United States team opened the third period in rapid fashion in a bid to tie the score, but Joseph Czarnota drew two minutes in the box for elbowing. Czarnota, whom the capacity crowd hadn't forgotten for his rough play in the match against the Swiss Tuesday, was booed.

The American team generally drew little applause with the stands full of Swedes rooting for their team and the few Americans among the spectators hopelessly drowned out. Despite the fury of the American attack, the Swedes opened the scoring in the last period, making it 2—0 as Goesta Johansson placed a beautiful shot right behind Donald Whiston.

Eight minutes later, Johansson again drove the puck into America's cage, but in another minute the Americans scored their first goal, Ken Yackel picking up Robert Rompre's pass and neatly evading the defense. With Aake Andersson off for hooking, the Americans were quick to take advantage of a weakened defense as Clifford Harrison quickly added the record goal, but Sweden retaliated in the twelfth minute.

Jeannette Altwegg, British brunette who won the Olympic figure-skating title last night, said she was retiring from competition and would not defend her world title in Paris next week. Jeannette does not plan to turn professional, as her predecessors, Canada's Barbara Ann Scott and Norway's Sonja Henie, did.

Miss Altwegg, from Streatham, began skating at the age of 6. She celebrated her victory by having chocolate ice cream, her favorite dish.

### Button Captivates Judges

OSLO, Feb. 21 (UP)—Dick Button, America's incomparable figure skater, retained his Olympic championship tonight with one of the most glittering performances of his career.

Despite one stumble during a difficult spin, the handsome, 21-year-old Harvard senior from Englewood, N. J., captivated the stern judges with the daring of his free-skating routine.

Placed first by all nine judges, Button earned fourth United States gold medal of the games. With a total of 17 points picked up by the figure skaters, the Americans had a firm grip on second place in the unofficial team standings with 73½ points. Norway leads with 101, Austria is third with 56, Finland fourth at 41 and Germany fifth with 28.

Button was happy but not satisfied. His near fall piqued him.

"The ice is never bad," he said. "It's my own fault. Don't blame it on anything else."

But his veteran trainer, Gus Lussi, did blame the fumble on cracked ice as Button was executing one of the most difficult maneuvers on skates—three consecutive double axels.

Clad in a specially tailored white mess jacket and black trousers, Button skated with confidence to a recording of the "Rumanian Rhapsody" by Enesco.

Mrs. Andrea Mead Lawrence, who captured the women's slalom title on Wednesday at Oslo after having taken the giant slalom on Feb. 14, was not the first American ever to win twice in the same Winter Olympic Games, as was reported in The New York Times yesterday. She was, however, the first woman to do so.

Doubles in speed skating were scored by both Irving Jaffee and Jack Shea in 1932. Jaffee prevailed in the 5,000 and 10,000 meter tests, while Shea won in the 500 and 1,500 meter events.

February 22, 1952

# Germans Take Four-Man Bobsled and Pairs Figure Skating at Winter Games

## AMERICANS SECOND IN 2 OLYMPIC TESTS

### Benham's Crew Runner-Up as Germans Complete Sweep of the Bobsled Events

### OSTLER IS WINNING PILOT

### Falks Beat Kennedy Pair In Skating—U. S. Is Now 16½ Points Behind Norway

**By GEORGE AXELSSON**
Special to THE NEW YORK TIMES.

OSLO, Feb. 22—West Germany won both of the Olympic events that were decided today, the four-man bobsled and pairs figure skating. At Bislett Stadium this evening the West German anthem hence was played twice, and 20,000 Norwegians in the stands cheered the German winners sportingly as they mounted the platform to receive their gold medals.

Americans were runners-up in both events. The United States bobsled team No. 1 beat the Swiss No. 1 team in the final heats, run off on Frognersetern Hill today, and in the skating competition Karol Kennedy and Peter Kennedy gave the German pair of Ria and Paul Falk what seemed a close race for the title—actually the American couple gathered 11.178 points to the Germans' 11.400.

Marianna and Lazlo Nagy of Hungary placed third with 10.828 points for the first medal any Iron Curtain country has captured in these Winter Games. The United States' second fancy-skating pair, Miss Janet Gerhauser and John Nightingale, added one point to America's score in the over-all count by placing sixth with 10.289.

**Snowfall Aids Victors**

The American bobsled team, captained by Stan Benham, had bad luck indeed in placing second. After yesterday's two heats, Benham's crew trailed Germany's No. 1 sled by a fraction of a second. In the third heat today, the Americans lost another fraction to the Germans, a handicap that was not insurmountable.

But the luck of the draw was such that the United States bob had to start after the Germans. No sooner had the Germans, captained by Andreas Ostler, completed their run than snow began falling. This meant a handicap of entire seconds to the unlucky competitors who had yet to run their heat. So while Benham's team ran its first heat today in 1 minute 16.72 seconds, the final heat required 1:18.54.

The Americans were lucky to take second place, because the Swiss No. 1 team was almost a second faster on its final heat. But the Swiss were behind so much on their first-leg run yesterday that in the final score they finished a minute behind the United States No. 1 team.

An additional factor in the German victory was weight. The Reich team totaled some 1,050 pounds against the Americans' 915 pounds. Weight being the factor it is in the bobsled sport, the International Bobsled Association meeting here has just ruled that henceforth the aggregate weight for two-man bob teams must not exceed 440 pounds and for four-man teams 880.

After the Kennedys, who were drawn as No. 2 in tonight's competition, had skated well in their five minutes on the Bislett ice, it looked as if there were a chance for an American gold medal. But the Falk couple brought such hopes to an end.

Their turn was perhaps not so spectacular nor so varied as that of the Kennedys but their smoothness, elegance and precision were such that the nine judges gave them the gold medal.

**Canadian Six Wins**

The Canadian ice hockey team defeated Sweden, 3—2, to remain unbeaten and the United States six turned back Poland, 5—2.

The United States raised its point total to 84½ but trailed Norway, leader in the unofficial team standing, by 16½ tallies. Third-place Austria has 58.

Only three events, plus ice hockey, are still to be decided. These three are ski jumping, the 10-kilometer cross-country ski race for women and the 40-kilometer relay cross-country ski race. In none of the ski events can the American team reasonably hope to win medals. Therefore the United States' point tally probably will not rise much higher than it is today.

The competition will end Sunday with the Holmenkollen ski jump and the last four matches of the hockey tournament, among which the United States vs. Canada engagement stands out.

**Sets Bobsled Record**

OSLO, Feb. 22 (UP)—Winter sports stars from Germany, competing for the first time since World War II, won two gold medals in the Olympic Games today. Andreas Ostler completed a sweep of bobsled events and a sparkling duo won the pairs figure skating crown.

Ostler, 32-year-old innkeeper who won the two-man bob title last Friday, piloted his four-man crew through the slushy chutes in record time at Frognerseteren and lifted the Olympic championship from the United States with a

Associated Press Radiophoto

Andreas Ostler piloting his German four-man sled to win the gold medal at yesterday's Olympic competition at Frognerseteren. The American team finished second. The Germans, right to left, are Ostler, Fritz Kuhn, Laurenz Nieberl and Franz Kemser.

crew assembled only a few days befor the competition began.

Under the lights tonight before 20,000 fans at Bislett Stadium, Ria and Paul Falk of Germany danced on skates to victory in the pairs figures. Karol and Peter Kennedy, sister-brother team from Seattle, were superb in a more difficult routine and finished a close second.

Ostler piloted his four-man team down the 1,500 meters (120 yards less than a mile) to a new track record on one heat and defeated the top United States sled driven by Stan Benham of Lake Placid, N. Y., by 2.64 seconds in total time for four heats. Two heats were run yesterday and the Germans held a .79-second lead going into today's final two heats.

**Track Record on Third Run**

Ostler, with Laurenz Nieberl and Fritz Kuhn riding and Franz Kemser at the brake, compiled a total time of 5 minutes 07.84 seconds for four runs, including a track record of 1:16.55 on the third heat. The 38-year-old Benham captured second with 5:10.48. Swiss teams were third and fourth, Austria fifth and Sweden sixth.

Big Jim Bickford of Saranac Lake, N. Y., who raced in poor luck yesterday when his foot stirrups broke on each run, finished in ninth place among fifteen entries in 5:19.68. He raced without mishap today.

Ostler's double victory in the two and four-man bobs was the second in Olympic history and the first since American teams accomplished the feat on their home course at Lake Placid, N. Y., twenty years ago.

It was all the more remarkable because Coach Karl Braun, in a daring move to put Germany's best men on one sled, had demoted two members of the original crack crew and replaced them with a pair from Germany's No. 2 sled. The No. 2 sled then was dropped from competition.

Riding with Benham were Pat Martin of Massena, N. Y., Howard Crossett of Bradford, N. H., and Jim Atkinson of Hamilton, N. Y.

The veteran driver hurtled down the course in 1:16.72 on the third heat, the first run today, with a drive that brought gasps and cheers from the crowd. But Ostler roared down in 1:16.55, a new track record, hardly believable because of the slush and bumps.

# FINLAND'S SKIERS SWEEP 2 RACES IN OLYMPIC GAMES

## Capture First Three Places in Women's Cross-Country— Men Triumph in Relay

By The United Press.

OSLO, Feb. 23—Little Finland's durable distance skiers won everything in sight in the sixth Winter Olympic Games program today, but Norway virtually clinched the team championship with only two more events remaining tomorrow.

Undefeated Canada clinched the hockey championship for all practical purposes with an 11-2 conquest of Norway. The once-beaten United States downed Czechoslovakia, 6—3, and plays the Canadians in the final game tomorrow. Even in the case of a tie, goal totals will decide the championship and Canada is way in front with 68 to 48 for once-beaten Sweden, which topped Switzerland, 5—2, today.

The hardy Finns, both men and women, dominated the next-to-last day of the 1952 games by racing off with the gruelling 40-kilometer (24 miles) cross-country men's relay and scoring a grand slam of all three medals in the women's 10-kilometer (six miles) cross-country race run as an Olympic event for the first time.

### Cheers for Americans

A plucky United States men's relay team, cheered mightily for its courage and Olympic spirit although hopelessly outclassed, finished last among the twelve nation's that completed the exhausting test. Even Finland's first three women skiers, headed by blond Lydia Videman, toured the identical distance on the same course in faster times than any of the four Americans on the relay team.

Finland picked up 31 points, zooming from fifth to third place with a total of 72, but American forces still held a tight grip on second place with 84½. Norway added six more points for the lead at 107 and only a complete disaster tomorrow could prevent it from winning the team title.

Norwegian special ski jumpers are prohibitive favorites to dominate that colorful event at Holmenkollen. The Americans, however, still can gain scattered points in hockey and in the jump in which Art Tokle of Brooklyn is a threat. They were almost certain to hold second place when the competition ends.

The Finns were magnificent today in their specialty, sweeping every medal they possibly could.

Before 60,000 fans, many of them on skis at vantage points along the course, Finland's relay team of Heikki Hasu, Paavo Lonkila, Urpo Korhonen and Tapio Maekaele led every step of the 40 kilometers for a victory by two minutes and fifty-five seconds over Norway. Sweden was third, France fourth, Austria fifth and Italy sixth.

### Hovland on U. S. Team

The Finns whipped over the course in 2 hours 20 minutes 16 seconds, more than a half hour ahead of the American team of George Hovland, Duluth, Minn.; John Burton of Wayzata, Minn.; Ted Farwell of Montague City, Mass., and Wendall Broomhall of Rumford, Me.

The only American consolation was the fact that Bulgaria's anchor man broke a ski and couldn't finish, thus placing the United States twelfth instead of thirteenth.

But the Scandinavians paid the courageous Yanks a tremendous compliment—those few who remained to see anchor-man Broomhall cross the finish line as he had vowed to do "if it takes me all night.'

A half-dozen fans lifted Broomhall in their arms and three times tossed him high into the air, a Nordic tribute normally reserved for winners.

"It was a great race at that," Broomhall said with a smile. "I got a great kick out of it."

Miss Videman, comely laboratory assistant, won the women's ten-kilometer test, which Finland had tried for years to get onto the Olympic program despite pleas from some other nations that it was "unladylike."

She toured the six miles in 41 minutes 40 seconds, with Mirja Hietamies of Finland second in 42:39, Siiri Rantenen of Finland third in 42:50, Marta Nordberg of Sweden fourth at 42:53, then Sirkka Polkunen of Finland at 43:07 and Rakel Wahl of Norway in 44:54. No American women were entered.

The first four finishers topped the best time by American men in the relay race. Hovland, American lead-off man, had an upset stomach at the start, lost four minutes in the first mile and struggled home almost exhausted on snow-caked skis in 44:01. Burton made 43:23 on the second leg. Farwell 43:06 on the third and Broomhall had the best American time of 42:58 as anchor man.

### Skis Become Caked

Hovland said he used the wrong ski wax and his skis became so heavily caked with snow he barely could drag them, finishing the leg virtually on courage alone.

Hasu, lead-off man for Finland, outsprinted the dozen others through the first 200 yards to the main track with the pack at his heels as they disappeared into the forest. He emerged again a full minute in the lead with a time of 35 minutes 1 second.

Lonkila took over with a run of 35:22 and completed his leg two and one half minutes ahead of Sweden and Norway, which were neck and neck for second place. Norway's great Martin Stokken then took over second place on the third leg but scarcely closed the gap on Finland's Korhonen, who was clocked in 35:47.

Maekaele, skiing the anchor leg, compiled the fastest time of the four Finns in 34:06 and won the event easily.

February 24, 1952

# *Norway Wins Sixth Winter Olympic Games, With United States Next, at Oslo*

## 120,000 FANS WATCH BERGMANN TRIUMPH

### By GEORGE AXELSSON
Special to THE NEW YORK TIMES.

OSLO, Feb. 24—The major competition of the Winter Games of the Sixth Olympic ended today in a brilliant victory for Norway. The host country's ski jumping team captured the first two places at Holmenkollen and was wildly applauded by a record crowd, variously estimated between 120,000 and 140,000 spectators head-ed by King Haakon, his family and Swedish and Belgian royalty. The victory gave the Norsemen the title with 125 ½ points.

The "blue ribbon" event of the games, in the eyes of the public, was conceded beforehand to the Nordic athletes, who specialize in this breakneck sport. An intrepid Norwegian "flyer," Arnfinn Bergmann, seconded by a compatriot, Thorbjoern Falkanger, proved the experts right in placing first and second with 226 and 221.5 points, respectively.

Sweden's Karl Holmstroem secured third place with 219.5 points and German Toni Brutscher tied for fourth place with Halvor Naes of Norway. Arne Hoel, also of Norway, was sixth.

The best Finn, Antti Hyvaerinen, was seventh and Pentti Uotinen of Finland shared the eighth place with Sepp Weiler of Germany.

### Undaunted by Accident

The four Americans in the competition made an honorable showing. Young Keith Wegeman of Denver, undaunted by a training accident which had laid him up for several days, placed twelfth, with 204.5 points. He beat all of the Swiss and Austrian skiers in the process.

Art Devlin of Lake Placid, N.Y., managed to gain fifteenth place, Art Tokle of Brooklyn eighteenth and Willis S. Olson of Eau Claire, Wis., twenty-second in a field of forty-four competitors.

Holmenkollen is a "slow" course because its 272-foot run at a thirty-three degree incline down to the take-off in the past has not permitted jumps above 233 feet. This record was untouched today, despite the fact that some of the competitors have surpassed 400 feet on the Continent.

Bergmann and Falkanger both reached 223 feet today.

Wegeman, best of the Americans, did 203 feet 7 inches in his top performance, while Devlin had 206 feet 9 inches. Wegeman obtained the higher score on style, however, one of the five judges giving him as much as 18.5 (20 points are the maximum, a rare occurrence), whereas Devlin did not get better than 17.

By comparison Bergmann scored

an average of 18.5 points, with 19.5 his top; runner-up Falkanger —normally Norway's best ski jumper but handicapped today by a recent shoulder injury suffered in practice, posted an 18 average and 19 high.

### Basis for Judging

The style judges consider take-off form, deportment during the aerial portion of the journey, manner of landing and the degree to which a jumper keeps his skis parallel. A fall in landing, while not a mortal sin if the skier manages to get up again, naturally loses many points.

The Holmenkollen jumping was seen by roughly 5 per cent of Norway's entire population. It marked the first appearance in public of King Haakon VII since his return from the funeral of King George VI of England.

From a portable platform just below the take-off, the King, Crown Prince Olaf and two of the latter's children, together with Swedish Prince Bertil and Belgium's Princess Josephine-Charlotte, acknowledged the plaudits of the mammoth crowd, which shouted in unison "welcome back."

The Royal party then mounted the tribune of honor, where America's Avery Brundage stood next to King Haakon throughout the hour and a half of ski jumping.

Access to Holmenkollen, beautifully situated above Oslo with a magnificent view over two fjords, was so limited that some of the hardier ski enthusiasts went up last evening, spending the night in sleeping bags out in the snow.

The United States and Canada tied, 3—3, in tonight's ice hockey match at Jordal Stadium, but Canada won the Olympic championship gold medal by virtue of its unblemished record in previous matches.

### 10,000 at Hockey Game

By tying Canada, the United States clinched the second-place silver medal, and the 5 points thus gained maintained America's hold on second place in the overall Olympic point scoring, behind Norway and ahead of Finland. The United States finished with 89½ points, while Finland had 73.

Before more than 10,000 spectators, a record attendance for the Jordal Arena, Canada started out strongly against the United States. In the first period the Canadians piled up a 2-0 lead, Billie Dawe and Robert Dickson scoring.

In the second period the Americans reduced the edge to 2—1 as John Mulhern countered just after the thirteenth minute. Half a minute later the United States equalized on a goal by Kenneth Yackel. Shortly before the end of the period Canada jumped into the lead again on Husky Donald Gauf's goal.

In the final period, both teams staged dangerous attacks, but none resulted in a goal until James Sedin connected for the United States to tie the score with two minutes of play left.

The match was correct and unmarred by incidents, only a few minor penalties being meted out.

The Canadians celebrated their acquiring of the Olympic title by tossing their trainer into the air several times and singing "For he's a jolly good fellow."

At this point several hundred youngsters engaged the police in a battle to reach the Canadians. The kids' wedge pierced the police lines and the Canadian players gave the lucky first-comers their hockey sticks as souvenirs.

Earlier in the day Sweden lost to the Czech sextet, 4—0. Under the Olympic rules governing ice hockey, the Swedes and Czechs must play off tomorrow for the third-place bronze medal, each team having won six matches and lost two in the round-robin tourney.

February 25, 1952

---

## Dick Button Turns Pro in $150,000 Deal

—The world and Olympic figure-skating champion signing contract with Norman Frescott, general manager of Ice Capades.

Dick Button, twice an Olympic figure skating champion, turned professional yesterday. The 22-year-old Harvard Law student signed a contract for $150,000 for limited appearances with the "Ice Capades of 1953," and he will make his salaried debut at Madison Square Garden on the night of Sept. 11. Mr. Button, who has captured five world, seven American, three North American and one European championship, in addition to his Olympic conquests, will continue his studies at Harvard. He left yesterday for Atlantic City to rehearse with the "Ice Capades" group.

The contract calls for the Englewood (N. J.) youth to headline the show at the Garden, Sept. 11 through Sept. 21. His following appearances will be at Pittsburgh, the Boston Garden and wherever the show may be during the Christmas and Easter holidays.

Button's intricate and spectacular free skating maneuvers have won the fancy of spectators everywhere. Last winter Dick, a James E. Sullivan Award winner, introduced the triple loop and triple double Axel.

The graceful athlete, a skater since he was 12 years old, stole the show here last winter, when he appeared at the Olympic Fund benefit program.

August 29, 1952

---

## Endrich Killed, Two Injured In Garmisch Bobsled Spill

By The Associated Press.

GARMISCH-PARTENKIRCHEN, Germany, Jan. 31—A Swiss bobsled hurtled over a fifteen-foot wall of ice on Garmisch's notorious "dead man's curve" today and crashed into a tree, killing its world champion driver and seriously injuring two of the three other riders.

Killed almost instantly was Felix Endrich, 32-year-old Zurich salesman who last week-end guided his two-man sled to the world championship over this same treacherous course.

He and his crew were on an

IN FATAL ACCIDENT: Felix Endrich of Switzerland, wearing goggles, who was killed yesterday at Garmisch-Partenkirchen, Germany, is shown here in a recent photo with Brakeman Fritz Stoeckli, who escaped injuries in same crash.

early-morning practice run for the four-man championship, scheduled to start today, when the sled going at fifty miles an hour, spun over the wall and flew forty feet through the air.

It sheared a flagpole and bounced off one tree before it crashed into another, sending fragments of steel and splintered wood over the icy slope.

**Wife Among Spectators**

While his bride of a month watched horror-stricken, Endrich's body was removed from the wreckage. His neck was broken, and he had internal injuries. He was dead on arrival at Garmisch Hospital.

The middle men, Aby Gartmann and René Heiland, were badly injured but the brakeman, Fritz Stoeckli, escaped by leaping from his back seat as the sled soared through the air. He landed on an American jeep, shaken but unhurt.

Heiland suffered a broken leg and possible spinal injuries. Gartmann's right shoulder was broken.

Today's opening heats in the four-man championship immediately were canceled and officials announced tentative plans to have the title determined by tomorrow's two heats. Normally the championship is decided by the accumulated time of four heats.

It was over this same 1936 Olympic course, that Gen. Matthew B. Ridgway, Supreme Commander of Allied Forces in Europe, and his wife, Penny, took a "thrill ride" last Monday behind Lloyd Johnson of Rapid City, S. D.

Johnson is one of two United States drivers shooting for the championship. The other is Stan Benham of Lake Placid, N. Y., winner of two world titles.

This morning's accident occurred on the Bavarian Curve about halfway down the 1,650-meter course, made dangerously slick by early thaws and an overnight freeze.

It was the same curve, known to the daring sledders as "dead man's curve," on which Sweden's Rudolph Odenrich was killed two years ago. The curve was rebuilt to reduce its hazards but was still regarded as the most treacherous corner on the track.

Endrich, an experienced international bobsledder, knew the course as well as any man. He had made scores of trips down the icy chutes.

Several racers had expressed concern about Endrich's safety because of his recklessness in speeding around the Bavarian Curve. Donna Fox of New York, United States team manager, has suggested the wall be built higher for safety.

Endrich nearly always skidded close to the top before but always managed to bring his sled down at the right time.

His wife was in the spectator's stands when Endrich set off on the practice run. Using the old-fashioned rope method for guiding instead of the modern steering wheel, the Swiss daredevil was going down the track at record-breaking speed when tragedy struck.

The sled hit the sharp turn going about fifty miles an hour, skidded up the retaining wall and shot over the top at full speed.

February 1, 1953

## Jenkins Victor in Figure Skating, Outclassing Grogan in Free-Style

DAVOS, Switzerland, Feb. 10 (AP)—Hayes Alan Jenkins of Akron, Ohio, succeeded to the crown of Dick Button today by outskating his teammate, Jimmy Grogan, to win the world figure-skating title.

It was the first time since 1948 that Button, now a profesional, had not skated away with the prize. Jenkins, a 19-year-old sophomore at Colorado College, had been trying to take the championship for three years.

Jenkins trailed Grogan, a 21-year-old G. I., from Colorado Springs, going into today's freestyle skating. When he skated out before the nine judges today, however, he put on a performance so daring and so precise that five of the judges awarded first place to him and the four others gave him second.

The lanky Grogan, who had won five firsts in the compulsory figures yesterday, received four firsts, three seconds and two thirds. One judge gave Jenkins a perfect score for execution today—a rare tribute.

Carlo Fassi of Italy, European champion, finished in third place, slightly ahead of Ronald Robertson, 15-year-old high school sophomore from Long Beach, Calif. Ronnie's repertoire today, including a difficult double loop, compared favorably with those of the older skaters.

Alain Giletti of France, who is 13 years old and skates with all the confidence if not quite the finesse of Jenkins, finished fifth. Alain found the big Davos rink a bit too tiring for his little legs.

Jenkins, after receiving a joyful kiss from his mother, Mrs. Hayes Jenkins Sr., of Akron, said he felt "numb."

He said he had no intention of turning professional, as four of last year's world champions have done in the past year. "I am much more interested in college than in turning professional," Jenkins said. He is studying business.

He said he "felt good" while going through his program but "wouldn't want to have to do it over again." There was one moment of near disaster, he said, when he was doing a difficult "double axle." Jenkins finished a little off balance and the crowd held its breath for a moment until he recovered.

Private Grogan took his narrow defeat in stride, and will go to Germany from here to resume his duties with the army.

February 11, 1953

## Boston Girl, a 1947 Polio Victim, Wins World Figure Skating Title

*Tenley Albright, 17, Is First United States Competitor to Take Women's Honors*

By The United Press.

DAVOS, Switzerland, Feb. 15— Tenley Albright, 17-year-old ice ballerina from Boston, became the first United States girl ever to win the world figure-skating championship today. She received the unanimous vote of a seven-man panel of judges.

Miss Albright's performance, which she herself described as her "best," gave the United States a sweep of the two world individual figure-skating crowns. Hayes Alan Jenkins of Akron, Ohio, won the men's competition last Tuesday.

A crowd of 4,000 saw the graceful American girl outclass nineteen other competitors from eight countries in the free-skating maneuvers, which concluded the championship program. The Boston girl began today's free-skating competition with a wide lead carried over from the compulsory figures.

Miss Albright's victory capped a courageous six-year comeback from polio. The blonde American girl, who has been skating since she was 9, was stricken in 1947. Last year she placed second in the Olympic championship behind Jeanette Altwegg of England.

So difficult were the free-skating figures which Miss Albright selected and so brilliant was her execution that all seven judges placed her first. For her maneuvers she chose the double axel, double loop, double rittberger and double solchow.

"I was at my best today," smilingly commented Miss Albright after her performance. "The ice was much better than it had been last week. It was a wonderful day."

Never before had a skater from the United States placed higher than second in the women's competition.

Of the three other American girls entered, 13-year-old Carol Heiss of Ozone Park, N. Y., finished fourth; Margaret Anne Graham of Tulsa, Okla., was seventh, and Miggs Dean of Detroit was sixteenth. Miss Heiss might have placed third but for a technicality in the scoring system.

Gundi Busch, 17-year-old German champion, placed second and Valda Osborn of England was third. Suzanne Morrow of Canada ruined her chances for a higher placing when she fell and finished in fifth place. Vevi Smith of Canada was sixth.

An ovation greeted Miss Albright's superb performance on the open-air Davos rink. Experts said she executed her tricky double jumps and pirouettes "as they have never been performed before." Miss Albright skated in a

Associated Press
**Tenley Albright**

purple dress to an Offenbach fantasy.

Although Miss Albright's performance was expected to bring her numerous attractive professional offers, her father, a Boston surgeon, said she would not accept any.

"Tenley has to go to college and is too young to become a professional star," Dr. Hollis Albright said.

Miss Albright added: "I love skating for skating. I want to continue as an amateur."

Miss Albright and Miss Heiss will give exhibitions in Switzerland and in Paris later this week before returning home for the national and North American championships.

Miss Heiss, who complained that the strong breeze hampered her breathing, actually received higher placings and a greater point score than Miss Osborn, who finished third. However, the judges gave the English girl third place because she received a majority of the third place votes cast by the judges.

February 16, 1953

## Miss Albright Keeps U. S. Skating Crown

### By LINCOLN A. WERDEN

Special to THE NEW YORK TIMES.

HERSHEY, Pa., March 28—Tenley Albright of Boston completed her own grand slam in figure skating tonight by retaining her United States crown at the Hershey Arena tonight.

An enthusiastic gathering greeted the efforts of the 17-year-old ballerina who won her third championship in the space of two months. Her triumph here completed the bid which began last February with the victory of the world's title, the first that had ever been won by a woman skater from this country. Then came the North American championship a few weeks ago at Cleveland.

Finally, the young lady, in a shimmering white costume with a blue sash, concluded the record-winning streak tonight. After she had finished skating to the music of Offenbach's "Fantasy," the crowd realized the importance of her triumph, the first of its kind in American annals. From all parts of the arena, waves of applause greeted the smiling girl long before the judges walked out on the ice with raised score cards that signified authentic approval in proper mathematical fashion.

The judges were unanimous in acclaiming Miss Albright's efforts. She received better than a 9.5 (ten is perfection) rating from each of the five officials for the program she skated. The excellence of her skating, and the intricacies which had required years of study were combined in a coordinated exhibition. The official observers were in accord on this, too, for their reaction was to give her marks averaging over 9.6. One believed that Miss Albright was so close to perfection that he rated her 9.9 on his card.

Second to the international champion was 13-year-old Carol Heiss of Ozone Park, N. Y., skating at high tempo and dashing through a program containing a succession of spins and breathtaking jumps, the little girl again demonstrated she is one of the world's best, notwithstanding her youth. Fourth best in the world tourney when Miss Albright won at Davos, the youngster, who skates three hours before going to school each day, won the acclaim of the gathering.

### Miss Graham Takes 3d Place

Margaret Anne Graham, Tulsa University senior, captured third place with a fine free-skating routine. She had been third in the figures standing on Wednesday, trailing the Misses Albright and Heiss.

Miggs Dean of Detroit was fourth, Kay Servatius of Colorado Springs fifth and Nancy Mineard of Akron, Ohio, placed sixth. The judges gave Miss Albright 1,806.4 points and Miss Heiss 1,735.2, although the latter did not receive a unanimous second-place vote. One official gave a second-place ballot to Miss Graham. The Tulsa girl, who is also a college cheer leader, accounted for 1,674.2 points. Miss Dean had

1,630.9, Miss Servatius 1,628.1 and Miss Mineard 1,582.6.

Dave Jenkins, 16-year-old younger brother of Hayes Jenkins, won the junior men's title with a performance that included thrilling jumps and dance steps.

The triumph was especially significant since young Jenkins moved from fourth place, which he occupied at the conclusion of the school figures that count 60 per cent toward the championship. In the final computation, four of the five judges gave Jenkins first place. One of them placed him second.

Jenkins represents the Cleveland Skating Club but attends school in Colorado Springs. His victory means that he and his brother will be able to represent the United States in the 1953 world championship.

Second place went to Bill Nick of Tacoma, the rangy six-footer who led in the figures. Nick was awarded only one first place. Tim Brown of Glendora, Calif., placed third, while Noel Ledin of Chicago was fourth. Peter Pender of Philadelphia was next, then came Ray Blommer of Milwaukee. Charles Foster of Fargo, N. D., was seventh.

Jenkins was the last of the juniors to skate, but he did so with apparent confidence, going into a triple-loop jump to attract immediate attention. He skated a mature program which was diversified and contained elements of both fast and slow tempo moods.

But it was his jumping and spinning, flawlessly done, that was exceptional. One judge gave him a 9.5 for content of program and 9.7 for performance.

The point tabulation for the men's junior gave Jenkins 1,165.04,

Nick 1,140.06. Brown 1,139.1, and Ledin 1,129.5.

The senior pairs laurels went to the representatives of the Skating Club of Fresno, Calif., as Carole Ormaca and Robin Greiner, Pacific Coast champions, executed a smooth, graceful routine. The Tulsa, Okla., sister and brother entry of Margaret Anne Graham and Hugh C. Graham Jr. was second. A fall on one of their difficult jumps spoiled their chance of taking a senior title to their home city for the first time. Kay Servatius and Sully Kothman of Colorado Springs, the other pair in this event, took third place.

### Capital Duo Takes Dance Title

Carol Ann Peters and Daniel Ryan of the Washington, D. C. Figure Skating Club won the gold dance championship. This victory followed their triumph earlier in the month in the North American championships.

Second in this event were Virginia Hoyns and Donald Jacoby of Philadelphia. Third place went to Mr. and Mrs. Edward Bodel of Berkeley, Calif. Phyllis Schroeder of New York and Martin Forney of Hershey were fourth while Janet Williams of New Haven and William Kipp of Allentown, Pa., were fifth.

The Harned Trophy, awarded to the city whose representatives performed the best in the championship, will be shared by Los Angeles and Boston. The Oscar Richard Cup for the outstanding performer was awarded to Ronnie Robertson of Colorado Springs, who finished second to Hayes Jenkins in the men's senior. Nancy Mineard of Akron was awarded the trophy for the most artistic skater.

March 29, 1953

## JENKINS BROTHERS DOMINATE SKATING

### Hayes, 20, Finishes First and David, 17, Second in U. S. Figure Tests on Coast

LOS ANGELES, March 21 (AP)—A family entry and a hometown girl starred in the concluding events last night of the United States figure-skating championship.

Hayes Alan Jenkins, who won't be 21 until later this month and already is twice a world champion, retained his men's senior singles title with a clean sweep of first-place votes.

The other half of the Jenkins family entry from Colorado Springs, Colo., 17-year-old David, finished in the runner-up spot. Such a one, two finish in this competition is believed unprecedented.

The Los Angeles girl whose dynamic rhythms in free skating brought her the women's junior championship, Catherine Machado, has an ambition to skate in the 1956 Olympics. It wouldn't surprise any of the approximately 1,600 fans who saw her in the Polar Palace if she reached that goal.

The 17-year-old high school senior also won the Oscar L. Richard award for the most artistic free skating performance in junior and senior ladies' classes.

March 22, 1954

### LEO, ALDRINE LEBEL STAR

#### They Better World Standards for Barrel-Jumping

GROSSINGER, N.Y., Jan. 8 (UP)—Leo and Aldrine Lebel, a brother and sister act from Lake Placid, N.Y., set world records today in winning the fifth annual men's and women's world barrel-jumping championships at the Grossinger Country Club.

Leo cleared fifteen barrels for a distance of 28 feet 7 inches to better the previous record of fifteen barrels for 28 feet 3 inches set by Terry Browne of Detroit in 1952.

Browne, who held the title from 1951, placed sixth today with a hurdle of thirteen barrels for 25 feet 2 inches.

In the women's division, Aldrine retained her title and bettered her world record with a jump of eight barrels for 18 feet 3 inches. Her previous record, set last year, was 15 feet 2 inches over seven barrels.

Yvon Jolin of Montreal, the Canadian champion, placed second in the men's event, clearing fourteen barrels for 25 feet 11 inches. Ron Gerrity of Daly City, Calif., was third and Paul Bonafe of Quebec was fourth.

January 9, 1955

## Werner, 17, Takes Downhill and Becomes First U. S. Skier to Win at Holmenkollen

OPPDAL, Norway, Feb. 19 (AP)—Wallace (Buddy) Werner, a 17-year-old high school boy from Steamboat Springs, Colo., who has been skiing ever since he was big enough to stand on barrel staves, today became the first American ever to win a race in the world famous Holmenkollen festival.

He zipped over the downhill course in competition with the world's best Alpine skiers in the good time of 2 minutes 13.2 seconds.

His margin of victory in the opening event of the festival was one-tenth of a second over Martin Strolz of the powerful Austrian team. Ernie McCullough of Canada was third in 2:14.4. The course ran 3,000 meters (about two miles) down a mountain near this central Norway village.

Werner's sister, Gladys, tied for tenth in the women's downhill race, in which Austrians swept the first three places.

Buddy was not included in the original list of United States entries for the world championships at Are, Sweden, starting late this month. He was hustled to Europe as an alternate, however, when Bill Beck of Kingston, R. I., broke his leg.

Louis Jaretz was the best of

the Austrians in the women's event with a time of 1:55. Trude Klecker was second in 1:56.4 and Erika Mahringer third in 1:56.7. Jeannette Burr of Seattle, Wash., finished fourth in 1:57.3. Miss Werner tied with Imogene Opton of North Conway, N. H., at 1:59.8.

In the men's event, Ralph Miller of Hanover, N. H., was the first United States entry behind Werner. He finished sixth in 2:16.1. The other American finishers were Brooks Dodge, Pinkham Notch, N. H., fourteenth; Verne Goodwin, Pittsfield, Mass., seventeenth, and Doug Burden, New York, twenty-sixth.

Katy Rodolph of Hayden, Colo., finished seventeenth in the women's race.

February 20, 1954

# Hayes Alan Jenkins Takes World Figure-Skating Title Third Straight Time

## AMERICA SWEEPS TOP THREE PLACES

### Hayes Jenkins Followed by Robertson and D. Jenkins —Miss Albright Leads

VIENNA, Feb. 16 (AP)—Hayes Alan Jenkins swept to his third straight men's world figure-skating title tonight. Tenley Albright took a strong lead in the women's division, which virtually assured a United States sweep of individual honors in the championships.

Jenkins, a 20-year-old competitor from Colorado Springs, put on a dazzling exhibition of free skating in Vienna's open-air rink to complete his victory over thirteen of the world's top performers.

His third championship, however, left him short of Richard Button's feat of ringing up five world titles and two Olympic crowns before turning professional in 1952.

### Crowd Hails Winner

Jenkins capped his performance to the tune of Gershwin's Rhapsody in Blue, spinning through a series of leaps and whirls that brought the crowd of 6,500 to its feet. He received a standing ovation when he skated off, not even breathing hard.

Ronald Robertson of Los Angeles was second and the champion's younger brother, David, was third.

Nine judges voted Hayes Alan Jenkins 203.7 points. Robertson received 201.12 and David Jenkins 196.69, France's 1955 European champion, 15-year-old Alain Giletti, was fourth with 190.64.

Earlier, Miss Albright, a 19-year-old Newton, Mass., premedical student, gave an exacting and brilliant performance in the first four of her compulsory figures. Observers said only a mishap could keep her from the crown she won in 1953.

### Two Figures Remaining

In compulsory figures, a skater must follow a series of set patterns. In the free skating category, he makes up his own routines. He is judged on the originality and perfection of the execution.

Miss Albright must complete the final two figures of her compulsory skating tomorrow morning. The free skating exhibition will be given tomorrow night.

Her closest rivals are two Austrians—the European champion, Tanna Eigel, and Ingrid Wendl. Both had a lot of ground to make up to catch the New England star.

Miss Albright had 563.3 points for the first four figures compared with 537.9 for Miss Eigel and 535.4 for Miss Wendl. Carol Heiss of New York was sixth with 522.7.

February 17, 1955

# Ossi Reichert of Germany and Finland's Hakulinen Win in Olympic Skiing

## U.S. COMPETITORS FALTER IN CORTINA

### Fraeulein Reichert Annexes Giant Slalom—Hakulinen Is 30-Kilometer Victor

#### By FRED TUPPER
Special to The New York Times.

CORTINA D'AMPEZZO, Italy, Jan. 27—An innkeeper's apple-cheeked daughter and a baldish forest ranger won first places for Germany and Finland, respectively, as the seventh Olympic Winter Games moved into high gear today.

Also, a jet pilot from Nergano—with a build like a ballet dancer—virtually guaranteed a gold medal for Italy tomorrow. There were thin pickings left for the United States.

The defending champion, Mrs. Andrea Mead Lawrence, tied for fourth in the women's giant slalom skiing, the American two-man bobsledders were a disappointing fifth and sixth at the halfway stage, the hockey team lost to Czechoslovakia, 4 to 3, and there wasn't one American in the top thirty-five in the thirty-kilometer (18 miles, 1,125 yards) cross-country skiing.

A few snowflakes were falling on Mount Tofana this morning, coating the breathtaking women's slalom run with its traverses, flushes and gates

rigged downward over a precipitous mile.

Ossi Reichert of Germany was away first, almost before the straggling spectators had panted up the mountainside.

Her style is deceptively simple and her control magnificent. She plunged into the early gates, shading the flags and burst over the last rise into the "arrivo" wide open. Her time was 1 minute 56.5 seconds. Not another competitor was near that clocking.

For the 30-year-old Fraeulein Reichert it had been a long, often exasperating wait. She took a silver medal (second place) in the special slalom at the Winter Olympics at Oslo, Norway, in 1952, but has never won a German championship because of injuries.

All morning she was nervously crossing her fingers waiting for the field to finish. "That snowfall helped," she said. "I could jerk through the gates without slowing up. The other girls had to brake after it got icy."

The fine runs today generally were made early. But blonde Josefine Frandl of Austria, who started midway, skimmed through in 1:57.8 for second place. Four athletes were bunched less than a second behind her.

#### U. S. Star Hesitates

Another Austrian, Dorothea Hochleitner, was third in 1:58.2 and Mrs. Lawrence, 23, of Parshall, Colo., tied for fourth in 1:58.3. Helmet askew and her long bun of hair streaming, Andy made up time at the finish but had hesitated a trifle earlier on.

Ossi Reichert of Germany, right, is warmly congratulated by Mrs. Andrea Mead Lawrence after winning women's giant slalom. Mrs. Lawrence of Parshall, Colo., tied for fourth.

"The course was excellent and my turns seemed perfect. Guess I was slow in the stretches," Mrs. Lawrence said.

Even with her was Madeleine Berthod of Switzerland, the favorite, who slid on the upper slopes and stopped dead to avoid missing a gate.

Sixth was freckle-faced Lucille Wheeler, daughter of a Laurentian, Canada, resort owner. She first wore skis at 14 months and celebrated her twenty-first birthday this month. Her time was 1:58.6.

Down the line were Gladys Werner of Steamboat Springs, Colo., twenty-second, and Penelope Pitou, 17, of Laconia, N. H., thirty-fourth. There were forty-four competitors from fifteen countries.

"The old woodchopper again, again," yelled the Finns as 31-year-old Veikko Hakulinen wearily slid and pushed down the last, long mile to win the thirty-kilometer cross-country race, a tortuous run uphill and downhill over wooded terrain. His time was 1 hour 44 minutes 6 seconds.

### Finn Tossed in Air

In exultation, the Finns tossed Hakulinen in the air a dozen times. Veikko won the fifty-kilometer title at Oslo and most of the long-distance international events since.

Second was the smiling Sixten Jernberg of Sweden. Six seconds ahead at the ten-kilometer check point, he gradually slipped behind and was clocked in 1:44.30.

The 26-year-old mechanic seemed the fresher at the end, though, and was one of the few to walk away unaided.

Vladimir Kuzin of Russia, a strong hope, was fifth, sandwiched among a Russian quartet.

Pavel Koltchin, third, had an incipient cramp and was massaged as he stumbled in. Anatoli Schelyukhin, fourth, resembled a snowman, with hair wreathed in icicles over his steaming brow. Fedor Terentyev was sixth.

Two Americans, Andrew Miller and Lynn Levy of the Camp Hale (Colo.) Ski Club finished thirty-eighth and fiftieth.

As anticipated, the brilliant Italians insured a runaway victory in the two-man, two-day bobsled event. The only surprise today was the order of the finish.

Eugenio Monti, a red-headed lumberman who lives in Cortina, had proved the better driver in trials over the past fortnight. This morning Lamberto Dalla Costa, the Italian Air Force pilot, thundered down the icy mile twice for a total time of 2:44.45 to shade Monti, who posted 2:45.26. Nobody else was even remotely close.

And yet, Dalla Costa's first run nearly didn't come off. There was fresh snow on the starting line, with ice underneath, and Dalla Costa slid attempting to get on.

As the Italian spectators groaned, he suddenly wrenched the sled to a halt before reaching the electric starting eye. He was permitted to begin again and his time, 1:22, was the fastest of the day.

Behind the Italians was Max Angst of Switzerland, who had improved greatly in the trials. Fourth was the debonair Alfonso Cabeza De Kavaca, Marquis of Portago, a gentleman racing driver who lives in Paris, once went to Lawrenceville School in New Jersey and had not been on a bobsled until a month ago. He wore football shoes, which helped him on the icy start, and drove like a demon.

The Americans, Waightman Washbond of East Hartford, Conn., and Art Tyler of Rochester, N. Y., were fifth and sixth and unhappy about it. Washbond lost two seconds on his first run as the sled slithered off the track at the start.

### Named World Champion Also

CORTINA D'AMPEZZO, Italy, Jan. 27 (UP)—Finland's Veikko Hakulinen, winner of the Olympic 30-kilometer ski race tonight received his gold medal and a diploma as the 1956 world champion.

For the first time in skiing history, the Olympic champion also was proclaimed world champion. The International Ski Federation decided at its 1953 meeting that the Olympic skiing competition also would be recognized as the world championships provided the rules for participation were the same as the general federation regulations.

A snowstorm, which had swirled over the stadium during the preceding hockey match, stopped for the medal presentation.

The stadium was darkened and eight heralds in medieval dress, their green cloaks swirling in the breeze, stepped on to the rostrum carrying long golden trumpets.

Suddenly the rostrum was bathed in lights from a battery of searchlights and standing behind the dais were the first three in the men's cross-country race.

Avery Brundage of Chicago, president of the International Olympic Committee, stepped forward, coatless despite the cold but wearing a Tyrolean hat.

As the athletes stood motionless, he took their medals and certificates from three girls in Italian national costume, presented them to the athletes and shook hands.

January 28, 1956

# RUSSIANS WIN 2 EVENTS TO LEAD IN WINTER OLYMPICS

## SKATE RECORD SET

### Grishin Races 500 in 0:40.2 and a Soviet Woman Skier Wins

#### By FRED TUPPER
Special to The New York Times.

CORTINA D'AMPEZZO, Italy, Jan. 28—A listed world record was broken, an Olympic record smashed and the marks of a dozen nations shattered here in one of the greatest days of speed skating in history.

When all the reports were in, it was the Russians who swept the ice on Lake Misurina with a first, second and fourth in the 500-meter race.

In another awesome display of power the Soviet athletes scored identically, 1, 2, 4, in the woman's ten-kilometer cross-country skiing, and are already in a position to dominate completely the Olympic Winter Games in their first crack at them.

Russia's team point total in the unofficial standing is 46. Finland and Italy follow at 15 points each. Germany has 10, Austria and Sweden 9 each and the United States and Switzerland 6½ each.

The unofficial scoring system awards 10 points for first place, 5 for second, 4 for third, 3 for fourth, 2 for fifth and 1 for sixth.

The spectacular Italians, hoarsely cheered by a huge dawn turnout, won the two-man bobsled, the third event on today's program. Finland and Germany earned gold medals yesterday.

Misurina is 5,500 feet high in the Dolomites and, though the crowd stripped outer garments under the bright sun, the ice on the rink was hard and smooth.

#### Grishin Called First

Yevgeni Grishin was called first, drawn against Johnny Cronsleu of Great Britain in the two-lane competition used in international skating.

Just last Sunday Grishin had unofficially broken the world record of 40.8 seconds by six-tenths of a second and was obviously the man to beat in this outstanding field.

His start was perfect and he churned down the first straightaway, arms flying, and slid into the turn, leaning left, to hug the corner.

Skates just scraping the snow line, he was around now, his style fluid and his speed tremendous. Another turn and then he shot into the stretch and was by the post.

There were yells from the Russians before the time went up. It was announced as 0:40.2, the same as his clocking last Sunday and more than two seconds better than the Olympic record set by Finn Helgesen of Norway in 1948. A half-dozen husky Russian officials rushed out of the stands and kissed him on the cheek.

Rafael Grach of Russia was drawn against Ken Henry, the Chicago schoolteacher defending the crown he won at the Oslo games in 1952.

Grach is even more slightly built than Grishin and nearly as fast. He finished in 0:40.8, with Henry twenty yards and two seconds behind. Henry tied for seventeenth. Alv Gjestvang of Norway was third with 0:41.

Yuri Sergeyev of Russia was fourth in 0:41.1; Toivo Salinen of Finland fifth in 0:41.7, and Bill Carow, Madison (Wis.) fireman, sixth in 0:41.8.

After two false starts Carow missed his stride slightly in cutting ahead of Sweden's Gunnar Strom as they crossed lanes on the far side and then he faded slightly in the homestretch.

"I thought Bill might break 41 seconds," said Del Lamb, the American coach from Milwaukee. "The lane cross slowed him up."

Yuri Miklailov, the Russian who set the world mark for the 1,500 meters at Davos, Switzerland, last week, caromed off the snow wall. Canadian Johnny Sands had tripped earlier in the same place.

John Werket of Minneapolis tied for eleventh and Don McDermott of Englewood Cliffs, N. J., for twenty-fifth.

In all, a dozen skaters from all over the globe broke their native national records on this lightning fast surface.

The Finns, men and women alike, have long been recognized as the world's best on skis over hill and trail. They play that way and even fight that way. They have won almost every long-distance event in every Olympics. But they were no match for Lyubov Kozyreva of the Soviet Union in the ten-kilometer cross-country today.

The slight, blonde Leningrad student with bulging leg muscles covered the six-mile-376-yard course in 38 minutes 11 seconds and, even with that sparkling time, was only a few yards ahead of a team-mate, Radiya Yeroshima, at the end.

Sonja Edstroem, a nurse from Luleaa, Sweden, and all rigged out in white, was third in 38:23, and Alevatina Kolchina of Russia fourth in 38:46.

Two Finns, Siiri Rantanen and Mirja Hietamies, were far behind in fifth and sixth places.

Huge headlines in the Italian press had been proclaiming the

certain victory of its bobsledders for days and the hummocks along the icy run were jammed with peasants from the mountain towns and high society from Rome.

### Dalla Costa Fastest Again

On his red sled, half upright to watch for ruts, Lamberto Dalla Costa turned in the fastest heats again today. The Italian jet pilot has raced only at Cortina and knows every inch of the run.

The total time for his four

heats was 5:30.14, a second or so better than Eugenio Monti, a lumberman from the Dolomites. Their joint performances outclassed the field.

The immaculate Marquis De Portago, a Spanish grandee who rides race horses, drives racing cars and has just taken up bobsledding, hit a deep rut on the treacherous Belvedere Curve and finished in fourth place behind Max Angst of Switzerland.

The marquis' wife, a South Carolinian, was more than pleased. "Now he's doing some-

thing for his country," she said.

Waightman (Bud) Washbond of East Hartford, Conn., and Art Tyler of Rochester, N. Y., were fifth and sixth.

Tyler's brakeman, Ed Seymour, tore ligaments in his leg when the sled bounced off Christallo Curve in the last heat and shook him partly loose.

The American hockey team remained in the running by defeating Poland, 4 to 0, in a preliminary round game.

January 29, 1956

# Sailer of Austria and Shilkov of Russia Triumph in the Winter Olympics

## LEAD IN SKATING TO HAYES JENKINS

### By FRED TUPPER
Special to The New York Times.

CORTINA D'AMPEZZO, Italy, Jan. 29—Anton (Toni) Sailer, a 21-year-old Austrian plumber, made a farce of the giant slalom and Boris Shilkov, a Russian dam-builder, skated to an Olympic record for the 5,000 meters in the only events decided at the Winter Games today.

The United States, snowed

under so far, apparently had a hammerlock on the men's figure skating. A brilliant trio, Hayes Alan Jenkins, world champion; his brother, David, and Ronald Robertson were in the top three places at the end of the compulsory figures. The free skating is scheduled for Wednesday.

Another split-day event ended in an international grab bag. A Russian, Yuri Moschkin, led the jumpers in the combined, and a Norwegian, a Swede, an Austrian, a Japanese and a Pole followed in that order.

Moschkin made a tremendous leap of more than 252 feet on his second jump in the combined and totaled 217.5 points for first place half-way through this

jumping-cross-country competition.

Sverre Stenersen of Norway had 215 points; Bengt Eriksson of Sweden, 214; Sepp Schiffner of Austria, 211.5, and Hiroshi Yoshisawa of Japan and Aleksander Kowalski of Poland, 210.5 each.

Marvin Crawford of Denver led the United States group with 200 points. Charles Tremblay of Keene, N. H., scored 185.5; Ted Farwell of Montague City, Mass., had 175.5, and Lynn Levy of New Orleans was last with 165.5 in the field of thirty-six.

At nightfall of the third day of competition, Russia had three gold medals and an unofficial point total of 60 in its first

appearance at the Winter Olympics.

Austria was next with 29 points; Finland, Italy and Sweden, with 15 each, followed. Then came Germany, 10; Switzerland and the U. S. 6½ each; France and The Netherlands, 5 each; Norway, 4; Spain, 3, and Canada 1.

### How Points Are Compiled

The points are compiled on a 10-5-4-3-2-1 basis for six places.

The giant slalom was staged on the slopes of Mount Faloria, some 7,000 feet up in the Dolomite Alps. The trail plummets downward for a mile and three-quarters through sixty-nine gates and broadens to a finish

Associated Press Radiophotos

Toni Sailer of Austria gliding over the snow at Cortina d'Ampezzo yesterday in the giant slalom ski championship.

Boris Shilkov of Russia during the 5,000-meter skating race on Lake Misurina. His time of 7:48.7 set an Olympic mark.

through tall pine trees 600 yards below.

Ralph Miller, an American Army private from Hanover, N. H., started first and fell almost at once. As the third skier, Ernst Hinterseer of Austria, came down, an avalanche broke over the run and he was ordered back. The event was postponed until the trail was cleared.

By this time a weary crowd of several thousand, unable to obtain sufficient transportation, had trekked up the mountain side and blanketed the sides of the slalom.

Sailer started as No. 18. The roars of the crowd could be heard below as he thundered down the mountain. A multilingual announcer, unable to restrain her enthusiasm, shouted "Wunderbar," "magnifico" and "formidable" as she reeled off his times at the various check points.

Toni was whipping through the gates without braking, and shot off the last ridge in a sixty-mile-an-hour schuss through the straight, white teeth gleaming in his bronzed face.

**'Sensational,' Says Announcer**

"Sensational," added the announcer as she gave the incredible clocking of 3:00.1. Not another skiier was remotely close to those figures.

A group of Austrian patriots, some of whom had skied all the way from the border, broke through the snow fence, tore off Sailer's white stocking cap and lifted him to their shoulders, skis and all.

"The run was perfect." Sailer shouted over the loudspeaker. "I did a few gelaendesprungs (jumps). They gave me more speed." Earlier this month he won the Austrian downhill at Kitzbuhel and had taken four European championships last winter.

Later, Chancellor Julius Raab of Austria wired congratulations to Sailer.

It was an Austrian triumph. Andreas Molterer was second. Walter Schuster was third and Hinterseer, the man who started over, was sixth. Adrien Duvillard and Charles Bozon of France were fourth and fifth, respectively.

The Americans finished far back. Despite his fall, Miller was thirteenth, Tom Corcoran of Westfield, N. J., fourteenth and Brooks Dodge of Gorham, N. H., fifteenth, all less than a second apart.

Wallace Werner of Steamboat Springs, Colo., whose forte is the downhill, fell twice and was twenty-first.

The Russians showed the world how they could skate yesterday by winning the 500 meters. They proved it again today in the 5,000. Shilkov flashed around in 7:48.7 for his specialty, twenty-two seconds better than the Olympic record.

And yet that time was old hat to the 28-year-old engineer. Shilkov had done three seconds better himself earlier this winter on the Alma Ata rink in central Asia.

Reports had been drifting around this mountain village all

week that Shilkov was "burned out" and might not enter. His victory was so easy that it points the way to Soviet medals in the 1,500 and 10,000-meter races to come.

The world champion, Sigge Ericsson of Sweden, was second on the glazed Mismurina rink in 7:56.7. He had been sidelined most of the winter with a liver ailment. "My short strokes were just too choppy," he said later.

Third was Oleg Goncharenko, a Russian, in 7:57.5. A pair from The Netherlands, Kees Broekman and Willem De Graaf, shared fourth place. Ronald Aas of Norway was sixth.

The records for twelve countries—Australia, Czechoslovakia, Great Britain, Canada, France, The Netherlands, Japan, Korea, Norway, Sweden, Switzerland and the United States—were bettered by their skaters in this race, a tribute to the Misurina ice.

**American Timed in 8:10.6**

Pat McNamara of Minneapolis, who was seventeenth, tied the old Olympic mark of 8:10.6 and snapped the American one by fifteen seconds.

Eugene Sandvig of Minneapolis was thirty-first, Art Longsjo of Fitchburg, Mass., was fortieth and Charles Burke of Chicago was forty-third. There were forty-six competitors.

In the figure skating, three-time world title-holder Hayes Jenkins, a slightly-built Colorado College student, held a narrow lead over Robertson of Long Beach, Calif., at the end of the compulsory figures. Third was

Hayes' 19 - year - old younger brother, David, and fourth was Alain Giletti, the European champion from France.

"We're just where we should be," said Eddie Scholden, who coaches the Jenkins brothers. "Hayes is in front and his free style is pure artistry based on a definite composition."

"We're pleased the way things stand," said Gus Lucy of Asbury Park, coach of the Californian. "Ronny is the best free skater alive." The free skating counts 40 per cent, compulsory figures 60.

The skaters, wearing work clothes, spent all day on five figures, "the counter," "double 3 change double 3 forward," "rocker," "loop" and "bracket change bracket."

"It's the best bracket I've ever done in competition," said the 18-year-old Robertson. Nevertheless, Hayes Jenkins scored higher points. Hayes Jenkins finished with 852.2 points. Robertson had 840.1, David Jenkins 837.3 and Giletti 822.5.

In two brilliant practice runs the Italians outclassed the four-man bobsled field and seem certain to duplicate their one, two victory in the two-man bob.

Art Tyler of Rochester was among the first half-dozen, but Jim Bickford of Saranac Lake hit an icy patch on the second run and overturned. The crew was shaken but unhurt.

January 30, 1956

---

# Russia, Norway and Switzerland Are Victors in Winter Olympics at Cortina

## SOVIET SKATERS CUT WORLD MARK

### Grishin and Mikhailov Timed in 2:08.6 for 1,500—Miss Albright Takes Lead

**By FRED TUPPER**
Special to The New York Times.

CORTINA D'AMPEZZO, Italy, Jan. 30—Two great winter sports nations, Norway and Switzerland, finally got into the act at the Winter Olympics today.

Norseman Hallgeir Brenden, a 26-year-old farmer who skis to work, won the fifteen kilometer cross-country event, and Renee Colliard of Switzerland, college student from Geneva, convincingly trounced an international field in the women's special slalom.

Norway won the Winter Olympics at Oslo in 1952, Switzerland won at St. Moritz in 1948. Until

today, neither had won a gold medal here.

They shared honors with Russia, which inevitably captured its third skating title, the 1,500 meters, in as many tries.

The world record holder, Yevgeni Grishin, and the unofficial holder, Yuri Mikhailov, were roundly bussed by Nikolai Romanov, the Soviet sports minister, after jointly careening around the Misurina rink in the world record time of 2:08.6.

**Ten Events Completed**

Russia now has four gold medals in the ten events completed so far and a whopping 85 points in the unofficial team standing.

Austria has 36 points, Finland 25, Sweden 20, Norway 19, Italy 18, Switzerland 16½, Germany 10 and the United States 6½.

The Netherlands and France, with 5 each; Spain, 3, and Canada 1, followed. The points are compiled on a 10-5-4-3-2-1-basis for six places.

The United States took a commanding lead in the women's figure skating as two-time world champion Tenley Albright of Newton Center, Mass., and 16-year-old Carol Heiss of Ozone

Park, Queens, placed one, two in the first day of the compulsory figures.

In competition for the first time since she gashed a half-inch hole below her right ankle nine days ago, the 21-year-old Radcliffe College girl scored a total of 623.1 points on three school figures.

Miss Heiss, the blonde with the pony tail, had 614.5 points. Far behind were Ingrid Wendl of Austria, the European champion, and Yvonne Sugden of Great Britain. Catherine Machado of Los Angeles was tenth.

"It's still difficult to push off my right foot," said Tenley, "as I had to in the third figure. But I'm resting it as much as I can and it feels good." She was heavily taped.

**Two Figures Tomorrow**

The other two compulsory figures will be run off tomorrow and the free skating on Thursday. School figures rate 60 per cent of the total points.

An American hockey team drubbed the Germans, 7 to 2.

Snow was falling intermittently this morning on the women's slalom course, a wide, white scar on the side of Col Druscie, one

of the splintered Dolomite peaks. It barely coated the hard, frozen surface that ribbons down for a 500-yard drop.

Spread out over the descent were red, yellow and blue flags. This marked the eighty-six gates in two parallel lanes the girls had to pass through to finish.

The slalom is a downhill race through gates. The gates (two flagged poles about ten feet apart) are placed so that the skier is almost constantly turning or twisting, putting a premium on timing and control.

Miss Colliard, jauntily outfitted in red, started first, a definite advantage under these snow conditions. She tore through her initial run in 0:55.6, the best time of the day.

Those going off the top early made good clockings. Mrs. Andrea Mead Lawrence of Parshall, Colo., who started at No. 15, had a fine swing in 0:57.5. It placed her fifth at the halfway mark, though by now the ice had come through.

**This Girl 'Forgot Skates'**

After that it was a carnage. One series of gates was repeatedly wiped out and the hill was

**WOMEN'S SPECIAL SLALOM:** Renee Colliard of Switzerland winning the 500-yard contest in a total time of 1 minute 52.3 seconds. Mrs. Andrea Mead Lawrence, America's defending champion, fell and finished far behind.

the Russian ace, was a surprise. Kuzin was second at five kilometers and fourth at ten, but trailed off badly to finish tenth. Andy Miller of McCall, Idaho, was forty-first and Larry Damon of Burlington, Vt., was fifty-first.

The world record of 2:09.8 for the 1,500-meter skating was set by Grishin in Asia earlier this year, but Mikhailov lowered it unofficially to 2:09..1 at Davos last week. They both needed record clocking to beat the

Finns, Juhani Harvenin and Toivo Salonen, who both sliced tenths off Grishin's record.

The Soviet's Robert Merculov was fifth and Sigge Ericsson of Sweden was sixth. The Americans were well down in the ruck. Pat McNamara, John Werket and Gene Sandvig, all of Minneapolis, finished twentieth, twenty-fifth and thirtieth. Don McDermott of Englewood Cliffs, N. J., was thirty-seventh.

January 31, 1956

# Sailer Captures Special Slalom For 2d Gold Medal in Games

### Igaya of Japan Is Runner-Up to Austrian, but U. S. Claims He Fouled—Sweden's Ericsson Sets Skate Record

By FRED TUPPER
Special to The New York Times.

CORTINA D'AMPEZZO, Italy, Jan. 31—Brooks Dodge of Pinkham Notch, N. H., finished fourth in the men's special slalom at the Winter Olympics today. However, Dodge may move up to third place and become the United States' first medal winner of the Games if a protest against the second-place finisher is allowed.

Chiharu (Chick) Igaya, a Japanese studying at Dartmouth, was the runner-up behind Anton (Toni) Sailer of Austria, but the American and Swedish coaches claimed Igaya had straddled the sixth gate near the top of the course. A slalom is a downhill race through gates consisting of two flagged poles about ten feet apart. The gates are placed so that the skier is almost constantly turning.

Bob Sheehan of the United States team and Bibbo Nordenskiold of the Swedish squad called the referee and the Italian ski trainer into the jury room as witnesses. The gate judge reported no infraction and the protest was rejected, with one proviso.

#### TV Films to Decide

If TV film taken of the race confirms the protest, Igaya will lose his medal. Fourteen days were granted to produce film evidence.

In that case Dodge, a Dartmouth graduate, would receive the bronze medal. Dodge's surprise showing was in the way of a celebration. He announced his engagement today to Ann Schafer of Washington, a Smith College graduate. They intend to be married in Zurich after the Games.

Aside from the protest, the program today was featured by a brilliant showing by athletes of the smaller countries. Sailer, a skiing great at 21, hurtled down treacherous Col Druscie hill to outclass a field of ninety-five in the slalom and become the first athlete to win two gold medals outright at Cortina.

Sverre Stenersen, a 29-year-old competitor from the northern tip of Norway, took the Nordic combined as three Norsemen finished in the first six. Sigvard Sigge Ericsson, a Swedish sporting goods salesman, broke the Russian monopoly of the speed-skating events with a victory in the 10,000-meter race.

#### Moschkin Fades in Race

Russia's march to its first winter Olympics crown was abruptly slowed. In addition to the Russians' failure in skating, Yuri Moschkin, who had led the Nordic combined at the end of the jumping phase, faded in the cross-country test. The Nordic combined consists of a ski-jumping contest and a cross-country ski race, with the best combined score taking the title.

With the games half through, the Soviet athletes lead, with four gold medals and an unofficial total of 89 points. Austria has 46 points, Norway 41, Sweden 39, Finland 28, Switzerland 18½, Italy 18, Germany 10, United States 9½, Netherlands 7, France 6, Japan 5, Poland 4, Spain 3 and Canada 1. Thirteen of the twenty-four events have been completed.

The United States seems assured of the women's figure skating gold medal, if 21-year-old Tenley Albright of Newton Center, Mass., can last through the free skating on Thursday. Skating on an injured ankle and nursing a cold, Miss Albright won the compulsory figures phase of the test today, enjoying a slight margin over 16-year-old Carol Heiss of Ozone Park, Queens.

The two Americans were far ahead of the European champion, Ingrid Wendl of Austria. The United States chances are so bright because both Miss Albright and Miss Heiss are particularly expert in the free skating.

Miss Albright, in a chartreuse skirt and a crimson sweater, gained 1,071.7 points in the school figures. Miss Heiss had 1,054.9; Fraulein Wendl, 1,008.1;

awash with falling bodies. Penelope Pitou, the Laconia, N. H., youngster, stumbled down among the last. "Yell for the coach," she said, "and tell him I forgot my skates."

A further distraction was the appearance of Sophia Loren, the Italian movie actress. Miss Loren is from Naples and does not ski. But, dazzlingly attired in a ski outfit of mustard yellow with a white swagger jacket, she attracted a crowd of photographers, who surged around the finish line as the competitors were coming down. Later she went down the mountain pursued by a mob of spectators.

The parallel lane for the second leg was in better shape, though bare ground showed toward the end. Again Miss Colliard was off first and skied beautifully to register a 1:52.3 clocking for her two runs. She knew it was good enough.

"I can't believe it was me," Miss Colliard yelled, throwing her arms around her coach, Bubi Roberti. "It's the first time I've ever skied for my country."

Twenty-year-old Regina Schopf of Austria was second and Yevgeniya Sidorova of Russia was third. The Russian girl made a brilliant recovery after falling.

Giuliana Minuzzo Chenal, the Italian champion, was fourth and fifth was Josefine Frandl, the Austrian fashion designer who placed second in the giant slalom. The first five places went to those who had started in the first dozen.

In a desperate attempt to make up lost time on the first

run, Mrs. Lawrence forfeited the title she won at Oslo when she fell heavily on the second. She finished twenty-fifth.

Dorothy Surgenor of Seattle was twentieth. Dorothy replaced Betsy Snite of Norwich, Vt., who was out with a sprained ligament. Gladys Werner of Steamboat Springs, Colo., was twenty-seventh and Miss Pitou was disqualified.

Norway has always specialized in the short cross-country races and one of its finest athletes, Brenden, outgalloped the sixty-one-man field in the fifteen-kilometer race.

Brenden came out of the woods poling down to the finish in 49.39 and his superb time was twenty-five seconds faster than Sixten Jernberg's of Sweden. The handsome farmer won the eighteen-kilometer race at Oslo and has since received the Egeberg Trophy, Norway's highest athletic honor.

"My wax was good," Brenden said. "Mine was not," said Jernberg. "I waxed for conditions below freezing. It was above."

#### Russian Ace Is Tenth

Earlier this week Jernberg finished second in the thirty-kilometer cross-country. The winner of that race, Veikko Hakulinen of Finland, was fourth today, just behind Pavel Koltchin of Russia, who lost a pole and valuable time en route. Hakon Brusveen and Martin Stokken of Norway were fifth and sixth, respectively.

The failure of Vladimir Kuzin,

Yvonne Sugden of Great Britain, 991.4; Hanna Eigel of Austria, 978.8, and Carole Jane Pachl of Canada, 953.7. Catherine Machado of Los Angeles was tenth with 930.4 points.

"My foot hurt today," said Miss Albright, who has twice been the world champion. "But I've got a day of rest and a lot of faith."

It was freezing cold on Col Druscie this morning and clouds shrouded the top of the men's slalom course. The ski run pitches sheerly down for 650 yards through a forest of 170 colored flags that marked the trail of the competitors.

As usual, the top rated athletes went off first. The great Sailer could be heard zooming down. A low roar of "Ooooh"—the Austrians' victory chant—swelled to a crescendo as Sailer thudded across the finish in 1 minute 27.3 seconds.

Dodge, who was nearly omitted from the Olympic team followed in 1:27.6 and Americans from all over hastily formed a cheering section.

It took three hours for the field to complete the first run. The spectators were numbed with the cold and jeered the tail-enders, most of them too inept to be allowed on this dangerous course.

Then Sailer made his second run. Shoulders and hips swinging, the Austrian plumber thrust out his chest like a sprinter as he scored in 1:47.4. His total time of 3:14.7 was best by four seconds.

**Favored for Third Medal**

Earlier this week, Sailer had taken the giant slalom. He is an overwhelming favorite to win a third gold medal in the downhill race.

"That I do good," he said. "Better than this. Today I must brake too much."

Igaya was second in 3:18.7. The little Japanese with the weaving style made the best run of his life. "I ski better when I'm nervous, and I was plenty scared," he said.

Stig Sollander, the Swede who beat Dodge for fifth place in the giant slalom at Oslo in 1952, finished ahead of him again today. Sollander's time was 3:20.2, Dodge's was 3:21.8.

Georges Schneider of Switzerland and Gerard Pasquier of France were fifth and sixth, respectively. Thomas Corcoran of Westfield, N. J., and Ralph Miller of Hanover, N. H., both from Dartmouth, finished nineteenth and twenty-second, respectively. Wallace Werner of Steamboat Springs, Colo., fell too often and was disqualified.

Throughout the games one man has consistently dominated his specialty. Stenerson did that in the Nordic combined. He won in the 15-kilometer (9.3 mile) cross-country race in 56:18. That, with his second place in the jumping, gained 455 points.

There was no one anywhere near him. The tall, thin Norwegian took the Holmenkollen gold medal for the best athletic performance in Norway last year.

**Ericsson Is Second**

Far behind, but within two points of each other were Bengt Ericsson, the Swedish woodchopper; Francis Gron Gasienica of Poland; Paavo Korhonen, a Finnish electrician; Arne Barhaugen, a Norwegian carpenter, and Tormod Knutsen, who works in an Oslo office. There were no Americans in the first twenty.

In the 10,000 meter speed skating race, a cold mist from the Dolomite peaks frosted Lake Misurina and slowed what is considered the fastest ice in the world, where the Russians have been setting new standards all week. Even so, Ericsson was timed in 16:35.9, an Olympic record and just three seconds back of Norseman Hjalmar Andersen's world record.

"I changed my style for this one," said Ericsson hoarsely, his throat raw from the weather. "I shortened my strokes. It worked, but I was so tired that I lost two seconds on the last lap."

The Swede lasted just long enough to beat Knut Johannsen, a 23-year-old Norwegian electrician who was timed in 16:36.9. Oleg Goutcharenko of Russia was third, as he was against Ericsson in Moscow last winter.

Norway's Sverre Haugli was fourth, Kees Broekman of the Netherlands fifth and the old wonder, Hjalmar Andersen, thrice a gold medal winner at Oslo, was sixth.

Matt McNamara of Minneapolis was twenty-seventh.

Tomorrow, with Hayes Alan Jenkins and Ronald Robertson on deck in the men's figure skating, America should win its first gold medal.

February 1, 1956

# U. S. Sweeps Men's Figure Skating, Swiss Girl Olympic Downhill Ski Victor

## H. A. JENKINS WINS, ROBERTSON IS NEXT

### Colorado Star Gains Title, but Coast Youth Excels in Free-Skating Phase

**By FRED TUPPER**
Special to The New York Times.

CORTINA D'AMPEZZO, Italy, Feb. 1—The strains of The Star Spangled Banner swelled over the Winter Olympic ice stadium tonight. At long last the United States had won its first event, the men's figure skating, sweeping all three medals.

In a finish so close that the judges calculated with slide rules for two hours, Hayes Alan Jenkins, the three-time world champion from Colorado Springs, edged the 18-year-old marvel, Ronnie Robertson of Los Angeles.

It was the polished technician against a master showman on the hard, bumpy rink in the fading light of this chilly afternoon. Jenkins skated flawlessly. Robertson performed his private bag of tricks and, as the crowd watched in amazement, shot into the triple Salchow—a jump that only three men in the world have

MEN'S FIGURE SKATING STARS: This trio gave the U. S. her first gold, silver, and bronze medals at the 1956 Olympics in Italy. Left to right: Hayes Alan Jenkins, who took top honors; Ronald Robertson, second, and David Jenkins, Hayes' brother, who was third.

The United States dominated men's figure skating at the 1956 Olympics. Hayes Alan Jenkins is shown here on his way to a first place finish. Ronnie Robertson took second and Jenkins' brother, David, was third.

In 1947, Tenley Albright was stricken with polio. In 1953, she became the first American woman to win the world's figure skating championship, which she won again in 1956. She was U.S. champion, 1952–1956, and is shown here being scrutinized by judges at the 1956 Olympics. The judges evidently liked what they saw: she was awarded first place.

Austria's Toni Sailer dominated Alpine skiing at the 1956 Olympics. He won in the slalom, giant slalom and downhill.

attempted in such competition. Robertson's extraordinary leaps and spins earned him the nod in the free-skating, but Jenkins had enough of a margin in the compulsory figures to gain the victory.

David Jenkins, Hayes' kid brother, was third. The trio received their awards tonight in a Stadium ceremony.

In other events, a Swiss milkmaid, Madeleine Berthod, celebrated her twenty-fifth birthday by winning the women's downhill ski race, and the Finnish team rallied in the last mile to take the women's 15-kilometer (9.3-mile) cross-country relay.

Earlier in the day, Art Tyler, the 40-year-old Rochester (N. Y.) physicist, piloted his four-man bobsled to the first place in the time trials. This was the first time—in practice or in competition—that any country had scored ahead of Italy in bobsledding at Cortina. However, this was still practice; the competition begins Friday.

At the close of the sixth day of the Winter Games, Russia leads with four gold medals and an unofficial point score of 94. Austria has 48½, Norway 44, Sweden 43, Finland 38, Switzerland 33½, the United States 28⅞, Italy 21½, Germany 10, France 9, Netherlands 7, Poland 6, Canada 5, Japan 5, Spain 3, Czechoslovakia 3 and Great Britain 1.

After the figure-skating judges had ended their prolonged huddle, Hayes Jenkins was declared the winner of the Olympic crown by only a fraction of a point. The waiting was torture and the anxious parents were in as much of a dither as were the competitors.

David Jenkins was so wrought up that he shouted to Hayes: "If they take this one away from you, I'll never skate again."

**Robertson Opens Program**

Robertson went on first. He had nothing to lose and decided to throw in his whole repetoire.

But the ice was against him, scratched and slippery.

He started smoothly and slowly as a showman should, getting the feel of the ice and the feel of the audience. Suddenly he spun into a double flip and double Axel and then faster, into a camel with jump sit, all intricate figures that he executed with ease.

Then, building speed again, the Californian leaped into the triple loop—a jump only America's Dick Button had done before him and a feat so dangerous that no European skater had ever tried it. The leap didn't quite come off, but Robertson recovered quickly and burst into the triple Salchow as the crowd roared.

In a smash finish, Robertson rolled into the flying sit and spin that has made him famous.

Robertson's maneuvers were among the most complex in figure skating. A Salchow is a jump made from the inside back edge of one foot, followed by a nearly complete revolution in the air, with the landing on the outside back edge of the opposite foot.

An Axel is a jump in which the skater takes off from an outer forward edge, does one and one-half turns in the air and lands on the outer backward edge of the other skate. It is therefore a waltz jump with a complete turn in the air added. Doing a double Axel consists of two such maneuvers in succession.

A loop in skating is a small elliptical figure turned on one leg without change of edge inside a larger circle. The flying sit and spin consists of a leap to one skate and then a spin until the skater finally sinks to a sitting position.

Jenkins left the dressing room knowing that Robertson had done brilliantly. The figures had been posted and now he, too, had to go all out.

As a champion must, Jenkins took the gamble. He called on the smooth, sound technique

built through years of practice, the waltzing glide that developed into a double Axel, then the double flip, and warming up, quickly the double-toed loop and the double Lutz.

A flip is a jump from the outer backward edge to the inner forward edge of the same skate. A Lutz is a jump in which the take-off is from the outside back edge with the toe of the free foot jabbed into the ice directly behind the skating heel. A complete rotation is made in the air, the skater landing on the outside back edge of the other foot.

There was no hesitation, no awkwardness in Jenkins' skating. When his five minutes were up, the applause was warm and appreciative.

The official results gave Robertson the free skating phase by 651.9 points to 645.5. Jenkins had a 12-point lead in the compulsory figures.

However, other complex calculations were involved. When it was all over, Jenkins had 166.4 points, Robertson 165.7. The world champion had won his biggest victory.

David Jenkins was third with 162.8 points after a fine, free exhibition. The European champion, the gay, gifted Alain Giletti of France was fourth. Karel Divin, the Czech youngster, and Michael Booker of Great Britain tied for fifth.

Miss Berthod, considered the best woman's skier in Europe, won the downhill after disappointments in two earlier races. She missed a gate in the giant slalom that cost her the crown and spilled helplessly in the slalom.

Today she roared down the fast, mile-long Canalone track faster than any girl had ever done it. Around the turn and down the last long stretch she zoomed, crouched low on her skies with her arms pumping to gain the last split-second of speed.

Her time was 1:40.7, more than four seconds ahead of the

clocking of her nearest rival.

Another Swiss mountain girl, Frieda Danzer, cracked an injury jinx that had dogged her since she began competing. Three years ago she broke a leg and had fallen or been hurt in nearly every big race since. Today the 23-year-old skier from Bern Canton finished in 1:45.4 to take second place.

Lucille Wheeler of Canada was third. The daughter of a Quebec innkeeper and a skier since she could toddle, Miss Wheeler had a great run at the top, but admitted to losing ground in the stretches.

**Signora Minuzzo Fourth**

Giuliana Minuzzo, an Italian signora, was fourth. The Austrian housemaid, Hilde Hofherr, was fifth, and Clara Marchelli of Italy sixth.

Gladys (Skeeter) Werner of Steamboat Springs, Colo., finished tenth, Mrs. Andrea Mead Lawrence of Parshall, Colo., thirtieth and Penelope Pitou of Laconia, N. H., thirty-fifth. Mrs. Dorothy Surgenor of Seattle was thirty-eighth.

Russia was in front and the Finns a shaky third after two kilometers of the women's relay, a rugged test of speed and endurance. Russia was still ahead and the Finns second after twelve kilometers.

Then ash-blonde Mme. Siiri Rantanen, a 30-year old mother, made her bid. She passed Radija Yeroshina, lost the lead and finally regained it again and pulled steadily away to win by 100 yards. The Russian girl was so exhausted that she stumbled over her poles and had to be helped after reaching the finish.

The Finns were clocked in 1:09.01, the Russians in 1:09.28. A fine last lap, the fastest of the morning, by Sonja Edstroem, put the Swedes third.

February 2, 1956

---

# Tenley Albright and Miss Heiss Finish One, Two in Olympic Figure Skating

## JERNBERG VICTOR IN SKI MARATHON

### Swede First in 50-Kilometer Test—Miss Albright Brings U. S. Second Gold Medal

**By FRED TUPPER**
Special to The New York Times.

CORTINA D'AMPEZZO, Italy, Feb. 2—A long time ago a little American girl conquered polio. This afternoon, ten years later, she fought off the agony of a

throbbing ankle to win another test—the women's figure skating championship of the seventh Winter Olympic Games.

Tenley Albright twice has been world champion and four times champion of the United States. This was the big one she had never won, and she was ready. Then ten days ago she gashed a half-inch hole in her right ankle while practicing and the wound refused to heal.

Launching the double loop jump—a high point in her repertoire—she twinged that ankle again competing today.

There was a moment's hesitation, then she went on like a trouper and finished with the top score in the free-skating field.

A double loop is a jump in which the skater takes off from

the outside edge of either skate, makes two full revolutions in the air and lands back on the outside edge of the skate on the jumping foot.

It was the second gold medal for the United States here and almost a duplication of the victory yesterday when Hayes Alan Jenkins, Ronnie Robertson and David Jenkins placed one, two, three in the men's figure skating.

#### Miss Machado Eighth

Little Carol Heiss, the New York teen-ager from Ozone Park, Queens, skated magnificently to finish second, and Catherine Machado of Los Angeles, who was third in the free, after having lost points in the compulsory phase, took eighth place.

In the fifty-kilometer (31 miles 120 yards) cross-country

skiing, one of the most grueling tests of skill, strength and stamina ever devised in the name of sport, Sixten Jernberg beat the Finnish and Russian threats to push Sweden into third place in the unofficial team standings.

Tonight Russia led with 101 points. Austria had 54½, Sweden 53; Finland, 46; Norway, 44; United States, 43½; Switzerland, 33½; Italy, 21½; Germany, 10; France, 9; the Netherlands, 7; Canada, 6; Poland, 6; Japan, 5; Great Britain, 4; Spain, 3, and Czechoslovakia, 3.

The points are computed on a 10-5-4-3-2-1 basis for six places.

Under Olympic scoring Russia had four gold medals, and Austria, Finland, Norway, Sweden, Switzerland and the United States two each. Germany and Italy had one each. There are six

Associated Press Radiophotos

A FAST MAN ON SKIS: Sixten Jernberg of Sweden entering stadium to win the rigorous 50-kilometer cross-country ski-marathon in 2 hours 50 minutes 27 seconds.

events left on the program.

The American hockey team drubbed Sweden, 6 to 1, tonight and now shares the lead with Russia. Each team has three victories in as many starts, with two games to go. The leaders will meet tomorrow.

**Standing Room Only**

A warm sun shone on the rink of the Olympic ice stadium, and there was standing room only in the wooden bleachers when Miss Albright appeared on the ice.

She was dressed in a dark rose wool sweater, with red flowers in her straight blond hair, and seemed poised and confident. She shook hands with the referee and bowed three times to the crowd of 10,000. Then the music started, and she swung into her routine.

Smiling, Tenley executed a stag and then, spinning, went into the one-and-a-half turn delayed Axel that has made her famous. She was skating beautifully now and danced the length of the ice.

The stag maneuver is entered in a backward position, jumped from the toe point with a half-turn in the air. The trailing leg is extended and the back arched. The landing is normally forward.

An Axel is a jump in which the skater takes off from an outer forward edge, does one and one-half turns in the air and lands on the outer backward edge of the other skate.

Now it was time for the double-loop jump. She leaped into it and her ankle turned. The pause was barely noticeable. She skated out of trouble and stretched out in a series of splits.

**Whirls to the Finish**

The tempo quickened and Tenley was all out, flying into a double-toe loop and a cross-foot spin. She spun up, whirling to the finish, and the spectators let out a long roar.

The double-toe loop is executed from the forward outside edge of the figure 3. The opposite foot takes the ice on the outside back edge and the foot that executed the 3 is extended to the rear. The skater jabs the opposite foot into the ice, jumps into the air and makes two full revolutions in the direction of the 3 turn. The landing is made on the foot opposite the one on which the 3 turn was made.

In a cross-foot spin the spinning is done on the outside back edges of both skates while legs are crossed.

The judges came out, holding their cards high. The scores were almost uniform in their excellence. Tenley had averaged just under 5.8, an impeccable performance under such pressure. Six is tops.

There was only one girl that had a chance to beat Tenley—Miss Heiss.

The sun was gone now, hidden by the Dolomites, when Carol appeared in a dress of aquamarine, with green helmet and black gloves.

Light and fast on her skates, Carol built up speed for the dou-

ble loop double loop—a tremendous figure—and broke out of it into a full split.

The double loop double loop is two double-loop jumps executed in sequence without an intervening step.

A rhythmic swing of the hips and she was down ice again, dancing delightfully to soft music. Up went the beat and she plunged into the sit spin and out, a thin, revolving blur as her pony tail whipped around her head like a plane's propeller.

A sit spin is done on a full knee bend on one leg, the other foot extended to the front. Out means to come up and finish with a stand-up spin.

It was all over and cheers rang incessantly down the rink as Carol skated off and hugged her mother.

Then jeers rose as the judges posted their figures. "Six, six, six," the spectators cried.

With all the free skating marks in, Carol had scored 794 points and Tenley 795.7.

By the complex calculations of the judges, it was determined that in the over-all scoring Miss Albright had 13 ordinals or placements and 169.6 points and Miss Heiss 20 ordinals and 168.1 points.

"We call her (Carol) the bridesmaid," said Mrs. Heiss, "always second to Tenley."

The press crowded around Miss Albright, who was limping slightly.

"It's like fighting with one arm tied behind your back," said the Radcliffe College junior from Newton Center, Mass.

"You were dead game," said her coach, Maribel Y. Vinson, an American champion for years.

Tenley has a fortnight to rest before defending her world title at Garmisch-Partenkirchen, Germany.

**European Champion Third**

Third today was Ingrid Wendl, the European champion from Vienna, who had scored so well in the compulsory figures. Fourth was Yvonne de Monfort Sugden, the 16-year-old brunette from Great Britain, and then followed Austria's Hanna Eigel, the European titleholder in 1954, and

Carole Jane Pachl of Canada.

With the temperature fifteen degrees below freezing, thirty rugged athletes skied off at dawn over the fifty-kilometer course that winds almost endlessly up and down these mountains.

The marathon over twenty-six miles is considered the ultimate trial of endurance in foot racing, yet this looping trial runs thirty-one miles under even tougher conditions. Today the snow was well-packed and the track fast.

Jernberg took the lead at the first check point and held grimly to it hour after hour. Just after 11 this morning, he spurted out of the woods. Down past the last white chalet and into the sloping straight.

A wide grin on his tanned face and a red stocking hat perched precariously on his corn-colored hair, he poled furiously to the finish.

A small army of compatriots shouted "heia, heia, Sverige"—a battle cry reserved for Sweden's heroes. They grabbed Jernberg as he poled out and tossed him into the air.

Jernberg is a woodsman from the hamlet of Limaa, some 300 miles north of Stockholm on the Arctic Circle. In spare moments, he runs or skis and is in superb condition the year round.

His time today was 2 hours 50 minutes 27 seconds, more than a minute ahead of his long-time rival, Veikko Hakulinen of Finland. Last Friday "Weikko the Woodchopper" won the 30-kilometer race and Sixten was second.

The clocking was more than 43 minutes faster than when Veikko won the race at the 1952 Olympics at Oslo, Norway.

Eero Kolehmainen of Finland, second then, was fourth today behind the 20-year-old Moscow pediatrics student, Fyodor Terentiev. Anatoli Schelyukhin and Pavel Kolchin, whose wife skied for Russia in the relay, were fifth and sixth.

"I had said before the race that who starts last will finish first," said Jernberg. That was where he was drawn. And that's all he said.

*February 3, 1956*

---

# Austrians Take Downhill Skiing And Pair Figure-Skating Titles

## Sailer Completes Sweep of Three Alpine Tests—Elisabeth Schwarz and Oppelt Defeat Canadian World Champions

**By FRED TUPPER**
Special to The New York Times.

CORTINA D'AMPEZZO, Italy, Feb. 3—Anton (Toni) Sailer entered the hall of the Olympic immortals today. The bronzed 20-year-old Austrian glazier—who looks like a movie star and skis like a dream—roared down the plunging two-mile Tofana

run wide open to win in an unwieldy field of seventy-five in the downhill race, the last Alpine event of the Winter Games.

His clear-cut triumph gave him the "hat trick." It was the first time any man had captured all three Alpine events in the

Winter Olympics. It elevated him to the stature of the other athletic giants who at one time ruled the world.

Jesse Owens of America took both foot-racing sprints, the broad jump and anchored the winning relay team at the Berlin Summer Olympics in 1936.

Thorlief Haugh, a Norwegian skier, won three events in the cross-country and jumping back in 1924. Hjalmar Andersen of Norway swept the three speed-skating titles at Oslo, Norway, in 1952 and the fabulous Czech, Emil Zatopek, won the 5,000 and 10,000-meter runs and the marathon at Helsinki, Finland, that summer.

Their names forever are written in the history of sport. Add that of Toni Sailer.

### Waltzers From Vienna

Elisabeth Schwarz and Kurt Oppelt, the waltzers from Vienna, staged a dazzling · display before 13,000—the largest crowd of the games—to capture the pair figure-skating crown.

So tonight, with two days to go, Austria has rocketed into a tie with Russia for the Winter Olympic championship. Under this scoring, only first places count. Austria has four, so has Russia.

Under the unofficial point scoring—a newspaper device to record the first six places on a 10-5-4-3-2-1 basis—Russia leads with 101 points. Austria has 78½, Sweden, 53; Finland, 46; United States, 45½; Norway, 44; Switzerland, 41½; Italy, 22½; Germany, 15.

Also, Canada, 12; France, 9; the Netherlands, 7; Poland, 6; Japan, 5; Great Britain, 4; Hungary, 4; Spain, 3, and Czechoslovakia, 3.

Early in the morning a Swiss mechanic piloted his four-man bobsled down the icy Pista di Ronco mile chute in record time to take the first two heats in that precarious exercise. The No. 2 Swiss team was second and the United States third. Two heats wind it up tomorrow.

The downhill run on Tofana is dangerous and devilish, a 3,500-yard ribbon that starts up among the splintered Dolomite crags and stretches straight down mountain for a half-mile. It was so fast today that the first half-dozen skiers either fell or failed to finish.

#### Travels at Full Speed

Sailer was No. 14. He hit the first precipice at full speed, driving between two rocky needles visible from the whole valley, and burst out into the open at an Alpine hut.

He was gone again into the woods and careened around two big bends. Then the Austrian hit the Italian "Suicide Six," a washboard roller-coaster where the Japanese, Chick Igaya, had already come to grief and the Frenchman, Rene Collet, had smashed a ski.

Toni teetered here, off-balance, then recovered and broke into sight. Suddenly he was on the last summit, schussing into the straight at better than a mile a minute.

As he flashed by, the Austrian mountain men who blanket the slopes here let out a full-throated roar that died instantly as they waited for the time. It was 2 minutes 52.2 seconds.

Sailer is a legend wherever skiers gather in the Alps. He has entered two dozen races in the past two years and won nearly every one. At Cortina he first took the giant slalom, added the slalom and then capped his feats with the downhill. Not a man was within striking distance of him in any one of them.

"This was the toughest," he said, as he skied up from the finish to take the plaudits of his admirers. "I almost fell back there," he added, pointing with a pole to the horror he had gone over.

Nearly everybody else did. Spectators checking their cards missed whole blocks of numbers where the skiers had come a cropper and were carted away in stretchers or ambulances. Forty-seven finished, some of them battered and bruised.

A Swiss, Raymond Fellay, a substitute starter, was next in 2:55.7; an Austrian truck driver, Andreas Molterer, was third; Roger Staub of Switzerland fourth; Hans Peter Laing of Germany fifth and Gino Burrini of Italy sixth.

Only one of the four American starters finished and he fell en route. He was Wallace (Bud) Werner of Steamboat Springs, Colo., and he tied for eleventh.

The world champion, Fritz Kapus, settled a personal feud with the Cortina bobsled run today. In 1954 he suffered a back injury so serious that he had to withdraw and was hospitalized.

Now 46 and hearty, he shot his sled down the glazed slide in 1:17.19 to smash all existing records. His two-heat total was a fraction of a second better than that of a team-mate, Max Angst, a Zurich butcher.

Last night the run had been sprayed with water to make it faster. The result was horrendous. The French tore a huge hole on the hairpin Christallo Curve and there buried their chances.

The Polish No. 2 sled hit the gash next and its brakeman cracked a rib. Art Tyler, the Rochester (N. Y.) physicist, tore through and bounced off the cement underneath.

#### American Sled Third

The Americans wore shoe coats of steel mesh to help their push start and wound up third. Then the referee stopped the racing for a half hour to fill the hole.

The second American sled, driven by Jim Bickford of Saranac Lake, N. Y., was twentieth and next to last.

From the start of the pair figure skating it was the Austrian European champions or the Canadian world champions to win. But the scoring is so complex that again the chilly stadium was deserted before a decision was reached.

The Austrians skated in white and black, Fraeulein Schwarz in lamé with a Juliet rhinestone helmet and Oppelt in a dark edged suit. They swung away in a series of spirals and lifts and built up speed for the immensely difficult double Salchows and loops.

To the delight of the Austrians, now down from the hills, they switched to waltz time and then broke out in a death spiral, with Elisabeth's blonde curls revolving inches off the ice. It was gay, gifted skating of the highest order.

There were dark shadows on the ice as Frances Dafoe and Norris Bowden appeared for Canada. Racing down rink, they wove from loops to floats, from split jumps to stags in a perfectly meshed treat of free, fast skating. A last, blinding spin and Frances leaped into Bowden's arms and they spiraled to cheers.

When the returns were in, the Austrians had just made it, winners by point fractions.

The only two Hungarians to appear at the Winter Games—Marianna and Laslo Nagy—were third on the strength of their spectacular overhead lifts.

Twelve-year-old Marika Kilius and 17-year-old Franz Ningel of Germany were fourth and their superb routine caused such a stir that when the judges flashed low figures, the unruly crowd booed for ten minutes. Oranges, bread crumbs and a chianti bottle hurtled down from the terraces.

February 4, 1956

# RUSSIANS WIN HOCKEY TITLE AND WINTER OLYMPICS

## SOVIET SKI VICTOR

### First in 40-Kilometer Relay—Swiss Take 4-Man Bob Title

**By FRED TUPPER**
Special to The New York Times.

CORTINA D'AMPEZZO, Italy, Feb. 4—A middle-aged mechanic with massive shoulders and hands of iron and four upright young men from the Soviet Union entered the fading spotlight of the Olympic Winter Games today.

The mechanic was Franz Kapus, 46, who works in a Zurich flour mill. He hurtled his red Swiss thunderbolt down the icy Pista di Ronco run in record time to swamp the four-man bob competition.

The four young men, Fyodor Terentiev, Pavel Kolchin, Nikolai Anikin and Vladimir Kuzin, skied with determination over twenty-five miles of rugged mountain terrain and brought victory to Russia in the forty-kilometer cross-country relay test. Each man raced ten kilometers.

That laudable feat, rewarded by an embrace from the Soviet Minister of Sport, gave Russia her fifth gold medal. As a result, Russia clinched the Winter Olympics championship in her first attempt.

Russia defeated Canada, 2—0, to take the hockey title and her sixth gold medal. The United States sextet finished in second place by beating Czechoslovakia, 9 to 4.

#### Austrian Total a Surprise

On an unofficial point-score basis, Russia had 121 points and Austria, with a population less than that of New York City, surprisingly had 78½ on the strength of Anton (Toni) Sailer's magnificent triple in the slalom, giant slalom and downhill skiing and the narrow triumph of those gay waltzers, Elisabeth Schwarz and Kurt Oppelt, in the pair figure skating.

Sweden had 60, Switzerland and the United States, 54½ each; Finland, 51; Norway, 47; Italy, 31½; Germany, 17; Canada, 16; France, 10; the Netherlands, 7; Poland, 6; Japan and Czechoslovakia, 5 each; Great Britain and Hungary, 4 each, and Spain, 3.

The points are reckoned on a 10-5-4-3-2-1 basis for six places.

Left on the card was the ski jumping tomorrow. More than 30,000 enthusiasts from all over the Alps are expected to stampede the slopes for the jumping, traditionally the highlight of these games.

The Winter Olympic closing ceremony will be staged later in the afternoon.

The mercury was low and the

Associated Press Radiophotos

**CLOSE TO DISASTER:** Driver Max Angst had to work hard to keep control of the No. 2 Swiss bobsled yesterday at this point. The team finished fourth. The No. 1 Swiss unit won.

sun was still shielded by the Dolomite peaks when the twenty-one bobsled quartets opened their last two assaults on this treacherous mile.

Kapus in the Swiss No. 1 sled had the overnight lead on his record 1:17.19 second run. A fraction of a second behind was Max Anget in the Swiss No. 2 sled, and within striking distance were Art Tyler of Rochester, N. Y., and the brilliant Eugenio Monti, the carrot-topped Italian lumberman.

Cortina is considered one of the two fastest bob runs in the world—the other is Lake Placid, N. Y.—and certainly the trickiest.

After the sleds had torn gaping holes in its fifteen-foot banks yesterday and an injured Pole had been taken to the hospital, a small army of men moved in blocks of ice, setting them in tile fashion along the walls and cementing them with slush.

The times were moderate today until Kapus made his great run from the last position. The weather-beaten Swiss mechanic, with Gottfried Diener, Robert Alt and Heinrich Angst behind him, were ready.

They were shod in soles of steel mesh to get better footing. As Franz shouted, they rocked the red sled and sprinted for the electric eye start. Kapus was in the sled now, hands of whipcord on the steering ropes. Then

they were all aboard and off.

By now the curves had been slashed by the steel runners, and slabs of ice—the size of gigantic cubes—were strewn down the chute. The tile design was a crazy mosaic of potholes and there were zigzag ruts all down the line.

Kapus shot into the Stries Curve, high up on the course, his team upright and alert behind him. They were all straining to see, to think and to shift with danger.

Through the goggles under their football helmets they caught sight of a crater in the labyrinth sector. Kapus tugged his ropes, they leaned left and raced through at a mile a minute.

**Takes Curve Low**

The green light shot up on the scoreboard. Kapus was at the split now—on Belvedere Curve —and the time was sensational. The throng in the stands at Antelao Hairpin had barely time to beat frozen hands together when Kapus had come and gone, ricocheting into Cristallo Curve. He took it low—as a great driver should—and thundered down the stretch.

A roar echoed up the mountainside as his clocking figures blared forth from the loud speaker. They were 1:17.09—a record for the run. That run did it.

At the bottom Kapus shouted: "the course is too dangerous." The next time down he took it easier. He could afford to. His four-heat total was 5:10.44 and he had an important second and a half to spare.

"It's my last run ever," he

said later. "I've won and I'm done. Too old."

Franz had waited a long time for this. He had been fifth at St. Moritz, Switzerland, in 1948, fourth at the Oslo (Norway) Olympics in 1952 and he cracked his back so seriously at Cortina in 1954 that he was forced to hand over the reins to another driver.

At 46, he had beaten his private jinx and brought the Olympic crown back to Switzerland.

Monti was next. The daredevil Italian, who broke his leg skiing and turned to bobbing, made perfect slush straddles on both runs to finish second. He already had taken the two-man title.

Third was Tyler, a physicist and a deliberate man, who had tested his sled in a New York University wind tunnel and plotted every move of his sled like a chess master. At 40, he, too, thought he'd had enough.

The Swiss No. 2, the Italian No. 1 and the German No. 1 sleds finished in that order behind Tyler.

Russia had come to Cortina with a colossal reputation in both speed skating and cross-country skiing. In skating, it was justified. They won three events and a total of 53 points on the ice at Lake Misurina. In cross-country skiing, they had been bilked and balked.

Hallgeir Brenden of Norway had won the fifteen-kilometer event, Sixten Jernberg of Sweden had taken the thirty and the "old woodchopper," Veikko Hakulinen of Finland had skied

away with the fifty. Today the Russians strung together their four best.

Terentiev, the 20-year-old Moscow pediatrics student, got off slowly. His wax was sticking slightly and at the first check point—a mile out—he was behind Hakon Brusveen of Norway and Sepp Schneeberger of Austria.

Then he made his move in the woods, poling down through the rough terrain with a long spurt. A Swede, Lennart Larsson, fell when a Yugoslav's ski pole stuck in his shoe binding and dropped half a minute wrenching it loose. His ten - kilometer stint over, Terentiev was a minute and a half in front of August Kiuru of Finland.

Pavel Kolchin took over. He was in tremendous fettle. Swinging steadily along, he built up speed for the downhill leg and came home in 33:05 for the six-mile stint, the best time of the day. The Russians had nearly three minutes on the field, a huge margin.

Arvo Viitanen of Finland cut it down on the third stage, gaining a minute on Anikin, and the Swedes, a bad sixth in the early stages, were now driving along in third.

Vladimir Kuzin, probably the biggest disappointment of the Russian team, was anchor. At the games here, he had done nothing and had been sidelined in bed with fever only two days ago.

He was out there in front and strung out behind were those menaces, Hakulinen and Jernberg. But the lead was too much.

When Kuzin poled into the stretch, snow sticking to his red sweater, he had 150 yards in hand. The woodchopper and the Swede had picked up a minute but the gap was too great.

The United States quartet of Ted Farwell, Montague City, Mass.; Andrew Miller, McCall, Idaho; Larry Damon, Burlington, Vt., and Marvin Crawford of Denver was twelfth in the field of fourteen. Coach Al Merrill of Lebanon, N. H., appeared satisfied.

"This sport," he said, "doesn't seem to fit into the American standard of living."

February 5, 1956

# U.S.S.R. SIX BEATS CANADIANS, 2 TO 0

## Russians Capture Sixth Gold Medal in Cortina Games— U. S. Second in Hockey

**By The United Press.**

CORTINA D'AMPEZZO, Italy, Feb. 4—Russia won the hockey championship and her sixth gold medal of the Winter Olympics by defeating Canada, 2—0, tonight. The United States, which had figured to be merely an also-ran, wound up with the second-place silver medal by beating Czechoslovakia, 9—4.

After America had beaten the Czechs and the United States coach, Johnny Mariucci, declared he was "proud as hell" of his team, the Russians thrilled a capacity crowd of 12,700 at Olympic Stadium by shutting out the Canadians. It was the fifth straight triumph for the U. S. S. R. in the final round of the hockey tournament.

Russia, making her first appearance in Olympic hockey competition, swept eight games. The Soviet Union skaters won all three of their preliminary-round contests in addition to the five they captured in the championship round.

The five final-round victories gave first place in hockey to the Russians with 10 points. The United States, which won four games and lost only to Russia, finished second with eight. Canada, the pre-tournament favorite, won the third-place bronze medal with 6 points on three

victories and two defeats.

Sweden, which played a 1-1 tie with Germany earlier in the day, was fourth in the hockey standings with one victory, one tie and three losses for 3 points. Czechoslovakia was fifth with 2 points on the basis of one victory and four losses. Germany, which lost four games and played one tie, finished last with a lone point.

There were two heroes in the victory that made the Soviet Union skaters the world hockey champions. They were Valentin Kuzin, a reserve forward who had a hand in both goals, and Nikolai Puchkov, who turned in his third shutout in the nets.

Puchkov, who had made twenty-four saves against the Canadians, previously had blanked the United States and Germany.

The Russians went ahead in the second period of the pay-off game at 5:25. Yuri Khrylov took a pass from Kuzin to beat the Canadian goalie, Keith Woodall, whose vision was obscured on the shot.

Russia added her insurance

goal fifty-five seconds after the start of the third period. Kuzin, who was stationed near the sideboards about five feet inside the Canadian blue line, latched on to Alexander Uvarov's pass and drilled it past Woodall from fifteen feet out.

The surprising United States team gained its fourth victory in the five games played in the championship flight and avenged a 4-3 beating the Americans took from Czechoslovakia in the preliminaries.

### Dougherty Nets 4 Goals

The Americans poured it on from the start. Richard Dougherty, a defense man from International Falls, Minn., led the team. He scored four goals, all in the third period.

The other United States scorers were Gordon Christian of Warroad, Minn., with two; Weldon Olson of Marquette, Mich.; William Cleary of Cambridge, Mass., and Richard Meredith of Minneapolis.

Olson gave the United States a 1-0 lead after twelve minutes of play. He took a pass from Kenneth Purpur of Grand Forks, N. D., and beat the Czech goalie, Jan Vodicka.

Christian made it 2-0 thirty seconds after the second period

opened. He converted a pass from Daniel McKinnon of Williams, Minn.

Then the Czechs scored their first goal. Slavomir Barton took a pass from Vlastimil Bubnik, who figured in all the Czech goals, and beat Donald Rigazio of Cambridge, Mass.

Christian scored his second goal at 4:20 on an assist from Cleary and then, after Vlastimil Bubnik had scored for the Czechs, Cleary converted Christian's relay to make it 4—2 for the United States at the end of the second period.

Dougherty tallied on a pass from John Mayasich of Eveleth, Minn., at 4:20 and then made it 6—2 at 9:35 when he scored unassisted. Twenty-four seconds later Meredith, on an assist from Mayasich, made it 7—2.

After Capt. Katl Gut of the Czechs made it 7—3, Dougherty scored two more goals, the first at 17:10 on passes from Meredith and Mayasich and the second forty seconds later on a pass from Mayasich.

Vlastimil Bubnik, who had assisted on Gut's goal, then notched his second goal with fifty seconds of play remaining.

*February 5, 1956*

# *Finns Finish One, Two in Ski Jump at Cortina as Olympic Winter Games End*

## HYVARINEN FIRST WITH 227 POINTS

### His Second Leap of 275 Feet Decides — Kallakorpi Next —Games' Success Hailed

**By FRED TUPPER**
Special to The New York Times.

CORTINA D'AMPEZZO, Italy, Feb. 5—The sun set on the seventh Winter Olympics tonight. To uproarious applause, the flag-bearers of the thirty-two competing nations marched into the crowded ice stadium for the closing ceremony.

Expressing his deepest gratitude to Giovanni Gronchi. President of the Italian Republic, and to the organizers of the Games, Avery Brundage of the United States, president of the International Olympic Committee, officially declared the Games closed.

Brundage also called upon the "youth of every country to assemble in four years at Squaw Valley (California) for the Winter Games of the seventeenth Olympiad."

Trumpets blared, the stadium lights were dimmed and, precisely at 6 o'clock, the five-ringed Olympic flag was lowered to the music of the Olympic hymn.

A thunderous barrage echoed through the frosty mountain valley as the flagbearers marched out, and then a blaze of fireworks lit up the rocky crags of the Dolomites.

### Brundage Presents Medal

Earlier, Brundage had presented the gold medal for ski-jumping—last athletic event on the program—to Antti Hyvarinen, a 23-year-old Finnish salesman from Lapland. Hyvarinen had made a prodigious jump of 84 meters (275 feet) and his flawless style and form clearly marked him the winner. It was the first time ever that Norway had failed to dominate this event.

Russia, winner in the hockey competition with a record of 5—0, received its sixth gold medal. Under Olympic scoring, which counts first places only, the Soviet had won the Winter Games on its initial attempt. Its other victories were in the 500, 1,500 and 5,000-meter skating; the 40-kilometer cross-country relay and the women's 10-kilometer cross-country.

Austria had four firsts. Toni Sailer's hat trick in the Alpine skiing events and the pair figure skating. Finland took the ski-jumping, 30-kilometer cross-country and women's 15-kilometer cross-country relay, and Switzerland won the four-man bobsled, the women's slalom and downhill.

Norway scored in the 15-kilometer cross-country and classic combined, and Sweden triumphed in the 50-kilometer

cross-country and 10,000 meter skating.

Hayes Alan Jenkins of Colorado Springs, winner in the men's figure skating, and Tenley Albright of Newton Center, Mass., victor in the women's figure skating, triumphed for the United States.

Italy captured the two-man bobsled and Germany the women's giant slalom.

### A Convincing Triumph

By the unofficial point system, the Russian margin was even more convincing. Russia scored a tremendous total of 121 points, followed by Austria with 78½, Finland 66, Sweden 62. Switzerland 55½, the United States 54½, Norway 47, Italy 31½, Germany 24, Canada 16, France 10, the Netherlands 7, Poland 6. Japan 5, Czechoslavakia 5, Hungary 4, Great Britain 4 and Spain 3.

The points were awarded on a 10-5-4-3-2-1 basis for the first six places in the twenty-four events.

Harry Glass, an East German who suddenly joined the ski-jumping elite earlier this winter by winning the Campari Cup at Cortina, led at the end of the first jump today. He soared 83.5 meters (273 feet 11 inches) and his form rating was a scant half point higher than Aulis Kallakorpi of Finland. The latter also leaped 83.5 meters on his first try.

Form judging is rated on the skier's position before take-off, on take-off itself, correctness during flight and, above all, safe-

ness in landing. Ideally, the jumper should be as parallel to the slope as possible when in the air. Form, style and distance all count in the judging.

Today the Trampolino hill was laid out so that 74 meters was considered the safest landing point and 89 meters was just possible, if dangerous. As the slope flattens out beyond, any longer jump meant certain injury.

### Bronze Medal or Gold

All through the Games, the Finns have shown tremendous courage under pressure. Hyvarinen made a courageous decision. Third at the end of the first round, he had the choice of playing safe for a bronze medal or going all out for the gold. He gambled and won.

By virtue of his second leap, Hyvarinen's total point score was 227. This was just short of perfection.

Glass had another jump to come. It was a fine effort and, arms out in swan dive position, he struck snow at 80.5 meters, far short of his first. Kallakorpi was right behind him. The distance was exactly the same but the Finn's form was better.

White mittens forward, Kallakorpi leaned far forward, his whole body immobile. That jump meant the difference. The 26-year-old Finnish electrician had half a point margin over Glass for second place.

Max Bolkart, another German, was fourth, and Sven Pettersson of Sweden was fifth. Eino Kirjonen of Finland and Andreas

Daescher of Switzerland finished in a virtual tie for sixth.

Dick Rahoi of Iron City, Mich., made the longest jump of the Americans. But he spilled, slid far down the stretch and was badly shaken. He finished last.

Art Devlin of Lake Placid was twenty-first, Roy Sherwood of New Canaan, Conn., thirty-sixth, and Willis Olson of Denver forty-third. The American jumps were short and their form mediocre.

Nikolai Kamenski and Koba Tsokadze, the Russians with the revolutionary forward lean style, fared poorly. Kamenski did 83.5 meters on his initial jump but he fell. Tsokadze leaped 82 meters on his second, but he collapsed, too, and snowballed down the slope.

In all, Italy spent $87,500,000, most of it taken from its soccer pool, to stage the Winter Games. They were an unqualified success. The contests were run quickly, well and on time. Press facilities were better than at other post-war Olympics.

There were a few complaints about public transportation to events. But the spectators, mostly Alpine people, good-naturedly walked miles up the mountains and occasionally skied down.

Because Cortina is difficult to approach from major European terminals and partly because the town's accommodations were reported sold out—as at all Olympics—attendance was disappointing. There were 1,800 vacant beds in Cortina all through the Games.

The eighth Winter Olympics are scheduled for Squaw Valley, Calif., in 1960, provided the California Legislature approves a $5,000,000 grant before April.

February 6, 1956

TOP OLYMPIC SKI JUMPERS: Antti Hyvarinen, center, of Finland, who won championship in closing event of yesterday's games at Cortina d'Ampezzo. Aulis Kallakorpi, right, also of Finland, was second, and Harry Glass of East Germany took the third-place prize.

# CAROL HEISS WINS SKATING

## U. S. ACES ONE, TWO

### Carol Heiss Dethrones Tenley Albright in World Skating

By The United Press.

GARMISCH-PARTENKIRCHEN, Germany, Feb. 18—Carol Heiss, a 16-year-old New Yorker, tonight became the world figure skating champion by defeating her arch-rival, Tenley Albright of Newton Center, Mass, the defender, for the first time.

The honey blonde, who turned 16 on Jan. 30, is the second youngest woman to win the world crown. Sonja Henie won it when she was 15.

Carol had been runner-up to Tenley in every major championship of the last two years. But tonight, with her pony-tail hairdo whirling like a propeller in the falling snow, the New Yorker from Ozone Park, Queens, would not be denied.

The determination that took Carol to the rink atop Madison Square Garden at 5 o'clock every morning to practice finally paid off before 8,000 cheering spectators in the Olympic stadium that Adolf Hitler built in this Bavarian resort.

Carol is the second American to win the crown. Miss Albright, who won in 1953 and last year, was the first United States skater to triumph since the women's championships began in 1906.

Miss Heiss won with six first and three second placings from the nine-member jury. Tenley was second with three firsts and six seconds. Ingrid Wendl of Austria was third.

#### British Skater Is Fourth

This margin in the free skating gave Carol the over-all title with 13 placings and 195.19 points. Miss Albright received 14 placings and 194.74 points.

Fraulein Wendl, third in the Olympics also, had 33 placings and 183.83 points. Yvonne Sugden of Britain was fourth with 37 and 182.27.

The Americans swept the individual titles for the second straight year. Hayes Alan Jenkins of Colorado Springs captured the men's crown last night.

The championships will end tomorrow with the dancing pairs title to be decided.

Tenley had forced Carol to take second place in the 1955 world, North American and United States championships and in the Olympic competition in Italy two weeks ago.

It looked as if it would be the same story again this time. The 20-year-old Miss Albright, as grim and devoted to training as Miss Heiss, rallied to take a narrow lead yesterday after four of the six complicated compulsory figures.

But this morning, Carol fought back and took a slight edge over Tenley when the last of the compulsory figures were completed.

The New Yorker never before had beaten her Massachusetts rival in the difficult school figure phase and she pressed her advantage in the free figures tonight.

Miss Albright performed first. Skating to the music of Jacques Offenbach's "Orpheus in Hades," she gave a nearly flawless performance that included a double Axel, double loop and many brilliant spins. But it wasn't good enough this time.

Carol, wearing an emerald green dress, took the crowd and the judges by storm. She unreeled a dazzling series of two double Axels, a double flip, double loops, a flying sit spin and other difficult figures. She skated to Adolphe Adam's "If I Were King."

For four minutes, she jumped so high and spun so fast that

her pony-tail cut the air like a whip. It stood out horizontally behind her as she completed her routine and the crowd, which had braved sub-zero weather, rose and cheered.

Long after Carol, crying with happiness, had gone into her locker room, the crowd was chanting "six, six, six, six," thus asking the jury to give her the maximum mark. Actually, Carol got nine 5.9's in the free skating while Tenley got only one 5.9.

Miss Albright, who fought off polio at 11 and a painful ankle injury recently to win the 1956 Olympic competition, took her defeat like a champion.

"Carol was great, better than ever," she said. "I have absolutely no complaints. The judging was okay."

Both girls said they would skate in the coming United States championships. They said they had no plans as yet to turn professional.

Hanna Eigel of Austria finished fifth with 48 placings and 179.91 points. Catherine Machado of Los Angeles was sixth with 49 and 179.41.

Ann Johnston of Canada was ninth with 72 placings and 175.26 points. Mary Ann Dorsey of Minneapolis, the other American entry, took tenth in the field of twenty-one with 9⁻ placings and 170.39 points.

Miss Albright congratulated Miss Heiss as soon as the decision was announced. Maribel Y. Vinson, Tenley's coach, burst into tears.

Miss Vinson said she had hoped Tenley would catch up tonight but that Carol had skated a "supreme free program." She believed the decision hinged on the first compulsory figure yesterday—a counter forward. Tenley failed to execute it perfectly.

The compulsory figures—complicated figure eights that require tremendous precision skating—count 60 per cent toward the title while the free skating counts 40.

Miss Heiss chalked up 989.5 points for the six compulsory figures, 1.5 points fewer than Miss Albright's 991. But the New Yorker had an ordinal 1 point better than her rival, and it gave her a slim lead in the complicated system used to determine the standing.

Carol had an ordinal or placing of 13, which meant five of the nine judges gave her first place. The others gave her second. Tenley had four firsts and five seconds for an ordinal of 14.

The defending champion started the final two school figures with a slight lead. But Miss Heiss pulled even by winning the fifth maneuver, a forward bracket change bracket. Carol then surpassed Tenley in the final compulsory, a loop change loop, to edge to the front and Tenley never caught up.

February 19, 1956

## TENLEY ALBRIGHT RETAINS U.S. TITLE
### Olympic Queen Beats Carol Heiss in Figure Skating— Miss Machado Third

*By WILLIAM R. CONKLIN*
Special to The New York Times

PHILADELPHIA, March 16— In a decimal-close contest Tenley Albright of Newton Center, Mass. won her fifth consecutive women's national figure-skating title tonight by defeating Carol Heiss of Ozone Park, Queens, at the Philadelphia Arena.

The 20-year-old Olympic champion retained the crown with the stately poise and fluidity of her performance. She swirled through an impressive free-skating routine. On Thursday she had taken the lead in the compulsory school figures, which count 60 per cent toward the total score.

Tonight's meeting was the ninth between Tenley and Carol in the last three years. In these, Tenley has won eight times, Carol triumphing in the world championship last month in Germany.

The 16-year-old junior at the Professional Children's School skated tonight with fire and verve—but not enough to overcome Tenley's lead.

#### Coast Performer Third

Third place went to Catharine Machado of Los Angeles, who had placed third in the school figure. The Californian executed impressive split jumps and cross-foot spins. Her performance, however, ranked well below the two top contenders.

With 10 as a possible perfect mark, Tenley scored 9.5, 9.7, 9.7, 9.8 and 9.7 with five judges on the content of her display. On performance they rated her 9.7, 9.8, 9.9, 9.8 and 9.7. Carol had content scores of 9.5, 9.2, 9.7, 9.7 and 9.8. On performance Carol was rated 9.6, 9.2, 9.7, 9.6. and 9.9.

Judging from the applause, Tenley won the popular verdict as well as the judge's decision. She drew round after round of hand-clapping and yells. Her split jumps, delayed jumps and crossfoot spins, almost flawless in execution, caught the crowd's enthusiasm. The rivals congratulated

each other before the result was announced.

Skating with fire and determination, Carol Heiss drew repeated applause from a crowd of 4,500. She skimmed through her free routine to the recorded music of Alphonse Adams' "If I Were King."

Tenley, according to Dr. Hollis L. Albright, her brain-surgeon father, suffered pain in her right ankle up to four days ago.

#### Brewer Takes Junior Test

She arrived in Philadelphia this week with a bandage over the ankle she gouged in practice last January at Cortina. In all her competitions here she has skated without the bandage. Her music was Jacques Offenbach's "Fantasy."

In other competition, Robert L., Brewer, 17, of the Blade and Edge Club of Pasadena, Calif., won the men's junior event. He had led that class yesterday in school figures.

Barlow Nelson of the Dartmouth Skating Club, Hanover, N.H., was second. He moved up in the final figures from an earlier third place. Bradley R. Lord of Boston was next.

March 17, 1956

# Hayes Jenkins Keeps Skating Title

## Ace Beats Robertson for 4th Straight U. S. Crown

*By WILLIAM R. CONKLIN*
Special to The New York Times.

PHILADELPHIA, March 17— Hayes Alan Jenkins, the Olympic and world figure-skating champion, added his fourth straight national championship to his laurels at the Arena tonight.

It was his last competition before he enters Harvard Law School this fall.

Jenkins, 22, triumphed once more over his closest rival, 18-year-old Ronald Robertson of Long Beach, Calif., who skated with his eligibility under an official protest. The German Skating Federation in charges filed with the United States Figure Skating Association, has charged that an unnamed representative of Robertson had sought excess- of Robertson had sought excessive expenses for exhibitions

Robertson's second place in the men's singles was awarded provisionally. Should the charges be disproved, he will be confirmed officially as the runner-up. If they are proved his second place will be disallowed on the ground of ineligibility as an amateur. He was runner-up to Hayes Jenkins in the Olympics and the world championships this year.

David W. Jenkins, 18, younger

Associated Press Wirephoto

Carol Heiss, left, and Tenley Albright hold trophies awarded to them last Friday night at national figure skating tourney. Skaters have been keen competitors in the world rinks.

brother of Hayes, took his customary third place. He finished in the show spot in the Winter Olympics at Cortina d'Ampezzo, Italy, in January and in the world competition last month at Garmisch - Partenkirchen, Germany.

In the school-figure competition yesterday, the Jenkins-Robertson - Jenkins order had prevailed again. All five judges were unanimously agreed on that ranking. The order was confirmed tonight in the free-skating competition, counting 40 per cent of the score. The top trio led Tim Brown of Los Angeles, Tom Moore of Seattle and Raymond Blommer of Philadelphia, in the final rankings.

Kenneth L. Brown, the U. S. F. S. A., president, says the charges against Ronnie must be settled before his national standing becomes official. As the fourday championships came to an end, it seemed likely that no decision would be made before the association meets on May 4 in San Francisco.

Brown held out one other possibility. The challenge to Robertson's amateur status could be determined by a mail vote after affidavits arrive from Germany, Brown said.

Meanwhile, popular interest still centered on last night's sparkling duel for the top wo-

men's senior honors between Tenley E. Albright of Boston and Carol E. Heiss of Ozone Park, Queens. Though the tall, poetically-graceful Radcliffe College student won, 16-year-old Carol put on a thrilling freeskating exhibition.

Tenley, 20 years old and a head taller than her rival, racked up 1,712.02 total points and 5 ordinal points. Five judges had her first in a unanimous vote. Carol's point total was 1,691.67, with 10 ordinals and a unanimous placing for second. Catherine Machado of Los Angeles placed third with 1,620.23 points and 15 ordinals. All five judges gave her the show spot.

**Claralyn Lewis Fourth**

From there down it was Claralyn Lewis of Colorado Springs,

who moved up from sixth to place fourth in the final; Nancy Heiss, Carol's 14-year-old sister, who held her fifth-spot placing; Mary Ann Dorsey of Colorado Springs and Charlene Adams of Chicago.

In winning, Tenley retained a title she first won in 1952. She held it through 1953, 1954 and 1955. The pre-medical student won the Olympic title last January, but placed second to Carol for the world title at Garmisch. In all the two have met nine times, Tenley has won eight times since 1953, Carol once.

Ronnie's father talked on the telephone with Mrs. Robertson in Long Beach, Calif. tonight and obtained her permission for her son to turn professional.

"We've had nothing but trouble since we started with ama-

teur skating," Robertson quoted his wife as saying. "I'll leave the decision up to you and Ronnie."

**Robertson Turns Pro**

The senior Robertson made it abundantly clear that the United States figure association's "completely false charges" against his son led to the decision that Ronnie should turn professional.

The father and son agreed tonight to a two-year contract with "Ice Capades" at more than $100,000. John Harris, president of the ice show, said the contract would be for a oneyear and would carry a one-year renewal option.

March 18, 1956

# Carol Heiss Takes Fourth Straight Women's World Figure Skating Title

## QUEENS GIRL WINS BY RECORD MARGIN

### Hannah Walter of Austria Is Second to Carol Heiss— Tim Brown Leads

COLORADO SPRINGS, Colo., Feb. 26 (AP)—Carol Heiss of Ozone Park, Queens, easily won her fourth straight women's world figure skating championship tonight.

Challenged by exciting performaances by flame-haired Ina Bauer of West Germany and Sjoujke Dijkstra of the Netherlands, the pretty, 19-year-old New York University student gave one of her finest exhibitions of free skating in the final phase of the competition.

The Ice Palace crowd of 3,000 applauded repeatedly as Carol leaped and spun through her dramatic routine. Smiling broadly, she skated off the ice to the cheers and whistles of the standing-room-only crowd.

Miss Heiss began her program with an opening axel in which she soared higher than any of her challengers. She did a fast step up the ice, followed by a double loop jump. Then she flowed into her next step.

There never was a break or a pause in her four-minute routine. She scored several 5.8 and 5.7 marks under a system in which 6 is perfect.

Hanna Walter of Austria, the European title-holder, finished second although she fell midway in her routine. Third place went to Miss Jijkstra. Fraulein Bauer was fourth and 17-yearold Barbara Roles of Temple City, Calif., fifth.

Miss Heiss won by the largest margin of her career in bigtime skating, scoring 1,358.4 points to 1,225.1 for Fraulein Walter. Her margin of 133.3 surpassed the previous high of 105 in the world event last year and she was the first-place choice of all seven judges.

Miss Dijkstra had 1,223.2 points, Miss Bauer 1,193.8 and Miss Roles 1,200.9. Carol Finnegan of Boston was sixth with 1,066.6 and Nancy Heiss, Carol's younger sister, eighth with 1,131.1.

Earlier in the day, Tim Brown of Sacramento, Calif., gained the lead over the defending champion, David Jenkins of Colorado Springs, in the school figures of the men's championship.

Brown, a University of California pre-medical student, took a 7.8-point edge over Jenkins, who is seeking his third straight title, through the first three of six compulsory figures.

Brown had a total of 291.0 points, compared with 283.2 for Jenkins, who appeared more tense and well below the form he showed in the national championships at Rochester, N. Y., earlier this year.

**Results Not Surprising**

However, the day's results were no great surprise. Brown, a polished figure skater, has beaten Jenkins several times in this phase of the competition, including the world event last year, but the nimble Colorado athlete inevitably triumphs with

his superior free skating.

The compulsory figures call for tracing involved figure eights on the ice. They count 60 per cent toward the title, with free skating worth 40 per cent.

The final three figures, tougher and worth more in points, will be skated tomorrow, with the free skating Saturday night.

Brown, skating confidently, led Jenkins in the scoring of six of the eight judges, with the seventh judge calling it a tie. The judges gave only four scores of 5 and better in the more than 100 cards held up. Brown and Jenkins had two each.

February 27, 1959

# Jernberg Ski Victor; Paul Pair Takes Skating

## Swede Triumphs in Cross-Country— Russian Out

By MICHAEL STRAUSS
Special to The New York Times.

SQUAW VALLEY, Calif., Feb. 19—The Soviet Union's hopes to gain the jump on its rivals in the Winter Olympics failed to materialize today. Sweden and Canada took the first two gold medals.

Sixten Jernberg, the 31-yearold ski salesman, put Sweden in the élite class by winning the thirty-kilometer (18.64 miles) skiing contest with a time of 1 hour 51 minutes 3.9 seconds. Barbara Wagner and Robert Paul of Canada triumphed in the pairs figure skating.

Neither victory was a surprise. Jernberg, known as the "cross-country king of the world" in Europe, has been the top long-distance ski artist for several years. He excels in all four of the regulation distances (ten to fifty kilometers). As for the Canadian skaters, they hold the world championship for pairs.

The Soviet Union's cause in the cross-country received an unexpected jolt when Pavel Kolchin, an ace long-distance man, was unable to start. Kolchin was suffering from a cold. He elected to pass up the contest, hoping to get back in shape for the remaining crosscountry events.

Kolchin, it was felt, would have provided a strong threat to Jernberg today. The Russian finished third in the thirty-kilometer event at the 1956 Olym-

## Miss Wagner Helps Canada Capture Gold Medal

pics at Cortina and was considered to be in top form. Last year, in the pre-Olympic trials here, he captured the fifteenkilometer competition.

The big surprise in the event was the poor showing of Veikko Hakulinen of Finland, winner of the event in 1956. The Finn never got untracked. He trailed the leaders in time all the way and finished sixth.

While Hakulinen was having his troubles (it was said he used the wrong wax), Jernberg raced over the McKinney Creek course, which is about seventeen miles from here.

Jernberg was pursued by a

team-mate, Rolf Ramgard, a 26-year-old forester from Alvadlen. Ramgard, a comparative unknown to the international picture, threatened to take it all. At the end of ten kilometers, he trailed Jernberg by only twenty-two seconds. After two-thirds of the trek, the difference in time was unchanged.

"I really was worried about Ramgard," Jernberg said, after completing his trip over the scenic course. "It was a hard race and the air up here (6,266 feet at the start) is thin. I found the breathing was not so difficult near the end."

Jernberg's official winning margin was only thirteen seconds. In third place, 1 minute 11.3 seconds behind the runner-up was the Soviet Union's Nikolai Anikin.

The Soviet's Gennadi Vaganov placed fourth (1:52:49.2), followed by Lennart Larrson (Sweden) and Hakulinen, in that order. Mack Miller, the first American to place, finished twenty-seventh in 2:03:05.4.

Most of the athletes in the field of forty-eight appeared in excellent condition after the contest, despite the high altitude. Cross-country racing is a grueling business. Courses are laid out so that a racer is required to climb, go down hill and ski on the level in about equal proportions.

### Narrow Skis Used

The skis used are extremely narrow (about two and a half inches wide), thin and light and have a special binding that allows freedom of foot movement, particularly at the heels.

Since they are started at one-minute intervals, racers frequently overtake one another on the course. When this happens, a competitor shouts "track" and the overtaken skier must step aside and let him pass. Jernberg or Ramgard weren't bothered in that department today. They did the passing.

Wax, as usually is the case, proved an important factor. The skies were overcast at the start and many competitors greased their runners, contemplating a sunless session. However, the clouds opened halfway through the race, and those who had waxed in anticipation that some of the terrain might become slower because of sun benefited.

Jernberg seemed to guess everything correctly. He had no trouble with his skis at any time and paced himself superbly. His clocking for the first ten kilometers (thirty-six minutes) was the best in the race. Rangard had the second fastest time for the first third (36:22), while Vaganov was third in this department (36:30).

### U. S. Coach Pleased

The back-of-the-pack showing by Miller, America's top long-distance man, was not received with gloom in the United States camp. Indeed, Sven Wiik, the coach, seemed pleased by his man's performance.

"We've never been strong in this sport," said Wiik. "The closest we've ever been to the leader in this Olympic race was sixteen minutes. Today, it was

less than thirteen minutes."

In the figure skating, there seemed little doubt that the Canadians were going to score their first Olympic success as they w nt through their performance. They executed their five-minute, three-song dance routine almost flawlessly. When the bowed at the end, they received a standing ovation from the crowd of 1,500 in the Blyth arena.

Attired in a gray flannel, pleated skirt with a fitted bodice, Miss Wagner made a fetching partner for Paul. Their skill evoked repeated bursts of approval from the spectators.

Particularly pleasing to the crowd was the pair's interpretation of the "Death Spiral," in which Paul, in a crouch, held his partner's foot in one hand while spinning her with her head down.

The victors were credited with a record Olympic total of 80.4 points (84 is perfect) for their inspiring performance and finished comfortably ahead of their nearest rivals, Marika Kilius and Hans Baumler of Germany (76.8).

Third was the United States' husband-and-wife pair, Nancy and Ronald Ludington, who brought the first medal to our country in these games.

February 20, 1960

# Heidi Biebl Wins Downhill, With Penny Pitou Second

### By MICHAEL STRAUSS
#### Special to The New York Times.

SQUAW VALLEY, Calif., Feb. 20—Heidi Biebl, a 19-year-old factory worker from West Germany, and Frau Helga Haase, a 25-year-old bookkeeper from East Germany, provided the big surprises in the Winter Olympics today.

The women registered brilliant performances that moved the combined German team into second place in the unofficial point-standings. Fraeulein Biebl triumphed in the women's downhill ski race on KT-22 Peak and Frau Haase captured the 500-meter speed-skating crown.

The United States, with the formidable quartet of Penny Pitou, Betsy Snite, Linda Meyers and Joan Hannah, was favored in the downhill. In skating the Soviets were expected to take at least three of the first four places.

The United States was able to gain only second place in the downhill (Miss Pitou) while the Russians placed only second (Natalija Donchenko) and fourth (Tamara Rylova) in the skating.

The developments were so surprising that they even surprised the winners. Fraeulein Biebl seemed extremely unhappy after completing her 5,997-foot run. She felt she had made many mistakes and made no secret of it.

It wasn't until her clocking of 1:37.6 was announced that she brightened. Then she was told she had beaten Miss Pitou by a full second and her face lit up for the first time.

Frau Haase, by her own admission, nurtured little hope of winning. Her practice sessions had been impressive here but almost no one thought the Russians could be beaten.

Spills suffered by three of the four American starters were the factors that put the final damper to America's hopes to sweep the gold medals in the Alpine (downhill, slalom and giant slalom) contests.

Although Miss Pitou was considered the strongest member of the downhill contingent, it was felt that any of the other three girls had enough daring and speed to take first place today. Indeed, Miss Hannah was a definite threat to take it all halfway down the course. Her plunge had been that fast.

But Miss Hannah, the last of the American quartet to take the course—she was the twenty-sixth starter—went a cropper at the same "booby trap" hit by her two mates.

The terrain that caused the

Associated Press Wirephoto

BIG THREE: Medal winners in women's downhill race at Winter Olympics are, from left: Traudl Hecher, Austria, third; Penny Pitou, U. S., second; Heidi Biebl, Germany, first.

three Americans their woe was only three gates from the bottom. It was on the far end of what is referred to as an airplane turn. Skiers catapulting into this bend approached it in the same way that a plane makes that wide bank as it heads for an approach into an airport.

At least a dozen girls spilled at this point, and Miss Pitou, the first girl down the mountain, teetered momentarily.

Asked about her experiences at the trouble point, Miss Pitou caught her breath and looked up the slope with a scowl. She said, "I knew it meant trouble as soon as I began rounding that turn. But I kept saying to myself, 'This is the Olympics. You can't fall now.' Somehow I didn't; I guess someone heard me."

### Hard to Check Speed

The chief difficulty in the turn stemmed from the fact that racers came into it at full speed with skis flat. Many found it difficult to slow down. Those that didn't have a sensitive hand on the throttle spilled.

Fraeulein Biebl, the eighth girl on the course, had her

trouble spots but none of them was major. She showed extremely fine balance almost all the way and came down the final pitch to the finish line in that familiar crouch racers use to cut down wind resistance.

Halfway down the mountain, it appeared that the German girl would prove no threat to Miss Pitou. Her clocking for that distance was 42.4 seconds as compared to 41 seconds for the American. However, she speeded up, hit the airplane gracefully and came home under full control.

Apart from that one trouble spot, Miss Pitou handled the course masterfully. She streaked down the top part of the mountain at a speed estimated at 60 miles per hour and seemed to be in perfect control during the first two-thirds of the trip.

### Miss Snite Fails to Finish

Miss Snite was the only American who failed to finish. She hit the ground so heavily in her spill that she went into a momentary collapse. By the time she caught her breath, it

was too late to continue. Traudl Hecher of Austria, 16, finished third, but her high placing was no surprise. The green-eyed blonde is Austria's national slalom and combined champion and has consistently placed high in tune-up European meets.

She was clocked in 1:38.9 to beat Pia Riva and Jerta Schir of Italy who finished fourth and fifth in that order. Miss Hannah, the second American in the final order, was twenty-first and Miss Meyer thirty-third.

The downhill course started at an altitude of 8,028 feet and had a drop 1,815 feet. A good downhill course is designed to provide extreme technical difficulties in the form of bumps, high-speed turns, sudden drops and transitions.

In the interest of safety, today's layout was made comfortably wide so that the girls could reduce their speed without danger of hitting trees or other obstacles.

The track seemed to be in as good a condition after the race

as it had been at the start. A downhill course deteriorates after the first dozen or so racers speed over it.

In speed skating, Frau Haase won by only one-tenth of a second. Miss Donchenko was followed in the finishes by Jeanne Ashworth, a 22-year-old Tufts student.

Although she had won ten North American and national indoor speed skating titles, Miss Ashworth's high placing also was a surprise. She raced over the strip in 46.1 seconds to top Miss Rylova by one-tenth of a second.

Miss Pitou, who is 21, announced tonight that this would be her last season of competitive racing.

"As you know I'm a matriculated student at Middlebury College," she said. "I want to return there and resume my studies. After all, I'm getting too old to just keep racing."

February 21, 1960

# 47,000 See Switzerland, Sweden and Soviet Union Win in Olympic Games

## CORCORAN OF U.S. 4TH IN SKI EVENT

### American Olympian Excels in Giant Slalom—Carol Heiss Skating Leader

**By GLADWIN HILL**
Special to The New York Times.

SQUAW VALLEY, Calif., Feb. 21—The United States' snow and ice athletes had to take a far-back seat to foreigners today, the fourth day of the VIII Olympic Winter Games.

They had to settle for a modest fourth place in the hair-raising, mile-long men's giant slalom skiing race. Competitors from overseas swept top honors in this contest, along with the women's 1,500-meter speed skating and the new biathlon event, which consists of cross-country skiing and shooting.

The Soviet Union set an unofficial world record in the women's skating and stretched its big lead in the unofficial team standing in the Games despite an unexpected setback from Sweden and Finland in the biathlon. Switzerland won the giant slalom, a serpentine downhill race-against-time through dozens of paired-pole "gates."

The gold jousting took place before a throng officially estimated at 47,000, the largest of

these Games, and possibly the largest gallery in United States winter sports history.

### Traffic At A Crawl

They flocked into this isolated little Sierra Nevada valley in a monstrous cavalcade of some 9,000 automobiles and 300 snorting buses that stretched bumper to bumper up to twelve miles along approach roads, crawling at ten miles an hour. It took one bus 1 hour 45 minutes to cover the eighteen miles from Kings Beach at the north end of near-by Lake Tahoe.

The United States' fourth place in the giant slalom was the work of Tom Corcoran, a 28-year-old American citizen, who lives in Beaconsfield, Que., and a 1956 Winter Olympian.

Although he finished slower than Roger Staub of Switzerland and Pepi Stiegler and Ernst Hinterseer, his placing still was a noteworthy accomplishment in an event in which Europeans are traditionally superior.

Carol Heiss of Ozone Park, Queens, and Barbara Ann Roles of Temple City, Calif., maintained first and third places among twenty-six contestants in the women's figure-skating competition.

### U. S. Jumpers Far Back

The United States had a chance to garner some glory in ski jumping, but the initial performances were inconclusive. The day's jumping — in which United States entries wound up twenty-seventh, twenty-eighth, thirtieth and thirty-first — was the first installment of the Nordic combined competition, which will be completed with a fifteen-kilometer cross-country ski race tomorrow.

**DRIVING FINISH:** Lidiya Skoblikova of Soviet Union, who won gold medal in women's 1,500-meter speed skating.

At the end of the day's three completed events, the Soviet Union had a three-day score of 63½ points under the unofficial 10-5-4-3-2-1 ranking system for the first six places in each event. Sweden stood second with 29. Germany had 28, the United States 16.

In the women's speed skating, Lidiya Skoblikova, a 20-year-old physiology student from Chel-

jabinsk in the Urals, did the 1,500 meters in 2 minutes 25.2 seconds, three-tenths of a second under the 1953 world record of Khalida Schegolewa, also from the Soviet Union.

Jeanne Ashworth of Wilmington, Mass., an unexpected third in yesterday's 500-meter women's speed skating, and Barbara Lockhart of Park Ridge, Ill., came in eleventh and eighteenth in the 1,500-meter event, raced in pairs against time on a 400-meter outdoor artificial ice rink.

**Soviet Skiers Again Beaten**

Another blank was drawn by the United States in the biathlon, with its four entries finishing fourteenth, twenty-first, twenty-third and twenty-fourth in a field of thirty men from nine nations.

The event was won by Klas Lestander, a 28-year-old carpenter from Laengviken, Sweden, who skied the twelve and a half miles and executed twenty

rounds of target shooting without a miss in 1 hour 33 minutes 21.6 seconds. A Finn, Antti Tyrvainen, was second.

It was the second time Sweden had nosed out the favored Soviet team in a cross-country skiing event. Sweden took first and second places in the men's thirty-kilometer race Friday, leaving the Soviet Union as today, third and fourth.

The Soviet Union swept third, fourth, fifth and sixth places in the biathlon. In the unofficial national point scoring, that was worth as much as a first place.

"If this were a world cham-

pionship," Semyon Bogachev, a Soviet Ski Federation official remarked, "we would be the team champions. But," he added, punctiliously alluding to the Olympics' nominal nonnational format, "this is an individual competition so our men merely finished third, fourth, fifth and sixth."

No Soviet skiers entered the giant slalom, the biggest event of the Games so far with sixty-five competitors from twenty-one nations.

It was staged on the side of 8,900-foot KT-22 Peak, over an extended version of the course

used in yesterday's women's downhill ski competition.

Staub's victory, in 1:48.3, accounted for Switzerland's first points in the team scoring.

The field also included Liechtenstein's three-man contingent, which got to the Olympics only after a governmental hassle in the tiny European principality. There were also entries from Turkey, Lebanon, Korea, Iceland, New Zealand, Argentina, Chile, Bulgaria and Spain.

February 22, 1960

# *France, Germany and Soviet Union Take Gold Medals in Winter Olympics*

## VUARNET IS FIRST IN DOWNHILL RACE

### Frenchman Olympic Victor —German Skier, Soviet Speed Skater Win

**By MICHAEL STRAUSS**
Special to The New York Times.

SQUAW VALLEY, Calif., Feb. 22—Germany took a first place and two seconds today in the day's three major events of the VIII Olympic Winter Games.

Occupying the spotlight, however, was a Frenchman, Jean Vuarnet, a 27-year-old hotel operator. Showing no fear of the perilous 10,154-foot course on Squaw Peak that dropped 2,487 feet, the innkeeper captured the men's downhill skiing event impressively. Hanspeter Lanig of Germany was second.

The other major victories were scored by Georg Thoma, a mailman from Hinterzarten, Germany, and Klara Guseva of the Soviet Union. Thoma paired his first-place finish in the 60-meter jump yesterday with a good effort in the fifteen-kilometer cross-country race today to capture the Nordic combined honors.

Miss Guseva's success came in a sport in which the Soviet Union excels — speed skating. She was clocked in 1 minute 34.1 seconds in leading her team to a one, three, four finish in the 1,000-meter speed-skating contest. A German, Frau Helga Haase, was second.

In the $3,500,000 Blyth Arena, Carol Heiss, the pretty blonde from Ozone Park, Queens, continued to set the groundwork for an American victory in figure skating. She completed the compulsory figures leading Sjoukje Dijkstra of the Netherlands by a comfortable margin.

As a result of the fine performances by Thoma, Lanig

Jean Vuarnet of France avoids bump as he races on Squaw Peak in men's downhill event yesterday. Vuarnet finished the race in 2 minutes 6 seconds and captured first place.

and Frau Haase, Germany moved ahead of Sweden into second place in the unofficial team standing. The Germans now have 48 points to 86½ for the first-place Soviet Union squad. Sweden is third with 29, followed by the United States with 16 and Switzerland and France with 15 poits each.

Although Thoma supplied the big surprise by taking the combined Gold Medal, the victory

by Vuarnet was the day's big item. Cross-country is not a spectator sport. This morning, only a few hundred spectators saw Thoma cover the course of about nine miles in 59 minutes 23.8 seconds.

His time was not the best but it didn't have to be. He had built up such a big lead in yesterday's jump that he was able to win by more than 4 points. Tormod Knutsen of

Norway placed second in the combined competition and Nikolai Gusakov of the Soviet Union was third.

More than 15,000 persons— the day's attendance was 18,500 —watched under a warm sun as Vuarnet made his dazzling descent of precipitous Squaw Peak. The crowd was strung up the peak as far as the eye could see.

Vuarnet, the tenth man down

the course, tore along at speeds as high as 60 miles an hour. He was in complete control all the way and never seemed to swerve from his determination to reach the finish as soon as gravity and his pumping legs could get him there.

When his official time (2:06) was announced, the crowd did not seem surprised. Everyone knew Vuarnet had been traveling fast. What some didn't know, however, was that he had used metal skis. This type runner proved ideal for the conditions. Later, it was learned that all four French skiers had performed on metal.

This strategy not only netted the French a gold medal but also brought them a bronze one, too. Guy Perillat, a 20-year-old skier from La Clusaz, placed third, four-tenth of a second behind Lanig. Following Peril-

lat were Willi Forrer and Roger Staub, both of Switzerland.

The day had its repercussions. Austrian officials, disappointed because their men have been doing poorly in events in which they always have excelled, changed their line-up for the special slalom on Wednesday. Karl Schranz and Anderl Molterer, among the world's best, were replaced.

Schranz finished only seventh in the downhill. Molterer was nineteenth. In the giant slalom yesterday, Schranz was seventh and Molterer twelfth. Only Josef (Pepi) Stiegler was able to save the day for the Austrians in the giant slalom. He placed second behind Staub.

Considering that the Austrians were expected to finish second in the unofficial point standings mainly because of their strength in the Alpine

events (they are tied for seventh place), the changes were no surprise.

The new Austrian starters in slalom, Ernst Hinterseer and Ernst Oberaigner, will join Stiegler and Leitner. But Austria no longer can finish second in the standing. Too much ground must be made up.

The use of metal skis in the downhill was not new. The French and Swiss have been experimenting with them for at least a year. Most of the other skiers in the downhill used run-of-the-mill laminated wooden skis. They traveled slower.

In winning, Vuarnet — and Perillat, for that matter—didn't even use wax. The metal ski doesn't require it on fast snow and the Frenchmen knew it. The Austrians applied wax to their hickory runners but apparently picked the wrong wax.

All of them seemed to lack their customary speed.

The United States lived up to expectations in the downhill. It fared poorly. The first American to finish was Dave Goruch, who was fourteenth.

Elwira Seroczynska of Poland almost won the women's speed-skating event. Rounding the last turn, her time was the best in the field. Then her skate bumped against the dividing line between lanes. She fell and failed to finish.

The dividing lines normally are made of snow. She said she thought her skate had struck ice rather than snow.

In this race, as in all other Olympic speed-skating events, two contestants raced at a time. The final placings were determined on a time basis.

February 23, 1960

# Carol Heiss Captures Figure-Skating Title and First Gold Medal for U. S.

## WORLD CHAMPION WINS IN OLYMPICS

Miss Heiss First in Figure Skating—Miss Pitou Is Second in Ski Race

By MICHAEL STRAUSS
Special to The New York Times.

SQUAW VALLEY, Calif., Feb. 23—After pursuing a first-place award for four days, the United States finally struck gold today.

Performing with the same confidence and skill that had carried her to four world championships, 20-year-old Carol Heiss won the women's figure skating crown for America's first gold medal of the Winter Olympic Games.

Her exhibition in the free-skating phase of the competition brought wild applause from the crowd of 8,500 at the Blyth ice arena. Her performance, paired with the superb one she had given in the school-figure programs earlier in the week, enabled her to win by a comfortable margin.

Miss Heiss totaled 1,490.1 points. Sjoukje Dijkstra of the Netherlands was next with 1,424.8. Barbara Roles of the United States had 1,414.9 for third place. Jana Mrazkova of Czechoslovakia followed with 1,338.7.

Miss Heiss' triumph followed a near-miss by Penny Pitou. The blonde New England girl, after a sparkling performance, placed second in the giant slalom, only one-tenth of a second behind the winner, Yvonne Ruegg of Switzerland.

Compared to their meager pickings of the first four days, the Americans had a bonanza today. They emerged with 23 points after having amassed only 16 previously.

Besides the contributions of Miss Heiss and Miss Pitou, Miss Roles added 4 points with her third place in figure skating and R. Laurence Owen scored one for finishing sixth. Betsy Snite registered 3 by placing fourth in the giant slalom.

As a result the United States advanced from fourth to third place in the unofficial standings. The Soviet Union still leads

with 104 points and Germany is second with 49½. The United States has 9, Sweden 36, Switzerland 25 and Finland 20.

The Soviet Union and Norway triumphed in the day's other medal events. The Russians continued to dominate speed skating when Lidija Skoblikova, a 21-year-old student, took the 3,000-meter championship for her second gold medal. Norway's gold medalist was Hakon Brusveen. He won the rugged fifteen-kilometer cross-country competition.

The weather again was ideal.

There wasn't a cloud to be seen. The courses for the giant slalom, cross-country and speed-skating races were extremely fast. Even the indoor rink was in peak condition—better by far than it had been since the games began.

Miss Heiss appeared in a fetching tangerine-colored outfit with a high collar. The Ozone Park (Queens) girl performed her tricky routines with grace and ease.

She breezed through such acrobatics as the Axel Paulsen (one and a half reverse in the air), the spread eagle and the

**ANOTHER SWISS TRIUMPH:** Yvonne Ruegg speeds through gate on her way to victory in women's giant slalom. Roger Staub, fellow-countryman, won men's giant slalom Sunday.

Arabesque Spin (spinning on her toes).

### High Scores From All

When she had finished, the nine judges credited her with top-heavy scores. Six points from an official is considered perfect. Perfection apparently is not considered attainable, but Miss Heiss came close. Two officials scored her at 5.9. Three gave her 5.8. No one scored her less than 5.5.

Miss Heiss said afterwards that she definitely would not turn professional.

"I have won every prize I ever hoped for," she said. "I may compete next year, but I'm not interested in becoming a pro.

"I'm tired of living out of a suitcase. I have a year and a half to go in school (New York University) and I'm going to finish. But first I'm going on a tour of Europe.

"I want to study French and German in school, primarily French, so I can understand what they're yelling about when I don't do a perfect delayed Axel."

In the giant slalom, only a brilliant descent by Miss Ruegg on the fifty-seven staggered-gate course of about three-quarters of a mile deprived the United States and Miss Pitou of a gold medal. The Swiss miss tore down Little Papoose Peak without faltering once.

The giant slalom differs from a special slalom in that the course is much longer and the gates much farther apart. A skier, therefore, can move the throttle up considerably without too much fear of being caught going too fast on the turns. Miss Ruegg proved to be a daring chauffeur. She rarely applied the brakes.

Despite her outstanding performance, the Swiss star didn't outclass the field. Less than a second separated the first seven finishers. After Miss Ruegg and Miss Pitou, in order, came Giuliana Minuzzo-Chanel of Italy, Betsy Snite of the United States, Carla Marchelli of Italy, Anneliese Meggl of Germany and Therese Leduc of France.

### Californian Is Injured

Although Miss Snite's fourth-place finish gave the Americans a total of 8 points for the event, the team's showing was a disappointment. The Americans had been expected to dominate the race with their triple threat of the Misses Pitou, Snite and Linda Meyers.

In justice to the Americans, it must be mentioned that Miss Pitou was competing with a bad cold—she found it difficult to breathe—and Miss Snite was bothered by an ailing ankle and bruised ribs. Miss Meyers was bothered by nothing as she started down the course, but trouble was waiting.

The Californian fell on the upper slopes and fractured her collarbone. She was removed to the Olympic Village infirmary and will be unable to compete in the special slalom on Friday.

Beverly Anderson, the fourth member of the American contingent, also encountered trouble. The University of Washington senior crashed into a gate near the top and lost the pole as well as her prescription skiing glasses. Nevertheless, she concluded her run and finished thirty-sixth.

Miss Pitou was a runner-up for the second time in the games. Last Saturday, she finished second to Heidi Biebl of Germany in the downhill race.

Despite her failure to win either of the first two Alpine events, Miss Pitou was in an excellent position to gain the world championship Alpine combined crown. Although there is no combined gold medal in the Olympics, the Federation Internationale de Ski recognizes such a title based on placings in the slalom, giant slalom and downhill.

Brusveen's gold medal in cross-country was Norway's first top award in the games. Brusveen, a ski-store owner and farmer, sped over the McKinney Creek layout in 51 minutes 55.5 seconds.

He upset Sixten Jernberg of Sweden (51:58.6), a seasoned Olympian considered by Europeans as the all-round cross-country champion of the world.

"I never hoped for a medal, or even a top position," Brusveen said. "But as I went out today, I felt great and felt that this might be my day. I found everything along the trail real easy."

February 24, 1960

# 27 Disqualified in Slalom Event Won by Austrian; Soviet Skater Triumphs

## HINTERSEER GAINS LAURELS IN SKIING

### Disqualifications Later Alter Placings From 7th Down —Grishin Wins for Soviet

**By MICHAEL STRAUSS**
Special to The New York Times.

SQUAW VALLEY, Calif., Feb. 24—In a dramatic comeback that had a crowd of 4,000 roaring, Austria regained some of her lost skiing prestige today.

Unable to win in the downhill and giant slalom earlier this week, the Austrians scored a one-two coup in the special slalom on the sixth day of competition in the VIII Olympic Winter Games.

The men who returned Austria to Alpine racing prominence were Ernst Hinterseer and Mathias Leitner. Hinterseer, a 27-year-old farmer from Kitzbuehel, gained the gold medal with a two-run total clocking of 2 minutes 8.9 seconds. Leitner was second in 2:10.3.

The Austrian comeback wasn't easy. At the end of the first run, Hinterseer and Leitner were fourth and fifth, respectively. But each turned in a remarkable second effort.

For two hours after the end of the event, the slalom jury listened to protests and studied photos of the competition, then announced the disqualification of twenty-seven of the sixty-seven racers. The jury gave official sanction to the first five finishers only.

The disqualifications included those who fell and did not finish, as well as skiers who missed one or more turns through the required gates. The highest-placed competitor to be disqualified was Francois Bonlieu of France, who had finished seventh.

Hinterseer registered the fastest time in the second set (0:58.2) while Leitner's time was 0:59.2. Amazement was expressed on all sides when their clockings were announced.

As a result Austria, picked to finish second behind the Soviet Union in the total scoring, advanced to fifth place in the unofficial point standing. A fifth place by their Josef Stiegler in the slalom earned them 17 points for the event and brought their total to 30.

The Soviet Union, meanwhile, added to its lead on the scintillating performance of Yevgeni Grishin in the 500-meter speed-skating contest. Grishin beat Bill Disney of the United States by a tenth of a second. He would have won by more had he not slipped momentarily as he tore around the final turn.

The stumble cost the Soviet star a world record. In making the once-and-a-quarter tour of the slick, speed-skating oval, the winner was timed in 40.2 seconds. The performance tied the mark he had set in the 1956 Olympics at Cortina d'Ampezzo, Italy.

Paced by Grishin's triumph, the Soviet Union increased its point total to 120. Germany remained second with 52½. Then came the United States (44), Sweden (39) and Austria. The competition ends Sunday.

### Not So Restful

The day had been expected to be a relatively quiet one in this picturesque Sierra Nevada valley, but it wasn't. Protests started coming soon after the slalom on KT22 Mountain, while near-by at the racing oval, Irving Jaffee, a former American Olympic speed-skating champion, was threatened bodily.

Protests are part of the normal procedure in Alpine racing. If a gate-keeper sees a racer miss a gate, it is his duty to report it to the contest jury. However, the incident involving Jaffee needed several referees rather than a jury.

The stage for the disturbance was set two days ago when Jaffee, who is working with United Press International here, reported that American speed skaters were complaining about mistreatment and mishandling. United States officials angrily denied the charge and demanded that Jaffee prove it.

Today, when the one-time Olympic star appeared at rinkside to report on the speed-skating race, he was ordered away by Phil Krum, the secretary of the Amateur Skating Union of the United States. Another official threatened, "I'll punch you in the nose."

The officials asked police to remove Jaffee, but Jaffee showed his press credentials and stood his ground. Finally, on the advice of friends, he walked to the press box and watched the races from there.

### Results Held Up

The protests involving the special slalom race held up the official results for more than three hours. Two hours after the competition was over, officials finally sent out word that the placings for the first five men had been confirmed.

During the delay, the United States and Germany were able to complete their hockey game at the $3,500,000 Blyth Arena. The Americans again proved strong contenders for the gold medal with an impressive 9-1 triumph. The unbeaten Americans have three more games to play in the six-country championship round-robin.

The special slalom turned into a tense struggle among twenty of the world's best Alpine performers. Most of the other starters didn't figure.

The leader at the end of the first run was Willy Bogner, a tall, slim bundle of energy from Germany who was later among those disqualified. Bogner came tearing down the tight, sixty-six-gate course, arms pumping at the poles and legs grinding on the edges. He was clocked in 1:08.8.

Bogner was the first man on the course, and no other competitor approached him. When the first round was over the German had a full second advantage. Tied for second were Bonlieu and another French skier, and Charles Bozon.

The second run was held over a different course. This course, adjacent to the first one, had sixty-nine gates. It was trickier and more dangerous. It called for more precision and more rhythm. And there was a precipitous pitch near the top hanging on what golfers would call an "uneven lie."

It was this hanging portion of the course that proved Bogner's undoing. Eager to bolster his lead, he took too many chances. He hit the "uneven lie" at too great a speed and went crashing. By the time he was, able to arise, his chances for victory had flown.

Bonlieu, who had been tied with Bozon for second at 1:09.8, also came a cropper at the hang. His recovery was better than Bogner's, however, and he managed to place seventh. Bogner finished twenty-second.

With these two racers out of contention, the job was made easier for Hinterseer and Leitner. They capitalized on their chance superbly. Hinterseer, the seventh starter, zigged and zagged through the gates superbly.

He took lots of chances, but that is what slalom racing calls for. As he weaved through the gates, his body nudged the poles, knocking some over. But the Austrian made no legal missteps.

**Leitner Also Excels**

Leitner, the eleventh man to face the starter, also had at least a half-dozen near-misses. But he kept his edges grinding when grinding was needed the most.

His efforts enabled him to top Bozon in the final scoring by one-tenth of a second. The same margin separated the fourth-placed Ludwig Leitner of Germany (not related to the Austrian) from Bozon.

A notable finish was registered by Tommy Corcoran, who led the four American entrants. Corcoran, who had placed fourth in the giant slalom, came home tenth.

The showing in the two events

by the former Exeter and Dartmouth ace was one of the top combination performances by an American in Olympic Alpine history.

At the ice arena, there was some uneasiness for the United States when David Jenkins, the favorite in the men's figure skating, was placed third after three of the five required school figures. In first place at the end of the day was Karol Divin of Czechoslovakia. Alain Giletti of France was second. Jenkins, however, was still the choice to win it all.

February 25, 1960

# U.S. Upsets Canada in Hockey; Finland and Soviet Union Win Gold Medals

## M'CARTAN EXCELS IN 2-TO-1 SUCCESS

### Goalie Helps in U.S. Olympic Victory—Jenkins Gains in Figure Skating

**By MICHAEL STRAUSS**
Special to The New York Times.

SQUAW VALLEY, Calif., Feb. 25—The chances of the United States to gain its first hockey gold medal in Winter Olympic history went skyrocketing tonight when the host team defeated Canada, 2—1, at Blyth Arena.

The outcome was a surprise. The Dominion team has been favored to regain the championship it lost to the Soviet Union at Cortina, Italy, in 1956. The United States was ranked third behind the Russians.

The United States also gained in another sport. David Jenkins, the favorite in men's figure skating, climbed to second place at the finish of the compulsory figures.

The only gold medals of the day went to Finland and the Soviet Union. Finland barely beat Norway in the forty-kilometer cross-country ski race. The Soviet Union continued its domination of speed skating when Viktor Kosichkin won the men's 5,000-meter race.

**U. S. Takes 2-0 Lead**

The United States team has been playing great hockey. This time, it gained the jump on Canada and made a front-running effort of it. Going into the last period, the United States had a 2-0 lead.

The United States' chances for the gold medal now appear rosy. The home team, winner of three games in the round-robin finals, now faces the Soviet Union (tied once) and

**DECISIVE GOAL: Paul Johnson (15) of U. S. six scoring against Canada in yesterday's Olympic game. Canadian players are Harry Sinden (2), Jack Douglas (5) and Don Head.**

Czechoslovakia (beaten twice).

The player who put the United States on the victory trail was Bob Cleary, a former Harvard all-American from Westwood, Mass. Cleary scooped up a pass from John Mayasich and drummed home the game's first goal at 12:47 of the opening period.

In the second period, Paul Johnson, a former University of Minnesota star, broke loose and outfeinted the Canadian goalie at 14:00.

Turning in a great effort was John McCartan, a 200-pound goal-tender from St. Paul. The United States goalie made thirty-nine saves.

Jim Connelly was the only Canadian to beat him to the punch. Connelly registered at 13:07 of the last period.

The Soviet Union stayed close to the top of the standing by

beating Germany, 7 to 1.

Czechoslovakia scored a 3-1 victory over Sweden in the final hockey game of the day in the championship round.

**Half Ski Length Decides**

By the margin of only a half ski length, Finland won its first gold medal here. The triumph in the cross-country relay race was one of the closest in Winter Olympic history. With 10 yards to go, the outcome was still in doubt.

Battling at the finish were two of the world's top overland skiers, Veikko Hakulinen, a 35-year-old lumberjack from Finland, and Hakon Brusveen, a 32-year-old star from Vingrom, Norway. Brusveen led by 200 yards going into the final leg of about six and a quarter miles.

But the Finn, who won the

thirty-kilometer crown in the 1955 Olympics, began whittling away at his rival's lead immediately. He put a big dent in it at the last big uphill portion of the up-and-down course. Then, with a mile to go, he caught up and took the lead.

The Norwegian, who had won the fifteen-kilometer crown earlier this week, refused to give up. He kept on Hakulinen's ski tracks for the rest of the trip, never trailing by more than a few yards.

With 200 yards to go, the Norwegian tried to put on a spurt. But he didn't have enough left.

"I just didn't have the strength to get ahead of him in the home stretch," said Brusveen. "That fella just refused to get tired."

The outcome was the signal

for jubilation among Hakulinen's team-mates. They lifted him to their shoulders and carried him from the ski stadium. Few football heroes have ever received greater on-the-spot acclaim.

Finland's time was 2 hours 18 minutes 45.6 seconds. Norway was eight-tenths of a second behind. Third at the end of the long run (about twenty-five miles) was the Soviet Union (2:21:21.6), followed by Sweden (2:21:31.8). The United States was eleventh and last.

The Russians added 17 points to their unofficial team score. They now lead with 137 points, with three days of competition remaining. Germany is second with 52½, followed by the United States (44), Sweden (42) and Norway (32½).

Jenkins was able to gain slightly on 23-year-old Karol Divin of Czechoslovakia as the compulsory figures were concluded. At the end of the five required figures, the 5-foot 10-inch Divin, born in Bratislava, had 797.7 points. Jenkins, who also is 23, had 775.2.

Divin, however, was far from confident of victory. He doubted that he could beat Jenkins in the free-style skating tomorrow.

"The best I think I can do is second," he said as he watched Jenkins perform. "But I'll be happy with that. After all, it would make me the top European."

The sandy-haired Kosichkin, who celebrated his twenty-second birthday today, had to cope with a wind of twenty-five miles an hour in the speed-skating race. But he registered an impressive 7:51.3 for the three-and-an-eighth-mile contest. His triumph was the Soviet Union's fifth in speed skating.

Kosichkin finished 9.5 seconds faster than his nearest rival, Knut Johannesen of Norway. Jan Pesman of the Netherlands, who paired with Kosichkin (two skaters race at a time), was helped by the Russian's fast pace. Pesman was third in the final standing in 8:05.1.

February 26, 1960

## SCORING COMPLEX IN FIGURE SKATING

### Esoteric Subject 'Clarified,' but a Good Bookkeeper Is Needed in Olympics

**By GLADWIN HILL**
Special to The New York Times.

SQUAW VALLEY, Calif., Feb. 25—The chances are just about 10,000,000 to 1 that you will never have to score a figure-skating competition. But knowing how it's done can be a great social asset, not to say a secret weapon.

It is one of the most esoteric matters in the field of sport. Figure skating got its name, one may presume, from the fact that, in Olympic competition for instance, approximately 140 different numbers go into figuring a skater's final standing. It is possibly the only sport in which a competitor can come out ahead of one with a better point score.

Thus, in this week's women's figure skating at the Olympic Winter Games, Laurence Owen of Winchester, Mass., placed sixth, even though she had 1,343 points to 1,331 for Joan Haanappel of the Netherlands, who placed fifth.

An understanding of such anomalies obviously provides a fine opportunity for conversational one-upmanship over the wretch who has just rattled off Zack Wheat's batting averages in 1909 through 1926 or let drop: "Of course at Sebring I was driving a Lancia."

#### A Recondite Subject

You just lead the conversation around to Olympics and remark drily: "I thought the judges did rather poorly by the Slobbovian girl in the figure skating." From there on, no one can say you nay. Fewer people know about figure-skating scoring than about Chinese mortuary jade.

Its seeming complexity is rooted in the fact that in Olympic competition there are nine judges. Everybody respects them, but nobody trusts them too far. A system of checks and balances has been developed so that no one judge's ratings, if unconscious bias should creep in, can have too much effect on a skater's final standing.

On each of five required figures from the traditional repertoire, each judge gives a rating based on the mystic perfection figure of 6; e. g., 5.5 for very good. This obviously yields forty-five numbers.

On a skater's optional-figure performance, each judge gives two ratings, one for content and one for execution. Eighteen more numbers.

The six ice figures (five compulsory, one optional) are weighted differently in final importance. So each rating on the respective ice figures is multiplied by a weighting factor, such as 3 or 4—producing a new crop of figures.

#### Judges' Rankings Checked

That is about half the battle. Next the ratings of the judges for each skater are checked for where they rank that skater in the field. Judge No. 1's performance point awards may put a skater in first rank. With Judge No. 2, the same individual may rank only second.

Here the principal of majority rule comes into play. A skater is given an ordinal score, denoting his or her standing with the whole panel of judges. Thus last Tuesday Carol Heiss' ordinal points were 1-1-1-1-1-1-1-1-1, meaning unanimous first rank.

But Laurence Owen's ordinal points were 6-3-6-13-7-5-4-9-4, meaning the performance point awards placed her anywhere from third to thirteenth in rank. Miss Haanappel's ordinals were 7-5-7-6-6-6-6-4-5, obviously a higher ranking. So, despite her lower aggregate point score, Miss Haanappel placed ahead of Miss Owen.

But it can be turned into a great ploy against the man who "drove a Lancia at Sebring."

February 26, 1960

---

# Jenkins of U. S. Wins Olympic Figure Skating; Russians Protest Ski Loss

## SWEDEN TRIUMPHS IN CROSS-COUNTRY

### But Soviet Women's Team Protests—Anne Heggtveit of Canada Wins Slalom

**By MICHAEL STRAUSS**
Special to The New York Times.

SQUAW VALLEY, Calif., Feb. 26—In a performance that earned one of the highest ratings for men's free figure skating in Olympic Winter Games history, David Jenkins of Colorado Springs won a gold medal for the United States today.

Jenkins, who has held the world championship for three years, had a near-capacity crowd of 8,000 at Blyth Arena enthralled as he skated through his five-minute performance to the strains of the Grieg Concerto.

When he had finished, the enthusiastic crowd rose for a standing ovation. The nine judges thought Jenkins' effort was exceptional, too. One even gave a perfect score of 6—a rare item.

The skating competition was one of four finals during the day as the VIII Olympic Winter Games neared completion. Decided this morning at Papoose Peak was the women's special slalom, won by Anne Heggtvait of Canada.

In the men's 1,500-meter speed-skating competition, Roald Edgar Aas of Norway tied Yevgeni Grishin of the Soviet Union. In the fifteen-kilometer, three-woman cross-country ski relay at McKinley Creek, Sweden upset the Russians, who then filed a protest.

#### Relay Finish Close

Less than a minute separated the Swedes and the heavily favored Russians, who were second. The winning time was 1 hour 4 minutes 21.4 seconds. The Swedish team was made up of Irma Johansson, Britt Strandberg and Sonja Ruthstrom.

An accident marked the race. Radia Eroshina, leading off for the Russians, fell shortly after the start and lost a ski. Siiri Rantanen of Finland, close behind her, was unable to stop in time to avoid a collision.

"It was just an accident," explained Miss Rantanen later. "The Russian girl fell in front of me. I couldn't stop in time and fell over her."

Miss Eroshina then borrowed a ski from a Soviet official on the trail and continued.

The Soviet Union filed a protest against Sweden after the women's relay race.

The Russians said that Miss Johansson, leading off for Sweden, cut to her right from the outside track to the inside track as the skiers were making a right turn after leaving the cross-country stadium. The Russians said she stepped on the skis of Miss Eroshina, causing the Russian girl to fall.

The Russians also said that Finnish and Polish skiers had fallen over Miss Eroshina.

The chief official of the race, Wendall Broomhall, said that the competition jury would make no decision until it viewed films of the incident. Efforts were being made to have the film processed—probably in San Francisco—as rapidly as possible.

As a result of Jenkins' success (plus a fifth place in the same event by Tim Brown), the United States moved into second place for the first time with 61 points. The Soviet Union leads in the unofficial team scoring with 153½. Germany is third with 58½.

#### Jenkins Rallies to Win

In winning, Jenkins had to rally. He trailed Karol Divin of Czechoslovakia at the end of yesterday's compulsory figures. But even Divin had conceded that Jenkins would outscore him in the closing program. Jenkins excels in free skating.

The American lived up to expectations. He went from the simple single axel (taking off

Associated Press Wirephotos

David Jenkins of the U. S. displays his prowess in the free figure-skating contest. He won the men's championship.

on one foot and making one and a half turns) to the more complicated simple loop (taking off on his left backward skate and making three complete revolutions) with an ease and grace that evoked repeated applause.

When he had finished his routine, the officials gave the final testimonial to what had been an almost flawless performa. . . For sporting merit, only one judge rated the winner as low as 5.8. Seven awarded 5.9 points and the remaining one gave the perfect mark.

Jenkins received almost the same high rating for general impression. Three judges scored 5.9, the rest 5.8. Jenkins finished with 1,440.2 points to Divin's 1,414.3.

Beaten by Miss Heggtveit in the special slalom for women was Betsy Snite, the pretty blonde from Norwich, Vt., who rates as one of the top slalom artists in the world. The American, who accounted for the competition's fastest time—55.5 seconds—in the second heat, placed second over-all in 1 minute 52.9 seconds. Miss Heggtveit's time was 1:49.6.

With Miss Snite's defeat passed one of the United States' greatest opportunities since the Winter Olympics began in 1924 to score a coup in women's Alpine (slalom, giant slalom and downhill) competition. In the three events, Americans were favored. In all three, they finished second.

The day produced another

major disappointment. Blond Penny Pitou of Gilford, N. H., second in the downhill and giant slalom, crashed in her second run of the slalom. Had she remained erect, she undoubtedly would have carried off the Federation Internationale de Ski combined championship.

The women's slalom provided plenty of spills. The two courses on Papoose Peak, each with fifty-three gates, were in perfect condition. The weather was cold and windy and the powder hard, packed and fast. If a skier let down her guard even momentarily, there was trouble ahead.

**Course Drops 610 Feet**

Miss Heggtveit proved that her reflexes are top drawer. She raced down the 1,575-foot hill that drops 610 feet in the excellent time of 0:54 on her first run. Even the inexpert in the crowd of 3,000 that lined both sides of the course knew that this was fast going. Only Marianne Jahn of Austria was able to approach this clocking.

Miss Jahn, timed in 0:55.5 for her first effort, ran into trouble during her second trip and was out of contention. Her trouble came only four gates from the finish. Down she went into the snow and down she went in the standing.

After the first series, Miss Snite was tied for fourth with Giuliana Chenal-Minuzzo of Italy and Barbi Henneberger of Germany. All three had finished the run in 0:57.4. In third place

was Inger Bjornbakken of Norway in 0:57.3.

Miss Heggtveit and Miss Snite, the first and second to face the starter, set a mark for the rest of the field of forty-three on their second runs.

The Canadian, declining to play it safe, flashed down the incline in 0:55.6. Miss Snite finished in 0:55.5. Nobody else was able to approach that kind of speed.

As a result of her brilliant second run, Miss Snite captured second place by a big margin. Fraeulein Henneberger was third in 1:56:6, followed by Therese Leduc of France (1:57.-4) and Hilde Hofherr of Austria and Liselotte Michel of Switzerland (each 1:58).

Miss Pitou, racing in pigtails, fell near the top of the second run after finishing her first run in 0:58.5, a performance that made her a contender for at least some points in the team scoring. She arose and completed the race but appeared to limp as she moved to the sidelines.

**Renie Cox Ninth**

Renie Cox and Beverly Anderson were the other Americans in the race. Miss Cox placed ninth and Miss Anderson twenty-sixth.

The Soviet Union speed skaters, who had been performing as if they owned the sport, had to settle for a first-place tie in the men's 1,500-meter race.

Grishin, their ace, and Aas, the Norwegian, skated to the first gold-medal tie in the Games when each finished in 2:10.4. The gold medal was the third in three skating events for the Russians.

Dick Hunt of Los Angeles, the leading American, was seventeenth in 2:17.7.

February 27, 1960

Knut Johannesen of Norway speeds around rink at the Winter Olympics to set world and Olympic records for 10,000-meter race. The Oslo carpenter's time was 15:46.6.

# Norway and Finland Take Squaw Valley Gold Medals

Special to The New York Times.

SQUAW VALLEY, Calif., Feb. 27—Speed skaters from five nations did a smashing job on the world and Olympic 10,000-meter records today as the penultimate session in the VIII Olympic Winter Games was completed.

Four skaters bettered the world record of 16 minutes 32.6 seconds for the race, about six and a quarter miles.

Eight broke the Olympic mark. It was one of the greatest attacks on speed-skating records in years.

Heading the parade of record-breakers was Knut Johannesen, a 27-year-old carpenter from Oslo. The Norwegian scooted around the 400-meter course twenty-five times in 15:46.6. Viktor Kosichkin of the Soviet Union was second in 15:49.2.

The big demonstration by the skaters took the play away from an outstanding performance by Kalevi Hamalainen, a 27-year-old forester from Finland. He won the grueling fifty-kilometer (thirty-one-mile) cross-country ski competition at McKinney Creek.

### 4-Minute Mile of Skating

For years, speed-skating officials have placed the sixteen-minute 10,000-meter race in the same high realm that track and field experts used to place the four-minute mile. Nobody had ever come close.

But this was a great day for skating. The weather was cold and the oval in top condition. Even the early starters had impressive times. Johannesen skated in the fourth pair. When he finished, the crowd of about 5,000 roared its approval.

As usual for Olympic competition, two skaters raced at a time. The final standing was based on time.

Joining Johannesen and Kosichkin in bettering the world record were Kjell Backman of Sweden (16:14.2) and Ivar Nilsson of Sweden (16:26). Terence Monaghan of Britain tied the world mark.

Torstein Seiersten of Norway (16:33.4), Olle Dahlberg of Sweden (16:34.6) and Jouko Jarvinen of Finland (16:35.4) also got into the record-breaking picture. They surpassed the old Olympic mark of 16:35.9 set at Cortina in 1956.

In the ski race, Hamalainen finished under a full head of speed and in excellent condition. He was timed in 2 hours 59 minutes 6.3 seconds. His triumph gave a second gold medal to Finland. The Finns captured their other first-place award in the four-man forty-kilometer relay.

Second to Hamalainen under cloudless skies was Veikko Hakulinen, also of Finland. Hakulinen, who has won two Olympic gold medals, lost by only 20 seconds.

The 35-year-old Finn had trouble at some of the uphill stretches. Then he found he could not overtake the pacemaker because of the soft snow near the finish.

Third place went to young Rolf Ramgard of Sweden in 3:02:47. His countryman, Lennart Larsson, who broke a ski at the start and borrowed a new one from friends, finished fourth in 3:03:28. He placed ahead of the fleet-footed Sixten Jernberg, the defending champion from Sweden.

Jernberg, who has been suffering from a slight throat infection, seemed to have waxing problems at the thirty-three-kilometer point. He just didn't seem to make his skis move at their usual speed.

Hamalainen, the world champion at thirty kilometers in 1958, seemed surprised at his victory here. This was his fifth time in a race of this length. Never before had he won.

"Four kilometers before the end," he said, "I felt very tired. I had chest pains but they seemed to ease off as I continued with the running. When I finished, I had my second wind and felt great."

The big point in the long-distance contest came at the fifteen-kilometer mark. Jernberg, considered Europe's best all-round cross-country man, began to tire.

Then Hamalainen, a 5-foot 8-inch, 160-pound racer from Paapela, took the lead. Hakulinen provided Hamalainen with the greatest contention most of the way but never threatened the winner.

In the speed skating, Johannesen took his success in stride. After completing his performance, he skated around the oval five times to keep his muscles limber. Then he went back to his quarters in the Olympic Village. He said he was going to take a nap.

The Norwegian wasn't confident of victory until the last man had skated.

"There are yet good men to skate," he kept saying. "But I am very happy and I hope nobody beats me. Conditions were wonderful. It's too bad we didn't have these kind of conditions for some of our previous races."

The competition continued for two hours after Johannesen completed his stint. But only Kosichkin came close to the Norwegian's time.

Johannesen's victory ended the Soviet monopoly in men's speed skating. In three previous Olympic races, gold medals went to Russians. In yesterday's 1,500-meter speed skating, however, a Norwegian, Roald Edgar Aas, tied Yevgeni Grishin of the Soviet Union for first place. Each earned a gold medal.

February 28, 1960

# U.S. Captures Hockey Title and German Ski Jumper Wins as Olympics End

## CZECHOSLOVAK SIX DROPS 9-4 CONTEST

### Six-Goal Third Period Wins for U.S.—Recknagel First, Finnish Jumper Second

**By MICHAEL STRAUSS**
Special to The New York Times.

SQUAW VALLEY, Calif., Feb. 28—In an amazing comeback, the United States hockey team defeated Czechoslovakia, 9-4, today for this country's first hockey gold medal in the history of the Olympic Winter Games.

Six American goals in the third period capped one of the finest showings by any squad since the first winter games at Chamonix, France, in 1924. Few thought before the games that the Americans could win the hockey championship.

Today's triumph was in keeping with the brilliance the team has shown throughout the competition. Trailing, 4—3, after two periods, the Americans proceeded to overwhelm their rivals.

Associated Press Wirephoto
**VICTORY YELL: Jubilant U. S. hockey team after winning gold medal yesterday**

Associated Press Wirephotos

**VICTORIOUS:** Helmut Recknagel of Germany is carried by two of his countrymen after winning the 80-meter ski-jumping championship, held on Papoose Peak.

In one sixty-seven-second span, they scored three goals.

The American victory provided a breathtaking start for the final day of competition, in which the special eighty-meter ski-jumping event shared feature billing. The ski jump, held immediately after the hockey match, was won by Helmut Recknagel of Germany.

### Two Superb Leaps

Two superb leaps by Recknagel (306 feet and 277 feet) won by a comfortable margin for the 26-year-old toolmaker. Niilo Halonen of Finland was second, with 222.6 points to the winner's 227.2. Otto Leodolter was third and Nikolai Kamenskiy of the Soviet Union fourth.

The jumping competition, in ideal weather, drew a crowd of 28,000. The hill was in perfect shape, although the starting point had to be shortened for the second round because the in-run (take-off hill) had become too fast. The sun had turned some of the packed powder into icy granular particles.

For a time it appeared that this would be a big day in ski jumping, too, for the United States. Ansten Samuelstuen, an electronics engineer from Steamboat Springs, Colo., was among the leaders most of the way. But several of the later performers did so well that Samuelstuen was shuffled back to seventh in the final standing with 211.5 points.

Despite the appeal that ski jumping has for sports-minded winter crowds, there was little doubt that hockey was today's big attraction in this picturesque Sierra Nevada valley.

The hockey hero for the United States was Roger Christian, who scored four goals and poked home the tying tally from twenty feet after 5:59 of the third period. Bob Cleary put the home forces ahead at 7:40 with a rebound from in front of the cage.

### 67 Hectic Seconds

At 11:01, Rudolf Potsch, a Czechoslovakian defense man, drew a two-minute penalty for interference. It was a signal for the Americans to start their mopping-up operations. Bob Cleary, Roger Christian and Bill Cleary put together the three goals in sixty-seven seconds that wrapped up the decision.

The first two periods were trying ones for the Americans. They had won four championship round-robin games and two preliminary contests and they seemed weary.

Several of them said later that they had been unable to sleep because of the excitement and tension resulting from their 3-2 upset triumph over the Soviet Union last night. John McCartan, the former University of Minnesota all-America goalie who had done a remarkable job in the nets throughout the competition, reported he had seen nothing but pucks flying at him all night.

The Czechoslovakians were ready to take advantage of any situation. They scored after only eight seconds of play. Miroslav Vlach registered from in close after Frantisek Tikal and Josef Golonka had set him up.

Weldon Olson evened matters at 4:19 and Bob McVey put the Americans ahead at 9:32 when he broke behind the rival defense after receiving a Johnny-on-the-spot pass from Bob Cleary. The score was tied again shortly thereafter when Vlastimil Bubnik registered on a pass from Karel Gut.

Bubnik's goal provided substantial evidence that the Americans were not playing wide-awake hockey. The goal was set up when Gut stole a pass on defensive ice while the Czechoslovakians were short two players.

In 13:33 of the first period, Roger Christian's first goal broke the 2-2 tie. Sixty-seven seconds later, there was a 3-3 tie. The equalizer was provided by Frantisek Vanek.

Early in the second period, Czechoslovakia gained the upper hand. Vlach got the disk in center ice on a pass from Jan Kasper, faked an American defenseman and rifled the puck past McCartan on a 15-footer. It was the only scoring of the period.

Distances suffered in the second series of ski jumps because of the shortened in-run. Under Olympic rules, whenever leaps exceed a hill's critical point (the longest distance considered safe for jumping) the in-run has to be reduced to cut speed.

All jumping hills are built with the critical point in mind. At Squaw Valley the critical point is eighty-three meters (about 272 feet). Officials, however, are allowed a margin of 8 per cent more, which would bring the danger point to about ninety-eight and one-half meters (323 feet). In the first round four competitors stretched out for ninety meters (293 feet) or better.

It was because of the critical-point angle that engineers constructed ten starting platforms, one meter apart, for the big hill here. Today the field of forty-five started from the next-to-last platform from the bottom. For the second series, the bottom platform was used.

Recknagel's 306-foot jump was the longest effort of the first round. Though his second effort was only 277 feet, his style points averaged 18 out of a possible 20 and that gave him his cushion.

The longest distance of the second series was posted by Torbjorn Yggeseth of Norway. The Norwegian went 290 feet and averaged 17 points on style. This, paired with a 290-footer on his first try, placed him fifth with 216.1 points.

Leodolter, in third place, had 219.4 points, while Kamenskiy, in fourth, had 216.9. Samuelstuen had leaps of 295 and 259 feet for his total of 211.5 points. He finished only 1.1 point out of sixth place, which was taken by Max Bolkart of Germany.

The other Americans fared poorly. Jan St. Andre was twenty-eighth, Bob Wedin thirty-second and Gene Kotlarek forty-second. Kotlarek was involved in one of the two spills of the program.

Canada finished second in the hockey standing, defeating the Soviet Union, 8—5, in the tourney's final game. The victory was the fourth for the Canadians in five starts. In the day's other hockey encounter, Sweden scored its first success in the round-robin by topping last-place Germany, 8—2.

February 29, 1960

## FIRST PRO SLALOM TAKEN BY PRAVDA

### Sun Valley Instructor Wins $1,500 by Outskiing 12 Others in Aspen Event

ASPEN, Colo., Jan. 29 (AP) —An Austrian, Christian Pravda, a long-time instructor at Sun Valley, Idaho, won the world's first professional ski race on Buttermilk Mountain today.

The race was staged by the newly formed International Ski Racers Association. Twelve contestants paid entrance fees of $20 each and competed for cash prizes before a paid gallery. They made two runs over a mile-long slalom course with sixteen gates. The seven who qualified on the first run skied for prize money on the second. Winners were chosen on their combined time for both runs.

Pravda, who had placed third on the first run, recovered on the second to win $1,000 in prize money plus $500 as his share of a $1,000 net gate paid by 2,000 spectators.

The six other finishers all are staff members of the Aspen Ski School. The runner-up was Andrel Molterer, who won $400 in prize money and $200 from gate receipts.

**THE FINISHERS**

|  | First Race. | Second Race. | Total Time. |
|---|---|---|---|
| Christian Pravda | 1:01.5 | 1:01.3 | 2:02.8 |
| Andrel Molterer | 1:01.3 | 1:01.7 | 2:03 |
| Tony Spiess | 1:01.4 | 1:02 | 2:03.4 |
| Hans Klimmer | 1:04.9 | 1:04.9 | 2:09.8 |
| Sigurd Rockne | 1:06 | 1:04.1 | 2:10.1 |
| Pierre Jalbert | 1:06.5 | 1:04.8 | 2:11.3 |
| Hans Zurslüh | 1:06.2 | 1:06 | 2:12.2 |

January 30, 1961

# *Monti Retains World Two-Man Bobsled Crown Before 8,000 at Lake Placid*

## ITALIAN IS VICTOR 5TH YEAR IN ROW

### Monti and Siorpaes Crash After Record Final Run —American Sled 2d

**By MICHAEL STRAUSS**
Special to The New York Times.

LAKE PLACID, N. Y., Feb. 12—Eugenio Monti, the amazing Italian, today raced to his fifth straight world two-man bobsled championship.

To prove his theory that anything anyone does he can do faster, Monti and his brakeman, Sergio Siorpaes, roared down the perilous sixteen-curve Mount Van Hoevenberg run in record time. The two daredevils were clocked in an almost unbelievable 1:09.22 for the mile run, their second of two today.

The winners, well in the lead after three heats—two were held yesterday—didn't have to travel as fast as they did in the finale to triumph. Monti, however, is a colorful racer who believes in finishing with a flourish. Today, he gave the crowd of 8,000 more of a thrill than even he had anticipated.

As his sled swept down the last straightaway at more than a mile a minute, he turned slightly to Siorpaes and ordered the brake applied. Apparently the brakeman took his teammate too literally. Down went the sled's jagged teeth into the out-run and out of control went the sled.

#### Monti's Head Hits Cowl

The big iron sled veered crazily to the right, went over a little bank and drove into a tree. The brakeman was tossed clear, but Monti's head struck the cowl.

Fortunately, the sled had slowed considerably and the Italian star suffered only minor facial cuts. A doctor patched him with a stitch near the nose.

Monti's final outing, following a trip that required 1:11.17 — only the fourth fastest in the third heat — gave him a combined time of 4:42.67 for the four-race contest. It easily surpassed the 4:45.74 clocking by Gary Sheffield and Jerry Tennant of the United States, who finished second.

Behind the first two came Italy's No. 2 combination of Sergio Zardini and Romano Bonagura (4:46.62), Germany's No. 1 duo of Franz Schelle and Otto Gobl (4:47.66) and Switzerland's No. 1 pair of Max Angst and Gopf Kottman (4:47.73).

There was one bad accident. Involved were Hans Roesch, of Germany. a former world four-man champion, and his brakeman, Theo Bauer. The pair slammed into a wall between the last two curves.

Bauer, thrown from the sled, escaped without injury. Roesch, however, who was slated to drive for Germany in next week-end's four-man championship, received a severe blow on the right elbow. He was taken to the Lake Placid Memorial Hospital, where it was reported he had suffered a compound fracture.

Sheffield and Tennant, both corporals in the Marine Corps, registered the second fastest time of the day—1:10.47—in the fourth heat.

All of Monti's split times were better than any that had ever been recorded here. He was timed in 5 seconds for the first fifty yards, 0:39.96 for the half-mile and 0:56.34 for the three-quarters.

February 13, 1961

# *18 U.S. SKATERS AMONG 73 DEAD IN A JET CRASH*

**By HARRY GILROY**
Special to The New York Times.

BRUSSELS, Belgium, Feb. 15 —A Sabena Airlines Boeing 707 jet crashed near the Brussels Airport early today, killing seventy-three persons, including the eighteen members of the United States figure-skating team.

The plane, en route from New York, plunged to earth after it had twice circled the airport. The dead included the sixty-one passengers, the crew of eleven, and a farmer in the field where the plane fell.

The passengers included forty-nine Americans, a Swiss, a Frenchman, a German, a Canadian, a Nicaraguan and seven Belgians.

The American figure-skating team was on its way to a world championship meet in Prague. Its members included Mrs. Maribel Vinson Owen, 49 years old, of Winchester, Mass., and her two daughters, both of them champions. Mrs. Owen was the United States figure-skating champion nine times. On the current trip she was the coach for her daughters.

The crash was the worst ever suffered by Sabena. It also

Associated Press

**ON FATAL FLIGHT:** Members of U. S. figure-skating team at Idlewild Tuesday before departure for Brussels. Front row, from left: Deane McMinn, coach; Laurence Owen, Stephanie Westerfield and Rhode Michelson. Others, bottom to top, from left: Douglas Ramsey, Gregory Kelley, Bradley Lord, Maribel Owen, Dudley S. Richards, William H. Hickox, Kay Hadley, Laurice Hickox, Dallas Pierce, Ila Hadley, Roger Campbell, Diane Sherbloom, Donna Lee Carrier, Robert Dineen and Patricia Dineen. Plane was Sabena jet.

marked the first time any passengers had been killed in a Boeing 707 accident. The last serious Sabena crash occurred May 18, 1958, when a DC-7C crashed at Casablanca, killing fifty-six passengers and nine crew members.

The four-engine jet came in sight of the control tower shortly before 10 A. M. in a cloudless sky. The plane, which had left New York at 7:30 P. M. yesterday, would have landed at once except that another plane was moving along the runway to take off, an airport official said.

Persons in the little farming hamlet of Berg, northeast of Brussels, saw the airliner circling overhead at an altitude of about 600 feet. Officials at the control tower were also watching the plane with field glasses.

Suddenly the plane fell. An airport official placed the time at 10:05 A. M.

### Plane Strikes Farmer

The plane came down at a 70 degree angle onto a small farm field. It plunged into a grove of trees, narrowly missing three houses. It struck Theo de Laet, a young farmer noted as an amateur cyclist, killing him. A piece of debris tore a leg off another farmer, Marcel Lauwers.

Parts of the plane were thrown 200 yards but the bulk of the airliner burst into flames, preventing anyone from approaching until firemen arrived from the airport.

February 16, 1961

## U. S. GROUP URGES TITLE MEET GO ON

### Skating Official Estimates Plane Disaster Set Back Sport Here 2 to 4 Years

Despite the sudden and tragic loss of the entire United States team in the crash of a Sabena airliner, the United States Figure Skating Association asked yesterday that the world championships, at Prague, Czechoslovakia, be held on schedule.

There were conflicting reports about the question of cancellation. When reports of the crash reached F. Ritter Shumway of Rochester, vice president of the skating organization, he immediately cabled a request to Dr. Jacob Koch, president of the International Skating Union, that he "carry on." Earlier, a dispatch from Europe had said

that the championships would be canceled.

"We appreciated the tribute to our skaters," explained Mr. Ritter, the top ranking United States skating official since the recent death of Hobart Herbert, former president of the United States Association. "But we thought the competition should continue as the skaters, I know, would want it that way. Accordingly I cabled Dr. Koch."

### Cancellation Is Urged

In Geneva, Dr. Koch called for a cancellation of the championships. However, the Czechslovak association was in favoring of carrying on and the question was put to a vote of the executive committee.

A United Press International dispatch from Davos, Switzerland, quoted George Haelser, secretary general of the International Skating Union as having said that the championships "will be canceled." However, a Reuters report from Prague stated "the championships will go ahead as scheduled."

Mr. Ritter asserted the "personal tragedy" of the crash had "overwhelmed him."

He said he believed that the United States would require "two to four years" to recover its international competitive strength in this sport.

Three of the first five finishers in the United States men's championships two weeks ago in Colorado Springs were on the plane. They were Bradley Lord of Boston, who finished first, Greg Kelley of Colorado Springs, second, and Doug Ramsey of Detroit, fourth.

The third-place finisher, Tim Brown of Berkeley, Calif., and 16-year-old Bruce Heiss of Ozone Park, Queens, who finished fifth, were not named to the team for the Prague event.

Laurence Owen, Stephanie Westerfield and Rohe Michelson, who placed one, two, three, respectively, the United States women's singles, also were

aboard the plane. Miss Owen won the women's title in the North American championships Sunday in Philadelphia.

### A 6 to 10 Year Task

"Skating has received an incalculable setback", asserted Pierre Brunet, coach of the Olympic champion, Mrs. Carol Heiss Jenkins, who is now a professional. Mr. Brunet planned to leave on Friday for Prague as the tutor of Donald Jackson, the Canadian who won the North American championship.

In Mr. Brunet's view the future of figure skating in the United States depends on the development of 14 and 15 year olds.

Mr. Brown is studying medicine and Bruce Heiss will be starting college in the fall. That means they will be unable to devote as much time to skating.

"To become an expert skater," Mr. Brunet said, "takes from six to ten years, depending on the individual. You have to practice three hours daily, summer or winter, if you want to climb to the top."

One of the requisites is the ability to trace on ice what are known as "school figures." They have a value of approximately 60 per cent when tabulations are made in deciding a championship.

The other phase of the test consists of "free skating," which is skated to music. This can have spectacular and artistic overtones, depending upon the competitor.

"There are ninety-six school figures that have to be skated by the time you reach senior competition," explained Mr. Brunet. "They are skated on both the right and left foot and are done forward and then backward."

Mr. Brunet said that it was possible that Nancy Heiss, Mrs. Jenkins' sister, might return to competition. Miss Heiss, who is 18 years old, is a sophomore at Michigan State. She has

been out of major competition for two seasons since breaking a bone in her foot.

### Top Prospect Retired

Two weeks ago, Miss Heiss gave an exhibition of free skating at the Dartmouth winter carnival in Hanover, N. H. Nancy Heiss finished second to her sister in the 1959 United States championship.

Mrs. Barbara Ann Pursley, the former Barbara Ann Roles of Los Angeles, who finished third in the 1960 Olympics, has retired from skating competitions. She could be a leading prospect in the women's ranks, according to Mrs. Howard Meredith, official and skating judge for more than twenty years. However, Mrs. Meredith thinks the real hope for the sport depends on how quickly the youngsters can mature.

Loraine Hanlon, a 15-year-old Boston girl, and recent winner of the national junior title; Carol Noir, 14, of West Orange, N. J., holder of the Eastern senior title; Tina Noyes, 12, of Boston, national novice champion, and Joya Utermohlin, 14, of New York, Eastern junior champion, were listed as likely prospects by Mrs. Meredith.

In the men's ranks, Monty Hoyt, 16, of Denver, national junior champion, and Scott Ethan Allen, 16, of New York, are regarded among the top young skaters.

February 16, 1961

# GETTING THE JUMP ON WINTER

## Mechanized Weather Becomes a Standard Fixture in Ski Centers Of the East and Guarantees Snow Regardless of Nature

### By MICHAEL STRAUSS

ONCE upon a time ski area operators, having cleared the stumps and rocks from their slopes and oiled up the rope tow machinery, had to sit around and wait for winter to come and to bring with it enough snow to make skiing possible. Mechanization has finally run rampant across the ski fields and today's ski resort operators no longer wait on nature; instead they are already getting the jump on the season by turning on their snow-making machines.

Last winter's spotty snow season is largely responsible for the big spurt in snow machine installations. Many a resort area sat

chilled but snowless last winter, sans skiers and sans profit, while competitive areas turned on their machines and enjoyed skiing and prosperity without any help from nature.

The most crushing rejection of nature was the giant installation recently of artificial snow machines at the New York State ski center on Whiteface Mountain. This center opened last year and sat out most of the winter in the heart of the Adirondack Mountains, within sight of Lake Placid where America's present ski boom began thirty years ago, without

enough snow or skiers to make it worth while.

### Snow Almost Guaranteed

Snow machines are now so prevalent that this winter's skiers will be able to leave home with the almost guaranteed assurance that somewhere near by they will find snow-covered slopes. The natural snowfall or lack of same will be immaterial; all that will matter is that the temperature be below freezing so the manufactured snow will stay snow and not revert to water.

Artificial snow is, of course, not new. Such southerly Catskill Mountain resorts as the Concord Hotel ski area at Kiamesha Lake, and the Grossinger, at Ferndale near Liberty, have been utilizing custom-made snow for a decade. But it was the tremendous success the machines made last year at such resorts as Bousquet at Pittsfield in the Berkshire Hills of Massachusetts; Mount Ascutney in Vermont, and the Mittersill in New Hampshire—places where there was good skiing last winter while elsewhere in the Northeast ski resorts had bare slopes—that gave the machinery installers their big season of 1961.

### Augmenting Nature

The machines simply do, on command, what nature sometimes refuses to do—put enough moisture into cold air to turn it into snow. The apparatus consists of pumps to bring water to the slopes and air compressors to push the water through fine nozzles under high pressure, turning it into a fine, fog-like mist.

When the mixture is just right and the temperature of the air is firmly below 32 degrees Fahrenheit, the spray shot into the air returns to earth in the form of snow. As long as the earth and the air are cold enough to prevent its melting, the synthetic snow will support skiers and ski resort operators.

Almost everywhere today the accent seems to be on this new type of snow insurance, a type entirely foreign to policy underwriters. This winter for the first time, there will be artificial snow at resorts in the United States as far north as Cascade Mountain near Portage, Wis.; Walloon Lake in Michigan's Lower Peninsula and Buck Hill and Lookout Mountain in Minnesota.

The snow machines, too, have enabled resorts even south of the Mason-Dixon Line to enter the winter sports field. Indeed, there will be some heavy ski traffic as far south as the North Carolina-Tennessee border this year. New ski areas in the Great Smokies region will use snow-making machines. The resorts are at Blowing Rock, N. C., and Gatlinburg in Tennessee.

Ever since the 1932 Winter Olympics at Lake Placid started the ski boom in the United States, ski resort operators have been alert for substitutes for real snow. Through the years they tried cocoa mats, granulated plastic, crushed ice, pine needles and even soap chips. In Germany, one enterprising resort operator is using a special type of crushed rock with fair success.

Snow machines use about ten gallons of water a minute for every 100-foot stretch of slope. Operators have been known to cover an area 1,000 feet long and 250 feet wide in one day with only a dozen nozzles.

Although the owner of the ski center at Jiminy Peak in the Berk-

shires estimates that it costs him only $110 to cover an area of 200,-000 square feet with six inches of snow, the price of the machines is not low. It costs something like $5,000 to equip a small slope and as much as $125,000 for a big ski

area. The manufacturers, however, use a telling point to help sell their product; they emphasize that a snowless season costs a resort without a machine even more.

December 3, 1961

---

# Hoyt, Denver Youth, Gains U.S. Figure-Skating Title

### By LINCOLN A. WERDEN
#### Special to The New York Times.

BOSTON, Feb. 3—Monty Hoyt, a slim 17-year-old 6-footer from Denver, became the men's national figure skating champion today. Before a capacity gathering of 3,000 at the Boston College rink, the high school senior completed a smooth free-skating routine to assure himself of the title.

A 12-year-old adversary, Scott Allen of Smoke Rise, N. J., furnished the chief challenge today, just as he did in the compulsory figure tests on Thursday.

The victory lifted Hoyt in one year from junior champion to the top in the men's senior ranks, depleted by the fatal airplane crash of Feb. 15, 1961. The 1961 champion, Bradley

Lord of Swampscott, Mass. was among the victims. The last to achieve the quick step from junior to senior champion was Dick Button, who won those honors successively in 1945 and 1946.

Hoyt will have the honor of leading the men's squad in the forthcoming world championship at Prague, March 14 through 16.

Among those to congratulate the new titleholder, who swept off with all five first-place votes of the judges, was Mrs. Gertrude Vinson, 81-year-old mother of Mrs. Maribel Vinson Owen.

Mrs. Owen, a former champion, and her daughters, Laurence and Maribee, were among those lost in the plane crash.

Allen, 5-footer, did his best to close the gap that existed between himself and Hoyt before their performances today. The little fellow skated from slow to rapid tempo, specializing in jumps and interpretive steps.

Officials gave him second by unanimous decision. He is one of the youngest ever to scale those heights in the men's ranks. He was trying for a record of being the youngest champion. Rubin Lee, who won this honor at the age of 15, was the youngest ever to do so.

Dave Edwards, a 17-year-old schoolboy from Philadelphia, was third. The other contestant was 23-year-old James Short of Alhambra, Calif., on Army furlough.

Some fine music appreciation was shown by Hoyt in his interpretative skating. His skate had an easy flow over the glistening surface and he interspersed double-loop jumps with his dance steps.

"He's one of the most intelligent skaters I've ever seen," commented his coach, Carlo Fassi, formerly of Cortina, Italy. "He skates with his head as well as his heart."

Fassi has been instructor at the Broadmoor Skating Club, Colorado Springs, where Hoyt trains on week-ends after leaving school in Denver on Friday afternoons. Fassi took over Hoyt's skating tutelage following the death of Ed Scholdan, Hoyt's former coach, in the tragic crash.

"I'm thrilled to have done so well in free skating," said Hoyt after he was declared the winner. "The five minutes is a killer, or has been for me, because you have to learn to pace yourself through the program." Allen was also second to Hoyt in the national juniors last year. Three brothers share Monty's skating enthusiasm.

The new champion speaks five languages, including a bit of Czech, which he said: "May help me get around in Prague."

Allen is virtually certain to get a berth on the men's world team, which will be announced tomorrow following the close of the championships. The women's senior event is on the final-day's schedule.

Hoyt, who is considering the diplomatic service as a career, has no intention of becoming a skating professional. Since the day he won the novice crown in 1959, his goal has been to be the United States champion.

February 4, 1962

United Press International Telephoto

CHAMPIONS: Monty Hoyt of Denver, who won the senior men's figure-skating crown, and Christine Haigler of Colorado Springs, Colo., victorious in the junior ladies' contest, skate off together after their triumphs in Boston.

## Canadian's Brilliant Rally Wins World Figure-Skating Laurels

### Jackson Performs First Triple Jump in History of Sport to Defeat Divin— Hoyt of U. S. Places Sixth

PRAGUE; Czechoslovakia, March 15 (AP)—Donald Jackson of Canada captured the world figure-skating championship tonight with the first series of triple jumps in figure-skating competition. He rallied to overtake Karol Divin of Czechoslovakia.

The 21-year-old Jackson thrilled a crowd of 18,500 with his dazzling leaps and spins in the freestyle competition.

Divin, the Olympic silver medalist at Squaw Valley, Calif., in 1960, had taken a 45.8-point lead over the Canadian in compulsory figures.

But the 25-year-old Czechoslovak was unable to match Jackson's daring and his imaginative performance in freestyle skating.

Jackson's victory gave Canada its second world title. Maria and Otto Jelinek took the pairs yesterday.

According to Associated Press tabulations, Jackson scored 2,277.1 points against Divin's 2,255.

The nine-man jury awarded Jackson five first-place votes. Divin had the other four.

The American champion, Monty Hoyt of Denver, placed sixth with 2,059.1 while the national runner-up Scotty Allen of Smoke Rise, N.J., was ninth with 2,002.

A graceful Dutch girl, Sjoukje Dijkstra gained the lead after the first two of six compulsory figures in women's singles, but America's hope, Mrs. Barbara Roles Pursely of Arcadia, Calif., remained in a strong position in fourth.

Mrs. Pursely, 20-year-old mother who was bronze medalist in the 1960 Olympics, is rated one of the world's best free skaters. The free skating counts 40 per cent in the final judging, against 60 per cent for compulsory figures.

Through the first two figures, Miss Sjkstra, had 349.2 points. Regine Heitzer of Austria followed with 338 and then came Wendy Griner of Canada with 335.6. Mrs. Pursely had 334.

Vicky Fisher, 18, of Minneapolis was seventh and 16-year-old Lorraine Hanlon of Boston was tenth.

Christine and Jean Paul Guhel of France invaded Britain's traditional ice-dance realm by capturing the compulsory figures.

Virginia Thompson and William McLachlan of Canada were second and Eva and Pavel Romanov of Czechoslovakia third.

The French couple piled up 187.4 points to 185.1 for the Canadians and 184.6 for the Czechs. Canada also got a fourth place with Paulette Doan and Kenneth Ormsby, who scored 182.9.

Britain's best couple, Linda Shearman and Michael Philips, wound up sixth with 182.2 points.
March 16, 1962

---

## SWEDE, 19, FIRST IN SPEED SKATING

### Nilsson, Setting 2 Records, Wins Men's World Title

KARUIZAWA, Japan, Feb. 24 (AP)—Jonny Nilsson of Sweden smashed two world records and became the youngest men's world speed-skating champion in history.

Nilsson skated against the near blizzard, snapped the mark for 10,000 meters today, to go with his record-breaking performance yesterday in the 5,-000. He had a record point total for the two-day, four-event grind.

The 19-year-old engineering student skated 10,000 meters in 15 minutes 46.6 seconds. He broke the record of 15:57.1 set in the 1960 Olympics at Squaw Valley, Calif.

Nilsson skated against the old record-holder Knut Johannesen, in the two-man heats of the 10,000. He whipped the Norwegian by three-quarters of a lap.

Lu Chik-uan of Communist China won the other event today, the 1,500 meters, in 2:09.2.

Nilsson's point total of 178.447 was 2.113 under the pending world mark. Johannesen, who finished second in the over-all standings, also bettered the old mark with 179.598 as did Norway's Nils Aaness, the former record-holder, who was third with 180.405.

The two American contestants, Edward Rudolph Jr., of Northbrook, Ill., and Arnold Urlass of Elmhurst, Queens, did not qualify for the final race. It was limited to the top 16 in over-all points.

February 25, 1963

---

# 2 Gates Added to Olympic Ski Run for Safety

### Few Call Course Dangerous Despite the Fatality—Girls' Track Shortened

INNSBRUCK, Austria, Jan. 26 (AP)—Extra safety precautions were ordered at the 1964 Winter Olympics today following a tragic series of training accidents that have cost two lives and caused several serious injuries.

Ross Milne, a 19-year-old Australian skier, was killed yesterday when he lost control on the downhill course on Mount Patscherkofel and crashed into a tree. On Wednesday, a 58-year-old British toboggan racer, Kazimierz (Kay) Skrzypeski, died of injuries received when his sled careened off the chute.

The gloom cast by the accidents was somewhat lightened today by the news that Sepp Fleischmann, a German bobsledder, had recovered consciousness for the first time since he was injured six days ago.

When his partner, Sepp Linz, appeared at his bedside with both arms in plaster casts, Fleischmann opened his eyes and said, "Sepp, is it you?"

#### Women's Course Shortened

The ski jury ordered two extra compulsory gates along the Patscherkofel men's downhill course to guide skiers and to help them avoid veering off the course. The trunks of hundreds of trees lining the course were heavily padded with straw. Milne's head struck a tree above the padding previously installed.

The women's downhill course at Lizum was shortened because of lack of snow at the top rather than as a precaution. Three more compulsory gates, however, were added.

New lips had previously been ordered for the dangerous curves of the toboggan run.

Experts declared that although the men's downhill run was one of the toughest in Olympic history, lack of safety precautions could not be blamed for the tragedy. They maintained that the track was dangerous only for inexpert skiers trying to compete against the experts.

"The course is real good, fast and very well prepared," said Bud Werner of Steamboat Springs, Colo. "Most of all, I would say it is safe."

A Soviet trainer described the trail as safe, but "very interesting."

The Austrian organizers announced that a team of three doctors would be in readiness at every finish line. The courses will be patrolled by rescue squads equipped with ski stretchers, snow vehicles and jeeps. A helicopter is available for difficult rescues.

Practice on the men's run will be resumed tomorrow. Meanwhile, the girls tested the shortened Lizum run carefully today and said they found it in good condition and not dangerous.

Undeterred by the death of one of their teammates, a pair of British bobsledders hurtled their two-man sled down the track in record time in the first of the official training runs.

Anthony Nash and Robin Dixon made one run in 1 minute 6.06 seconds, breaking the mark of 1:06.42 made by Eugenio Monti of Italy in last year's world championships on the Olympic run at nearby Igls. They also made the best over-all time for two runs, 2:13.20.

Stan Benham, the United States bobsled team captain, tentatively picked Larry McKillip of Saranac Lake, N. Y., and Garry Sheffield of Lake Placid, N. Y., as the drivers of the United States' two-man sleds after a single qualification run.

Art Tokle of Lake Telemark, N. J., the coach of the United States ski jumpers, said he would wait until Tuesday to decide whether Gene Kotlarek of Duluth, Minn., would take part in the Nordic combined jumping event on the 70-meter hill at Seefeld on Friday. Kotlarek has an injured left ankle

and he doesn't like the 70-meter hill.

John Balfanz of Minneapolis made a stylish jump of 251 feet in practice, but his distance didn't match that reached by some newly-arrived Norwegians.

American women speed skaters trailed far behind the Soviet women in a pair of pre-Olympic races. Lidia Skobilikova, the Soviet Union's double gold medalist at the 1960 Squaw Valley games, bettered her own Olympic record in winning the 1,500 meters. Irina Yegorova took the 500 meters.

#### Marie Lawler Is Fifth

The highest placed American in the 500 was Marie Lawler of Minneapolis, who finished fifth in 46.8 seconds. Janice Smith, a promising 18-year-old competitor from Rochester, was a half-second slower in sixth place. The winner was timed in 0:46.

In the 1,500, Jeanne Ashworth of Lake Placid, N. Y., a bronze medalist at Squaw Valley, was the first American, finishing eighth. Miss Smith was ninth.

Torgeir Brandtzaeg, a 22-year-old salesman from Trondheim, Norway, amazed the crowd at the ski jump when he made four impressive leaps ranging from 254 to 257 feet the first time he tried the hill. Thorbjoern Yggeseth was close behind with a best jump of 252 feet.

Dave Hicks, a 19-year-old jumper from Duluth, was back in action, but he was stiff after a fall a few days ago. His best jump was 246 feet, which was matched by Amsten Samuel-stuen of Boulder, Colo.

Al Merrill, the head United States ski coach, said of Kotlarek, "He doesn't like the hill here any more, and personally I feel he should wait for the Berg Isel hill competition on Feb. 9 where the big special jump will be held."

January 27, 1964

# SOVIET SKATERS WIN GOLD MEDAL

### Protopopov-Belousova Pair Upsets World Champions

INNSBRUCK, Austria, Jan. 29 (AP)—Oleg Protopopov and Ludmila Belousova of the Soviet Union tonight won the pairs figure skating gold medal in the IX Winter Olympic

Games—the first gold medal of the competition.

It was the first time the Soviet Union had won an Olympic gold medal in figure skating.

The experienced Soviet competitors won first-place decision from five of the nine judges with a difficult skating program executed with ballet-like grace.

They narrowly upset the world champions, Marika Kilius and Hans-Juergen Baeumler of Germany.

The total points for the Soviet skaters were 104.4. The Germans had 103.6.

Debbi Wilkes and Guy Revell of Canada took the bronze medal with 98.5 points.

The ordinal points, based on the placings given by the judges, were 13 for the Soviet skaters and 15 for the Germans.

Miss Wilkes and Revell had 35.5 ordinal points.

They took third from Vivian and Ronald Joseph of Highland Park, Ill., by the slender margin of 98.5 to 98.2 in the total points.

The Soviet Union's husband and wife pair were runners-up to the Germans in the World Championships last year. They placed only

ninth in the 1960 Olympics at Squaw Valley, Calif.

Miss Kilius and her partner smiled and applauded with the crowd as Avery Brundage, the president of the International Olympic Committee, hung the gold medals around the necks of the winners.

Protopopov and his wife, who skates under her maiden name were certain winners after the judges posted their point totals following their performance. He is 31 years old and she is 28.

They gave a remarkably smooth and precise performance, going through a complicated routine with graceful lifts and jumps. Their spins were made with ballet-like gestures that delighted the 11,000 spectators.

The youthful American skaters made surprisingly good showing in spite of their lack of experience. Judianne and Jerry Fotheringill of Tacoma, Wash., took seventh place with 69.5 ordinals and 94.7 total pints and Cynthia and Ronald Kaufmann of Seattle, finished eighth with 74 ordinals and 92.8 total points.

January 30, 1964

of 45 seconds was an Olympic record and her closest rivals were two other Russian skaters.

Another gold medal went to Eero Maentyranta of Finland, who won the men's 30-kilometer skiing event in 1 hour 30 minutes 50.7 seconds.

The women's figure-skating opened with the first two of five compulsory figures and the leader, as expected, was Sjoukje Dijkstra of the Netherlands, the world champion. Three more figures are scheduled tomorrow, with the final on Sunday.

The United States was idle in the hockey competition after its 5-1 loss to the Soviet team yesterday. In today's games, Canada won for the second time by defeating Sweden, 3—1, and Switzerland lost for the second time when it bowed to Finland, 4—0.

The first heats in men's and women's tobogganing also were held. Germany finished one, two, three in the men's competition, with Thomas Koehler the winner. Ortrun Enderlein, also of Germany, was the women's winner.

In the downhill, Zimmermann rocketed off the mark and picked up his margin early. A giant-slalom specialist, he was shaving the gates and gathering speed for the almsot vertical plunges along the route.

He drove sharply into the curves and came hurtling out of the forest wide open, huddled as if in prayer for the final long schuss into the straight. There was that one flickering bobble, but then he was safe and clear.

"I had to win," Zimmermann said, "and I knew I had." He moved off to shake the Mayor's hand and was nearly mobbed by the 30,000 spectators who had been toiling up the sides of the mountain since dawn. A squad of policemen pulled him free.

"Egon is in a class by him-

# Zimmermann of Austria Wins Olympic Downhill

## SKI VICTOR RACES TO COURSE RECORD

### Zimmermann Is Joined as A Winner by Soviet Speed Skater Mrs. Skoblikova

**By FRED TUPPER**

Special to The New York Times

INNSBRUCK, Austria, Jan. 30 — Egon Zimmermann, a sandy-haired skier from the Arlberg in West Austria, today won the Winter Olympic gold medal that means more than any other.

The 24-year-old Zimmermann roared down the lightning-fast Patscherkofel in 2 minutes 18.6 seconds, a record for the 3,412-yard slope, and captured the downhill prize on the second day of the IX Winter Olympic Games.

For a split second, it was a near thing for the sturdy representative of this nation where Alpine skiing was born. He teetered and almost fell about 50 yards from the finish. But he recovered, and he won.

No American was in the first 10. The leading American finisher was Annibale (Ni) Orsi of Stockton,

Calif., who placed 14th in 2:21.59. The 19-year-old Orsi was not in the seeded group of 16, who had the advantage of covering the course first.

And so the United States was shut out of the first, second and

third place medal ceremonies in this event, as it has been in every event at the games so far.

The Soviet Union won its second gold medal when Mrs. Lidiya Skoblikova took the women's 500-meter skating race. Her time

**Egon Zimmermann of Austria sweeps down the Patscherkofel course to take the men's downhill event. Leo Lacroix of France was second, Wolfgang Bartels of Germany third.**

self," said Marc Hodler of Switzerland, who heads the World Federation of Skiing. "This year, right now, he's as good as Toni Sailer was when he swept the board at Cortina in 1956."

The young Austrian is the son of a hotel-keeper in Lech, a hamlet of fewer than 200 persons. Lech has produced two other gold-medalists in Othmar Schneider, who took the slalom at Oslo in 1952, and Trude Beiser, the women's downhill winner that year.

Zimmerman is an all-round athlete who trained as a chef in Paris but dabbles in motor-car racing and water skiing. He won the world giant slalom at Chamonix in 1962.

Second in this glamour event of the games was Leo Lacroix of France, who makes skis when he isn't skiing. It was his first Olympic bid. Lacroix, who is 26, admitted that "I forced too hard at the start and didn't have any strength when I needed it."

Third was Wolfgang Bartels of Germany, the son of a Bavarian hotel-keeper. Joos Minsch of Switzerland was fourth. He trailed Bartels by six-hundredths of a second.

"The only difference between me and a bronze was a blink of the eye," Minsch said. "Next time I remember not to blink."

Thus the "big four" in Alpine skiing—Austria, France, Germany and Switzerland—finished in that order, taking the first 13 places.

As for the American skiers, Orsi was unhappy with his 14th-place finish and said so. Billy Kidd of Stowe, Vt., and Bud Werner of Steamboat Springs, Colo., had nothing to say at all. They finished 16th and 17th, though both were in the high seeded group. Chuck Ferries of Houghton, Mich., was 20th.

There had been a hubbub most of the winter about the American skiers being seeded too low. The rankings were reversed earlier this week and Kidd and Werner were placed in the first 16. Kidd was the first starter and took a gate too wide toward the finish. Werner lost time high up when he swerved off the track.

Prince Karim, the Aga Khan, competed for Iran and placed 59th of the 77 who finished. He was pleased.

The Soviet Union's winner today was the world's finest women's speed-skater. Mrs. Skoblikova made a shambles of the record book in the 500-meter. Mrs. Skoblikova, who electrified the Squaw Valley Olympics by skating away with the 1,500 and 3,000 meters, whizzed around the Ice Stadium track in breaking the Olympic mark by nine-tenths of a second. The old mark, 0:45.9, was set by Helga Haase of Germany at Squaw Valley. Helga was eighth today in 0:47.2.

With her arms flailing and her body bent nearly parallel to the ground, Mrs. Skoblikova finished to the sound of cheers and put her hands over her eyes to hide the tears.

Irina Yegorova and Tatyana Sidorova took the silver and bronze medals for the Soviet and they, too, beat Miss Haase's 1960 time.

The Americans had bad luck. Jeanne Ashworth, a 25-year-old school teacher from Lake Placid, N. Y., was balked at the start. Then she hit the ice separating the lanes halfway around and hit it again on the final bend. She finished fourth in 0:46.2.

"After four years of drudgery, why should I make simple mistakes now?" she said.

Janice Smith of Rochester, N. Y., drew the outside lane against Hei Sook Kim of South Korea and had to hesitate a fraction of a second in the cross-over behind Miss Kim. Nevertheless, Miss Smith tied Miss Ashworth's time for fourth place.

The skaters raced in pairs, with times deciding the placings.

Marie Lawler of Minneapolis had an attack of shin splints and had to soak her left leg for hours before the race. She was seventh behind Gunilla Jacobsson of Sweden.

Maentyranta, a guard who patrols a Finnish border on skis, spreadeagled a huge field in winning the 30-kilometer cross-country ski run over the ribboned track at Seefeld.

Maentyranta was ahead after passing the man he feared the most, Sixten Jernberg of Sweden. Poling powerfully into the stretch, he came home in 1:30:50.7, which cracked all records for the event.

Jernberg, who had won this event at Squaw Valley and the 50-kilometer at Cortina, nearly caught the Finn at 16 kilometers. "My legs were good, but my stomach muscles were weak," said the 34-year-old Swede, who finished fifth.

The Americans were far down the line. Michael Elliott of Durango, Colo., was 30th; Richard Taylor of Laconia, N. H., 42d; Larry Damon, a three-time Olympian from Burlington, Vt., 46th, and James Shea of Lake Placid, 48th.

*January 31, 1964*

## Everything's Done To Make Downhill Faster and Faster

### By ROBERT DALEY
Special to The New York Times

INNSBUCK, Austria, Jan. 30 —Egon Zimmermann of Austria today won the Olympic downhill, the queen event of winter sports, over an unusually fast course.

Year by year, here and elsewhere, ski racers plunge down mountains faster and faster, and by next winter this race may seem slow. Zimmerman broke the course record, set last year, by five seconds.

Eight winters ago, at Cortina d'Ampezzo, Italy, Toni Sailer of Austria won three Olympic gold medals and was called a wonder skier. But the Sailer of 1956 would not have finished in the first 20 today. Technique, the courses, the skis have changed. And the racers have changed.

In 1960, aerodynamic principles were first applied seriously to the position racers try to hold—the tight crouch, the arms tucked in under the ribs. Previously skiers, including Sailer, were acrobats, always teetering at high speed. Now they are missiles.

The skin-tight stretch parts are recent, and at high speeds are worth fractions of seconds in reduced drag. Metal skis were introduced in 1960. They are worth seconds, too. Only Karl Schranz of Austria still races on wood, and he was 11th today. He does not prefer wood, but must use it because he works for the Kneissl ski factory, which does not yet make metal skis.

The courses were changed in 1959 following two fatal crashes in downhill races. Bulldozers and dynamiters moved onto the mountains. Anything a racer might strike was removed or blasted. Courses became "safe."

Downhill racers often touch speeds of 60 miles an hour. When they fall at such speed on tracks as steep as the Patscherkofel here, they bound and slide down the mountainside for hundreds of yards. The bumps pound them. They bound down the mountain in a cloud of snow, their skis can be seen flailing above their heads as they fight to keep from getting their legs broken.

Finally, they come to a stop. Downhillers have always crashed a lot, but on the new safe courses they can risk crashes they never could have risked in the past.

Training has changed. Nowadays, all top teams begin training on dry land in September or even in August. By the time they get out on the snow, they are as hard and indefatigable as prize fighters. They can hold positions for 2½ minutes against the tremendous forces of their own speed, which former skiers never could have held.

And so they can go faster.

The skiers are tougher mentally each year. Each year, the competition is keener. Zimmermann crashed twice at high speed in training last year. He was dragged off by stretcher with concussions, and he missed many races.

But today he criticized himself for being "too technical." He said he had won because other skiers had been even more "technical" than he.

Why didn't they risk a little more, he asked.

For all these reasons, downhill racing is faster than ever, but today there was one extra reason: The Patscherkofel was a particularly artifical and carefully prepared course.

Because there was not enough snow, the track was packed by hand by soldiers who moved about 8,000 cubic meters of snow onto it. They raked this snow, smoothed it and sprayed enough water on to keep it in place, though not enough to produce glare ice.

A natural snowfall will smooth out all but the most exaggerated features of the terrain. But on the Patscherkofel, every single stone or rut was faithfully reproduced on the surface of the track.

Thus, this was a bumpy track, and the racers were in the air frequently.

**The temperature was about 25 degrees, perfect for sliding, and this added to the speed, too.**

*January 31, 1964*

---

## Olympic Games Continue at Innsbruck

INNSBRUCK, Austria, Jan. 30 (AP)—Two New York girls, Jeanne Ashworth of Lake Placid and Janice Smith of Rochester, made the best showings of any Americans in today's Olympic competition. Competing in the 500-meter skating race, they finished in a tie for fourth.

The winner in this event was Mrs. Lidiya Skoblikova, who led a Russian sweep of the first three places. Her time was 45 seconds, an Olympic record.

The Misses Ashworth and Smith were clocked in 0:46.2.

Marie Lawler of Minneapolis, the other American competitor, registered 0:46.6 despite an overnight attack of shin splints. She was seventh after preparing for the race by soaking her left leg in hot and cold water for several hours.

Shin splints is an ailment in which the muscle separates from the leg bone.

"Every step in the race hurt," Miss Lawler said, "but it was worth it. I was pleased with my time."

Miss Ashworth threw everything into her race and literally flung herself over the finish line. She was cheered wildly by the crowd of 3,000 at the finish.

The women raced in pairs against the clock, and the 18-year-old Miss Smith was 18 yards ahead of Hei Sook Kim, a South Korean.

Miss Ashworth, who stumbled twice on her way around the oval, said:

"The only thing that disappointed me is that I have skated better and could have skated better."

The team manager, Philip Krumm of Kenosha, Wis., said he was pleased with the showing of the girls.

"After all, we're the amateurs." he said. "The Russians are the pros."

*January 31, 1964*

# Finn Takes Ski Jump, Mrs. Skoblikova Wins Skating and U.S. Fails Again

## LAST LEAP PLACES KANKKONEN FIRST

### He Overtakes 2 Norwegians With a Flawless Effort— Speed-Skating Mark Set

**By FRED TUPPER**
Special to The New York Times

INNSBRUCK, Austria, Jan. 31 Veikko Kankkonen of Finland grabbed a gold medal in the ski jump with a fantastic final leap, Lidiya Skoblikova of the Soviet Union took the 1,500-meter speed-skating event by smashing her Olympic record and a team from Britain, where snow is frowned on, surprisingly led halfway through the two-man bobsledding competition.

These were the highlights today of the third day of the IX Winter Olympics. And on a negative note, the United States still had no medal of any kind.

The Americans, however, do have hopes for one tomorrow. Jean Saubert of Ogden, Utah, who swept five pre-Alpine events, is a favorite in the women's slalom.

In other action today, Sjoukje Dijkstra of the Netherlands continued to lead women's figure skating, Thomas Kuehler and Ortrun Enderlein stayed in front after the second of four heats in men's and women's tobogganing, and the United States and the Soviet Union scored round-robin hockey victories.

The movie men never could have outdone today's script. It was the last jump of the program in the 70-meter (229.66 feet) special ski jump. At stake was the gold medal and the world championship, too. Thousands were streaming home from Berg Isel, and with reason. Josef Matous of Czechoslovakia had smashed the hill record on his first attempt with a prodigious 80.5-meter leap and looked like the winner even though he had faltered later.

### Brandtzaeg Challenges

Then Torgeir Brandtzaeg of Norway came into the running with leaps of 79 and 78 meters. But this threat lasted only until the world champion, Toralf Engan of Norway, made his third attempt of the competition, which is decided on each contestant's two best leaps. Engan touched 79 meters and his form was flawless. His 226.3 points seemed unbelievable.

It was time for Kankkonen, the last of the 53 entrants, to jump. His first leap had been wretched, and he had been placed 29th. His second had been near perfect. His third had to be perfect to win.

The square-jawed Finnish sports instructor tore down the slide at breakneck speed. He was in the air now, legs straight, arms clasped to his side and head bent flat over the tips of his parallel skis. Out and out he soared. He hit the steep slope in the classic landing position and swung to a stop. He had soared 79 meters and finished with 229.90 points.

The spectators knew at once. They vaulted over the barriers and ran after Veikko. They hoisted him high. Three times they lifted him as the Finn grinned and waved and laughed. He had won. Second and third were the Norwegians. John Balfranz of Minneapolis was 10th and Gene Kotlarek of Duluth, Minn., 14th.

Another Olympic speed-skating record vanished when Mrs. Skoblikova tore around the 1,-500 meters in 2 minutes 22.6 seconds to smash her 1960 mark of 2:50.2 at Squaw Valley, Calif.

Four of the world's best managed to match her time for the first two laps, but then the graceful Siberian switched on the power. Body nearly parallel to the ice, she glided into the far turn and started her sprint. Arms flailing wide, the 24-year-old teacher thundered down the stretch to wild cheers.

"It was better than I thought," she said, "and the ice was perfect." Lidiya, who won the 500 meter yesterday, was being kind. She had tripped and nearly floundered at the start of the second lap. And the ice, firm enough earlier, had softened under the sun by the time she got away.

Kaija Mustonen of Finland stuck her pug nose over the line in 2:25.5 to finish second. The 22-year-old Helsinki typist was superb. She cracked her best former mark by five seconds and finished strongly ahead of Berta Kolokoltseva, 26, of Moscow who took the bronze medal.

The Americans bogged down. They were fast enough on the first lap, but their stamina failed in the stretch. Judy Morstein, 20, of Butte, Mont., was in the first half-dozen halfway around but finished 15th. Marie Lawler of Minneapolis, still troubled with shin splints, was 19th, and Janice Smith of Rochester 24th in a field of 30.

The 18-year-old Miss Smith crash-dived at the finish, slid 40 feet into a snowbank and was carried out on a stretcher. She recovered quickly.

Mrs. Skoblikova now is a good bet to take four gold medals, a feat never before accomplished in the Olympics. Hjalmar Anderson of Norway won three in speed skating at Oslo, Norway, in 1952, and Toni Sailer had three in Alpine skiing at Cortina, Italy, in 1956. Mrs.

Veikko Kankkonen of Finland displays form as he soars in the special 70-meter ski jump at Innsbruck, Austria.

Skoblikova has the 1,000 and 3,000 meters to go, and there is nobody around remotely in her class.

Thanks to a fine sporting gesture by Eugenio Monti of Italy, a couple of game Britons were leading the two-man bob event at the halfway mark.

Anthony Nash, 27, and his brakeman, Robin Dixon, 28, whipped their bright blue sled down the 1,506-meter ice-banked run in 1:05.3. Then a nut popped loose on the rear axle. Monti, an eight-time world champion but not yet an Olympic winner, removed the nut from his own sled and sent it over.

The British finished their two heats in 2:10.63 and Monti, despite a record-breaking second descent in 1:04.90 with Sergio Siopaes, was third behind the Italian second team of Sergio Zardini and Romano Bonagura.

"It was jolly decent of Monti," said Nash, "particularly when he was behind and not ahead of us."

Victor Emery and Peter Kirby of Canada were fourth, the United States No. 2 team of Charles McDonald of Malone, N. Y., and Charles Pandolph of Saranac Lake, N. Y., fifth and James Lamy of Lake Placid, N. Y., and Lawrence McKillip of Saranac Lake sixth. The

final two rounds will be completed tomorrow.

**A Commanding Lead**

Miss Dijkstra had a commanding lead at the end of the compulsory figures in women's figure skating. The two-time world champion, who rises at dawn, practices for hours daily and goes to bed at 8:30 P.M., leads Regine Heitzer of Austria and little Petra Burka of Canada by a wide margin. Two American girls—Peggy Fleming of Pasadena, Calif., and Christine Haigler of Colorado Springs—are eighth and sixth, respectively.

In the accident-marred tobog-

ganing competition, which saw a number of skids on the icy trails, Koehler held the lead despite a strong challenge from a teammate, Klaus Michael Bonsack. Another German, Hans Plenk, was third. Ilse Geisler of Germany was second behind Miss Enderlein and Helene Thurner of Austria was third.

The United States hockey team brought its record even at 1—1 by routing Germany, 8—0, while the Soviet Union remained in a first-place tie with Canada at 2—0 by defeating Czechoslovakia, 7—5.

February 1, 1964

# FRENCH SISTERS 1,2 IN SLALOM; JEAN SAUBERT NEXT; SOVIET WOMAN TAKES THIRD GOLD MEDAL IN SKATING

## UTAH GIRL STARS

### Oregon State Junior Gives U.S. Its First Medal in Olympics

**By FRED TUPPER**
Special to The New York Times

INNSBRUCK, Austria, Feb. 1—Christine, who was not supposed to win, beat Marielle, who was, as the gay Goitschel sisters dived and darted today through the awkward gates to take the women's slalom for France on an Olympic course considered too dangerous for girls.

They finished 1, 2 to the roars of a huge crowd at the Alpine resort of Lizum. Jean Saubert of Ogden, Utah, had a brilliant second run to grab third place.

There was some question whether the 21-year-old Oregon State University coed had missed a gate. The judges looked at film and said she hadn't. Her bronze medal was the first for the United States in these IX Winter Olympic Games.

Christine Goitschel, 19, had never won a ski race of consequence. Marielle, 18, raced off with the Alpine combined at the world championships in Chamonix two years ago.

**History Is Made**

Marielle was the strong favorite today. She and Christine became the first sister act to score in winter Olympic history.

And the first woman ever to win three gold medals in a single Olympic is Lidiya Skoblikova, the 24-year-old school teacher from Siberia. She was at her matchless best this morning, thrashing a star field to win the 1,000-meter (1,093.3 yards) speed-skating and crack another Olympic record. She's a certainty for her fourth gold when she competes in the 3,000 meters tomorrow. Irina Yegorova of the Soviet Union was second and Kaija Mustonen, the Finnish typist, third.

The Russians were 1, 2, 3 on the winding forest trail at Seefeld this morning. Claudia Boyarskikii, a tiny teacher from the Siberian wilds, stemmed into her turn and poled mightily uphill to edge Eudokia Mekshilo by two seconds for the women's 10-kilometer cross-country crown. Maria Gusakova, who won at Squaw Valley, Calif., in 1960, was third.

It was a banner day for the British. Tony Nash, a company director, and Capt. Robin Dixon, recently of the Grenadier Guards, took the two-man bobsled by coming from behind with a daring assault down the 1,500-meter run of icy curves.

A dawn delegation that had flown from London greeted their

surprising triumph with whoops of oy as Eugenio Monti of Italy, the daredevil eight-time world champion, found the course too slow on his last attempt. Sergio Zardini and Romano Bonagura of joy as Eugenio Monti of Italy, and Sergio Siepeas of Italy third. The Canadian team of Victor Emery and Peter Kirby was fourth and the United States No. 1 team of Lawrence McKillip of Saranac Lake, N. Y., and James Lamy of Lake Placid, N. Y., fifth.

At the end of the fourth day of competition, the Russians had five gold medals, three silver and four bronze. Finland had two golds, a silver and a bronze, France a gold and two silver, Austria and Britain a gold, Norway two silvers and a gold each, Norway two silvers and a bronze, Germany and Italy a silver and a bronze each and Canada and the United States a bronze each.

In hockey, the United States bowed to Sweden, 7—4. The Soviet Union took its third straight in the eight-team round robin by trouncing Switzerland, 15—0, while Czechoslovakia whipped Finland, 4—0.

"The slalom is a killer for girls unless they widen the gates," said Toni Sailer, the Austrian who had taken three gold medals at Cortina, Italy. The first course was a brute, laid out over a 350-meter course (416.13 yards) with a 150-meter drop that was particularly steep at the finish.

Marielle Goitschel was off

first, hipping and swinging through the early gates with confidence. She found the line quickly and began to thread the needle, darting through the holes while her speed increased. Half a hundred gates later, she burst into the clear with the fastest run of the day, in 43.85 seconds. The crowd howled, and a man high up in a 100-foot pine fell off in excitement.

**Miss Saubert's Turn**

Jean Saubert was off in eighth position. As the pre-Alpine champion over this winter's circuit, she figured to have a good chance. But she was not loose and took the gates too wide.

"I couldn't see, but it was my own fault," she said, as she trundled in.

She was sixth after the first run. Christine, seeded down at 14th, was superlative. The course was cut up now, and the ice showing through. She roared down, perfectly in control, in 0:43.85, the best time after her sister.

She had the break in heat 2 as the seeded group of 15 switched order. Christine started second and was bursting with eagerness. As the spectators cheered her down, she flashed flawlessly through the 56 gates of the course, set up by Austrian ski coach, Herman Gamon. Her time was 0:46.01, and the only one remotely near her was Miss Saubert.

The Oregon State junior was angry now, and she gave it the big try. Closer and closer she edged toward the gates, and then she hurtled down, ripping down into high, ripping down in 0:46.58. It was a brilliant run under pressure.

The rest of field was having trouble, cascading through the gates and falling. Marielle tried hard, but the course had slowed and ice spots were in evidence. She had her second place

### She Does It Again

Mrs. Skoblikova did it again as she made a mockery of the 1,000-meter speed-skating run. For the third time in as many days she pulverized a high-class field.

Mrs. Skoblikova skates effortlessly. With a pronounced forward lean, she is bent parallel to the ice and she stays there, whether gliding or cornering or sprinting.

For a time, Irina Yegorova looked like the winner. She finished second in the world championship last year and led Lidiya in time until the last 200 meters. After that, she flailed her arms a little and set about going faster. Irina's time was 1:34.3 and Miss Mustonen's was 1:34.8.

Janice Smith of Rochester, who fell yesterday, was seventh, Barbara Lockart of Chicago 10th and Jeanne Ashworth of Lake Placid, N. Y., 11th. The American girls are not good at distances over 500 meters. They start fast, but don't stay.

The Russians do, and they proved it again in the grueling 10-kilometer cross-country grind. Strangely enough, Alvetina Kolchina was odds-on to win it, and she did not get in the first half-dozen. Perhaps the track was slow when she started near the end. It made no difference. The Russians took the first three places.

February 2, 1964

# BRITONS CAPTURE 2-MAN SLED TITLE

## Nash and Dixon Triumph by Narrow Margin After 4 Heats—Italians Next

### By ROBERT DALEY
Special to The New York Times

INNSBRUCK, Austria, Feb. 1—By .12 of a second, two astonished Englishmen, Tony Nash and Robin Dixon, today won the Olympic two-man bobsled race.

It was only the third time a gold medal was won by Britain in the history of the Winter Olympics.

Previously, a British girl won the figure-skating title in 1952, and a British hockey team, with a Canadian accent, won in 1936. That's all.

Nash and Dixon had led after two runs yesterday, but had dropped to second after the third run today. Their fourth and final run this morning was, they thought, disastrous.

They stood morosely at the bottom of the mountain waiting to congratulate the several other sleds they were certain would finish ahead of them.

But sled after sled plunged noisily down the mile long, twisting, glazed ice chute, banging into and out of 14 turns at an average speed of close to 60 miles an hour.

Sled after sled failed to beat what the two Englishmen considered their own mediocre run. At last their forlorn faces began to glow and then to grin. They became hopeful, and hope was the most painful emotion they went through. As each new clocking was announced, they scarcely dared breathe.

When the final sled was down

they were still first, they leaped and shrieked with glee.

Second place went to the Italian sled of Sergio Zardini and Romano Bonagura. Eugenio Monti and Sergio Siorpaes, also of Italy, were third, Vic Emery and Peter Kirby of Canada, fourth, and Larry McKillip and Jim Lamy of the United States, fifth.

The second American sled, driven by Charles McDonald, with Charles Pandolph riding brake, slipped to seventh after a weak final run.

Nash and Dixon completed the four-run event in 4 minutes 21.90 seconds. Zardini and Bonagura had a time of 4:22.02.

Nash is 27 years old and Dixon 28. Both are from prosperous families. Both took up bobsled racing at St. Moritz, Switzerland, in 1957. They had never finished better than third in any previous major race.

Neither expected to win. Their lead at the half-way point was already more than they hoped for.

As Dixon paced nervously about the starting area before the final run he remarked: "If I knew we would finish third, I'd be satisfied."

"No you wouldn't," a friend said.

Dixon bit his lip. "We haven't made a perfect run yet," he said.

"Nor a bad one," said the friend.

Today's event had started nearly an hour early because the morning was gray and warm. The run would deteriorate fast under the pounding of the sleds, and the idea was to get the race finished before the sun came up over Patscherkofel Mountain.

After three runs, Zardini led, and Monti was only .23 of a second behind in third place. Monti, the world champion eight times in the last 10 years, was the man all feared.

### A Nervous Wait

During the long interval between the final two runs, the 21 sleds from 11 nations were brought up on trucks, unloaded with great care and laid upside down on sawhorses. Men endlessly honed and polished the gleaming runners. Bolts were tightened. The alignment of runners was checked with instruments.

Monti sat in the contestants' hut, staring at the floor. Ward, burly and baldish, nervously gave a radio interview. Zardini paced up and down. The two Italians are small men. Monti is 36, with red hair now graying at the sides, his face scarred by a bobsled crash. Zardini is 32, and also a former world champion. They wore the cheerful Italian uniform: red stockings, blue knickers, blue parka and red stocking cap.

But neither felt cheerful.

The Englishmen were called to the starting line. Nine other Englishmen carried the heavy, clumsy sled to the line, and tenderly laid it down. Nash and Dixon rocked it back and forth, then with a shout pushed it, running hard alongside pushing, down the chute. They leaped aboard, rocketed into the first turn, and were gone.

They got done in 1 minute 5.88 seconds, slow time. About 20,000 persons, most of them peering down into hairpin turns, sighed with disappointment.

At the starting line an Englishman said disgustedly: "It's a toddle for Zardini now."

Zardini's sled was carried to the line by eight burly Italians. They were singing something from opera.

Off went Zardini. Presently the loud speaker gave his time: 1:06.05. The Englishmen still led.

The run was getting soft fast, and many more sleds went down before Monti. The tension built up all that time, and then the friendly little Italian with the broken face pushed off, running his sled down the chute, then leaping aboard.

His time was 1:06.45. Nash and Dixon had won.

Monti did not blame the softening run. He said he had driven badly all the way down. He warmly congratulated the Britons and kissed them on both cheeks.

The Englishmen drove off on a truck with their sled. They were heading for a party. The British bobsled team came here in an antique Bentley car with a bar in the back. Bobsledding is that type of sport, and probably the last of same.

February 2, 1964

# *Mrs. Skoblikova's Five Skating Gold Medals in Two Olympics Set Mark*

## 1,000-METER TIME IS ALSO A RECORD

INNSBRUCK, Austria, Feb. 1 (UPI)—Mrs. Lidiya Skoblikova's victory in the Olympic 1,000-meter speed skating race today was a record accomplishment in more ways than one.

The triumph made the 24-year-old Soviet school teacher the first woman to win three gold medals in one Winter Olympics. She also became the first athlete—man or woman—to win five gold medals in overall Olympic competition. Her time was a record, too, the third straight race in which the blonde from Siberia broke an Olympic mark.

And she isn't done yet. She'll be after more of the same tomorrow in the 3,000-meter event.

Her time today was 1 minute 33.2 seconds. The old mark was 1:34.1, set by Klara Guseva of the Soviet Union at Squaw Valley, Calif., in 1960.

### Two Against the Clock

As usual, the women raced against the clock in pairs. Mrs. Soblikova's partner was Doreen Ryan of Edmonton, Alberta. Miss Ryan's time was 1:38.7, which eventually earned her a tie for 11th place with Jeanne Ashworth of Lake Placid, N. Y.

There were 14 pairs in all for

the race of approximately 1,100 yards.

Irina Yegorova of the Soviet Union was second in 1:34.3 and Kaija Mustonen of Finland was third in 1:34.8. Then came Helga Haase of Germany in 1:35.7.

Janice Smith of Rochester, who fell across the finish line after finishing 24th in the 1,500-meter yesterday, led the United States by finishing seventh in 1:36.7. Barbara Lockhart of Park Ridge, Ill., was 10th in 1:38.6.

Judges at the 1960 Olympics watch a master at work. They awarded Carol Heiss a gold medal. Heiss was world's champion, 1956–1960 and U.S. champion 1957–1960. From 1954–1956, she battled Tenley Albright in the world competition, finishing second the first two years and finally beginning her own string of victories in 1956.

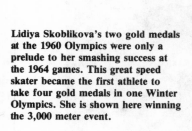

Lidiya Skoblikova's two gold medals at the 1960 Olympics were only a prelude to her smashing success at the 1964 games. This great speed skater became the first athlete to take four gold medals in one Winter Olympics. She is shown here winning the 3,000 meter event.

Mrs. Skoblikova's time was outside her world record of 1:31.8.

### Sailer's Record Tied

Mrs. Skoblikova also had set Olympic records in the 500 and the 1,500. Her third gold medal tied the accomplishment of an Austrian skier, Toni Sailer, at Cortina, Italy, in 1956. The two other gold medals in her set of five came in the 1,500 and 3,000 meters at Squaw Valley.

Clas Thunberg, also a speedskater, had been the recordholder with four gold medals. He won two medals for Finland in the 1924 winter games and two in 1928.

The only other woman to win three Olympic gold medals was Sonja Henie, the Norwegian figure skater who did it in three Olympics—1928, 1932 and 1936.

Mrs. Skoblikova had the crowd of more than 8,000 cheering only for her, and the spectators ticked off the seconds from the large clock as she completed the race. She was greeted by such loud cheering that the announcement of her time had to be made five times, and even then most of the crowd was unable to hear.

February 2, 1964

# Mrs. Skoblikova Skates to 4th Gold Medal at Innsbruck for Olympic Mark

## Soviet Woman Skater Is First To Win Four Olympic Events

### By FRED TUPPER
Special to The New York Times

INNSBRUCK, Austria, Feb. 2—Mrs. Lidiya Skoblikova made more Olympic history today. She streaked around a puddled rink in 5 minutes 14.9 seconds to take the 3,000-meter speed-skating crown and become the first athlete ever to win four gold medals in one Olympics.

Yesterday she became the first woman to win three gold medals in one Olympics. She won the 500, 1,000 and 1,500 meter titles, breaking an Olympic mark each time.

The 24-year-old teacher missed a record today by a fraction of a second because the sun was hot and the artificial ice too wet and slow. The old record was her own, anyway.

François Bonlieu roared down the 1,500-meter Lizum slope with its precipitous plunges and 75 contrived gates to take the giant slalom for France.

Eero Maentyranta, the Finn with the legs of steel and the heart of oak, fought off exhaustion in the early stages to win the 15-kilometer cross-country ski event. He beat Harald Groenningen, the Norwegian farmer, the same man he defeated last week for the 30-kilometer gold medal.

Then Georg Thoma, a German mailman, took a narrow lead at the end of the jumping in the Nordic combined over his old rival, Tormod Knutsen of Norway. They placed first and second at Squaw Valley, Calif., in 1960.

And the two-time world champion, Skoukje Dijkstra of the Netherlands, electrified a standing-room crowd at the ice stadium by winning the women's figure skating.

In the round-robin hockey tournament, Sweden trounced Finland, 7-0, and Canada defeated Germany, 4-2.

Mrs. Skoblikova had her mind on great things today. She was gunning for a time under five minutes, unheard of in the 3,000-meter event. She already has a world record pending of 5:04.3, made in her home town, Chelyabinsk, and she set the Olympic record of 5:14.3 at Squaw Valley in 1960.

But the sun was against her. The early skaters found the ice firm and fast, but by noon pools of water dappled the rink. In such conditions, there was doubt she could match the time of her teammate Valentina Stenina, who had clocked 5:18.5.

Halfway through the race she was half a second ahead. Then she really poured it on. In a furious final lap, Mrs. Skoblikova, her head down and her arms swinging, roared across the finish as the crowd waved and screamed.

The last girl out, tiny Pil Hwa Han of North Korea, then put on a show of her own. To the astonishment of the onlookers, she was even with Mrs. Skoblikova on the

**MEDALISTS—FOR SOVIET UNION:** Lidiya Skoblikova wins the 3,000-meter speed-skating event to become first athlete in Winter Olympics history to win four gold medals.

first lap, then the second, the third and the fourth. The spectators were in a frenzy, cheering her on. She was a second behind the Soviet woman's time with a lap to go. But she couldn't do it, faltering in the home drive to tie with Miss Stenina for second. The applause was tremendous.

And so Mrs. Skoblikova passed Ivar Ballangrud of Norway, who took three skating gold medals in 1936; Hjalmar Anderson of Norway, who won three in 1952, and Toni Sailer of Austria, who won three Alpine events of Cortina d'Ampezzo, Italy, in 1960. She has six gold medals over all, breaking a record she set yesterday.

### A Running Fight

Bonlieu's victory in the giant slalom followed the 1, 2 finish yesterday of Christine and Marielle Goitschel. Bonlieu has been in a running fight with his coach all winter and nearly left the team. The mountain guide wanted to ski on American skis and did so at Laubersorn. Coach Horne Bonnet wanted him to use French skis, which he did today.

Self-taught, Bonlieu was a wonder at 16 and is considered the finest technical slalomer in the world. He proved it.

"I took every chance," he said. "I have never seen François smile like this before," said Bonnet.

The 26-year-old Frenchman drew the perfect position, starting No. 2 before the man-made track started to crumble. He swung and swiveled and had a fine line through the gates, zooming into the stretch for a superb time of 1:46.71.

Karl Schranz of Austria, the world downhill champion, was second at 1:47.09, and Josef Stiegler, the Austrian photographer, third at 1:48.05.

The Americans were supposed to do well in this one. Jim Heuga of Tahoe City, Calif., unofficially finished fifth and then was disqualified for having missed a gate. Wallace (Bud) Werner of steamboat Springs, Colo., unofficially finished 14th and was disqualified, too. Billy Kidd of Stowe, Vt., finished seventh and Bill Marolt of Aspen, Colo., was 12th

"I was ragged," said Marolt. The Americans protested that three Austrian skiers had walked down the course before the race started and should be disqualified.

"It was agreed last night that no skier could," said Coach Bob Beattie of the American team.

The judges threw out the protest.

### Second Gold Medal

Maentyranta took his second gold medal, over the rugged Seefeld cross-country course this morning. His time was 50:54.1 to Groenningen's 51:34.8.

He had his problems however. "My pulse beat is 44 normally," he said. "Today it raced so fast I was frightened. I was tired at seven kilometers and more tired at 10."

"Nonsense," said Groenningen, "Eero is the best long-distance skier in the world. He will win the 50-kilometer as well."

"You will," said Eero as they hugged each other at the finish.

Sixten Jernberg, who won the 50 kilometers at Cortina d'Ampezzo in 1956 and the 30 kilometers at

Squaw Valley in 1960, had a third for Sweden. Mike Gallagher of Killington, Vt., was the first American home; he was 38th.

February 3, 1964

# DUTCH GIRL FIRST IN FIGURE SKATING

## Miss Dijkstra Easy Victor— U.S. Entrants 6th, 7th, 8th

Special to The New York Times

INNSBRUCK, Austria, Feb. 2—Sjoukje Dijkstra, a 22-year-old sturdily-built Dutch girl, leaped and spun on the ice and then walked away with the Olympic gold medal in figure skating tonight before a wildly applauding capacity crowd at the Ice Stadium.

The Ice Stadium holds 10,500 spectators, almost 3,000 of them standees. Tickets are sold until there are no more buyers, but the police close the place when it is full. Latecomers are advised to try for a refund tomorrow.

But for those who came early and waited for 27 other girls from 13 countries to perform, Miss Dijkstra was very much in demand. She had already landed a commanding lead after the compulsory school figures last week. Her victory was virtually a foregone

conclusion. She won with nine ordinals and 2,018.5 points.

Nonetheless, she won big. She is a heavy girl, but graceful for all that. She wore a turquoise costume with a shawl collar and there was confidence in every movement she made. Only once did she falter. On a double-axel jump she nearly fell to the ice, but she recovered.

The best score from the judges is 6. When the nine score cards were held up at the end of Sjoukje's four-minute program, they all showed 5.8 or 5.9, both for content and for execution.

No one else did nearly so well, and so Miss Dijkstra joins Carol Heiss, Tenley Albright, Barbara Ann Scott and Sonja Henie and others as Olympic champion. Miss Dijkstra was second to Carol Heiss at Squaw Valley in the 1960 Winter Olympics.

Regine Heitzer of Austria was second, Petra Burka of Canada was third, and fourth was Nicole Hassler of France, who is a magnificent spinner, the best of all tonight. Miwa Fukuhara of Japan was fifth, despite a flaw.

The three American girls, Peggy Fleming, Christine Haigler and Tina Noyes finished sixth, seventh and eighth, respectively.

Miss Fleming is a tall, slender girl, and there is a wondrous lightness to the way she lands after leaps and spins. She fell once, but bounced up undismayed. She gives every indication of being the champion of the future. ROBERT DALEY.

February 3, 1964

# Jean Saubert Ties for Second Behind Marielle Goitschel in Giant Slalom

## FRENCH SISTERS STAND OUT AGAIN

### Christine Goitschel Shares Runner-Up Honors as U.S. Gains 2d Olympic Medal

#### By FRED TUPPER
Special to The New York Times

INNSBRUCK, Austria, Feb. 3 —It was the kid sister's turn today as 18-year-old Marielle, the younger of the amazing Goitschel sisters, charged down the icy slopes of Lizum in 1 minute 52.24 seconds to win the women's giant slalom Olympic crown for France.

Christine Goitschel, 19, tied with Jean Saubert of the United States for second place in a mathematical fluke as the computers caught them both in the time of 1:53.11.

Two days ago, Christine won the women's slalom, with the favored Marielle second and Miss Saubert third in a blanket finish.

With the IX Winter Games half over, the United States has won only two medals, one silver and one bronze, courtesy of Miss Saubert.

#### Tobogganing Put Off

The 32-year-old Norwegian lumber clerk, Tormod Knutsen, placed third in the 15-kilometer (9.32 miles) cross-country skiing, high enough to win the Nordic combined. Georg Thoma, the previous champion from Germany, had the lead after the ski-jumping yesterday.

Manfred Schnelldorfer, who won his first German championship at the age of 12 and hasn't been beaten since, held a slight figure-skating margin over Karol Divin of Czechoslovakia after two of the five compulsory figures.

The toboggan singles for men and women were postponed as the south wind from Italy slipped through the Tyrolean

peaks and sent temperatures hurtling into the 40's. Bobsled practice was called off with the run awash.

Canada defeated the United States in the round-robin hockey tournament, 8-6.

For a few frantic minutes today, it was touch and go in the women's giant slalom. Christine had drawn the No. 3 slot, probably the best position, and had fled fluently down the 1,530-meter slope through 59 gates. Her time at gate 13 had been 0:32.3.

There were yells of delight from the American delegation when Miss Saubert, already on the course, was timed in 0:31.9 at the intermediate position. She roared down the plunging slope, swinging slightly wide 10 gates from the finish and came pouring into the finish gate huddled in a crouch. Her time was identical to Christine's, her run spectacular.

"I jammed up a bit back there," she said breathlessly. "I couldn't get my skis straight."

The great Alpine skiers were rushing down the slope and the

times were slower as the slide became slippery and the track crumbled. Marielle was the only threat left, drawn badly at No. 14.

The younger Goitschel knew what she had to do. She had heard the times, and she was determined to go all out.

She ran it straight. A roar went up as she was clocked at 0:31.7 on the big red board, and the noise swelled as she swung sharply into the last curve and rocketed into the finish.

Fourth was Christl Haas of Austria, who is the favorite for the downhill Thursday, fifth was Anine Famose of France and sixth was Edith Zimmermann of Austria. Madeleine Bochatay, the fourth French entry, spilled heavily. She somersaulted off the course early and was lucky not to fall over a cliff.

The other Americans, drawn badly, were far back. Barbara Ferries of Houghton, Mich., was 20th, Joan Lee Hannah of Franconia, N. H., 27th and

Linda Meyers of Bishop, Calif. 31st.

Norway took its first gold medal as Knutzen found the right waxing combination for his cross-country skis, 6-by-8 inches long and only 2½ inches wide. He was fourth in 50:58.6 for 469.28 points over all. The course was difficult and dangerous this morning, with icy patches on the higher hills and water on the lower parts. Oddmund Jensen, the Norwegian waxing expert, had three of his men in the first four.

The winner today was Alois Kaelin of Switzerland at 49:12.8.

Victory had been a long time coming for Knutsen. He finished sixth in the Nordic combined at Cortina d'Ampezzo, Italy, and was second to Thoma at the 1960 Games in Squaw Valley, Calif. Thoma, a mailman, had a terrible time. His wax was wrong, he fell down three times and he panted in 10th, dead tired.

He dropped to third place at 452.88 points behind Nikolai Kiselev of Leningrad, who had 453.04. Nikolai Gusakov of the Soviet Union was fourth. His wife, Maria, did better. She won the bronze medal in the women's 10-kilometer cross-country Saturday.

An Army lieutenant, John Ford Bower, 24, of Auburn, Me., made America's best showing ever in this event. He finished with a terrific spurt to take ninth in the cross-country and 15th in the combined. Jim Shea of Lake Placid, N. Y., was 19th in the cross-country and 27th over all.

At the halfway stage, the Soviet Union has six gold medals, France and Finland three each and Austria, the Netherlands, Britain and Norway one each.

February 4, 1964

# McDermott Wins Skating Race for First U.S. Gold Medal

## AMERICAN SCORES AN OLYMPIC UPSET

### McDermott Sets 500-Meter Record in Outspeeding Grishin of Soviet

**By FRED TUPPER**
Special to The New York Times

INNSBRUCK, Austria, Feb. 4 — The United States has won a gold medal. With a roaring drive down the stretch, Terry McDermott catapulted to the Olympic 500-meter speed-skating championship today. His time of 40.1 seconds smashed an Olympic record.

McDermott beat Yevgeny Grishin, the great Soviet skater who had held the Olympic mark of 0:40.2 and has the world record of 0:39.5. The margin of the 23-year old barber from Essexville, Mich., was half a second over Grishin and two others for the 547-yard distance.

Grishin, racing in the second heat, had slipped slightly on the first turn, and though he recovered quickly he lost valuable time.

In speed-skating, the competitors race against the clock in pairs. McDermott's partner was Andre Kouprianoff of France. In all, 44 skaters from 19 nations competed.

**Three Men to Beat**

When McDermott took the ice, Grishin was tied for first place with Vladimir Orlov of the Soviet team and gangling Alv Gjestvang of Norway. Gjestvang had been third at the distance in the 1956 games at Cortina, Italy, and sixth in the 1960 games at Squaw Valley, Calif.

McDermott's medal was the third for the United States in the IX Winter Olympic Games. The other two—a silver and a bronze—had been won by Jean Saubert of Ogden, Utah, in the women's giant slalom and the slalom.

McDermott is essentially a sprinter. He will not go on to the world championships in Finland. Instead, he'll return home to his wife, Virginia, whom he married four months ago.

"My wife doesn't skate," McDermott said. "She works in a bank. Right now she's back home meeting the payments on our house."

Just before McDermott's turn on the ice, Fumio Nagakubo of Japan fell at the finish of his heat and crashed into the official timing device. In the five-minute intermission for repairs, the sun broke through, softening the artificial ice and making it speedier.

Then McDermott stood ready. He lunged. It was a false start. The pressure was agonizing. He was off again, sprinting down the straight and he hit the 100-meter mark in 10 seconds, a tenth of a second behind Grishin's time at that stage.

Terry galvanized into top gear around the turn. His body was bent far forward, his knees tucked well under and his power was tremendous. He was around the last bank now as the seconds flashed off the big red board. He was ahead.

As the crowd went wild, he flailed his arms wide and thundered down the home stretch. The electric numbers whirled to a stop at 40.1 seconds. He had done it. He had his gold medal.

**German Tobogganists Triumph**

The Germans swept the tobogganing, a new event in the Olympics. Thomas Koehler and Klaus Michael Bonsack of East Germany and Hans Plenk from the West were one, two, three in the men's singles. Ortrun Enderlin and Ilse Geisler were one, two in the women's singles and a 25-year-old Australian housemaid, Helene Thurner, was third.

The Russians won their seventh gold medal by taking the biathlon, which combines 20-kilometer (12½-mile) cross-country skiing with marksmanship.

The three-time world champion, Vladimir Melanin, was around the course in 1 hour 20 minutes 26.8 seconds. Melanin defeated a teammate, Aleksandr Privalov. Each had a perfect target score of 20 bullseyes, but Melanin completed the job in faster time.

The German champion, 19-year-old Manfred Schnelldorfer, had a slight lead in the figure-skating at the end of the compulsory school figures. Next is the free skating, which is not Schnelldorfer's forte. Karol Divin of Czechoslovakia, now second, or Alain Calmat, the world and European champion from France, who is now third, could win the title left open by the retirement of David Jenkins, the American who triumphed at Squaw Valley.

Scott Ethan Allen of Smoke Rise, N. J., who won't be 15 until Saturday, was fourth. Nineteen-year-old Monty Hoyt of Highland Park Ill. was sixth.

The American speed-skaters had come to Europe carrying a bagful of near-world marks achieved in the rarefied altitude of Colorado Springs, where the team trained in December. Tom Gray, 19, of Bloomington, Minn., had a 39.5-second 500-meter time to his credit and was accorded a fine chance when he opened the program today. But Gray was around in a mediocre 0:41.5 and his final placing was No. 14.

Then it was Grishin's turn. For years the 32-year-old Soviet star has been in a class of his own at 500 meters. He set the Olympic mark at Cortina and he tied it at Squaw Valley. He won the world sprint championship in Japan a year ago and he set his world standard of 0:39.5 in the secret Central Asian rink at Alma-Ata. He was the foregone favorite.

The first-turn skid threw him off balance and upset his rhythm. His time of 0:40.6 was so slow for him that the ice must have been slow, too. Minutes later Orlov, a 25-year-old Moscow student, tied him. Orlov never had broken 0:40.9 until this year. He had an 0:40.5 in a preliminary meet here for a first-place tie with McDermott.

Then Gjestvang got into the act. In a last-second lunge the Norwegian was through the timer in 0:40.6, too, and the crowd whistled in surprise.

Eddie Rudolph of Northbrook, Ill., had a respectable 0:40.9. Then Nagabuko took his dive, tearing his left leg as he plummeted into the timer.

**Big Chance for Terry**

It was wide open now for McDermott. The sun was out, the ice was faster and the flags around the stadium were lying limp against the masts. Conditions were ideal. The rest is in the record book.

"I knew I could win," said McDermott. "I'd borrowed coach's skates and they were longer and better for gliding."

"He's learned how to sit down," said Coach Leo Freisinger. "He gets well over and he sits down lower on his skates. It gives him enormous speed and power. Terry can do the 100 meters in 0:09.7, but he's learned to go slower at first and save his strength for the stretch."

The Soviet coach, Konstantin Koudratchev, dropped over after the race to pay his respects. "You have fine young skaters," he told Freisinger.

Some American skaters who haven't been doing so "fine"— the men of the hockey team— were idle today. The big game on the program resulted in a 10-0 Soviet victory over Finland. This gave the Russians first place in the eight-team round-robin.

February 5, 1964

## Germans Take 2 Gold Medals In Dominating Toboggan Events

IGLS, Austria, Feb. 4 (UPI) —Germany captured the men's and women's singles tobogganing events today, winning five of the six medals at stake in the events.

Thomas Koehler led a one, two, three German finish in the men's division and Ortrun Enderlein set a record to win the women's race. Only Helene Thurner of Austria broke the German monopoly, finishing third behind Miss Enderlein and Ilse Geisler.

The toboggan event, considered one of the most dangerous of all snow sports, is being staged for the first time in the Olympics. The race took place on the same Alpine slopes where the British tobogganist, Kazimierz Kay-Skrzypeski, was killed during a training run two weeks ago.

Koehler had runs of 51.50 and 52.47 seconds on today's runs over the icy 1,064-meter track for a four-heat total of 3 minutes 26.77 seconds. He was followed by his countrymen, Klaus Michael Bonsack, with 3:27.04 and Hans Plenk with 3:30.15.

The inexperienced Americans could do no better than 13th in the men's singles as Francis (Buddy) Feltman of Idaho Falls had a composite clocking of 3:35.05. Tom Neely of Arlington, Va., was 17th in 3:40.18; Mike Hessel of Eugene, Ore., was 22d in 3:43.30; and George Farmer of Seattle, was 29th in 4:16.60.

Mrs. Dorothy Ann Hirschland of Boston, the only United States entry in the women's competition, dropped out of the race after a slow first heat last week.

Warm weather had prevented the final two heats from being run yesterday as scheduled, but the temperature dropped below freezing last night and the track held well for the completion of the events.

Miss Enderlein, a blonde mechanic, had an aggregate time of 3:24.67 for a record on the women's 964-meter course. Her victory was considered a mild upset over Miss Geisler, the world champion in 1962-1963.

"I am very happy that everything is over," Miss Enderlein said. "From the first I found the right line, even in training."

Miss Geisler, a dimpled 23-year-old teacher whose time was 3:27.42, said: "I'm not sad that my friend Ortrun won the gold medal. I'm happy with the silver."

February 5, 1964

Associated Press Cablephoto

**HEADING FOR VICTORY:** Thomas Koehler, 24, German university student, flashes down the chute at Igls, Austria, to win the men's tobogganing event in the Olympics.

# Sweden, Norway, Soviet Union and Austria Capture Olympic Gold Medals

## JERNBERG IS FIRST IN SKI MARATHON

### Johannesen Takes Skating Medal—Mrs. Boyarskikh and Austrian Pair Win

**By FRED TUPPER**
Special to The New York Times

INNSBRUCK, Austria, Feb. 5 — It was a great day for the oldsters at the IX Winter Olympic Games today.

Stonefaced Sixten Jernberg, who will be 35 tomorrow, poured on the pace to win the 50-kilometer cross-country ski race for Sweden and Knut Johannesen, a 30-year-old Norwegian, took the 5,000-meter speed-skating crown in Olympic record time.

Their triumphs were right out of the history book. Jernberg, a lumberjack and a Swedish national hero, won his third gold medal in three Olympics. He may be the finest Nordic skier of any time. Johannesen, an Oslo carpenter, is a 10,000-meter gold-medalist from the 1960 games in Squaw Valley, Calif.

Prince Bertil of Sweden was in the stands at Seefeld for Jernberg's victory on the grueling 31-mile course, and Prince Harald of Norway wrung Johannesen's hand after the frantic finish of the 3 1/10-mile skating race.

Today's other gold-medal winners were Mrs. Claudia Boyarskikh of the Soviet Union in the five-kilometer women's ski race and the Austrian team of Josef Feistmantl and Manfred Stengl in the two-man tobogganing.

### Soviet Far Ahead

After seven days of competition in the 12-day Olympiad, the Soviet team leads in gold medals with eight. France and Finland are closest in the 36-nation field with three each. The United States has one.

In the hockey round-robin, the Soviet and Canadian teams stayed at the top by winning their fifth game each. The Russians defeated Germany, 10—0. Canada turned back Finland, 6—2. The United States lost to Czechoslovakia, 7—1. Sweden crushed Switzerland, 12—0.

There were yells of protest when the officials switched the five-kilometer women's ski race to a course deemed more suitable in today's snow-melting weather. But it made little difference to Mrs. Boyarskikh, who captured her second gold here.

The Soviet school teacher had taken the 10-kilometer cross-country race last week. Today she defeated a Finnish milkmaid, Mirja Lehtonen, and another Russian, Mrs. Alvetina Kolchina, who were closest in a field of 33.

A dream came true for an Austrian schoolboy, Manfred Stengl. The 18-yearold Stengl and Josef Feistmantl won the two-seater toboggan. Austria also won the silver medal and Italy the bronze.

### A Record for Canada

The Canadian entry broke the course record in the four-man bobsled when Victor Emery of Montreal rammed his sled through the 14 tortuous curves in 1 minute 2.99 seconds on the first of two runs. Four runs will decide.

The Canadians had a slight halfway lead over the favored Italian team headed by Eugenio (Redtop) Monti, eight times the world champion and notoriously unlucky in Olympic competition. As the course disintegrates with cracked walls and slushy straightaways, officials may call the competition off right here.

In the 50-kilometer ski event, Jernberg ran the kind of race he loves. The man to beat, he knew, was Kalevi Haemaelaeinen, the 1960 Olympic champion from Finland. Sixten was 20 seconds behind the Finn at 10 kilometers, 55 seconds behind at the halfway and 20 seconds again at 35 kilometers.

"I could see that he was breaking up," Jernberg said. Piston legs at the churn, the Swede was by Haemaelaeinen after 40 kilometers and came home, fresh and smiling, to a hero's welcome. Haemaelaeinen slumped to 16th, and Assar Roennlund, a clerk from Sweden was second. Arto Tiainen of Finland was third.

"Not bad for an old man," shouted Jernberg as he sprinted away from the crowd that had hoisted him on a pedestal. He plans to retire from ski competition this year.

Jernberg won this race at Cortina, d'Ampezzo, Italy, in 1956, took the 30-kilometer at Squaw Valley and, over the years, has captured a bagful of silver and bronze medals. He is the world champion in the 50-kilometer event, but until today

**STILL THE CHAMPION:** Sixten Jernberg of Sweden displays his winning form during the 50-kilometer cross-country ski race at Seefeld, Austria. He won the event for third time in three Olympics. Assar Roennlund of Sweden was second in the 31-mile event.

he hadn't won a race this season.

For the past two Olympics, the Russians have dominated the 5,000-meter speed-skating taking over where the Norwegians left off. Then last year Jonny Nilsson of Sweden set a world record at Karuizawa, Japan. His time was a brilliant 7 minutes 34.3 seconds. Nilsson was in the field of 42 this morning.

The Olympic mark was 7:48.7 set in 1956 by Boris Shilkov, who now coaches the Russian women skaters. This mark was cracked right off when Hermann Strutz of Austria went around four-tenths of a second faster.

Then Viktor Kosichkin of the Soviet Union knocked 2.9 seconds off the old mark. It was cold and cloudy on the rink but there was no wind and the ice seemed fast. As usual, the competitors skated in pairs against the clock.

It was time for the 19-year-old Norwegian star, Per Ivar Moe. He was a delight to watch. Starting like a frightened deer, he fled around the track in sensational style. Norwegian flags waved and an impromptu cheering section yelled him on.

Moe was gliding powerfully and cornering perfectly, picking up the seconds as he shortened stride and dug in round the turns. To a burst of applause he was home in 7:38.6, the second-fastest 5,000 meters ever.

Nilsson holds the world records for the 3,000 and 10,000 meters, too, but he didn't have

what he needed today. As the announcer tolled off the laps, the Swede fell farther and farther behind Moe's time, and he finished, straining a little, nearly 10 seconds slower.

There were cheers again for Fred Anton Maier, a 25-year-old clerk from Torstag, Norway, who was making his first Olympic bid. A huge man, he took right out after Moe's mark. But the seconds drifted off and he was clocked in 7:42.

The race seemed over. But Moe was far from sure. "I'm afraid of Johannesen," he said. "He can win."

Knut was not fast away. He was a second behind Moe's time at two laps, three behind at seven. It was time to hurry and the Norwegian cheering section was in full cry as a forest of flags fluttered up and down the line.

Body bent over the ice, legs churning at the banks, the great Norwegian made his bid. He was a second behind at eight laps and all even with one to go. Ten thousand spectators were on their feet, cheering and yelling and driving him on.

Johannesen leaned still lower, nose over the ice, legs forcing the pace. He was in the stretch now, arms at full swing, and he dived over the line. The clock read 7:38.7, and there were sighs.

Then came a roar as a correction went up. Johannesen had done it. His time was 7:38.4 and Norway had swept it with Johannesen, Moe and Maier.

*February 6, 1964*

## AUSTRIANS TAKE TOBOGGAN RACING

### Feistmantl-Stengl Triumph
### —U.S. Team in Crash

IGLS, Austria, Feb. 5 (UPI)—Josef Feitmantl and Manfred Stengl of Austria won the gold medal and another Austrian team took the silver medal today in the two-man Olympic tobogganing race. The event was marred by a crash in which two American tobogannists narrowly escaped injury.

The accident involved the team of Ronnie D. Walters of Garden Grove, Calif., and Jim Higgins of San Gabriel, Calif., whose toboggan was going down the treacherous 1,064-meter chute at 45 miles an hour when it slammed into an ice wall, spun out of the track and crashed into the frozen snow.

Higgins, a 27-year-old soldier, was knocked unconscious, but neither racer suffered serious injury. Higgins said at first he thought he had injured his back. "It's all right now but I won't be able to sit down for a couple of weeks," he said.

Feistmantl and Stengl, an 18-year-old high school student, took first place with a clocking of 1 minute 41.62 seconds. Their countrymen, Reinhold Senn and Helmut Thaler, finished second.

The Italian team of Walter Ausserdorfer and Sigisfredo Mair took third in the two-heat race down the 18-curve course. The German team of Walter

Eggert and Helmut Vollprecht placed fourth.

The second United States toboggan, with Ray Fales of Royal Oak, Mich., and Nick Mastromatteo of San Mateo, Calif., finished last in the 13-team field.

The Polish world champions, Lucjan Kudzia and Ruzszard Pedrak, were pre-race favorites, but finished fifth, behind the second-choice German team.

Several experts had picked the German team of Thomas Koehler and Klaus Bonsack, the first and second place winners in the men's singles tobogganing race, to take the two-man gold medal but they didn't compete in the second heat after a poor 0:53.13 clocking on their first ride.

Tobogganing differs from bobsledding in that a bobsled has movable runners and a steering apparatus to help the drivers guide the sled. In tobogganing there is no steering apparatus and the driver must shift his body weight from one side to the other in directing the vehicle.

*February 6, 1964*

## RUSSIAN WOMAN FIRST IN SKI RACE

SEEFELD, Austria, Feb. 5 (UPI)—Mrs. Claudia Boyarskikh, a schoolteacher, won her second gold medal and the eighth for the Soviet Union in the Winter Olympic Games today by winning the women's 5,000-meter (3.1 miles) cross-country ski race.

Mrs. Boyarskikh, 24 years old, swept over the course, which in places was turning brown and green because of the recent mild weather, with the same power and ease she displayed in winning the 10,000-meter race last Saturday. The course today was changed from the one originally scheduled to be used.

The star was timed in 17 minutes 50.5 seconds, a record because the event was being held in the Olympics for the first time.

But the one, two, three sweep of the medals predicted for the Russians in the event was turned into a one, three, four finish instead when Mirja Lehtonen, a powerfully built Finnish girl, took the silver medal for second place with a clocking of 17:52.9.

Mrs. Alvectina Kolchina of the Soviet Union was thrid, with a time of 18:08.4. Eudokia Mekshilo, also of the Soviet Union, was fourth in 18:16.7.

Fifth place went to Toini Poeysti of Finland in 18:25.5, followed by Toini Gustafson of Sweden in 18:25.7.

*February 6, 1964*

# Austria Captures First Three Places in Women's Olympic Downhill Skiing

## MISS HAAS VICTOR; AMERICAN IS 26TH

### Jean Saubert and Marielle Goitschel Fail to Threaten —Soviet Skater Scores

**By FRED TUPPER**

Special to The New York Times

INNSBRUCK, Austria, Feb. 6 Three angry Austrians swept the women's downhill today, and a 25-year-old Estonian student named Ants Antson gave the Soviet Union its ninth gold medal of the IX Winter Olympic Games by winning the 1,500-meter speed-skating title.

A bobsled quartet from Canada, which doesn't have a bob run, increased its lead afer its third run down the scarred, putty course with one run remaining. Two runs were made yesterday.

Scott Allen of Smoke Rise, N.J.,

won the fourth medal for the United States by finishing third in men's figure skating. Manfred Schnelldorfer of Germany won the gold medal, and Alain Calmat of France was second.

Christl Haas, an Amazon of a girl, ran away with the down-mountain skiiing race. It was high time, the natives felt. The fantastic French sisters—Marielle and Christine Goitschel—with an assist from Jean Saubert of the United States, had made a shambles of the Alpine events.

Marielle had won the giant slalom, and Christine the slalom. When they hadn't won, they finished second. Miss Saubert had tied for second in one event and placed third in another, with no medals for the Austrians.

### Sailer Critical

So the Austrian girls were angry, particularly at Toni Sailer, the Austrian skiing great who won all three alpine events at Cortina d'Ampezzo, Italy, in 1956 and is now a journalist.

"Our girls have no fight spirit," he had said.

Miss Haas proceeded to take the course apart. Edith Zimmermann and Traudl Hecher, both Austrians, finished second and third.

This course is built for Christl, and she is built for the course. It starts a few hundred yards under the snow-dusted peak of Mount Hoadl and plummets 7,050 feet down mountain with a drop of 1,570 feet through 24 gates. It takes a big, strong girl to handle its plunges, curves and straightaways.

Christl stands just under 6 feet, weighs 170 pounds and is muscular. The timers caught her at average speeds in the early stages, but then Christl found her pace at the halfway mark.

Up and down the huge slope were 10,000 Austrians. They were there to see their girls win and were roaring for their favorite.

The noise reverberated down the mountain as Miss Haas passed gate 21 and thundered into the final schuss to the Ziel. She was through in 1 minute 55.39 seconds, winning by more than a second. She had gone down in a crouch all the way, the only girl strong enough to do it.

### A Big Grin

Christl swiveled about, took her glasses off and looked at the time flickering in lights on the red board. She grinned like a gamin and then bent double in excitement.

"I found the best line down," she said. "The skis did the rest."

Miss Zimmerman came up to kiss her. Toni Sailer came up to congratulate both of them. They weren't angry anymore.

Marielle Goitschel placed 10th and Jean Saubert 26th. Christine Goitchel did not compete. Starr Walton of Sacramento, Calif., was 14th and Joan Lee Hannah of Franconia, N.H., 15th.

Marielle was confirmed as the winner of the women's world Alpine combined title with 34.82 points. Miss Haas was second, Miss Zimmerman third and Miss Saubert fourth.

All the names that have made skating news were in the men's 1,500 meter (1.640.41-yard) speed race this morning. There was Yevgeny Grishin of the Soviet Union, who set the Olympic record of 2:08.6 at Cortina in 1956; Juhani Jaervinen of Finland, who set a world mark of 2:06.3 at Squaw Valley, Calif., in 1959; Lev Zaitsev of the Soviet Union, who tied it a few weeks ago on the Central Asian rink at Alma-Ata, and Rutgerus Liebrechts of the Netherlands, who won here in a speed trial five days ago in 2:07.9.

Not one of them placed for a medal. Clouds hung low over the rink, the ice was dead and

United Press International Radiophoto

**CLEAN SWEEP: Christl Haas** waves triumphantly after winning women's downhill ski race at the Olympics at Innsbruck, Austria. Her teammates, **Edith Zimmermann,** right, and **Traudl Hecher,** finished second and third, respectively.

a north wind buffeted the skaters as they wheeled into the east curve. The contestants skate in pairs against the clock.

Liebrechts was off first. He was timed in 2:12.8, and it was apparent that no marks would be broken. Eduard Matusevich of the Soviet Union knocked off six-tenths of a second, Jaervinen had a 2:12.4.

A spot of sun broke through as Antson came on the ice. He was in form. At the Bislet rink in Oslo, Norway, three weeks ago, he won the combined European skating championship. What's more, he has won the 1,500 meters outright.

He was down the first stretch in 0:28, the first lap in 1:01 and the next in 1:35, good but not great times. Then he went to work. He glided powerfully into the far turn and turned on the sprint, arms swinging, body low, legs thrashing into the straight. With a last lunge, he was through in 2:10.3.

Snowflakes were drifting down as Villy Haugen of Norway made his bid. A storm of cheers from the Norwegian stands sent him pelting into the sprint position for the whole last lap. The 19-year-old Trondheim plumber was timed in 2:11.2 for the bronze medal.

**Furious Last Lap**

The 33-year-old Grishin gave it a final fling. His time for the first lap was 0:26.8, fastest of the day and he was 1:00 at lap 2. Then the wind hit him. His form fell apart. The snap went out of his legs and he finished far out of the running.

Zaitsev was in line. He hit the last lap in 1:34, best time to that point. He looked like a winner, but he labored down the stretch and was fifth.

There was just one more possibility, a 22-year-old bartender from the Netherlands who was not ranked high.

But Cornelius Verkerk raced a furious last lap as the Dutch cheering section flung banners, and when the figures flashed to a stop they showed 2:10.6 for second place. Dick Hunt of La Crescenta, Calif., was 15th at 2:14.4.

"We spread the gap a little more," said Victor Emery of Montreal this morning after he had piloted the Canadian four-man sled down the ragged, rackety run at Igls in 1:03.64. Austria was second and Italy third.

The plastic wheel of the American No. 2 bob spun, the axle broke, the wheel finally fell off during a pilot run and the team withdrew. The Belgians cut an ice strip six feet wide out of the bank and the concrete wall showed through. The bobsled event winds up tomorrow if the run can be repaired in time and the teams want to race.

With three days to go, the Games look like a Russian benefit. They have nine gold medals, eight silver and five bronze for a total of 22, a record. They had 21 at Squaw Valley.

February 7, 1964

# GERMAN WINNER IN FIGURE SKATING

Schnelldorfer Takes Gold Medal—Allen of U.S. 3d

**By ROBERT DALEY**
Special to The New York Times

INNSBRUCK, Austria, Feb. 6 — Manfred Schnelldorfer of Germany, a solidly built 6-footer, is the Olympic figure-skating champion. He won the gold medal tonight before 10,000 wildly applauding fans with a flawless five-minute free-skating routine full of leaps and bounds and intricate, mincing dance steps at top speed.

Second was Alain Calmat of France, the world champion and the favorite, who crashed to the ice twice but finished his routine outwardly undismayed.

Then came small, skinny Scott Allen of Smoke Rise, N. J., who won't be 15 years old until the

day after tomorrow. He missed second place over all by only 4 ordinals and by 3 judges' points.

Fourth was Karol Divin of Czechoslovakia, and fifth was Emerich Janzer of Austria.

**Litz Places Sixth**

Sixth was Tommy Litz from Hershey, Pa., who started the evening in 13th place after having skated his compulsory figures poorly earlier this week. The judges rated Litz second best in free skating.

Schnelldorfer, 6-2 and 180 pounds, is 20 years old and comes from Munich where he is a student in architecture. He started as a roller-skating champion and was skating in top competition in West Germany, where roller skating is big time, when he was only 12.

At 15, he was the roller-skating champion of the nation. Then he switched to ice. His trainers were and are his parents.

He is fond of good literature, photography and weight-lifting, not necessarily in that order, and he went on a strenuous diet last year to trim 10 pounds.

He had been known as a fine technician in the school figures, but from poor to terrible in free skating. He looked heavy on the ice, and he usually tired fast toward the end of his five-minute program.

Five minutes is a long time to skate at top speed, and if one doesn't skate at top speed and put excitement into every second of the routine, he doesn't win.

All the other skaters looked exhausted at the end—some were red-faced and huffing— but Schnelldorfer was calm and relaxed. His program was smooth and artistic and he was so in control from beginning to end that apparently the effort took less out of him than the others.

After the school figures, Schnelldorfer led, with Divin second, Calmat third and Allen fourth. Schnelldorfer had 17 ordinal points, Divin 20, Calmat 23 and Allen 32. The compulsory figures count 60 per cent toward the final score and free skating 40 per cent.

The smart money was on Calmat, a tall, thin, 23-year-old medical student. Calmat excels in free skating, and it was felt that Schnelldorfer did not.

The book on Schnelldorfer was that he would start with a double Axel jump. The double Axel is difficult at any time, but murderous early when the skater is not warmed up.

It was said that if Schnelldorfer missed his double Axel, he would go to pieces.

Of the four contenders, Divin skated first. He tried a triple loop, missed it and sprawled on the ice. This was the only triple he tried, and he blew it. It took the starch out of him.

Then came Calmat. He started with a rhythmic hop and skip dance down the ice. Applause rang out. He leaped into a double lutz, missed it and fell. He tried a triple loop and fell. He tried the double lutz again, lost control and settled for a single lutz.

But as he warmed up he got better, and he never gave up hope, although by now his cause looked hopeless. He came on strong and tried to end with a double axel jump. He barely managed it. The crowd expected low marks, but Calmat got high ones and the crowd hooted the nine judges for some time.

Allen, 5-4 and 135 pounds, came on and skated most of his routine with a big grin on his face. The crowd loved him and applauded throughout. Once Allen waved as he skated, and once, not paying attention, he tripped and nearly fell while skating in a straight line. His marks ranged between 5.6 and 5.8 of a possible 6, and the pressure was squarely on Schnelldorfer.

The German moved down the ice to the Toreador song from "Carmen." He leaped into his double axel and made it and from then on he simply got stronger. He did not try a single triple, perhaps feeling confident that he could win without a triple and might lose if he tried one and fell.

February 7, 1964

# *Four-Man Bobsled Team Wins Canada's First Gold Medal in Olympic Upset*

## SOVIET TRIUMPHS IN WOMEN'S SKIING

**BY FRED TUPPER**
Special to The New York Times

INNSBRUCK, Austria, Feb. 7 —Canada entered the lists of the gold medal winners today in the IX Winter Olympic Games. Victory Emery of Montreal drove his light blue sled through the twisting curves of the Igls course to win the four-man bobsled championship.

The Canadian sled steered by the 30-year-old Emery hurtled down the mile-long run to defeat Austria by a total of 1.02 seconds for four descents. The Maple Leaf quartet had the fastest time in the final heat.

Neither Canada nor Britain, which won the two-man event, has a bob run and their stunning triumphs have created a sensation in the bobsled world.

The Soviet Union and Sweden also won gold medals today. The Russians took the women's 15-kilometer cross-country race for their 10th victory in the 10 days

of the games so far and clinched the major share of the gold medals.

The Swedes accounted for their second gold medal in the men's 10,000-meter speed-skating event.

In hockey, the Soviet team beat Sweden, 4—2; the Czechoslovak squad upset Canada, 3—1; Finland downed the United States, 3—2, and Germany topped Switzerland, 6—5.

It was the third gold medal in a row in the cross-country for the strapping Mrs. Claudia Boyarskikh. She teamed with Eudokia Mekshilo and Mrs. Alyetina Kolchina to take the 15-kilometer

relay title. Finland and Sweden were next. The Sverdlovsk school teacher already holds the 5 and 10 kilometer cross-country titles.

Jonny Nilsson of Sweden, the world record-holder in the 10,000-meter speed-skating, made a comeback at the age of 20 to trounce the great Norwegians, Fred Anton Maier and Knut Johannesen.

As real snow came late to this Tyrolean town, all the men who matter in Alpine skiing qualified for the men's slalom tomorrow. Moody Francois Bonlieu of France, winner of the giant slalom,

Associated Press Cablephoto

**SHOT BLOCKED: Pat Rupp, U. S. goalie, stops a shot on goal by Jarmo Wasama of Finland in Olympic hockey game.**

United Press International Radiophoto

**JUBILANT: Doug Anakin tosses his helmet high as four-man bobsled team celebrates Canada's first gold medal.**

turned in the best time. Jim Heuga and Bud Werner of the United States finished fifth and sixth, Billy Kidd was 12th and Charles Ferries 27th.

In the spirit of friendship, the Russians invited the Americans to a party and suggested a dual meet in winter sports. The Americans stalled tactfully and asked for a dual meet in swimming. The Russians accepted.

The Canadians were gunning for the gold today. With three of the four runs gone, their lead was less than a second. They were afraid of the Austrians, who were in second place, and downright frightened of Eugenio Monti, the old Italian master, who was third.

### Course in Fine Shape

The course was in their favor. For once, it was in fine shape. Austrian soldiers had swept away the snow and packed it overnight. The Canadians took a trial run and decided to change runners on the sled.

Their target was 63 seconds, just over their record time established earlier in the week. Emery was in the driver's seat, 33-year-old Doug (Mickey Mouse) Anakin at No. 2, Emery's brother, John at No. 3 and the taciturn Peter Kirby on brakes.

They pushed off, Kirby jumping aboard as the sled gained momentum, and careened down the course. The sled ripped through the curves, sounding like a jet

plane on takeoff. The time was good and Emery dead on track.

Disaster loomed at the 12th curve. The sled hit the curve high and Kirby's elbow struck the ice. Emery tried to come out low and hit the wall. Precious hundredths of a second were wasted and the time target was gone. It didn't matter. The clock read 1:04:01 at the finish. They had won with a total time of 4 minutes 14.46 seconds for the four runs.

The other bobbers rushed over and hoisted the Canadians high. Little Anakin pulled off his crash helmet and flung it wide. It hit a spectator on the forehead. Emery jumped up and down and then went over to shake hands with Monti. "You taught us," he said.

### Monti Says He Is Through

"I'm through," said Monti, now 36 years old. The Italian, eight-time world champion in the two-man and twice champion in the four-man, had won everything but an Olympic gold medal.

Sergio Zardini, the other fine Italian driver, was fourth, Germany fifth and the United States sixth with Bill Hickey at the helm. The steering wheel on the other American sled snapped yesterday.

Nilsson set his world speed-skating record just a year ago at Karuizawa, Japan, with a clocking of 15:33. Jonny has done little since. He was first on the ice this morning and caromed around the 25 laps in 15:50.1, good but not sensational time. The crowd of 8,000 milled around most of the day in the expectation that

somebody would beat it. The skaters went out in pairs and raced against the clock.

Nothing much happened. For tedium this event has few equals in sport. Thirty-three racers skated more than 214 miles over five hours. Lieut. Col. Pavel Popovich, the Russian cosmonaut who went a great deal further faster, dropped in for an hour and left, bored stiff.

A wind came up and made the times slower. An ice-clearing machine groaned around the rink now and then. The Russians and Norwegians protested. It is harder to skate without loose particles on the ice, they said.

The referee pointed out that the rink had to be cleared and that it had been decided beforehand when it would be. Not just before our men skate, pleaded the Russians and Norwegians.

The day rolled on. Rutgerus Liebrechts of the Netherlands had turned in a time of 16:08.7, then Ants Antson of Russia, the 1,500-meter gold medal winner, clocked 16:08.8. Antson's time was corrected to 16:08.7, the same as the Dutchman's. Then Liebrechts time was corrected to 16:08.6.

### Johannesen Is Third

Knut Johannesen took a crack at winning. He is the olympic record-holder with a mark of 15:46.6 set at Squaw Valley, Calif., in 1960.

He did 15:42.9 at the Bislet rink in Oslo last month and he won the 5,000 meters in good style two days ago. As he start-

ed, the wind freshened. At the end of a dozen laps the Norwegian was ahead of Jonny's time by one second. Then the wind slowed him. To the cheers of the Norwegians still there, Fred Maier trundled around in 16:06 to beat Johannesen for second place.

There was some grumbling by the world's better Alpine skiers about having to qualify for the slalom. François Bonlieu was irritated enough to win the first heat in 0:51.23 and will be the favorite tomorrow. Jean-Claude Killy, another Frenchman, rode down cautiously and did not qualify. So he tried again in the second group and had the best time.

Wolfgang Bartels, the best of the Germans, fell down and went again. He finished eighth. Hias Leitner of Austria was halfway down when the Chilean coach, Pierre Hallaut, slipped and fell on the course, dragging The Aga Khan with him. Leitner was miffed and stopped. The judges met and told him to try it again. He qualified.

February 8, 1964

# U. S. TAKES SILVER AND BRONZE MEDALS IN SLALOM

## AUSTRIAN IS FIRST

### Stiegler Wins Slalom —Kidd, Heuga Next in Olympic Event

**By FRED TUPPER**
Special to The New York Times

INNSBRUCK, Austria, Feb. 8—Austria took the slalom today, but the United States placed second and third for its first men's Alpine skiing medals in Olympic competition.

Leading after the first run, Josef (Pepi) Stiegler finished strongly enough on his second to stave off the furious challenge of William Winston Kidd and James Heuga, two 20-year-old Americans, on the next-to-last day of the IX Winter Olympic Games.

"Billy the Kid" of Stowe, Vt., made the afternoon run in 60.31 seconds, dancing through the gates for a combined time just 14/100ths of a second behind that of the stocky blond Austrian.

Heuga's third-place finish was incredible. In slalom skiing, the draw is vital. The unseeded Californian started 24th and then 22d on his runs, when the track was rutted and the icy slopes laid bare.

#### Third Each Time

As a crowd of 15,000 whooped it up and the Americans went wild, Heuga was third on each run on the way to his bronze medal behind Stiegler's gold and Kidd's silver.

"He's a tremendous come-from-behind skier," said the American ski coach, Bob Beattie, "so the spot was ready-made for him."

Kidd's performance placed him third in the Alpine combined standing behind Ludwig Leitner of Germany and Gerhard Nenning of Austria. The combined standing determines the world's best skier. It is based on over-all showings in the Olympic downhill, giant slalom and slalom. Kidd's position was the best ever for the United States.

#### Sweden Wins Relay

Sweden also won a gold medal today. In a story-book finish that saw Norway and

Associated Press Cablephoto

**THE THREE WHO LED: Men's Olympic slalom medalists after event near Innsbruck. They are, from the left: Billy Kidd of Stowe, Vt., who finished second; Josef Stiegler of Austria, who was first, and Jimmy Heuga, of Tahoe City, Calif., who took third place.**

then the Soviet Union ahead in the stretch, Assar Roennlund stormed from behind to give a Swedish foursome the 40-kilometer cross-country relay. Finland was eight seconds behind.

The Soviet Union clinched the hockey championship for its 11th gold medal of the games. The United States had one gold, Terry McDermott in the 500-meter speed-skating; two silver, Kidd in the slalom and Jean Saubert in the women's giant slalom, and three bronze, Heuga, Miss Saubert in the slalom and Scott Allen in the figure-skating.

The competition winds up tomorrow with ski-jumping on Bergisl and closing ceremonies in the ice stadium.

The first slalom run was held on the Kalkkoegal course, which plunges 500 yards through 78 gates on Birgitkoepfl. New snow had fall overnight and a blizzard whipped across the run as Leitner led off. He caught a ski on a gate and was timed in 0:71.19. It gave the others a mark to shoot at.

Then disaster struck. Jean-Claude Killy of France piled up and stopped. Guy Perillat of France, who had won the 1960 combined at Squaw Valley, Calif., caught a gate near the finish and had to retrack. Chuck Ferries of the United States sprawled far

down and went through the finish on his nose.

Gerhard Nenning, an Austrian, had 0:70.29 and Karl Schranz, the world downhill champion who is also from Austria, had 0:70.04. Then it was time for the 26-year-old Stiegler, a photographer from Linz.

He was lucky to be there at all. Twice he had been removed from the team by Austrian ski officials and replaced by Egon Zimmermann, this year's Olympic gold-medalist in the downhill. Skiers, ski fans and newspapers complained and the president of the Austrian Ski Association put him back just before the draw.

With Austria one, two ahead of him (Schranz and Nenning) and the French almost out of it, Pepi charged the run. The course was tight, with half the gates set in the fall line, and it demanded perfect control. Pepi had it. He caught the short way down, swiveling and poling, and he skated through the ziel (finish) in a wondrous 0:69.03.

The crowd yelled and howled and stamped feet.

#### Kidd Makes the Trip

Now it was up to Kidd. The Stowe hotelier gave it a fine try. He was down in 0:70.96, braking too hard near the finish. Bud Werner of Steamboat Springs, Colo., had 0:71.64, skidding off line halfway down.

Then the spectators caught a breath for François Bonlieu. The morose Frenchman had won the giant slalom and vowed he would

win this. The tip of a ski crashed a gate and he rolled down the mountain.

The great ones had gone and the second group was coming up.

The bare-headed Heuga, a University of Colorado student from Tahoe City, Calif., ripped down the mountain. His run was superb, his time tremendous. He was clocked in 0:70.16 and was third behind Stiegler and Schranz.

The initial afternoon run was easier, the course more open with fewer gates. Kidd tore it apart. He was timed in 0:60.31 and there was nobody close to him that mattered until Stiegler made his bid.

Stiegler's run was coolly and carefully done, again a triumph of control. Pepi clocked 0:62.10, only seventh best in the afternoon. But good enough over-all.

#### Easy Does It

"Keep calm, Pepi," Stiegler had said to himself," and you will win," He had. The margin was minuscule.

Then Heuga skied into the record book.

"Boy, did I make it?" he said, peering at the red clock. "You did, you did," said Werner, breaking through the crowd.

Werner was worth a cheer, too. He had finished eighth.

Heuga grabbed Kidd and pointed to the board. "You see that, Billy?" It's you and me."

"We did it," said Coach Beattie," We finally did it."

"That puts the States up with the European best in the slalom," said Toni Sailer, the Austrian wonder who swept the Alpine at Cortina, Italy, in 1956.

The American men never had won a medal in the Alpine. The girls have. Pig-tailed Gretchen Fraser took the slalom at St. Moritz, Switzerland, in 1948 and Vermonter, Andrea Mead, won the slalom and giant slalom at Oslo in 1952.

February 9, 1964

## Kidd, Heuga Give U.S. a Shining Hour

### By The Associated Press

INNSBRUCK, Austria, Feb. 8—Billy Kidd and Jimmy Heuga today turned the IX Winter Olympic Games from a series of frustrations, disappointments and disasters into the finest hour of American skiing.

They did it by finishing second and third in the slalom race. An Austrian, Josef (Pepi) Stiegler, was ahead of them, but the showing of the two 20-year-olds was more than even the most optimistic American rooter had envisioned.

Kidd is 5 feet 8 inches tall and weighs 150 pounds. He is quiet and serious and inclined to brood when things go bad. He started to ski when he was 4 years old.

He first came into prominence in 1962, when he went to Europe with an American team and finished eighth in the world championship slalom.

Heuga got an even earlier start. He was 2 when he first climbed on skis at Tahoe City, Calif. At his high school classes regularly let out on Wednesday afternoon so the student body could go skiing. He chose the University of Colorado because it had a good ski program.

Heuga was fifth in the 1952 world championship combined

standings and also won the St. Moritz, Switzerland, slalom that year. He is 5 foot 6, 145 pounds, and smiles more easily than Kidd.

Along with Bill Marolt, also 20, of Aspen, Colo., they are expected to lead the new wave of American skiing, replacing the 27-year-old Buddy Werner, who probably will retire soon.

Werner hovered around the top of world skiing for eight years, but never was able to score a breakthrough.

"Now it has come. We'll never have to prove ourselves again," said Bob Beattie, the American Alpine coach.

Stiegler paid tribute to the Americans. He said:

"The Americans have been very strong and today they showed they are excellent skiers. We all have known that before but it wasn't until the final race that they were able to overcome the bad luck."

"I wish I had skied faster on the first run," said Kidd. "I could have won the whole thing."

And this from Beattie:

"There were a thousand American supporters in the crowd, all yelling. All our boys were crying when they hit the first gate, they were so choked up over the American support."

February 9, 1964

## RUSSIANS' SEXTET WINS GOLD MEDAL

### Subdues Canadians, 3-2— U.S. and Swedes Score

### By United Press International

INNSBRUCK, Austria, Feb. 8 — The Soviet Union scored a 3—2 victory tonight over Canada and won the Olympic gold medal in hockey for the second time in three attempts.

The United States the pre-

vious winner, ended its dismal showing with a 7—3 victory over Switzerland and finished the seven-game round-robin tournament in a tie for fifth place with Germany and Finland. Sweden routed Czechoslovakia, 8—3, in the final game to win the silver medal. Czechoslovakia took third place and Canada fourth.

The Soviet Union outplayed and outshot the young and inexperienced Canadians from the start but didn't go ahead until Veniamin Alexandrov scored at 1:36 of the third period. The goal came against Seth Martin, who had replaced Ken Broderick at the start of the third period in a move the Rev. David Bauer, the Canadian coach, hoped would give his team "a lift."

The Canadians had gone ahead, 1-0, when George Swarbrick converted a pass from Marshall Johnson at 5:57 of the first period and led, 2-1, on a goal by Bob Forhan at 13:40 of the third period.

#### Maiorov Scores

Boris Maiorov scored the first Soviet goal at 10:49 of the second period and Vyacheslav Starshinov tallied the second Soviet goal at 18:18 of the second period. Starshinov's goal came on a power play while Reg Conacher was serving two minutes in the penalty box.

Alexandrov quickly put the Russians ahead for the first time when he beat Martin at 1:36 of the third period on a pass from Alexandr Almetov. The Russians kept the Canadians off balance with a swarming attack and totaled 20 shots at Martin during the period.

"We held them for most of the game," said Father Bauer, "but we made a couple of slips and they got on top of us."

"We are not talking about the National Hockey League, but the Russians are a good, really good amateur club. We hoped, of course, when we came here we would catch them on a bad day the way they have caught us in the past. But we

just didn't make it."

Father Bauer explained why he had replaced Broderick with Martin.

"Kenny played a whale of a game for us, and there is no criticism of his play," he said. "I talked it over with him, and we agreed that Seth might give us the lift we needed for that important goal."

#### Referees Criticized

Art Potter, the president of the Canadian Amateur Hockey Association, said the refusal of the referees to call penalties against the Russians had cost Canada the game. But Father Bauer and his brother, Bobby, a member of the Boston Bruins' famous line of the 1930's and 1940's and the coach of Canada's losing Olympic entries in 1956 and 1960, said the refereeing had been sloppy but not unfair.

The Russians completed the tournament with a 7-0 record and 54 goals against 10 by their opponents. The Russians scored more goals and allowed fewer than any other team.

Pat Rupp of Detroit, substituting for Tom Yurkovich, yielded two early goals to Switzerland, but the United States had a 3-2 lead after the first period on goals by Bill Reichart of Rochester, Minn., Paul Johnson of West St. Paul, Minn., and Gary Schmalzbauer of St. Paul. Rog Christian of Warroad, Minn., and Dave Brooks of St. Paul tallied in the second period, and Herb Brooks of St. Paul and Dates Fryberger of Duluth, Minn., added goals in the third session.

#### Two Men Ejected

Dave Brooks and Rog Christian were thrown out of the game, Brooks following a scuffle along the boards with a Swiss defenseman, Max Ruegg, in the second period and Christian for tapping Referee Boris Staravoitov of the Soviet Union on the shins with his stick after having drawn a tripping penalty in the first period.

February 9, 1964

# Engan of Norway Captures 90-Meter Ski Jumping as Winter Olympics End

## KANKKONEN FALLS ON FINAL ATTEMPT

### By FRED TUPPER
#### Special to The New York Times

INNSBRUCK, Austria, Feb. 9 — Toralf Engan, a slightly built salesman with legs of steel, won the 90-meter ski jump at Bergisel today for Norway's third gold medal as the ninth Olympic Winter Games ended.

An entranced crowd of 70,000, the largest of the 12-day competition, saw Veikko Kankkonen, the Finnish sports instructor from Lahti, finish second. Third was Torgeir Brandtzaeg, a 22-year-old salesman from Steinkjer, Norway. Each of the 52 jumpers was allowed three attempts, with the two best making up his score. Engan's best jumps measured 307 and 297 feet, and he scored 230.7 points. Kankkonen sailed 313 and 297 feet for 228.9 points. Brandtzaeg's jumps of 302 and 295 feet earned 227.2 points. They were far ahead of the others.

The script was familiar, but the ending was switched. Last week, the 27-year-old Engan almost had the gold medal for the 70-meter-hill jumping in his pocket. There was only one man left to jump—Kankkonen. That time, the Finn gave it the hero treatment. His leap was tremendous and his form impeccable. He won.

This time, Kankkonen had the day's best jump on his first attempt, a prodigious effort that carried him 313 feet. The markings on his form by the five judges were near perfect. He led at the end of the first round.

An east wind was blowing directly across the hill, disturbing the balance of the jumpers. A vast throng that ribboned up the slope shrieked and sighed as the landings became more hazardous and the spills more frequent. The jumping platform was lowered for safety.

Engan was silhouetted against the sky at the top of the chute for his second attempt. He pushed into the run and crouched low, his hands clasped as if in prayer.

He exploded off the ramp, legs straight, arms flat against his sides in the new airfoil position and body rigidly parallel to the skis. He struck the slope beautifully at the 297-foot level. The form markings flashed on the red board. Cheers echoed up and down the mountain. The Norwegian led.

Kankkonen was down at the bottom of the draw, the 47th to jump. He was far out in a perfect arc, but his skis were unsteady. He landed wavering on the 297-foot mark, but one judge ruled that a hand had touched the slope. He had slipped to second.

### Down Goes the Platform

Brandtzaeg had won the bronze medal on the small hill at Seefeld and he was aiming for higher things. The platform had been lowered again and the Norwegian needed distance. He reached 285 feet. The judges were in accord, each giving him 18 points out of 20 for form. It was the best jump of the third round so far.

Engan had his last attempt. The Norwegian won the world championship in small - hill jumping two years ago in Poland. He had taken 24 of his last 27 meets. He was the hope to regain the Olympic crown that Norway had worn in six consecutive winter games through 1952.

Engan hesitated too long on the ramp. His form was poor, and he windmilled his arms to keep from falling.

The scenario was ready for camera. It was Kankkonen's last attempt. He had made it before. Breathlessly the crowd surged, straining to see the takeoff.

The Finn was flat against his skis, etched against the horizon. It was a beautiful jump — 288 feet — and the best of round three.

Kankkonen hit the slope hard. He couldn't hold it. He fell. It was all over, and Norway had its Olympic title.

### First American is 24th

"My only fear was the winds," said the Trondheim auto salesman. "When I saw the flags blowing, I knew I had to concentrate."

Dieter Bokeloh of Germany was fourth, Kjell Sjoeberg of Sweden fifth and Alexander Ivannikov of the Soviet Union sixth. Gene Kotlarek of Duluth, Minn., was the first American at 24th. Dave Hicks was 29th, Ansten Samuelstuen 33d and John Balfanz, supposedly the best of the lot, 41st.

And so the Winter Olympics ended. They were a runaway for the Russians, who scored

their third consecutive victory in the unofficial standing since they appeared at Cortina d'Ampezzo in 1956. The Soviet Union won 11 gold medals, eight silver and six bronze.

Its women won seven of those gold medals. Four went to Mrs. Lidiya Skoblikova, the dimpled blonde from beyond the Urals, who took all the speed skating titles and set three Olympic records. Her feat was never achieved before in the Olympics.

Mrs. Claudia Byarskikh took three gold medals, winning the women's 5 and 10 kilometer cross-country races and anchoring the Soviet Union's 15-kilometer relay team.

The Scandinavian skiers won the Nordic titles as they were expected to. The Norwegians staged a speed skating comeback, sweeping the 5,000 meters and finishing second and third to Jonny Nilsson of Sweden in the 10,000.

France and Austria, the two great European Alpine skiing nations, divided the spoils. The United States, long an orphan, bagged two medals in the men's slalom with Bill Kidd and Jim Heuga. Jean Saubert, the Oregon State coed, took a silver medal in the women's giant slalom and a bronze in the slalom. She is world class and, on her day, perhaps the best of them all.

Over all, the American showing was disappointing. The United States has done worse— in 1924 and 1936—but there were fewer events then. Terry McDermott, the 23 - year - old barber from Bunny's Shop in Bay City, Mich., won America's only gold medal by setting an Olympic record of 40.1 seconds in the 500-meter speed skating.

Fourteen-year-old Scott Allen of Smoke Rise, N. J., took third in figure skating and seems destined for the heights.

America had skill but not stamina all along the line. The slalom demands skill; it did well there. The downhill and giant slalom demand stamina;

America did not place. McDermott's gold medal was won over the short haul. The other American skaters were far back in the longer races and, according to Coach Leo Freisinger, may not compete in those distances in the future.

"We need a series of refrigerated rinks all over the States," said Freisinger, "and we need Government support to build them."

The United States got nowhere in Nordic events, through lack of stamina. There are athletes in America now who can run the mile and two-mile. Certainly, there are men who can be trained to ski those distances and longer ones.

The American hockey team won in 1960 at Squaw Valley, Calif. It took two games and lost five here, finishing in a tie for fifth.

The story is familiar. The Russians are called professionals, the Americans are amateurs. Presumably, the Americans are amateurs in tennis, golf, track and swimming. They beat the world in those sports.

The ski jumpers were supposed to do well. They did not. Gene Kotlarek twisted an ankle. John Balfanz finished 10th on the 70-meter hill.

The toboggan teams were shut out. "Luge," as the French call the sled, is a new sport in the Olympics. The Germans and Austrians have trained at it for years; America has not.

The bobsledders did poorly. For some time now, bobbing has been an upper-New York State monopoly. It needs new blood. There was no finer evidence of the real amateur spirit than the surprising triumphs of Britain in the two-man and Canada in the four-man bob events. Neither nation has a bob run.

February 10, 1964

United Press International Radiophoto

**WINS FINAL OLYMPIC EVENT: Toralf Engan of Norway in the 90-meter special ski jump near Innsbruck. He was first with leaps of 307 and 297 feet for 230.7 points.**

## Peggy Fleming Takes U.S. Title In Figure Skating for 3d Time

### Colorado Girl Is First Triple Winner Since Carol Heiss —Miss Noyes Runner-Up

By United Press International

BERKELEY, Calif., Jan. 29

Peggy Fleming won the national women's figure skating title last night for the third straight time.

The 17-year-old Miss Fleming is the first three-time winner since Carol Heiss, who had a string of four victories from 1957 through 1960. Miss Fleming, a slim Colorado Springs brunette, received the first-place votes of all five judges in the free-skating competition, matching her marks in the

school figures a day earlier.

The runner-up was Albertina Noyes of Arlington, Mass. Miss Noyes, who has been training in Los Angeles for three months, made a determined bid in the free skating, but finished second on the cards of all judges.

Pamela Schneider, 17, of Lincroft, N. J., took third place, ahead of Sheri Bates of Oakland, Calif., whose free-skating brought her from seventh to fourth. Miss Schneider was second to Miss Bates in the national junior ladies competition last year.

Scott Allen of Smoke Rise N. J., moved ahead of the defending champion. Gary Visconti of Detroit, in the men's competition.

Dolly Rodenbaugh, 17, and Thomas Lescinski, 27, of Pittsburgh, won the Silver Dance title tonight.

The national junior men's title was won by John Misha Petkevich, a powerful 16-year-old skater from Great Falls, Mont. Petkevich was the unanimous choice of the five judges in the free-skating competition. He had held a slight lead at the end of the compulsory figures.

Second place went to James Disbor of Troy, Ohio, who moved up from fourth place on the strength of his free skating. W. Patrick Lalor of Talleyville, Del., dropped to third place, ahead of two Californians, Barry Munns of Walnut Creek

and Johnny Moore of Fullerton.

As expected, Cynthia and Roland Kauffmann of Seattle won the senior pairs easily. The Kauffmanns, second in the nationals and sixth in the world championship last year, skated against only two other teams, both graduates of 1965 junior competition.

Susan Berens of Pasadena. Calif., and Roy Wagelein of Los Angeles were second, followed by Page Paulsen and Larry Dusich of Downey, Calif.

The Kauffmanns were left as America's leading pairs team when Vivian and Ronald Joseph of Chicago decided to retire.

January 30, 1966

# Miss Fleming of U.S. Captures Gold Medal in World Title Figure Skating

## MISS BURKA FAILS TO RETAIN CROWN

### Canadian Girl Finishes 3d

### Lowest of Any Defender

### —Miss Seyfert Second

DAVOS, Switzerland, Feb. 27 (AP)—Peggy Fleming, an attractive, dark-haired 17-year-old high school senior from Colorado Springs, gave the United States a world figure-skating gold medal today with a dazzling victory in the women's competition.

Miss Fleming's medal was the fifth won by the Americans, who have rebuilt their figure-skating forces since the entire United States team of 18 skaters was killed in a plane crash in Brussels five years ago.

Miss Fleming was awarded first place on the cards of all nine judges after her flawless free-skating performance. She took a commanding lead in the compulsory phase of six school figures yesterday, then outclassed the rest of the field under a bright sun in the outdoor rink today.

"I did my whole program and it worked out wonderfully," the joyous, but tired Miss Fleming said. "Nothing was missing. The only trouble was with my eyes, the sun was too bright."

Mrs. Albert Fleming, beaming at her daughter, said, "I am speechless. I've never even dared to dream of it."

#### Defender Falters

Petra Burka of Canada slipped to third place behind Gabriele Seyfert of East Germany, marking the first time in the history of the championships that a defending titleholder finished that low.

Associated Press Cablephoto

**POISED, GRACEFUL, VICTORIOUS: Peggy Fleming of Colorado Springs performing during free-skating phase of the women's world figure-skating championships at Davos, Switzerland. Miss Fleming, 17, won the title.**

Miss Fleming, going ahead by 49 points in the compulsory figures that slanted 60 per cent toward the title, finished with a 62.3 edge over Miss Seyfert.

Miss Fleming totaled 2,291 points and was awarded the perfect score of nine ordinals, which are based on the judges' placing—1 for first, 2 for second and so forth.

Miss Seyfert moved into second ahead of Miss Burka, getting 2,228.7 points and 22 ordinals to 2,226.2 and 23 ordinals for the Canadian girl.

Albertina Noyes of Boston was ninth and Pamela Schneider of Lincroft, N.J., was 12th among the 20 skaters.

In the men's competition, the United States suffered a disappointment when Scott Ethan Allen of Smoke Rise, N.J., finished fourth in the finals last Friday, but Gary Visconti of Detroit took the bronze medal for third. Emmerich Danzer of Austria won the event. Wolfgang Schwartz of Austria was second.

Kristin Fortune and Dennis Sveum

won the silver medal in ice dancing, while Lorna Dyer and John Carrell of Seattle, took the bronze. The title went to Diana Towler and Bernhard Ford of Britain.

Ludmilla Belousova and her husband, Oleg Protopopov, the Soviet Union team, won the pairs championship, with Cynthia and Ronald Kauffman of Seattle placing third.

On the Davos rink today, rimmed by glittering, snow-covered mountains, Miss Fleming was a beautiful figure in purple as she glided and pirouetted on the ice.

She was a tense, lip-biting girl as she went before the capacity crowd of 5,000 and was fatigued after she had captivated the spectators with her spectacular performance.

"The big scare is over," she said later.

February 28, 1966

# *Killy Captures Alpine Combined Title*

## FRENCH DOMINATE WORLD SKI MEET

### Killy's Victory One of 6 for Team—Noisy Night Party Piques Austrian Squad

PORTILLO, Chile, Aug. 14 (AP)—Jean-Claude Killy won the men's combined Alpine championship today and brought France a record-tying harvest of six gold medals at the world Alpine skiing championships.

Killy, who won the downhill event and finished fifth in the giant slalom, capped his performances with a conservative two runs in the special slalom, finishing eighth with a combined time of 104.40 seconds.

Carlo Senoner of Italy won the special slalom—the final event of the championships—with an aggregate time of 101.56 seconds.

The top American finisher in the special slalom was Jimmy Heuga of Tahoe City, Calif., who was sixth in 103.69 after runs of 55.43 and 48.26. The two other United States hopes, Jere Elliott of Steamboat Springs, Colo., and Bill Marolt of Aspen, Colo., were disqualified.

Seven coaches said they would protest the final standing. Stanislaus Ziobrzynski of Poland, technical delegate of the Fédération Internationale de Ski, said the bottom part of the list was incorrect.

The protest later was upheld, jumbling the standings from ninth place on down. The leading French, Austrian and American competitors were not affected, but the ruling came after the awards of prizes and caused some embarrassed exchanges of certificates.

**Party Upsets Austrians**

Killy's triumph in the combined event—generally considered the world championship of skiing—came after an early morning party that kept the Austrian team, with some of Killy's main challengers, awake for several hours.

The Austrian team was kept from sleeping when women skiers from the British team and men skiers from the Brazilian team went for a postmidnight swim at the Hotel Portillo pool.

Hotel guests asked the party-goers to be quiet and eventually emphasized their demands by hurling glass objects from the hotel windows.

Austrian team leaders said they called the military police, but the police told them they could not deal with the matter. The Austrians finally went to the pool and scuffled with the swimmers as they tried to pull them out. Two hours later, ho-

tel officials restored quiet.

One of the Austrian skiers, Karl Schranz, was Killy's closest rival for the combined title. On his first run in the special slalom, Schranz missed a gate about one-third down the run, fell and injured his shoulder.

Killy went down in 54.65 seconds, then in 49.75. That gave France its sixth gold medal in the eight events. Senoner and Erika Shinegger of Austria were the only two skiers who broke French domination. Second place in the combined went to Leo LaCroix of France, with Ludwig Leitner of West Germany third.

Guy Perillat of France, with a time of 102.25, was second in the special slalom and another Frenchman, Louis Jauffret, was third in 102.58.

August 15, 1966

## *Skating Title Kept By Peggy Fleming*

By United Press International

VIENNA, March 4 -- Peggy Fleming retained her world figure skating title here tonight with a brilliant performance that drew ovations from the crowd and was labelled extremely graceful" by international skating experts.

A capacity crowd of 4,000 gave the 18-year-old girl from Colorado Springs a big hand despite the fact that she took a spill right at the start of her program after a double axel jump.

"I slipped after the takeoff and could not regain control in the air," Peggy said after her performance. "But I don't think it hurt the over-all impression very much."

Gabriele Seyfert of East Germany, the 1967 European champion, took second place and Hana Maskova of Czechoslovakia was third.

Experts confirmed that Miss Fleming's 4-minute free-style program was outstanding in grace, skill and composure despite the fall.

Two of Peggy's main rivals, Miss Seyfert and Valerie Jones of Toronto, also took spills during their free-style programs.

Dressed in a pink bejewelled costume, the Colorado freshman presented a sparkling repertoire to the tunes of two Italian operas and a Tchaikowski concerto.

Her program included all the double-jumps in the business— double axels, double flips, double loops and several single jumps presented with remarkable ease and beautiful grace.

A series of fast-moving pirouettes showed that she deserved her nickname of a "skating whirlwind."

Miss Fleming had piled up a huge lead of 69.2 points over her nearest challenger, Miss Jones, after the compulsory figures that count 60 per cent towards the title.

Miss Fleming clinched her second world title with the ideal ordinal number of nine, which indicates that the nine-judge panel was unanimous in awarding her first place.

She scored a total of 2273.4 points, followed by Miss Seyfert's 21 ordinals and 2179.4 points. Miss Maskova had 29 ordinals and 2151 points.

Miss Jones, who was in second place after the intricate school figures, fell back to fourth position after a poor free-skating performance, with 35 ordinals and 2143.2 points.

Kumiko Okawa of Japan moved up one place after the compulsory skating and was fifth by virtue of a magnificent free-skating program marked by high double jumps and excellent footwork.

The second Japanese entry, Miss Miwa Fukuhara, who was in seventh place after the compulsory figures, had to withdraw because she fell ill on the eve of the free skating.

Tina Noyes, 18, of Arlington, Mass., took seventh place and 17-year-old Jennie Walsh of Torrance, Calif., was eighth.

Miss Noyes was particularly impressive with a solid free-skating repertoire earning her marks between 5.5 and 5.8.

March 5, 1967.

## 'SKIING' IN A CART NEW SNOW THRILL

### Motorized Sport Is Infusing Economic Life Into Quiet Winter Adirondacks

Special to The New York Times

SPECULATOR, N. Y., March 12—An economic boom is putt-putting into the remote fringes of the Adirondack Forest Preserve these days on the rubber tracks and diminutive skis of the snowmobile.

Some restaurants, banks, gasoline stations and grocery stores, long accustomed to depressingly quiet winters in this snowfast region, now are doing a volume of business that reminds them of days in July and August.

Each weekend, some 11,000 snowmobilists fan out from Albany, Schnectady, Troy and the downstate areas for a day or two of picnicking and racing on the lakes and mountains of Warren, Oneida, Herkimer, Lewis, Franklin, St. Lawrence and Hamilton Counties.

One enthusiast estimates there will be 100,000 snowmobiles in New York State within a few years.

A snowmobile is basically a bobsled mounted on two small skis, which are used for steering. Propelled by a small gasoline engine that drives a flanged rubber track, it can go about 25 or 30 miles an hour on level ground and twice that on a downhill slope.

Its invasion of the Adirondacks has not been entirely an unmixed blessing.

A snowmobile operator recently was arrested in Massena for drunken driving. Burglars using one of the sleek little vehicles pushed nine miles through snowbound country to break into a summer camp in Franklin County and steal $300 worth of equipment.

Still, the local residents of such villages as Speculator are happy to see the winter weekenders trundling along the highways with their snowmobiles cradled on trailers behind their cars.

"Most winters we used not to make expenses," said Howard Romaine, a restaurant proprietor here. "But with these snowmobile people coming in, the millenium has arrived."

Booneville was host to 8,000 snowmobilists and their friends a few weeks ago. Wells, another community near here, is enjoying a similar boom.

And this is only the beginning, if John B. Knox and the newly formed 900-member

Walter Grishkot for The New York Times

**Mr. and Mrs. John B. Knox and daughters enjoy a pair. That's an iron deer at upper left.**

Adirondack Snow Travelers Association have their way.

Mr. Knox, president of the gelatin company that bears his name and an avid snowmobilist, is pushing for state legislation to open the woodland trails of the Adirondack Forest Preserve to snowmobiles for a $5-a-year user's fee.

"Within a few years there will be 100,000 snowmobiles in use in New York State alone," he says. "This would mean $500,000 a year for the state government."

March 13, 1967

# *Killy and Nancy Greene Take Vail Trophy Giant Slalom*

## FRENCH SKI STAR DEFEATS HEUGA

### Killy Gains 7th Victory in U.S. During Snowstorm— Miss Goitschel Sixth

**By MICHAEL STRAUSS**
Special to The New York Times

VAIL, Colo., March 19—Even a major snowstorm failed to stop Jean-Claude Killy today as the French superstar streaked through blinding snowflakes with ease to capture the Vail Trophy giant slalom.

The victory was Jean-Claude's seventh in a row since coming to the United States 11 days ago, a string that never has been matched in top international Alpine competition.

"Now, we've seen him here racing in all types of conditions," commented a United States Ski Association official

"Probably he could win on mud, too."

Killy gave another of his sparkling exhibitions in finishing ahead of Jimmy Heuga. The Frenchman was clocked in 1 minute 42.83 seconds to top the American ace by 1.82 seconds. Two Austrians, Heini Messner and Karl Schranz, placed third and fourth respectively.

The contest, a World Cup event, held on a mile course that plunged 1,300 feet and which started at an altitude of 9,500 feet, set the stage for an additional Killy milestone. It enabled him to finish his campaign for the cup, which he previously had clinched, with a perfect score of 225 points.

**Women's Result Undecided**

In contrast, the cup competition in the women's division remained undecided. Marielle Goitschel of France, the leader, lost her pole for the second time in four days and finished sixth after posting the fastest time of 32.3 seconds at the halfway mark.

Her misfortune cleared the way for a split-second victory by Canada's Nancy Greene. Miss Greene, clocked in 1:16.14 over a shortened course, triumphed over Erika Schinegger of Austria. The margin was .54 seconds.

The outcome left Miss Greene with an outside chance to win the World Cup. The winner will be decided at the Wild West Classic at Jackson Hole, Wyo. during which the concluding cup giant slalom and slalom events will be held.

In topping the men's field of 52 skiers, who represented Norway, Chile, England, Austria, Switzerland, Canada as well as the United States and France, Killy again proved that at least part of his success stems from his ability to adapt himself to all conditions.

Just before the half-way mark, his goggles fogged as he sped over a small stretch of flat at about 50 miles an hour. Without the loss of speed and with his poles dangling from his wrists, he wiped his glasses.

**Let the Skis Steer**

"It was nothing really," said Jean-Claude later. "My skis were doing a good job. I let them do the steering for the few moments."

Several other skiers were reluctant to duplicate Killy's feat. They simply removed their glasses and cast them aside. Jim Hoeschler of La Crosse,

Wis., who finished 39th, was among those who came home without them.

A 30-minute delay between races to set up the women's course proved particularly advantageous. The snowfall had stopped. As a result, the girls were provided with excellent visibility as the sun shone during most of the race.

Miss Greene posted a half-way time of 32.4 Miss Goitschel, who said yesterday the French were getting tired because of the winter-long campaign, reached the same point in 32.3. However, her pole caught as she rounded the 10th gate and her speed slackened.

"I do not know what happened," she said at the finish line. "Suddenly, I am without the pole."

March 20, 1967

# *Franco Nones of Italy Takes Cross-Country Ski Race in an Olympic Upset*

**FIRST GOLD MEDAL** of the Winter Olympics at Grenoble, France, went to Franco Nones of Italy, who won the 30-kilometer cross-country ski race

## SKATERS ARE LED BY MISS FLEMING

### U.S. Girl Flawless in First 2 Figures—Scandinavian Hold Broken in Skiing

**By FRED TUPPER**
Special to The New York Times

GRENOBLE, France, Feb. 7—Peggy Fleming of the United States took a commanding lead in the figure skating and Franco Nones, an Italian customs officer astounded the world of Nordic skiing today by humiliating all the great Scandinavian racers in winning the 30-kilometer cross-country race for the first gold medal of the Winter Olympic Games.

Dark, diminutive Peggy skated almost flawlessly this morning and built a 30.4-point margin over her most dangerous rival, blonde Gaby Seyfert of East Germany.

The 19-year-old Colorado State College freshman, a vision in powder blue with white skates, cut her two-lobe and three-lobe figures (a lobe is a complete circle) with such assurance and authority that the crowd gave her

warm applause before the judges even held up her high markings.

Miss Fleming, the world champion, had a total of 373.4 points to 343 for Miss Seyfert, the runner-up to her a year ago. Third was Beatrix Schuba of Austria with 340.7 and a delighted fourth was red-headed Tina Noyes of Arlington, Mass., with 332.5, just ahead of the European champion, Hana Maskova of Czechoslovakia. Halfway down the list at 16th was 14-year-old Janet Lynn of Rockford, Ill.

### Relay News Conference

Miss Fleming was sealed off from newsmen. Questions were answered through her "interpreter," John R. Shoemaker of San Francisco, manager of the United States team.

"I am pleased with my position" he said she said. "My skating is adequately satisfactory."

Asked if it had been easier for her because she was skating the same group of figures that won her the national title at Philadelphia last month, Shoemaker answered, "She skated on a different foot in Philadelphia."

In the mysterious phrases of figure-skating, the figures were known as figure 3-left back, paragraph 3 and right forward inside rocker. All compulsory figures are based on the figure 8. There are three more compulsory

figures to be skated tomorrow, and then Miss Fleming will be permitted to be interviewed. The free-skating finale takes place Saturday evening.

### Scandinavian Hold Broken

The victory of Nones, the 27-year-old customs officer, was the first scored in a cross-country event by anyone but a Scandinavian since the Winter Games started in 1924.

The short, slender Italian from Catella di Fiemma, a hamlet near Trento in the Dolomites, won by the astonishing margin of 400 yards, finishing the 30 kilometers (18.6 miles) strongly in 1 hour 35 minutes 39.2 second. That was nearly 50 seconds faster than Odd Martinsen of Norway. Eero Maentyranta of Finland, a double gold-medal winner at Innsbruck, Austria, in 1964, was a badly tuckered-out third.

Nones, who started in the 26th position, led all the way. Months of backbreaking training in the hills of northern Sweden under the guidance of a Swedish coach, Bengt-Herman Nilsson, had made him strong and fit and he had intelligently waxed for the weather.

"I thought I could win it last night when it turned colder," he said. "I'm always better on fast snow."

It was clear and cold at 8:30

this morning when the competitors started out. Nones's chief danger, he thought, would be Maentryranta, and at 20 kilometers he led the Finn by a scant four seconds. But Maentyranta faded badly.

"I had nothing more to give," he said, "I had to stop and be sick."

### Wild Yell of Victory

The numbers in the teens were finishing when Nones hit the last hill leading into the trail to the stadium. Teammates checking by radio had told him his lead seemed safe, so the Italian gave a wild yell of victory as he plunged down the last slope and barreled across the line.

The first American to finish was Michael Gallagher of Killington, Vt., 27th in a field of 63.

"The toughest course I've ever raced on; all uphill for the first 10 kilometers," said Gallagher. "I'm satisfied, but I think I could have gone faster. My wax was not right for the snow near the finish."

Michael Elliott of Durango, Colo., was 29th, a spot higher than his placing at Innsbruck.

"There I lost by 10 minutes, now I've cut it down to six something," he said, "And I've been out of training for a year."

February 8, 1968

# Killy Wins Olympic Downhill Gold Medal and Calls It 'Great Honor for Me'

## 3 U.S. WOMEN TIE FOR 2D IN SKATING

### They Trail Soviet Winner —Miss Gustafsson First in Cross-Country Ski

**By FRED TUPPER**

Special to The New York Times

GRENOBLE, France, Feb. 9— Jean-Claude Killy won the downhill gold medal as the French placed one, two today in this classic Winter Olympic event. The darkly handsome 24-year-old idol of France beat the experienced Guy Perillat in a frantic finish by eight one-hundredths of a second to uproarious acclaim. Killy will now shoot for the Alpine grand slam, first made by Toni Sailer of Austria 12 years ago at Cortina, Italy. Billy Kidd of the United States was an also-ran.

The United States took three silvers, its most medals ever in one Winter Olympic event as Jenny Fish, Dianne Holum and Mary Margaret Meyers incredibly tied for second behind Ludmilla Titova of the Soviet Union in the 500-meter speed skating.

Then blonde Toni Gustafsson, a 29-year-old Finnish born gym instructor from Sweden, ran away from the field to win by 68 seconds in the 10-kilometer women's cross-country. Russian domination of the event for 16 years was broken as Scandinavians took the first five places.

The speed-skating race was a cliffhanger. An early 46.3-second clocking by Miss Meyers, who is from St. Paul, seemed unimportant at the time. Although she had won the world title a year ago, Mary had been a bit off form recently and her reading this morning was slower than many practice times and far behind the unofficial world record of 44.7 turned in at Davos last week by the 1968 world champion, Ion Tatiana Sidorova of the Soviet Union.

But Miss Sidorova was timed in 46.9 for the lap-and-a-quarter race and 16 of the 28 competitors had finished without offering a challenge. Then Miss Titova came to the start, drawn against Misae Takeda of Japan. They were nervous and overeager, with many false starts.

United Press International

**SPARKLING PERFORMANCE: Jean-Claude Killy of France sends snowflakes flying as he soars over a bump on the way to victory in 2,890-meter ski event in the Olympics.**

Miss Titova broke fast, and arms windmilling, hit the 100-meter mark in 11.8. The 21-year-old from Chita rode with the northeast wind down the back straight and, head down and legs and arms churning, roared through the blue timing markers in 46.1 as the Soviet contingent waved handkerchiefs.

It was time now for 16-year-old Miss Holum of Northbrook, Ill., third in the world last year and

second this year. She was off like a rocket and passed the 100-meter mark in 11.6, the fastest yet. The impromptu American cheering section was yelling, "Go, Go, Go" as she ate up the meters and there she was in the stretch with the race in her grasp. Her strength was waning now and she reached home in 46.3. "I died at the end," she said. "My legs tightened up."

Little drops of rain were spattering on the ice as the last couple

came up to the start. Eighteen-year-old Miss Fish of Strongville, Ohio, was paired with Irina Egorova of the Soviet Union. Jenny was away badly, nervous and off balance. When she reached the 100-meter mark, 12 precious seconds had gone and the ice was slower now. Then she made her charge. In a tremendous finish she was up and through the markers in 46.3, the Russian wilting behind.

This was the breakthrough.

Three Americans had tied for second place and the silver medals. The United States had placed in women's skating for the first time. And yet, Miss Titova held the title won the last time by the great Lydia Skoblikova, four times a gold medalist at Innsbruck. The slow times had been caused by the wind sweeping down from the mountains. "We had to skate into it twice, both at the start and finish," said Miss Meyers.

As all France had prayed he would do, Killy won his gold medal. He rocketed down the twisting Chambrousse course—2,890 meters with a vertical drop of 840—in 1:59.85, though it was whisker close with 29-year-old Perillat at the end.

A bronze medalist eight years ago at Squaw Valley, Calif., Perillat was the first man away, often an advantage. Coolly in control, his time over the early stages was 48.45 as compared with 48.61 for Killy. He was timed in under two minutes, a mark the great Alpine aces challenged in vain. Gerhard Nenning of Austria was ninth and a co-favorite, Edmund

Bruggman of Switzerland, 10th. Kidd, from Stowe, Vt., had come and gone, far off the pace, when Killy made his run. The Frenchman knew what he had to do. "When I heard Guy's time, I was sure I could beat it without strain. But it was slippery up top. No trouble after that."

February 10, 1968

# MISS FLEMING OF U.S. WINS OLYMPIC FIGURE SKATING

## Colorado Girl's Triumph First for American Team

### By FRED TUPPER
Special to The New York Times

GRENOBLE, France, Feb. 10—Peggy Fleming won an Olympic Games gold medal for the United States tonight and became enshrined among the figure-skating immortals. At 19 years of age her delicate artistry and subtle movement have brought her all the laurels that count—an Olympic championship, two world titles and five American titles.

Deafening applause rolled round the rafters of the Stade de Glace as she whirled and pirouetted, jumped and danced through four minutes of inspired free-skating, capping the prohibitive 77.2-point margin she had established earlier in the week over Gaby Seyfert of East Germany, the runner-up to the United States' first gold-medal winner in the games.

Miss Fleming took the ice midway through the three-hour spectacle, her fragile dark beauty accentuated in a chartreuse dress, rhinestones glittering under the arc lights.

Her opening set the scene for the performance to come. She was quickly into a double-toe loop jump and out into a delayed axel, seemingly hanging in air. Two waltz steps and she was flying down the ice and into her repertory. The names of the jumps were meaningless, but the execution was breathless.

Here they were one after another—the double loop, the double axel, the Wally jump, the ballet jump, another Wally, the flying camel and the double lutz.

The music softened. In intricate patterns she was into a camel spin, head down, twirling like a top. Then she leaped from a combination into a double axel—or 2½ revolutions—the most difficult jump in figure skating. The Colorado College student spun down the ice.

Peggy was nearing the end now—her skates flowing onto the ice and there suddenly was the finale—a half-toe loop, one-and-a-half toe loop, then a double-toe loop, perfectly conceived, perfectly executed. One last leap into a flying sit spin and then a blur as she dissolved into her spin turns.

That was it. The applause came down. Up went the judges' cards.

February 11, 1968

## Peggy Fleming Acclaimed as Ballerina on Ice

### Her Success Viewed as Triumph Over 'Follies' Skaters

#### By LLOYD GARRISON
Special to The New York Times

GRENOBLE, France, Feb. 10—Peggy Fleming's victory in the Olympic figure skating tonight was not only a personal triumph, it was also a victory of the ballet over the Ice Follies approach to figure skating.

For traditional aficionados, her victory had all the ingredients of a Good Guy whipping the Bad Guys in an Italian-made Western, in which the film is no good unless the Good Guy guns down at least a posse of black-hatted hombres in the first reel.

Tonight, the Colorado State college girl with a weakness for chocolate cake and whipped cream took on no fewer than 32 competitors and knocked them all dead.

Until Miss Fleming came along, the women's figure skating threatened to be dominated by those whom Dick Button calls the Diana Dorses of the sport—"the razzle-dazzle girls who are all flash and no depth."

#### Audrey Hepburn of Skating

Earlier tonight America's two-time Olympic winner in the men's figures described Peggy Fleming as the Audrey Hepburn of skating "and Audrey Hepburn is not a Diana Dors and never will be. She isn't deliberately flashy. She doesn't blast you. She's subtle."

The Diana Dorses are not unpretty to look at, but to observers like Button, they resemble overgrown chorus girls with the legs of a Green Bay linebacker.

"You see a lot of Peggy's competition clumping around, skating fast like hockey players, flailing the ice with

A graceful Peggy Fleming captures the Olympic gold medal at Grenoble in 1968. She was also women's world champion, 1966–1968, and holder of the U.S. title, 1964–1968.

quick stops, trying to overpower you with gimmicks. The crowd may like it but it's not beautiful and it's not good skating."

Button has compared figure skating to high diving. "You can do a triple flip and touch your toes, but if you don't enter the water cleanly, it's not a good dive and the judges know it.

"Position and recovery are just as important in skating," he said. "With Peggy, there's not a misplaced move. She's always in perfect position going in and out of her jumps."

The "Ice Follies" analogy

was coined by Miss Fleming herself. "I primarily represent the ballet approach," she said the other day. "That is, where the movements are more graceful and everything blends smoothly as you flow across the ice."

Being polite, she describes the "Ice Follies" school as being merely more "athletic." But the other girls got the point.

"Peggy," says Gabrielle Seyfert of East Germany, "has no weaknesses. I know I am the more athletic type and I'm trying to overcome it. Peggy lands softly and everything she does is connected. It's pure ballerina."

At 5 feet 4 inches and currently weighing only 108 pounds, Peggy has occasionally gotten up to 112—with her penchant for desserts. But such rare lapses account for her breaks in discipline in a sport with incredible physical and psyhcological demands.

While at times exuding a sorority girl's impishness, on the ice she's all poise, a very worldly black-haired and dark-eyed beauty.

At last year's world championships in Vienna, the Austrian press tried to pin down Miss Fleming's appeal both as a skater and as a young woman.

Some described her as "classic." Others compared her to a Grecian beauty. The Express finally tabbed her as "America's Shy Bambi."

Few would quibble with any one of these descriptions. But Miss Fleming is refreshingly unconcerned about image-making.

Before the finals here, she had her usual double-decker sandwich. After she had won and was finished with the interviews and the congratulations, she had her chocolate cake. And at last, with tonight's triumph, a few pounds more or less wouldn't matter.

February 11, 1968

# Olga Pall and Groenningen Capture Olympic Ski Races

## OLGA PALL TAKES DOWNHILL EVENT

### Austrians Gain 3 of First 4 Places—Groenningen Cross-Country Victor

Special to The New York Times

GRENOBLE, France, Feb. 10—Olga Pall, a freckled-faced brunette from the heart of the Tyrol won the Olympic Games womens downhill race from Isabelle Mir of France today as the Austrians took three of the first four places in their struggle with the French for Alpine skiing supremacy.

A surprise sixth was Felicity Field of England, where there's hardly a hill or snow to slide on. The World Cup winner, Nancy Greene of Canada, was 10th, apparently a victim of bad waxing.

Harold Groenningen, a rugged Norwegian farmer who had been three times a silver medalist, upset his old nemesis, Eero Maentyranta of Finland, in the home stretch by a couple of seconds in taking the 15-kilometer cross-country. It was a reverse of their placings in the 1964 Olympics.

A blonde, 26-year-old Finnish typist, Kaija Mustonen, ruined Lydia Skoblikova's bid for a seventh gold medal and broke the Soviet athlete's Olympic record in taking the 1,500-meter speed skating in a surging finish. The resurgent Dutch finished second and third and Lydia trailed sadly—out of the first 10.

First on the ice this gray, misty morning was Ludmila Titova, one of Lydia's teammates. There was no spark in her sprint, but the time

of 2 minutes 26.8 seconds—over four seconds off the Olympic mark—seemed good, considering her slow 46.1-second victory clocking in the 500 meters yesterday.

The favorite was, the world champion, Stein Kaiser, a big, strong skater from the Netherlands. Arms moving like propellers, she tore down the straight and was through the blue marker in 2:24.5. Surely, that was good enough.

Miss Mustonen was paired with Dianne Holum, the pert 16-year-old American who won a silver medal yesterday. Dianne was around the first 300 meters in 29 seconds, the Finn right on her heels, moving effortlessly, hands knit behind her back, long, gliding strokes eating up the ice.

#### Finish Is Powerful

Kaija hit the bell lap in 1:43, still gliding, and then began to windmill her arms on the far turn as she poured on the power. Her time was 2:22.4, a fifth of a second under Miss Skoblikova's record, set at Innsbruck in 1964. The ice was fast, the wind nonexistent today.

"She was so far ahead that I began to think I wasn't trying," said the exhausted Dianne, who finished 13th. Jeanne Ashworth of Burlington, Vt., and 36-year-old Jeanne Omelenchuk of Warren, Mich., were far down the field of 30.

Carolina Geijssen, a 20-year-old Amsterdam secretary who skates to work, made a final

bid. With half a lap to go and blares from Dutch horns urging her on, her time was identical with the winner. But she took the turn too wide and was second in 2:22.7.

Then came Lydia—two gold medals at Squaw Valley, Calif., in 1960, a sweep of four at Innsbruck. Today she was 11th.

#### Big Year for Olga

An occasional first-10 finisher a year ago, Olga Pall burst into the limelight this year when she won a race at Val d'Isere and then took a big one at Bad Gastein against the world's elite.

Shapely, strong and a natural athlete, she has a distinct assurance and style that prompted the local press reluctantly to pick her as the chief danger to the great French quartet that had swept the slopes for the last year.

It had looked all Austria as the contestants rocketed down the 2,160-meter Chamrousse course fast and relatively firm today over the 600-meter plunge to the bottom.

The Olympic champion, Christl Haas, had come out of temporary retirement to finish fast. Back of her was Brigitte Seiwald. Most of the French had floundered and the world champion, Miss Greene, was dismally slow, for her, from a bad choice of wax.

Karen Budge, the best of the Americans, had collided before the start and dislocated a shoulder, another victim of the injuries that have plagued the United States Alpine squad.

#### Isabelle Flashes Across

Stocky, redheaded Isabelle Mir was poised at the top, blue helmet gleaming in the sun. She flew down the course, bent deep in the tuck position and roared through the finish sign in 1 minute 41.33 seconds as the crowd roared. After Jean-Claude Killy's downhill victory

yesterday, this would set the seal for France.

Olga heard the time and charged, ripping into the first turn, slipping slightly on the second. But her line was true and her control superb. She shot out of the last left turn and across the line in 1:40.87, saw the time and threw her arms wide in delight.

The Americans did little. Suzanne Chaffee had lost her struggle early, unable to move with her sticking wax.

"Have them change it!" she shouted.

Sixteen-year-old Kiki Cutter did better and wound up 17th, with Sandra Shellworth 21st.

February 11, 1968

## FINNISH GIRL WINS IN SPEED SKATING

### Miss Mustonen Sets Olympic Mark of 2:22.4 in 1,500

GRENOBLE, France, Feb. 10 (UPI) — Kaija Mustonen, a bright-eyed Finnish secretary, broke the Soviet Union's domination of women's speed skating today by winning the gold medal in the 1,500-meter event in an Olympic record time of 2 minutes 22.4 seconds.

Miss Mustonen, 26 years old, also upset two Dutch rivals, Carolina Geijssen and Christina Kaiser. Miss Geijssen, fastest girl in the 1,500 meters this season, took the silver medal with a time of 2:22.7 and Miss Kaiser, a two-time world champion, won the bronze, in 2:24.5.

The United States, which reached a milestone yesterday when three girls tied for second place in the 500 meters, was nowhere in contention in the 1,500. Dianne Holum of Northbrook, Ill., finished 13th in 2:28.5, Jeanne Ashworth of Wilmington, N.Y., was 16th in 2:30.3 and Jeanne Omelenchuk of Warren, Mich., was 25th in 2:35.5.

Crown Princess Beatrix of The Netherlands and Prince Claus were among the 1,000 spectators who watched the race. The heiress to the Dutch throne and her husband took the silver and bronze winners to lunch.

But if the Dutch were disappointed, the biggest disappointment was suffered by the Russians, who had won eight of nine Olympic women's speed skating gold medals, including the 500-meter event won by Ludmila Titova yesterday.

Lidyia Skoblikova, who won six of the Russian gold medals and set the previous Olympic record of 2:22.6 for 1,500 meters four years ago at Innsbruck, Austria, finished 11th with a time of 2:27.6.

The top-ranking Russian today with Lasma Kaouniste, who finshed fifth with a time of 2:25.4, behind Norway's Sigrid Sunby, whose fourth-place time was 2:25.2. Miss Titova was seventh in 2:26.8.

The Finnish team mobbed Miss Mustonen when her record time was posted, jubilantly certain she had won even though there were still nine pairs to race, including Miss Geijssen and Miss Skoblikova.

"I guess those two black cats I saw in the street Friday were lucky for me. I set my own pace and didn't worry about Dianne [Holum]. It's the fastest time I've ever recorded for the distance and I can't get over it," Miss Mustonen said.

February 11, 1968

## U.S. GIRL IS THIRD IN SPEED SKATING

### Monti of Italy Gains Gold Medal in 2-Man Bobsled —Raska Wins Ski Jump

**By FRED TUPPER**
Special to The New York Times

GRENOBLE, France, Feb. 11—Jean-Claude Killy is halfway there in his quest for the three-event Alpine skiing grand slam. The idol of France romped through the first heat of the giant slalom today with an enormous 1.2-second margin and must be the favorite to add this title to his downhill victory for a second gold medal tomorrow. The United States was still in the running with Jimmy Heuga in seventh place and Billy Kidd in eighth.

After Peggy Fleming's sublime free skating for a gold medal in the Stade de Glace last night, 16-year-old Dianne Holum picked up a bronze medal today. The smiling Illinois skater finished behind Carolina Geijssen of the Netherlands and Ludmila Titova of the Soviet Union in the 1,000-meter speed skating race for her second medal in the 10th Winter Olympic Games.

Dianne was one of three Americans to tie for second place in the 500-meter event.

Eugenio Monti of Italy finally has won a gold medal. He has been trying for 12 years and has won nine world championships along the way, but the Olympic prize always eluded him. The 39-year-old redhead from the craggy peaks of the Dolomites piloted his sled, with Luciano DePaolis on the brakes, down the last run of the twisting 1,600-meter ice chute in 1:10.05 just before dawn this morning. "Luciano gave it a devilish push," said Monti. It was the fastest run.

That was important, because Italy and West Germany finished the four heats of the two-man bobsled event tied at 4 minutes 41.54 seconds.

Each team would receive a gold medal, it was decided at first. Then the officials reversed the decision. The judges based their verdict on world bobsled competition rules. The Germans protested because they contended there is no provision in Olympic rules for the breaking of a tie.

Bobsled racers have a deep affection for Monti. He is patched together with bits of tape. As a skier he broke the tendons of both knees. He has cracked up as a racing driver. He has twice had plastic surgery performed on his face.

"Speed must be in my veins instead of blood," he once said. Monti has never stopped trying. He won both sivler medals in the bobsled events at Cortina in 1956. He took both bronze medals in 1964. And he loaned Tony Nash and Robin Dixon a steel runner that enabled them to win the gold medal at Innsbruck. For that gesture UNESCO gave him its first Fair Play Trophy.

"I'm done now," he said. "I'm satisfied. I'll retire peacefully."

The blessings of sportsmen throughout the world go with him.

Horst Floth and Pepi Bader of West Germany were then second, Ion Panturu and Nicolae Meagoe of Rumania third, with Nash and Dixon in fourth place and the American first sled of Paul Lamey and Robert Huscher sixth.

Franz Keller, a 23-year-old army sergeant, won the combined Nordic gold medal for West Germany. Keller led the ski jumping event yesterday, but Alois Kaelin of Switzerland won the 15-kilometer cross-country race today. Keller's over-all point total was highest.John Bower of the United States finished 13th.

The Scandinavians surprisingly were shut out in the 70-meter or small hill jump. Jiri Raska, 27, of Czechoslovakia, won the gold medal with Reinhold Bachler and Preim Baldur of Austria taking the silver and bronze medals. John Balfanz of the United States was 40th.

Manfred Schmid, a 23-year-old Austrian locksmith, leads halfway through the luge or toboggan competition with Tom Koehler of East Germany, a gold medal winner at Innsbruck, second.

February 12, 1968

---

# Killy Wins Giant Slalom for 2d Olympic Gold Medal, but Kidd Takes Heat

## U.S. SKIER IS FIFTH IN OVER-ALL SCORE

### Killy Will Seek 'Grand Slam' Saturday—Dutch Girl Sets World Record in Skating

**By FRED TUPPER**
Special to The New York Times

GRENOBLE, France, Feb. 12—Jean-Claude Killy has done it again. The 24-year-old French customs officer with the moviestar profile won the giant slalom today and a second gold medal in his bid for the Winter Olympic triple crown of Alpine skiing, a feat accomplished only by Toni Sailer of Austria in 1956 at Cortina, Italy.

Jean-Claude shattered the field with a 2.22-second margin in the combined two-heat standings, but Billy Kidd had the fastest time today. Back in the superlative form that placed him with Killy on a pedestal two years ago, the Vermonter darted and danced through the 57 gates over the 1,780-meter Chamrousse run in the lightning time of 1 minute 46.46 seconds to finish eight-hundredths of a second ahead of Killy.

"I had to take more chances—and I did," said Billy, "and there's still the special slalom to come." Kidd's comeback has been the talk of the skiing world. He strained an ankle in Kitzbuhel in 1966, broke a leg in Chile and then bruised the same ankle again in training last week. At that time it was thought he was out of the Games.

#### Heuga Finishes 10th

Jimmy Heuga was 10th, Spider Sabich 13th and Rick Chaffee 15th for the United States.

A drifting fog and flakes of snow made the skiing tougher this morning. Visibility was poor.

Killy came down near the end of the first flight of 15, when the course was rutted. He had Kidd's time to shoot for and was soon in attack position, with skis far forward, hips swiveling through the gates. Impatient near the end, trying to drum up speed, he whipped the snow incessantly with his left pole and shaved the last flag before hurtling through the "arrivee" gate.

A roar from 20,000 throats echoed off the peaks as Killy's time came up at 1:46.54. Today, for once, it was second best.

"I didn't care about the fog, I just go," said Killy in English. "For this one, I've been waiting since 10 years."

#### De Gaulle Is Expected

President de Gaulle is expected Saturday to see Killy try for the grand slam.

"He'll be more nervous than I," said Jean-Claude.

Red-capped Willy Favre of Switzerland, his knees pumping frantically down the last schuss, was second, and Heinie Messner of Austria moved fast enough to pass Guy Perillat of France and take third place.

The women's special slalom will be held over two heats tomorrow. Add to the rising

**Jean-Claude Kily of France racing through the second heat of the men's giant slalom event at Chambrousse, France. He won second straight medal by a margin of 2.22 seconds.**

American ailing list the name of Kiki Cutter, 18, the top American finisher in the downhill. Miss Cutter has measles, but she will ski anyway.

The great Lidia Skoblikova had her Olympic swan song today. Holder of six gold medals, the Russian skated the 3,000 meters. Blonde hair streaming, red mittens clasped behind her back, she got round the 7½ laps fast enough to break her own Olympic record by more than six seconds. The trouble was 10 other girls broke the mark, too, and Lidia wound up in sixth place.

The winner was Johanna Schut, a 23-year-old curly-haired brunette from Apeldoorn in the country of canals. The husky Dutch girl, world champion this year, fairly flew round the rink. With the now-familiar cowhorns blaring, she was through the first timing stage three seconds faster than the field and, gliding powerfully, had the same margin at the bell lap.

Arms windmilling and head low, she charged down the stretch for a 4:56.2 timing, 18 seconds under the Olympic record and one-tenth of a second below the world mark set by her teammate, Stien Kaiser, who finished third.

Wilhelmina Burgmeijer was fifth as the Dutch were sandwiched round two Finns, Kaija Mustonen, the gold medalist in the 1,500 meters, was second and Kaija Keskivitkka fourth. Jeanne Ashworth of the United States was 10th.

In its skating renaissance, the Netherlands supplanted the Soviet Union in Olympic women's competition, taking two gold medals—the nation's first ever—a silver and two bronze in the four events.

At the Games' halfway stage, Norway had its second gold, too, to join France, Italy and The Netherlands. It was a surprise to Magnar Soldberg, and to his coach, too, for the 31-year-old policeman from Trondheim was new to the Olympic scene and had been beaten many times by the elite group he mastered this morning.

"I was full of fighting spirit," he said, "and ready to run," He won the biathlon, a combination of skiing and shooting, by finishing second over the 20-kilometer cross-country course and first in rifle-shooting.

February 13, 1968

# *Miss Goitschel of France Takes Olympic Slalom as Miss Nagel Loses Lead*

## U.S. GIRL FALLS ON HER 2D RUN

### Misses Chance After Skiing Fastest Heat—French Put Three in First 5 Places

**By FRED TUPPER**
Special to The New York Times

GRENOBLE, France, Feb. 13 —Apple-cheeked Marielle Goitschel won the Olympic women's slalom for France with a two-heat combined time of 85.-86 seconds today after 16-year-old Judy Ann Nagel of Enumclaw, Wash., had thrown the Alpine ski world into a fit by taking the first-run lead in the fastest time of the day.

Miss Nagel fell the next time down, though, and the great

**Marielle Goitschel of France flashes through the gates on the way to victory in the slalom**

Miss Goitschel had the title vacated by her sister, Christine, with a half-second margin over Nancy Greene of Canada, as France put three women in the first five places. Annie Famose was third, Gina Hathorn of Britain a surprise fourth and Isabelle Mir fifth.

For a while America's hopes soared as its quartet placed 1, 2, 4, 6 on the scoreboard after the first heat. It was too good to be true. And it wasn't. Wendy Allen, Kiki Cutter and Rosie Fortna were disqualified for having missed gates high on the course.

But Miss Nagel led the field. The little high school junior had not even made the American team until a fortnight ago.

On the first descent she had a margin of eight-hundredths of a second over Miss Goitschel, but in that do-or-die second run she died nine seconds out, tumbling at the second and third gates.

Miss Goitschel was superb. She lives in Val D'Isere, a snowball throw from Jean-Claude Killy, and she skis in the same powerful, relentless style. Chomping on a wad of gum, she shot through 56 gates so placed on this extremely fast course that it was difficult to attack.

"I attack, I attack, I attack!" she said. "It was the race I wanted most in the world."

She had been second to her sister in the Olympics at Innsbruck in 1964 and second to Miss Famose in the 1966 world championships.

### No More a Runner-Up

"I was tired of second in this race," she said.

This was her second gold medal. She reversed placings with her sister, now retired, to take the giant slalom at Innsbruck and holds the world title in that event.

The red-sweatered Miss Greene took the second heat in the effortless, commanding manner that won her the World Cup last year. The 24-year-old student at Notre Dame in British Columbia picked up nine-tenths of a second on the way.

"I lost speed on that earlier run," she said. "And I'm sorry for the Americans. They were very good, but they need more experience."

"Three ruddy hundredths of a second cost me a medal"! exclaimed Miss Hathorn. It could have been Britain's first Alpine medal ever, but a nervously crossed ski on the first run made the difference.

Toini Gustafsson started last and finished first in the five-kilometer cross-country race to take her second gold medal for Sweden. She won the 10-kilometer last week.

For her everything was perfect today. She rose early, cooked some strong coffee—and nothing else—and waxed her skis.

From her back position among the 34 starters, she knew how she stood and what she had to do. The 29-year-old gymnasium teacher was 10 seconds behind at one stage, but she felt strong and knew that she could stay the route as the leaders tired and tumbled on

the fast downhill runs toward the end.

With a kilometer to go, she was four seconds off the pace of the Soviet Union's Galina Koulakova, but a brave schuss down the last slope brought the Swede home in 16:45.2 with time to spare.

It was a tight finish for most of the others, though, with the next seven separated by a total of 12 seconds.

### Two Russians Next

Miss Koulakova was second and her teammate, Alevtina Koltchina, snow-crusted by a spill four kilometers out, finished third. Barbro Martinsson of Sweden was a couple of seconds in front of Miss Koltchina, but faded toward the end.

With a bronze medal in plain view, Marjatta Kajosma of Finland tottered and dropped with only 700 meters to go, finally finishing fifth.

"I was so tired," she said, "and there I was on my nose."

Three East German girls who had placed among the first four were disqualified in the luge or toboggan event for having heated their sled runners illegally. They were Ortrun Enderlein, who had led at the halfway stage of four heats in 2:28.04; Anna-Maria Mueller, in second place, and Angela Knoesel, fourth.

The disqualifications moved Erica Lechner of Italy to the top after three heats.

Warming runners is a serious violation of rules of the International Luge Federation. The rules require the runners to be of the same temperature as the

air at the track.

Emmerich Danzer of Austria, the world and European champion, squeaked ahead of his teammate, Wolfgang Schwarz, after two of five compulsories in the men's figure skating. The compulsories were the backward paragraph "3" with a right-foot start and the outside rocker off the left foot. Tim Wood of Highland Park, Mich., the American champion, was fourth behind Patrick Pera of France.

"I did a lousy first figure," he said. "I wasn't quite awake." (Competition starts shortly before dawn.)

Wood, who started skating as a 2½-year-old toddler in Detroit, figures he can catch up with Pera. He said: "I beat him in the free skating here in Europe last fall."

Gary Visconti of Detroit was sixth and John Petkevich of Minneapolis, whose scintillating free skating had ousted Scotty Allen, the 1964 bronze-medal winner from the squad, was 13th.

At nightfall France was the first to have three gold medals. Prime Minister Georges Pompidou of France saw Miss Goitschel take the slalom, and Prince Bertil of Sweden handed Miss Gustafsson a bouquet of roses and kissed her on both cheeks after her victory.

As Miss Gustafsson knew this morning, it was her perfect day.

February 14, 1968

# McDermott Wins a Silver Medal for U.S. Team in Olympic Speed Skating

## WOOD MOVES UP IN FIGURES EVENT

### U.S. Skater in Second Place —Norwegian Skiers Gain Their Third Gold Medal

**By FRED TUPPER**
Special to The New York Times

GRENOBLE, France, Feb. 14—A challenge of raw courage by the experienced Terry McDermott in speed skating and some superb figure skating by young Tim Wood brought the United States back into the medal hunt as the favorites won their specialties today at the Winter Olympic Games.

The 27-year-old McDermott, the only gold medalist for the United States at the 1964 Innsbruck Games, raced last when

the sun was hot and the ice was slow. He charged through the timers a fifth of a second behind Erhard Keller of West Germany and took a silver medal in the 500-meter sprint by tying Magne Thomassen of Norway.

Wood, an indifferent fifth in the two tracings yesterday, soared past a two-time world and European champion, Emmerich Danzer of Austria, and wound up second to another Austrian, Wolfgang Schwartz.

"I'm going for the gold," said the elated Wood after scoring highest in one of the three difficult final compulsory figures. The free-skating finale will be on Friday.

### Killy Goes for Three

Still searching for the triple crown in Alpine skiing, Jean-Claude Killy had the best time in the special slalom eliminations. The French superstar coasted through an annoying qualification heat in 45.89 seconds on the 63-gate, 520-meter course in his quest to add the

slalom gold to those won in the downhill and giant slalom.

Norway, the revelation of these Games, took the 40-kilometer cross-country ski relay for its third gold medal. Its rugged quartet of Odd Martinsen, Pall Tyldum, Harald Groenningen and Ole Ellefsaeter had nearly two minutes in hand over the Swedes and the Finns. Finland's two-time gold medalist, Eero Maentyranta, stormed from behind down the stretch to nip Viatches Vedenine of the Soviet Union for the bronze medal by half a second. After Mike Gallagher had doggedly raced into sixth place on the first leg, the United States slumped to 12th in the field of 15.

The sun had climbed over the side of an Alp and was glancing across the ice when Thomassen, a slightly built bank clerk from Trondheim, Norway, made his bid in the 500-meter skating. A red stocking cap wobbling on his head, he had a mediocre 10.5 sec-

onds for the first 100 meters, picked up speed as he hit the final bend and flashed down the home stretch in 40.5, a clocking that proved more important as time went on.

The world-record holder, Yevgane Grishin, was next. The 28-year-old, durable Russian had won four skating golds over the years from Cortina in 1956 and was second to McDermott at Innsbruck. A stylist, Grishin had 10.2 for the 100 and, bent low, skated round the turns in 40.6.

Good for starters, said the crowd that had overflowed the bleachers. But the experts had already decided the winner would be either Keller, who has an amazing 39.2 world mark waiting to be ratified, or Keiichi Suzuki of Japan, the reigning world champion.

Keller was champing at the bit, ready to go. He springs off the crouch to pick up starting speed. Like that other West German, Armin Hary, who won the 100-meter track dash at the Rome Olympics, he was de-

Erhard Keller of West Germany speeding to a gold medal in the men's 500-meter speed skating event at Grenoble.

Terry McDermott of Birmingham, Mich., won silver medal despite starting last in heat when ice was churned up.

termined to jump the gun.

He was called back for one false start, but then he was away beautifully. Through the first mark at 10.2, he fairly tore around the saucer. With German horns giving him wings, he dived though the timers in 40.3 and skated a lap of honor in bedlam.

Suzuki, a 25-year-old office manager who wears black horn-rimmed glasses as he skates, was 10.2 on the first leg. But disaster struck on the far turn as he missed his stride and nearly fell. Still game, he was clocked in 40.8, out of the hunt.

The sun was higher now, and pools of water were forming on the practice infield. The times were rising as the ice slowed. John Wurster had a 40.7 early on and Neil Blatchford, supposedly America's best, was on deck. He had 10.1 at 100, the fastest clocking yet and he was up with Keller when he, too, messed up a stride on the far turn. Recovering, he did 40.7.

The ice was cleaned again for Tom Gray of the United States and Valery Muratov, the

Soviet sprint champion. Their times were poor. It seemed all over now. McDermott was to race last. He was 10 pounds heavier than at Innsbruck. The father of three children, for two years he had been in retirement. Now the luck of the draw seemed to have left him no hope.

But Terry was determined to give it a go. His technique is an obsolete stand-up position and he skates that way. It makes no difference. He has power and speed and desire. He made a memorable run, skating bare-headed. There was a slight slip at the start before he gained speed and then the crowd became electric, yelling him on.

He had the fastest time at three quarters, moving like a steam engine, but there was still that agonizing last stretch. The legs were failing, but he battled on, sheer courage getting him home in 40.5, a joint second with Thomassen.

He was at the interview table then, gray flecks in his hair, a grin showing his pleasure.

"It was a gutsy race," a man said.

"That's the way I skate," said McDermott.

Over the last year, Wood has

struck top class. Third a year ago in the American nationals, he winged by Gary Visconti and Scott Allen to win at Philadelphia last month, taking a month off from college to polish up his figures and routine.

Fifth yesterday after two compulsories, Tim had good marks on the first today—a paragraph double 3 forward, explainable as two circles with turns toward the center skated on one foot.

He had top marks of all in the change loop backward and finished the third figure-A paragraph forward, in which the turns were made outward in two circles, in second place. Over all he had 992.4 points and 21 ordinals. Wolfgang Schwartz led with 1,006.6 points and 16.5 ordinals.

February 15, 1968

# PAIRS TITLE GOES TO SOVIET COUPLE

### Beloussova-Protopopov Duo First in Figure Skating

GRENOBLE, France, Feb. 14 (AP) — The husband-and-wife team Ludmila Beloussova and Oleg Protopopov of the Soviet Union, the 1964 winners, put on a near-flawless performance to-night to win the Olympic pairs figure-skating championship.

The Protopopovs, she is 33 and he is 36, are regarded as the oldsters of skating competition. They emphasized grace rather than athletic ability by skating to fairly slow music, but doing it with such perfect unison that the crowd of 12,-000 was cheering them through-out.

The judges gave them high scores for both technical ability and artistic showing.

The second-place silver medal went to another Soviet couple

—Tatiana Joukchesternava and Aleksandr Gorelik, while West Germany's Margot Glockshuber and Wolfgang Danne were third.

**Kauffmans Are Sixth**

The best the top American couple of Ronald and Cynthia Kauffman of Seattle could do was sixth.

Sandi Switzer of Burbank, Calif., and Roy Wagelein of Los Angeles were seventh and Alicia Starbuck and Ken Shelley of Downey, Calif., finished 13th.

The only imperfection in the masterly skating exhibition of the Soviet gold medalists was a final jump that forced Ludmila to land on both skates instead of one.

They finished with 315.2 points and 10 ordinals to the 312.3 points and 17 ordinals of the runners-up. The Glockshuber-Danne duo had 304.4 points and 31 ordinals for the bronze medal.

The Kauffmans had one of the best performances of the night underway when Ron suddenly fell as he went into a death spiral. He slid across the ice for a moment before he could recover.

The fall apparently upset his sister, because she fell a moment later on a held butterfly seconds before the end of the performance.

February 15, 1968

# Nancy Greene of Canada Takes Giant Slalom in Winter Olympics

## SECOND CAPTURED BY MISS FAMOSE

### By FRED TUPPER
Special to The New York Times

GRENOBLE, France, Feb. 15 — Nancy Greene has taken the giant slalom in the Winter Olympic Games for Canada, just as she was supposed to do. The blue-eyed beauty from British Columbia ripped and slashed down the 1,610-meter,

63-gate Chamrousse course in 1 minute 51.97 seconds to win by an incredible 2.64 seconds from Annie Famose as France had its entire quartet in the first seven.

It was the first Alpine skiing gold medal for Canada since Ann Heggtveit took the slalom at Squaw Valley, Calif., in 1960.

It was time for Miss Greene to win this one. She has won nearly everything else. The fiery competitor rallied to take the World Cup last year from Marielle Goitschel. Her victories listed nine giant sla-

loms in all, the names reading like a tourist guide. But an injury had bogged her down before the Olympics. Was she fit, was she mentally ready?

### She Shaves Gates

Most of the names that mattered had gone down before Nancy started in ninth position. White cap jaunty over her bangs, she jumped through the timing gate and charged the course.

Every move, every thought was designed to increase speed. Quick anticipation lined her in position to shave the gates rushing at her.

The half-way time told the story. Her margin was building up. To Nancy, more effort seemed needed. She flipped her poles to gain time as she threaded the holes ahead. Her technique was flawless, control complete. She flew through the last few gates, barely wriggling her hips in disdain.

When her time lighted up the scoreboard the crowd massed deep over the slopes whistled in disbelief.

The race was hers, of course, but Marielle was still to come. Last in the favored first 15, Miss Goitschel had heavier

Associated Press

**Nancy Greene of Canada is carried by Robert Swan, left, and Bill McKay, teammates, after winning the giant slalom. At far left is Annie Famose of France, who was second. Fernande Bochatay of Switzerland holds Miss Greene's hand.**

132

weather to face. The course was breaking up a bit, ruts clearly etched in the snow. For Marielle, the time was slow.

Nancy was overjoyed, wiping away the tears, the smile wide on her freckled face. "I guess I worked harder on the course," she said. "I skated and I poled and I pushed."

**Miss Famose Is Second**

The silver medal went to Miss Famose and the bronze to tiny Fernande Bochatay of Switzerland, who nipped Florence Steurer of France by one hundredth of a second. "I sewed the starting number on my back," she said. "It made the difference."

Fifth was the downhill winner, Olga Pall of Austria, with Isabelle Mir and Marielle following for France. The 16-year-old Judy Nagel of Enumclaw, Wash., who had startled the Alpine world with the fastest heat in the slalom, was 12th as she crashed beyond the finish line.

It is two medals now for the girl they call "Tiger" from Rossland, British Columbia, six miles from the United States border. Miss Greene was second to Miss Goitschel in the slalom.

In the Alpine combination results for slalom, giant slalom and downhill, Nancy leads the French. She has 16.31 F.I.S. (Federation of International Skiing) points to 36.00 for Marielle, 36.19 for Miss Famose and 40.78 for Isabelle Mir.

Fred Anton Maier of Norway is the world record-holder in two long-distance skating events but he finds it tougher all the time to stay on top.

A couple of weeks ago his 10,000-meter mark was broken

by a teammate, Per William Guttormsen, at the European championships in Oslo. Eighteen minutes later the 29-year-old clerk from Notteroy had taken it back again.

Maier's record for the 5,000-meter event was up for grabs this morning and it didn't last long. Cornelis (Kees) Verkerk, a 25-year-old Dutchman who rides a stationary bicycle two hours daily to develop leg muscles, attacked it at once.

Bent low over his skates, one arm firmly tucked behind his orange jersey, he monotonously reeled off lap after lap in 36 seconds, a killing pace that soon made a farce out of the old Olympic mark.

As a fervent Dutch section blew horns and shook cowbells, Verkerk glided through the timers in 7:23.2, three seconds under the world mark.

The craggy-faced Norwegian was on the starting line 10 minutes later, the lap marks clear in his mind. As he wheeled around the track, the announcer called out the times.

"The same as Verkerk," he said, as lap after lap went by.

Maier was confident and picked up the pace a little. He had two seconds in hand at the fifth lap, three seconds at the half-way mark. But the strain was telling.

With the bell coming up, he had a full two seconds to spare but he couldn't summon a sprint. Flailing now, he lunged up the long stretch and across the mark in 7:22.4. His world record had come home again. He had broken the Olympic time by 16 seconds.

Petrus Nottet of the Netherlands was third, Per Willy fourth. The two countries domi-

nate long-distance skating, and train together in Norway. Even the press conference was held in Norwegian.

"I knew he'd beat me," said Verkerk.

"Maybe never again," said Maier, who is thinking of quitting.

Despite a heroic effort by Magnar Solberg, who had won the individual biathlon, Norway was licked today by the four-man Soviet relay team.

In this combination of skiing and shooting, Solberg had the best time of all but the Russians won their first Nordic medal of the games in 2:13:02.4 with more than a minute's margin. Norway took the silver, Sweden the bronze as the United States finished eighth among the 13 entries.

February 16, 1968

## LUGE EVENT ENDS AFTER THREE RUNS

**Schmid and Miss Lechner Named Singles Winners**

VILLARD DE LANS, France, Feb. 15 (UPI) — Manfred Schmid of Austria and Erica Lechner of Italy won the Olympic men's and women's luge titles today when the International Luge Federation scrapped the fourth and final heat and declared winners on the basis of three runs.

Two German riders shared the other medals in the sled events, which were curtailed

because of warm weather.

Christa Schmuck and Angelika Duenhaupt of West Germany took the silver and the bronze medal in the women's competition. the defending champion, Thomas Koehler, and Klaus Bonsack of East Germany finished two, three in the men's event.

**Two Girls Disqualified**

Miss Lechner moved from third spot to the top after three heats only because two East German girls, Ortrun Enderlein, the defending champion, and Anne Maria Mueller, were disqualified for illegally heating the metal runners of their toboggans. Angela Knoesel, in fourth position, also was disqualified.

But Miss Lechner never had to fight for her lead anymore. She won the gold medal while walking in the streets of this Alpine resort when the final heat was canceled.

There was no doubt about the shine of Schmid's gold medal. He led the favored Koehler by eighteen-hundredths of a second in the final standing.

Six teams, including the United States, had demanded that the entire East German team be barred from further competition for cheating. This was turned down by the Federation Internationale de Luge because none of the six teams could prove that East German officials had a part in the heating.

Officials said they hoped to go through with the men's doubles before the closing ceremonies Sunday.

February 16, 1968

# Verkerk Wins Olympic Speed Skating; Schwarz Takes Figure Title

## DUTCH STAR SETS 1,500-METER MARK

**Verkerk Timed in 2:03.4 — Wood of U.S. Is Second in Figures—Norway Wins**

**By FRED TUPPER**
Special to The New York Times

GRENOBLE, France, Feb. 16 —Kees Verkerk, who held a world record in the 5,000 meters for just 20 minutes yesterday, broke his own today as he captured the Olympic 1,500-meter speed-skating event.

The 25-year-old bartender

from Puttershoek—short, dark, and compact—flailed through the finish in 2 minutes 3.4 seconds, half a second under his world mark, as the supposedly phlegmatic Dutch did everything but tear up the seats in their frenzy. Nineteen men, including Dick Wurster of Schenectady, N. Y., cracked the old Olympic record of 2:08.6.

Tim Wood of the United States took the silver medal, but it was Wolfgang Schwarz, the perennial runner-up, who became the new Olympic figure-skating champion.

Schwarz's lead in the compulsory figures, which count 60 per cent, and a second in the free-skating behind a fellow Austrian, Emmerich Danzer—the man who always beat him before—enabled him to whip Wood narrowly at count-

ing time tonight.

Schwarz scored 1,904.1 points and 13.0 ordinals, while the pencil-thin Wood, from Bloomfield Hills, Mich., had 1,891.6 points and 17 ordinals. Patrick Pera of France was third.

Danzer, twice world and four times European champion, was fourth, with Gary Visconti of Detroit fifth and John Petkevich of Minneapolis sixth.

It was desperately close at the finish. For a time Wood thought he had won. An American figure skater, Tina Noyes, brought him the news.

"Tough luck," she said. "Saw it on the I.B.M. standings on TV."

A vote for Wood by the Canadian judge would have meant the difference.

"My program was strong," said Wood, "but not superb."

A triple salchow brought the house down. (A triple salchow

is a jump in which the skater takes off from the back inside edge of the skating foot, turns three times laterally and lands on the back outside edge of the original foot).

"Schwarz was great," said Tim.

Babben Enger Damon, wife of a Vermonter, snatched a second leg lead back from a Soviet skier as Norway won its first Olympic 15-kilometer cross-country relay from Sweden and the Soviet Union to top all teams with five gold medals in the fading days of these Winter Olympic Games.

That old daredevil, Eugenio (Red) Monti of Italy rode the high wall for the fastest time in the four-man bobsled race, with the second and final heat coming up tomorrow. The two United States teams were not in the first 10.

Jean-Claude Killy got the

break he wanted in his quest for the triple crown of Alpine skiing. Fog canceled the qualification races the French superman thought unnecessary for starting positions as he rates in the top 15 on merit in the special slalom tomorrow, with Billy Kidd of Stowe, Vt., is one of his chief contenders.

The hockey world is in an uproar. With the Soviet Union's defeat in world and Olympic competition for the first time since 1963 by Czechoslovakia, the gold medal rests on the final games tomorrow between Canada and the Soviet Union and between Czechoslovakia and Sweden. The first three are tied with five victories and a loss. The combinations to work out the victor are numerous, but if the Canadians win, they have the gold medal regardless.

The Norwegians started faster but the Dutch finished stronger in the classic 1,500-meter speed race. Ard Schenk, a 23-year-old physical therapy.

student, set the pattern early on ice shiny with rain. Striking out powerfully he was through the timing stages in 26, 58 and 91 seconds and came home in 2:05 to better the Olympic mark by more than three seconds.

Verkerk was on the starting mark, out of his crouch and sprinting to the turn. Into the slide now, bent low, one arm riveted behind his orange jersey, Kees had the same time at halfway. With horns and bells imploring him on, he hit the bell lap in 90 flat and held his form down the stretch to clock his 2:03.4 world-record time.

The Dutch rooters went berserk. They marched up and down carrying banners inscribed "Heya Keesie." They yelled and pounded one another in deafening din. Arms linked, swaying, they even sang the words of "Daisy Bell," more familiarly known as "A Bicycle Built For Two," perhaps be-

cause two hours a day on an anchored cycle has built up Verkerk's strength.

The race was by no means over. The three Norwegians were to come and the main threat was Magne Thomassen. Thomassen had tied for second with Terry McDermott of the United States in the 500 meters and two weeks ago had set a 2:02.5 world mark at Davos that is up for ratification.

The Norwegian was a second faster at halftime and even with Verkerk at the bell but the pace had been killing and he faded to 2:05.1. Bjoern Tveter had 2:05.2 and Ivar Eriksen, struggling, was timed in 2:05 and shared second place with Schenk.

There was a sentimental cheer for Ants Antson, the Russian who had beaten Verkerk for the gold at Innsbruck. Today he was 12th. Wurster was 19th.

Norway has been the star of these games but its gold in the women's cross-country

came as a surprise. The Soviet Union had won at Innsbruck and had taken the world championships in 1966 at Oslo.

Except for those last few seconds two kilometers out on the second lap, when Rita Achkina headed Babben Damon, it was Norway all the way. Inger Aufles handed Mrs. Damon a big lead but her greatest danger was Toini Gustafsson, a 29-year-old Finnish-born competitor who had taken golds here for Sweden in both Nordic races.

Toini had the fastest lap, moving Sweden to second place, but Barbro Martinsson, an Oslo policewoman, found the answer on the final leg. She ordered herself off the track to the outside, where the snow was faster.

"It's easier to make turns on the track," she said, "but I took the risk. I am strong in the arms, you see."

February 17, 1968

# KILLY GAINS OLYMPIC TRIPLE

## VICTOR IN SLALOM

### Frenchman Is Placed First After 2 Rivals Are Disqualified

**By FRED TUPPER**
Special to The New York Times

GRENOBLE, France, Feb. 17 —Jean-Claude Killy won the triple crown of Alpine skiing at the Winter Olympics today, but it took a jury's decision to make it official.

In the slalom race the idol of France, who had previously won the downhill and giant slalom, plunged through 131 gates on the 1,040-meter course in dense, icy fog for a two-heat time of 99.75 seconds.

He had the fastest time in the first heat, from which he had started in the 15th position.

In the second he was the first man down. Now all he could do was wait. It was agonizing.

Haakon Mjoen of Norway had better times, but was disqualified for having missed gates. The other men who might have beaten Killy had come and gone, and the thousands of fans peering through the mists were waiting for the seasoned Karl Schranz of Austria. He could be the danger.

Schranz had been third in the first heat. A spectator inter-

fered on his second run and Schranz pulled off the course. He sidestepped back to the top and was given permission to go again.

This time he was spectacular, darting and swiveling through the flags with such controlled abandon that his two-heat time was 99.22.

That should have been it. The Austrian had won. But had he?

He was reported for missing a gate before the interference by the spectator. If so he would automatically be disqualified, and that was the way the jury ruled in the end. The bulletin was flashed two hours after the race.

So Killy, the darkly handsome customs officer from Val D'Isere, has brought all those magazine covers back to life. He has won the triple, a memorable feat achieved only by Toni Sailer of Austria in 1956 at Cortina.

The Austrians, who were still protesting the decision, got the silver and bronze medals, anyway. Hubert Huber was timed in 9.82 and the youngster, Alfred Matt, in 100.09.

From an almost impossible starting position in the second 15, Spider Sabich of Kyburz, Calif., finished fifth. Jim Heuga of Squaw Valley, Calif., was seventh and Rick Chaffee of Rutland, Vt., ninth.

At the Games in Innsbruck four years ago, Billy Kidd of Stowe, Vt., and Heuga were second and third, respectively, as the United States took four medals in Alpine skiing. This time it won none. Kidd caught a ski tip and crashed today on the first run.

There were other heroes. That wonderful redhead, Eugenio Monti, had done it again. The 40-year-old ski-lift operator from Cortina, a miracle of

plastic surgery after his years of derring-do, piloted his way smoothly down the twisting over the 1,600-meter ice chute to give the Italian four-man

Associated Press

**Jean-Claude Killy swings through a gate during the men's slalom. He finished third, but was awarded gold medal when the leaders were disqualified for missing gates.**

bobsled team a victory in the two-heat time of 2:17.39, nine-hundredths of a second faster than Ervin Thaler and the Austrian sled.

The Swiss, driven by Jean Wicki, were third, with a course record in the second heat.

The accolade was expected. Monti is loved by the men who ride sleds.

"The best bobber there is," said Thaler. "If we must lose, we're glad it's to Monti."

"I came here to learn from the master," said Boris Said of Fair Haven, Vt., pilot of the American sled that came in 10th.

"My men did it," said Monti, pointing to Roberto Zardonella, Mario Armand and the brakeman, Luciano de Paoles.

"We're going to do it tonight," said Armand. "After all these weeks of no wine, there will be rivers of Chianti flowing."

And so the old redhead now retires. He had two bronze medals at Innsbruck, two silvers at Cortina and now, with his first in the two-man sled here, the two golds he had always longed for. In between he has won nine world championships.

Norway, the medal leader, had its sixth gold one as Ole Ellefsaeter won the 50-kilometer cross-country, the most grueling race in all sport.

A tree-chopper from Nybygda, Ole panted and poled over those 30-odd miles and was still running on his skis at the end, long after the field had disappeared behind him.

Down that last right turn out of the pine trees he came, legs of steel pistoning for the gate. He was through in 2:28:45.8, the leader from the 15-kilometer post onward.

"My skis were soaked," said Ole. "The wax was torn off in the last few kilometers and it was slow going."

Viatches Vendenine had been gaining rapidly. Tenth halfway and third at 40 kilometers, the Russian had faster wax but lost time passing the also-rans and was 17 seconds behind at the end.

Josef Haas of Switzerland won the bronze medal for third, and Mike Gallagher of Killington, Vt., finished 22d.

An icy wind was blowing down from the peaks and across the speed-skating rink this morning. The world record-holder, Fred Anton Maier of Norway, was reputedly the man to beat in the 10,000-meter race. He started first, wheeling steadily around in the cold, with a schedule to meet of 37 seconds per lap. He came home flying in 15:25.9, the Olympic and his own world marks shattered.

Surprisingly, it wasn't good enough. The other great names attacked it and failed, but Johnny Hoeglin of Sweden had picked up a second on Maier's

time along the way, when the gusts died down, and still had that margin at the bell lap. And he beat Maier with 15:23.6.

"I was hoping for fifth," he said. "I've never been under 15:40 in my life." Hoeglin was not well enough to compete in the European championships two weeks ago.

Third was Oerjan Sandler, also of Sweden, as the Dutch, for once, did not get a medal. Bill Lanigan of the Bronx, New York, was 21st, exactly tying the old Olympic mark of 16:50.1.

With only one more event, the 90-meter ski jump, scheduled for the final day tomorrow, Norway has won the Games. Her six gold medals cannot be matched by any other country, and in Olympic competition only first places count.

February 18, 1968

# SOVIET HOCKEY VICTOR

## CANADA BOWS, 5-0, IN DECIDING GAME

---

### Russians Take Gold Medal —U.S. Six Ties Finns, 1-1, and Finishes 6th

---

**By MICHAEL STRAUSS**
Special to The New York Times

GRENOBLE, France, Feb. 17 —The winner is still champion, for the sixth straight year.

A scrappy, fast Soviet Union sextet kept the world amateur ice-hockey crown and won an Olympic gold medal tonight by

beating Canada, 5-0, in a one-sided contest.

The game, the final Olympic event in the Ice Stadium, drew an enthusiastic standing-room crowd of 13,000. Tomorrow the final ceremonies of the Winter Games will be held under the same roof.

Earlier Czechoslovakia blew its chance to dethrone the red-shirted Russians by playing a 2-2 tie with Sweden. A victory would have given the Czechs the title regardless of the Soviet-Canada finale.

The Canadians put up a stubborn fight for one and a half periods, then started wilting. The Russians, after having scored a goal in each of the first two periods, broke the game open in the final session with a three-goal burst.

Before tonight's action the Soviet Union, Canada and Czechoslovakia were tied for first with five victories and one loss apiece. But in the technical standing the Russians were in trouble because they had been beaten by the Czechs.

Then, with the Czechs out of the way as a result of their tie, the Russians took up their task quickly. They scored the first goal shortly after the halfway mark in the opening session, although outnumbered on the ice by one man. The tally was made by Anatoli Firsov, who also got the final goal.

#### Shoot from up Close

All the goals were scored from up close, after the Russians had worked the puck in. That's the usual Soviet technique.

In contrast the Canadians did

most of their attacking from outside. In the second period they put the pressure on the champions, storming the net repeatedly.

But Viktor Konovalenko, the Soviet goalie, was invincible. He stopped shots sent at him from all directions, using his stick, skates and gloves.

The Canadians made their peak effort in the second period, during which the action became so wild that seven sticks were broken within four minutes.

As for the United States, it was held to a 1-1 tie by Finland in the battle for fifth place. By finishing sixth, the Americans posted their poorest record in Olympic hockey—two victories, four defeats and a tie.

The second-place silver medal went to the Czechs and the Canadians won the bronze.

February 18, 1968

Associated Press
**OUTNUMBERED:** Russia's Eugeny Michalov, dark jersey, was heading for Canadian goal, right, but he couldn't maneuver past Ken Broderick, Canadian goalie, and two defenders.

# *Beloussov Wins 90-Meter Ski Jump*

Soviet Union's Vladimir Beloussov in mid-flight during the 90-meter jumping event at Olympics. He won gold medal.

Associated Press

## EAST GERMAN PAIR TAKE LUGE EVENT

### Victory of Beloussov Gives Soviet Union Its First Gold Medal in Jumping

#### By FRED TUPPER
Special to The New York Times

GRENOBLE, France, Feb. 18 —Black-haired Vladimir Beloussov won the 90-meter ski jump for the Soviet Union today in the final event of the 10th Winter Olympic Games. The 21-year-old locksmith roared down the chute, hung suspended briefly in space and landed with hands raised high over his head.

Beloussov knew he had won. He leaped into the air with his skis, kicked them off and leaped again. The Russian had 231.3 points on jumps of 101.5 and 98.5 meters (333 and 323 feet) to beat Jiri Raska, a locksmith from Czechoslovakia, whose point total was 229.4 with jumps of 101 and 98 meters. The bronze medal went to Lars Grini of Norway with 214.3 points.

It was the Soviet Union's first gold medal in ski jumping and Beloussov's first international competition. A few years ago, the Russians were ready to hurl themselves into the back of beyond at the risk of disaster. Beloussov's form to-day was flawless.

Earlier, Thomas Koehler and Klaus Bonsack of East Germany, the world champions, had taken the luge (two-man toboggan) event with a combined time of 1:35.85., with Austria second and West Germany third.

The star of the 10th Olympic games was Jean-Claude Killy. The best skier of his time, aggressive, swashbuckling and good-looking, the 24-year-old idol of France, bagged the triple crown of Alpine skiing. He won the downhill, the giant slalom and finally, the special slalom, on a jury decision that disqualified the Austrian Karl Schranz, for missing a couple of gates.

#### France Hails Killy's Feat

When that momentous news was flashed, girls sighed, headlines screamed and people all over France hugged and kissed each other in delight, Killy had achieved what was once thought to have been impossible, and the man who had said so was Toni Sailer of Austria, who at Cortina 12 years earlier was the only one who had done it before.

Then raven-haired Peggy Fleming, featherlight on her silver skates, capped a marvelous score in the compulsory figures with a free-skating routine of such inspiration and grace that the score for artistic impression that flashed on the scoreboard was a solid row of 5.9's. She had won everything, this fragile 19-year-old miss from Colorado Springs, the national and world championships and, in this moment of triumph, the gold medal that was the highest accolade of all.

To the sentimentalists the victories of 40-year-old Eugenio Monti of Italy in the two-man and four-man bobsled events will be memorable. The old red-head said he had "speed not blood" in his veins. His face, a miracle of plastic surgery, Monti, who once shattered the tendons in both legs, hurtled his sled down the dangerous ice chutes for two gold medals, and the men who applauded most were those he raced against.

#### Her Prince Charming

Toni Gustafsson won three medals, two gold in the cross-country, and a silver for her fastest lap in the Nordic relay that put Sweden ahead of Finland and Russia. The blond 29-year-old gym teacher had other thrills she prized as much—a bouquet of roses and a kiss from Prince Bertil.

Those leathery tough athletes from Norway were the revelation of the games. In the long-distance Nordic and skating events, where preparation pays, Norway won six gold medals and six silver. Over the years they have dominated the Winter Olympics, explainable perhaps by Magnar Solberg, who won the biathlon by hitting the bullseye with every shot, a feat he had never performed before.

"I have the fighting spirit," he said. "It's a national characteristic."

And from Italy came Franco Nones to surprise the Nordic nations by winning the 30-kilometer cross-country, once considered the exclusive property of the Scandinavian countries.

The Soviet Union is faltering. In the three previous

games the nation had won 25 golds, including a whopping 11 at Innsbruck, Austria. Her seasoned performers appear to have passed their peak. Lydia Skoblikova had previously won four golds in speed skating, this time she got none. Eugeny Grishin had won four golds at Cortina and Squaw Valley, a silver behind Terry McDermott in Innsbruck. Now at 38, he had a bronze medal within his grasp in the 500-meter race until that last electric moment when McDermott, heavier now, had flashed around the soggy track to tie for second place and win a silver medal.

#### Soviet Wins 5 Gold Medals

In the current Olympics the Soviet Union has taken five golds, including the hockey medal last night after being beaten earlier in the games by Czechoslovakia, her first loss in world or Olympic hockey competition since 1963.

How did the United States fare? By any estimate, just so so. At Innsbruck the United States had a gold by McDermott; a silver and bronze by Jean Saubert in women's Alpine skiing; a silver by Billy Kidd and a bronze by Jimmy Heuga in the men's Alpine; and a bronze by Scott Allen in the men's figure skating. There were rumblings then about the paucity of medals and promises of better facilities and intensified training.

What has materialized?

This time the United States has taken seven medals instead of six, primarily by a timing fluke. And all of them are in skating events. Miss Fleming had her gold and young Tim

Wood a silver in the free skating. McDermott had his silver and 16-year-old Dianne Holum a bronze in speed skating and then there was a shower of three silver medals in the 500-meter race as Dianne, Jenny Fish and Mary Margaret Meyers tied for second.

The Alpine team was out of the medal category, mainly because of wretched luck. Robin Morning broke her leg before the games began. James Barrow broke a hip, and Jere Elliott sustained two sprained ankles and a shoulder injury. Kidd, the best skier, bruised his ankle and finished fifth in the giant slalom after taking the fastest heat, and then fell in the slalom yesterday. Sixteen-year-old Judy Nagel fell, too, after posting the fastest heat in the women's slalom with three other American girls disqualified for missing gates. Spider Sabich had a fifth in Killy's disputed slalom yesterday.

In the other events, the United States was unimpressive.

February 19, 1968

## Winter Olympics End in Controversy Over Killy's Medal

By The Associated Press

GRENOBLE, France, Feb. 18 —The Olympic flame was snuffed out today in a spangled spectacle of booming cannons and parachuted roses, but the controversy over the outstanding performance of the Winter Games increased in intensity.

A crowd of 12,000 here and millions on television watched the athletes from 37 nations parade from the stadium as sirens sounded. However, the final ceremony failed to detract attention from the question raised in yesterday's triumph by Jean-Claude Killy:

Was the Austrian, Karl Schranz, deprived of first place in the men's special slalom so the French hero, Killy, could complete his coveted "grand slam" of skiing?

"It was an unjust decision," the Austrian said today in a hastily called news conference at the Centre de Presse.

His accusation touched off an international dispute that led to British intervention and a variety of name-dropping: e.g., President de Gaulle, Avery Brundage, the Olympic Committee president, and even the Common Market.

French and Austrian journalists screamed at one another. The British berated a French press officer, and the officer hit back with the comment:

"General de Gaulle kept you British out of the Common Mar-

ket and you can get out of here as well. I am de Gaulle."

Once the two interpreters, English and German, walked out in a huff on a French charge they were butchering the interpretation of the questions and answers. They had to be begged to come back.

Charges and countercharges were hurled across the floor, but the major questions were left unanswered:

Who was the mysterious man in black who strode across Schranz's trail on the vital second run at Chamrousse Saturday?

Why wasn't Schranz permitted to take his case to the jury?

Was the controversy really set off by commercial pressure —as the French charged?

"It makes us think that Mr. Brundage is correct in his stand that Alpine skiing is saturated with commercialism," a Frenchman said.

The news conference was called by Frank Kneissl, an Austrian ski manufacturer. He said Schranz worked for him.

The French said Kneissl had no right to call a news conference because he wasn't an official of the Austrian team. Kneissl said anybody could call a news conference, if somebody wanted to listen.

Two members of Austria's ski administration were there to back Schranz—Dr. Karl-Heinz Klee, president of the Austrian Ski Federation, and Prof. Franz Hoppichler, team manager.

Klee said they had no hope of having the gold medal taken from Killy, but the Federation Internationale de Ski could award Schranz the world championship.

The controversy began yesterday after Killy had made his two runs in the slalom, in 1 minute 39.73 seconds.

Norway's Haakon Mjoen was clocked half a second faster, but was disqualified—without dispute — for having taken a short cut on the second run.

Schranz, given a second chance on the second run because he said a spectator had stepped in his path, was clocked in a brilliant 1:39.23, enough to make him the winner. He was first declared unofficial winner. Later Killy was named the unofficial winner. The Austrians protested.

The jury ruled that Schranz had missed two gates before the spectator crossed his path, so actually he was disqualified before the interference.

Schranz insisted his run "was interfered with."

"It was a man in black overalls," he said. "He was on skis. He was slow and sluggish. He stood for some time."

He said the distance was very narrow between the 19th gate, the second he was charged with missing, and the 22d, where the spectator crossed his path.

Schranz said an East German, a Russian and a Yugoslav, who witnessed the incident, appeared before the jury

to confirm that he had been distracted.

"Do you consider it sport to obtain a medal through protest?" someone asked the Austrian.

Schranz replied: "Do you think it right to lose a medal through interference?"

February 19, 1968

TAKES WORLD TITLE: Peggy Fleming of Colorado Springs, who won women's world figure skating championship for the third time.

## SKATE TITLE WON BY MISS FLEMING

### Colorado Girl Announces Retirement After Taking 3d World Crown in Row

By THOMAS J. HAMILTON
Special to The New York Times

GENEVA, March 2 — Peggy Fleming won her third world figure skating title tonight with a superb performance, then announced her retirement from competitive skating to devote full time to her college studies.

Already the holder of the Olympic and American titles, the 19-year-old Colorado Springs girl took her third straight world championship with elegant command of the intricate jumps in her free skating program.

Seasoned skating enthusiasts said that her two rivals, Gabriele Seyfert of East Germany, who came in second, and Hana Maskova of Czechoslovakia, who finished third, had never skated better.

However, Miss Fleming, surpassing her performance at Grenoble, was the unanimous choice of the nine judges for first place with 9 ordinals and 2,269.7 points. Miss Seyfert had 19 ordinals and 2,179.8 points. Miss Maskova, who finished third, had 29 ordinals and 2,121.5 points.

The results thus reproduced the figure skating standings in the Olympics.

After receiving the title, Miss Fleming disclosed at a news conference that she would not defend it when the world championships were held in Colorado Springs, her home town, next year. Miss Fleming explained that she had a scholarship at Colorado College and wanted to prepare herself for a career as an elementary school teacher. She also said that she might get married. And it is understood that she has a boy friend in Texas. She said she had not considered the question of turning professional as "yet."

The Colorado Springs freshman went on the ice tonight with such a commanding lead in the compulsory figures, which count 60 per cent, that some of her advisers counseled her to delete one or two of the most difficult jumps from her program.

They warned her that a couple of falls could still prevent her from making a clean sweep of the titles open to her this year, whereas — as one Swiss correspondent wrote—she could take the title if she did her free skating "knitting in a chair."

However, as Carlos Rossi, Miss Fleming's trainer, told the story, Miss Seyfert and Miss Maskova, who skated just ahead of her, had done so well that a play-safe strategy might have ended with one of them taking the free-skating event, though Miss Fleming won the championship.

According to Rossi, Miss Fleming said that she did not want the championship if that was the way she had to win it, and decided to go ahead with her full program.

During her warming-up period Miss Fleming had appeared rather nervous, but after she had made her opening bow to the judges she was again her self-possessed and imperturbable self.

With Tschaikowsky's "Sixth Symphony" as her accompaniment, she embarked upon an impeccable rendering of the double axle, the spread, the split jump and the double flip.

She was wearing a salmon-pink costume, with white daisies appliqued on the bodice.

Some in the audience thought

that grace and precision would have established an equally high position for her in ballet.

Everything went exactly as she had planned it. And the audience roared its applause when she gave the traditional farewell salute to the judges with a fly split spin, followed by a fast spin, which was too fast to count the number of times she spun round.

On technique, Miss Fleming rated 5.9 of a possible 6 points from all the judges except two, who gave her 5.8. On artistry it was 5.9 again, except for two judges who assigned her the coveted 6 as the crowd cheered its approval.

The world championships produced exactly the same winners as the two preceding world championships and Miss Fleming has also won the United States championship five times and the North American championship once.

As to the possibility of her turning professional, Miss Fleming said she would do it "at the right time."

The champion's mother, Mrs. Doris Fleming, said later that Miss Fleming almost retired from competition after her father, a newspaper pressman, died two years ago.

### Money Is a Factor

Mrs. Flemming said she had three other children to bring up and indicated that the financial strain was a factor—she said she had made all of her daughter's skating costumes, including the one she had worn tonight.

In addition, Mrs. Fleming said, the Colorado college authorities had informed her daughter that she would have to attend regularly to retain her scholarship. Miss Fleming missed the spring and winter terms to compete in the Olympic skating championships and to take part in an impending tour of the Soviet Union and other European countries by leading skaters.

Miss Fleming, who led Miss Seyfert by 9 ordinals and 1,209.7 points to 20 ordinals and 1,134.8 points at the end of the compulsory figures, beat her East German rival on the over-all score by 90 points, the same margin as she gained in her victory in the Olympics.

Miss Seyfert said she was "happy to be second," but that she did not think Miss Fleming deserved the two 6-point scores tonight for artistry.

"In her skating expression she is very good," Miss Seyfert said, "but technically I think I am as good as she is."

Miss Maskova, in a white lace costume that emphasized her dark hair, won her third place with a fine display tonight, which enabled her to overcome the considerable lead Beatrix Schuba of Austria had piled up against her in the compulsory figures. Miss Schuba took fourth place.

Albertina Noyes, 19, of Arlington, Mass., was sixth and

the youngest American entrant, Janet Lynn, 14, of Rockford, Ill., achieved a remarkable eighth-place finish.

Indeed there are some experts who see her as another world's champion by the time she reaches Miss Fleming's age.

### Champagne Comes Early

When she left the ice after her title-winning appearance, a smile was on Miss Fleming's lips, and she said she was heading for a champagne party. The champagne came sooner than scheduled, brought to her dressing room by Emmerich Danzer, the Austrian winner of the men's figure skating, who also gave her a congratulatory kiss.

The others who were awarded titles during the championships were: the husband-and-wife pair of Oleg Protopopov and Ludmila Belousova of the Soviet Union in the pairs, and Bernard Ford and Diane Towler of Britain in the ice-dancing. Tim Wood, an American, had come in second to Danzer last night in the men's figure skating.

Wood said today that he did not believe his mishap during a difficult jump, the triple shaltow—he had to put his hand on the ice to steady himself when he landed—had had anything to do with his defeat.

March 3, 1968

# WOOD CAPTURES TITLE IN SKATING

### World Crown Returns to U.S. First Time in 10 Years

COLORADO SPRINGS, Colo., Feb. 28 (AP)—Tim Wood of Detroit gave a dynamic exhibition in free skating tonight and brought the world men's figure skating championship back to the United States for the first time in 10 years.

The 20-year-old prelaw student from John Carroll University, a silver medalist in the 1968 Winter Olympics, skated with such verve and daring that he piled up a more than 100-point lead over Ondrej Netla of Czechoslovakia, the European champion.

For the first time in the event, judges gave the American star a three scores of 6, designating perfection. For technical merit, he received eight scores of 5.9 and one of 5.8 from a Canadian judge which drew loud boos from the gallery.

Scored on artistic impression, the slender dark-haired Detroiter received three perfect scores and five of 5.9.

The final placing was delayed since there were four more contending skaters to perform, but none within reach of the new champion. These included John Misha Petkevich of Great Falls,

United Press International

**Gabriele Seyfert of East Germany competing in women's world figure-skating championship Thursday night. The tourney took place at Broadmoor Arena, Colorado Springs.**

Mont., East Germany's Gunther Zoller, Patrick Pera of France and Jay Humphrey of Canada.

Three former champions — the only ones America has had in the 46 years of the championship—were in the crowd of 5,000 at the Broadmoor arena to watch the sensational young Wood bring the title home.

They were Dick Button, who won five titles between 1948 and 1952; Hayes Alan Jenkins, who captured four between 1953 and 1956, and his brother, David, winner of three from 1957 through 1959.

Wood gave a dramatic performance, skating flashily to the music of Pagliacci and Tchaikowsky. He swept across the ice, pirouetting, doing double axels, split lutzes, triple salchows and triple loops.

The three-man American team all skated brilliantly. Game little Gary Visconti, 23, possibly making his swan song in world competition, also put on a stirring show, marked by bouncy music, triple salchows and three double axels. He had two new jump combinations in his program.

Haig Oundjian of Great Britain, first skater on the evening's program, collapsed midway

through his program and had to be carried to the dressing room. A doctor later said he had fully recovered.

Petkevich, a Harvard University student and one of the flashiest free skaters in the world, highlighted his program with a triple salchow, which brought loud cheers from the crowd. However, he started the evening in seventh place from school figures.

March 1, 1969

## Schranz Triumphs For World Ski Cup

### By MICHAEL STRAUSS
Special to The New York Times

BEAUPRE, Quebec, March 15—Karl Schranz, Austria's old man of the mountain, who keeps improving with age, capped a colorful career today by clinching the World Cup skiing crown.

The 30-year-old star from the high Arlberg village of St. Anton, put the finishing touches to his fantastic winter campaign by winning the two-run du Maurier Cup international giant slalom, which was concluded this afternoon. Dumeng Giovanoli of Switzerland was second in the event.

Schranz, who gained a substantial edge yesterday in the opening round with a time of 1 minute 41.4 seconds, sped down a 5,500-foot layout that dropped 1,590 feet in the third fastest time today of 1:47.87. His total of 3:29.27 gave him a 1.61-second edge over Giovanoli.

"I could have raced faster," said Schranz, the owner of a plush Alpine hotel. "But with the big lead I held yesterday, I asked myself: 'Why hurry?' And, I didn't."

The victory, worth 14 points in the complicated World Cup scoring system, sent Schranz's total soaring to 177. The only people who can catch up with him now are possibly the custom officials when he brings home his hard-earned silver trophies after next week's final races at Waterville (N.H.) Valley.

### Kiki Cutter Triumphs

Earlier in the day, Kiki Cutter, the little brunette with the big racing heart, brought victory to the United States with a blazing-second run that enabled her to take the two-run du Maurier World Cup special slalom event, along with combined honors for the two days of competition.

The 19-year-old skier from Bend, Ore., won in a squeaker. She was separated from Ingrid Lafforgue of France by the smallest possible margin in Alpine ski racing—one-hundredth of a second. Florence Steurer also of France, was third, followed by blond-haired Barbara Cochran of Richmond, Vt.

Both triumphs were witnessed by a few thousand spectators who hiked more than a mile up the sunny slopes of the modest-sized 2,625-foot high Mont-Ste. Anne, which overlooks the ice-locked St. Lawrence River. In an enthusiastic demonstration of nonpartisanship, they applauded the two winners.

The fastest plunge in the men's event today was posted by the rapidly improving Henri Duvillard of France. The 20-year-old younger brother of Adrien, a former Olympian, tore over surfaces made firmer by

the use of "snow cement" in 1:47.59.

But Duvillard, who had a clocking of only 1:44.34 yesterday, which berthed him in 13th place, was no threat to Schranz. The Frenchman from Megeve wound up sixth with a time that was 2.64 seconds slower than the total registered by the Austrian ace.

Giovonali, who was 12th in World Cup competition (54 points), posted the afternoon's second fastest time of 1:47.83 to total 3:30.88. Jakob Tischauser, also of Switzerland, placed third in the final order, with Heini Messner of Austria fourth, and the surprising Claudio Detassis of Italy fifth.

Reinhard Tritscher, second in the World Cup standings with 108 points, wound up eighth.

In taking the women's event, Miss Cutter, who weighs 100 pounds, ended a victory drought. Her previous triumph had been scored in a giant slalom at Oberstaufen, Germany, in early January. She had been unable to click in subsequent appearances in Switzerland, Austria, Italy, Czechoslovakia and California.

Today, however, she was not to be denied. Berthed sixth after the first round with a clocking of 36.02, she snaked through a 43-gate course that

dropped 550 feet in 33.78 to post a time of 1:09.8. Her whirlwind finale was the fastest of the round.

"I decided to try and take it all," she said after her second run? "I know I had an outside chance. I also knew I had to go all-out if I hoped to win. So, I went all-out.

For Miss Lafforgue, who put together trips of 35.94 and 33.87, the day was doubly frustrating. Apart from losing by the smallest possible ski-racing fraction, the blonde from the Luchon Mountain country of France saw her chance to overtake Gertrud Gabl of France in the World Cup race vanish.

This disappointment came on the heels of another major one yesterday in which the French star was disqualified from second place in the giant slalom for allegedly missing a gate. The French coaching staff, in its protest, presented a strong case in Miss Lafforgue's behalf before the jury, but to no avail.

As a result, only Wiltrud Drexel of Austria (107 points) and the astonishing teen-age Michele Jacot (92 points) remained in the running to catch Miss Gabl (131 points) for the World Cup crown. Miss Gabl fell today after leading at the end of the first run.

March 16, 1969

# Kidd, in Last Race as an Amateur, Captures Alpine Combined World Title

## FRANCE'S RUSSEL FINISHES SECOND

### U.S. Scores First Combined Victory on Kidd's Tie for 5th Place in Downhill

VAL GARDENA, Italy, Feb. 15 (AP)—Billy Kidd, in his last race as an amateur, gave the United States its first Alpine combined gold medal today by finishing tied for fifth place in the downhill. Bernhard Russi of Switzerland was the surprise winner in the final event of the world ski championships.

Wearing a back corset, Kidd, of Stowe, Vt., totaled 21.25 points in the combined standings to beat Patrick Russel of France, who had 50.15 points.

Kidd, the ace of the United States men's squad, entered the final race as one of the favorites for the combined title after placing 15th in the giant slalom and third in the special slalom earlier in the week.

He thus capped the best American showing since the Inns-

United Press International
**ELATION: Billy Kidd after his skiing victory in Italy.**

bruck Olympics in 1964 as the Americans captured four medals, two of them by Kidd.

Kidd's time through the 26 gates of the 3,750-meter track was 2 minutes 25.52 seconds, less than a second behind Russi's 2:24.57.

Immediately after his victory, Kidd announced he was dropping out of amateur skiing.

"I don't know yet whether I'll turn pro or go to work," he said. "Everyone knows, though, that I have been considering this decision for quite a while now, and it is only natural, as I am 26 and I have chronic back trouble.

"I had to race in the men's downhill today with a corset. It did not bother me too much, but it has edged me out of amateur racing. I just needed another medal today to quit on the winning side."

### Pyles of U.S. Finishes 11th

The other American finishers were Rudd Pyles of Frisco, Colo., who placed 11th in 2:27.13; Bobby Cochran of Richmond, Vt., who was 26th in 2:29.9, and Mike Lafferty of Eugene, Ore., who was 31st in 2:30.58.

Russi, a 21-year-old industrial designer, flashed down a heavy track for his nation's second gold medal, exploiting his 15th starting number and waxing mistakes made by the world's top aces, including Kidd.

Russi's best finish this season had been fourth in the Kandahar downhill two weeks ago.

The steadily hardening snow that fell overnight prompted numerous surprises. Favorites, such as Karl Schranz of Austria, Henri Duvillard of France, Jean Daniel Daetwyler of Switzerland and Heini Messner of Austria, finished far back.

Late-starting unknowns fared much better as Karl Cordin of Austria took second in 2:24.79 and Malcolm Milne took third in 2:25.09 for Australia's first medal in the world championships.

Schranz was clocked in 2:25.46 and Kidd tied with Marcello Varallo of Italy.

Schranz retained his World Cup lead with 142 points as Russel, tied for second with Gustav Thoeni of Italy at 140 points, placed a dismal 43d.

February 16, 1970

# Janet Lynn Captures Women's Senior Figure Skating Title for 3d Year in Row

## MISS HOLMES WINS RUNNER-UP HONORS

Special to The New York Times

BUFFALO, Jan. 30—Janet Lynn, a 17-year-old high school girl from Rockford, Ill., shook off a fall earlier in her free-skating program today and won the United States senior women's figure skating championship for the third straight time. Miss Lynn, skating last in a field of 12, delighted the crowd of 6,000 in War Memorial Auditorium with her performance.

The petite blonde from the Wagon Wheel Figure Skating Club, skating in a purple outfit, fell while attempting a triple toe loop, her second jump in the four-minute program. However, Miss Lynn continued and won marks of 5.6 to 5.9 from the seven judges.

"I would have liked to have done it. I've been doing it in practice all the time. However, I just got up and forgot about it and continued to skate," the champion said after the competition. "For some reason I didn't feel up to it. Maybe I didn't have enough faith in myself at the beginning."

### 6 First-Place Votes Won

Trailing Julie Holmes of Tulsa. Okla., following the compulsory school figures, Miss Lynn captured the over-all first-place votes of six of the seven judges. Miss Lynn thus retained the title she first won in Seattle two years ago and retained last year in Tulsa. Each time Miss Holmes was the runner-up as she was today.

Miss Holmes, with a bright green headband matching her skating outfit, lost her balance on a double Lutz jump to ruin an otherwise good program.

Moving up to third place and gaining a spot on the world team was Suna Murray of South Orange, N. J. She earned the only standing ovation for her free skating. Her exhibition, second only in scores to Miss Lynn, helped her to advance from fourth place after the school figures.

In an early afternoon event, David Santee of Park Ridge, Ill., won the junior men's championship. Mahlon Bradley of Boston was second.

In the compulsory round of the gold dance which was completed this afternoon, three time champions Judy Schwomeyer of Indianapolis, and Jim Sladky of Syracuse, N. Y., were far ahead. The pair, who was the runner-up in the world championships last year by a tenth of a point to a Soviet couple, held first place vote by unanimous decision of the judges.

The completion of the Gold Dance will be tomorrow afternoon as well as the final of the junior ladies event.

In Friday night's competition, John Misha Petkevich of Great Falls. Mont., despite a fall and faulty, music, won the senior men's title. He scored the first perfect mark in free-skating since receiving one in 1968. Petkevich had been the runner-up the last two years to Tim Wood, now retired.

Skating to a Rachmaninoff concerto, Petkevich had to alter his routine on the ice when the record missed and cut out some 12 seconds of music. Taking out two planned jumps and putting in another while trying to get back in time with the music didn't hurt his chances as he received a 6.0 from one judge for interpretation.

### Difficult Jump Fails

Chances for a perfect mark in the technical aspects of his skating vanished when he fell on his final jump—a double Axel directly into a sitspin, an extremely difficult combination.

Petkevich was the last man to receive a 6.0 in a national championship when he got one in Philadelphia as he qualified for the Olympics. With a spectacular performance then he gained the third spot on the American team.

This year Petkevich, Ken Shelley of Downey, Calif., and Gordon McKellen of Lake Placid will make up the national team that will compete in Canada and France.

January 31, 1971

Associated Press

Janet Lynn of Rockford, Ill., performing a layback spin. The 17-year-old won her third straight national title.

---

## Report on Rise in Ski Injuries Is Disputed by Area Operators

### By MICHAEL STRAUSS

A report from Aspen, Colo., last Saturday, during a get-together of 300 medical specialists, announcing that ski injuries are reaching epidemic proportions has puzzled many observers close to the sport.

Statistics presented by two orthopedic surgeons estimated that there are between 180,-000 to 200,000 injuries each winter. However, no breakdown was offered as to the nature of the injuries or their seriousness.

Ski area operators, and others interested in the sport, feel the statistics are misleading. It is well known, for example, that when a skier reports a cut finger, that injury, though a minor one, becomes part of the statistics.

"A cut finger doesn't sound very serious to me," said Sepp Ruschp, the highly regarded head of the Mount Mansfield Company which operates the two ski complexes at Stowe, Vt. "In my opinion perecntagewise, ski injuries have been decreasing. Skiers today have better equipment and more know-how generally than in past years."

Ralph (Doc) Des Roches, executive director of Ski Industries America, an organi-

:ation of manufacturers, said:

The statistics quoted in Aspen are not realistic. Apparently they have no definitive study available. We know skiers get hurt. But, in how many cases are such injuries severe enough to cause more than brief discomfort? A breakdown of that statistic is what I'd like to see."

•

Some evidence to dispute the "epidemic' charge made in the Aspen report was gathered after inquiries were made yesterday at New England ski areas.

George Webster, assistant ski patrol director at Stratton (Vt.) Mountain, said:

"I'd say as a rule, three of five skiers entering our first-aid room, walk out on their own. We had 25 accidents reported last week. Less than three were fractures."

Damon Gadd, the president of the large Sugarbush center in Warren, Vt., and Hans Thorner, the president of Magic Mountain, agreed that serious injuries—at least in the East—were on the decline. Said Thorner:

"We list every injury in our statistics from a split toe nail or a frozen ear lobe to a fracture. Fractures at our area are at an all-time low. I'd say that this is true generally of the entire East which is noted for its well-manicured slopes and trails.

"As for that Aspen statistic, I'd say it's nothing less than sheer sensationalism."

February 11, 1971

# SCHRANZ BARRED FROM OLYMPICS

### I.O.C. Cites Pro Activity of Austrian Skiing Ace as Ground for Expulsion

SAPPORO, Japan, Monday, Jan. 31 (UPI)—The International Olympic Committee today declared the Austrian skiing star, Karl Schranz, ineligible to compete in the Winter Olympics because of his professional activities. The Games open here Thursday.

In a statement following a meeting, the committee said that "considering the activities and influence of Karl Schranz, the way he has permitted the use of his name and pictures, it has been decided that he will be ineligible to participate in the Winter Olympics."

Avery Brundage of Chicago, the I.O.C. president, who led a

fight to oust several Alpine and Nordic skiers he considered professionals receiving payment from sporting goods companies and other sources, said there would be no appeal.

Schranz was not called before the committee, which passed the resolution ousting him by a vote of 28-14.

"We don't deal with individuals," Brundage said.

He said Schranz had been ruled ineligible because of "the manner in which he has been acting for the past several years and for the statements he has made in the press since his arrival here." He did not elaborate.

#### Was Favored to Win

For Schranz, the "old man" of Alpine skiing, it was a blow. Although world champion a number of times he had never won an Olympic gold medal. In pre-Olympic races he had been in top form, winning several downhills, and was the favorite for the Olympic downhill.

"This is impossible. I don't believe it," he declared.

His expulsion and not that of any other skier appeared to be a compromise of what Brundage had wanted and the attitude of other committee members. They had felt it was unfair to go after just the skiers while other athletes—such as those from Communist countries—made their living from athletics while retaining their classification as amateurs.

Schranz was training on the downhill course when word of his expulsion came at the Park Hotel in downtown Sapporo where the I.O.C. was meeting. The Austrians had said they would pull out their whole team if Schranz was expelled.

Edgar Fried, secretary general of the Austrian Olympic Committee, said that "we have no immediate reaction to the I.O.C. decision."

"I don't want to comment on reports that we may pull out of the games," he added.

Schranz is a phenomenon in world skiing if for no reason other than his longevity as an amateur. He won his first international races in 1954 when he was 18 years old, and has captured every major international race at least once over the years.

The I.O.C. statement added:

"The International Ski Federation (F.I.S.) has been invited to confer with the executive board of the International Olympic Committee on the subject of enforcement by national Olympic committees of F.I.S. rules on eligibility."

#### Austrians Are Shocked

SAPPORO, Monday, Jan. 31 (AP)—The decision on Karl Schranz came as a shock to other Austrians today.

"I can't believe it," said Dr. Karl Heinz Klee of the Austrian Ski Federation. "We'll launch any appeals that are possible against this."

"There is no doubt that Karl

is just a scapegoat,' an Austrian official commented.

With the move of Jean-Claude Killy to pro ranks, Schranz became the most famous of the World Cup Alpine stars. He was reported to have earned $40,000 to $50,000 a year from his ski connections. Schranz never denied this, but contended that he was be-

Associated Press
**Karl Schranz in Sapporo**

ing punished for a crime of which all athletes were guilty.

"The Russians are subsidized by their own government and all international athletes get help from one source or another," he said earlier this week.

"It's an emphasis on the wrong principle. I think the Olympics should be a contest of all sportsmen, with no regrad for color, race or wealth."

Schranz's father was a poor railway worker who died young and left Schranz's mother to raise a family of five. The ski ace now owns a hotel.

January 31, 1972

# AUSTRIA, HEEDING SCHRANZ'S APPEAL, REMAINS IN GAMES

### Decision to Disqualify Him Wrong, Ace Skier Insists in Exhorting Teammates

SAPPORO, Japan, Wednesday, Feb. 2 (UPI)—The Austrian ski team, heeding a personal plea from Karl Schranz, decided this morning to remain in the Winter Olympics despite the International Olympic Committee's decision to disqualify Schranz from the Games because of professional activities.

Schranz, 33 years old, appeared at a news conference to ask that Austria's Alpine and Nordic teams, which had decided to withdraw in protest of the I.O.C. decision, remain in the Games.

"I don't want my country to be excluded from the Olympic Games because of me," Schranz said. "A wrong decision concerning me should not prevent other Austrian skiers from competing.

"I also feel that Olympic ski races without participants from Austria would lose some of the thrill," Schranz, who has been favored to win the downhill race, said.

Karl-Heinz Klee, president of the Austrian Ski Federation, said the Austrian team would accept Schranz's plea and stay in the Games.

The I.O.C., by a vote of 28-14, decided Monday that Schranz should be barred from the games because he allowed his name and picture to be used for commercial purposes. The I.O.C., at a meeting yesterday, turned down an Austrian appeal without a vote.

Avery Brundage, president of the I.O.C., said yesterday that Schranz was singled out for discipline because "he was the most blatant and verbose skier."

Schranz had not been permitted to speak in his own defense, Brundage said, explaining. "We don't deal with individuals. We deal with national Olympic committees. An Austrian member was present throughout our discussions..."

#### Brundage Is Angered

Special to The New York Times

SAPPORO, Japan, Feb. 2—Karl Schranz, the Austrian ski star who was disqualified from the Winter Olympic Games on charges of commercialism, was accused today by Avery Brundage, president of the International Olympic Committee, of being "disrespectful to the Olympic movement."

Appearing at a news conference at the Sapporo Park Hotel, Brundage said the Olympic Committee had not accepted the appeal of the Austrian Ski Federation for Schranz's reinstatement.

Brundage, going well beyond his vague criticism yesterday, said Schranz had repeatedly violated Olympic eligibility rules by appearing in advertisements and making a great deal of money from skiing.

But the 84-year-old Olympic official, who has made a fetish of his crusade for amateurism in Alpine events, appeared disturbed particularly by an interview Schranz had given The Associated Press.

In the interview Schranz was quoted as denouncing the I.O.C. for its "Nineteenth-Century attitudes" and as an organization "favoring rich competitors over poor ones." Brundage said such remarks were "very ill-advised," since they would "give young people an erroneous impression of the Olympic movement."

When asked whether any prominent skier could comply with the Olympic eligibility rules, Brundage replied of Schranz, "he was worse than all the others put together—almost." He said personal advertising was an indignity and immoral.

"All we are trying to do, Brundage said, "is to keep the respect of the public by keeping the Olympic Games clean, pure and honest. That's our obligation."

February 2, 1972

# Soviet Skier Wins at Olympics

## Vedenine First Gold Medalist— Schenk Scores

SAPPORO, Japan, Friday, Feb. 4 (AP)—Ard Schenk, the flying Dutchman of speed skating ,and Vyacheslav Vedenine, one of the aces of the Soviet Union's powerful Nordic skiing team, won the first gold medals of the Winter Olympic Games today.

Schenk won the 5,000-meter speed-skating race while Vedenine, a 30-year-old soldier, took his gold in the 30-kilometer cross-country skiing race.

They were the only two events to be decided on the first full day of competition.

The 23-year-old Schenk, the world champion who is given an excellent chance of also winning gold medals in the 1,500 and 10,000 meters, skated first in heavy snow but still won easily although later rivals skated in clear weather.

Schenk's time of 7 minutes 23.61 seconds was close to the Olympic record of 7:22.40 set by Fred Anton Maier of Norway in 1968 at Grenoble but was far off Schenk's world record of 7:12.00.

Roar Gronvold of Norway took the silver medal in 7:28.18 and Sten Stensen of Norway got the bronze in 7:33.39. Goran Claesson of Sweden finished fourth in 7:37.17 and Willy Olsen of Norway was fifth in 7:36.7.

The best American finish was 10th by Dan Carrell of St. Louis in 7:44.12.

Vedenine lay comfortably back in the early going of the cross-country race but surged from seventh into the lead and held off Pall Tyldum of Norway to win.

### Norwegians 2d and 3d

Vedenine was timed in 1 hour 36 minutes 31.15 seconds to 1:37.25.30 for Tyldum for the 30 kilometers which is 18.6 miles. Johns Harviken of Norway was third in 1:37.32.44 and Gunnar Larsson of Sweden was fourth in 1:37.33.27, followed by Walter Demel of West Germany in 1:45.53.

Franco Nones of Italy, the 1968 Olympic champion in 18.6-mile cross-country, was in Sapporo but did not enter the race, which was held over rolling terrain in periods of snow and sunshine.

One of the favorites for the race this year, Gerhard Grimmer of East Germany, dropped out just before the start of the race because of a bad cold he developed overnight.

### American Is 26th

The best United States finish as Verdenine became the second non-Scandinavian to win a gold medal in individual Olympic cross-country ski racing was a 26th by Mke Elliott of Durango, Colo., who was timed in 1:43.15.03.

Wolfgang Zimmerer and Peter Utzschneider of West Germany took the lead after two of four runs in the two-man bobsled. The final two runs will be held tomorrow.

Zimmerer and Utzschneider zipped down the 1,563-meter Mount Teine course in 1 minute 14.81 seconds and 1:14.56 for a total of 2:29.37. Jean Wicki and Edy Hubacher of Switzerland were second in 2:30.97, and Horst Floth and Pepi Bader of West Germany were third in 2:31.42.

The best American bobsled showing was a 13th in 2:34.57 by Boris Said of New York and Thomas Beck of Plattsburgh, N.Y.

Hideki Nakano of Japan took the lead in the Nordic combined by winning the 70-meter ski jump with leaps of 269 and 266 feet for 220.5 points. Rauno Miettinen of Finland was second with 254 and 259 for 210 points and Alexandre Nossov of the Soviet Union was third with 261 and 254 for 201.3.

The 15-kilometer cross-country race will complete the Nordic combined tomorrow.

Czechoslovakia and Sweden began their pursuit of the Soviet Union's defending champion ice hockey team with decisive elimination-round victories that thrust them into Class A competition.

Czechoslovakia defeated Japan, 8-2, and Sweden defeated Yugoslavia, 8-1. The results of the Games' initial competition placed the Czechs and Swedes alongside the Russians, who drew a bye.

February 4, 1972

# Miss Nadig, Swiss Skier, Wins Downhill With Miss Proell Next

## Susan Corrock of U.S. Takes Third Place

SAPPORO, Japan, Saturday, Feb. 5 (AP)—Marie Therese Nadig of Switzerland won the women's downhill ski race today as Susan Corrock of Ketchum, Idaho, finished third and gained the first medal for the United States in the 11th Winter Olympic Games.

Miss Nadig, a 17-year-old student, flashed down the course in 1 minute 36.68 seconds and beat Annemarie Proell of Austria, the favorite by 32 hundreths of a second. The women's World Cup leader, finished in 1:37 with Miss Corrock taking the Bronze medal in 1:37.68.

The performance of the 22-year-old Miss Corrock, who has been skiing in international competition just two years, also brought the United States its first Olympic medal in Alpine skiing since 1964.

In those games at Innsbruck, Austria, Jean Saubert won a silver medal in the women's giant slalom and a bronze in the slalom and Billy Kidd won a silver medal and Jimmy Heuga, a bronze in the men's slalom.

West Germany took two of the other three titles at stake today and East Germany gained the other. Erhard Keller of West Germany set a record in regaining the Olympic 500-meter speed skating crown. The other West German victory was in the two-man bobsled.

East Germany received a gold medal when 19-year-old Ulrich Wehling finished third in the 15-kilometer cross-country ski race and won the Nordic combined championship. He had placed fourth in the jumping yesterday.

Wolfgang Zimmere and Peter Utzschneider of West Germany won the gold medal in the two-man bobsled championship.

Keller, who won the 500 meters race at the 1968 Winter Games at Grenoble, France, was timed in 39.44 seconds. His time bettered that of Hasse Borjes of Sweden, who finished second. Borjes, who skated a few minutes before Keller, was timed in 39.69, breaking the Olympic mark. The record was held by Terry McDermott of the United States.

Valeri Mouratov of the Soviet Union, the bronze medalist, finished in 39.80, and Per Bjoran of Norway in 39.91 for fourth place.

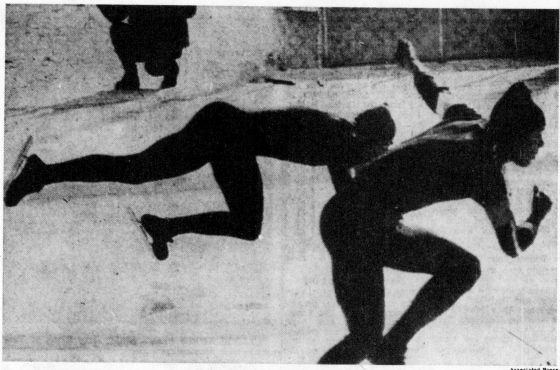

Associated Press

**SPEED SKATER SLIPS:** Ard Schenk of the Netherlands falters at start of 500-meter Olympic event this morning. His time was 43.4 seconds. At right is Neil Blatchford of the U.S., who finished 15th with a time of 40.67 seconds.

The United States athletes did not do well. A weary American hockey team, which was playing its second game in 16 hours, was defeated by Sweden, 5-1.

Goals by Tommie Bergman and Inge Hammarstrom in the third period clinched the game. They offset any possible protest from the United States team after the Finnish referee had disallowed two American goals.

The official ruled that on both occasions an American player had preceded the puck into the Swedish goal crease.

Lars Nelsson, Thommy Abrahamsson and Tord Lundstrom were the other Swedish scorers. Kevin Ahearn of Milton, Mass., scored for the United States at 8:04 of the first period.

Karl-Heinz Luck of East Germany finished first in the 15-kilometer country race in 48:24.9. Urban Hettich of West Germany was second in 49:00.4 and Wehling third in 49:15.3.

Other top finishers in the cross-country race were Erkkie Kilpinen of Finland, fourth in 49:52.6; Ralph Pohland of West Germany, fifth in 49:55.6 and Michael Devecka of Government Camp, Ore., fifth in 50:00.

Wehling finished with an over-all point score of 413.340, Miettinen in second place with 405.505 and Luck in third place, 398.800.

After the jumping Friday, Wehling was trailing Miettinen by 9.1 points and had to beat the Finn by 1 minute 1 second to overtake him. The young German, who is a high school student from Halle, beat the Finnish baker by 1 minute 52 seconds.

Wehling started his international career two years ago by winning the Socialist Countries Junior Cup in Bulgaria. Last year he won the European junior championship.

The United States hockey team had gained a pairing against third-ranked Sweden by defeating Switzerland, 5-3, for a place in the six-team championship round-robin.

Goals by Tim Sheehy, his second of the game, Stuart Ir-ving in the third period broke a 3-3 deadlock before a near capacity house of 5,600, including Emperor Hirohito and his official party.

Kevin Ahearn also scored twice for the Americans.

February 5, 1972

# Ard Schenk: Speed and Power on Ice

### By FRED TUPPER

Special to The New York Times

SAPPORO, Japan, Feb. 4—The Olympic men's 5,000-meter speed-skating event turned out to be treat for the Dutch.

It was won, as it was supposed to be, by 23-year-old Ard Schenk of the Netherlands, the finest skater of his time and the world record-holder in all three distance events.

He set a 5,000-meter world standard of 7 minutes 12 seconds in the European championships at Davos, Switzerland, a year ago. But there was no way that he could break it today or the Olympic record either — though he came close to it.

Schenk was off first in a driving blizzard that coated the ice and made visibility difficult.

"It was hard on the last few laps," he said, "the snow was blowing in my eyes. And my legs were worse."

But he romped in. His margin was nearly five seconds over Roar Gronvold of Norway and about 10 seconds over Sten Stensen, the Norwegian who finished third. The time was 7:23.61, compared with the Olympic mark of 7:22.4 set by F. Anton Maier of Norway in Grenoble France.

"I didn't know what the Olympic record was," said the 6-foot-2-inch, 194-pound physiotherapy student. "It was more important to win the medal."

"The only medal I didn't have," he said, with a wide smile. The hulking Dutchman, blue-eyed and very blond, was questioned repeatedly by girl reporters.

One skater looks much like another in world class: the quick digging in of the skates at the start, the right-arm swing to provide the push round the turns and the easy glide with hands be-hind the back down the stretches, and finally the two arm swing of the sprint down the homestretch.

Schenk is more powerful than the rest and his strides are longer.

His studies in physiotherapy help: "Maybe because I know more how the human body works."

He was going to try for the the four golds. But he fell during the 500-meter race and finished with a time of 43.40 seconds. Erhard Keller set an Olympics record of 39.44 in the event.

"He's [Schenk] just the best." said Gronvold. "I knew his times and tried to keep up. After four laps it was useless."

Dan Carroll of St. Louis finished 10th in the 5,000, among the 28 starters, the best result yet for an American over this distance.

February 5, 1972

# SCHENK TAKES HIS 2D OLYMPIC SPEED-SKATING TITLE

## TRIUMPHS IN 1,500

### Dutch Ace Sets Mark for Games—Japan Gains First Title

**By The Associated Press**

SAPPORO, Japan, Sunday, Feb. 6 — Japan captured its first Winter Olympic gold medal ever and Ard Schenk of the Netherlands flashed to an Olympic-record victory for his second speed-skating gold at the 11th Winter Games today.

The Soviet Union's crack skiers claimed their second gold in the only other medal event, the women's 10-kilometer cross-country.

Yukio Kasaya sent the Japanese fans into a frenzy, taking the 70-meter ski jump with leaps of 275.58 and 264.10 feet while Emperor Hirohito watched.

Japan swept the silver and bronze medals for the event as well, the first nation to take all three places in any competition at these Games. Akitsugu Konno was second and Seiji Aochi third.

Kasaya had 244.2 points, Kanno 234.8 and Aochi 229.5. Jerry Martin of Minneapolis was the best American finisher with 197.2 points for 34th place.

#### Well Off World Record

Schenk, who won the 5,000-meter race Friday, shattered the Olympic standard for the 1,500 meters, dashing around the rink in 2 minutes 2.96 seconds. The time was well off Schenk's world record of 1:58.70.

The silver medal went to Roar Gronvold of Norway in 2:04.26. Gronvold was also second to Schenk in the 5,000-meter. Goran Claesson of Sweden was third in 2:05.89.

Dan Carroll of St. Louis was the top American finisher in the speed skating with his 2:07.24, good enough for seventh place.

Schenk will try to complete an Olympic speed-skating triple crown tomorrow in the 10,000-meter test.

**Associated Press**

**SETS OLYMPIC MARK: Ard Schenk of the Netherlands in 1,500-meter speed skating**

Salina Koulakova, a 29-year-old school teacher, gave the Soviets the gold medal in the cross-country race. She covered the 6.2-mile course in 34 minutes 17.82 seconds, beating Alevtina Olunina, a teammate, who took the silver medal in 34:54.11.

The bronze medal went to Finland's Marjatta Kajosmaa, who was timed in 34:56.45. The top American finisher was Martha Rockwell of Putney, Vt., who was timed in 36:34.22 for 16th place.

Miss Koulakova's victory in the 10-kilometer event followed Vyacheslav Vedenin's triumph in the men's 30-kilometer cross-country race on Friday. The Soviets won only one gold medal in Nordic skiing at the last Winter Olympics at Grenoble, France, in 1968.

Miss Koulakova finished sixth in the same event at Grenoble but was never challenged today, leading the race from start to finish.

Other American finishers were Alison Owen of East Wenatchee, Wash., 35th in 38:50.05; Margie Mahoney of Anchorage, Alaska, 36th in 39:27.95, and Trina Hosmer of Santa Monica, Calif., 41st in 40:40.56.

Later today, America's Jo Jo Starbuck and Ken Shelley of Downey, Calif., began their medal quest in pairs figure skating with the start of the compulsory figures portion of the competition. Favored in the event were the Soviet team of Irina Rodnina and Alexei Ulanov, the world champions.

Janet Lynn, continually frustrated in her bid for international honors despite her four-year reign as the United States champion, appeared hopelessly out of the gold medal chase in figure skating on the eve of the free skating competition.

The pretty, quiet blonde from Rockford, Ill., faltered on her fifth of six compulsory figures and then had to rally on the final figure to move from sixth place to fourth in the field of 19.

Although Miss Lynn is considered by many as the world's foremost free skater, she appeared much too far behind the leader, Beatrix Schuba, to overtake the Austrian world champion in tomorrow night's concluding program. Miss Schuba is considered relatively weak in free skating, but she carries 1,247.0 points into this portion of the competition to 1,074.6 points for Miss Lynn.

Miss Lynn's best hope appears to move up at least one notch and earn a medal, but even this can prove difficult.

Julie Lynn Holmes of North Hollywood, Calif., skating with confidence and poise, stands second with 1,128.5 points and the North American champion, Karen Magnussen of Canada, is third with 1,105.7. Miss Magnussen also is an excellent free skater and isn't likely to yield much ground to Miss Lynn.

It was reported that Miss Lynn felt ill, but the American

star refused to comment on this or any other matter. After saying that she would be available for an interview once the point totals were announced, Miss Lynn was taken by the arm and whisked quickly away by her manager, Slavka Kohout. Miss Kohout said that Miss Lynn would talk to no one.

Miss Lynn was well received by the small audience at the Mikaho indoor rink and appeared primed for a good day when she received fine marks for her first figure, the paragraph double three.

But then she weakened on the next figure, a change loop, which dropped her back to sixth place. The highest mark she received for this figure was a 3.9 (of a possible 6), and her total ranged as low as 3.4. In contrast, Miss Schuba's marks ranged from 4.4 to 4.8 for this figure and Miss Holmes ranged from 4.0 to 4.4.

A slight recovery on the final figure, the paragraph bracket, in which she received a high score of 4.1, moved Miss Lynn back into contention.

Following the compulsory portion of the 1968 Olympics at Grenoble, Miss Lynn was 14th, eventually moving up to ninth in the free skating. Miss Schuba was fifth in that competition, won by Peggy Fleming of the United States.

February 6, 1972

# Schenk Victor in 10,000 Meters For Third Speed-Skating Title

## Dutch Ace Sets Olympic Mark —Russi Captures Downhill

SAPPORO, Japan, Monday, Feb. 7 (AP)—Ard Schenk of the Netherlands set an Olympic record in the 10,000-meter speed-skating race today and became the first triple gold-medal winner of the 11th Winter Games.

Schenk, skating in the final twosome, won in 15 minutes 1.35 seconds, adding the 10,000-meter title to those he had won in the 1,500 and 5,000 meters.

Bernhard Russi won the men's downhill, giving Switzerland a sweep of the Alpine skiing event. He was timed in 1 minute 51.43 seconds over the 2,640-meter course, with a vertical drop of 772 meters. Marie Theresa Nadig of Switzerland previously won the women's downhill.

Roland Collombin, also of Switzerland, placed second in 1:52.40. Heinrich Messner of Austria finished third in 1:53.19.

The best the United States could do was an eighth-place finish by Robert Cochran of Richmond, Vt., who was clocked in 1:53.39. Other American placings were Michael Lafferty of Eugene, Ore., 14th; David Currier of Madison, N.H., 17th, and Hank Kashiwa of Old Forge, N.Y., 25th.

Sweden got its first gold medal of the Games when Sven-Ake Lundback, a 24-year-old electrician, won the 15-kilometer cross-country ski race.

Schenk beat a teammate, Cees Verkerk, timed in 15:04.70, in the 10,000. Sten Stensen of Norway finished third in 15:07.08. The three medalists and two others broke the previous Olympic record of 15:23.60 set by Johnny Hoglin of Sweden in 1968.

Hoglin, due to race today, did not appear and was scratched. He was believed to be suffering from a throat infection.

Jan Bols of the Netherlands was fourth in 15:17.99 and Valeri Lavrouchkin of the Soviet Union was fifth in 15:20.08, both under the old standard.

Schenk, a 27-year-old bachelor, missed out in only the 500-meter race, one which he had not been expected to win. Ernard Keller of West Germany was the 500 winner.

Dan Carroll of St. Louis was ninth in the 10,000 in 15:44.41.

Lundback led from the start of the 15-kilometer cross-country race and was timed in 45 minutes 28.24 seconds. Fedor Simaschov of the Soviet Union was second at the end of the 9.3 miles. He was clocked in 46:00.84 to 46:02.68 for Ivar Formo of Norway, who finished third.

In hockey, an underdog Swedish team scored three goals in the final period to tie the strong Soviet Union, 3-3, and throw the competition into a scramble.

Russia held a 2-0 lead going into the third period.

The tie upset pre-tournament predictions that the Russians would win all their games and retain their Olympic title. Sweden and the strong Czechoslovaka team are now in a position to win the championship.

The Soviet star, Valerii Charlamov, figured in all his team's scoring, with two goals and one assist.

The Swedish goals were scored by Bjorn Palmqvist, Inge Hammarstrom and Hakan Wickberg.

The Swedish goalie, Christer Abrahamsson, put on a spectacular display in the third period to keep the Russians from scoring. In the final 10 minutes he stopped several point-blank thrusts.

For the first two periods, Swden skated hard and often carried the play, but the Swedes were unable to control the puck in the Russian end. They played far better in the

Associated Press

**FIRST TRIPLE MEDAL WINNER:** Ard Schenk, shaking hands after 1,500-meter race, won 10,000-meter today.

third period, however, and forced the Russians to adopt a defensive style of play.

The Swedes also resorted to heavy checking to contain the Russians. But the Russians countered with an equally bruising style, something they don't often do.

In the second period, play was held up several minutes after both teams nearly came to blows. The confrontation started when a Swedish forward, Stig-Goran (Stisse) Johansson, piled into the Russian goalie, Vladislav Tretiak.

Seconds afterward, Charlamov blatantly speared Bert-Ola Norlander and both teams spilled onto the ice. But the referees stepped in and broke it up before a full-scale brawl could start.

American expectations received a mild jolt yesterday when two Soviet couples finished first and second, followed by East Germans, in the compulsory phase of the pairs figure-skating competition.

The United States hoped for a silver or a bronze from its national championship pair, Ken Shelley and JoJo Starbuck of Downey, Calif., and the brother-sister team of Mark and Melissa Millitano of Dix Hills, L. I.

Irina Rodnina and Alexei Ulanov of the Soviet Union, the world's best although they are not on speaking terms, missed a couple of steps in the compulsory routine, and there was some grumbling that the judges, who awarded them 13 ordinal points, had their minds made up ahead of time.

Ludmila Smirnova and Andrei Souraikin of the Soviet Union were next with 144, followed by Manuela Gross and Uwe Kagelmann of East Germany with 34.5.

Miss Starbuck and Shelley were fourth with 37.5 and the Militanos were eighth with 75.5 The compulsories count 25 per cent toward the pairs' championship. Both United States couples are sensational free skaters, but so are the Soviets.

February 7, 1972

# Miss Nadig Takes Giant Slalom For Her 2d Olympic Gold Medal

## Figure Skating Crown Goes to Miss Schuba

SAPPORO, Japan, Tuesday, Feb. 8 (AP)--Maria Therese Nadig of Switzerland captured her second gold medal of the 11th Winter Olympics today with a convincing victory in the women's giant slalom ski race in a heavy snowstorm.

The 17-year-old star, who had scored an upset in taking the downhill race, covered the 1,240-meter course in 1 minute 29.90 seconds.

Annemarie Proell of Austria finished second, as she had in the downhill, with a time of 1:30.75. Her Austrian team-mate, Wiltrud Drexel, took third in 1:32.35.

Last night Beatrix Schuba brightened a bleak week for Austria by winning the gold medal in figure skating. In second place was Karen Magnussen of Canada. Janet Lynn of the United States placed third for the bronze medal and Julie Holmes of the United States finished fourth.

Miss Nadig's victory made her the first woman Alpine ski-ing double champion since Andrea Mead Lawrence of the United States took the slalom and giant slalom in the 1952 Games.

### Visibility Decreases

She was the 10th starter in the race and the course deteriorated quickly with visibility and speed decreasing.

In fourth place was Laurie Kreiner of Canada, 1:32.48. Then came Rosie Speiser of West Germany, 1:32.56, and Florence Steurer of France, 1:32.59.

American girls were a disappointed crew. The best time among them was 1:33.16 by Barbara Cochran of Richmond, Vt., who finished 11th.

Three other Americans were far down the list. Karen Budge of Jackson Hole, Wyo., clocked 1:35.57 and commented dejectedly: "I don't want to talk. I couldn't see one thing."

Sandy Poulsen of Olympic Valley, Calif., missed a gate and was disqualified. She said, "The snow was slow and the course was slow." Marilyn Cochran, Barbara's sister, was timed in 1:35.27.

Ondrej Nepela, the world champion from Czechoslovakia, unofficialy took the lead in the first half of the men's figure skating copulsory event with 10 ordinals, eight firsts and one second.

In the women's skating, Miss Schuba, 21-year-old world champion, had a total of 9 ordinals to 23 for Miss Magnusen and 27 for Miss Lynn. The big blonde from Vienna built such a commanding lead in the compulsories earlier in the week that no one could catch her even though she finished only seventh in the free-skating finale.

A large Austrian contingent cheered her as she became the first Austrian to win the figure skating title since Mrs. Heima von Szabo-Planck in 1924, the inaugural year for the Winter Games.

"It was great to have the Austrian ski teams along to encourage me like that after all the disappointments they have suffered here in Sapporo," said Miss Schuba, glowing as much as the silver glitter in her royal blue skating dress.

Other Austrian gold medal hopes were dashed when the Alpine ski ace, Karl Schranz, was disqualified on charges of professionalism and the World Cup leader, Annemarie Proell, was beaten in the women's downhill by Marie Therese Nadig of Switzerland.

Miss Lynn, a petite 18-year-old from Rockford, Ill., dressed in hot pink, was No. 1 in the free-skating segment despite one spill.

"I jumped up to go into a sit spin and I just sort of sat instead," she said. "It happens all the time. This is a slippery sport."

It was because of Janet's compulsories, in which she finished fourth, that the silver medal was slipped around Miss Magnussen's neck. Karen, tiny and blonde like Janet, but not nearly so effervescent on the ice, was No. 2 overall with a second in free skating and a third in figure eights.

Miss Holmes, 20, of North Hollywood, Calif., was second after the compulsories, but plummeted to fourth over all after she had landed badly coming out of a jump, and was rated eighth for the evening.

"I don't know what I did," she said, her red chiffon skating dress wrapped in a fur coat to ward off the chill. "I was a little nervous, as always."

Suna Murray, a 16-year-old schoolgirl from South Orange, N. J., the United States' only other woman figure skater in the Games, wound up 13th.

In ice hockey Mike Curran's alert goaltending was the decisive factor in a 5-1 upset by the United States over Czechoslovakia yesterday.

February 8, 1972

---

# Miss Holum Wins Skate Race, Giving U.S. First Gold Medal

## American Sets Games Mark in the 1,500

SAPPORO, Japan, Wednesday, Feb. 9 (AP)—Dianne Holum of Northbrook, Ill., flashed to an Olympic record in the women's 1,500-meter speed skating race today and gave the United States its first gold medal of the 11th Winter Olympic Games.

The 20-year-old Miss Holum, the teen-age darling of the United States team in the 1968 Games when she won a silver medal and a bronze, took the lead about midway in the race, in which the previous Olympic mark was broken by the first five finishers.

Miss Holum smashed the 1968 mark of 2 minutes 22.40 seconds by Finland's Kaija Mustonen with a clocking of 2:20.85. The world record-holder, Stein Baas-Kaiser of the Netherlands, was timed in 2:21.05 for the silver medal.

The bronze went to Atje Keulen-Deelstra of the Netherlands in 2:22.05.

### Miss Koulakova Victor

In today's other finals, Galina Koulakova of the Soviet Union won the gold in the women's 5-kilometer cross-country race and Magner Solberg of Norway took the gold in the grueling individual biathlon.

A Norwegian, Erik Haaker, clocked the best time in the first heat of the men's giant slalom. The second heat will be run tomorrow.

Haaker flashed down the extremely steep, 1,034-meter (3,420-foot) course on Mt. Tiene in one minute 31.70 seconds. Second was Alfred Hagn of West Germany in 1:31.78. The world champion, Gustavo Thoeni of Italy, was third in 1:32.19. France's Henri Duvillard, leader in the World Cup standing, caught a ski on a gate and fell.

The best United States time was the 1:35.39 by Bobby Cochran of Richmond, Vt., who finished far down the list.

Ondrej Nepela of Czechoslovakia took the lead in the men's figure skatin by winning the compulsory figures. Patrick Pera of France was second and Sergei Tchetveroukhin of the Soviet Union was third.

Nepala's original score was 9.0 perfect — from the nine judges. Pera finished with 20.0 ordinals and Tchetveroukhin had 26.0.

For Miss Holum, a dedicated speed skater who trained in the Netherlands last fall, the victory marked a high in a career that saw her finish third in over-all world championships as a 15-year-old in 1967. She won a silver medal in the 1,000 meters and a bronze in the 500 meters at the Winter Olympics in Grenoble, France, four years ago.

"Everybody told me that the 1,000 meters was my best distance, but I knew I could win this race," said Miss Holum.

"I thought it all out carefully and I remember every detail of it from start to finish."

The United States also got a seventh place in the opening race of the women's speed skating program when Connie

Carpenter of Madison, Wis., was timed in 2:23.93.

Miss Holum's victory put the United States in an excellent position to top the gold medal output of one each in the last two Olympics. Anne Henning, also of Northbrook, is favored in the 1,000 and the 500.

Miss Koulakova, who had won the 10-kilometer race, became the third multiple gold medal winner of these Games when she won the 5-kilometer cross-country race in 17 minutes 0.50 seconds. Mariatta Kajosma of Finland raced the 3.1 miles in 17:05.50 for the silver medal and Helena Sikolova of Czechoslovakia took the bronze in 17:07.32.

The Alpine skier, Marie Theresa Nadig of Switzerland, also has won two gold medals and the speed skater Ard Schenk of the Netherlands, has won three.

Miss Koulakova, a 29-year-old physical education teacher is the current world 5-kilometer champion.

The 30-year-old Solberg was timed in 1:15:15.5 for the biathlon, in which a competitor skis cross-country 20 kilometers with a rifle on his back, stopping at four designated areas to fire five shots at a target 150 meters away. Solberg, the 1968 Olympic biathlon champion, had a two-minute penalty for two target misses added to his time.

Hansjorg Knauthe of East Germany got the silver medal, covering the 12.4 miles in 1:16:07.6, including a one-minute penalty. LarsGoran Arwidson of Sweden got the bronze in 1:16:27.0, including a two-minute penalty.

The Soviet Union won a gold medal last night when the world champions, Irina Rodnina and Alexei Ulanov, danced to victory in the pairs figure skating.

The No. 2 Soviet pair, Ludmila Smirnova and Andrei Suraikhin, took the silver medal and East Germany, with Manuela Gross and Uwe Kagelmann, placed third.

United States hopes for a medal died as Jo Jo Starbuck and Kenneth Shelley of Downey, Calif., were awarded fourth. They put on a stirring exhibition that drew a rafter-rocking ovation from the 10,000 spectators at the indoor Makomanai rink.

Melissa and Mark Militano of Dix Hills, L.I., finished seventh, while Barbara Brown and Douglas Berndt of Denver were 12th.

Meanwhile, in the Alpine competition, Miss Nadig of Switzerland, whose favorite pastime when not skiing is playing soccer with boys, stands poised for a triple. If she can win the ordinary slalom Friday, she will be the first woman in Olympic history to take all three Alpine skiing gold medals.

Swiss officials believe she is in such tremendous form that she can do it.

Her victory in the giant slalom yesterday gave Switzerland a sweep of all three Alpine events so far. The Swiss could make it four in a row in the men's giant slalom. Werner Mattle, winner of two European giant slalom races last month, leads the challenge.

The Soviet Union seemed sure of the gold medal in last night's pairs skating. The two Soviet pairs had a convincing lead after the compulsory section Sunday, and the only thing in doubt was which couple would win.

But Miss Rodnina and Ulanov had some anxious moments before they clinched the title. The 22-year-old Miss Rodnina faltered in an early jump, but immediately regained her stance and entranced the crowd.

The two Russian couples showed no outward signs of tension, although bad feelings had been reported between them over romantic entanglements.

This marked the third straight Olympic victory in the pairs for the Soviet Union. Ludmila Belousova and Oleg Protopopov won in 1964 and 1968.

The Militanos skated in mod blue lavender costumes. Instead of the normal tight-fitting jacket, Mark wore a loose, open-throated shirt.

They pleased the crowd, but their advanced approach to the conservative rites of figure skating automatically lowered their rating.

February 9, 1972

# Miss Henning Skates to Victory

## U.S. Star, 16, Sets Mark at 500 Meters

Special to The New York Times

SAPPORO, Japan, Thursday, Feb. 10—The American skating superstar, Anne Henning, won the Olympic 500-meter sprint today, but for a dreaded second or two the issue was in doubt.

The world record-holder from Northbrook, Ill., had rounded into the backstretch in the outside lane and was preparing to make a change-over to the inside. Right there in her path was Sylvia Burka of Canada. Collision seemed certain. Miss Henning did what she had to do, broke stride, straightened up, lost her arm rhythm and then dug in again.

"Don't lose it," she said to herself. "Don't blow it now. Keep going."

Pouring it on, she finished in 43.73 seconds, the best time then and an Olympic record.

In speed skating the skater moving from the outside to the inside has the right of way. Miss Burka was disqualified under International Skating Union regulations. Miss Henning had the option of skating again. She made the decision to do so. Although the confused crowd of 30,000 thought her first time was invalid, it was not. Under the rules, she could skate again and pick the faster time.

And so — for the first time — a skater beat an Olympic record twice in the same race. On her second chance, cheered to the echo, Miss Henning set another record, 0:43.33, racing by herself. The previous mark of 45 seconds flat was established by the great Lidia Skoblikova of the Soviet Union, holder of six golds, at Innsbruck, Austria, in 1964.

### The Youngest Winner

Miss Henning, at 16 years, is the youngest winner in these Games and the victory gave the United States its second gold medal. Her teammate and idol, 20-year-old Dianne Holum, also of Northbrook, Ill., won the 1500-meter race yesterday.

Button-nose, cheery Vera Krasnova of the Soviet Union was second today in 44.01 and the Olympic defending champion, Ludmila Titova of the Soviet Union, was third in

Associated Press

AMERICAN GOLD: Dianne Holum, left, of Northbrook, Ill., winning the women's 1,500-meter speed skating at Sapporo, Japan, yesterday. Nina Statkevitch, U.S.S.R., at right.

44.45, edging Sheila Young of Detroit by .08 of a second.

Conditions were ideal. A pale cold sun shone out of a blue sky and the Olympic flags lay flat against their poles.

It had been hoped that Miss Henning could break her world mark of 42.5.

Miss Henning was away beautifully on the first start, hit the 100 meters in 10.77 and was in top gear when she was forced to pull up.

"We were almost even," said green-eyed, blond Miss Henning, "but I was sorta behind, so I dropped back, stood up and let her go. Then I had to get into hard stroking again."

Could she have set a world record? "Maybe. The times were not that fast. Maybe I lost a second."

Was she psyched up the second time? "It was a hard decision. It had to be a letdown. I tried hard to get back up."

A year ago Miss Henning had some blazing times, but Mrs. Ruth Budzisch of East Germany, then Miss Ruth Schleirmacher, took the world sprint title and Nina Statkevich of the Soviet Union edged out Miss Henning for the over all world championship.

Anne's rise since has been meteoric. Half a dozen times she has shattered her 1971 world mark of 42.75, culminating with a 42.5 only weeks ago.

The Northbrook Skating Club gang of 50 was in full cry today. It was their cheers, said Anne, that kept her going the second time round.

"They're fantastic," she said. "They pulled me up off the floor and got me going."

### A 16-Year-Old 'Killer'

Her mother, Joanna, was a self-confessed nervous wreck. Superstitious, she had assembled a four-leaf clover, Japanese beads, a Christmas ornament and two American flags for good-luck charms. "She's going to win," she said fervently during the race. "I feel it—all the way. Go, girl, go—you're tough. Win, win." Husband Bill was more restrained. "How's that, Ma?" he said when Anne finally made it.

Ma was in tears. "She always listens to her mother except when I tell her to pick up her room. She's a loving girl but when she gets on that ice, she has icewater in her veins."

"She's a killer," said Bill Henning.

### A Gold For Italy

In other finals Paal Tyldum, a 30-year-old farmer from Norway, won the grueling 50-kilometer cross country skiing in 2 hours 43 minutes 14.75 seconds, and Italy's Gustavo Thoeni captured the men's giant slalom with a two-run total of 3 minutes 9.62 seconds.

Magne Myrmo of Norway was second and Vyacheslav Vedenin of the Soviet Union third in the 31-mile skiing test. Tyldum was second to Vedenin in the 30-kilometer cross-country earlier in the Games.

Thoeni won the slalom when Erik Haaker of Norway, leader after the first run, fell. Edmund Bruggman of Switzerland took the silver medal and another Swiss skier, Werner Mattle, won the bronze.

February 10, 1972

# Barbara Cochran of U. S. Wins Slalom

SAPPORO, Japan, Friday, Feb. 11 (AP)—Barbara Cochran of Richmond, Vt., twisted through a heavy snow today to win the women's special slalom and give the United States its first Olympic gold medal in Alpine skiing since 1952.

Miss Cochran's stunning victory came about two hours after Anne Henning and Dianne Holum, both of Northbrook, Ill., the other United States gold medalists of these 11th Winter Games, failed to win the 1,000-meter speed-skating race. Miss Henning finished third, less than a quarter of a second behind the winner, Monika Pflug of West Germany.

Miss Cochran, whose older sister, Marilyn, fell and was disqualified in the first of two runs, had a total time of 1 minute 31.24 seconds in giving the United States its third gold medal, the most since 1950 and its first in skiing since Andrea Meade Lawrence was a double gold medalist in 1952.

### Miss Fraser Won in '48

Gretchen Fraser won an Alpine gold for the United States in 1948 but American men have not won an Olympic Alpine race.

Miss Cochran had the fastest time of 46:05 seconds on the first run. She then had the second fastest time of 45.19 on the second run to give her a

Barbara Cochran being carried on shoulders of her brother, Bob, left, and Rick Chaffee after she won first place in women's slalom. This gave the United States its first gold medal in Alpine skiing in twenty years.

winning margin of two one-hundredths of a second over the silver medalist, Danielle Debernard of France.

Miss Debernard had runs of 46.08 and 45.18 for a total of 1:31.26 while the bronze medalist, Florence Steurer, also of France, had times of 46.57, 46.12 for 1:32.69.

Miss Pflug was timed in 1:31.40 in winning the 1,000-meters speed-skating final. The silver medalist, Atje Keulen-Deelstra, of the Netherlands, was clocked in 1:31.61 to 1:31.62 for Miss Henning.

Miss Holum, who won the gold medal in the 1,500-meter event Wednesday, the day before Miss Henning won the 500, finished sixth in 1:32.51, also under the old Olympic record of 1:32.60 set by Carry Guyssen of the Netherlands at Grenoble, France, in 1968.

The United States speed skaters were upset about a delay in Miss Holum's start that was caused when Lisbeth Berg of Norway, the other girl in the pairing, lost an armband. Miss Holum had to wait for several minutes.

"It looked like gamesmanship," said Miss Holum's father, Edward. "Dianne was all keyed up and ready to go."

Wojciech Fortuna of Poland leaped a tremendous 111 meters —364 feet 2 inches—on his first jump and was just good enough

on his second to win the 90-meter ski jumping title by the narrowest of margins.

Fortuna went 87.5 meters—287 feet 1 inch—on his second jump and with form points scored a total of 219.9. Walter Steiner of Switzerland was second with 219.8 and Rainer Schmidt of East Germany was third with 219.3.

### U.S. Sextet Hopeful

The gold medal in the biathlon relay was won by the defending champion Soviet Union, with Finland second and East Germany third. The United States finished sixth in its best performance ever in the event.

The Soviet Union team of Alexandre Tikhonov, Rinnat Safine, Ivan Biakov and Victor Mamatov was timed in 1:41.-44.9 for the biathlon relay, which consisted of an 18.6-mile cross-country race and target shooting.

Switzerland's four-man bobsled team held the lead after two of the four runs. The last two runs will be held tomorrow.

The Swiss team of Jean Wicki, Hans Leutemiger, Edy Hubacher and Werner Camichel turned in runs of 1:10.71 and 1:11.44 for a total of 2 minutes 22.15 seconds. West Germany was second and Italy third going into the final two runs.

A United States sled was dis-

qualified when its members fell off while going around the fifth curve of the 1,563-meter course.

The driver, John James Hickey, an Air Force sergeant from Keene, N.Y., suffered a possible broken rib. James Bridges, an airman from Plattsburgh, N.Y., suffered a bruised shoulder. Thomas Becker, an Air Force sergeant from Indianapolis, and Howard Siler of Auburn, N.Y., were not hurt.

The United States had a second team in the race. It clocked 1:12.31 for 12th place in the first run.

In ice hockeyl, the United States kept its chances for a bronze medal alive by beating Finland, 4-1, for its second victory against two defeats. The once-tied Soviet Union crushed Poland, 9-3, and remained in first place in the round-robin Class A tournament, one point ahead of Czechoslovakia, which edged Sweden, 2-1.

If the United States can come up with another "bad" game against Poland tomorrow night, the Americans will be in excelent position to claim their first Olympic medal in hockey since 1960.

If the United States wins and the Soviet Union beats Czechoslovakia on Sunday afternoon, the Americans will win the bronze medal. This would be almost as incredible a feat as their gold medal suc-

cess at Squaw Valley, Calif., in 1960.

"We felt all along we were going to take a medal," said Henry Boucha, who scored a goal and two assists against Finland. "We're a young team and it was natural to think positive. The desire was always there and now it looks as though we'll get that medal."

Mike Curran, the United States goalie who made 35 saves, agreed, saying, "We came here thinking positive and there's no reason to believe we won't do our part by beating Poland."

Oddly, Coach Murray Williamson, who had heaped lavish praise on his squad after it dropped a 7-2 decision to the Soviet Union the previous night, felt the club was below par against Finland.

"One thing I was very worried about two days ago was playing Russia and Finland, two powerful clubs, back to back," said Williamson. "I thought the Russian game would take too much out of us and it did. The boys didn't have their legs against Finland, but they played with their hearts.

"We couldn't get a jump on the puck, we were loggy, our passes were a little off. They have a good club and we were lucky to get all the breaks."

February 11, 1972

---

# Miss Holum Is 2d in 3,000 Skate Final

SAPPORO, Japan, Saturday, Feb. 12 (AP)—Dianne Holum of Northbrook, Ill., captured the United States' first silver medal at the 11th Winter Olympic Games today, finishing second to Stien Baas-Kaiser of the Netherlands in the grueling 3,000-meter speed-skating test.

Miss Holum, bidding for a second gold medal to go with her 1,500-meter crown, was timed in 4 minutes 58.67 seconds and led through most of the event until the Dutch skater took her turn. Mrs. Baas-Kaiser then sped around the Makomanai outdoor rink in an Olympic-record time of 4:52.14.

Third place went to another Dutch girl, Atje Keulen-Deelstra, timed in 4:59.91.

The previous Olympic record for the event was 4:56.20, set by Ans Schut of the Netherlands in 1968 at Grenoble, France. Mrs. Baas-Kaiser holds the world mark of 4:46.50.

Earlier, Galina Koulacova, a 29-year-old teacher, anchored the Soviet Union to the 15-kilometer women's cross-country skiing championship and Jean Wicki piloted Switzerland's four-man bobsledders to victory.

The cross-country gold medal was the third at these games for Miss Koulacova, who had captured the 5-kilometer and 10-kilometer individual races

earlier in the week.

The Soviet women took the lead from the start with Lubov Moukhatcheva jumping ahead on the first leg. Alevtina Olyunina maintained the lead on the second leg and Miss Koulacova clinched the victory.

The winning time for the Soviet was 48 minutes 46.15 seconds for the 9.4-mile course.

Finland earned the silver medal in 49:19.37 and Norway took the bronze in 49:51.49. The United States team finished 11th, timed in 53:38.60.

Wicki, a 10-year bobsledding veteran who earlier earned a bronze medal in the two-man event, guided Switzerland's four-man crew into the lead in the first of four heats and was never threatened.

The rest of his crew was Edy Hubacher, Hans Leutenegger and Werner Camichel. Their combined time for the four heats was 4 minutes 43.07 seconds.

The silver medal went to Italy's No. 1 sled, timed in 4:43.83, and West Germany took the bronze in 4:43.92. Wolfgang Zimmerer, gold medalist in the two-man bobsled earlier, piloted the West German sled.

In figure skating yesterday, American men failed to win, place or show for the first time in 36 years.

The best Ken Shelley and John Misha Petkevich could manage against the Europeans in the final stretch was to overtake 16-year-old Jan Hoffman of East Germany, who was No. 4 after the compulsories.

Shelley, No. 1 in the United States, and Petkevich, No. 2, finished fourth and fifth behind the winner, Ondrej Nepela of Czechoslovakia; Sergei Chetveroukhin of the Soviet Union, who was second, and Patrick Pera of France, who was third.

"I saw nothing in the American performance that anyone need be ashamed of," said Shelley's coach, John Nicks, whose hopes for a medal were dashed twice during the 11th Winter Games.

Nicks also coaches Shelley and Jo Jo Starbuck, the United States pairs champions, who were fourth on Wednesday night.

The sentiment of many American backers was that the three East Europeans on the panel of nine judges stacked the deck against the United States.

"It is not a question of unfair bias by the East Europeans," said the British-born Nicks. "They are a little restricted in their experience of free skating. They see only one type of skating, and they are slow to appreciate other types."

Shelley, a 21-year-old political science student from Downey, Calif., who turned in a dynamic free-skating performance, as did Petkevich, agreed.

"I think they think in a certain way, and the only thing to do is go out and do your best."

Petkevich, 22, of Great Falls, Mont., and Harvard, said he didn't think his countrymen were given full credit for their choreographics, which sparkled, in comparison to the medal winners.

"This was my best skating in about four years," said the blond pre-med student. "Both Shelley and Gordon McKellen did some very nice figures and I didn't see anything superior, except possibly from the Russian boy, Yuri Ovyvhinnikov."

McKellen, an 18-year-old Lake Placid, N.Y., youth who is ranked third in the United States, finished 10th in the Olympics and the Russian 12th.

Not since 1936, with two Winter Games cancelled because of World War II, has an American man failed to win a figure skating medal.

American gold medalists include Dick Button in 1948 and 1952; Hayes Alan Jenkins, 1956, and David Jenkins, 1960. Scott Allen won a bronze medal in 1964 and Tim Wood a silver medal in 1968.

February 12, 1972

# SOVIET SIX CAPTURES OLYMPIC TITLE, U.S. FINISHES 2D

## CZECHS LOSE, 5 TO 2

### Finland Tops Sweden, Helping U.S. to Gain the Silver Medal

**By The Associated Press**

SAPPORO, Japan, Sunday, Feb. 13 — The Soviet Union's powerful ice hockey team completed the competition at the 11th Winter Olympic Games today with a gold-medal victory that also gave the silver medal to the United States, the Americans' first hockey medal since their upset triumph in 1960.

For surprises, the United States hockey team had to share the spotlight with Francisco Fernandez Ochoa's stunning upset victory in the men's special slalom that gave Spain its first medal of any kind in Winter Olympic history.

Russia's winning the Olympic hockey title for the third straight time since being upset by the Americans at Squaw Valley, Calif., built up a 4-0 lead over Czechoslovakia and then held on for the 5-2 victory.

**Records Are Identical**

The loss left Czechoslovakia with a 3-2 won-lost record and 6 points, the same as the United States, but the Americans got the silver because they had beaten the Czechs.

The United States silver was set up when Finland upset Sweden, 4-3, earlier today, giving the Swedes a 2-2-1 mark and five points.

The silver medal was a tremendous accomplishment for the young United States team that had to beat Switzerland the day before official Olympic competition opened to even qualify for Group A and a chance at a medal.

The other gold medal handed out on the final day went to the Soviet Union's men's cross-country skiing team, which won when Vyacheslav Vedenin, the 30-kilometer gold medalist, surged from behind in the last few hundred meters.

**Cousins Are 2d and 3d**

Ochoa beat Italian cousins Gustavo and Rolando Thoeni in

pulling his Alpine surprise.

Ochoa, one-third of the Spanish Winter Olympic team —the other two members also are Alpine skiers—took the lead after the first run with a time of 55.36 seconds and kept it when he completed the second run in 53.91 for a total time of 1:49.27.

Gustavo Thoeni, winner of the giant slalom who was eighth after the first run in 56.69, took the silver medal when he whipped down the course in the fastest time of the day, 53.59, for a 1:50.28 total.

Rolando Thoeni placed third in 1:50.30.

The Soviet Union cross-country relay team earned its gold with a time of 2 hours 4 minutes 47.49 seconds for the 40 kilo-

meters or 24.8 miles. Norway was second in 2:04.57.06 and the bronze medal went to Switzerland in 2:07.00.06.

It was a fantastic triumph for the Russians and Vedenin, who was trailing Norway's anchorman, Johs Harvigen, by more than a minute as they started the final leg.

Vedenin's strong finish was a big disappointment to Norway, which was the defending Olympic champion. The United States finished 12th.

The Americans zipped off to a fast start against the Poles. With assists from Stuart Irving, 23, of Beverly Farms, Mass., and Robbie Ftorek, 20, of Needham, Mass., Tim Sheey, 23, of International Falls, Minn., jammed the puck past the Polish goalie 57 seconds after the opening face-off.

Craig Sarner, 22, of St. Paul scored two goals and one assist and moved into a tie for second place in the Class A scoring race with nine points. Valerii Kharlamov of the Soviet Union leads with 15.

One of Sarner's linemates, Kevin Ahearn, 23, of Milton, Mass., had three assists yesterday and ranks fifth in scoring with seven points. The third man on that line, Henry Boucha, 20, of Warroad, Minn., had one goal and one assist and is in a tie for eighth with five points.

Tadeusz Obloj ruined the bid for a shutout by the spectacular United States goalie, Michael Curran, 27, of Green Bay, Wis. The Pole scored on a 30-foot slap shot over Curran's shoulder early in the last period.

February 13, 1972

---

## Schenk Equals 1912 Feat On Speed-Skating Sweep

OSLO, Norway, Feb. 20 (AP) — Ard Schenk, three-time gold medalist at the recent Winter Olympic Games, won the 1,500 and 10,000 meter races today and became the first speed skater in 60 years to win all four events of the men's world championships.

The 27-year-old Dutchman's domination of the 66th championships also made him only the third man to win three consecutive over-all world titles.

Schenk broke his championship record of 2 minutes 4.80

seconds in the 1,500 meters by zipping home in 2:03.6, and then won the 10,000 meters in 15:22.09.

Schenk, who had a tulip named after him as an honor by the Netherlands, began his sweep yesterday by finishing in a tie for first with Roar Groenvold of Norway in the 500 meters and winning the 5,000 meters.

Groenvold finished second in the 1,500 meters in 2:04.40 and Eddy Verheyen of the Nether-

lands was third. Jan Bols of the Netherlands was second in the 10,000 meters in 15:26.52, and Sten Stensen of Norway was third.

Schenk's over-all point total was 171.594. Groenvold was next with 174.305, followed by Bols, 174.493, and Stensen, 175.446.

Gary Jonland of Park Ridge, Ill., was 11th in the 1,500 meters in 2:08.89 and Dan Carroll of St. Louis 16th in 2:09.34. Carroll was 16th in the 10,000 in 16:21.11 and 15th over all with 179.509 points.

In 1912, Oscar Mathiesen of Norway won all four world championship races.

February 21, 1972

---

## New Cult Developing In Skiing: The Acrobatics

**By WILLIAM N. WALLACE**
Special to The New York Times

SUN VALLEY, Idaho, March 25—There is the back scratcher, the worm, the outrigger, the bun buster and Polish wedlen. If you can do these, on skis, then you belong to a new cult rapidly achieving status in skiing. You are a hot dog and you are something special.

Acrobatic skiing has made significant advances in this ski season now drawing to a close. National competition in hot-dog skiing—exhibition skiing is the more formal title—was held this month at Waterville Valley, N.H., Sun Valley and Vail,

Colo. Scott Brooksbank of Vail emerged from the national championships at Vail last Tuesday and Wednesday as the king of the hot doggers.

Furthermore, skiing may have found something that the sport has long sought, a spectator event that can draw and hold the attention of viewers far better than jumping, or downhill and slalom racing as in the Olympic Games or on the professional circuit. It has not escaped the promoters that exhibition skiing may be better suited for television than the conventional racing.

"The crowd really went wild," said Gor-

Jim Stelling of Sun Valley doing cartwheel in ballet part

Greg Litschke of the ski patrol doing a full gainer or back flip off a bump in the aerial competition section.

don Butterfield, director of the Sun Valley Ski Club and one of the judges in the Western Division championships held here 10 days ago. "It was some of the most exciting skiing I've ever seen."

Showing off on skis has been part of the sport for a long time, especially among youthful, skillful participants to whom the mere act of going up on a lift and then skiing down is not quite enough. The recent technological advances in boots and skis and smoothing out of terrain has considerably widened the scope of the expert skier.

Organization of the exhibitionists—the hot dogs—seemed inevitable.

A year ago, Doug Pfeiffer, editor of Skiing magazine, and Tom Corcoran, the former Olympic downhill racer now running Waterville Valley, thought it worthwhile to find who out there was really the best trick or stunt skier.

They knew there were hundreds of crack young skiers who either had no interest in formal Alpine racing (downhill, giant slalom and slalom), or who were former racers and who much preferred the euphoria of free skiing in any style and manner they wished. The disciplines of racing against a clock were not for them. Some were ski patrolmen, a few might be instructors, but most worked around areas in various capacities and skied every day.

So Waterville Valley staged the first competition a year ago. It was such a success that the program was extended to three championships this year and Chevrolet provided promotional and prize money.

Brooksbank at Vail last week won a $6,300 Corvette automobile and there was $6,000 in cash prizes for other winners.

There were three categories in these championships. The first was stunt or ballet skiing done on a smooth open and rather gentle slope. Each competitor was required to make up a routine which he performed before five judges, similar to the free skating event in figure skating competition.

Here is where one gets the dance steps, doing a version of the Charleston on skis for example, or the outrigger in which one ski is extended far out to one side. Bob Mann of Aspen, Colo., has a specialty called the slow dog noodle in which at very slow speeds he sits on the back of his skis and does a series of 90-degree turns.

The second event was aerial acrobatic skiing done off a series of six built-up jumps. The judges were not interested in distance off the jump but in length of time in the air plus variety and difficulty of acrobatic leaps. It is in this competition that one finds the back scratcher. The skier touches his back at the shoulder

blades with the tails of the skis while in the air. Others like the bun buster, Polish wedeln and the worm all but defy description.

The third event, run down the steep heavily moguled Exhibition slope here was the free-style in which anything goes. The judges looked for general excellence of fast, fall line skiing over the most difficult terrain. Falls were acceptable as long as the skier recovered without breaking the continuity of his run.

The judging, purely subjective and in need of further refinement, was based on a point score of zero to 20. A skier making 17 to 20 points was "super hot"; 10-13 "cool," and 0-5 "super cold."

Hot-dog skiing has its critics. There are those who say it encourages wild, out-of-control skiing among youngsters that endangers others sharing the same slopes. The criticism may have validity, but there seems no holding this new phase of the sport once the drumbeats of promotion get going.

Movies, sponsored by Chevrolet, equipment manufacturers and experienced ski movie makers like Dick Barrymore, are in the works and seem certain to have a tremendous appeal to young, competent skiers seeking more thrills Areas in search of promotional outlets and paying spectators are likely to sponsor their own tournaments as skiing takes off in another new dimension.

March 26, 1972

## Soviet Union Ice Dancing Pair Takes 4th World Title in Row

BRATISLAVA, Czechoslovakia, March 2 (AP) — Ludmila Pakhomova and Alexander Gorshkov of the Soviet Union won their fourth consecutive dance title today and Ondrej Nepela held a commanding lead for the men's crown in the world figure skating championships.

The victory in the ice dance, a specialty once dominated by the British, provided the second over-all gold medal for Soviet Union skaters, who earlier had

won the pairs event.

The blue-clad husband and wife team whirled through a brilliant performance in the free-skating dance final and drew the No. 1 vote from all nine judges.

The silver medal for second place went to the West German brother-sister team of Angelika and Erich Buck. The bronze medal was won by Hilary Green and Glen Watts of Britain.

Toller Cranston of Toronto won the compulsory free-skating event today but failed to overtake Nefela, the defending

champion, in the battle for the men's title which will be decided tomorrow.

After the compulsory figures and the short program today, Nepela, a Bratislava University law student, maintained the lead over second-place Sergei Cheverukhin, of the Soviet Union. Cranston took third, with Gordon McKellen Jr., of Lake Placid, N.Y., the American champion fourth.

In the compulsory free skating, a new exercise in world competition, Cranston scored 78.95 points and had 16.5 ordinals. Nepela had 78.51 points but 27.5 ordinals, which are the judge's placings and the real barometer of scoring.

### 2 Perfect Marks Given

Cranston received one of the two perfect marks of 6 for the six required moves. Chetverukhin got the other.

The 19-year-old McKellen skated a brief program of 1 minute 24 seconds—faster than any of his rivals.

"I'm satisfied with my skating," he said. "but I felt a bit unsure on some of my landings. My skates need sharpening."

After completing his routine, McKellen was given a big hug and kiss by his Rockford, (Ill.), College schoolmate, Janet Lynn, the silver medalist in the ladies' competition.

March 3, 1973

## Nepela Takes Title In Figure Skating 3d Straight Year

BRATISLAVA, Czechoslovakia, March 3 (UPI)—Ondrej Nepela captured the men's world figure skating title today for the third straight year to the thunderous applause of an excited crowd in his hometown.

Nepela, the 23-year-old civil law student, was covered with flowers thrown on the ice by his supporters when he had finished his routine that earned him a top mark of 6.0—his first ever—from a Rumanian judge.

He got higher marks for his free-skating performance than Toller Cranston, the Canadian, who fell at a triple salchow and skated slightly below expectations.

Nepela, clearly ahead after the school figures and the compulsory free skating, appeared never in danger of losing the title as he skated to the music of the Russian composers, Kachaturian and Tchaikowski.

He finished his performance with a clean triple jump and was given nothing less than 5.8 and 5.9 for the technical merit of his program.

The Rumanian judge awarded him a 6 for composition and style while the Canadian and Italian judges rated this part of his program only at 5.7.

"I am glad I did it again," Nepela said. "But this was definitely the last time. My skating career was long enough."

Nepela has been skating in competition for 16 years. He made his international debut in 1964 at the Olympic Games in Innsbruck at the age of 13. He took part in 10 world championships.

He wanted to quit skating after winning the world and Olympic titles last year but was urged by Czechoslovak authorities to postpone his retirement for another year to give his farewell performance in his hometown.

International experts believed Nepela skated well and deserved to retain his title, but was not good enough to warrant a top mark of 6.

Nepela's performance was witnessed by Gustav Husak, the secretary general of the Czeshoslovak Communist Party, and other top party and government leaders.

The 12,000 spectators in the capacity packed ice stadium waved little Czechoslovak flags and chanted choruses of "Ondrej, Ondrej" as the champion finished his program and was assured of his third title.

Nepela skated right after Cranston, who is considered the world's most spectacular free skater, and was expected to remain in the shadow of the Canadian Champion's performance.

But Cranston, skating to Liszt's Hungarian Rhapsody, fell in trying a triple salchow and remained nervous for the rest of his program.

Cranston opened with a huge split jump, followed by a double axel and then went on to a triple loop before he fell at his second triple jump.

He immediately resumed but did not quite live up to expectations although the choreography of his performance was outstanding among all the competitors.

Cranston, a 23-year-old professional painter from Toronto, had not fallen in competition in the last three years. He is considered the most consistent competitor in international skating.

March 4, 1973

# Thoeni Captures Ski Title

**By BERNARD KIRSCH**
Special to The New York Times

ST. MORITZ, Switzerland, Feb. 5—The Italian Army, led by Sgt. Gustavo Thoeni, attacked on skis today and won the battle of the men's giant slalom in the world Alpine championships.

Thoeni, who wins the big races, beat an Austrian, Hans Hinterseer, by almost a second today, while three other Italians dominated the top 10 places. Pvt. Piero Gros was third, Helmuth Schmalzl was fourth and Erwin Stricker sixth. The Italian men have had a good season, and today's results were expected.

Nothing exciting was expected from the American civilians, however, and, after a good first run, that's what they produced. Cary Adgate, 20 years old, from Boyne City, Mich., finished 14th; Greg Jones, 20, of Tahoe City, Calif., finished 18th; Geoff Bruce, 20, of Corning, N. Y., was 26th, and Bob Cochran, 22, of Richmond, Vt., didn't finish the second heat.

Thoeni, 22, had the fastest first heat with a 1-minute-36.71-second clocking. Then he had a "prudent" second run of 1:31.21 for a total time of 3:07.92 to Hinterseer's 3:08.84.

Thoeni knows exactly what to do when it comes to winning titles, and the Italian Ski Association knows exactly what to do when it comes to building a winning team: Join the Army.

Mario Cotelli, the coach of the Italians, said last week that the ski team had "an agreement" with the military. When a skier makes the national team, he is conveniently allowed to join the army and is not given a gun. His weapons are skis and poles, and he serves the cause by winning races.

The Italian success story opened during the 1970-71 season when Thoeni became the first Italian to win the World Cup. He kept up the habit the following two seasons, and in 1972 he won the Olympic gold medal in the giant slalom and the silver medal in the special slalom.

Cotelli explained that when Thoeni began to win he brought up the level of the entire ski team. "A team rises and falls with its best," said Cotelli. Also, stories started drifting off the mountains tops about a reported $50,000 to $70,000 a year Thoeni was making from people in the "ski industry." That, too, helped to inspire many a young boy.

This season, the Italian men have won five World Cup races, once sweeping the top five places in a giant slalom.

Hinterseer has usually been the intruder into the Italians' domination. The son of Ernst Hinterseer, the slalom gold medalist in the 1960 Olympics in Squaw Valley, Calif., had one victory, a second and two thirds in past giant slaloms this season.

For the American men, all civilians, the giant slalom continued to be their weakest event, though Adgate's performance made him the skier of the future. After a good

Associated Press

**Gustavo Thoeni in the giant slalom event yesterday in St. Moritz, Switzerland**

first run, on the 1,290-meter course, Adgate said: "I guess I clutched. It was a bad race to learn in, but it will help me at lot."

Another pair of learning skiers in the field of 116 were Hwang Wei-Chung and Edwin Yeh of Taiwan, who finished 67th and 68th. The only skiers they beat were the 48 who failed to finish both heats. They included Yun-Ming Chen, also of Taiwan, a land that discovered skiing just 12 years ago.

February 6, 1974

## Miss Proell Clinches 5th Ski Cup Title

NAEBA, Japan, Feb. 23 (AP)—Annemarie Proell of Austria won a women's giant slalom race today and clinched her fifth consecutive World Cup Alpine skiing championship.

Miss Proell was timed in 1 minute 27.57 seconds for the single-run race, defeating Monika Kaserer of Austria, who was clocked in 1:28.29.

The 4-year-old Austrian ace earned 25 points for the victory, giving her 268 in the World Cup standing and putting her out of reach of her nearest challengers in the season's six remaining cup races.

Christina Tinot of Italy was third in 1:28.45 and Michelle Jacot of France fourth in 1:28.60.

The top American was Viki Fleckenstein of Syracuse, who finished fifth in 1:28.90. Cindy Nelson of Lutsen, Minn., was eighth in 1:29.33 and Becky Dorsey of Wenham, Mass., was ninth in 1:29.35.

Earlier, another Austrian, Hans Hinterseer, scored a narrow victory over Ingemar Stenmark of Sweden in the men's slalom race.

Hinterseer had runs of 42.58 and 43.88 seconds for a combined total of 1:26.46. Stenmark had a combined time of 1:26.52, with Christian Neureuther of West Germany third at 1:26.87.

In the battle for the men's World Cup title, the three-time champion, Gustavo Thoeni of Italy, increased his lead. Thoeni held a 198-190 lead over Franz Klammer before the race, finished fifth in 1:27.53, and raised his point total to 206 with six races left in the 24-race season. Klammer finished 17th in 1:31.99.

February 24, 1975

# Koch, Skier, and Miss Young, Skater, Take Olympic Silver Medals for U.S.

## Klammer Wins Downhill Race At Innsbruck

### By FRED TUPPER
Special to The New York Times

INNSBRUCK, Austria, Feb. 5—Austria and the Soviet Union won opening day gold medals as they were supposed to do in the Winter Olympics but three astonishing performances by Americans today produced two silver medals and an undreamed of sixth place.

The United States has its first cross-country skiing medal. Bill Koch of Guilford, Vt., who said he would have been happy to make the first 10, was second to Sergei Saveliev a Russian soldier, over the demanding 30-kilometer Nordic event. He was only 28.46 seconds back of the winner, who was timed in 1 hour 30 minutes 29.38 seconds.

"The silver medal was much better than I could expect," said the blue-eyed, pink-cheeked 20-year-old Vermonter from a village of 1,100, a few miles south of Brattleboro. "You push yourself to the limit and hold on to do the best you can." Koch was in fourth or fifth place most of the way but turned it on down the stretch. His muscles were cramping at the finish.

"He's mentally and physically exhausted," said Coach Marty Hall. "He should be in bed."

With this feat Koch became the youngest silver medalist

Associated Press

Franz Klammer, left, the Austrian downhill gold medal winner, relaxes at news conference with Bill Koch, U.S., who won silver medal in 30-kilometer cross-country event.

over this distance in Olympic history.

### Scores in "Warmup"

Sheila Young of Detroit took the silver medal in 1,500-meter speed skating, an event not her distance. There have been hopes all along that the 25-year-old brunette would take the 500 meters, in which she set a world record five days ago at Davos, Switzerland.

The 1,500 was supposed to be a warmup. "I thought it would be good to skate another distance first," she said, "and the conditions were really fantastic." She opened up and let it rip, diving low through the finish in 2:17.06, an infinitesimal eight-one hundredths of a second behind the Soviet Union's Galina Stepanskaya.

Favored Franz Klammer, the idol of this ski-mad country, survived several near spills in taking the downhill, long the glamour event of the Games. As the yells of "hopp auf (go on) thundered and reverberated as 45,000 jammed around the 3,020-

meter course, the golden boy, now 22, came from third at the interval in a driving run that had the crowd in hysterics.

"I thought I was going to crash all the way," he said breathlessly later, after roaring through the clock in 1:45.73, arms raised high in victory. Second was Bernhard Russi of Switzerland, the gold medalist at Sapporo, Japan, in the 1972 Games.

Andy Mill of Aspen, Colo.,

who will be 23 next week, finished sixth, "the best in 20 years for an American downhiller," said Hank Tauber, the United States director of Alpine skiing. Mill has gone through hell. He had an operation last year on his right knee in March and another on his left knee in May. He was bruised and contused before takeoff today. A sore leg was packed with ice before the launch, and a piece of cardboard inserted into the boot to prevent chafing the raw skin.

"It's the first time I've been in the top 15 this year," said Andy.

"Any time you have athletes that give everything they have to try and be the best," Tauber said, "then you've got to love them."

Mill's performance wasn't the only one that Tauber loved. Greg Jones of Tahoe City, Calif., finished 11th and Pete Patterson of Sun Valley, Idaho took 13th place. With three Americans in the top 15, Tauber was very happy. "We've always had guys falling, but this time I think we showed how far the United States has come."

The fourth American, Karl Anderson of Greene, Me., after a mistake at the beginning, wound up in 24th place.

Miss Young goes for that coveted 500-meter crown tomorrow but it will be a time before she forgets that charge down the last straight today. Tatyana Averina, the world record-holder from the Soviet Union, was the favorite, because of her time 2:09.9 made at the rink near Alma Ata. Perhaps the second favorite was Leah Poulos of Northbrook, Ill.

A hot sun shone and it was thought that the pairs starting early would have the advantage before the ice began to soften. In the end it made no difference. What did, though, was a swirling wind that often has made the Innsbruck rink an unhappy place at which to compete. It came and went.

Miss Stepanskaya, a 27-year-old from Leningrad, got the good break. She skated just after the half-time intermission with the ice cleared, the flags flat against their poles with no wind at all. That meant the difference and the Russian skated beautifully, making up time every meter of the way and finishing strongly in 2:16.58, an Olympic record.

The Misses Averina and Poulos had varying winds, Tatyana, slow earlier, Leah fading slightly toward the end. To Miss Young, who once fell here, the "conditions were fantastic. I had no problems. There was a slight disadvantage finishing on the outer [lane] and maybe I was struggling a bit there in the last 200."

Her father, Clair, was ec-

static. "I'm overwhelmed, to say the least." The hundred or so skating buffs from the West Allis, Wis., area, one of the nation's leading skating centers, tooted horns and waved American flags. "Go, Sheila, go," they screamed, but they're really waiting for tomorrow. So is everybody else.

Third place went to Miss Averina and Miss Poulos finished sixth. The American champion's time was 2:19.11.

### U. S. Dancers 3d

The American ice dancers, Colleen O'Connor and James Millns of Colorado Springs, held on to third place. They trailed two couples from the

Soviet Union but were close enough to the second-place pair to make a silver medal possible in the final Monday night. In first place were Lyudmila Pakhomova and Aleksandr Gorshkov, the world champions who appeared certain to win the first Olympic title. The event was added to the games this year.

The leaders have 9 ordinals and 103.72 points. The second-place duo, Irina Moiseyeva and Andrei Minenkov, had 21 ordinals and 100.08 points and the Americans are next with 26 ordinals and 99.84 points.

The pair skating began with Irina Rodnina and Aleksandr Zaitsev of the Soviet Union took the lead as expected.

The American champions, Tai Babilonia, 15, and Randy Gardner, 17, of Los Angeles were in fifth place.

### Luge Record Broken

In luge, Josef Fendt of West Germany broke the track record but was in second place after a 51.933 run over the 1,217-meter course. The leader was Detlef Guenther of East Germany after two of the four runs. The best of the Americans was Jim Murray of Steamboat Springs, Colo., in 29th place.

Monika Scheftschik of West Germany led the women. Kathy Homestead of Goleta, Calif., was 21st and Maura Jo Haponski of Lake Placid, N. Y., 24th.

*February 6, 1976*

# Miss Young Captures Olympic Skating Title

**By FRED TUPPER**
Special to The New York Times

INNSBRUCK, Austria, Feb. 6—Sheila Young, the 25-year-old speed skating marvel from Detroit, made a shambles of the 500-meter sprint, her speciality, today in winning the gold medal in the Olympic Winter Games. Her triumph was the first for an American in the competition that started yesterday.

Her time for the lap and a half race was 42.76 seconds, superb in low clouds and fog over the ice, she smashed the 43.33 Olympic mark set at Sapporo, Japan, in 1972 by Anne Henning, another American, and bettered the 43.18 Innsbruck record that happened to be Miss Young's own.

Second was Cathy Priestner of the Calgary (Alberta) Skating Club, in 43.12 seconds and third was Tatyana Averina, of the Soviet Union, a former world record-holder. The Russian came through at the end in 43.17 to snatch the bronze medal from Leah Poulos of Northbrook, Ill., by four one-hundredths of a second.

Miss Young described her thoughts at the start and on her way round the rink:

"Oh, my God; good start. Here I go; 10.82 at the 100. That's pretty good. Round the turn. I could hear Peter [the coach] yelling, and my fiancé yelling. 'Fight, fight, fight.' Try to go faster. Legs starting to go."

### Crowd Cheers Victor

Then she was making the last turn, her body parallel to the ice, pony tail stream-

United Press International

**Sheila Young waves to crowd after receiving the silver medal for her performance in 1,500-meter competition.**

ing. The stretch ahead, the test of strength and stamina. Head bent low, arms swinging, legs pumping, she came home with the crowd rising to cheer her, the gang from the Midwest bellowing "Go, Go, Go." A final surge and the clock high on the electric

scoreboard stopped, flashing the magic 42.76.

Miss Young came into the interview room carrying a bunch of yellow daffodils. "I didn't like to go early. The warmup conditions were terrible. The ice was bad, then good," she said. "I thought it would be nice for the sun to come out for my ice."

She skated without socks, she explained, "so I could move my toes around. It gives me better rapport with my skates. It wasn't a perfect race. I drifted out on the turn. My last hundred meters, I was coming back on my heels."

The waiting for the remainder of the contestants to take their turns was agony. Miss Young refused to take her skates off. The ice was clear half-way through, long after she had skated. The buffs say that the second skater after intermission gets the best ice. She was Vera Krasnova, the best of the Russians on reputation.

Miss Krasnova was clocked at 10.64 seconds at the 100-meter mark, 1.8 seconds faster than Miss Young. "Oh, no. Here it goes," the American thought. "I saw her 200, her 300, her 400. Saw I still had a chance." The Russian finished in 43.23 seconds and in fifth place.

"It was weird. I wasn't sure till the end. Then I got this rush through my whole body," the Detroit woman said.

Tomorrow Miss Young skates in the 1,000-meter event. Yesterday she had placed second in the 1,500, not her favorite distance. Six days ago she had set up an unimaginable world record time of 40.91 seconds at

Davos, Switzerland, a rink at an altitude of 1,600 meters (1,000 meters higher than Innsbruck) where the air resistance is less and faster times result.

It had been a long wait for a gold medal. Just as Miss Poulos was nipped today, so Miss Young had lost what seemed like a sure bronze at Sapporo to Miss Averina.

"I thought I'd quit," Miss Young said, she did odd jobs. She worked as a waitress. Then she took up cycling to build up her leg muscles. She crashed twice in the world cycling championships at San Sebastian, Spain, in 1973. Her legs bled. Her arms were bandaged. Half a dozen stitches were sewed into her scalp. "She must have been the toughest girl in the world," said a correspondent who was there and she won.

Miss Young plans to compete in the world cycling this summer in Italy. She wants that championship again.

"And I'll predict she'll win," said her father, Clair. "She puts her heart and full self into it."

Miss Henning, now a commentator with ABC, hugged Shelia. "She's the best. The best ever? They learn all the time. They know more now. They skate faster. She's the best."

The Soviet Union took its third gold medal when a 25-year-old Army Officer, Nikolai Kruglov, took the individual 20-kilometer biathlon event on the Seefeld course.

Heikki Ikola of Finlnad, who led until near the finish was second. The Russian's winning time was 1 hour 14 minutes 12.26 seconds. He and Ikola each had 2 minutes in penalties added to the racing time for missing in target shooting.

The medal supposedly should have gone to Aleksandr Tikhonov, second at Grenoble in 1968 and fourth at Sapporo in 1972, but he failed on his final shots, receiving six penalty minutes. He finished fifth. Aleksandr Elizarov, of the Soviet Union was third.

The United States had an unhappy day. Capt. Lyle Nelson of Boise, Idaho, wound up 35th with 10 penalty minutes after a good start.

The American hockey team held the Russians to a 6-2 victory, today a sterling performance for amateur collegians considering the 5-2-1 record the Soviet Central Army and Wings rang up against the National Hockey League teams.

After the first two runs for the two-man bobsled title, Fritz Sperling and Andreas Schwab of Austria had squeezed out a three-one hundredths of a second edge over the favored East German team of Meinhard Nehmer and Bernhard Germeshausen. The West German sled of Wolfgang Zimmrcer andManfred Schumann was third The leading time for two runs was 1:52.25. Final runs will be held tomorrow.

The best American showing was that of Jim Morgan, a driver from Saranac, N.Y., and Tom Becker of Indianapolis. They were in 15th place. Brent Rushlaw of Saranac Lake and John Proctor of Plattsburgh were 20th.

East Germans led in men's and women's luge, the coasting competition with the little sleds. Detlef Guenther retained the lead in the men's division with another record performance over the 1,217-meter track. He covered it in 51.418 seconds bettering the mark Josef Fendt of West Germany made yesterday. Fendt was still in second place over all. Hans Rinn of East Germany was third.

Margit Schumann, the world champion from East Germany, went into the lead in the women's division. She set a track record for the 870-meter women's run in 42.28 seconds. She went ahead of Monika Scheftschik of West Germany, who had steering problems and wound up ninth in the day's run and dropped to seventh place. However, another West German, Elisabeth Demleitner, moved into second place over all.

The Americans were still far down. Kathy Homstad of Goleta, Calif., was 23d. Richard Cavanaugh of Hermosa Beach, Calif., was 27th in the men's competition.

February 7, 1976

# Sheila Young Takes 3d Olympic Medal; East Germans and Russians Triumph

*Detroit Skater Is 3d—Leah Poulos 2d*

**By FRED TUPPER**
Special to The New York Times

INNSBRUCK, Austria, Feb. 7—Sheila Young's hopes of two gold medals were shattered today as the Russians and East Germans dominated the third day of the Winter Olympics.

Tatyana Averina of the Soviet Union set an Olympic record in the 1,000-meter speed skating event, with Leah Poulos of Northbrook, Ill., second and Miss Young, an overnight household heroine, making a late charge for third as the ice conditions deteriorated.

Now with a first, a second

Associated Press

Sheila Young talking on the phone with her family in Detroit after winning her third Olympic prize, a bronze medal in the 1,000-meter speed skating event.

Associated Press

Leah Poulos of Northbrook, Ill., was in good mood after winning the silver medal in 1,000-meter speed-skating competition. Tatyana Averina of U.S.S.R. won event.

and a third place in the skating events, the 25-year-old Detroit brunette became the first American to win three medals in the Winter Olympics. Yesterday she ran away from the field in a record-breaking 500-meter sprint after she had taken second in the 1,500-meter behind another Russian on Thursday.

"Not bad so far for a country that has 150 speed skaters," said Philip Krumm, the president of the United States Olympic Committee, "compared to the 50,000 that skate in Russia."

The East Germans were overpowering in the luge competition. With Detlef Guenther and Margit Schumann winning the golds, they took four of the six medals. Richard Cavanaugh of Hermosa Beach, Calif., was the first American at 25th, while Kathleen Homstad of Miles City, Mont., led American women, three places ahead of her sister, Karen Roberts.

Hans-Georg Aschenbach, the world champion who was sidelined a year ago by knee surgery took a third gold medal for East Germany in the 70-meter ski jump. He leaped 276 and 269 feet for 252 points. His teammate, Jochen Danneberg, was second.

His total included jumps of 274 and 271 feet for 246.2 points. Karl Schnabl of Austria took third place. Jim Denney of Duluth, Minn., was in 21st place.

Like Miss Young, Olympic great Galina Kulakova was frustrated in her attempt for a victory today. Three times a winner at Sapporo, Japan, in the 1972 Nordic events, the Russian, now 33, finished third in the five-kilometer cross-country race. Helena Takalo of Finland captured the first gold medal for her country in 15:48.69 with Raisa Smetanina of the Soviet Union second.

There had been predictions that Martha Rockwell, 31, of West Lebanon, N.H., would finish in the first 10 but she wound up 29th. She was seven stages ahead of Jana Hlavaty, a former Czech who acquired American citizenship by a unanimous vote of Congress last month.

Looking "for a near perfect performance" in the 1,000-meter event, Miss Poulos almost brought it off. Angry at the starters, who, she said, "let us stand there freezing so long that we put our warmup suits back on," Miss Poulos skated brilliantly until the last turn.

"I didn't lean into it as good as I could. You can let up on your speed and tempo."

She finished in 1:28.57 and led the field, throwing the delegation of fans from the midwest into an uproar. But Miss Averina, the world record holder was next, she was faster at 200 meters and though her margin was whittled down, she raced past the timers with a .17 second edge.

"You always expect more of yourself than others do and there's room to improve," said Miss Poulos, dark and disappointed. "I couldn't hear my coach calling the times because the people were screaming. Then I made that turn mistake and knew what it cost me."

**Associated Press**
Helena Takalo of Finland wins gold medal in five-kilometer cross-country.

Asked if she would do it differently next time, the silver medalist thought that an earlier arrival here was mandatory. "I needed the adjustment," she said. There were no recriminations. She was happy with the result.

Peter Mueller, her fiancé who is a sprint skater, thought it good enough to win.

"If I do something wrong, he's the first to tell me," she says. They have been engaged for two years. They've dropped out of college temporarily to pursue skating.

"That may be as worthwhile, says Miss Poulos." I took French for nine years and am still shaky. I learned Dutch just by skating on those rinks."

She says no date has been set for the wedding. "We need money in the bank."

It seemed Miss Young had the perfect draw. She likes the sun on her face and it broke out of the foggy gloom after intermission. The villain was the ice-restructuring machine, believes Coach Peter Schotting—"too much water on the ice and there's softer frosting that can slow you down."

The Detroit woman started slowly and was nearly a second behind at 600 meters. The adrenalin flowed and the rhythm came. In a furious lap, the fastest of the day, she came home in 1:29.14 to warm applause.

For Miss Young, the glory days are nearly over. One of the best women athletes of her time, a world champion in two sports, this is her last year of competition. There are a few dates still to keep: the world speed skating championships in Norway, the world sprints at Berlin and a last shot in the world cycling championship. Then comes marriage.

In the world first 10 a year ago and rated eighth now, Cindy Nelson has a chance for a medal in the women's downhill competition tomorrow. Her confidence has been shaken. "I've got a lot of things to work out. I just can't seem to get it together." In the final practice today the 20-year-old skier from Lutsen, Minn., missed a gate halfway down mountain and dropped out. She has drawn the 10th starting position. Susie Patterson of Sun Valley, Idaho, a rapid improver, finished 12th in today's run, "and I can do better," she says.

To nobody's surprise, Irina Rodnina won her second Olympic title, this time paired with husband, Aleksandr Zaitsev. Her first one at Sapporo was with Alexei Ulanov. In all the superb Russian skater has won seven world titles, four with Ulanov, three with Zaitsev.

The gold medal was the fifth for the Soviet Union.

East Germany has four, all earned today as it snatched the two-man bobsled championship from the Austrians.

East Germany gained second and third in the pair skating and the youngsters from Los Angeles, Tai Babilonia, 15, and Randy Gardner, 17, gave a sound, mature performance that gave them fifth place and promises well for their future.

February 8, 1976

# German Jumpers Are 1, 2

**By MICHAEL STRAUSS**
Special to The New York Times

SEEFELD, Austria, Feb. 7—In this little Tyrolean resort village where Vermont's Bill Koch two days ago electrified the Nordic skiing world by winning an Olympic silver medal in cross-country, the United States failed to provide anything resembling a surprise today.

With the Alpine racers idle in Innsbruck, two Nordic events — jumping and women's cross-country — took the spotlight in a Christmas card scene under cloudless skies. The United States could not place an athlete among the first twenty in either event.

The East Germans produced a one-two finish in the jumping on the well-shaded, 70-meter hill, confounding many Austrians in the crowd estimated at 25,000. Hans-Georg Aschenbach and Jochen Danneberg finished first and second, respectively. Both were injured a few months ago.

"I think perhaps the Austrians were a little too confident," said Aschenbach, who beat his teammate by a whopping 5.8 points.

**Miss Takola Triumphs**

In the five-kilometer cross-country event (about three miles) Finland's Helena Takalo was the winner, followed by three stalwarts from the Soviet Union—Raisa Smetania, Galina Kulakova and Nina Baldicheva. Miss Kulakova, almost 19 seconds slower than the winner, was the defending champion.

Jim Denney, a 19-year-old who was crowned champion at Squaw Valley, Calif., last month in his first Class A national event, led the Americans by placing 21st. The best finish for an American in the women's race was Martha Rockwell's 29th.

Glenn Kotlarek of Duluth, Minn., the American jumping coach, was enthusiastic, saying:

"Over all, our four men, I am told scored the greatest total points for an American Olympic team. Denney certainly was impressive. He's only a newcomer to international jumping, still he traveled 79 meters [about 259 feet] in his first trip. A veteran like Aschenbach, in making the meet's longest flight, went 276 feet."

Jerry Martin, who, like Denney, comes from Minnesota, was the second best American with a 27th placing. He did 256 on his first flight, but only 245 on his second.

Denney traveled 251 feet the second time, and was disappointed. But Martin, a seasoned hand who now has been on two Olympic squads, felt the youngster had made outstanding progress in the few weeks with the team.

"Trying to put together a jumping team that can match the East Germans or Austrians is a tough assignment," said Martin, who competes despite being almost sightless in one eye.

Jana Hlavaty, a Czechoslovak who recently became an American citizen, was second-best among her teammates with a 36th placing in the cross-country.

"I think Jana was nervous," said Tom Upham, the American women's coach. About Miss Rockwell, he said: "Martha was hit by flu a few weeks ago and it slowed her training. Besides, she's better at 10 kilometers."

Miss Rockwell said:

"The uphills are what hurt me most. I went as fast as I could, but my fast wasn't fast enough."

Mrs. Hlavaty, a tall blond whose long legs and intensive poling give her somewhat the appearance of a spider in motion was very unhappy.

Miss Takalo, victory was no surprise. She has been improving constantly. But the powerful showing by Aschenbach and Danneberg stunned the Austrians in the crowd. They had expected more from their athletes. They had to be content with a third by Carl Schnabl and sixth, seventh and eighth placings by his teammates.

The slim Aschenbach, who jumped 276 and 269 feet against 274 and 271 for Dannenberg, said while eating a frankfurter without a roll:

"I felt good after my first jump. I skied right out of the outrun and headed for the woods so the photographers wouldn't find me. I wanted to be left alone."

After coming to a swishing stop at the end of his second flight, the East German raised both hands into the air in an expression of delight. He seemed certain he would win although 15 jumpers followed him.

Last August Aschenbach underwent a knee operation and had to stop training for two months. Danneberg, until recently, had been plagued with an ailing shoulder.

Said Ron Mackenzie of Lake Placid, N.Y., head of that Winter Olympics scheduled for that Adirondack resort in 1980:

"I wonder how much better those two Germans would have done had they been able to keep training at all all?"

February 8, 1976

---

# Rosi Mittermaier Captures Downhill, Miss Nelson of U.S. Third at Olympics

## Czechoslovaks Top Americans in Hockey, 5-0

**By FRED TUPPER**
Special to The New York Times

INNSBRUCK, Austria, Feb. 8—Rosi Mittermaier, the captivating West German skier, won the women's downhill, star attraction of the Winter Olympic Games, today. Ten years on the circuit, three times an Olympian, "Mama" finally did it.

The 25-year-old Miss Mittermaier scooted down the mountain in 1 minute 46.16 seconds to beat the hot favorite, Brigitte Totschnig of Austria. Cindy Nelson of the United States was a remarkable third.

The United States hockey team battled the highly rated Czechoslovaks on nearly even terms for two periods tonight before succumbing to a third-period onslaught in a 5-0 loss. It was the Americans' second straight defeat.

Milan Novy tallied in the first and third periods for Czechoslovakia, whose goalie, Jiri Holecek, was brilliant.

The American collegians, got a strong game from their goaltender, Jim Warden. He and his teammates held the Czechoslovaks to two goals in the first two periods.

In other games in the round-robin medal tournament, the Soviet Union, heavily favored for the gold medal, routed Poland, 16-1, and Finland defeated West Germany, 5-3.

Although she has done most everything else, today's downhill victory was Rosi's first ever. "I can't believe that it's me who has won," said the bronzed brunette with the flashing smile. "I'd had bad experiences in Olympics before."

Miss Mittermaier leads the World Cup standing for 1976 with 224 points and six events to go in the United States and Canada.

Cindy could hardly believe it either. The blue-eyed 20-year-old from Lutsen, Minn., had been off form of late, falling yesterday in her last practice run and making it to the bottom only three times in nine tries.

### She Bemoans Mistake

"I skied well," Miss Nelson said, "but 1 made a mistake that cost me time. I had to make a turn to get back on my line, a thing you should never do in downhill."

"I've been telling the world for two years that she was that good," said the United States director of Alpine skiing, Hank Tauber. "They knocked me at first. Now they know."

That bronze gives the United States six medals, one-two-three finishes by Sheila Young and a second by Leah Poulos in speed skating plus a second by Bill Koch in the 30-kilometer cross-country.

The 20-year-old Koch wound up only sixth today in the 15-kilometer cross-country, won by little-known Nikolai Bajukov of the Soviet Union, with the Vermonter

Rosi Mittermaier of West Germany after finishing her winning run in women's downhill in course-record time.

drooping with three laps to go.

Bajukov was clocked in 43:58.47 for the 9.3 miles. Evgeny Belisev of the Soviet Union was second and Arto Koivisto of Finland was third.

Ulrich Wehling, East Germany's defending champion in the Nordic combined, led today with 225.5 points in the jumping.

Fourth after the first figure, Sergei Volkov of the Soviet Union vaulted into the lead with a well-traced back outside paragraph bracket and forward outside paragraph loop, figures in the

eerie world of compulsories that must be completed before they can get at the free skating that packs the crowds in nightly. The current European champion, John Curry of Britain, who lives in New York, is a slight favorite. He was second after today's competition. Dave Santee of Park Ridge, Ill., is in fifth position.

By a blink of an eyelash, Tatiana Averina became the first athlete to win two gold medals. The great Soviet skater, who holds two world records in the middle distances, took the long 3,000-meter event by four one-hundredths of a seconds from Andrea Mitscherlice of East Germany, with Lisbeth Kors-

mo of Norway a finger snap behind. The winning time was 4:45.19, an Olympic mark.

Only the legendary Lydia Skoblikova has done better. The Russian took all four golds at Squaw Valley and picked up two more on this Innsbruck rink in 1964.

Ice conditions were perfect on this slow rink. The sun shone, the Alps were out in their finery and the times were tremendous. Nancy Swider did her best ever but saw her third place disintegrate at the end with a rush by unknown East Germans.

The skater from Park Ridge, Ill., was near tears. "I lost two seconds on the second leg and never got them back." she said.

Beth Heiden, 16, of Madison, Wisc., a mere slip of a girl at 85 pounds and five foot nothing, came along later at 11th. Asked if longer legs would help in skating, she said "I don't know. I never had longer legs."

Miss Mitscherlich, the 15-year-old doll from Dresden, had it all wrapped up. With a lap to go, she was leading Miss Averina by an enormous 1.74 seconds. She slowed, strength waning and form crumbling. The Russian had done the loop in 38.50, Andrea in 40.31. Remember the name though. She'll be heard of again.

February 9, 1976

# Thoeni Leads in Giant Slalom, Phil Mahre 4th at Innsbruck

## U.S. Twosome Gets Bronze in Dance

**By FRED TUPPER**
Special to The New York Times

INNSBRUCK, Austria, Feb. 9—Gustavo Thoeni of Italy, the defending Olympic champion in the giant slalom, raced into the lead in his specialty, as expected, today at the 12th Winter Games, but the big surprise was the fourth-place finish of Phil Mahre.

The young American eclipsed such skiing giants as Sweden's Ingemar Stenmark and Italy's Piero Gros, one, two this year in the World Cup rankings, after the first runs over the icy and extremely tricky Hoadl course.

The United States picked up a bronze medal in the ice dancing event when Colleen O'Connor and James Millns of Colorado Springs placed third after the final phase was completed today. Lyudmila Pakhomova and Aleksandr Gorshkov of the Soviet Union won the gold and Irine Moiseeva and Andrei Minenkov, also of the Soviet Union, took the silver.

Starting among the top 15 for the first time in his life, the 18-year-old Mahre, from White Pass, Wash., flashed through the timers behind Thoeni and two Swiss racers, Ernst Good and Heini Hemmi, 1.39 seconds off the pace.

Mahre was beside himself, hoping for a medal. "You've really got to go for it, make the turn and a ride a good ski," he said. He's happy

**Associated Press**
Philip Mahre from White Pass, Wash., racing to a fourth-place finish on the first run of the giant slalom competition yesterday. Event is scheduled to be completed today.

about the hill they race on tomorrow in the giant slalom's final leg. "It's a little steeper, not sidehill and has gates close together."

Mahre's identical twin, Steve, was 14th.

"You've just seen the beginning of these Mahres," said the United States Alpine director, Hank Tauber.

"They're unbelievable."

Two years ago Phil broke a leg in an avalanche. Last year he did it again, sliding down an amusement park chute. A delegation of hometown folk has flown over to see him go tomorrow. He started sixth today, has seventh position on his next run.

Thoeni, however, is no shoo-in. The gold medalist at Sapporo and four times World Cup champion, he is chiefly threatened by Stenmark, eighth today, and Gros, fifth. Time and again the 19-year-old, freckle-faced Swede has gone from far back to snatch the victory. Gros was World Cup champion the only year—1974—that Thoeni wasn't.

"I'm nervous," admitted Thoeni, "but I still think I'll sleep."

Ulrich Wehling of East Germany has his second gold medal in the Nordic combined. With a huge lead after the jumping yesterday, he was strong enough to finish 13th in the cross-country today to win the event.

For the 23-year-old from Halle, it was a struggle. "Nerve pressure was my worst enemy," he said. "It was much easier to win at Sapporo when I was not the favorite." Only 19 then, he was the youngest man ever to win the Nordic event, long the property of the Norwegians.

West Germany's Urban Hettich gave Wehling a good run for it, sprinting away from the field over the 15-kilometer course. "I knew how fast he was going," said Wehling. "Then I used all my strength."

Hettich was second and Konrad Winkler of East Germany third.

Jim Galanes of Brattleboro, Vt., confessed he picked the wrong skis after finishing 17th, best for an American in this event.

"I used a soft ski. It dragged, so I had to push that much harder than I usually do. It gave me a backache. I got tight and could not ski a relaxed race."

Galanes improved his position, though, advancing from 25th place in yesterday's 70-meter jumping.

Mrs. Galina Kulakova of the Soviet Union, a three-time gold medalist, was disqualified from keeping the bronze medal in the five-kilometer cross-country race. She took nose drops the night before the race, but the medication, ephedrine, is on the list of banned drugs.

John Curry of Britain, a four-year resident of the United States, is now the favorite to win the gold in free skating.

Second to Sergei Volkov of the Soviet Union after the comprehensive figures, Curry put on a two-minute short performance today that had the judges averaging 5.8 for technical merit and an almost solid line of 5.9's for artistic impression.

Only the three-time world champion, Toller Cranston of Canada, had higher marks but he had been buried in the figures.

"He's elegant," said the retired two-time gold medallist, Dick Button. "He has an extraordinary style." Translated, it means that Curry is the best spinner in the business where jumping is now the rage.

Volkov was solid but not spectacular. Another Soviet skater, Vladimir Kovalev,

chickened out of a triple salchow and was low-marked on his double, and Jan Hoffman, the East German who was been called the best skater in the world "from the waist down" for his pure jumping, spinning and clear

landing, marred that reputation today. He blew a double axle, which was mandatory in the program, and was moved down to third place.

February 10, 1976

# E. German Skier Keeps Nordic-Combined Title

Special to The New York Times

INNSBRUCK, Austria, Feb. 9—Ulrich Wehling of East Germany who broke protocol in 1972 by becoming the first non-Scandinavian to win the Nordic-combined skiing championship in the Olympics, retained the title today. But his closest competitors were a West German and an East German teammate.

It was the West German, Urban Hettich, who finished first in today's phase of the dual event, the 15-kilometer cross-country ski race. He skimmed home more than a minute ahead of Stein Erik Gullikstad of Norway in 48 minutes 1.55 seconds. Several more came in ahead of Wehling who was 13th.

However, Wehling had won the jumping phase yesterday by a large margin and those points gave him the over-all lead with a total of 423.39 points. Hettich, 11th in the jump, had 418.9, enough to win the silver medal. The bronze medal went to Konrad Winkler of East Germany with 417.7. The best of the Scandinavians was Rauno Miettinen of Finland, who was second in 1972 at Sapporo, Japan. He had 411.30 points this time.

When Wehling took the honors away from the Scandinavians in 1972 he was fourth in the jumping and third in the race.

Those competing in the cross-country race at Seefeld saw some snow fall for the first time since the Games began. It was little more than a light dusting, but it caused problems for those who had waxed for a "fast" track.

"It gave me trouble," said Wehling. "It went fine up to about five or six kilometers. Then my skis went slippery and I had trouble in the uphill parts of the course."

By the time the first run in today's giant slalom was starting—about three hours later — at Axamer Lizum which overlooks this city, the sun was back again.

Although the extremely icy course deteriorated quickly turning into a surface of light granular snow, there were

few spills. A performer who took a header was Thomas Hauser of Austria. He went sprawling near the end of the run after allowing himself to sit back too much, thereby missing connections with a gate.

February 10, 1976

# Soviet Skier Loses Medal Over a Drug

**By MICHAEL STRAUSS**
Special to The New York Times

INNSBRUCK, Austria, Feb. 9—The first penalty for use of an unauthorized drug was imposed today at the 12th Winter Olympics.

Urine tests taken last Saturday from Mrs. Galina Kulakova of the Soviet Union immediately after the women's five-kilometer cross-country race at nearby Seefeld were found to contain ephedrine. The Russian star, who had placed third in the event, was disqualified this morning.

The Soviet Union, however, didn't suffer in the medal standing because its Nina Baldicheva was advanced from her fourth-place finish to receive the bronze medal.

Associated Press

**Galina Kulakova of the Soviet Union winning a bronze medal in cross-country race Saturday. Medal was taken from her yesterday because she had taken banned drug.**

Prince Alexandre de Merode of Belgium, president of the International Olympic Committee's medical commission, in announcing his group's decision, expressed his regrets, indicating there had been some reluctance in making the decision.

"It is almost an injustice to take the medal away from this fine Russian athlete," he said. "It seemed such an innocent act by Mrs. Kulakova. But if we are to have rules, we must enforce them."

The Nordic event star (she holds the Order of Lenin and was the winner of gold medals in all three 1972 cross-country events at Sapporo, Japan) said she had not realized she was violating a rule in taking the drug.

"My nose was stuffed at about 3 o'clock in the morning on the day of the race," she was said to have told

the medical commission. "I didn't think it necessary to consult a physician."

Dr. Fred Schoonmaker of Denver, who is on the American Olympic team's staff, said ephedrine was of the same type that could be purchased at drug stores in the United States without a prescription.

"Just how long it takes for it not to show up in an examination depends on how large a dose is taken," he explained. "Even a small amount might still appear in a test after as long a time as 24 hours."

Members of the American Olympic Committee here recalled that during the 1972 Summer Olympics at Munich, one of their own swimmers—Rick de Mont—had been made to return a gold medal in a similar situation. He had taken medication before his winning effort

because he was suffering from asthma.

"A list of forbidden drugs was issued to all team doctors before our Olympics began here," said Prince de Merode. "Our decision should be a warning to all athletes to consult their team physicians before taking any kind of medication.

"In agreement with the International Ski Federation," he concluded, "no further sanction will be taken in this case. Mrs. Kulakova is not prevented from partaking in further competition in these Olympics."

**Swiss Skier Isolated**

INNSBRUCK, Austria, Feb. 9 (AP)—Lise-Marie Morerod, the Swiss skier, was put in isolation today to be protected from a flu virus going around in the Olympic Village that has affected many athletes.

Among those taken ill were players of the Czechoslovak

hockey squad, the Austrian Alpine skier, Anton Steiner, and the 1972 Olympic downhill champion, Marie-Therese Nadig of Switzerland.

Miss Nadig ran a fever and had to stay in bed yesterday while West Germany's Rosi Mittermaier won the downhill.

To safeguard Miss Morerod, she was taken to Schuls in the Engandin Valley where she will await the start of the slalom race, scheduled for Wednesday.

The 118 Americans at the Games have escaped the virus and are enjoying an epidemic of health," said Dr. Tenley Albright, a former Olympic gold medalist. "Our team has been very lucky, I think mainly because of the very clean hygiene conditions in the village."

February 10, 1976

---

# U.S. Third in Men's Speed Skating, Wins in Hockey; Swiss Skiing Victor

**By FRED TUPPER**
Special to The New York Times

INNSBRUCK, Austria, Feb. 10—Dorothy Hamill, the United States figure skater, made a start toward a gold medal at the Winter Olympics today, Dan Immerfall snatched a bronze by two-hundredths of a second in speed skating and astonishing Phil Mahre, yesterday's headliner, followed the world's two best giant slalom racers home only to find that a pair of Swiss had stolen the show.

Erase any epitaph for the United States hockey team. In the dying moments of the last period, which produced three goals in 31 seconds, the Americans held on to edge Finland, 5-4. There is a bronze medal ahead if they can beat Poland and West Germany.

"It's our biggest victory of the year, a super effort," said Coach Bob Johnson, whose team was drubbed twice, 9-2 and 9-3, by Finland before the Games.

"Our forwards played well, the defense was strong and Jim Warden [goalkeeper] had another great day."

Depending on who was counting, it was announced that the Soviet Union had passed brave Norway in the number of gold medals won at all Winter Olympics, 48-47, getting its ninth and 10th here in speed skating and cross-country today.

The United States is still looking for its second gold medal, and it may be that Miss Hamill has traced the winning line. First on the ice this morning, she led the world champion, Dianne de Leeuw, in the three compulsories. A year ago she was fifth and the Dutch woman from Los Angeles first in this phase, as they eventually finished one, two.

The compulsory that mattered most was a "forward outside counter," which

prompted praise from her coach, Carlo Fassi, who guided Peggy Fleming to a gold medal at Grenoble, France, in 1968.

"Beating de Leeuw in the figures is as good as winning the gold," said Fassi, normally a reticent man.

The giant slalom was decided yesterday, many persons thought. Gustavo Thoeni of Italy, the best there is, led after the first heat. Piero Gros of Italy, the

World Cup leader, was a threat, as was 19-year-old Ingemar Stenmark of Sweden, in eighth place.

Two Swiss were near the leaders and then there was 18-year-old Phil Mahre.

The United States Alpine director, Hank Tauber, was hoarsely yelling for Mahre at the finish. "The best intermediate time!" he shouted, "two more gates to go! He's coming! He's coming down! He's got it!"

For just a crazy minute Phil had it, then Stenmark ran amok. The Swede's time was 1:40.90, untouchable all day. Thoeni faded along the way.

And there were the Swiss in a familiar role. Four years ago Marie-Therese Nadig had beaten the unbeatable Annemarie Proell, and Bernhard Russi had taken the downhill.

Now Heini Hemmi, 27, was first and the new champion on combined time for yesterday's and today's runs. In six years of World Cup competition he had never won a race. Ernest Good, 26, was second. He had never won either. Stenmark finished third, Thoeni fourth and Mahre fifth.

Yevgeny Kulikov of the Soviet Union holds the world 500-meter sprint record of 37 seconds flat, an almost unbelievable figure in the skating world. And now he holds the Olympic record.

Associated Press

**Phil Mahre of White Pass, Wash., on his way to a fifth-place finish in the giant slalom yesterday.**

But for a time he doubted it.

Plagued with the sweeping flu and with a fever of over 100, he was unhappy with his early 39.17 clocking on the slow rink. Earlier the United States hope, Peter Mueller, had 39.57 and a little later Mats Wallberg of Sweden had 39.56.

After intermission, the sun broke out and the flags indolently lay against their poles. Conditions were perfect for the low-altitude rink.

Moscow's Valery Muratov was around in 39.25 for second. After early trouble, Immerfall of Madison, Wis., chased him home in 39.54, nipping the Swede and Mueller for the bronze medal.

"I almost fell", said Immerfall. "After about 75 meters, I hit my right heel with my left skate. I picked up good around the first turn and then slipped going into the last inner. In the last 100 I picked up."

His mother, Irene Immerfall, was out on the ice in rhapsody, kissing him and waving a little American flag at the same time. As a widow, it's been a struggle for her. By day she's a secretary, by night a key-punch operator.

February 11, 1976

# Miss Mittermaier Captures Olympic Slalom

**By FRED TUPPER**
Special to The New York Times

INNSBRUCK, Austria, Feb. 11—Mama has done it again.

With the smile of an angel and a devil's daring, Rosi Mittermaier won the women's slalom race at the Olympics today. She now has two gold medals in Alpine skiing, joining such immortals as Marie-Therese Nadig of Switzerland, who lost a pole today at the start and surrendered, and Andrea Mead Lawrence of Rutland, Vt.

Down icy tracks, for which she had been praying, the 25-year-old West German finished second in the first heat and first in the second for a combined time of 1 minute 30.54 seconds. She beat 20-year-old Claudia Giordani of Italy, long a slalom specialist, by 33-hundredths of a second. Hanny Wenzel of Liechtenstein was third and Linda Cochran of Richmond, Vt., sister of Barbara, slalom gold-winner at the 1972 Olympics, was sixth.

Over her 10-year career on the world circuit, Miss Mittermaier has won countless slaloms. Last Sunday she took the downhill, a race she had never before won.

"I wanted a fast, icy track and I got it both times," said the beaming victor. "They were beautiful."

Faster and fitter, she found the best line to hold all the way.

"Nobody could have beaten Rosi, but the ski cap fell over my eyes and I had to throw it away, losing time," said Miss Giordani.

John Curry, the 25-year-old Briton, who trains at the Broadmoor in Colorado Springs and lives in New York, won the men's gold medal in figure skating. It was Britain's first medal in the Games.

Vladimir Kovalev of the Soviet Union took the silver medal and Toller Cranston of Canada the bronze. David Santee of Park Ridge, Ill., finished sixth and the United States champion, Terry Kubicka of Cypress, Calif., placed seventh.

Dorothy Hamill was on her way to a gold medal in figure skating. Performing in the two-minute compulsories, she passed Isabel de Navarre of West Germany with a faultless program that produced a rarity, a perfect 6.0 score.

Miss Hamill posted much higher figures for technical merit and artistic impression than the world champion, Dianne de Leeuw of the Netherlands, who lives in Paramount, a Los Angeles suburb.

A row of 5.9's and 5.8's flashed in lights on the scoreboard, and Miss Hamill blinked in delight. The best spinner in free skating, the 19-year-old from Riverside, Conn., leaped into a delayed axel, then a double axel and in succession executed a flying sitspin, a double flip, then a double toe loop. The audience was all hers now, and she wound up with dazzling stepwork and a layback spin.

There were boos from the crowded house when Miss de Leeuw, who gave a solid if not spectacular program, was marked in the 5.8-5.7 area. The exception was the United States judge, Yvonne McGowan, who gave her 5.3 and 5.2.

"I think she was right," said Emmerich Danzer of Austria, three times the men's world champion in the mid-1960's, of the McGowan tally. On a jump combination, Miss de Leeuw slid a bit between the down and up.

Nothing is certain. In the early warmup Miss Hamill fell in doing a flying sitspin, a variation of the move that tumbled Janet Lynn and led to her receiving only a bronze medal at Sapporo four years ago.

At the two minute finish Miss Hamill had 10 places and 88.40 points, mumbo-jumbo except to the experts. Miss de Leeuw was second. second, Miss de Navarre third and two East Germans, Christine Errath and Anett Poesch, fourth and fifth. Then came Wendy Burge of Garden Grove, Calif., and Linda Fratianne, the 15-year-old jumping wonder from Northridge, Calif.

And somewhere near the middle of the list was Elena Voderoezova, the 12-year-old Russian with potential for greatness.

With 36 hours to go before the next phase, Miss Hamill was asked if she would be scared.

"No, I won't be scared, but I will be nervous," she replied. "The rest will be nervous, too. If I don't foul up, I shall do it."

Usually strong in speed skating, the United States bogged down in the interminable 5,000 meters, held in wretched conditions. Not an Alp appeared. Snow, sleet, and rain fell and there was no wind to clear the area.

Thirteen laps round the track on crusty ice, the event inevitably is disputed between the Norwegians and Dutch. The world record-holder is Hans van Helden of the Netherlands, who recently set a time of 7:07.82 in the rarified atmosphere of Davos, Switzerland, where there is less air resistance. The man the Norwegians thought could beat him was

United Press International
**Dorothy Hamill of Riverside, Conn., during figure skating competition yesterday at Innsbruck, Austria.**

Sten Stensen, an army lieutenant, and he did.

Van Helden skated in icy conditions, Stensen after the rink had been cleared.

"It was like skating on sandpaper," said a Canadian competitor. "Hard to push."

The Dutchman started fast ("Too fast," he said later. "I tired."). Stensen loped around in 7:26.54, not so good as the record set by a teammate, Fred Anton Maier, eight years ago. The Norwegians didn't care. They blew horns, whistles and yelled, not only for their men in red, but also for everybody else.

In the end Piet Kleine of the Netherlands had the silver medal and van Helden the bronze.

Dan Carroll of St. Louis, who has skated in three Olympics, is making a comeback. But he was recovering from flu and wound up sixth.

**Finland Takes Relay**

INNSBRUCK, Feb. 11 (AP) —Finland won the gold medal in the 40-kilometer cross-country ski relay today. The United States, despite a superb performance by 20-year-old Bill Koch, finished sixth. Koch had the best time in the third lap, briefly pulling his team into third place. Norway was second and the Soviet Union third.

February 12, 1976

# Rosi Mittermaier: Relaxed, Quick and Efficient

United Press International

**Rosi Mittermaier of West Germany winning the women's slalom yesterday at Innsbruck, Austria. It was her second gold medal. She also won the women's downhill.**

**Innsbruck Olympic Slalom Course**

START

**Solid line is course attempted by better skier**

**Dotted line is course a weaker skier would take**

FINISH

The New York Times/Feb. 12, 1976

**By MICHAEL STRAUSS**
Special to The New York Times

INNSBRUCK, Austria, Feb. 11—If anyone had told Rosi Mittermaier as recently as two weeks ago that she would win two gold medals and possibly three in the Winter Olympics, she would have disregarded the notion as a crazy dream.

She has never had illusions about herself. Considered one of the best technical skiers on the world circuit for years, she has had lots of poor luck.

Still, as the Winter Olympics moved toward the last four sessions the West German star was on the threshold of accomplishing what no woman had ever done— score an Olympic Alpine grand slam. Only Toni Sailer of Austria and France's Jean-Claude Killy have accomplished it among the men.

Although she has been on two world championship teams and this is her third appearance in the Olympics, Rosi had never won a medal. Only once was she reasonably close. In 1972 she finished sixth in the downhill at Sapporo, Japan.

To what can her sudden successes this winter—she is also leading in the World Cup scoring—be attributed? What does she do differently that raises her above the other skiers?

"Not difficult to explain," says Klaus Mayr, West Germany's women's coach since 1968. "Rosi has matured. She's learned concentration.

"For many years she would have a great run on part of a course, only to make a mistake that cost split seconds or made her spill. Too often she worried about what times her opponents had made and the possible problems that lay ahead. Today she knows there will be problems and is prepared for them."

Claudia Giordani, the slim Italian who finished second in the race, held in a snowstorm, gives Rosi a plus in a department that is particularly important in both the slalom and grand slalom.

"She is fantastic in her ability to adjust," said Miss Giordani. "If she makes a mistake by leaning too far in one direction and is in danger of missing a gate, she has the strength and technique to correct herself instantly."

Hank Tauber, director of the United States Alpine squad who has seen Miss Mittermaier perform since she was a teen-ager, puts the reason for her recent successes more simply:

"She has acquired the knack of finding the shortest way down. "Keeping tight to those gates in making turns, whether the discipline be downhill or either of the slaloms, is the real name of this game. She has legs that she can bend in extreme angles to clip past those gates with remarkable efficiency."

He added:

"A big asset is her attitude. After all these years on the circuit, she approaches a race with almost no tension—a trait younger racers find difficult to acquire. Rosi swings her legs and shoulders as if they were being motivated by a precision machine. And she goes all out in attacking a course. She is no stranger

to failure and is willing to take chances."

Although she is the only active skier left who scored World Cup points in 1967, the year of the cup's inception, she seldom has won individual events. Injuries have impeded her career.

She was struck by a surfboard in Hawaii in 1973 while "shooting the waves." Last February she was back in a hospital, this time having been crashed into by a tourist skiing on the Axamer Lizum slopes on which she triumphed today.

In gaining her second gold medal Miss Mittermaier pro-

duced two sparkling efforts typical of her suddenly improved form. After the first run on the precipitous, icy course, which had sent 11 starters sprawling, Rosi found herself in second place.

Then she set out after Pamela Behr, a teammate who had led by only nine-hundredths of a second after the first run. Miss Mittermaier, attacking the course fiercely, turned in the second run's fastest clocking, 43.77.

Asked whether she felt that improved technical ability

was suddenly helping her to win medals, she replied:

"I'd say no, but I now have concentration and I'm more relaxed. I love ski racing and since I'm doing what I enjoy, I no longer worry about not doing well.

"Experience also has taught me to plan my attack of the course wisely. If I feel I am being challenged or about to be challenged, my poling in slalom and giant slalom becomes more determined and my leg action more pronounced."

February 12, 1976

# Mueller Gives U.S. a Second Gold Medal

## Skater Takes 1,000 Meters at Innsbruck

### By FRED TUPPER
Special to The New York Times

INNSBRUCK, Austria, Feb. 12—The United States speed skating team was whooping it up tonight, celebrating its second gold medal.

It was won by Peter Mueller, this time in the 1,000 meters, a new event in these Winter Olympics. And the only surprise was the enormous margin of victory. Sheila Young won the other gold medal in the women's 500 meters, and wound up one, two, three in the sprints.

Starting early, when the surface was fast, the Wisconsin whiz got around the 2½ laps in 1 minute 19.32 seconds, more than a second faster than anybody else and in the process snapped the rink record.

That Mueller was capable of sensational performances has been said repeatedly by the American men's coach, Peter Schotting. Mueller had been frustrated earlier this week in the 500 meters when it was Dan Immerfall who grabbed a bronze medal, with Peter an unhappy fifth a measly four-hundredths of a second off the pace.

Nobody really gave him a challenge today. Mats Wallberg of Sweden and two Russians, the world-record holder, Valery Muratov, and Aleksandr Safranov, had faster times halfway round the first lap but Mueller had a slight margin with a lap to go and ran away from the classy field with the ferocity of his final sprint.

### 'Happy It's Over'

"My coach thought we should go early," said Mueller. "I was pretty stiff after 200 meters, then from 200 to 800 it went good. I thought 1:19 would win it and I'm just happy it's over."

"For that last 200 I was just biting my nails", said

his Fiancée Leah Poulos of Northbrook, Ill., who had taken a silver medal in the 1,000 for women. "But I knew he could do it, and I wanted him to get a better medal than I did."

Mueller admitted he was a nervous wreck before the race. "I haven't eaten for

two days," said the 22-year-old from Mequon, Wis. Asked what chance he had of winning the gold, the light-haired athlete, who has a 3 handicap in golf and played both football and baseball in high school, said:

"I must have lost eight pounds worrying, but I've been beating the Russians in the 1,000 all year."

"Olympics has been a dream of his for years," said his mother, Rita Mueller, "and I had my worries about his skating the second pair. His father, training to be a glider pilot in the Luftwaffe during World War II, cracked

United Press International

**Peter Mueller of the U.S. on his way to a gold medal in the 1,000-meter event**

up in a snowstorm and was given a desk job. He moved to the States in 1952 and now is a service mechanic for German cars.

The ice was fast at first today with no wind, but the sun warmed it after a while and when it was resurfaced halfway through, it became slow and watery.

It's been a financial sacrifice for Peter and Leah to compete. "With no ice in the States, we had to spend six weeks in Berlin. I guess it cost us $10,000 in all. My dad helped. The Russians get about $12,000 for top skaters," he added," and the U.S.A. gives us about $1,000. "Why compete?"

"I enjoy it", he said, "and Dad pushed".

The United States hockey team swept by Poland, 7-2, and needs to beat West Germany on Saturday to get a bronze medal.

The second case of doping in four days involved Frantisek Pospisil, Czechoslovakia's hockey captain, who was given codeine by the team doctor before his team beat Poland, 7-1, on Tuesday. The International Olympic Committee said the Czechoslovaks would forfeit that game but that Pospisil "will be allowed to play on since the responsibility of the athlete was not being questioned in this case."

The team doctor, however, will be banned and "shall not be permitted to be a member of any delegations in the future."

The Czechoslovaks defeated West Germany, 7-4 today, and the Soviet Union beat Finland, 7-2.

Tomorrow there's almost a promise of a third American gold in the women's figure skating. Dorothy Hamill of Riverside, Conn., has a large lead over her formidable rival, Dianne de Leeuw

of Los Angeles, who skates for the Netherlands.

It thus appears the United States will have its best record since those long ago days at Oslo in 1952. And then the Russians and East Germans weren't around. To date, the Americans have nine medals: two golds, three silvers with the Misses Young and Poulos and Bill Koch in the 30-kilometer cross-country, and four bronze with Cindy Nelson in the downhill, Immerfall, Miss Young in the 1,000 and Jim Millns and Colleen O'Connor in the ice dancing. In Sapporo, Japan, last time out there were eight, including three golds.

There was another event today, the Nordic 20-kilometer cross-country relay for women. Nine teams entered. The Soviet Union won it, the Untied States finished ninth.

February 13, 1976

# Miss Hamill Skates to Gold Medal in Olympics

## Miss de Leeuw Is Runner-Up; Norwegian Wins Speed Event

### BY FRED TUPPER
Special to The New York Times

Associated Press
**Dorothy Hamill displaying her gold medal in Innsbruck**

INNSBRUCK, Austria, Feb. 13—Dorothy Hamill has won her Olympic gold medal and all is right in the figure skating world. In four minutes of triumphant merchandising at the Winter Games, tonight, she put together a package to pleasure the eye and pound the heart.

Starting in the 14th slot, or first in the last seven, she had to convince judges who are inclined to save the high marks for the end. Not this time. She delighted them as much as the crowd, who rained down bouquets of spring flowers onto the rink at the Olympic Ice Hall.

It was near to flawless, but nothing is. It was solid, sound and eye-catching. Look for a mistake and there was no big one, and that the marks confirmed. She had eight 5.8's and a 5.9 in technical merit and a roar of acclaim as a solid line of 5.9's flashed on the board for artistic interpretation. Nobody was even close.

Dianne de Leeuw of Paramount, Calif., who skates for the Netherlands came nearest but there was not a 5.9 on her card, nor on anybody else's.

The stunning victory, rich in American tradition, gave the United States its third gold medal of these games and if there is a medal for coaching, it would be the

third, too, for Carlo Fassi, her coach.

He guided Peggy Fleming to the championship and stardom at Grenoble, France, in 1968 and piloted John Curry of Britain to his first place Wednesday night.

Before that Tenley Albright had won at Cortina, Italy, in 1956 and Carol Heiss (always a bridesmaid and never a bride, according to her mother) took the precious gold in 1964 at Squaw Valley, Calif., for the United States.

The final scores were Miss Hamill 9 in ordinals, which meant that all the judges voted her first and 193.80 points, with Miss de Leeuw 20 ordinals and 190.24 and Christine Errath of East Germany third with 28 and 188.16, her fine performance marred with two stumbles and a fall.

Here's the way Miss Hamill's four minutes were spent: on ice in a low-cut, red dress she leaped into a delayed axel, a walley jump into a double-axel, a double-toe loop, a camel spin, a double-lutz into a back spiral, a double-axel, a double-salchow, a split, a double-toe loop and a butterfly, just slightly off color; then a layback spin, delayed double-salchow, a Bauer spiral into a double-lutz, a walley, then another with the crowd humming along to her Russian music, a split, a split again and an exit on her signature that has become so memorable, the Hamill camel (camel spin into a sitspin) with a spin coming out.

Then the marks went up to prolonged cheers. They were pretty special for the 19-year-old brunette from Riverside, Conn., who does most things left-handed but skates right.

"I felt good skating right after my warmup," she said. "I saw a sign for me and started to cry because I was so nervous and didn't want to let anybody down. I felt good skating, not uncomfortable but I was sort of blank. I can't remember anything. All my jumps were very consistent [she tried no triples] and I left out one jump. That didn't matter."

It was a double lutz near the end.

"It's not the best I've skated since I've been there, and not the worse, either," said the champion.

By a ridiculous 12 hundredths of a second, Rosi Mittermaier missed the grand slam of Alpine skiing. With the world yelling her on, she finished second to Kathy Kreiner, an 18-year-old Canadian who had won only one major race in her life. Third was Danielle Debernard of France as just this trio broke a minute and a half.

Little chance was given

Karl Schranz, one of Austria's greatest skiers, was a controversial figure in two Olympics. In 1968, his disqualification for missing a gate in the slalom event enabled Jean-Claude Killy to take the triple crown. Schranz was banned from the 1972 games because he was said to have turned professional.

Dorothy Hamill won every individual skating title worth winning in 1976. She took the world and U.S. titles *and* won the Olympic gold medal. This photo captures her superb form in the Olympics at Innsbruck, Austria.

Miss Kreiner. Her credentials had been sound in the past, this year she had a meagre 2 points in the World Cup standing. A Montreal newspaper had not even a man on the hill when the Canadian, starting first, found the perfect line, snakehipped past the intermediate timer in 58.95 seconds and roared home in 1.29.13.

"I was attacking all the way down," said Miss Kreiner from Timmins, Ontario, a skier at the age of 3, a racer at 7 and an Olympian at Sapporo, Japan, when 14, "and still hanging on at the finish. Then there was that terrible wait."

Miss Mittermaier was fourth in the order, an ideal position. An unexpected winner of the downhill, a justified favorite in the slalom, the West German charmer had everybody on her side, including a Toronto newspaper. The parents of Miss Kreiner are quoted as saying: "Wouldn't it be a shame if somebody prevented her from taking a triple?"

This is how close the German skier came: She had the fastest interval time at 58.41 seconds, and her line seemed faultless. "Lower down I made a tiny mistake," she said. "I skied into a gate too directly." That huge, Halloween smile lit up the scene. "I'm very happy with the silver. I had not counted on such success."

At 25 she may go on, she may not. "If I get the itch this summer, I could start training. I just don't know," she said.

Linda Cochran of Richmond, Vt., was 12th, the first of the Americans. "Those who started early had an advantage," said Hank Tauber, the United States Alpine director, normally an ebullient man. "But this is the first real disappointment that the United States has had in the games."

Miss Mittermaier is the third woman to win two of the three Alpine events and with her second-place finish came closest to a sweep. Andrea Mead Lawrence of the United States took both slalom events in 1952 but finished 17th in the downhill. In 1972, Marie-Terese Nadig of Switzerland won the downhill and giant slalom.

Jan Erik Storholt of Norway had been predicting he would win the 1,500 meter Olympic speed skating gold medal on his birthday. It may have sounded like bragadoccio since he'd never won a major race before.

Today was his birthday, his 27th, and he won. "Friday the 13th. I didn't know whether that would be lucky or not," he said grinning, minutes after the race.

The Trondheim engineer won it handily in 1:59.38, snapping the Olympic mark

of 2:02.96 set by Ard Schenk of the Netherlands at Sapporo and just fractions of a second off Schenk's world mark of 1:58.70.

He won it because he beat the man he was paired against, Juri Kondakev of the Soviet Union, after trailing at the first timing stage.

The worst winds of the games went every which way today, whipping the rinkside flags into frenzy, some came from the northwest, others from opposite and in between, gusting up to 45 miles an hour. The first four pairs had the best of it and that's where the three medals went, with the silver to Kondakov and the bronze to Hans Van Helden of the Netherlands.

The Norwegians exploded. All week they have occupied an entire stand, blowing horns, waving flags and singing, perpetually singing. Today they jumped out of those stands, reaching hands out to their hero. They had expected Sten Stenson to win the 5,000, they were nowhere so sure today.

Dan Carroll, 26, of St. Louis, was a disappointed fifth, his third time at the Olympics. Making the split at 700 meters, "I was hit by a blast and made a very bad turn. My last shot at it," he said, "that's the way it goes."

Eric Heidin, a 17-year-old skater from Madison, Wis., was delighted with his seventh. Skating only because

a teammate, Charles Gilmore, withdrew in his favor, Heidin was two-hundredths of a second behind Piet Kleine of the Netherlands who registered a protest to Referee Victor Kapitanov of the Soviet Union after the race. With five skaters scratched, the order was upset and Kleine was called from the dressing room to the track long before he was ready.

The last words were correctly expressed by Storholt, the winner.

"I skated," he said, "a perfect technical race." He started fast and finished fastest.

Russian skiers retained the championship in the biathlon relay, which combines cross-country racing and target shooting. Finland was second and East Germany third in the 30-kilometer event. The United States team finished 11th.

After the first two runs for four-man bobsleds, the East Germans were in front. Meninhard Nehmer, the winning driver in the two-man sleds, had the two fastest runs today, and a total of 1:49.07. Close behind was the West German crew led by Wolfgang Zimmerer, the 1974 world champions driver, in 1:49.69. Next was the Swiss sled of Erich Schaerer, the world champion, with a time of 1:49.77.

February 14, 1976

# *Kathy Kreiner Takes Giant Slalom for Canada*

## German Skier Second in Bid for 3 Titles

**By MICHAEL STRAUSS**
Special to The New York Times

INNSBRUCK, Austria, Feb. 13—You don't need such sophisticated uphill rides as a gondola or a chairlift—or long slopes—to start a career leading to an Olympic gold medal.

Kathy Kreiner, the 18-year-old Canadian with blonde tresses, proved again today that a creaky rope tow and gravity can provide the necessary training fundamentals.

Miss Kreiner's surprising success in winning the women's giant slalom—she was an extreme outsider in prerace estimates—brought to mind the elementary skiing education of the flying Coch-

rans of Richmond, Vt. In that ski-minded family all four children became American Olympians with a rope tow the chief spawning ingredient.

Barbara Ann Cochran was the gold medal winner in the 1972 slalom at Sapporo, Japan. She and her sisters, Marilyn and Lindy, and her brother Bob, all began on a small hill next to their home, helped by a tow built by their father.

### A Basic Education

Almost overlooked in the astonishment greeting Miss Kreiner's success today was that she had access only to a rope tow from the time she started at the age of 4 to about the time she was 12. Her 21-year-old sister, Laurie, who finished 27th in the giant slalom, said her elementary skiing education was gained the same way.

"Our city of Timmins [Ontario] is about 500 miles

north of Toronto," said Laurie. "Advanced uphill riding equipment was slow in arriving. We both learned on a tow that was in tandem. We would ride to the top of one and then ski over to start uphill on a tow that went to the top."

To the top? The ski hill at Timmins only offers a vertical drop of about 300 feet. The slope, the only "big bump" in the mining community of 42,000 residents, is not much longer than the ones to be found at such nearby New York City retreats as Silvermine at Bear Mountain or Mount Airy in the Poconos.

"A few deep breaths and you're down the hill," said an observer from Toronto who was at the outrun when Miss Kreiner's skis ground to a rooster-tail finish. "Lately, however, that same ski area in Timmins has come of age. It now has a T-bar lift."

Kathy, at the postrace news conference, while bearing up well under the questioning, seemed a little bewildered by it all. And it was small wonder. Despite her early start in skiing, her recent credentials had not been impressive.

"This was one of my best two races, ever," she said. "I won a World Cup giant slalom in West Germany two years ago. Otherwise, I've been strange to victories—so far."

For most of those crowded around the 1,225-meter (about 4,100 feet) course on the Axamer Lizum that has a vertical drop of 385 meters, it seemed Miss Kreiner, in plunging down the slope in 1:29.13 as the leadoff racer, merely had given some of the event's better known stars a mark at which to aim.

The Canadian had turned in a fluent descent and at no time had shown a sign of

United Press International

**Kathy Kreiner, giant slalom winner, is lifted on shoulders of Rosi Mittermaier of West Germany, left, who finished second, and Daniele Debernard of France, who was third.**

faltering. Although she had skimmed around the gates as close as was possible without knocking over the poles, the general feeling was that faster times were still to be posted.

There were Rosi Mittermaier, Daniele Debernard of France and the defending champion. Marie-Therese Nadig of Switzerland, among those still slated to face the starter. No one, however, went any faster. Rosi, losing by only 12 one-hundredths of a second, beat the 21-year-old Miss Debernard for the silver medal by only 70 one-hundredths of a second. Miss Nadig was fifth.

Nevertheless, Miss Mittermaier, expressing amazement hours after her second-place finish over the attention she had received as a result of her earlier victories in the downhill and slalom, emerged with the greatest overall Alpine performance for a woman in Olympic history.

February 14, 1976

# Russian Six Takes Title

### By FRED TUPPER
Special to The New York Times

INNSBRUCK, Austria, Feb. 14—United States hopes for a hockey medal in the 12th Winter Olympics were dashed today and the Soviet Union's expectations of winning the championship almost met the same fate.

But the Russians fought back from a two-goal deficit in the first period and went on to defeat a surprising Czechoslovak squad, 4-3, and take the gold medal. The Czechoslovaks took second place and the West Germans were third for their 4-1 triumph over the Americans.

The Czechoslovaks had taken a 3-2 edge in the third period but the Russians scored twice in the last five minutes for the victory. Aleksandr Yakushev tied the score then Valery Kharlamov knocked the disk into the net 24 seconds later for the decisive goal.

In the final full day of competition, hockey shared top billing with long-distance skiing and skating events that added gold medals to the Italian, Dutch and Norwegian totals. Piero Gros of Italy took the men's slalom

by defeating his celebrated teammate, Gustavo Thoeni; Piet Kleine of the Netherlands won the 10,000-meter speed skating and Ivar Formo of Norway posted the fastest time in the 50-kilometer ski race.

The only medal that the United States got was not Olympian although it will be remembered only for what might have been. Finishing behind Thoeni and Willy Frommelt of Liechtenstein, Greg Jones of Tahoe City, Calif., took the bronze F.I.S. (International Federation of Skiing) medal in the combined, which includes downhill, giant slalom and today the joint heats in the slalom.

The leader at the intermediate stage on the first heat today was Geoff Bruce, 23, of Corning, N.Y., thrashing through the gates and apparently headed for the fastest run. But he lost the line approaching the finish and ran out, and Gros emerged the winner.

Out in a blinding snowstorm was Bill Koch, the 20-year-old wonder from Guilford, Vt. who last week took a silver in the 30-kilometer

cross-country race, leading the field by eight seconds halfway through 50 kilometers (31 miles), considered the toughest race in sport. Only the second time he had run it, Koch had started too fast and began to drop away. He was fifth at the third stage and stumbled in 13th, certainly the best performance by an American in this Olympic event.

Almost inevitably the winner was from Norway for its third gold in successive Olympics as Formo of Oslo, a 24-year-old student, had over 43 seconds in hand against Gert-Dietmar Klause of East Germany with Benny Soedergren of Sweden a late third.

What rankled most was the beating given the United States in hockey. The team had looked good in its last two games against Finland and Poland and had commanded a large rooting section at the Olympic Stadium. Halfway through the game against West Germany today there was no score until Erich Kuehnhackl, a 6-foot-4-inch, 210-pound Czech born player made his presence felt. He blasted in a rebound for a 1-0 lead for the Germans at 30:30 and then assisted on the other three goals.

The American goal was scored on a solo effort by Buzz Schneider of Grand Rap-

ids, Mich., on a dash from the blue line. The American team was in a panic, changing its lines 29 times in the last 20 minutes and ending up with a man short and two sticks on the ice.

It was though that the soft, wet snow blanketing the ice rink would have made record times impossible in the 10,000-meter event, the contest supposedly was between Sten Stenson of Norway, who won the 5,000 and Hans Van Heldern of the Netherlands. Ard Schenk, the hero of the 1972 Winter Games at Safforo, Japan, holds both world and Olympic records in the 10,000.

Kleine, an unemployed 25-year-old Dutch carpenter beat both of them, destroyed the Olympic mark and can't quite believe it. He had registered a complaint to the Russian referee yesterday about hurrying his start, today he was ready to go. What he didn't know was that his coach kept giving him slower times to make him go faster. It worked. He broke the record by 28-hundredths of a second.

"All I need now is a job," he said. "So I'll try my luck as a mailman."

---

**E. German Sled Wins**

IGLS, Austria, Feb. 14 (UPI) — Meinhard Nehmer held off a late challenge from Eric Schaerer of Switzerland, the world champion, in the four-man bobsled competition today and posted a victory that gave East Germany a sweep of all the Olympic bobsled and Luge gold medals.

It was the second gold medal for Nehmer and Bernard Germeshausen, who earlier won the two-man event. Jochen Babok and Bernhard Lehmann completed the winning quartet, who forged a commanding lead during the first two runs on Friday.

The last Germans had an aggregate time of 3:40.89 for four runs and finished nearly a half a second ahead of the Switzerland sled which clocked 3:40.89.

February 15, 1976

# Austrian Skier Takes Final Olympic Event

**By BERNARD KIRSCH**
Special to The New York Times

INNSBRUCK, Austria, Feb. 15 — A graduate of a ski-jumping school received the highest honors today as the Austrians closed the Winter Olympic Games the same way they had opened them—in triumph.

Karl Schnabl, with jumps of 320 and 318 feet, received 234.8 points for his two jumps from the 90-meter hill. He beat his Austrian teammate, Anton Innauer, an undergraduate at the ski school, by 1.9 points for the gold medal. Henry Glass of East Germany won the bronze as the host nation and the East Germans filled the top eight spots.

The American skiers occupied places No. 18, 30, 32 and 36, with James Denny coming closest. The skier from Duluth, Minn., finished more than 42 points behind the winner on leaps of 292 and 279 feet.

The Austrians are serious about their jumping. About 60,000 people filled the jump stadium, not in use since the opening ceremonies, to watch the high flying. This was their Super Bowl; these were the men they chased for autographs.

Austria had not won a gold medal since Franz Klammer took the downhill ski race 10 days ago with several of their favorites failing or falling. But Schnabl spent four years learning to land on his feet. There is a university at Strams, Austria, that mixes higher education with winter sports for the specially endowed athletes. Schnabl, who is 22 years old and Innauer, 17, qualified, being carefully prepared for the Olympics. Schnabl took third place in the 70-meter jump.

The men went off the lip of the runway today at 55 miles an hour and when they landed and were slowed by the uphill grading on the lower slope, they came to a stop several feet in front of the Olympic Flame. Below the flame are a church and a graveyard.

The winners made it look easy, appearing at home in the air as they gained precious points for style, which is added on to the distance of the leap. Schnabl picked up points on the second jump to beat Innauer, who led after the first jump. The younger skier scored, 126.5 on his first leap of 337 feet to Schnabl's 117.5. Innauer disappointed his Austrian fans with a second leap of only 299 feet.

Terry Kern, also from Duluth, was 30th, Jerry Martin of Minneapolis 32d and James Maki of Bovey, Minn., 36th.

February 16, 1976

Associated Press

**Dorothy Hamill of Riverside, Conn., performing in the women's short-program event in Goteborg, Sweden, meet.**

# Hamill Wins Ice Crown

GOTEBORG, Sweden, March 6 (AP)—Dorothy Hamill of the United States, a 19-year old Olympic champion, won the women's world figure skating championship today. She is the first American to win the title in eight years.

Miss Hamill, from Riverside Conn., is coached by the same man, Carlos Fassi of Denver, who trained the last United States world champion, Peggy Fleming. She withstood challenges from the defending champion, Dianne de Leeuw, who lives in California but competes for the Netherlands, and the 1974 champion, Christine Errath of East Germany. Miss Errath, with strong free skating, overtook Miss de Leeuw for second place.

Miss Hamill, who has declared that this competition was to end her competitive career here, won both yesterday's short program and today's four-minute free skating.

She did not have as difficult a program as Miss Errath, the only woman who dared the difficult triple toe-loop, but she executed her program with competent double jumps and excellent spins, including her famous "Hamill Camel."

She got three near perfect scores of 5.9 for technical merit, including marks from the United States and Soviet judges, and a row of 5.9's from all but one judge for artistic impression. Miss Errath had 5.9's for technical merit but 5.8's for artistic flair. She also had a slight miss on one jump.

March 7, 1976

# Figure Skating Growing As a Performing Art

Twyla Tharp, the choreographer, instructing John Curry, the world and Olympic figure-skating champion, during practice at Madison Square Garden yesterday.

The New York Times/D. Gorton

### By NEIL AMDUR

When John Curry first approached Twyla Tharp about breaking the ice with him, it was almost worse than preparing for an Olympic final.

"I was a bit nervous about working with her," the world and Olympic figure-skating champion said yesterday, recalling his meeting with the queen of choreography. "I was afraid I wouldn't be able to do the routines well enough."

Miss Tharp, who has blazed revolutionary trails in ballet and modern dance, had never been on a pair of skates.

"I was able to ask, 'Can you?'" she said, dramatizing their earliest discussions. "He said, 'Here's how.'"

While 140 skaters from 6 to 11 years old were gliding across the ice yesterday afternoon at a rink in Westwood, N.J., Mr. Curry and Miss Tharp were putting the polish on his routine at Madison Square Garden.

Figure skating finally has come of age in the United States. And with more skaters, rinks and clubs catering to the ambitious demands of recreation-minded Americans, the time may be right for something dramatic in the sport, such as carrying it one step beyond, into the realm of performing art. Enter Mr. Curry and Miss Tharp and Super-

skates III, a fund-raising event for the United States Olympic Committee next Monday night at the Garden.

Free from the rigid confines of compulsory routines and the subjective views of judges, Mr. Curry, under the direction of Miss Tharp, has constructed a seven-minute routine that he believes will capture what skating is supposed to be, not what is packaged into the "uncreative atmosphere" of competitions and ice shows.

The routine will begin and end on traditional curves and include jumps and turns. But Miss Tharp's fascination with change of direction will be felt, along with her use of space and consideration for body movement.

"To skate this piece, it's like learning a whole new vocabulary," said Mr. Curry, who was associated with a classical style as an amateur. "There are elements and movements I haven't used before."

Many elements will be more subtle than dramatic, a chance for Mr. Curry to display how he feels about skating. But right-corner turns and a stress on making each move meaningful will eliminate what he feels is the tendency to create routines as "display places for tricks."

"I don't like ice shows at all," Mr. Curry said in an interview before his afternoon workout. "They're like vaudeville on ice. I don't think they use the skater well. They're aimed at a certain market and they succeed at that market. But for the skater, it's

not particularly exciting. Just because a person turns professional shouldn't become the end of that persons creative ability."

After having swept gold medals at the Winter Olympics in Innsbruck, Austria, and the world championships at Goteborg, Sweden, the 27-year-old Mr. Curry formed his own professional group. Because of his own love for dance, and a desire to develop and stretch his talent and also expand the sport's horizons, he got in touch with Miss Sharp.

### Picks a Baroque Work

They are an odd couple in an interesting way, after only three weeks together. Mr. Curry is British, has a somewhat self-effacing nature and looks like the boy next door in his navy blue pea coat. Miss Tharp, from Indiana, has been called "small, dark and intense" about her commitment toward what she calls "the artistic links between something possible and that which is beyond."

It was Miss Tharp who settled on the music for the routine, the Concerto for Trumpet in B Flat, a baroque work by Albinoni.

"The horn related to the imput of wind and the momentum of the skater," she said.

Mr. Curry's attempt to convey "what skating is all about" and a new tour headlined by Toller Cranston, the free-skating Canadian Olympian, could carry considerable long-range significance. In recent years much of the glamour in figure skating has gone to such gold-medal heroines as Peggy Fleming and Dorothy Hamill.

Figure-skating officials see a male push into the sport similar to the belated acceptance of tennis as something more than a "sissy sport." Roy Winder, executive director of the United States Figure Skating Association, said yesterday that registered or competitive skaters had increased from 29,000 to 35,000 in the last five years and the number of clubs from 275 to 372.

The number of recreational skaters has shot up from 3 million to almost 4 million, according to Fritz Dietl, a member of the Ice Skating Institute of America.

"There are at least 500 to 600 more rinks now," said Mr. Dietl, who operates the Dietl Skating Rink in Westwood. "And in my area alone, around Bergen County and North Jersey, we've had an increase from three to nine in the last two years."

From association headquarters in Boston, Mr. Winder said:

"There's been a big upturn, particularly among the men. We may not get into the high-test structure that goes with Olympic skaters, but among recreation skaters, there's a lot of them."

Mr. Curry was 7 years old when his mother took him skating for the first time, a feeling that "was love at first sight," he says.

**His Boots Were Not Too Big**

"My early skating was supervised and my boots were not four sizes too large," he said. "And my mom didn't push me. Skating was the big treat of the week, something I looked forward to."

Mr. Curry believes many goal-oriented American parents are too impatient and shoot for gold-medal greatness or nothing from their children by age 16.

"Skating should be enjoyable at all levels," he said. "For me, it's a total experience—mentally rewarding and esthetically pleasing. If these qualities are

not there, I wouldn't skate for very long. It would bore me."

Miss Tharp hardly needed any trips on the ice to satisfy her artistic appetitie. But the sense of venturing into the unknown "where angels fear to tread," with a known quantity prompted her acceptance. She has traded boots for pleasure skating five times since starting the project, and says proudly, "I can go forward very fast."

How good is the routine?

"I love it, it's very challenging," said Mr. Curry. "It's very well constructed and very rich in invention."

"I like it very much," added Miss Tharp, "and I don't often say that in advance."

Perhaps the most interesting comment came from a woman spectator at the workout.

"There's a certain attitude," she said while watching Mr. Curry execute. "He looks like one of her dancers now, and that takes some doing."

*November 11, 1976*

# *Could Sonja Henie Skate Circles Round Them All?*

**By NEIL AMDUR**

She opened her routine with two dazzling triple jumps in the first 40 seconds and closed with two Russian splits and three consecutive butterflies. And after Linda Fratianne received the crown as America's newest women's figure-skating queen last weekend, her grace and artistry were wrapped in superlatives.

But when it came to selecting the greatest woman figure skater in history, only one name emerged at the top in an informal survey of coaches and officials at the national championships last weekend in Hartford. And it was not Peggy Fleming, Tenley Albright, Janet Lynn, Carol Heiss, Dorothy Hamill, Barbara Ann Scott or Linda Fratianne.

"If I had to name one, said Dick Button, a former men's champion, whose name is synonomous with greatness in the sport, "it would be Sonja Henie. She had the most distinguished competitive career and she clearly affected the sport more than anyone before or after."

**'Revolutionized the Sport'**

"The greatest of all time has to be Sonja Henie," observed Sandra Stevenson, the skating correspondent for a British paper, The Manchester Guardian. "She revolutionized the sport, changing it from an amusing pastime indulged in by the upper classes in the elite winter watering spots to a highly competitive activity contested by teenagers."

"Sonja dominated the sport in her day far more than anybody before or since," said Ben Wright, a respected world referee and also a member of the technical committee of the International Skating Union.

With 10 world titles and three Olympic gold medals, Miss Henie was an overwhelming No. 1 choice. Most frequently bracketed behind her were Miss Fleming and Miss Albright, both Olympic champions although different

stylists. Surprisingly, Miss Hamill, the 1976 Olympic and world champion, was not among the top five selections of most coaches surveyed, although she was included in the list of Carlo Fassi, her coach.

Fassi named Misses Henie, Albright, Fleming and Hamill, although not necessarily in numerical order.

"Henie was the first one who brought skating to the world," said Fassi, who now is tutoring Barbie Smith of Denver, the runner-up last weekend to Miss Fratianne. "Albright was the first to get the choreography and jumping and put it all together. Fleming put art in skating, and Dorothy made a lot of people more aware of the sport."

Button's top five, behind Miss Henie,

*The New York Times*

Sonja Henie: World champion who revolutionized figure skating

Associated Press

**Peggy Fleming: Art in skating**

also included Miss Albright and Miss Fleming. But he added Janet Lynn, a five-time national champion, and Charlotte Oehlschlagel, a pioneer German exhibition skater, who performed in New York around 1915.

There was divided opinion on Miss Lynn's greatness. Two top coaches, Evy Scotvold and Mary Ludington of Rockford, Ill., felt Miss Lynn "had a profound effect on skating."

"Janet Lynn had more of an effect on skating than anyone," said Scotvold, who coached Terry Kubicka, last year's men's champion.

Yet others did not include Miss Lynn among their top five because they said she had not won an Olympic or world title. Miss Hamill's much-publicized, one-year achievements also lacked impact for many critics.

"My definition of a great skater," said Button, who serves as the analyst on ABC Sports skating telecasts, "is someone who not only reaches the top but leaves the sport better for having been in it."

### 'The Soft Doe'

Miss Stevenson's top five also offered another opinion. Behind Miss Henie, she listed Irina Rodnina of the Soviet Union, known primarily for pairs; Jacqueline Du Bief of France ("she brought a flamboyant artistry into play that has not been equaled"), Madge Syers Cave of Britain, the 1908 Olympic champion, who often competed against men, and Miss Fleming, the 1968 Olympic gold medalist.

"The Europeans called her the soft doe because of her balletic, effortless flow," Miss Stevenson said of Miss Fleming.

One professional skater from Los Angeles, who asked to remain anonymous, rated Miss Fleming ahead of Miss Henie, who competed internationally for Norway before being embraced by Hollywood moviemakers.

"Poor old Sonja's out of it," the pro said of his list. "At her best, the waltz jump was all she could do. She put skating on the map not because of what she could do on the ice but because of her brain."

Wright, the past-president of the United States Figure Skating Association, disagreed, adding "who knows what Sonja could have done with today's indoor areas and training facilities?

"It's like trying to compare Joe Louis and Jack Dempsey," Wright said. "I would say were Sonja competing today, I think she could have matched these girls. Don't forget, compulsory figures accounted for 60 percent of the scoring in her days. Today, the emphasis is on free skating."

Could Miss Henie have completed the difficult triples being tried by today's top skaters?

"I wouldn't assume she couldn't," Wright concluded.

February 8, 1977

# Heiden Is First U.S. Man to Take World Skating

HEERENVEEN, the Netherlands, Feb. 13 (AP)—Eric Heiden, an 18-year-old University of Wisconsin freshman, became today the first American to win the men's world speed-skating championship with a superb all-round performance.

"It's unbelievable. I just can't believe this is true," said Heiden as he came off the track to the cheers of the capacity crowd of 18,000.

The Madison, Wis., teen-ager eclipsed two experienced Norwegians, who had started the two-day event as favorites.

Heiden broke the track and world championship record, placing first in the 500-meter race yesterday. Then he finished third in the 1,500 meters. Today he was ninth in the 5,000 meters and third in the 10,000 meters for the best aggregate point total. He led the overall standings from start to finish.

The European champion, Jan-Egil Storholt of Norway, was second and his countryman, Sten Stensen, was third.

Heiden clinched the title with his performance in the exhausting 10,000 meters, where he had been expected to lose ground and let the Norwegians take over the lead.

Heiden was paired in the 10,000 against the defending world champion, Piet Kleine of the Netherlands, and this seemed to draw the best out of the young American. He matched his opponent stride-for-stride and won the heat by more than a second in 14 minutes 59.02 seconds. It was one of only three times under 15 minutes in the event.

"He is a worthy world champion, truly a great rider," Kleine said. "When a youngster can skate that well over all four distances he deserves to win."

However, Heiden said he didn't think his victory "will have any impact at all in promoting speed skating in the United States."

In an interview with the Norwegian State Radio, Heiden said: "People will read about it in the papers, and probably remember it for a week, but then they'll forget."

February 14, 1977

# *Miss Fratianne Takes World Figure Skating Championship*

TOKYO, March 3 (AP)—Linda Fratianne of Northridge, Calif., won the women's world figure skating championship today, saving herself with grace and technical control after a fall in the important free-skating event. The 16-year-old United States champion, received 10 ordinals and 189.26 points, which means that eight of the nine judges gave her first place and one gave her second.

Meanwhile, Vladimir Kovalev of the Soviet Union traced the best compulsory figures at the start of the men's competition and a Soviet pair was on its way to winning the ice dancing title after the third day of competition.

Miss Fratianne was beaten in the free skating by a 13-year-old girl, Yelena Vodorezova of the Soviet Union, after the damaging fall in attempting a triple salchow jump. She got up, however, and flew successfully into a triple toe loop.

Anett Poetzsch of East Germany, the European champion and an early leader in the women's event, was second with 22 ordinals and 185.18 points. Dagmar Lurz of West Germany took third place with 43 ordinals and 182.48 points after scores from the three events—compulsory figures, the short program and free skating—were computed.

Two other Americans were fourth and fifth, respectively. Barbie Smith of Denver finished fourth with 43 ordinals and 182.44 points and Wendy Burge of Garden Grove, Calif., wound up fifth with 41 ordinals and 182.90 points.

"I felt I was out of shape because I couldn't do my long program every day and I've been sick with a sore throat," said Miss Fratianne. "I haven't been eating well and have been very weak," she said. "It was hard for me to jump back after the fall and get going. I felt a little off balance."

### Trainer Explains Program Change

"I'm delighted," said Frank Carroll, her trainer, about the gold medal. "I was worried she couldn't complete her program and that she would stop in the middle from dizziness. I told her to stop if she felt sick. She looks frail, but she's a very tough kid. I think she's going to be a lot better next year."

Asked why Miss Fratianne's program was not as fast-moving as the skating she did a year ago, he said it was more lyrical and softer in feeling because "it's important to do a different thing every year."

He said Miss Fratianne was able to do more technically difficult moves than other American skating stars such as Janet Lynn and last year's world champion Dorothy Hamill, and said that Miss Fratianne skated more like Peggy Fleming, world champion from 1966 to 1968.

Kovalev, the runner-up in the last two world championships, received top marks for all three figures in gaining the lead. Jan Hoffman of East Germany, the 1974 world champion, was next, with Pekka Leskinen of Finland third.

For the three figures—outside counter, bracket and loop—the Soviet skater had a total of 12.5 ordinals and 44.40 points.

Hoffman, who placed third in the 1976 world championship after missing the 1975 competition because of a broken leg, remains favorite to win the overall title. He defeated Kovalev in the European championship in Finland. The 22-year-old East German had 28 ordinals and 42.52 points. Leskinen, a 23-year-old law student, finished third with 39.5 ordinals and 42.00 points.

### American Champion Is Fourth

David Santee of Park Ridge, Ill., who placed third in the United States championship, was in fourth place, followed by Charles Tickner of Littleton, Colo., the new American champion. Santee had 29.5 ordinals and 42.04 points and Tickner 55 ordinals and 39.52 points.

Earlier in the day, the Soviet pair of Irina Moiseyeva and Andrei Minenkov skated the best original set pattern dance and kept a tight hold on first place in the ice dancing competition.

Janet Thompson and Warren Maxwell of Britain were in second place with half the events finished. Kristina Regoeczy and Andraas Sallay of Hungary were third.

The free dance, which will determine 50 percent of the score, is scheduled for tomorrow night.

March 4, 1977

# Stenmark Again Wins World Cup

ARE, Sweden, March 20 (AP)—Ingemar Stenmark of Sweden captured the World Cup in Alpine skiing today for the second year in a row. He clinched the honor with a smashing victory by 1.59 seconds in the last slalom race of the series.

The impressive triumph in one of the toughest slalom events of the season—only 26 of the 53 starters finished the race—gave the Swede an insurmountable 61-point lead in the overall standing.

"It was more exciting to win this year," said Stenmark. "I'm glad I managed to clinch it in the slalom, my favorite event, and especially here near my home grounds."

More than 17,000 fans, a record crowd for an Alpine ski meet in Sweden, were on hand for Stenmark's big day. He did not let them down.

### Heidegger's Runs Are Slow

Skiing on an icy and tricky 600-meter course with a 170-meter drop, Franco Bieler of Italy turned in a surprising strong first run of 47.97 seconds and took the lead. Stenmark trailed by eighteen-hundreths of a second with Paul Frommelt of Liechtenstein third, two-hundreths of a second further behind. Just seven-tenths of a second separated the top 10 in the closely contested first run.

Klaus Heidegger of Austria was the only skier who had a chance to challenge Stenmark for the cup before this next to last stop of the circuit. But the 19-year old Austrian lost his slim chance on the first run, finishing 16th, 1.37 seconds behind Bieler. Heidegger came back strongly in the second run and tied for fifth with Piero Gros of Italy, the winner of the Cup in 1974, but it was not good enough.

The fifth-place finish gave him 8 points while Stenmark picked up 25 for his victory to take a 289-228 lead with only two giant sialom races to go.

Stenmark made it a one-man show with a fine second run and a time of 50.78 seconds, beating Bieler and the rest of the field by a wide margin. His total for the two runs was 1:93. Bieler finished with 1:40.52. Gustavo Thoeni of Italy, who clinched the first of four World Cups here six years ago, was third in 1:41.02.

March 21, 1977

# THE UNLONELINESS OF THE LONG-DISTANCE SKIER

Young skier in Putney, Vt., a center of cross-country racing in America.

Old-timers lament—with some
exaggeration—that the woodland solitude is
suddenly gone and there's a skier behind every tree.
But they delight in benefits that the new
popularity and prosperity
have brought to America's snowbelt.

## By Peter Wood

KILLINGTON, Vt. Adolf Delso, a retired Army mountaineering instructor, was seated behind a half-gallon jug of rosé at a table in a rough-and-ready lounge at the Mountain Meadows Ski Touring Center. "When I first came up here in 1964, I had the woods to myself," he said. "Now, there's a skier behind every tree." His lament reflects a warning issued by Rudi Mattesich, president of the Ski Touring Council and the unofficial dean of cross-country skiing in America. In an introduction to one of the many books that had begun appearing on the subject in the early 70's, he wrote: "Ski touring would be spoiled if too much emphasis is placed on the merchandising of fancy equipment, changing fashions, or organized area skiing, and on the promotion of the name resort." The words are a blueprint for the present state of the sport.

☐

Delso illustrates a typical dichotomy among seasoned cross-country hands. Just 10 minutes before he made those remarks last season about the solitude of 1964, he was speeding along on the finest of new equipment, crossing the finish line of a well-organized race, promoted by a name resort, in a thickly, if temporarily, populated area of the Vermont woods.

Though he and his friends mourn the passing of the good old days, they delight in the superiority of the new equipment that the new popularity and the prosperity have brought, and they're not above participating in the good-natured gregariousness of a Saturday-morning race.

☐

Moreover, Delso is an expansive type. He tends to exaggerate. There are probably not as many skiers in the world as there are trees in Vermont. So how could there be a skier behind every one?

Well, actual numbers were not his point. A decade ago, however many skiers there were, 99.9 percent of them

Peter Wood writes frequently about the outdoors.

could be expected to be Alpine skiers, a category that began to mean skiers who were crowded like sheep at the bottom of lift lines or jostling for position, often at high speeds, on wide, packed trails that pointed downhill. However the trails twisted and turned, they led inevitably to a cash register at the bottom. That left the rest of snow country to the handful of cognoscenti like Delso' and Mattesich, who took pleasure bushwhacking through leafless, snowbound forests and following old logging roads, or to the college and prep-school introverts who practiced the grueling and largely gloryless sport of cross-country racing.

Still, the actual numbers are impressive. In 1967, 12,000 pairs of cross-country skis were sold in the United States; last year, the figure was an estimated 415,000; this means that roughly a quarter of all skis sold in the United States were the light skinny ones designed for running—or walking, safely and sanely—on snow rather than booming down a mountain. Last year alone, 100 new cross-country centers opened in the snowbelt from Maine to California, putting the total number of centers at close to 400. Eighty more are in prospect for this season. (One of the major attractions from the promoters' point of view is the relatively low cost. Howard Peterson, president of the National Ski Touring Operators Association, estimates that to lay out 10 miles of touring trails, buy a snow cat to groom them, and put together 50 sets of rental skis, boots and poles need not cost more than $25,000. "You can't even build a small T-bar lift, for downhill skiing, these days for that kind of money." And this says nothing of increased costs of operating and maintaining the fuel-guzzling lifts.)

So perhaps because of the energy crisis, still snapping at our traces like a pack of ravening wolves, and because of the country's growing interest in matters ecological along with the current physical-fitness fad, some cross-country centers are actually having to turn skiers away on busy weekends. In fact, America's ski habits are in revolution, and, until the powder settles, patterns will be changing daily as to how cross-country is done, what equipment is used and where—whether it be on the narrow racing course, on the touring center's wider, smoothed-out trail for the nonracer, or simply on the open field or unplowed country road or even along the fairways of the suburban country club.

[ ]

Adolf Delso and others had gathered for the Mountain Meadows Saturday race. John Tidd of the Mountain Meadows Ski Touring Center sent these solitude lovers—all 26 of them—off in a

---

Behind the cross-country fad lies a growing concern for physical fitness, an interest in matters ecological and the energy crisis, still 'snapping at our traces like a pack of ravening wolves.'

---

mass start. The mob moved off in a clutter of poles and skis, swiftly gliding over the snow, barely touching the snow, toes attached to supple skis, waxed to grip and glide alternately. Settling into a rhythmic stride, they quickly fell into line according to relative speed, and they were moving rapidly as I watched them disappear over a hill and into a gap in the woods.

[ ]

Though the cross-country craze for racers and nonracers alike is young in the United States, the Scandinavians, of necessity, have been doing it for thousands of years. A 4,000-year-old carving on a rock wall on the island of Rodog off the coast of Norway unmistakably shows a man on skis. Early skis were strictly tools, used for travel. The first skiing done for pure sport was jumping. Using the same boards they walked about on, youngsters would streak straight downhill, hit a bump and become airborne. The one who flew the farthest was the winner. The sport of downhill skiing did not begin until a century ago when a native of Telemark, Norway, one Sondre Nordheim, a famous jumper in his time (who later emigrated to the United States), invented the leather toe piece and heel-strap binding that gave him lateral control over his skis. Little could Nordheim have imagined at the time the gaudy, plastic prosthetic boots and space-age safety bindings that would characterize our present method of welding a downhill skier to his boards—or rather, to his plastic laminates, for it has been some years now since any self-respecting downhill skier would be caught out on wooden skis. In any case, the application of modern engineering to skis would take place for the most part in the Alpine countries of Austria, Switzerland and France.

Meanwhile, the Scandinavians, attached only by their toes, went right on skiing cross-country, in track and out, uphill and down. And when new forms of transportation were invented, in the

---

normal course of progress, what had once been a necessity of life became a highly developed and immensely popular sport. In Norway, according to an official report, "one out of every four Norwegians is a regular, keen and skilled cross-country skier." That means that a quarter of the population enjoys trekking long distances in winter, from hut to hut, just as many hikers do each summer in America, and that they frequently compete in

races of anywhere from five to 50 miles. The ultimate in cross-country ski races, the Vasa-Loppet, is held each year in Sweden to commemorate Gustav Vasa, founder, in 1521, of the present kingdom. Upward of 10,000 skiers have competed at one time in the Vasa-Loppet, all starting at the same gun. The distance is 85 kilometers, or more than 50 miles, and many skiers finish in well under five hours.

During the 1950's and 1960's, the big development decades in America for Alpine skiing, cross-country (which, with jumping, belongs to the Nordic branch of the sport) was still ignored by all but a handful of recreational skiers like Delso and a few die-hard racers—die-hard, because in international competition against the Scandinavians and Eastern Europeans they fared so miserably. But they kept on trying.

☐

I could not now see Delso and his friends among the Mountain Meadows racers as they continued on their five-kilometer course that skirted through the woods around Lake Kent. But the 26 skiers were soon unbunched as they followed the leader, 17-year-old Scott Stevens, son of the owners of the Mountain Meadows lodge, along tracks set by Tidd that morning with a snowmobile, surging uphill and down with the rythym of a train. By now they were moving as fast as — and far more easily than — a champion distance runner, using their arms to pole and help propel themselves, utilizing almost every muscle of their bodies.

☐

For all-around conditioning the only sports that compare with cross-country are swimming and rowing. Harry Parker, an ex-Olympic oarsman and coach of the perennially strong Harvard varsity crew, took up cross-country for the first time a few years ago at the age of 43. He "likes the motion," he said. "It's less punishing on the body than running, yet ultimately more demanding. And it's exciting going downhill." Parker now encourages his oarsmen to follow his lead. ☐

The short shrift given cross-country on this side of the Atlantic after World War II can

*Cross-country marathon at Engadine, Switzerland*

be explained in part by its apparent lack of commercial attractiveness, its lack of any obvious turnstile at the bottom of a mountain. People crazy enough to exhaust themselves on equipment that was both cheaper and easier to master (meaning less work for instructors) than downhill gear simply had no appeal for the ski industry. Now, by dint of sheer numbers, they do.

By 1967, it was already apparent that with or without active promotion cross-country was a comer. Not only were vastly greater numbers of cross-country skis being sold, but the industry—both the American manufacturers, new in the field, and the more powerful European ski makers — were developing ways to stimulate the same sort of appetite for accessories and fancy clothing as they had done so successfully for downhill. Fiberglass skis were being suggested to replace wood. Fiberglass is stronger, lighter and — you guessed it — lots more expensive.

Skis that dispensed with the sometimes tedious and always-perplexing addition of wax were also getting a big

boost. Before the turn of the century, waxing of cross-country skis was unheard of. A newspaper account of a race in Norway in 1892 reported: "All the new snow and sunshine spoiled the day for most of the competitors. As much as six inches of snow accumulated on the bottoms of the skis, so that some of the competitors appeared to be walking on snowshoes." The waxing of skis for the sole purpose of streaking downhill, on the other hand, had been known to miners in the American West for some time before that. During the 70's and 80's those daredevils raced each other for purses and bets that amounted to many thousands of dollars. Streaking side by side straight down the mountain on ragged 12-foot-long boards, they reached speeds of up to 80 miles per hour. To get as much zip as possible they treated their skis with "dope" or "Sierra lightning." The formulas, always well-kept secrets, might contain anything from sperm oil and bear fat to tobacco juice and a variety of substances unmentionable in polite society.

The cross-country waxes,

developed in the Nordic countries, are a compromise. Their molecular structure is such that, when the ski is planted solidly, they snap down like tiny cleats that have a sharply braking effect in the snow, but, when the ski is pushed forward horizontally, they lie back smoothly. In other words, the skis adhere when the foot is planted for the "kick," yet slip for the "glide." But different snow conditions and different temperatures demand different waxes. The wax you put on in the morning is not likely to give you the grip you need to climb at noon, when the snow has warmed up. It is often the best-waxed rather than the smoothest or strongest skier who will win a race.

Waxless skis take advantage of some sort of mechanical device to effect the same dichotomy of grab and glide. Popular, but noisy, is a fish-scale pattern embossed in a plastic laminate on the ski bottom. Racers usually shun them, but for the recreational skier, waxless skis are here to stay. And they are popular with the industry because they represent a developing technology and therefore the opportunity to sell a new product each year to the skier who must have the best and the latest.

Choosing among cross-country skis can be a bewildering experience. At the annual ski trade show this summer 44 different manufacturers exhibited 276 models with price tags ranging from $45 for wooden laminates to a $350 racing ski by Epoke of Norway. The description of the latter, "a laminated wood and foam core wrapped in carbon fiber in a torsion box construction. Polyethylene base," illustrates just how far ski construction has come since the days of the simple grooved hickory board. You can take a ski like that and bend it tip to toe without its breaking. To build the same strength-to-weight ratio into a wooden ski is all but impossible, and in cross-country any extra weight is a burden.

Boots, bindings and poles have undergone similar transformations. A few years back, the industry introduced something called the Nordic Norm in an attempt to standardize the variety of different boot-binding combinations. In theory, any Nordic Norm boot should fit any Nordic Norm binding, and all manufacturers would conform to the measurements. A skier with his own boots could then rent skis wherever he wants without the sort of lengthy adjustments necessary with most downhill bindings. However, no sooner had the norm been promulgated, than the West German firm of Adidas came out with an improved boot and binding all its own, lighter in weight and narrower, so that in a fixed track there was less friction between the binding and the snow. The advantage was strictly for serious racers. But not to be outdone, other manufacturers copied the principle, calling it the Nordic Racing Norm. The design, which calls for a boot with a long lip projecting forward from the toe, is a good one, and more and more recreational skiers are adopting it.

These were the essentials. On ski-shop shelves, extras included such items as sleek nylon one-piece racing togs in jester's patterns and colors to replace the tried-and-true knickers and long stockings. The price tag on such an outfit, more and more of which are appearing on the trails, is anywhere from $50 to $100. At the other end of the scale, Doug Kreeger, proprietor of Kreeger and Sons, a New York City hiking and camping store, claims that all one needs to be adequately dressed for cross country is a pair of $13.95 gaiters, which protect the critical area between the top of the boot and the bottom of one's Levis.

As to where one might go to use such equipment in the orderly and convivial atmosphere that many skiers now desire—as opposed to just going off by oneself in the woods—one finds at the top of the list of "name resorts" the Trapp Family Lodge at Stowe, Vt. Built by the "Sound of Music" family, it claims to be the first establishment in the United States devoted entirely to cross-country skiing. Certainly its gingerbread decor, 75 miles of meticulously groomed trails and staff of 12 instructors, including one former Olympian, make it one of the most elaborate.

In the Middle West, there is Telemark Lodge in Wisconsin, a two-hour drive south of Duluth. Telemark boasts 93 kilometers of trails, and each year plays host to the country's largest citizens' race, the Birkebeiner, modeled on a famed Norwegian race (2,000 entrants last year, including 400 Norwegians who flew over just for the event). National parks, such as Bryce Canyon and Yellowstone, are getting increasing numbers of organized tours. Beyond that, the 1978 Guide to Cross-Country Skiing (newsstand price, $1.95) lists more than 375 touring centers and wilderness areas across the country, with trail, lodging, ski-school and price information.

Perhaps the most pleasant of all cross-country experiences presently available is skiing between country inns in the vicinity of Middlebury, Vt. Skiing inn to inn, or hut to hut, is common practice in Scandinavia. This New England version, in which your car and luggage are advanced day by day, was the brainchild of Tony Clark, proprietor with his wife, Martha, of probably the most successful of all New England's cross-country ski inns. In the past six years since they started taking in some 18 guests a night at Blue-berry Hill, in Goshen, Vt., feeding them sumptuously, treating them like family and turning them loose on 40 miles of ski trails through the Green Mountain National Forest and the Central Vermont Public Serivce Company lands, the Clarks have seen their business grow until they literally have had to beat customers away with sticks. Or so it seemed when I visited not long ago on an interinn tour. On the morning our group was supposed to ski down to the next way station, Churchill House, in Brandon, Vt., it was blowing a full gale. One of the Clark's barns had already collapsed and shingles and branches from an old sugar maple in front of the ski shop were falling thick as flack in a London air raid. Nevertheless, Tony pushed us out in the howling storm and clattering debris to complete our appointed rounds. He had more guests coming in to take our beds that night. By early afternoon, we reached Churchill House; all of us were crusted with wind-driven snow, though warm from exertion. We had experienced the woods in a rare fury, and to a man and woman we were glad we had gone.

At the other end of the spectrum is a new phenomenon that promises to catch on, urban cross-country. At Weston, Mass., just 12 miles from the Boston Common, on a 250-acre municipal golf course, Mike Farny has installed what until this year was the only snow-making equipment exclusively devoted to cross-country (Telemark Lodge in Wisconsin is installing snow equipment on 15 miles of its trails). This season will be Farny's fourth at Weston. The first, when there were still bugs in his $5,000 spray guns, he registered crowds of up to 300 skiers on a good Saturday or Sunday. Last year, he repeatedly has as many as 600 and 700, about the limit of the area. Hundreds also took advantage of the lights he installed to ski at night. "With all the snow we had right after Christmas," Farny recalls, "the demand was phenomenal around Boston. We've had as many as 150 people just waiting to rent skis" ($8 to rent boots, skis and poles all day; $2 trail fee if you bring your own).

For all the grass-roots support, American cross-country promoters lacked a star attraction. But then they found that, too, in a 20-year-old named Billy Koch of Gilford, Vt., who burst on the American sporting scene in 1976 via satellite from Seefeld, near Innsbruck, Austria, where the winter Olympics were being contested. There, under close scrutiny of a battery of ABC Sports television cameras, Koch took a silver medal in the 30-kilometer cross-country race. It was the first Olympic medal ever won by an American cross-country skier — the first time, in fact, that an American had placed higher than 15th.

At home the reaction was resounding. A near mystic in his dedication to his sport, yet with an appealing, clean-cut freshness, Koch returned to what in the ski world, at any rate, was a Lindberghlike welcome. Not since the South lost the Civil War has a second-place finisher been so warmly clasped to the American bosom. But in their enthusiasm to hail a new messiah the industry nearly crucified the young athlete.

*Waxing for a tour cross country—actually cross park in suburban Long Island.*

In the ensuing blizzard of interviews and adulations, endorsements and speaking engagements, requests to write articles and make personal appearances at races and resorts, two items bear mention. First, the Travelers Insurance Companies made a grant to the U.S. Ski Association—Eastern Division, which christened a snowy version of Little League baseball for boys and girls ages 6 to 13 as the Bill Koch Ski League. Second, the French ski-manufacturing firm Rossignol, already the quality leader in the downhill market and bent on gaining the same position in the burgeoning cross-country field, signed Koch to a contract to represent it at a yearly salary variously rumored at between $25,000 and $40,000. At Innsbruck, Koch had run on Austrian skis made by Fischer. In the world of cross-country, Rossignol's coup was as significant that year as ABC's theft of Barbara Walters from NBC.

In fact, Koch appears to have earned every penny Rossignol pays him. Like a lightening rod he drew attention to the sport and has given it the legitimacy and glamour that only the Olympics lend. As Teyck Weed, Nordic program director, N.S.S.A.—Eastern Division, put it, "Billy Koch has done more for cross-country in one year than all the other boosters of the sport put together."

One event that surely would not have transpired without Koch's second-place finish at Seefeld was the World Cup race last season at Telemark, Wis. In the past, World Class racers had disdained to participate in United States cross-country events. Last year for the first time, more than a dozen of the best Scandinavian and Eastern European racers flew to Wisconsin to compete. Ironically, Koch was suffering from a respiratory ailment brought on, those close to him say, by his overly demanding schedule, and he came in 27th in the 15-kilometer race out of a field of 72. That finish cost him a trip to Europe to compete on the World Cup circuit, though he retained his place on the U.S. National Team. Koch is training hard again this year, but as yet it is too early to tell whether he has regained his Olympic form.

His standard has been taken up, appropriately, by Tim Caldwell, son of the man who almost alone nursed American cross-country racing through sickly childhood and frail adolescence.

[ ]

For John Caldwell, the Putney School, in Putney, Vt.—private, expensive, progressive, set high on a windy hill above the Connecticut River Valley—has been home base ever since he arrived there in 1941 as a 13-year-old student. He was later graduated from Dartmouth, and returned to Putney to teach math and coach skiing, as he still does.

In 1952, Caldwell won a berth on the U.S. Nordic Olympic team. He finished last in cross-country (he had injured himself jumping and had raced with his shoulders taped). From there, for a stubborn man, there was nowhere to go but up. Under Caldwell's prodding, Putney became the nucleus of cross-country racing in America, producing its top teams through the 50's and 60's. In 1966, Caldwell was named United States Nordic coach, a position he held until 1972. His writings are considered the basic texts on the sport. Martha Rockwell, the best American woman racer, now retired, is a Putney product. So is Billy Koch, and, of course, Tim Caldwell.

I once visited this mecca before the snow season. The Caldwell house is a mile from the school. Final directions came from two boys on roller skis—devices with ratchetted wheels for training on paved roads. John and Tim were down by the sugar shed and sauna chopping wood beside a small pond. Caldwell, in a railroad engineer's cap and faded pink sweatshirt, put down a chain saw. Tim, of medium height, but with strikingly broad shoulders from a lifetime (he is 23) of poling on skis, went on swinging his splitting maul. The logs flew apart.

The elder Caldwell, cheery, easy, directed me to the anteroom of the sauna, where, sprawled on benches, we talked cross-country. From somewhere Caldwell produced two cold beers. Now and again one heard Tim toss a log into the furnace, stoking the sauna.

*Cross-country companions of the Vermont woods.*

It was a ritual, Caldwell, explained, every Wednesday. People count on it and drop in. Among other things, he talked about skiing in Australia. Australia? "You bet, fabulous." He talked about clinics at Putney with Scandianivan coaches, about the annual George Washington's Birthday Race at Putney. A classic (last year there were 1,100 runners). "It's really gotten out of hand." American prospects for the Lake Placid Olympics in 1980: clearly better in cross-country than they have ever been.

While he talked, two college-age joggers in training, one a male, the other a female, came in, stripped and entered the sauna. From the back, the female appeared every inch as athletic and muscular as the male; later, seen from the front, she appeared very much a woman: muscle mixed with grace and beauty—what more could one ask of a sport, I thought.

Fourteen minutes after my friend Delso and his fellow racers disappeared around the bend of Killington's Lake Kent, young Scott Sevens

reappeared, and the others began coming in two minutes later. Though not first, Delso did win his class—men 50 years and over—as he often does in races hereabouts. As each followed, Tidd encouraged him or her with verbal pats on the back: "Atta boy," or "You're looking good, Ruthie."

Despite the 14-degree temperature, Ruth was in fact looking quite hot, perspiring like a coal stoker, while the faces of those with mustaches and beards were hidden behind hoarfrost and icicles. Among the other finishers—in 11th and 12th place-- were a couple of friends—Jim Cutler and Ron Bruce, both Vermont engineers. Gaining the last steep uphill before the finish, they were within a couple of strides of each other and broke into a sprint. Form was forgotten and they collided, finishing the race in a cartwheel of skis, flying snow and laughter. Cutler, in his mid-20's, used to race downhill in high school. But he has mostly given that up now; he, too, was sick of fighting the crowds, and the cost of tows. To look at Cutler's icicle-rimmed smile, you knew he considered the $2 entry fee for the Mountain Meadows race to be money well spent.

A winner in her class, women over 50, was Peg Watt, a diminutive lady in Kelly-green ski togs. When she and her husband, both doctors, retired to Ely, N.H., a few years ago, they took up cross-country skiing, which neither had tried before. Dr. James Watt,

a former director of the National Heart Institute in Washington, is the walker in the family; "... as good a method for graduated exercise as I know of," he says. Peg Watt is the racer. She claims never to have entered a race in which she did not win her class—a fact that says as much about the number of senior women who compete in these citizens races as it is a

measure of her strength. Mrs. Watt's biggest race to date was the 1975 Canadian Marathon, between Montreal and Ottawa. The 190-mile distance is divided into 10-mile segments. She did not ski them all, but she did win the award for the oldest woman competitor. Mrs. Watts is 70.

Billy Koch says, "There is something very spiritual about

cross-country . . . Sometimes I see it as an art form." Anyone who has become proficient enough to have fallen under the spell of the easy rhythm and glide the sport imparts, or even anyone lucky enough to watch the finish of a race like the Mountain Medows will know what Koch is talking about. ∎

December 18, 1977

# Miss Fratianne Wins Figure-Skating Title

### By GERALD ESKENAZI
Special to The New York Times

CINCINNATI, Feb. 3 — Skating strongly in a new, sequined hot red outfit, and putting what her coach called "sex" into her routine, Linda Fratianne tonight captured her third straight United States women's figure-skating title.

And for the second straight year the 5-foot-1-inch, 96-pounder defeated her neighbor from Los Angeles, Lisa-Marie Allen.

Carrie Rugh, another Californian, was third, and the trio will represent the United States in the world championships that start at Vienna in five weeks.

Miss Fratienne finished second in the world event last year, behind Annett Poetsch of East Germany. When they meet again, Miss Fratianne will wear her new flashy costume and dance the same program that lifted her to the United States title tonight.

#### Music from 'Carmen'

She skated to "Carmen" in the freestyle phase of the championships, which was worth 50 percent. She was first on all seven judges' scoring cards, lengthening the lead that she had established earlier.

Before the women took the ice in the Coliseum, Charles Tickner of Littleton, Colo., the reigning world and national men's champion, increased his edge with an almost-perfect two minutes in the "short phase."

A misstep following a "double-flip combination" cost him what might have been a score of perfect 6's. Scott Cramer of Colorado Springs remained second, and David Santee of Park Ridge, Ill., was third. The men's competition ends tomorrow night.

It was apparent from the opening moments that the 18-year-old Miss Fratianne, a high school senior, was going to be strong.

In fact, it almost appeared as if she was rushing through the early part of the program. Then she smoothly went into jumps, spinning as she landed, then going through more difficult routines, and it as obvious she was in control.

"You've got it together tonight, baby," shouted the president of the Broadmoor Figure Skating Club, Jack Might.

That was precisely what her coach,

Frank Carroll, had hoped for.

"We wanted to sell the program to the audience," he said. "This was one of her best performances, better than last year's nationals."

If it is possible to think of something else when a national championship is at stake, Miss Fratianne apparently did.

After she had won, she was asked if she was ready for the world competition. She paused a few seconds and then said, "Yeah." She won the world title in 1977, and when she failed to repeat last year many skating observers believed she might not be able to come back this season.

But it is rare for a reigning United States champion to be dethroned — no one in the United States Figure Skating Association could recall when that last happened — but she did not back into the title tonight.

Although Miss Allen lost points when she had to steady herself by placing her hand on the ice after a double axel, it was unlikely she would have caught Miss Fratianne even if she had landed perfectly.

Miss Fratianne was not the only one

thinking about the world championships following victory here. Late last night 18-year-old Tai Babilonia and her 20-year-old partner, Randy Gardner, took their fourth straight national pairs title.

Although they are not considered well-rounded enought to surpass the Russians and East Germans, who finished 1, 2 ahead of them last year, the Americans could go into Vienna favored.

Irina Rodnina, who is married to her partner, Aleksander Zaitsev, is expecting a baby any day. Meanwhile, says Gardner, the East German team of Manuela Mager and Uewe Bewestdorf is injured. "We heard that either one or both of them suffered serious injuries," Gardner said. "But we also heard they're supposed to return soon."

Meanwhile, three women from the New York area appeared in the finale of the singles championship — Simone Grigoreson of the Skating Club of New York was seventh, Aimee Kravette of the Long Island Figure Skating Club was 10th, and Laura McDonald of the skating club of New York was 11th.

Another "New Yorker," Allen Schramm, was one of the most popular skaters tonight, although he was sixth among the men. But he brought squeals of delight from the young girls in the crowd with his routine.

Schramm is actually a Californian, but moved to New York where it was easier to qualify for the nationals.

February 3, 1979

# Skating: For Heiden, A 7th World Crown

OSLO, Feb. 11 (AP) — More convincing than ever, Eric Heiden of the United States captured his seventh world championship title in speed skating in three years today by winning all four races at Oslo's Olympic Bislet Stadium.

The 23-year-old Madison, Wis., star set a world record for a single meet and championship record of 162.973 points. He won the 1,500-meter race in 1 minute 56.05 seconds and set a world record in the 10,000-meter event in 14:43.11. Those two victories followed triumphs yesterday in the 500-meter contest (38.22 seconds) and the 5,000-meter event (6:59.15).

With his previous personal record of 0:37.90 for the 500 meters, he also climbed from a pre-meet ninth place to the top of the career points list with 162.653 points.

Speed skaters are scored on a basis of their actual 500-meter time and the average 500-meter times for the three longer distances.

Only one week ago, Eric's 19-year-old sister Beth also won all four races at the women's all-round championships at the Hague, the Netherlands, to win her first senior world title and the first world championship for the United States since Kit Klein won in 1936.

Next weekend Eric and Beth are fa-

178

vored to win the world sprint championship titles for men and women at the artificial ice rink at Inzell, West Germany.

Under ideal weather and ice conditions at Bislet's natural ice rink, Jan Egil Storholt, Norway's 1979 European all-round champion, placed second over all with 167.805 points. His compatriot, Kay Stenshjemmet, placed third with 167.903 points. Storholt held the previous world record for points in one meet with 163.221, and Heiden held the previous championship record of 167.831, both from 1977.

Heiden was not the only American doing well. Mike Woods clinched fourth place over all with 168.497 points by finishing 11th in the 1,500 meters and fourth in the 10,000 meters. Viktor Ljoskin of the Soviet Union was fifth with 168.660.

February 12, 1979

# World Cup Skiing Titles To Mrs. Moser, Luescher

FURANO, Japan, March 19 (AP)— Ingemar Stenmark of Sweden scored a record 13th victory by capturing the final World Cup Alpine ski race of the season today, but he had to settle for fifth place in the overall cup standing.

In an earlier race, Annemarie Proell Moser delivered under pressure on the second run of the final women's giant slalom and won a sixth overall World Cup championship.

Mrs. Moser, a downhill specialist from Austria, was sixth after the first run. But she rallied on the second run and finished second to Marie-Therese Nadig of Switzerland and captured the Cup by 3 points from Hanni Wenzel of Liechtenstein. Miss Wenzel was fifth today and failed to pick up any Cup points. Mrs. Moser's performance earned her 23 Cup points.

Stenmark's victory in 2 minutes 58.59 seconds gave him a sweep of the season's 10 giant slaloms—the Swede also won three slalomsw—and enabled him to break the season record of 12 victories set by Jean-Claude Killy of France.

But the three-time World Cup champion finished fifth over all in the cup standing because he did not enter downhill races, and new rules this season limited the number of points a skier could pick up in any one specialty. So Stenmark was limited to the maximum 150 points he could earn for the slalom and giant slalom.

The overall Cup title already had been clinched by Peter Luescher of Switzerland, who was seventh in the final race. Luescher finished with 186 points to 163 for Leonard Stock of Austria. Phil Mahre of White Pass, Wash., who missed the last six races because of a broken leg, finished third with 155 points and Piero Gros of Italy was fourth with 152.

Miss Wenzel, the defending overall champion who started the race with a 240-to-220-point lead over Mrs. Moser, was fourth after the first run today, then spun out on the second run and finished fifth. Irene Epple of West Germany, third in 2:51.52, finished third in Cup points with 189 and Cindy Nelson of Lutsen, Minn., sixth today in 2:52.03, was fourth with 168 points. Miss Nadig, the winner today in 2:46.03, finished fifth over all with 156 points.

Heidi Preuss of Lakeport, N.Y., who celebrated her 18th birthday yesterday, was the top American finisher in the women's giant slalom, fourth in 2:52.83. The top men's finisher was Pete Patterson of Sun Valley, Idaho, 12th, in 3:03.

Heini Hemmi, 30, an Olympic gold medalist from Switzerland, finished second today in 3:00.15 in the final race of his career.

March 20, 1979

**BOBSLEDDING,** bob sled-ing, is a fast and dangerous winter sport in which crews of two or four persons race steel sleds over an icy walled course. Each run by each sled is timed, and the sled with the lowest aggregate time is the winner.

**The Course.** To qualify for international competition, a course must have at least 15 banked curves linked by straight stretches, or straight-aways, with high walls to contain the sleds, and must be a minimum of 1,500 meters (about 1 mile) long. The pitch of the run cannot exceed 15% at any point and must average not less than 8%. The curves cannot be less than 18 meters (approximately 59 feet) in radius and must be between 2 meters (about 6 feet) and 7 meters (about 22 feet) high, according to their radius. Two of the better major runs are the Mt. van Hoevenberg at Lake Placid, N.Y., and Cortina d'Ampezzo, Italy. Mt. van Hoevenberg is 1 mile long with 16 curves, including the world famous Shady Curve, a hairpin 22-feet (7 meters) high. Cortina is 1⅐ miles (1,700 meters) long, with 16 challenging turns.

Other courses approved for international competition include Garmisch-Partenkirchen, West Germany; Innsbruck, Austria; St. Moritz, Switzerland; and l'Alpe d'Huez (Grenoble), France.

All critical points on a major course are connected by telephone, and spectators are kept informed of a sled's progress through a public address system. Each run is timed electrically.

**The Sled.** The modern bobsled is a highly specialized and complicated steel and aluminum machine, designed strictly for speed and safety. It has two solid axles, with two runners attached to each axle. The front axle turns for steering; the rear one is usually fastened solidly to the frame. The runners are approximately half-round, with a maximum width of 0.67 meter (about 2 feet 2⅐ inches) from center to center. Each runner acts independently of the others. Seats for the crew are barely 6 to 8 inches (15-20 cm) above the ice. Streamlined cowls on the front of the sled reduce wind resistance, and push handles on the sides help the crew get a fast start.

Sleds are steered with ropes attached to the front runners or with a steering wheel connected by cables to the front runners. Most Americans believe they have more control if they use the wheel. Europeans use ropes almost exclusively on the premise that greater sensitivity in feeling the track is

Sleds are steered with ropes attached to the front runners or with a steering wheel connected by cables to the front runners. Most Americans believe they have more control if they use the wheel. Europeans use ropes almost exclusively on the premise that greater sensitivity in feeling the track is gained in this way. Maximum steering capability results when

centrifugal force presses the sled against the ice wall of a curve. Because of the design of the runners and the icy surface of the run, practically no steering can be done in the straightaways.

The brake is situated between the rear runners. It is a hardened steel bar with a serrated edge for cutting into the ice. Two levers with handles, one on either side of the frame, act as a unit in operating the brake. No braking is allowed in competition, because the severe raking action of the brake's serrated teeth would cause ruts that would be dangerous for the next sled. (Brakes may be used in an emergency, but the sled that uses them is automatically disqualified from the competition.)

The maximum length for a 4-man sled is 12 feet 5 inches (3.8 meters); for a 2-man sled, 9 feet (2.7 meters). Because there is no official limit for weight, sleds may vary as much as 50 pounds (23 kg). The average 4-man sled, however, weighs about 507 pounds (230 kg); the average 2-man sled, about 353 pounds (160 kg).

In international competition the combined weight of sled and crew cannot exceed 1,389 pounds (630 kg) for the 4-man team and 827 pounds (375 kg) for the 2-man team. If the maximum weight is not attained, additional weight may be bolted to the sled to equalize the chances of a light crew against heavier opponents. Four-man sleds reach speeds up to 100 miles (160 km) per hour in competition. Two-man sleds run slightly slower.

**Competition.** Teams race the course against time, using a running start from a fixed point. A series of four heats, or runs, two on each of two consecutive days, is required of each team, with the low aggregate of all four times deciding final positions.

In 4-man competition, the team captain steers. The rear man, or brakeman, is responsible for checking skids and stopping the sled. The two middle men assist in starting and supply ballast. All ride the sled in such a manner that a smooth, straight "line" is followed all the way down the course, assuring a fast time. In 2-man competition, the two riders perform the duties of the front and rear members of the 4-man teams.

**History.** Bobsledding was originated during the latter part of the 19th century in Switzerland by tobogganers who added runners to their sleds and banked the turns on the slide to increase the speed and thrill of toboganning. The first artificial bobsled run was built at St. Moritz in 1904. Other winter sports centers soon followed. The first national bobsled championship competition was held in Austria in 1908 and the first European championships were decided in 1914.

The international governing body for the sport, the Fédération Internationale de Bobsleigh et Tobogganning, was organized in 1923 and conducted the first world championships in 1927 at St. Moritz. For the United States the governing body is the Amateur Athletic Union.

Bobsledding has been part of the Winter Olympic Games since 1924 (except for 1960).

**Famous Competitors.** Outstanding U.S. Olympic gold medal winners include William Fiske, J. Hubert Stevens, Curtis P. Stevens, Ivan E. Brown, Alan M. Washbond, William D'Amico, Edward Rimkus, Francis Tyler, and Patrick Martin. Arthur Tyler, James Bickford, Fred Fortune, and Stan Benham were internationally prominent during the late 1960's. Other famous names include Fritz Feierabend, Reto Capadrutt, Franz Kapus, and Frederich Endrich, Switzerland; Max Houben, Belgium; Hans Kilian, Andreas Ostler, and Antoni Pensberger, Germany; Eugenio Monti and Sergio Zardini, Italy; Tony Nash, Britain; and Victor Emery, Canada.

Joe Pete Wilson
*Lake Placid (N.Y.) Bobsled Team*

**Skating** is gliding over a surface by means of skates. In ice skating the skates are short metal runners attached to boots or shoes. In roller skating, wheels replace the runners. This article deals with the sport of ice skating. See also Hockey.

The main divisions of the sport of ice skating include speed skating and figure skating. National and international competitions are held in both. According to the branch he chooses, a skater may exercise sheer physical prowess, creative ability, artistic sense, or a combination of all three. The opportunity for beauty of movement in modern figure skating is so great that this branch has been raised to an art form comparable to the dance.

Skating appeals to people of all ages, whether as a pleasant recreation, as a discipline with competition as its goal, or as a profession. Increasingly comprehensive coverage of national and international events by television and the accelerated building of artificial ice rinks are visible indications of the sport's growing worldwide popularity.

**Equipment.** Strictly speaking, the term "skate" should be confined to the metal runner, which consists of a blade attached to sole and heel plates by vertical stanchions. In the United States, however, the word "skate" is used loosely to mean the combination of boot and runner, the latter being referred to as the "blade."

The difference between speed, figure, and hockey skates lies in the structure of both the blade and the boot. The figure blade projects only slightly at the toe and heel, the bottom of the blade being ground to a complex curve form front to back, the major part of which corresponds to a circle having a radius of between 6 and 7 feet (1.8-2.1 meters). The rounded front section contains a series of sharp serrations known as "toe rakes" or "toe picks," which are used in certain types of spins and jumps. The beginner's tendency to catch these in the ice is due to the faulty return of the foot after the thrust. Running the length of the bottom of the blade is a groove known as the "hollow," which serves to divide the cutting section into two distinct edges. The figure boot is sturdy and relatively high both in the shaft and heel. A stiffened section known as the "counter" supports the arch of the foot.

For speed skating the blade is thin, has relatively little curvature from front to back, projects considerably in front of the toe of the boot, and is ground completely flat. The boot is low and quite flexible. The ice hockey boot is also somewhat low but is quite tough, having a reinforced toecap and a vertical leather section at the back to protect the Achilles tendon. The blade is thin, is sharply curved at the front and rear, and has a middle section varying in curvature according to the player's preference.

Women's figure skating attire normally consists of tan, semi-sheer nylon tights, a short skirt or dress, and matching pants. Skating costumes, usually in stretch materials, are also obtainable in the form of a leotard with a brief skirt attached. A sweater and gloves are advisable for cold rinks. Boots are usually white. Hair, if long, should be tied back, and scarves and hats are not recommended. Figure skating attire for men is informal except during tests and competitions, when one-piece suits made of a stretch material are usual. Boots are traditionally black. For speed skating, black tights and black turtleneck sweaters are popular.

**Skating for Recreation.** A beginner's first object should be to learn to stroke correctly. A good stroke involves thrusting from the correct part of the blade, controlling knee action, and correctly transferring weight from one foot to the other, a subtle skill often taking several seasons to perfect. The following points should be observed in simple forward skating. The power thrust is made from the inside edge of the blade, never from the toe rake, and the direction of the thrust is sideways and slightly to the rear. A relatively upright posture is preserved throughout the thrust. When skating forward one should place his weight toward the rear of the blade. Backward skating should be learned as soon as possible. In the early stages the action consists of a two-footed movement.

Once a beginner decides what branch of skating most appeals to him—speed skating, figure skating, or hockey—practicing becomes more specialized. If figure skating is his goal, he should learn to make the curves, both forward and backward, on the inside and outside edges. He may also want to attempt the various jumps, spins, and general footwork, collectively known as "free style."

A skater may measure his progress in basic skating, figure skating, and free style by taking the official tests administered by the U.S. Figure Skating Association (USFSA). These consist of a series of 12 elementary tests available to the general public, plus a series of more advanced tests requiring membership in the USFSA, the eighth of which constitutes the gold medal and requires many years of hard training. It should be possible, however, for a reasonably athletic adult to master the 12 USFSA basic tests in one or two seasons if he is able to practice at least twice a week. The Ice Skating Institute of America (ISIA) is a professional organization consisting mainly of ice rink managements that aims at furthering recreational skating and technical knowledge of ice rink management. They administer a series of skating tests. The Professional Skaters Guild of America (PSGA) controls and classifies member professional figure skating instructors in the United States.

**Amateur Competition.** Amateur figure skating is regulated in the United States by the USFSA and speed skating by the American Skating Union (ASU). Both bodies are affiliated with the International Skating Union (ISU) and are members of the U.S. Olympic Committee. These regulating bodies organize championship competitions and trials, the results of which determine the composition of the teams representing the United States at the Olympic Winter Games and the world championship.

Figure skaters wishing to compete nationally must first qualify through regional and sectional competitions. It usually is necessary to join a local club affiliated with the USFSA. Selection of teams to compete internationally is based on the results of national competition. A speed skater may enter local competition by registering with his local association. International teams are selected at annual trials.

**Speed Skating.** Two forms of racing, known as Olympic style and American Pack or Mass Start style, exist in the United States. The basic difference is that in Olympic style racing the skater skates against the clock, while in the American Pack a number of skaters start together, competing against each other in a series of heats.

The Olympic Winter Games events and the world championship are held according to regulations laid down by the ISU. The distances are 500, 1,500, 5,000 and 10,000 meters for men, and 500, 1,000, 1,500 and 3,000 meters for women. Skaters reach speeds of over 28 miles (45 km) per hour in short races and maintain averages of over 25 miles (40 km) in longer events. The ISU also holds a competition known as the World Sprint Championship. A standard 400-meter track with two lanes is used, regulations permitting two skaters to skate simultaneously. At one point on the straightaway the tracks cross, thus enabling both skaters to take equal advantage of the inside track. Tracks used in American Pack style racing include the 6-lap (to the mile), the 8-lap, a 16-lap indoor track, and a 400-meter track adapted for this type of racing by the ASU. On occasions a 12-lap track is also used.

After a number of qualifying heats the winner of an American Pack style race is the skater who in the final round crosses the finishing line in the shortest time. The usual method of deciding the winner of the world championship is to take the total of each skater's times in seconds over all four distances, the longer distances having been proportionally reduced to reflect his time over 500 meters. The skater having the least number of seconds (points) against him is the winner. In the Olympic Winter Games each distance is treated as a separate event, and gold, silver, and bronze medals are awarded for each. The Olympic Games are not classified as championships.

Unlike the figure skater, the speed skater adopts a crouching posture, which reduces wind resistance and enables him to achieve a longer stroke. A strong rhythmic swing of the arms is used to increase momentum. As the tracks get smaller, increasing emphasis is laid on the ability to negotiate the curved ends of the track, such ability becoming of paramount importance on the 16-lap indoor track. The skater's lean to the inside of the circle may cause the edge of the boot to touch the ice. For this reason, and because all racing is in a counterclockwise direction, it is usual to set the blade well to the left edge of the boot.

The Olympic Winter Games held in Sapporo, Japan, in 1972 produced two outstanding American speed skaters. Anne Henning won the 500-meter event in record time and earned a bronze medal in the 1,000 meters. Dianne Holum skated to the gold medal for the 1,500 meters, also establishing a new Olympic record, and won a silver medal in the 3,000-meter event.

**Figure Skating.** Figure skating is a wide and loosely used term embracing three branches: figures and free style, pair skating, and ice dancing. All branches had their origin in the curves and turns that can be made on correctly designed figure skates.

**Fundamentals.** A figure blade possesses two physical edges. The one farther form the center line of the body is called the outside edge, and the one nearer the center line is the inside edge. If a skater leans to one side so as to rock his blade over onto an edge he will make a curve in that direction. Four curves may be skated on each foot, each curve being known as an "edge." The names of the edges on the right foot are: the right forward outside (RFO), right forward inside (RFI), right back outside (RBO), and right back inside (RBI). The edges on the left foot are similarly designated. The foot on which the skater is at any moment skating is known as the skating foot, while the foot in the air is known as the free foot. Corresponding terms are used for other parts of the body, and thus reference is made to the free arm, skating shoulder, and so on. The size of a curve depends on the skater's height, speed, and degree of lean.

Control of the edges is fundamental and vital to the proper performance of every movement contained in all branches of figure skating. The greatest difficulty confronting a beginner is the fact that his body tends to rotate in an uncontrolled manner in the direction of the edge being skated. When one skates a clockwise curve, for example, the body will rotate in a clockwise direction, soon producing an untenable position. To correct this the skater must learn to hold his body from the hips upward completely motionless both during and after the thrust, thereby preventing the

slightest rotation of any part of his body in the direction of the curve, which is achieved solely by leaning. The hips are almost invariably the last part of the body to be brought under control, and the help of an expert instructor is usually necessary.

The body should be erect, with the hands and arms extended from the body at approximately hip level and the knees always preserving some degree of flexibility. The skating knee is very rarely completely straight. All balance should be controlled by the muscles of the skating leg and not by the upper part of the body. Having achieved initial control of the edges, the skater must then learn to rotate his body in a controlled fashion around its vertical axis. In this way the various turns may be made.

The simple movement of rocking from one edge to another without turning the body is known as a "serpentine" or "change of edge." For example, a skater might be on a clockwise curve and then rock his body over onto the opposite edge to take him in a counter-clockwise direction, thus producing a serpentine line. Turns may be made from forward skating to backward or from backward skating to forward. One-footed turns are known as "threes" and "brackets" when turned on the circumference of a circle and as "rockers" and "counters" when made at the rockover point—the point where a change of edge is made—of a serpentine line. Turns involving a change of foot are known as "mohawks" when made on the circumference of a circle and as "choctaws" when made on a serpentine line. When executing threes and rockers, the skater turns the skating foot in the natural direction of the initial curve, while brackets and counters require him to turn the foot in the opposite direction. The direction of rotation of mohawks and choctaws is governed by the character of the initial edge.

**Competition.** Since a blade leaves a white mark, or tracing, on clean ice, edges and turns are used to make various geometric drawings known as "figures," all of which are based on the two-circle figure eight form or the three-circle serpentine form. There are 69 such figures in the ISU schedule, but only a selection is used for any one competition. Judging, on a scale of one to six, is based on various considerations, including symmetry, cleanness of turns, correctness of form and—inasmuch as each figure must be skated three times without pause (triple repetition)—the ability to place one tracing on top of the preceding one.

In addition to their use in the actual figures, the turns and edges may, in conjunction with various spins and jumps from one edge to another, be used to produce over the whole ice surface a continuous and harmonious series of free style movements that, when performed to music for a specified length of time, are known as a "program." Two sets of marks are awarded, the first for technical merit and the second for artistic impression. A short second free style program, containing compulsory free style moves, was introduced in 1973. Under the revised rules, freestyle skating counts for 40%, compulsory free style for 20%, and the figure section—also known as school figures—for 40% in competition.

One of the most attractive forms of skating to watch is pair skating, which consists of a free style program performed in unison by a mixed couple, with the addition of spectacular lifts by the man and various combined spins. There is a short second program containing compulsory moves. No figures are involved, and marking is on the same basis as for single skating.

The third branch, ice dancing, differs from pair skating in that a number of compulsory dances such as waltzes, foxtrots, and tangos must be performed, as well as an exhibition program known as "free dance," in which lifts, combined spins, and the separation of partners are severely restricted. Inventions for a compulsory type of dance may also be required. This branch of figure skating is not included in the Olympic Winter Games.

Famous names abound in figure skating, but undoubtedly those whose names are best known to the public are the former world champions Sonja Henie, Tenley Albright,

Peggy Fleming, Dick Button, and Oleg and Ljudmila Protopopov, a great Russian pair.

Robert Ogilvie
*Author of "Basic Ice Skating Skills"*

### Bibliography

**Amateur Skating Union of the United States,** *Official Handbook* (Amateur Skating Union).
**Brown, Nigel,** *Ice Skating, A History* (Barnes, A.S. 1959).
**Lussi, Gustave, and Richards, Maurice,** *Championship Figure Skating* (Barnes, A.S. 1951).
**Ogilvie, Robert S.,** *Basic Ice Skating Skills* (Lippincott 1968).
**Owen, Maribel Vinson,** *The Fun of Figure Skating* (Harper 1960).
**Richardson, T.D.,** *The Art of Figure Skating* (Barnes, A.S. 1962).
**U.S. Figure Skating Association,** *The Rulebook* (USFSA, biannually).
**U.S. Figure Skating Association,** *Evaluation of School Figure Errors, 7th ed.* (USFSA, 1970).

**SKIING.** Skiing has been practiced for over 4,000 years, but it did not become a popular recreational sport until the 20th century. The two main types of competitive skiing are Alpine and Nordic. Alpine skiing consists of downhill and slalom racing, while Nordic embraces jumping and cross-country events.

**Skis and Poles.** A ski is a long, flat runner turned up at the front end. Skis are made of a variety of materials, including wood, plastic, metal, and combinations of the three. Styles range from long for downhill racing, to heavy for jumping, to light for cross country. Wood skis, for many years the only type, are usually available in the lower price ranges. Metal and plastic skis have increased greatly in popularity as improved production methods have brought price reductions.

All skis should be cambered, or arched slightly in the middle, so the skier's weight will be distributed evenly when he steps on the skis. Plastic running surfaces reduce friction and increase speed, while metal edges permit good control on turns. Skis must be strong but should also be flexible and resilient. Finally, they must be able to withstand great variations in climate.

For ordinary skiers, all-purpose skis are suitable for most types of slopes and snow conditions. A common rule for ski lengths has been the distance between the ground and the skier's hand raised above his head but many instructors recommend shorter skis for beginners. For experts and professionals, skis vary to meet the needs of a particular event. Downhill skis are longer and heavier than slalom skis, which are used for turning quickly. Cross-country skis, even lighter and narrower, are usually made of wood. Different waxes are used for different snow conditions. Jumping skis are long, wide, and heavy.

Two poles are used, with light metal, such as an aluminum alloy, the most popular construction, although steel and fiberglass poles are not uncommon. The tip of a pole is sharp, and about 5 inches (13 cm) above it is a circular ring, interlaced with webbing. The ring and webbing prevent the pole from sinking into deep snow. At the top of the pole is a thong that fits around the wrist, so that the pole will not be dropped. Poles are an aid in climbing and pushing off, and sometimes help maintain balance. Downhill poles are shorter than the cross-country variety. Those for the average skier reach midway between the waist and armpit.

**Boots, Bindings, and Other Equipment.** Advances in plastic techniques have revolutionized ski-boot construction since the late 1960's. Rigid, waterproof plastic boots often with some leather parts, quickly surpassed all-leather boots in popularity. Double boots, consisting of a rigid outer boot and a more flexible inner one, are also available. Modern boots are fastened with buckles, which have almost completely replaced the traditional laced boots. Flexible, soft-leather boots are still preferred for cross-country skiing.

Until the 1950's, the only purpose of ski bindings was to hold the skier's feet firmly on the skis. However, injuries from falls were frequent, and designers developed several bindings that would release the feet in a fall and still provide good contact while skiing. Modern cross-country bindings hold the feet only at the toes. For Alpine skiing step-in bindings have practically replaced earlier release bindings that used cables. Safety straps, attached to the binding and the boot, are often used to prevent skis from "running away" when the boots are released from the bindings.

Ski clothing should be warm, lightweight, wind-resistant, and as moisture-proof as possible. Sunglasses and goggles help prevent eyestrain and protect the skier from ultraviolet rays. Various types of packs, in which to carry food, extra equipment, and clothing, are widely used.

**Alpine Skiing.** The primary objective of the casual skier is to enjoy the downhill run and to reach the bottom of the slope safely. Control is of the utmost importance, and the skier should be able to stop or turn. Checks and turns of the snowplow and stem variety—the ski tips close together, the heels relatively far apart—are the most elementary. For more advanced skiers there are variations of the Christiania, or Christie, where skis are parallel, and weight shift and body rotation are used. Experts can accomplish jump turns and other acrobatic maneuvers in the air.

For downhill racing, speed is the most important requirements, although not at the sacrifice of control, as slopes are uneven. Skiers do not race en masse, but separately, and each contestant is timed. Record times are obviously no criterion, since snow conditions vary, as well as the slope and length of the descent. Racing speeds sometimes exceed 80 miles (128 km) per hour.

The slalom form of downhill racing calls for great turning ability. The skier races against time through a number of pairs of flagged poles, each pair known as a gate, placed on the course so the skier must take a serpentine zigzag path down the slope. The faster the skier can change course and check his speed, the better he will do, but if he takes too great risks, he may fall or miss going through a gate. Judgment and control, as well as speed, are therefore of the utmost importance. The giant slalom, combining characteristics of the downhill and the slalom, has a longer course than the regular slalom, with gates set farther apart.

**Nordic Skiing.** Although the jumping part of Nordic skiing has always been popular, cross-country skiing was confined largely to Scandinavia until the late 1960's. For jumping, the ski is longer and heavier than other types and usually has three grooves in the bottom for better control. No poles are used. The skier glides down an elevated ramp, the in-run, and then takes off into the air, landing on the outrun, or sloping surface of the hill. He is marked for distance and for form, so the longest jump will not necessarily win first place. Jumps of over 540 feet (165 meters) have been made. Since the distance of the jump depends not only on the jumper's skill but also on the size of the slope and the snow conditions, records are not always meaningful. The most celebrated jumping meet is at Holmenkollen, Norway.

In cross-country racing the ski is somewhat narrower and lighter than the downhill ski. Bindings permit free up-and-down foot motion, and the boot soles are more flexible than downhill ones. Cross-country racing is over level terrain, climbs and descents, and the skier is often faed with obstacles like walls and wooded territory. When not skiing downhill, the competitor must depend on his stride and pole thrust to supply momentum, which makes cross country the most physically taxing type of skiing. In Sweden the long Dalarna cross-country race, which commemorates a historic journey of Gustav Vasa, attracts several thousand competitors.

**Competition.** Skiing is one of the most important sports in the Winter Olympic Games. For both men and women, the two basic divisions are Nordic and Alpine events. Women's

Nordic events are limited to cross-country races, while the men's division includes a variety of cross-country and jumping events, plus the biathlon, a combination of skiing and shooting. A Nordic Combined title, recognizing jumping and skiing excellence, is awarded in the men's division. In the Alpine category, men and women each compete in downhill, slalom, and giant slalom race. An Alpine Combined title was part of the competition through the 1948 games and has been unofficially awarded since then.

World championships, originally held annually, have been staged every four years since 1950 and are under the auspices of the Fédération Internationale de Ski (FIS). Topflight Alpine skiers compete for the World Cup, which is awarded annually to those who compile the most points in a series of international races. In addition, many countries stage national championships each year. Professional skiers hold a number of tournaments throughout the world.

**History.** Primitive skis over 4,000 years old have been found in Scandinavian bogs, and it is known that the Laplanders were early skiers. At the Battle of Oslo in 1200, Norwegian troops used skis, and military use of skis was made in other wars, including World Wars I and II. Ski lengths have varied greatly over the centuries, with skis as short as 3 feet (1 meter) being used in 16th century warfare.

In earlier times skiing was more often a military skill or a means of transportation than a sport. However, it assumed recreational status during the late 19th century, and in the 20th century it became a major winter sport wherever terrain and weather conditions permitted.

In 1862 the first officially recorded ski competition was held near Oslo, and in 1877 the Christiania Ski Club was organized in Norway. An indication of the country's importance in skiing progress is the large number of skiing terms that are in Norwegian. The Christiania—commonly shortened to Christie—designates a high-speed turn with parallel skis. Telemark, a turn in deep snow, and slalom are other skiing terms with Norwegian origins.

Scandinavians were instrumental in introducing the sport to the United States, with skis reported in the Middle West as early as 1840. The first ski club in the United States, eventually known as the Nansen Ski Club, was organized in 1882 in Berlin, N.H., for jumping and cross-country racing. In 1904 the National Ski Association was formed in Ishpeming, Mich. All the charter member clubs were from the Middle West.

Around 1880 skiing gained popularity in Austria and later in Switzerland, Germany, and France. In the late 19th century many Englishmen became ski enthusiasts during their travels on the Continent. The Ski Club of Great Britain, formed in 1903, became one of the world's largest. In general, West Europeans preferred downhill skiing to the jumping and cross-country racing favored by the Scandinavians.

Beginning in 1907, Hannes Schneider, an Austrian, began to teach skiing in the Arlberg section of the Alps. His Arlberg technique, which was an improvement of the methods of an instructor named Mathias Zdarsky, became extremely popular after World War I. Schneider taught a crouched style with forward lean that emphasized rotating the body into a turn. Schneider's techniques were relatively easy to learn and were instrumental in popularizing the sport. An additional spur was the development of rope tows, which eliminated the slow, arduous uphill climb and enabled skiers to make many more runs per day.

In North America, eastern Canadian colleges and the Dartmouth Outing Club in the United States made key contributions to early 20th century skiing. In 1931 the first snow train carried members of the Appalachian Mountain Club from Boston to the ski slopes of the White Mountains. This was followed by trains from New York, and many city dwellers were soon taking weekend or vacation excursions to ski resorts. In 1932 the Winter Olympics, held at Lake Placid, N.Y., did much to stimulate interest in the United States. Enthusiasts watched and read about jumping and cross country as well as downhill and slalom racing.

After World War II different types of techniques developed. The Austrians championed the wedeln, which emphasized short, connected parallel turns. Another school stressed counter-rotation of the body while turning. In an attempt to standardize instruction in the United States, the American Ski Technique was worked out and gained acceptance during the 1960's.

By the early 1970's there were approximately 4 million skiers, nearly half of them women, in the United States, compared with a total of 2 million about 20 years earlier. In addition to the traditional ski areas, some of them world famous, many new ski slopes open each year. Artificial snow-making machines supplement normal snowfalls at many ski slopes and have allowed skiing to be introduced into some areas where natural conditions make the sport impossible. The Northeast and Far West, with the advantages of cold winters and mountainous terrain, continue to be the most popular ski areas, but the sport is also growing rapidly in the Midwest, and some trails have been carved out of the mountains in the Southeast. Cross-country skiing, which had been out of favor in the United States, surged in the early 1970's as skiers enjoyed lighter equipment and the freedom from lift lines and increasingly crowded downhill slopes.

Although the most dramatic growth has been in the United States, enthusiasm for the sport has increased in Europe, South America, Japan, and other areas that have suitable conditions. To serve the multitudes of new skiers, the manufacture of skis and other equipment has burgeoned, and resort complexes have multiplied.

Parke Cummings
*Author of "The Dictionary of Sports"*

### Bibliography

Bradley, David et al, *Expert Skiing* (Grosset 1963).

Caldwell, John, *New Cross-Country Ski Book* (Greene 1971).

Jerome, John, and others, *Sports Illustrated Book of Skiing*, rev. ed. (Lippincott 1971).

Lederer, William J., and Wilson, Joe P., *Complete Cross-Country Skiing and Touring* (Norton 1970).

Lund, Morten, *Ski, G.L.M.: The Fastest and Safest Way to Learn* (Dial 1970).

Scharff, Robert, and others, eds., *Ski Magazine's Encyclopedia of Skiing* (Harper 1970).

**TOBOGGANING,** is the sport of coasting down a snow-covered slope or specially prepared track on a flat, runnerless sled called a toboggan. The vehicle was first used by the North American Indians for hauling supplies and game over the snow, and it serves the same purpose for campers and hunters today. In addition, many participants in winter sports use it for recreation.

Indians made the first toboggans of skins, which they attached to a frame. Later, two or three boards lashed together served as a base, with the front end curled up and backward, forming a "hood." A low railing around the sides and back helped keep the goods on the base. Toboggans were narrow so that they could be dragged through the forest by hand or by dogs.

The modern toboggan is constructed of hard, polished woods, and the boards are held together by crosspieces on the nongliding surface. A hand rope around the sides and back helps riders stay on the vehicle. Toboggans vary from 3 to 8 feet (0.91-2.43 meters) in length and from 1⅟ to 4 feet (0.45-1.21 meters) in width. The longest toboggan will support 4 or 5 riders seated one behind the other, with knees bent and feet straddling the rider ahead. The front rider braces his feet against the hood.

To keep the vehicle on a course without a prepared track or run, the rear rider must guide the toboggan by trailing a foot on one side or the other. Runs were first provided by resorts and country clubs late in the 19th century, the length depending on the terrain available. Rivalry in speed led to tobogganing competitions.

Bill Braddock, *New York "Times"*

## BIATHLON

| 1960 | Klas Lestander, Sweden | 1:33:21.6 |
| 1964 | Vladimir Melanin, USSR | 1:20:26.8 |
| 1968* | Magnar Solberg, Norway | 1:13:45.9 |
| 1972 | Magnar Solberg, Norway | 1:15:55.50 |
| 1976 | Nikolai Kruglov, USSR | 1:14:12.26 |

## BIATHLON RELAY

| 1968 | USSR | 2:13.02 |
| 1972* | USSR | 1:51.44 |
| 1976 | USSR | 1:57:55.67 |

## BOBSLED: 2-MAN BOB (winning driver)

| 1932 | U.S.A., Hubert Stevens | 8:14.74 |
| 1936 | U.S.A., Ivan Brown | 5:29.29 |
| 1948 | Switzerland, F. Endrich | 5:29.2 |
| 1952 | W. Germany, Andreas Ostler | 5:24.54 |
| 1956 | Italy, Dalla Costa | 5:30.14 |
| 1964 | Britain, Antony Nash | 4:21.90 |
| 1968 | Italy, Eugenio Monti | 4:41.54 |
| 1972 | W. Germany, Wolfgang Zimmerer | 4:47.07 |
| 1976* | E. Germany, Meinhard Nehmer | 3:40.43 |

## 4-MAN BOB (winning driver)

| 1924 | Switzerland, Edward Scherrer | 5:45.54 |
| 1928 | U.S.A., William Fiske | 3:20.5 |
| 1932 | U.S.A., William Fiske | 7:53:68 |
| 1936 | Switzerland, Perre Musy | 5:19.85 |
| 1948 | U.S.A., Edward Rimkus | 5:20.1 |
| 1952 | W. Germany, Andreas Ostler | 5:07.84 |
| 1956 | Switzerland, Franz Kapus | 5:10.44 |
| 1964 | Canada, Victor Emery | 4:14.46 |
| 1968* | Italy, Eugenio Monti | 2:17.39 |
| 1972 | Switzerland, Jean Wicki | 4:43.07 |
| 1976 | E. Germany, Meinhard Nehmer | 3:44.42 |

## ICE HOCKEY

| 1920 | Canada |
| 1924 | Canada |
| 1928 | Canada |
| 1932 | Canada |
| 1936 | Britain |
| 1948 | Canada |
| 1952 | Canada |
| 1956 | USSR |
| 1960 | U.S.A. |
| 1968 | USSR |
| 1972 | USSR |
| 1976 | USSR |

## FIGURE SKATING—MEN

| 1908 | Ulrich Salchow, Sweden |
| 1920 | Gillis Grafstrom, Sweden |
| 1924 | Gillis Grafstrom, Sweden |
| 1928 | Gillis Grafstrom, Sweden |
| 1932 | Karl Schafer, Austria |
| 1936 | Karl Schafer, Austria |
| 1948 | Richard Button, U.S.A. |
| 1952 | Richard Button, U.S.A. |
| 1956 | H.A. Jenkins, U.S.A. |
| 1960 | David Jenkins, U.S.A. |
| 1964 | Manfred Schnelldorfer, W. Germany |
| 1968 | Wolfgang Schwarz, Austria |
| 1972 | Ondrej Nepela, Czechoslovakia |
| 1976 | John Curry, Britain |

## FIGURE SKATING—WOMEN

| 1908 | Madge Syers, Britain |
| 1920 | Magda Julin-Mauroy, Sweden |
| 1924 | Heima von Szabo-Planck, Austria |
| 1928 | Sonja Henie, Norway |
| 1932 | Sonja Henie, Norway |
| 1936 | Sonja Henie, Norway |
| 1948 | Barbara Ann Scott, Canada |
| 1952 | Jeanette Altwegg, Britain |
| 1956 | Tenley Albright, U.S.A. |
| 1960 | Carol Heiss, U.S.A. |
| 1964 | Sjoukje Dijkstra, Netherlands |
| 1968 | Peggy Fleming, U.S.A. |
| 1972 | Beatrix Schuba, Austria |
| 1976 | Dorothy Hamill, U.S.A. |

## FIGURE SKATING—PARIS

| 1908 | Germany: Ann Hubler, Heinrich Burger |
| 1920 | Finland: Ludovika and Walter Jakobsson |
| 1924 | Austria: Helene Engelmann, Alfred Berger |
| 1928 | France: Andrée Joly, Pierre Brunet |
| 1932 | France: Andrée and Pierre Brunet |
| 1936 | Germany: Maxie Heber, Ernest Baier |
| 1952 | W. Germany: Ria and Paul Falk |
| 1956 | Austria: Elizabeth Schwarz, Kurt Oppelt |
| 1960 | Canada: Barbara Wagner, Robert Paul |
| 1964 | USSR: Ludmila Beloussova, Oleg Protopopov |
| 1968 | USSR: Ludmila Beloussova, Oleg Protopopov |
| 1972 | USSR: Irina Rodnina, Alexei Ulanov |
| 1976 | USSR: Irina Rodnina, Alexandr Zaitsev |

## SPEED SKATING—MEN: 500 METERS

| 1924 | Charles Jewtraw, U.S.A. | 0:44.0 |
| 1928 | Clas Thunberg, Finland, and Bernt Evensen, Norway (tie) | 0:43.4 |
| 1932 | John A. Shea, U.S.A. | 0:43.4 |
| 1936 | Ivar Ballangrud, Norway | 0:43.4 |
| 1948 | Finn Helgesen, Norway | 0:43.1 |
| 1952 | Kenneth Henry, U.S.A. | 0:43.2 |
| 1956 | Evgeniy Grishin, USSR | 0:40.20 |
| 1960 | Evgeniy Grishin, USSR | 0:40.20 |
| 1964 | Richard McDermott, U.S.A. | 0:40.10 |
| 1968 | Erhard Keller, W. Germany | 0:40.30 |
| 1972 | Erhard Keller, W. Germany | 0.39.40 |
| 1976* | Evgeny Kulikov, USSR | 0:39.17 |

## SPEED SKATING—WOMEN: 500 METERS

| 1932 | Jean Wilson, Canada | 0:58.0 |
| 1960 | Helga Haase, W. Germany | 0:45.9 |
| 1964 | Lydia Skoblikova, USSR | 0:45.0 |
| 1968 | Ludmila Titova, USSR | 0:46.1 |
| 1972 | Anne Henning, U.S.A. | 0:43.3 |
| 1976* | Sheila Young, U.S.A. | 0:42.76 |

## SPEED SKATING—MEN: 1,000 METERS

| 1976* | Peter Mueller, U.S.A. | 1:19.32 |

## SPEED SKATING—WOMEN: 1,000 METERS

| 1932 | Elizabeth Du Bois, U.S.A. | 2:04.0 |
| 1960 | Kara Guseva, USSR | 1:34.1 |
| 1964 | Lydia Skoblikova, USSR | 1:33.2 |
| 1968 | Carolina Geijssen, Netherlands | 1:32.60 |
| 1972 | Monika Pflug, W. Germany | 1:31.40 |
| 1976 | Tatiana Averina, USSR | 1:28.43 |

## SPEED SKATING—MEN: 1,500 METERS

| 1924 | Clas Thunberg, Finland | 2:20.8 |
| 1928 | Clas Thunberg, Finland | 2:21.1 |
| 1932 | John A. Shea, U.S.A. | 2:57.5 |
| 1936 | Charles Mathisen, Norway | 2:19.2 |
| 1948 | Sverre Farstad, Norway | 2:17.6 |
| 1952 | Hjalmar Anderson, Norway | 2:20.4 |
| 1956 | Evgeniy Grishin and Y. Mikhailov, USSR(tie) | 2:08.6 |
| 1960 | Edgar Roadaas, Norway, and Evgeniy Grishin, USSR (tie) | 2:10.4 |
| 1964 | Ants Antson, USSR | 2:10.3 |
| 1968 | Cornelis Verkerk, Netherlands | 2:03.4 |
| 1972 | Ard Schenk, Netherlands | 2:02.96 |
| 1976* | Jan-Egil Storholt, Norway | 1:59.38 |

## SPEED SKATING—WOMEN: 1,500 METERS

| 1932 | Kit Klein, U.S.A. | 3:06.0 |
| 1960 | Lidia Skoblikova, USSR | 2:52.2 |
| 1964 | Lidia Skoblikova, USSR | 2:22.6 |
| 1968 | Kaija Mustonen, Finland | 2:22.40 |
| 1972 | Dianne Holum, U.S.A. | 2:20.80 |
| 1976* | Galina Stepanskaya, USSR | 2:16.58 |

## SPEED SKATING—MEN: 5,000 METERS

| 1924 | Clas Thunberg, Finland | 8:39.0 |
| 1928 | Ivar Ballangrud, Norway | 8:50.5 |
| 1932 | Irving Jaffee, U.S.A. | 9:40.8 |
| 1936 | Ivar Ballangrud, Norway | 8:19.6 |
| 1948 | Reidar Liaklev, Norway | 8:29.4 |
| 1952 | Hjalmar Anderson, Norway | 8:10.6 |
| 1956 | Boris Shilkov, USSR | 7:48.70 |
| 1960 | Victor Kosichkin, USSR | 7:51.30 |
| 1964 | Knut Johannesen, Norway | 7:38.40 |
| 1968* | Fred Anton Maier, Norway | 7:22.40 |
| 1972 | Ard Schenck, Netherlands | 7:23.60 |
| 1976 | Sten Stenson, Norway | 7:24.48 |

## SPEED SKATING—WOMEN: 3,000 METERS

| 1960 | Lidia Skoblikova, USSR | 5:14.3 |
| 1964 | Lidia Skoblikova, USSR | 5:14.9 |
| 1968 | Johanna Schut, Netherlands | 4:56.2 |
| 1972 | Stien Kaiser-Baas, Netherlands | 4:52.14 |
| 1976* | Tatiana Averina, USSR | 4:45.19 |

## SPEED SKATING—MEN: 10,000 METERS

| 1924 | Julian Skutnabb, Finland | 18:04.8 |
| 1928 | No decision because of thawing ice | |
| 1932 | Irving Jaffee, U.S.A. | 19:13.6 |
| 1936 | Ivar Ballangrud, Norway | 17:24.3 |
| 1948 | Ake Seyffarth, Norway | 17:26.3 |
| 1952 | Hjalmar Anderson, Norway | 16:45.8 |
| 1956 | Sigvard Ericsson, Sweden | 16:35.9 |
| 1960 | Knut Johannsen, Norway | 15:46.6 |
| 1964 | Jonny Nilsson, Sweden | 15:50.1 |
| 1968 | Johnny Hoeglin, Sweden | 15:23.6 |
| 1972 | Ard Schenk, Netherlands | 15:01.35 |
| 1976* | Piet Kleine, Netherlands | 14:50.59 |

## SKIING: ALPINE—MEN: DOWNHILL

| 1948 | Henry Oreiller, France | 2:55.0 |
| 1952 | Zeno Colo, Italy | 2:30.8 |
| 1956 | Anton Sailer, Austria | 2:52.2 |
| 1960 | Jean Vuarnet, France | 2:06.0 |

| | | |
|---|---|---|
| 1964 | Egon Zimmermann, Austria | 2:18.16 |
| 1968 | Jean-Claude Killy, France | 1:59.85 |
| 1972 | Bernhard Russi, Switzerland | 1:51.43 |
| 1976* | Franz Klammer, Austria | 1:45.73 |

### ALPINE—WOMEN: DOWNHILL

| | | |
|---|---|---|
| 1948 | Hedi Schlunegger, Switzerland | 2:28.3 |
| 1952 | Trude Jochum-Beiser, Austria | 1:47.1 |
| 1956 | Madeleine Berthod, Switzerland | 1:40.7 |
| 1960 | Heidi Beibl, W. Germany | 1:37.6 |
| 1964 | Christi Haas, Austria | 1:55.3 |
| 1968 | Olga Pall, Austria | 1:40.8 |
| 1972* | Marie Therese Nadig, Switzerland | 1:36.68 |
| 1976 | Rosi Mittermaier, W. Germany | 1:46.16 |

### ALPINE—MEN: GIANT SLALOM

| | | |
|---|---|---|
| 1952 | Stein Eriksen, Norway | 2:25.0 |
| 1956 | Anton Sailer, Austria | 3:00.1 |
| 1960 | Roger Staub, Switzerland | 1:48.3 |
| 1964* | Francois Bonlieu, France | 1:46.7 |
| 1968 | Jean-Claude Killy, France | 3:29.28 |
| 1972 | Gustavo Thoeni, Italy | 3:09.62 |
| 1976 | Heimmii , Switzerland | 3:26.97 |

### ALPINE—WOMEN: GIANT SLALOM

| | | |
|---|---|---|
| 1952 | Andrea Mead Lawrence, U.S.A. | 2:06.8 |
| 1956 | Ossi Reichert, W. Germany | 1:56.5 |
| 1960 | Yvonne Ruegg, Switzerland | 1:39.9 |
| 1964 | Marielle Goitschel, France | 1:52.2 |
| 1968 | Nancy Greene, Canada | 1:51.97 |
| 1972 | Marie Therese Nadig, Switzerland | 1:29.90 |
| 1976* | Kathy Kreiner, Canada | 1:29.13 |

### ALPINE—MEN: SLALOM

| | | |
|---|---|---|
| 1948 | Edi Reinalter, Switzerland | 2:10.3 |
| 1952 | Othmar Schneider, Austria | 2:00.0 |
| 1956 | Anton Sailer, Austria | ———— |
| 1960 | Ernst Hinterseer, Austria | 2:08.9 |
| 1964 | Josef Stiegler, Austria | 2:11.13 |
| 1968 | Jean-Claude Killy, France | 1:39.73 |
| 1972* | Francisco Fernandez Ochoa, Spain | 1:09.27 |
| 1976 | Piero Gros, Italy | 2:03.29 |

### ALPINE—WOMEN: SLALOM

| | | |
|---|---|---|
| 1948 | Gretchen Fraser, U.S.A. | 1:57.2 |
| 1952 | Andrea Mead Lawrence, U.S.A. | 2:10.6 |
| 1956 | Renee Colliard, Switzerland | — |
| 1960 | Anne Heggtveigt, Canada | 1:49.6 |
| 1964 | Christine Goitschel, France | 1:29.8 |
| 1968* | Marielle Goitschel, France | 1:25.86 |
| 1972 | Barbara Cochran, U.S.A. | 1:31.24 |
| 1976 | Rosi Mittermaier, W. Germany | 1:30.54 |

### NORDIC—WOMEN: 5 KILOMETERS

| | | |
|---|---|---|
| 1964 | Claudia Boyarskikh, USSR | 17:50.5 |
| 1968 | Tolni Gustafsson, Sweden | 16:45.2 |
| 1972 | Galina Koulacova, USSR | 17:00.50 |
| 1976* | Helena Takalo, Finland | 15:48.69 |

### NORDIC—WOMEN: 10 KILOMETERS

| | | |
|---|---|---|
| 1952 | Lydia Wideman, Finland | 41:40.0 |
| 1956 | Ljubavi Kazyreva, USSR | 38:11.0 |
| 1960 | Marija Gusakova, USSR | 39:46.6 |
| 1964 | Claudia Boyarskikh, USSR | 4j0:24.3 |
| 1968 | Toini Gustafsson, Sweden | 36:46.50 |
| 1972 | Galina Koulacova, USSR | 34:17.80 |
| 1976* | Raisa Smetanina, USSR | 30:13.41 |

### NORDIC—WOMEN: 20-KILOMETER RELAY

| | | |
|---|---|---|
| 1956 | Finland | 1:09.01.0 |
| 1960 | Sweden | 1:04.21.4 |
| 1964 | USSR | 59:20.2 |
| 1968 | Norway | 57:30.00 |
| 1972* | USSR | 48:46.10 |
| 1976 | USSR | 1:07:49.75 |

### NORDIC—MEN: 15 KILOMETERS

| | | |
|---|---|---|
| 1956 | Hallgier Brenden, Norway | 49:39.0 |
| 1960 | Hakon Brusveen, Norway | 51:55.5 |
| 1964 | Eero Maentyranta, Finland | 50:54.1 |
| 1968 | Harald Groenningen, Norway | 47:54.20 |
| 1972 | Sven-Ake Lundback, Sweden | 45:28.20 |
| 1976* | N. Bashukov, USSR | 43:58.47 |

### NORDIC—MEN: 30 KILOMETERS

| | | |
|---|---|---|
| 1956 | Veikko Hakulinen, Finland | 1:44:06.0 |
| 1960 | Sixten Jernberg, Sweden | 1:51.03.9 |
| 1964 | Eero Maentyranta, Finland | 1:30:50.7 |
| 1968 | Franco Nones, Italy | 1:35:39.20 |
| 1972 | Vyacheslav Vedenin, USSR | 1:36:31.10 |
| 1976* | Sergei Saveliev, USSR | 1:30:29.38 |

### NORDIC—MEN: 50 KILOMETERS

| | | |
|---|---|---|
| 1924 | Thorlief Haug, Norway | 3:44:32.0 |
| 1928 | Per E. Hedlund, Sweden | 4:52.03.0 |
| 1932 | Veli Saarinen, Finland | 4:28:00.0 |
| 1936 | Elis Viklund, Sweden | 3:30:11.0 |
| 1948 | Nils Karlsson, Sweden | 3:47:48.0 |
| 1952 | Veikko Hakulinen, Finland | 3:33:33.0 |
| 1956 | Sixten Jernberg, Sweden | 2:50:27.00 |
| 1960 | Kalevi Hamalainen, Finland | 2:59:06.30 |
| 1964 | Sixten Jernberg, Sweden | 2:43:52.60 |
| 1968* | Ole Ellefsaeter, Norway | 2:28:45.80 |
| 1972 | Paal Tyldum, Norway | 2:43:14.75 |
| 1976 | Ivar Formo, Norway | 2:37:30.05 |

### NORDIC—MEN: 40-KILOMETER RELAY

| | | |
|---|---|---|
| 1936 | Finland | 2:41:33.0 |
| 1948 | Sweden | 2:32.08.0 |
| 1952 | Finland | 2:20:16.0 |
| 1956 | USSR | 2:15:30.0 |
| 1960 | Finland | 2:18:45.6 |
| 1964 | Sweden | 2:18:34.6 |
| 1968 | Norway | 2:08:33.50 |
| 1972* | USSR | **2:04:47.90** |
| 1976 | Finland | 2:07:59.72 |

### NORDIC—MEN: COMBINED CROSS COUNTRY AND JUMPING

| | | |
|---|---|---|
| 1924 | Thorlief Haug, Norway | 453.800 |
| 1928 | Johan Grottunsbraaten, Norway | 427.800 |
| 1932 | Johan Grottunsbraaten, Norway | 446.200 |
| 1936 | Oddbjorn Hagen, Norway | 430:300 |
| 194c | Heikki Hasu, Finland | 448.800 |
| 1952 | Simon Slattvik, Norway | 451.621 |
| 1956 | Sverre Stenersen, Norway | 455.000 |
| 1960 | Georg Thoma, W. Germany | 457.952 |
| 1964 | Tormod Knutsen, Norway | 469.280 |
| 1968 | Franz Keller, W. Germany | 449.040 |
| 1972 | Ulrich Wehling, E. Germany | 413.340 |
| 1976 | Ulrich Wehling, E. Germany | 423.390 |

### NORDIC—MEN: 90—METER SKI JUMPING

| | | |
|---|---|---|
| 1924 | Jacob Thams, Norway | 227.5 |
| 1928 | Alfred Andersen, Norway | 330.5 |
| 1932 | Birger Ruud, Norway | 228.0 |
| 1936 | Birger Ruud, Norway | 232.0 |
| 1948 | Petter Hugsted, Norway | 228.1 |
| 1952 | Arnfinn Bergmann, Norway | 226.0 |
| 1956 | Antti Hyvarinen, Finland | 227.0 |
| 1960 | Helmut Recknagel, W. Germany | 227.2 |
| 1964 | Toralf Engan, Norway | 230.7 |
| 1968 | Vladimir Beloussov, USSR | 231.3 |
| 1972 | Wojiech Fortuna, Poland | 219.9 |
| 1976 | Karl Schnabi, Austria | 234.8 |

### NORDIC—MEN: 70—METER SKI JUMPING

| | | |
|---|---|---|
| 1964 | Veikko Kankkonen, Finland | 229.9 |
| 1968 | Jiri Raska, Czechoslovakia | 216.5 |
| 1972 | Yukio Kasaya, Japan | 244.2 |
| 1976 | Hans-Georg Aschenbach, E. Germany | 252.0 |

### TOBOGGAN (LUGE)—MEN: SINGLES

| | | |
|---|---|---|
| 1964 | Thomas Koehler, W. Germany | 3:26.77 |
| 1968* | Manfred Schmid, Austria | 2:52.48 |
| 1972 | Wolfgang Scheidel. E. Germany | 3:27.58 |
| 1976 | Detlef Guenther, E. Germany | 3:27.688 |

### WOMEN: SINGLES

| | | |
|---|---|---|
| 1964 | Ortrun Enderlein, W. Germany | 3:24.67 |
| 1968* | Erica Lechner, Italy | 2:28.66 |
| 1972 | Anna Muller, E. Germany | 2:59.180 |
| 1976 | Margit Schumann, E. Germany | 2:50.621 |

### MEN: DOUBLES

| | | |
|---|---|---|
| 1964 | Austria: Josef Feistmanti, Manfred Stengl | 1:41.62 |
| 1968 | E. Germany: Klaus Bonsack, Thomas Koehler | 1:35.85 |
| 1972 | tie: Italy (Paul Hildegartner, Walter Plaikner) and E. Germany (Horst Hornlein, Reinhard Bredow) | 1:28.35 |
| 1976* | E. Germany: Hans Rinn, Norbert Hahn | 1:25.604 |